SCORPION IN THE HAND

SCORPION IN THE HAND

Brajbhasha Court Poetry from Central India around 1800

A Critical Edition of Ṭhākur's Kabittas

IMRE BANGHA

MANOHAR
2014

The publication of this book was supported by the John Fell Oxford University Press (OUP) Research Fund.

First published 2014

ISBN 978-81-7304-999-6

Published by

Ajay Kumar Jain *for*
Manohar Publishers & Distributors
4753/23 Ansari Road, Daryaganj
New Delhi 110 002

Typeset at

Digigrafics
New Delhi 110 049

Printed at

Salasar Imaging Systems
Delhi 110 035

To

the memory of

DR. KISHORILAL (1931-2012)

Contents

Acknowledgements 9

Note on the Transliteration and the Dates 11

Introduction 13

THE POET AND HIS TIMES 15
- Bundelkhand at the turn of the nineteenth century 15
- Ṭhākur's life in anecdotes and poems 16
- The many Ṭhākurs 23
- Conclusion 26

ṬHĀKUR'S QUATRAINS AND HINDI LITERATURE 29
- 'The dignity of Ṭhākur'—Early modern individualism 31
- Unconventional poetic forms 32
- Nature and love 33
- *Rītimukta* poetry 35
- Search for a new style: regionalism and idioms 37
- Style and reflection on the art 40
- Intertextuality 41
- Conclusion 48

THE TEXT 49
- Prosody 49
- Oral and written transmission 50
- The sources 58
- List of sources 69
- Concordance 79
- Editorial procedures 92
- Abbreviations 95

ṬHĀKUR-KABITTĀVALĪ: HINDI TEXT WITH CRITICAL APPARATUS AND NOTES 99
- *Bhakti aur līlā-varṇan* 101
- *Śṛṅgār* 141
- *Ṛtu-varṇan* 238
- *Saṁsār aur nīti* 282
- *Sandigdha kabitt* (Quatrains of uncertain authorship) 310
- *Prakīrṇak* (Miscellanea) 319

ENGLISH TRANSLATION OF SELECTED POEMS 325
- About the translation 325
- Devotion and God's sports in the world 326
- Love 330

The seasons 339
The world and proper conduct 346

Bibliography 351

Index of Poems 355

Index of Names and Works 367

Acknowledgements

I express my deepest gratitude to three learned teachers of Brajbhasha, the late Dr. Kishorilal in Naini, near Allahabad, the late Professor Govind Sharma in Vrindaban, and Professor Ramdeo Shukla in Gorakhpur, who during the years of my study of Ṭhākur selflessly offered their time and expertise in interpreting early Hindi texts. They have transmitted a knowledge accumulated over centuries, which is now the privilege of only a few. Our spirited discussions offered more instruction than any study in Europe could have possibly provided.

I am also grateful to Dr. Udaya Shanker Dubey from the remote village of Karerua in Uttar Pradesh for sharing the materials of his personal library and his sustained help in locating Ṭhākur manuscripts; to Dr. Daksha Mistry from M.S. University in Vadodara who helped me to copy several manuscripts and in the context of an overlapping project participated in various sessions discussing Ṭhākur's poetry with Brajbhasha experts. Two outstanding scholars directed my attention to new materials during my trip to Bundelkhand, Professor Krishna Bihari Lal Pandey in Datiya and Ganga Prasad 'Barsainya' in Chatarpur. Discussion with them provided further inspiration to undertake this research. My investigation also benefited from the friendly welcome of Mr. Raghuvir Singh in Chatarpur, who also allowed access to his manuscript collection. Dr. Jayesh Khandelwal in Vrindaban also granted me access to a rich collection and discussions with him helped me to understand better the deep roots of Brajbhasha love poetry in the devotional milieu of the land of Braj. Professor Balwant Singh Dhillon's help in getting access to some important manuscripts was indispensable as were Dr. Jeevan Singh Deol's indications on where to search for Hindi manuscripts in Panjab. Mr. Saheb Singh Dhesi, and Ms. Katalin Dobos located and checked important material for this project. My manuscript hunt also benefited from Professor Vishnuvirat Chaturvedi's search for Hindi manuscripts in Gujarat.

I also thank Professor Polly O'Hanlon (Oxford), Ms. Megan Robb (Oxford), Mr. Peter Diggle (Oxford) and Mr. Richard Williams (London) for their excellent suggestions on the manuscript. Lively conversations on early modern Hindi poetry at various parts of the globe with Professor Allison Busch (New York) and Professor Francesca Orsini (London) have contributed to form many ideas in the Introduction and helped to preserve my enthusiasm for a project dragging over more than a decade. I especially thank Professor Busch for her in-depth feedback at a very late stage. Reading Ṭhākur in the Oxford classroom with students like Saheb Singh Dhesi, Jaspreet Sanghera, Sophie-Jung Kim, Vanya Bhargav, Richard Williams and Vijay Ramnarace was a rewarding experience. The book has greatly benefited from their remarks as well as those of the participants of the Brajbhasha and Early Hindi Retreat in Miercurea Ciuc, Romania in 2011.

Access to manuscript and published material was granted at the Alwar, Bharatpur, Bikaner Jaipur, Jodhpur and Udaipur branches of the Rajasthan Oriental Research Institute, at the Khasmohar Collection of the Maharaja Sawai Mansingh II. Museum, Jaipur, the Sanjay Sharma Museum and the Acharya Shri Vinayanand Jnan Bhandar, Jaipur, the Abhay Jain Granthalaya and the Vidyamandir Shodh Pratishthan in Bikaner, the Rajasthani Research Institute in Chopasni, the Hindi Sahitya Sammelan in Allahabad, the Oriental Institute, Vadodara, the Nagaripracharini Sabha, Kashi, the Gujarat Vidya Sabha, and the L.D. Institute of Indology in Ahmadabad, the Bundela Shodh Sansthan in Seondha (M.P.), the Sukar Kshetr Shodh Sansthan in Kasganj (U.P.), the Vrindaban Research Institute, the Ras Bharati Sansthan and the Braj Cultural Research Institute in Vrindaban, Guru Nanak Dev University and the Sikh History Department of Khalsa College in Amritsar, the Vishveshvaranand Vedic Research Institute in Hoshiarpur, DAV College in Chandigarh, Punjabi University and the Government Language Department in Patiala. I am grateful to the directors and staff of these institutions as well as to the owners of private collections that provided manuscripts for inspection for this project.

The Max Mueller Memorial Fund, the Sub-Faculty of South and Inner Asian Studies and Wolfson College at the University of Oxford as well as the British Academy provided funding for several study tours in India, where among other matters I discussed early Hindi poems with local experts and extensively copied and consulted books and manuscripts. A British Academy Travelling Scholarship Grant for Dr. Kishorilal enabled me to discuss the text in Oxford with one of the most outstanding experts of Brajbhasha.

IMRE BANGHA

Note on the Transliteration and the Dates

Indian terms that are familiar in English and can be found in the *Oxford English Dictionary* as well as modern Indian names are normally spelt in English. This means that terms and names such as bhakti, sampradaya, Krishna, Shiva, etc. are treated as English words. Other technical terms, titles of works and quoted passages are italicised and spelt as in the original language with diacritics. Pre-nineteenth-century Indian proper names, including names of sects and institutions, are also transliterated with diacritics.

The transliteration for terms in Hindi follows that of R.S. McGregor's *The Oxford Hindi-English Dictionary* with a few deviations from his system. Whenever possible, *anusvāra*s are spelt out as the appropriate nasals. In other cases, the *anusvāra* sign is transliterated by an *ṁ* not with a subscript but with a superscript dot evoking the Devanagari form of the *anusvāra*. A vocalic *r̥* is marked with a subscript circlet instead of a dot. In this way, subscript dots consistently represent retroflex sounds. When *anusvāra*s stand for nasalisation and not for homorganic nasals, such as in final position in non-Sanskritic words or before nasals in manuscripts, they are marked as nasalisation with a tilde. In the transliteration of Hindi words, the indistinct final sound will be spelt as *a* after clusters of consonants with the exception of nasal-plosive combinations, such as *panth*, *aṅg* etc. If the same phenomenon happens in the middle of long words, the *a* may be spelt out. When Brajbhasha poetry is cited the modern silent *a* is always transliterated since it has a metrical value and is still pronounced in recitation. When, however, individual words are referred to, this *a* is treated as in modern standard Hindi words. Terms borrowed from Sanskrit will also retain the modern silent *a* in transliteration.

Dates in the book, if not indicated otherwise, refer to the Common Era. The *Vikram* Era—marked with the word *Saṁvat*—or other dating of manuscripts and works are indicated only occasionally. The Common Era years are achieved by subtracting 57 years from the *Vikram Saṁvat*, when no Indic month is specified with it.

Introduction

Hindi literature of the eighteenth and nineteenth centuries is a neglected but fascinating field to explore. Traditional Hindi poetry at that time was in its last phase of indigenous development unaffected by western modernity. Court literature was flourishing in smaller and bigger centres and with the mediation of oral transmission and manuscript culture—thriving as never before—transcended the limits of court patronage and reached out to the wide masses of learned people in the villages.[1] This literature was far from being 'frozen' 'waning' or 'decadent' as claimed by Hindi literary historians under the influence of colonialist or nationalist ideas.[2] Its themes and aesthetics expressed, along with an apparent awareness of classical values, a search for new ways of expression influenced by the increasingly marked presence of early modern ideas.

One of the most outstanding Hindi authors of these times was the poet who signed his poems as *Ṭhākur*, 'Lord'. The work of this once popular, but today little-known composer of courtly quatrains demonstrates the active force of creative tradition in Hindi literature in a time that scholars have long denounced as a dark age. Ṭhākur, one of the last Brajbhasha authors before the advent of western modernity, along with Padmākar (1753-1833), his more renowned contemporary, was amongst the favourites of nineteenth-century anthologists. In the twentieth century, Ṭhākur would be known as one of the few representatives of a personal voice in the highly stylised 'Era of Convention', the *Rītikāl*. He came to be celebrated as a 'true love poet' since the expression of personal sentiments was allegedly a driving force in his poetic work and not the illustration of poetic conventions, as considered usual in his times. He often expressed his love for independence and self-assertion through the voice of *gopīs*, the cowherd girls of the Krishna-lore. His poetry usually follows conventional Krishna-themes in Brajbhasha but his style is peculiar to him not simply because of his sporadic use of Bundelkhandi themes, vocabulary and morphology, but rather because of his fondness for proverbs. Anthologists and scholars referred to him as the 'Ṭhākur of the proverbs' *(maslāband* or *muhāvrāvālā Ṭhākur)*.

The importance of Ṭhākur, however, lies not in the fact that he was an innovative poet shifting the emphasis from one aspect of already existing conventions to others but rather in his not being an isolated phenomenon. He is one of the most powerful representatives of the early modern sensibility in Brajbhasha literature. In the expression of individual sentiments, he may well be indebted to Ānandghan (*c.* 1700-1757) while his search for a

[1] In the early 1800s the British army officer T.D. Broughton collected orally transmitted Hindi court poetry by Keśavdās, Dev, Bihārī and others from his sepoys hailing from the villages of Avadh. See I. Bangha, *The First Published Anthology of Hindi Poets: Thomas Duer Broughton's Selections from the Popular Poetry of the Hindoos, 1814*, New Delhi: Mahatma Gandhi International Hindi University and Rainbow Publishers, 2000.

[2] A reevaluation of Hindi court poetry in the light of post-colonial research is A. Busch, *Poetry of Kings: the Classical Hindi Literature of Mughal India,* New York: Oxford University Press, 2011. On nationalist attitudes towards court poetry see the subchapter "*Rīti* literature and its discontents" (pp. 3-6) and the chapter "The Fate of *Rīti* Literature in Colonial India' (pp. 202-39).

simple style distances him from the most celebrated poets of the early eighteenth century and puts him close to Padmākar. Moreover, Ṭhākur's poetry also demonstrates innovations usually associated with modern poets. He displays political contextualisation of the Krishna myth, as did Hariaudh in the first modern Hindi *mahākāvya*, the *Priy-pravās* (1914). He shows an increased sense of individuality so closely connected to the *Chāyāvād* poets of the 1920s and 1930s. His search for simple post-classicist style became a defining feature of poetry before the advent of colonial modernity.

The poetic output that can be reliably claimed to be his consists of three hundred and thirty quatrains (*ghanākṣarī kavitta*s and *savaiyā*s), referred to in Hindi generally as *kabitta*s, the most popular forms of Hindi court poetry. These quatrains are present in innumerable nineteenth-century anthologies—both handwritten and lithographed. His popularity in that century may well suggest that his move away from the ornamented Brajbhasha of Ānandghan and Dev (1673-1767) towards simplicity as well as his poetic self-assertion prepared the aesthetic sensibilities of Hindi audiences and readers for the acceptance of the more straightforward style and the more individualistic ideas of western literature. Ṭhākur's example shows that the appearance of these western ideas was not a radically new phenomenon in an otherwise dead literary tradition but rather the confirmation of already existing developments.

According to a generally held view, the largely normative and derivative Hindi poetry of the eighteenth century would only be revitalised by western influence from the middle of the nineteenth century onwards. A closer study of Ṭhākur's period can contribute to our better understanding of the transition from the early modern period to modernity.

The Poet and His Times

BUNDELKHAND AT THE TURN OF THE NINETEENTH CENTURY

There is a consensus in legends and modern scholarship that Ṭhākur lived in eastern Bundelkhand around the turn of nineteenth century. The ruling elite of this region, the Bundelas, originally a semi-pastoral and later a landholding clan that specialised as military employers, claimed Rajput status but were not recognised as such by the Rajputs of Rajasthan, the "Rajputs of the great tradition". Having acquired a foothold in the thirteenth century in what later became Bundelkhand, they served the Mughal Empire by recruiting soldiers in north India and leading them into war for the Mughals until the mid-eighteenth century.[1]

Eastern Bundelkhand, a large territory of what is today northern Madhya Pradesh, in the late eighteenth and early nineteenth centuries consisted of several small princely states ruled mostly by Bundela overlords. These rulers were the descendants of Chatrasāl (1649-1731), a chieftain originally in the service of the Mughals who after a revolt against his imperial employers became the overlord of Bundelkhand. Yet, conforming to the custom of the early eighteenth century, he never completely withdrew from the empire and accepted *mansabs* and titles.[2] Chatrasāl ruled from Panna and although in 1707 he founded his own capital, Chatarpur, Panna remained the symbolic centre of the Bundelas. Because of their resistance to the Mughals Chatrasāl and his followers were called *daṅgāhī* or 'revolting' Bundelas[3] as opposed to the *bādśāhī* or 'royalist' Bundelas of western Bundelkhand, who continued to serve the languishing empire.

The history of Bundelkhand became particularly troubled after Chatrasāl's death, when his empire fragmented. The eighteenth century was a time of the constant emergence and dissolution of political entities, fragile alliances, intrigue, small princely states, petty chieftains and adventurers, including a warlord of ascetics with an army of twenty thousand, *gosāīṁ* Anūpgiri, alias Himmat Bahādur.

Family lore connects Ṭhākur with princely centres in eastern Bundelkhand, namely Panna, Banda, Jaitpur and Bijawar. After Chatrasāl's death in 1731 the largest part of his kingdom, including his capital town Panna, was given to his eldest son, Hirde Śāh. One of Chatrasāl's temporary capitals, Jaitpur, fell to his third son, Jagat Rāj (d. 1757), who may have earlier been the founder of the town and from whom it seems to have taken its name.[4] In 1769, another successor state came into being. Bijawar, which until that time was part of the

[1] D.H.A. Kolff, *Naukar, Rajput and Sepoy: The Ethnohistory of the Military Labour Market in Hindustan, 1450-1850,* Cambridge: Cambridge University Press, 1990, p. 120.

[2] Ibid., pp. 143-4.

[3] *Imperial Gazetteer of India: Central India,* Calcutta: Superintendent of Government Printing, 1908, p. 365.

[4] W.W. Hunter, *Imperial Gazetteer of India (Indore to Kardang),* 2nd edn., vol. 7, London: Trübner & Co., 1886, p. 71.

Jaitpur State, was given to an illegitimate son of Jagat Rāj, Bīr Siṁh Dev, who extended his original holdings until he fell against Anūpgiri in 1793.[5]

This *gosāīṁ* warlord, Anūpgiri (*c.* 1734-1804), also known by his title Himmat Bahādur, who established himself in Bundelkhand in 1792 by defeating the Bundela chieftain Arjun Siṁh, was one of the most powerful figures towards the end of the eighteenth century.[6] In the words of the historian William R. Pinch,

> The more one examines the succession of events that marked Mughal (and Maratha) decline in the late eighteenth century, and the concomitant rise of British power, the more one sees the outline of Himmat Bahadur in the background. On several occasions he emerges into the light. He fought on the side of the Mughal emperor and the Afghans against the Marathas at Panipat in 1761; he was present with the Awadhi and Mughal forces against British forces at Buxar in 1764, and helped Shuja ud-Daula escape after his defeat; he was instrumental in the downfall of Bharatpur and the rise of Najaf Khan, the Persian adventurer, at Delhi in the 1770s; he engineered Mahadji Shinde's foray into Delhi politics in the 1780s; he was the force behind Ali Bahadur's conquest of Bundelkhand in the name of the peshwa in the 1790s. His last act, at the end of his life in 1803, was to enable the Maratha defeat at the hands of the British in Bundelkhand and the Doab and, thereby, the British capture of Delhi, an event that catapulted the Hon'ble Company into the role of paramount power in southern Asia—and ultimately the world.[7]

After the death of Himmat Bahādur the British entered Bundelkhand in 1804, and the Bundela principalities continued their existence as semi-independent princely states under British protectorate.

Kiśor Siṁh was the nominal ruler of the Panna State from 1798 though he was in exile. The British reinstated him with *sanad*s granted in 1807 and 1811 and then he ruled until 1840. Himmat Bahādur restored Bijawar to Kesrī Siṁh, the son of Bīr Siṁh, granting him a *sanad* in 1802. On the accession of the British to power, Kesrī Siṁh professed his allegiance. After his death, a dispute followed and a *sanad* was granted to his son Ratan Siṁh in 1811.[8] In the State of Jaitpur after the death of Gaj Siṁh the British gave a *sanad* in 1812 to Kesrī Siṁh, who was followed by Parīkṣit (Parichat).[9] In 1842 when Parīkṣit revolted against the Company, the British captured him and his territory reverted to them.[10]

ṬHĀKUR'S LIFE IN ANECDOTES AND POEMS

Apart from the poems preserved in the anthologies, no early written document about Ṭhākur has come to light. We have, however, at our disposal a stock of family lore and anecdotes contextualising some quatrains preserved by his descendants and others. It is the poems

[5] *Imperial Gazetteer of India: Central India,* p. 380.

[6] On Anūpgiri see W. Pinch, 'Who was Himmat Bahādur? Gosains, Rajputs and the British in Bundelkhand ca. 1800'. *The Indian Economic and Social History Review*, vol. 35, no. 3, 1998, pp. 293-335 and W. Pinch, *Warrior ascetics and Indian empires,* New York: Cambridge University Press, 2006. The battle at Ajaygarh took place on 18 April 1792. See B.R. Andhare, *Bundelkhand under the Marathas, 1720-1818 A.D : A study of Maratha-Bundela relations,* Nagpur: Vishwa Bharati Prakashan, 1984, p. 109.

[7] Pinch, *Warrior Ascetics and Indian Empires*, p. 4.

[8] *Imperial Gazetteer of India: Central India*, p. 380.

[9] Divan Pratipal Singh: *Bundelkaṇḍ kā itihās*, pp. 387-8. See G.P. 'Barsainya', 'Bundelkhaṇḍī kavi ṭhākur (ṭhākurdās kāyastha) aur unkā kāvya', *Bundelī basant*, 2002, p. 26.

[10] Hunter, *Imperial Gazetteer of India: Indore to Kardang,* p. 71.

and the anecdotes that serve as a basis for positioning Ṭhākur within north Indian history.

As has been mentioned, family lore links Ṭhākur to the political setting of the small princely centres of Jaitpur, Bijawar, Panna and Banda. Connection with several minor courts points towards the life-style of court poets, who often needed to move from one court to another one. Although the idea of a troubled Bundelkhand prior to the British conquest as well as the image of a court poet constantly changing patrons fit well into the colonial conception of Indian history, it should not be forgotten that the mere presence of court poets indicates that there were also peaceful and creative periods between military confrontations.

The greater part of the family lore on Ṭhākur was collected in the 1920s or earlier by Lala Bhagvandin, a professor at Banaras Hindu University, who was one of the most active Hindi scholars of his time.[11] In Bijawar with the help of the local headmaster, Lala Deviprasad, Bhagvandin met people who professed to be Ṭhākur's descendants, including a relative called Lala Harsevak and collected his material from them.[12] Since Bhagvandin does not mention any direct connection between the family and the poems, such as manuscripts or documents, there might always be some doubt that external material merged into his anecdotal evidence. Notwithstanding the exaggerations of early family history and the idealising traits in Ṭhākur's memory, it would be very hard to discard his entire evidence for Ṭhākur's life as ahistorical. This is not only because of the richness of the oral material he collected in a place where Ṭhākur claimed to have worked and the lack of such material elsewhere but also because by Bhagvandin's time Ṭhākur was a half forgotten figure of the literature of Bundelkhand.[13] Claiming any connection with him did not, therefore, involve any special increase in prestige. Moreover, family lore presents a fairly consistent geography and chronology with regards to the life of Ṭhākur.

The word *ṭhākura,* 'lord', tends to refer to members of the Bundela clan.[14] However, the family affirmed that the poet, originally called Ṭhākurdās, was a Kayastha from a family with roots in the village of Kakori in the district of Lucknow that claimed to have taken to soldery generations before Ṭhākur. His grandfather, Lālā Khaḍgarāy, is with some chronological inconsistency, claimed to have been a *mansabdār* of a fabulous 60,000 in Agra at the time of Emperor Akbar and arranged a lavish wedding for his son Gulābrāy with the daughter of a nobleman called Rāv Rājā from Orcha. The wedding was attended by 12,000 imperial horsemen. Their son, Ṭhākurdās, was born in Orcha in 1756. Since many relatives from Kakori settled down in eastern Bundelkhand, in the towns of Jaitpur and

[11] L. Bhagvandin, *Ṭhākur ṭhasak,* Benares: Sāhitya Sevak Kāryālay, 1924, 'Ṭhākur kavi kā jīvancarit' pp. 5-18. His earlier research on the poet's life published under the title 'Ṭhākur kavi kā jīvancarit' in the *Nāgarīpracāriṇī Patrikā,* Benares around 1914 is referred to in ibid. 'Vaktavya', p. 3.

[12] Ibid. 'Ṭhākur kavi kā jīvancarit', p. 8.

[13] His name and poetry is, for example, missing from the list of 385 representative Bundelkhandi poets given by Divan Pratipal Simh in his *Bundelkanḍ kā itihās* (pp. 256-310) although Ṭhākur's alleged son Daryāv Siṁh (Nr. 322) and grandson Śaṅkar Prasād (Nr. 327) are mentioned (see 'Barsainya', 'Bundelkhaṇḍī kavi ṭhākur', p. 26). It is also absent from the first version of a representative anthology of poets from Bundelkhand published around the years of Bhagvandin's research. See G.D. 'Shankar', *Bundel-vaibhav athavā bundelkhanḍ ke hindī kaviyõ kā sāṅgopāṅg itihās (sacitra aur saṭippaṇ)* 3 vols. vol. 1-2, Agra: Śānti Pres, 1935. However, under the influence of Bhagvandin's *Ṭhākur ṭhasak,* the poet made his way into the later third volume (pp. 345-7).

[14] *Imperial Gazetteer of India: Central India,* pp. 189, 373.

Bijawar, Ṭhākur also took up service at the court of Kesrī Siṁh in Jaitpur who appointed him as his court poet and assigned him the revenue from a village in Karaiya Pargana.[15] Ṭhākur also attended the court at Bijawar, since he had relatives settled in that town. At that time the ruler of Bijawar, also called Kesrī Siṁh, assigned him the revenue of a village called Rora. At a time of regency after the demise of Kesrī Siṁh of Jaitpur, Ṭhākur settled down in Bijawar. When, however, the new ruler in Jaitpur, Parīkṣit, reached adulthood, he called Ṭhākur back to his court and it was there that Ṭhākur became a famous poet. Parīkṣit is also remembered as a generous patron of poetry by his other poet-minister, Navaleś, who in one of his thirty-two compositions described the ruler's journey to Mathura.[16] Parīkṣit gave Ṭhākur the revenue of a village and bestowed upon him occasional donations. The now famous poet was invited to various courts, including that of Himmat Bahādur in Banda, who made him engage in contests with his own court poet Padmākar. According to an anecdote collected by Bhagvandin, Padmākar accused Ṭhākur of writing light poetry. In response Ṭhākur said that it was precisely why his poetry was flying all around.

Ṭhākur died around 1823. His son, Daryāv Siṁh, also wrote poetry under the pen-name 'Catur'. Daryāv Siṁh's daughter-in-law as well as several descendants of Khaḍgarāy were still alive in Bijawar at the time of Bhagvandin's visit. The Benares scholar does not mention any relatives of Ṭhākur in Jaitpur, the other centre to which the poet was closely linked since he probably did not visit that place. Some seventy years after Bhagvandin, Ganga Prasad 'Barsainya' found that the memory of the poet was hardly alive in Bijawar or in Jaitpur.[17]

A story recorded in the *Śivsiṁh Saroj* and the other anecdotes collected by Bhagvandin relate Ṭhākur to the Bundelkhand of the late eighteenth and early nineteenth centuries. Already in 1878, Śivsiṁh Seṅgar mentioned Ṭhākur's connection with Himmat Bahādur.[18] Śivsiṁh referred to an unnamed Bundelkhandi poet as the source of the story of how Ṭhākur received a reward from Himmat Bahādur by dissuading the disgruntled Bundelas assembled in Chatarpur from attempting to kill the warlord and exhorting them to accept the situation. The vehicle for this political action was a quatrain ostensibly about the distress of the cowherdesses abandoned by Krishna and denigrated by gossipers,

Now there is nothing left to say or to hear; don't be troubled by good or bad.
We must resign ourselves to remain always according to his wishes.
Ṭhākur says, this is the counsel to follow in order to see the Dear Child :
Living amongst these troublemakers, my friends, we should keep aloof from the bad times.[19] (Ś136)

Family lore did not preserve the memory of Ṭhākur's good relationship with the warlord. It rather related how the poet saved maharaja Parīkṣit from the trap of Himmat Bahādur in Banda by recounting the following *savaiyā*,

kaise sucitta bhae nikasau bihā̃sau bilasau hari dai galabā̃hī|

[15]The pargana of Karaia was the fourth isolated pargana of the state. *Ibid.*, p. 380.

[16]Andhare, *Bundelkhand under the Marathas, 1720-1818 A.D.: A study of Maratha-Bundela relations*, p. 164. According to Andhare the above work was to be published by Babulal Goswami.

[17]'Barsainya', 'Bundelkhaṇḍī kavi ṭhākur', p. 26.

[18]K. Gupta, *Saroj sarvekṣaṇ*, Allahabad: Hindustānī Ekeḍemī, 1967, p. 328.

[19]The word *vīra* translated as 'my friends' originally means 'hero(es)' and thus fits the context of the story associated with this poem.

ye chala-chidrana kī batiyā̃ chalatī china eka gharī pala mā̃hī̃|
ṭhākura, ve juri eka bhaī̃, racihaī̃ parapañca kachū braja mā̃hī̃|
hāla cavāina kau dahucāla, so, lāla, tumhaī̃ yā dikhāta kai nā̃hī̃|| cf. Ś139||[20]

How carelessly you set off, laugh and enjoy yourself, putting your arm on Hari's shoulder!
This fraudulent speech will deceive you in the twinkling of a moment.
Ṭhākur says, they have gathered and are about to make some plot in Braj.
My Dear Child, can you see the current wicked conduct of the slanderers or not?

The story here reveals that listeners did not always easily understand covert messages. In this case, the prince missed the meaning and Ṭhākur had to recite another quatrain to make his point clear.

nija mantra na aurana sõ kahane, apane cita coja bicārane hai|
puni neka ko neka, laṭo ko laṭo, yaha rīti sadā ura dhārane hai|
kaha ṭhākura, pyāre sujāna sunau, mana kī urajhī nirabārane hai|
cahū̃ ora se caucāda cāra uṭho, so bicāra ke, yāra, sā̃bhārane hai|| cf. Ś151||

You should not tell your own mantra to others but meditate on its wonder in your mind.
You should call good good and bad bad. This rule should always be born in your inner self.
Ṭhākur says, listen my dear connoisseur, remove the confusion from your heart.
Slander and slur arose all around, keep it in mind, my friend, and be careful.

Following this event Himmat Bahādur summoned Ṭhākur, whom he valued as a poet, and threatened him with jail. On this occasion, Ṭhākur recited a *kavitta*,

veī nara niranaya nidāna mẽ sarāhe jāta,
sukhana aghāta, pyālā prema ko piye rahaī̃|
hari rasa candana caḍhāya aṅga aṅgana maī̃
nīti ko tilaka bẽdī jasa kī diye rahaī̃|
ṭhākura kahata, mañju kañja tẽ mṛdula mana,
mohanī sarūpa dhāre, himmata hiye rahaī̃|
bhẽṭa bhae samaye-kusamaye, acāhe-cāhe
ora laū̃ nibāhaī̃, ā̃khaī̃ eka sī kiye rahaī̃|| cf. N28||

Those men are eventually praised and sated with happiness who keep drinking from the cup of love,
Who always apply the sandalwood of God's flavour on their every limb and put on the sectarian mark of good conduct and the bindi *of fame.*
Ṭhākur says, their minds are gentler than a delicate lotus; they hold in them the form of the Enchanter and keep courage [himmat] *in their heart.*
Whether they meet one at appropriate or inappropriate time, whether they wanted it or not, they carry out their ideas and view the world consistently.

[20]The text of the following contextualised poems is quoted as cited by Bhagavandin, *Ṭhākur ṭhasak*, pp. 'Ṭhākur kavi kā jīvancarit', pp. 2-23. However, if the Hindi version corresponds to the established text of my edition then the original is not given.

When Himmat Bahādur was not pacified by this reminder of equanimity Ṭhākur unsheathed his sword and uttered the following poem,

sevaka sipāhī hama una rajapūtana ke
dāna yuddha juribe mẽ neku je na murake|
nīti denavāre haĩ mahī ke mahipālana kaũ,
kavi unahĩ ke je sanehī sā̃ce ura ke|
ṭhākura kahata, hama bairī bevakūphana ke,
jālima damāda haĩ adāniyā̃ sasura ke|
cojana ke cora rasa-maujana ke pātasāha
ṭhākura kahāvata pai cākara catura ke|| cf. N25||

I'm the servant and soldier of Rajputs who do not turn the least away from gifts and battles.
I give prudent counsel to the kings of the earth; I'm the poet of the true-hearted lovers.
Ṭhākur says, I am the enemy of the stupid; the cruel son-in-law of the miserly father-in-law.
I'm the thief of wonders and the emperor of the surges of emotion; called Lord but I'm the servant of the intelligent.

At these words Himmat Bahādur changed his attitude and said that he only wanted to see whether Ṭhākur was just a poet or he also had the courage of his ancestors. Ṭhākur answered that "Courage *(himmat)* has always been devoting itself to me in an unparalleled *(anūp)* way. How would my courage fall *(gir)* away today?" Himmat Bahādur, alias Anūpgiri, was delighted by this clever word play on his names and, consoling the poet with a huge donation, allowed him to take leave.

In another setting, two *savaiyā*s were composed on the quandary of the forsaken *gopī*s and allegedly recited at the court of Kiśorī Siṁh of Panna, lamenting a state of affairs that had changed for the worse,

cāla na vā, caracā na vā cāturī vā, rasa rīti na prīti ko ḍhaura hai|
sā̃ca ghaṭo, baḍho jhū̃ṭha jahāna maĩ, lobha ke lāne jahā̃ tahā̃ daura hai|
ṭhākura, veī gopāla, vahī hama, vohī cabāva raho ika ṭhaura hai;
mereī dekhata, merī bhaṭū, sigaro braja hvai gayau aura ko aura hai|| cf. Ś109||

Manners are no longer the same; no talk is the same, no sharpness, not the same emotional manner and flow of love.
Truth decreased and falsity increased in the world—people run everywhere out of their greed.
The lord is the same, the Cowherd is the same, I am the same—there is still the same slander going on.
The whole Braj has changed for the worse, my sister, in front of my very eyes.

ve parabīna bicacchana loga bane pai samai kachu āna bhayo, rī|
cīkhe savāda jahāṁ ati mīṭhe so sīkhe svabhāva nayeī naye, rī|
ṭhākura, kauna sõ kā kahiye aba, o cita cāhave ve samaye, rī|
ve dina, ve sukha, vaise uchāha so, ve saba, bīra, herāya gaye, rī|| cf. Ś65||

He has turned clever and sagacious and the time has become somewhat different.
On tasting, he tastes very sweet but he's learnt to always change his nature.

Ṭhākur says, can I say anything to anyone now? That mind and that affection were at those times.
Those days, that happiness, such enthusiasm—all this, my companion, has been lost.

When Kiśorī Siṁh's youngest wife was so modest that she never lifted her veil even in front of her husband Ṭhākur gave the following *savaiyā* to the ruler to recite it to her when they were together,

yaũ tarasāibo kaune bado, mana tau mili go pai milai jala jaiso|
kauna durāva raho unasaũ, jinake saṅga sātha karau sukha aiso|
ṭhākura, yā niradhāra sunau, tumhaĩ kauna subhāva paro hai anaiso|
prānapiyā ghaṭa mẽ basi kai hãsi kai phira ghũghaṭa ghālibo kaiso|| cf. Ś103||

To whom did you make a vow to torment in this way? After all, your mind is united with him like water in milk.
What concealment remains from the one in whose company you enjoy such bliss?
Ṭhākur says, listen carefully, how did you acquire this undesirable behaviour?
Dear as my life, when you live in my heart why do you smile at me and yet keep your veil?

Upon hearing this quatrain, the wife gave up her habit of extreme shyness and honoured Ṭhākur with a gift. She became so devoted to her husband that when Kiśorī Siṁh died, she committed sati. Her memorial can still be seen in Panna.

In Bijawar, the poet became infatuated with a woman called Sujān. Whenever he met her in the streets, he composed a poem on her beauty and recited it aloud so that she could hear it. She did not reject his courting and listened to the poems with delight. When she fell ill and he was not able to see her for four days, he composed the following poem and recited it in the lane behind her house,

gati merī yahī nisavāsara hai, cita terī galīna ke gāhane hai|
cita kīnhaũ kaṭhora kahā itano, aba tohi nahī̃ yaha cāhane hai|
kavi ṭhākura, neku nahī̃ darasī, kapaṭīna ko kāha sarāhane hai||
mana bhāvai sujāna soī kariyau, hamaĩ neha ko nāto nibāhane hai|| cf. Ś116||

It is my condition day and night that my mind wanders in your lanes.
Why did you harden your mind so much? It is now not your wish either.
The poet Ṭhākur says, you haven't shown yourself to me; what good is it to be praised by deceivers?
Do, Sujān, what you please – I will fulfil my love's commitment.

Ṭhākur's affectionate poem had its effect and Sujān regained her health overnight. When people reported his illicit love for Sujān to the king, Ṭhākur asserted that he was an admirer of her beauty, nothing more. The king still confined him in his palace for a week, during which period the wells of Sujān's neighbourhood dried up and water returned to them only when the ruler released Ṭhākur. The poet, however, was angry and left Bijawar, never to return. After this incident, Sujān never put on any ornament.

According to another story, King Parīkṣit of Jaitpur used to watch people passing by his palace. His entourage noticed a modest *baniyā* lady who used to pass by veiled and with head bent down. A courtier challenged Ṭhākur to prompt the lady by a poem to raise her eyes to her onlookers. He composed the following quatrain,

Whenever I see you, I say to myself that you should keep increasing your love.
Radiant lady, give up your worry and enjoy delight—why go around with wounded pride?
Ṭhākur says, your Beautiful Boy is hiding somewhere among your co-wives—gain back your married bliss.
Appear before him and make him happy, let separation pass, look at him, look at him!
(Ś96)

The woman, who was herself a poet, was delighted and gave one of her golden bangles to Ṭhākur. The ruler in turn gave some gifts to the poetess.

The poet composed the following *kavitta* when he fell seriously ill. With the help of medication from the royal doctor and by repeatedly reciting this *kavitta* he was cured within a week,

rāma mere paṇḍita akhaṇḍita sudina sodhaĩ,
rāma mere guru japa mere rāma nāma haĩ|
rāma rāma gāvatahī rāma rāma dhyāvatahī
rāma rāma socata kaṭata āṭhau jāma haĩ|
ṭhākura kahata, sā̃cī āsa mohi rāmahī kī
rāmahī se kāma dhana dhāma mere rāma haĩ|
rāma mere baida bisarāma mero rāma sā̃co
rāma merī auṣadhi jatana mere rāma haĩ|| cf. B12||

Ram is my pandit who finds the entirely auspicious day for the medicine; Ram is my guru and I keep repeating the name of Ram.
I pass every hour of the day by singing Ram, by meditating on Ram and by thinking on Ram.
Ṭhākur says, I have true hope only for Ram, my only concern is Ram and my wealth and home is Ram.
Ram is my doctor and my true rest is Ram; Ram is my medicine and my efforts are for Ram.

Some of the above stories show Ṭhākur's moderately liberal attitude towards women. This is, however, contradicted by the contextualising story in which he rebuked a young wife who on her return to her father's house kept going around in the neighbourhood visiting friends,

laharaĩ uṭhaĩ aṅga umaṅgana kī, mada jobana ke laharāti phirai|
baḍarī akhiyāna citai tirīche, cita logana ke laharāti phirai|
kaha ṭhākura, hai ati opa kharī nirakhe na thirai, thaharāti phirai|
sira oḍhe uḍhonī, kase chatiyā̃, phariyā pahare phaharāti phirai||cf. Ś13||

Waves of enthusiasm rise on her body and she goes around radiating her intoxication of youth.
She looks sideways with her big eyes and she goes around exciting people.
Ṭhākur says, she has great lustre and she does not stop when observed, she goes around swaying.
Her head covered with her shawl, her breasts tight in her bodice she goes around flapping the smaller shawl she wears.

Apart from these contextualising stories, there is also a quatrain about Ṭhākur ostensibly by a certain Muslim poetess Śāhzādī who out of love for Ṭhākur becomes Hindu.[21]

allā, bisamillā, rahamā̃na o rahīma choṛa
pīra vo sahīdõ kī caracā na calāū̃gī|
sūtanā utāra, paira ghāgharõ ghumāvadāra,
phariā ko phāra sīsa cūnarī uṛāū̃gī|
kahata śāhajādī ṭhākura kabi paija kara
phaijābāda choṛa mẽ bṛndāvana jāū̃gī|
rādhe mahārānī jū kī bāndī banū̃gī jāya,
turakinī kahāya phera gopikā kahāū̃gī||

I will leave Allah, Bismillah, Rahman and Rahim behind and won't engage in talks of pirs and shahids.
Taking off my trousers I will put on a skirt in which spinning around is easy; I will tear my small, girl's skirt and cover my head with dyed, red cūnrī.
Śāhzādī says: I'll make a vow for the poet Ṭhākur and leaving Faizabad go to Vrindaban.
There, I will become the slave of Queen Radha—once known as Muslim woman now I will be called a gopī.

Composed in a mixture of Braj and Khari Boli, evoking Urdu, this *kavitta* alludes to (or maybe ridicules) Ṭhākur's implied involvement with Muslims, of which no trace is preserved in the legends. This latent tension towards Islamic culture can also be perceived from the transmission history of some quatrains. Scribes felt uneasy about *savaiyā*s Ś100 and Ś116 both addressing the beloved as *sujān*, a word with Persianate resonance used frequently by Ānandghan in the first half of the eighteenth century.[22]

THE MANY ṬHĀKURS

The name Ṭhākur 'Lord' is a common name especially among Rajputs, and Ṭhākurdās can be a name used by people belonging to a variety of castes. The existence of several poets who called themselves Ṭhākur is already noted in the anthology *Sudhāsar*, composed in 1838.[23] At the end of this massive compilation its compiler, the poet Navīn, gave a list of various poets who shared names. He stated that there were three Ṭhākurs, an old one *(prācīn)*, one who used proverbs *(maslāband)* and a Ṭhākurdās Brahman from Jhansi.[24]

Literary histories and manuscripts also preserve the memory of several other poets called Ṭhākur but none of them can be credited reasonably with writing quatrains.

A Brahmin Ṭhākur who claimed to have preceded our author lived not in Bundelkhand but in Asni near Benares. The earliest printed reference to him is in the *Śivsiṁh Saroj*, which not only gives his *floruit* as 1643 but also tells a story that links him to Himmat

[21]This poem is numbered as 42 on pages 7-8 in a handwritten book in Chatarpur in the private collection of Mr. Raghubir Singh. The book, called *Dohõ kī pustak*, includes a few poems by Ṭhākur.

[22]See the chapter on *Rītimukta* poetry below as well as the paragraph on the variants of Ś100 on p. 55.

[23]About this anthology, see below, pp. 60-9.

[24]Manuscripts S_1 f. 449v, S_3 f. 294v(83v), S_6 f. 416v, S_7 f. 284v. (S_1 does not separate the first two Ṭhākurs with a *virām* sign and leaves the impression as if there had been only two.)

Bahādur.[25] Relying on the *Saroj,* Grierson in his account of 'the poet Ṭhākur the elder' also gives his *floruit* as 1643 and mentions that according to one account he was a bard of the village Asni in the Fatehpur district and lived about the time of Muhammad Śāh (r. 1719-48), and according to another legend he was a *kāyastha* from Bundelkhand and was present at the time of Himmat Bahādur.[26] In another chapter Grierson mentioned one other Ṭhākur, whose *floruit* he assumed was 1743 but did not give any hint that he may be identical with the one from Asni.[27] Grierson did not indicate any source for the information on either of these early Ṭhākurs. Correcting the accounts of the *Saroj* and of Grierson, twentieth-century Hindi scholars, such as Lala Bhagvandin and Ramchand Shukla, accepted the existence of only one 'old' Ṭhākur, who lived in Asni, and attributed several quatrains to him. Bhagvandin claimed that his literary output was 'bound by conventions and confined within themes of the classification of heroines *(nāyikā-bheda)*, figures of sound and sense *(alaṅkāra)*, head-to-toe descriptions *(nakha-śikha varṇana)* and the depiction of the six seasons *(ṣaḍ-ṛtu varṇana)*', and made efforts to sort out which quatrain might have belonged to which Ṭhākur.[28]

The case was further complicated by the presence of yet another Ṭhākur, who was also a Brahmin Bhāṭ from Asni. The *Vāgvilās granth,* a book written by Kṛṣṇa, the nephew of this Ṭhākur's grandson, Sevak, tells us that the family was originally a family of priests (Miśra). An ancestor of Ṭhākur, however, composed and recited poetry for a royal wedding procession and accepted remuneration for it. Since then the family has been considered to be bards (Bhāṭ).[29] This Ṭhākur in 1804 (*Saṁvat* 1861) composed the *Satsaiyā varanārtha,* a commentary to the *Satsaī* of Bihārī, apparently in Benares.[30]

sasi rasa sidhi sasi sāla guru terasi badī asāḍha|
racaũ jathāmati maĩ tilaka āsaya sahita agāḍha|| 3||[31]

In the year of (one) Moon, (six) rasas, (eight) magical powers and (one) Moon, on Thursday, the 13th of the dark fortnight of the month of Āṣāṛh;
I am composing this ornament (commentary) to the best of my judgement under generous patronage.

Although verse 13 mentions a ruler, possibly Udit Narayan Singh of Benares (r. 1795-1835), this monumental work of 9700 verses is claimed to have been written under the patronage of a certain Bābū Devakīnandan of Benares and is often referred to as the *Devakīnandan* commentary.

[25] Gupta, *Saroj sarvekṣaṇ,* p. 328.

[26] G.A. Grierson, *The modern vernacular literature of Hindustan,* Calcutta: Asiatic Society, 1889, p. 71 (Nr. 173).

[27] Ibid. p. 103 (Nr. 434).

[28] Cf. Bhagvandin, *Ṭhākur ṭhasak,* 'Ṭhākur kavi kā jīvancarit' p. 1 and C. Mishra, ed. *Ṭhākur granthāvalī,* Varanasi: Nāgarīpracāriṇī Sabhā, 1973, 'Saṁkṣipt jīvanvṛtt' p. 1.

[29] S. Mathur, *Kavi ṭhākur aur unkā kāvya,* New Delhi: Young Asia Publications, 1969, p. 2.

[30] S. Das, *Annual Report on the Search for Hindi Manuscripts for the Year 1904,* Allahabad: United Provinces Government Press, 1907; reprint, Varanasi: Nāgarīpracāriṇī Sabhā, 1995, p. 22 (04-18) gives a description of a manuscript of this name, which was copied in *Saṁvat* 1891 (AD 1834) and in 1904 was deposited at the Library of the Maharaja of Benares.

[31] Ibid., p. 22.

putra sukavi riṣinātha ko haũ hai ṭhākura nāma|
asanī vāsī maĩ kahyau yā lakhi nṛpa guṇa dhāma|| 13||
saba jānata yaka īśvarai saba saba jānata hai na|
karata vinai līјau banai sukavi su kahata banai na|| 14||
banai su rādhā hari kṛpā yaha nihacai jiya jāna|
jo na banai so jānie nija mati anumāna|| 15||[32]

Named Ṭhākur, I am the son of the fine poet Riṣināth;
I am called "the one living in Asni". The king, abode of virtues, seeing that
God alone knows everything, people do not know all,
entreated me to make sense of this, since what the Poet (Bihārī) says is not clear.
Whatever is elucidated is done by the grace of Radha and Krishna ; know this with certainty in your heart;
If something does not make sense, take it as the conjecture of my mind.

Śivsiṁh Seṅgar, the author of the *Śivsiṁh Saroj* worked under the false impression that one of his sources, the '*Kālidās-hazārā*' was a collection from the eighteenth century and consequently assigned early dates to poets figuring in this *Hazārā.* Since quatrains by Ṭhākur were included into this anthology and at the same time Śivsiṁh was aware of a Bundelkhandi Ṭhākur present at the time of Himmat Bahādur in the late eighteenth century, he had to propose the idea of two different authors of quatrains called Ṭhākur: an early one from Asni and a later one from Bundelkhand. Kishorilal Gupta in his *Saroj Sarvekṣan* demonstrated that the '*Kālidās-hazārā*' was in fact a nineteenth-century compilation and, therefore, there are no two Ṭhākurs of Asni.[33]

Manuscript material does not support the partition of Ṭhākur's quatrain-corpus either and in most of the cases there is no ambiguity in deciding what belongs to the poetic oeuvre of our Ṭhākur and what does not.

There is no early mention that the author of the *Devakīnandan* commentary ever composed independent quatrains. Moreover, if there had been two poets of the same name, writing in the same genre, distant neither in time nor in space, it would have been easy to refer to at least one of them with an epithet to distinguish him from the other. Actually, this was the case with the *Sudhāsar* Ṭhākurs. With the exception of the *Sudhāsar* no early anthology attributes *kabittas* to multiple Ṭhākurs. Although the compiler Navīn was aware of an earlier poet called Ṭhākur, no quatrain was assigned to him in the anthology unless he is identical with the Ṭhākurdās credited with a *savaiyā* (U6) in the earliest version of the anthology (S_1) (and in manuscript S_5). This is suggested by the fact that Ṭhākurdās is not mentioned separately in Navīn's list of poets. However, this Ṭhākurdās might be identical with Navīn's third Ṭhākur to whom the compiler attributed two quatrains (eleventh and twelfth in the *Māninī* section) with the signature 'Brajbhūṣan' (S_1 ff. 92v-93r; S_7 ff. 64r [642], 148r [1409]). This Ṭhākur was introduced as *Ṭhākurdās brāhman sãjhīvāre* (or *jhāṁsīvāre*), Ṭhākurdās of Sanjhi (or of Jhansi). While in his case the poetic signature clearly indicates different authorship, it still remains unclear who the author of U6 was. The quatrain does not bear Ṭhākur's signature although later manuscripts (S_3 S_4 S_5) introduce it as a poem by Ṭhākur. The distinctive style—for instance, the sharp words of the cowherd women and the use of

[32]Ibid., p. 22.
[33]Gupta, *Saroj sarvekṣaṇ*, pp. 106, 328.

a strong idiom in the last line—would support this attribution. Also suggestive are select words and concepts recurring in the other quatrains of the Bundelkhandi Ṭhākur, such as *neha kī nīti, gaṁvār-, kapaṭ-, ḍhīṭh-*. Furthermore, Ṭhākurdās is the proposed full name of the Bundelkhandi poet.

There are several so far unpublished poets mentioned in manuscript searches who signed their work as Ṭhākur but none of them seem to have produced quatrains. One Ṭhākur wrote an epic poem based on the Mahabharata, the *Karnārjunī.*

sārada māratаï sapana dekhāvā| gaurīputra janu parabata pāvā|
mai ṭhākura puchata hau tohī| bhāratha kathā sunāvahu mohī|| 2||

sārada mātā ganapati dui mīlī kīnha pasāva|
ṭhākura budhī punīta ati bhāratha kathā sunāva|| 3||

Mother Sarasvati appeared to me in a dream and I received mountain-like Ganesha—
'I am asking you, Ṭhākur, to recite me the story of the Mahabharata.'
Both mother Sarasvati and Ganesha made this suggestion—
'Ṭhākur, recite the story of the Mahabharata with very pure mind.'

The only available manuscript of this work was copied in 1796 in a place called *Dhavanharā.*[34] A description of this *kaithī* manuscript was published in Khoj 41-89 and the compiler of the report suggested that its author may be identical with Ṭhākur of Asni.

Another Ṭhākur composed *pads* and signed his poems either as Ṭhākur or as Ṭhākurdās.[35] Two pads by Ṭhākurdās appear at the end of the text edition section of this volume numbered as M11 and M12. The *Khoj* Report of 1908 (p. 363) mentions a manuscript of the *Gobardhan līlā melā saḍan* by Ṭhākurdās Kāyastha, a native of Charkhari, which was copied in 1884. The name coincides with the one proposed by Bhagvandin. In addition, Charkhari is very close to Jaitpur, where Thakur was in service before his move to Bijawar. Unfortunately, the *Khoj* Report does not quote from the manuscript or offer any further information on the author or quotations from the manuscript. It is, therefore, impossible to determine whether the work belongs to the Ṭhākur of the subject of this study.

The *Khoj* Reports and various manuscript catalogues contain references to several other poets called Ṭhākurdās.[36] None of them, however, seems to have composed poems with the signature Ṭhākur that could be mistaken for the quatrains of our poet.

CONCLUSION

In sum, the geography and chronology of the family lore presents a consistent picture. All stories relate Ṭhākur to eastern Bundelkhand and place him in the courts of Kesrī Siṁh of

[34]Manuscript 918 at the Nāgarīpracāriṇī Sabhā.

[35]I found one *pad* with the signature Ṭhākurdās in the Sanjay Sharma Sangrahalay (nr. 933/727 f. 8rv) and a manuscript called *Ṭhākurdās padāvalī* with several *pads* in the Nāgarīpracāriṇī Sabhā (nr. 833). A manuscript at the Rajasthan Oriental Research Institute, Jodhpur (nr 6937[2], ff. 1-17, 36-7) also includes *pads* by Ṭhākur.

[36]A *Guṇ nāṭikā* was composed in 1666 (*Saṁvat* 1723) by Ṭhākurdās (Rajasthan Oriental Research Institute, Jodhpur, Nr 21349, 14ff). A relatively long (142ff) *Rāmcandra-vilās* was written by Lālā Ṭhākurdās of Ṭīkamgaṛh (Nāgarī Pracāriṇī Sabhā nr. 3327). Two manuscript copies of a *Rukminī-maṅgal* by Ṭhākurdās consisting of 147 *ślokas* are mentioned in *Khoj* 6-337. *Khoj* 41-90ka and kha describes a *Śabd satguru ke* and a *Jñāngītā* by Ṭhākur(dās) of Gauspur (P.O. Nizamabad, Ajamgarh).

Jaitpur (r. from 1812), Kesrī Siṁh of Bijawar (r. 1802-11) and Parīkṣit of Jaitpur (r. until 1842). The same sources mention that he met Anūpgiri a.k.a. Himmat Bahādur (*c*. 1734-1804*)* and his court poet Padmākar (1753-1833) in Banda, and Kiśor Siṁh of Panna (r. 1798-1840). Bhagvandin records the dates of Ṭhākur's birth and death on the basis of family lore as *c*. 1766 and *c*. 1823.[37] Although there is no evidence to prove the exactness of these dates, the persons appearing in the anecdotes as well as the occurrence of his distinctive quatrains in dated manuscripts from 1803 onwards indicate that Ṭhākur was active at the turn of nineteenth century and that the family tradition must be reasonably correct with regards to his date and place.[38] Some chonological inconsistencies, however, do appear. Contrary to the the family lore collected by Bhagvandin, Ṭhākur could not have gone to the court of Kesrī Siṁh of Bijawar after the death of Kesrī Siṁh of Jaitpur since the latter started to rule in 1812 and the former had died already by 1811. Similarly, the poet's later patron, Parīkṣit, started to rule long after the death of Anūpgiri, rendering their purported clash historically impossible.

By removing the apparent contradictions of the hearsays one can further speculate that Ṭhākur was more at home among the Bundelas than with Anūpgiri even though he might have been a supporter of a compromise. Furthermore, his stand was even appreciated by the *gosāīṁ* warlord. He might have exploited information he acquired in his court to save a Bundela chieftain from a trap. — All this, however, is speculation.

The anecdotes agree that Ṭhākur was in the service of the regional nobility. His poetry also speaks about the norms of rulership and service (N25-27). Recurring themes in his verse include praise of the generous lord (N33-35) and cursing of the miserly *(adāniyā)* (N14-15, N18, N21), suggesting that he was also trying to solicit donations from his patrons. Other quatrains express his martial and political standing and assertiveness, his *ṭhasak* or 'dignity'.

Some quatrains contain indirect references to living in difficult times (Ś65, Ś109, Ś136, Ś139). To counter this, the poems stress the need for steadfastness and remind the audience of the importance of rules (*prīti kī rīti, ras-rīti, braj-rīti* in Ś2, Ś25, Ś42, Ś59, Ś61, Ś93 etc.). This reminder is often couched within the framework of the cowherd women's love for Krishna. To emphasise that conventional rules *(cāl)* do apply in a community, poems may stress the commonwealth of lovers in the 'city of love' (B35) or 'bazaar of love' (Ś10).[39]

Judging from the family lore, Ṭhākur seems to have been not only a poet but also a courtier who undertook diplomatic missions. This was the case with other court poets, such as Sundar Kavirāy or Raslīn. However, unlike most of the Hindi court poets, he did not compose any work featuring the name of a patron; in this respect he resembles Bihārī. Composition for him was casual and oral rather than written. The anecdotes agree that he presented his poetry verbally and do not mention any written work by him.

Ṭhākur's poetry relies less on traditional taxonomies than that of his more conventional contemporaries, such as Padmākar. He seems to have produced only free-standing quatrains (*muktaka*s). No long historical poem or treatise on the classification of heroines, *nāyikā-*

[37]See Bhagavandin, *Ṭhākur ṭhasak,* 'Ṭhākur kavi kā jīvancarit', pp. 6 and 23.

[38]The earliest dated manuscript containing his quatrains, called M_1 in this edition, is Rajasthan Oriental Research Institute, Jodhpur, nr 13515(2), ff. 11-13. For its description see p. 73.

[39]The idea of the city of love was already present in the poetry of the mid-seventeenth century poet Bihārī. Interestingly, the couplet that refers to it (325 in *Bihari-Ratnākar)* shows Persionate influence both in its theme of a murderous beloved and in its vocabulary.

bheda,—two genres popular among court poets—survives under his name. While Padmākar, who wrote long compositions (*prabandhas*) on these themes, enjoyed the patronage of the most outstanding rulers of his times, such as Himmat Bahādur, Pratāp Siṁh and Jagat Siṁh of Jaipur, Ṭhākur circulated only in the smaller courts of Bundelkhand. It must be due to the lack of longer compositions that his fame did not spread as fast as that of Padmākar. His name, just as Padmākar's, is missing from both editions of Garcin de Tassy's *Histoire de la littérature hindoui et hindoustani* (1839-47 and 1870-1). However, as we are going to see, his poetry was very popular in nineteenth-century anthologies.

All this rather suggests that Ṭhākur may have been a courtier-politician who also composed poetry but did not make his living exclusively from his quatrains. In one poem he calls himself both a soldier and a poet in the service of thc Rajputs *(sukavi sipāhī hama una rajapūtana ke)* and also defines his role as the arbiter of moral behaviour *(nīti denahāra).* His literary independence may have contributed to the twentieth-century notion that he was not the author of conventional *rīti*-poetry.

Ṭhākur's Quatrains and Hindi Literature

Ṭhākur's Krishna-poetry was not limited to describing love scenes in a fantasized, mythological setting but was also a forceful vehicle for political ideas. In this respect, regardless of whether Ṭhākur wrote his poems on the occasions mentioned in the contextualising stories, tradition has perceived them as a mode of political engagement.

The fact that the tight framework of *rīti* literature served political purposes is not exceptional. There are already famous examples of political contextualisation considered under the traditional aesthetic rubric of 'saying something else', *anyokti*.[1] The practice of *anyokti* has a long tradition in Sanskrit. For instance, rhetoricians in the second millennium CE connected *anyokti* either to the *alaṅkāra*s or to *dhvani* 'suggestion'. In Hindi literature, in addition to Rahīm, Bihārī and Vṛnd, some minor poets also used this device. In the nineteenth century *anyokti* became the organizing force of the poetry of 'Bābā' Dīndayāl Giri (1802-65), who wrote about knowledge, renunciation and other virtues, through descriptions of seasons.[2]

Notwithstanding classical categories, a love poem could be contextualised on the spot and interpreted as *anyokti*. This was the case with Niẕām ul-Mulk, who in 1737 entreated Nādīr Śāh to stop his massacre of Delhi by reciting the following couplet about a cruel beloved in Persian:

Lay down your sword of pride, for none is left for you to slay
— Except you raise the dead to life that you may slay again.[3]

The relatively high number of politicised anecdotes regarding Ṭhākur's poems suggests that he used *anyokti* more regularly than his Hindi predecessors, who only have a few couplets with such contexts attached to them. Some instances of Ṭhākur's contextualisation may even seem to contradict each other. While Śivsiṁh indicated Ṭhākur's service to Anūpgiri, through which he earned a reward from the warlord, the anecdotes collected from Ṭhākur's descendants show rather the poet's opposition to him and do not mention the story cited by Śivsiṁh. However, even Bhagvandin's anecdotes admit that Ṭhākur had also been present in Himmat Bahādur's court and indicate the privileged status of a court poet to criticise his master. Several instances described in the contextualising stories in the previous

[1]A famous example of *anyokti* in Bihārī quoted by Lallū Lāl (S. Pandey, ed. *Bihārī satsaī: lālcandrikā se yukta* Varanasi: Nāgarīpracāriṇī Sabhā, 1977, p. 346) is a poem addressed to Jaisingh when he was infatuated with a young girl: *nahī parāga nahī madhura madhu, nahī bikāsa ihi kāla; alī, kalī hī te bandhyo, āge kauna havāla.* (630) 'No pollen, no sweet nectar, no blossoming yet; if the bee is caught up with the bud even, what will happen later [when it blooms]?' (Translation by R. Snell : R. Snell, *The Hindi Classical Tradition: A Braj Bhāṣā Reader*, London: School of Oriental and African Studies, 1991, p. 135).

[2]For a brief historical survey of *anyokti* see I. Bangha, 'Political Contextualisation, Individualism and Search for a New Style in Late Brajbhasha Court Poetry: The quatrains of Ṭhākur from Bundelkhand', in *Bhakti in Current Research 2000-2003: Procedings of the Ninth International Conference on Early Devotional Literature in New Indo-Aryan Languages, Heidelberg, 23-26 July 2003*, ed. Monika Horstmann, New Delhi: Manohar, 2006, pp. 3-5.

[3]K. Islam and R. Russell, *Three Mughal Poets*, London: Allen & Unwin, 1969, p. 230 (note).

chapter, such as saving a maharaja from a trap by recounting the plight of forsaken cowherd-girls against slanderers or the poem on the quandary of the forsaken *gopīs* lamenting the decline in the state of affairs, are examples of early modern political communication. C. A. Bayly in his monograph on intelligence gathering and social information in India mentions the nineteenth-century French scholar Garcin de Tassy's observation that Western distinctions between politics, history and literature did not really apply in the case of Hindi and Hindustani narratives.[4] Bayly states that "strong political messages could be conveyed through cultural performance which linked elite and populace in enjoyment."[5] For example, months before the Vellore mutiny in 1806, it was the puppeteers that carried the message that Tipu Sultan's sons were about to regain their power. The British scholar demonstrates that the heroic ballads of traditional bards, travelling puppet shows and theatrical performances were able to spread subversion, parody and political comment.[6] Since several of Ṭhākur's quatrains were also perceived as spreading political message, courtly Krishna poetry should also be added to Bayly's list.

One can observe a relatively simple pattern of contextualisation in these poems. The setting is Braj, the geographical sphere of the activities of the speaker and the addressee, while the absence of Krishna refers to the absence of favourable times. The speaker, a cowherd girl abandoned by Krishna, speaks to one or more girls of her community who share the same fate: they have to cope with both the unfavourable times and the enemies, the slanderers. Moreover, the enemies may be within one's inner circle—one's own in-laws. Bearing all this in mind, poems in which no explicit political context is mentioned lend themselves to contextualisation. Some poems strongly suggest moral attitudes that transcend the framework of Krishna-mythology, as is the case with the following quatrain,

I cannot live without seeing that enchanting face of the dear Enchanter.
Therefore, I listen to everything, good and bad in this world, and consider it as teaching.
Ṭhākur says, in order to see the Dear Child I do not reply to anyone.
What can I say when I have been entangled? I flatter all the people. (Ś83)

In a similar vein, the following poem laments the unpredictable behaviour of people with power apparently in connection with Krishna, but with the adverb *sadā* 'always' and with the emphatic progressive verbal form of *hotaī āe* 'have been (till the present)' the poet makes it explicit that his statement also refers to the lords of his times,

In Kabul, he sowed nuts in plenty—when he came to Vrindaban he planted caper bush.
Foregoing a fair woman like Radha—he fell in love with his hunchback.
He discarded Duryodhana's dry fruits—to eat the peels in the house of Vidura's wife.
Ṭhākur, what shall I say of my Lord? Lords have always been crazy. (N22)

These two poems present two attitudes of people who are subject to a lord but still expose their independent thinking. The first one about flattering also implies the subjugation of sentiments in order to gratify those in power. The second one does not present inimical

[4]Garcin de Tassy, *Histoire de la littérature hindoui et hindoustanie,* vols. 1-3, Paris, 1870-1; reprint, New York, Franklin, 1968, vol. I, pp. 9-10 quoted in C.A. Bayly, *Empire and Information: Intelligence Gathering and Social Communication in India, 1780-1870,* Cambridge: Cambridge University Press, 1996, p. 201.

[5]Bayly, *Empire and Information,* p. 207.

[6]Ibid., pp. 207-9.

superiors: although while criticising the lords in general, it accepts their eccentricity. Both of them suggest a policy of rational compromise.

'THE DIGNITY OF ṬHĀKUR'—EARLY MODERN INDIVIDUALISM

It is not only the covert political message in the garb of Krishna poetry that makes Ṭhākur peculiar. Both legends and his poetry suggest that Ṭhākur possessed an independent courtier's standing and assertiveness. According to Vishvanath Prasad Mishra, his pride influenced Bhāratendu Hariścandra.[7]

It is, therefore, not without reason that Bhagvandin published the collection of his poems under the name of *Ṭhākur ṭhasak* 'The pride of Ṭhākur'. Ṭhākur's standing and independence was usually channelled through traditional subject matters such as the lovelorn cowherd girls' passionate plight against Uddhav, Krishna's messenger. According to the legend, Krishna left the cowherdessess of Vrindaban for ever. At one point, however, he sent his friend, Uddhav, to comfort them with the message propagating an abstract religion and the doctrine of discipline, 'yoga'. Uddhav contended that since Krishna is the Absolute himself, he is present in everyone's heart. The girls vehemently rejected this, arguing that their love was for a god who has a form and whom humans can experience. Ṭhākur's other favourite theme was adulterous love disregarding all bonds—a further example of independent standing. While the Uddhav-poems, usually referred to as *Bhramargīt* 'bee songs', had been a favourite theme of the *bhakti* poets since the sixteenth century, in the time of poets like Sūrdās and Nandadās, devotional or classicist poets rarely emphasised the theme of explicit adulterous love. Although the situation might remind the listener or the reader that in many legends Radha, the exemplary beloved, was also the wife of someone else and not of Krishna, in these poems Ṭhākur uses almost no veneer of the Krishna legend. Since this theme was still easily inserted into the classical framework of the 'classification of heroines', the *nāyikā-bheda*, it could not be considered subversive. That is why some anthologies introduce such poems as examples of the category *parakīyā nāyikā*, 'the heroine who belongs to someone else'. Moreover, the *parakīyā nāyikā* class was not the only possibility of locating these poems within a *nāyikā-bheda* framework. The following quatrain, for example, in the anthology *Sudhāsar* was given as an illustration of *prītopālambha* 'complaint against love',[8]

> *I knew that my beloved is not my own but of someone else—this is what the Vedas sing.*
> *Neglecting this, I fell in love and discarded the family honour propagated by the elders.*
> *That lord has not become mine. Whom shall I blame for this, my sister?*
> *A bee is visible in the milk, my friend; I have drunk it though it was right before my eyes.* (Ś122)

The presentation of 'adulterous' poems in these conventional categories illustrate that in the same vein as Krishna mythology, the poet could exploit the *nāyikā-bheda* to express his individual attitudes.

[7] V. Mishra, *Hindī sāhitya kā atīt*, vol. 2, Varanasi: Vāṇī vitān, 1960, pp. 348-9.

[8] This is a rubric within the different types of complaint and is opposed to the categories of *virahopālambha* 'complaint against separation', *nāyak prati upālambha* 'complaint against the lover' and *kāmopālambha* 'complaint against erotic desire' in the *Sudhāsar*.

There is, however, a single poem apparently in a tone of realism, with no effort whatsoever to reduce the stigma of prostitution through the pretext of Krishna lore.

O my sister, whom should my husband approach to make money?
Not even a king's intellect can find a solution.
My body and wealth became lean, my mind fouled,
my soul, restless and troubled, is never at peace.
Ṭhākur says, compulsion overwhelms this world.
My mind is stained, show me some way out!
Now when I have nothing but oaths in my mouth, I can do nothing but sin,
I have disgrace to take and false love to give. (Ś131)

Although this poem is unique in the entire corpus, it shows that early modern literature could also experiment with the direct presentation of social problems.

UNCONVENTIONAL POETIC FORMS

Another, slightly unconventional attitude is when in the Indian aesthetic context of *purvā-nurāga* 'pining in love's first infatuation' poets present the sentiments of a male hero as is typical in Persian and Urdu ghazals. In the following *savaiyā* the closeness to Persianate aesthetics is also expressed by the rhyming pattern reminiscent of the rhyme-syllables (*qāfiya*, here *-ānati*) and end-rhymes (*radīf*, here *hvaihai*) of the ghazals. The presumptives in the rhymes introduce the doubts of a male hero between rejection and hope,

vā niramohini rūpa kī rāsi jo ūpara ke ura ānati hvaihai|
bārahū̃ bāra biloki gharī-gharī sūrata tau pahicānati hvaihai|
ṭhākura, yā mana kī paratīti hai jo pai saneha na mānati hvaihai|
āvata haĩ nita mere liye, itano tau biseṣahū jānati hvaihai|| Ś44||

That beautiful girl without love, who superficially probably thinks about me
looking at me again and again all the time must at least recognise my face.
Ṭhākur says, my mind trusts her yet she probably does not feel love for me.
She always appears for me— she must at least be aware of this.

Ṭhākur produced six other poems with a similar double rhyming pattern *(dohre kāfiye kā chand)* spreading over at least three syllables and often over two or more words.[9]

Ṭhākur's other experiments with forms popular in late Brajbhasha poetry include *rekhtā*, poetry using marked Persian vocabulary with Khari Boli grammar, such as B64 *(kūbarī kānhara kā ikalāsa kiyā, sabahī bidhi khūba hai allā).* He also produced poems playing on the abundant recurrence of one phrase, word or a sequence of sounds *(ek śreṇī ke chand)*, such as N37, quoted below on p. 36, repeating the phrase *sīkha līnho* or B12 repeating the word *rāma* over and over again. Another late form is the *siṁhāvalokan savaiyā*, in which the sequence of syllables at the end of a line is repeated at the beginning of the next one evoking the lion looking back time after time, as he advances. Unlike in the probably spurious U4, the words repeated at the end and then at the beginning of the next line in B6 (*rasa nā̃hī milyau hai. . .*) tend to be not repetition but puns called *sabhaṅga yamaka*s.

There are also poems with coded *(kūṭ)* usages that produce meaning through synonyms,

[9]Poems B32, Ś57, Ś79, Ś80, Ś146, R47 in this edition.

as was already done in Hindi poetry attributed to Sūrdās, Rahīm and others. In these poems, certain words or phrases do not fit into the syntax of the line. The reader or listener has to substitute them with a synonym, which has further meanings relevant to the poem. N37, for example, praises Tulsīdās's good writing with the unrelated word *hema* 'gold'. The meaning is reached by substituting it with the synonym *suvarna* 'gold', which can also mean 'good letters, good writing'. In a similar vein, *sītalā ko bāhan* 'the vehicle of the goddess Śītalā ' should be substituted with *gaddhā* 'donkey', in a poem about dullness (N16). In our corpus of poems with uncertain authorship, there are six *kūṭ kavitta*s (U11-16) built almost entirely on coded meanings.

Ṭhākur's description of good and bad people in the Nīti section was also a popular theme among late Brajbhasha poets as illustrated in the *Duṣṭajan aur sajjan kā varṇan* section in Hāfizullah Khān's *Hazārā* (1875). This theme was already present in early Hindi, for example, in the *sant-asant* verses of the *Rāmcaritmānas* (1, 4-6 and 7, 39-41).

NATURE AND LOVE

One of Ṭhākur's favourite themes is the description of love within the setting of a specific season *(ṛtu-varṇan)*, especially of spring and the monsoon. The poet posits love within transient time and aims to preserve a specific moment.

The favourable setting (*uddīpan*) for the emergence of a poetic emotion *(rasa)* is an important category of classical Indian aesthetics. In many poems, however, in spite of the presence of the favourable setting, the lover is absent and the evocation of the beauty of the world only underscores the sense that something is missing. The pang of separation in the absence of the lover (*viraha)* is a frequent theme of Brajbhasha literature. The words are put into the mouth of a lonely woman, the more vulnerable sex in her society. Often she expresses emotions unapproved by the community, which therefore weigh on her even more heavily: women have more to lose than men do. At the same time, the female horizon is more focussed on love than that of a man with duties and activities in the outer world. It is true that mostly males enjoyed and produced court literature but this poetry is more than the sexual fantasy of a male audience.[10] Heroines are preferred to male heroes because the description of their sentiments gains poetic intensity. The longing expressed in this poetry is rather an existential and transcendental longing, since the absent lover is the par excellence lover, Krishna, God himself. Just as many other poets, Ṭhākurs took on a female persona to express his deeper, psychological self, while he articulated his social self in the *nīti* 'conduct' poems closely related to one of his favourite themes, 'manliness'. Ṭhākur has produced far more poems from a woman's point of view than direct *nīti* poetry, but as noted above, he was able to express his opinion about the political world with the words of the cowherdesses. In his shifts between a female and a male poetic persona, Ṭhākur is similar to some early vernacular poets of the Krishna-devotion, such as Sūrdās. The corpus of Sūrdās includes songs in which cowherd-women speak and others, called *vinaya* perform a 'humble request', in which the poet addresses the god directly. Similarly, the fifteenth-century Telugu bhakti poet Annamayyā's *padam*s have been categorised either as *śṛṅgāra* 'love' or *adhyātma* 'metaphysical' or 'introspective'. The translators of Annamayyā note,

[10]On the male gaze see Chapter 2 in Busch, *Poetry of Kings*.

In the male mode, as we have seen, there is mostly conflict and disturbance; human life itself is burdened by a furious subjectivity, at war with the senses and the body. The vicissitudes of daily awareness with its moods and cognitive puzzles, occupy the centre of attention. In the female mode, almost infinitely elaborated, this same poet gives himself over to a harmonious and luxuriant erotic excess. In this state "he" is even capable of controlling the god, demanding his attention and enjoying his love. The listener cannot escape a clear-cut perception that the female *śṛṅgāra* persona is somehow more fulfilling, indeed more full. Perhaps it is not by chance that Annamayya wrote four times as many *śṛṅgāra* poems as *adhyātma* poems.[11]

Although Ṭhākur worked more in a courtly than in a bhakti environment, one cannot fail to observe that, like the other early modern Krishna poets, Ṭhākur was also more at home in talking about emotions expressed through a female mode than in taking up a more direct male voice.

Along with Ṭhākur's individualism, one can also perceive the importance lent to sensual perception and the realism in his descriptions of details especially in poems about the seasons. In these poems Ṭhākur may rely on visual or aural motifs as, for example, in the following one consoling a lovelorn woman, whose lover seems to have been hindered in the rains on his way home,

The earth turned green; the roads are invisible under streams of water: even things that do not flow do flow now.
Black clouds have caused darkness and no difference remained between day and night.
Ṭhākur, it is impossible to go from one house to another: I am deeply concerned.
How could they come? What can they do? My friend, is it the fault of the poor travellers? (R59)

Similar instances are frequent in Ṭhākur's quatrains although it is rare that he builds a *kavitta* exclusively on sensual descriptions. In most of the cases, description is only present in one or two lines and the rest of the poem would use traditional *alaṅkāras*.

In many quatrains poetic fantasy searches for new images in contemporary material culture, such as comparing the clouds to china bowls or to silk cloth (R55) or likening the rainy season to Kāma's frying pan (R56).

At other times, Ṭhākur evokes the season through onomatopoetic usages and impressive alliteration. A good example is R42, where the first line alliterates in *da-* evoking the swiftness of the lightning, the second in *gha-* for the rumbling of the clouds, the third in *pī-* for the cries of the cuckoo and the fourth in *jha-* for the pitter-patter of the rain. Although almost every word alliterates within a line, Ṭhākur does not force the alliteration throughout but makes allowances for a more natural meaning. The line about the rumbling of the clouds, for example, is as follows,

ghūmi-ghūmi, ghahari-ghahari ghana ghaharāta,
gheri-gheri ghora ghano sora sarasatu hai|

Gathering clouds lower and surge,
they encircle everything and their deep sounds increase.

In his description of nature, the poet may occasionally draw on mythological convention,

[11]See V.N. Rao and D. Shulman, *God on the Hill: Temple Poems from Tirupati,* New York: Oxford University Press, 2005, pp. 132-3.

such as in *śyāma ghaṭā deha jākī* . . . (R63), where clouds evoke Airāvat, the elephant of Indra, the God of rainfall. The above-mentioned cloud-elephant imagery may also relate to the popular myth of the seven elephants whom Bhīma hurled into the sky and who still wander there. The reference to Krishna eating the banana peels offered by Vidura's wife in N22 is a further development on an episode in the Mahabharata, which only briefly alluded to how Krishna accepted the hospitality of Vidura. Ṭhākur's mythological apparatus in a wider context, beyond the setting of Braj, tends not to be Puranic but rather related to later popular beliefs or hagiography. Similarly, the hagiographic references in N24 also point to popular concepts beyond the Puranas.

RĪTIMUKTA POETRY

The importance lent to individual sentiments and sensual perception as opposed to a more iconic and stereotypical representation of the earlier centuries may be due to the emulation of what is called the *maqtab-i wuqu'* "realistic style" of sixteenth-seventeenth-century Persian literature.[12] This literary style also fit well into an emerging individualism in South Asia. It was imitated in Urdu poetry and transmitted into Hindi most powerfully by Ānandghan, whose quatrains emphasised the immediacy of personal emotions.

In the twentieth century, this emerging pre-colonial individualism was conceptualised as a poetic current with a clear mission to express personal feelings. Literary historians presented several poets as adherents to this so-called *rītimukta kāvyadhārā,* 'poetic current free from convention'. The idea of *rītimukta* poetry is, however, a twentieth-century concept that developed parallel with the literary movement of *Chāyāvād.* It was convenient for critics who were enthusiastic about the idea of individualism so prominent in *Chāyāvād* to conceive of an earlier independent movement similar to the *Chāyāvād* in many of its ideas. Some critics grouped together Ālam, Ānandghan, Ṭhākur, Dvijdev and others and presented them as poets who wrote to express their individual love as though in romantic opposition to the classicist modalities of *Rīti*-poetry.[13] In order to bolster the idea of *rītimukta* poetry, scholars made efforts to find markedly *rītimukta* authors. One of their major problems was that although several *kabittas* by *rītimukta* authors display individualism, the authors have composed many others in which they clearly abided by conventions. Theoreticians of the *rītimukta* poetry were reluctant to accept the polyphony of particular poets who sometimes struck very individual notes.

Although, unlike with Ālam, Ānandghan, Bodhā (and even Raskhān), there is no significant love story credited as an inspirational force behind his poems, Ṭhākur was more personal in many of his quatrains than most of his contemporaries. Behind the veneer of the Krishna myths and classification of heroes and heroines one can feel a proud standing and independent spirit, which was maintained even at the price of confrontation. In a more realist vein, the poems demonstrate the need for political compromise during troubled years in Bundelkhand.

Poem N37 in its twentieth-century variant is often quoted as one of the fundaments of

[12]See e.g. P. Losensky, "Moḥtaśam Kāšānī", *Encyclopaedia Iranica* (2004), http://www.iranica.com/articles/mohtasham-kashani.

[13]About the development of the concept of *rītimukta* poetry see I. Bangha, 'Romantic poetry in the Era of Convention? The Emergence of the Idea of a Rītimukt Trend within Hindi Mannerist Literature', *South Asia Research*, vol. 25, no. 1, 2005, pp. 13-30.

the idea of poetry free from convention and is interpreted as a refutation of *Rīti*-poetry in favour of a more individualised literature,

sīkha līnho mīna mr̥ga khañjana kamala naina
  sīkha līnho jasa au pratāpa ko kahāno hai|
sīkha līno kalpabr̥kṣa kāmadhenu cintāmani
  sīkha līnho mera au kubera gira āno hai|
ṭhākura kahata yāki baṛī hai kaṭhina bāta
  vāko nahī̃ bhūli kahū̃ bā̃dhiyata bāno hai|
ḍela so banāya āya melata sabhā ke bīca
  logana kabitta kībo khela kara jāno hai|| cf. N37||

They have learnt eyes are like fish, deer, wagtail or lotus;
  They have learnt to say 'this is an epic tale of fame and valour';
They have learnt about the marvellous tree, the wish-granting cow or the wondrous jewel
  they have learnt to bring in Meru and the Mountain of Kuvera;
Ṭhākur says, poetry is a most difficult matter
  words can never, not even accidentally confine it;
Still they churn it out and introduce it to the assembly:
  people think composing poetry is an easy game.

It is easy to see that the *sīkha līnho* repetition in each of the first four lines is a kind of dramatic reinforcement of the inadequacy of merely repeating tradition itself. It should, however, be born in mind that in some places convention is as important to the poets classified as *rītimukta* as to the other *Rīti*-authors. What Ṭhākur has done is to move beyond the mastery of poetic customs as the sole measure of poetic genius. Rather than condemning classicism per se, he breathed new life into it.

Triggered by the idea of *rītimukta* poetry scholars have divided the Ṭhākur textual corpus between two or three different poets. The reason behind this division was that Ṭhākur was one of the chief representatives of *rītimukta* poets and yet there was an unquestionable presence of conventions in his poetry. Literary histories have earlier talked about several Ṭhākurs. Their poetic output was not always available for research and when it was, as in the case of the *Devakīnandan* commentary by Ṭhākur of Asni, it did not consist of quatrains. Yet scholars emphasising Ṭhākur's importance as a *rītimukta* poet had to attribute the more conventional Ṭhākur-quatrains to some of the other Ṭhākurs. In this way the editor of the influential *Ṭhākur ṭhasak,* Lala Bhagvandin, in his *Introduction* tried to assign several quatrains to three different poets called Ṭhākur. However, he himself was confused about their authorship since by also including many of these quatrains into the main corpus of his text he suggested that all belonged to the same poet. Similarly, Vishvanath Prasad Mishra and Chandrashekhar Mishra attributed the quatrains with Ṭhākur's signature to two different poets. Ṭhākur's most important edition, the *Ṭhākur granthāvalī* edited by Chandrashekhar Mishra noticeably under the influence of his father, Vishvanath Prasad Mishra, presented 219 and 51 quatrains under the conception of two different authors called Ṭhākur. They attributed the larger part of this corpus to the *rītimukta* Ṭhākur of Bundelkhand and they identified the author of what they perceived as the 51 conventional quatrains with the author of the *Devakīnandan ṭīkā* and called him *rītibaddha* Ṭhākur. It is, however, not only in the *rītibaddha* section of the *Granthāvalī* that we find conventional poetry. They figure in abundance also among the 219 quatrains that Mishra judged to belong to the *rītimukta* poet.

Ṭhākur's was not the only case when Vishvanath Prasad Mishra, with the intention of making his point on *rītimukta* poetry clearer, deprived a textual corpus of poems that seemed too conventional by attributing it to another poet. He had earlier proposed a similar separation in the case of Ānandghan and Ghanānand, where he artificially attributed the bhakti-poetry of a *rītimukta* author to an earlier Vaishnava poet, Ānandghan, and tried to present a markedly *rītimukta* Ghanānand. Facing more manuscript evidence, however, he abandoned his early idea.[14]

The figure of Ṭhākur was more complex than simply being an exponent of a poetic current. Through the use of proverbs and of little ornamentation he created a down-to-earth language; through his *gopīs*' cheeky replies to Uddhav and the laments of women in adulterous love he struck a more individual note than classicist poets. This, however, did not mean that he discarded conventional *Rīti*-poetry.

SEARCH FOR A NEW STYLE: REGIONALISM AND IDIOMS

Ṭhākur's realism, demonstrated in his description of nature, also manifests itself in his use of mimicry. Through a marked inclusion of local Bundelkhandi forms, as opposed to standard Braj, the poet evokes the rustic voice of the cowherds and localises his poetry in Bundelkhand.

LANGUAGE

Since the quatrains published in this book have already undergone phases of oral and written transmission we cannot be certain of their symmetry to Ṭhākur's originals. This uncertainty render it difficult to determinate their original language. Nevertheless, one can observe preference for certain grammatical features. Some of these feaures, such as the *-ibo kar-* frequentative/intensive structure (Ś79, Ś80, Ś139, Ś140), should be treated as reflecting stylistic rather than dialectal tendency.

It can also be observed that readings in the manuscripts normally vary between standardised Braj forms and less standardised forms with elements of what is considered Bundelkhandi and Khari Boli dialects. Ṭhākur's poems circulated in a wide area in north India as can be seen from the provenance of our manuscripts. It is likely that while oral transmission was open to the inclusion of local forms, written transmission and especially nineteenth-century print culture preferred to move from non-standard forms towards a more standardised Brajbhasha. Twentieth-century editors, however, conscious of Ṭhākur's Bundelkhandi origins, preferred Bundelkhandi forms.

The language of the quatrains is Brajbhasha. Many poems, however, are preserved not in the Brajbhasha of the poets who lived in Braj and whose works were transmitted primarily in Braj and eastern Rajasthan but in a variation of it, an extended Brajbhasha in which lexical and grammatical elements of the bordering areas, especially of Bundelkhand, feature

[14]The change in his approach can be observed through the comparison of V. Mishra, ed. *GhanĀnand aur Ānandghan (granthāvalī),* Varanasi: Vāṇī Vitān, 1945, 'Introduction', pp. 6-14 and in ———, ed. *Ghan Ānand (granthāvalī),* Varanasi: Vāṇī Vitān, 1952, 'Vānmukh' pp. 51-79, especially pp. 67-8.

prominently. Since Bundelkhandi characteristics have been current within the extended Brajbhasha, it is not always easy to point them out. The area of spoken Bundelkhandi borders the area of Braj, and in actual usage, it is hardly distinguishable from it. The few distinguishing traits are accepted among the wide range of variations within the extended literary Brajbhasha and may not always reflect Bundelkhandi rootedness.

Scholars have pointed out specifically Bundelkhandi forms in Ṭhākur. Due to the closeness of Braj and Bundelkhandi dialects, their decisions about the dialects are often arbitrary. Dictionaries give most dialectal labels based on written texts, which may not reflect actual regional usage. Moreover, Hindi dictionaries hardly ever distinguish specific Bundelkhandi usage. (I did not, for example, find any of Ṭhākur's words labelled as Bundelkhandi in the *Bṛhat hindī koś*, which according to its list of abbreviations pays attention to Bundelkhandi usage.)

Let us see a few examples. The word *chīnā* 'to touch' is designated as Braj since it is used in the *Sūrsāgar (Brajbhāṣā sūr koś)*, but the modern interpreter Dr. Kishorilal pointed out that it reflects Bundelkhandi usage in contrast with the standard Braj (and modern Hindi) *chū-*.[15] Ṭhākur-scholars also indicated certain lexical and grammatical elements as specific to Bundelkhand. For example, according to Krishna Chandra Varma *thigarī, ulaṅk, naiyā̃, ūmar, sahiyā, cakkarā, ūsaï, lod, ẽḍ, laphānā, cauvar, bodar, ghinocī* are Bundelkhandi words.[16] Bhagvandin also distinguished between words used in the central areas and others used in Bundelkhand.[17] Surendra Mathur distributed Ṭhākur's non-Braj words into five categories, Sanskrit, dialectal, Bundelkhandi, Perso-Arabic and those coined by the poet.[18] There is, however, no full overlap in what these three scholars considered as Bundelkhandi.

The poems reconstructed in this edition present several suffixes that do not figure in standard Brajbhasha.

-ena pl. obl. ending;
-iyata pass. used as active (cf. Varma 2000: 55-6);
-ne (hai) gerund ending (cf. Varma 2000: 55-6);
-iyā̃ (pahiyā̃, nahiyā̃, bahiyā̃, mahiyā̃) (cf. Varma 2000: 55-6);
-ibo for verbal nouns (cf. Varma 2000: 55-6);
-vārau / -vāre / -vārī in the sense of *kā / ke / kī*.

Ṭhākur's peculiar pronominal forms, *jauna* (H *jo*) and *tauna* (H *vah*), used in the Avadhi, Bhojpuri and Magehi dialects, also reflect eastern usage.[19] However, according to Kellogg and Grierson they are also Braj and Kannauji forms.[20] Their presence in the *Brajbhāṣā sūr*

[15]Personal communication on 17 Feb. 2011.

[16]K.C. Varma, *Kavivar ṭhākur*, Delhi: Niraj Book Centre, 2000, p. 55. Varma's list is repeated in V.S. Ray, *Svacchand kāvyadhārā aur kavi ṭhākur*, Varanasi: Manīś Prakāśan, 2008, p. 208.

[17]Bhagavandin, *Ṭhākur ṭhasak*, p. 5.

[18]Mathur, *Kavi ṭhākur aur unkā kāvya*, pp. 75-9.

[19]S. Varma, *G. A. Grierson's Linguistic Survey of India: A summary*, 3 vols., Hoshiarpur: Vishveshvaranand Institute, Panjab University, 1972, vol. 2., pp. 593, 599.

[20]S.H. Kellogg and T.G. Bailey, *A grammar of the Hindí language: in which are treated the high Hindí, Braj, and the eastern Hindí of the Rámáyan of Tulsí Dás: also the colloquial dialects of Rájputáná, Kumáon, Avadh, Ríwá, Bhojpúr, Magadha, Maithila, etc.: with copious philological notes*, 3rd edn., London: K. Paul, Trench, Trubner and co., Limited, 1938 and G.A. Grierson, *Linguistic Survey of India*, Calcutta: Office of

kos indicates that they were indeed not alien from literary Braj. There are many more words that some speakers of Braj would consider alien but their inclusion into the *Brajbhāṣā sūr koś* or the *Sāhityik brajbhāṣā koś* shows, that they are present in Brajbhasha, although perhaps peripherally. Such words include, *kaiyo* 'several, various', *nākha-* 'to throw away, to destroy', *agīta* 'in front', *pachīta* 'behind', *nāhinai* 'no', *laṭ-* 'bad', etc.

Some morphologic tendencies such as the *-o* ending of the masculine perfective participle instead of the standard Braj *-yo* or *-yau* are also perceived to be Bundelkhandi.[21] Such forms, however, tend to appear more in twentieth-century editions, especially in the *Ṭhasak,* than in some manuscripts which have preference for the Braj forms.[22]

The past tense of the verb 'to be' in Braj is *hau / ho; hī, he, hī̃*. Braj also uses the Kannauji *hutau, hutī, hute, hutī̃* forms, which it shares with Bundeli. Such forms are present in quatrains Ś12, Ś88, Ś105, Ś120, Ś123, Ś128 etc. Bundeli, however, can also have the forms *to, tī, te, tī̃*.[23] These occasionally occur in Ṭhākur's quatrains as in R51 *(dekhana gaī tī),* or in the rhymes of R27 and of B51. The transmission of this Bundeli form sometimes presented problems for the scribes. It seems that an early version of Ś19 having the Bundeli form, *haũ tau ina doina ke paharaī̃ rahī tī hāya* (present in E S_1 U), has been reworked into phrases with more standard Braj usages in later *Sudhāsar* and other manuscripts: *yaha kachu akatha kathā na mopai kahī jāti* (S_2 S_7), and *iha mopai akatha kathā na kachū kahī jāi* (H_e V_2).[24] Yet, this Bundeli verbal form was so closely associated with Ṭhākur that sometimes poems were reworked to present it. The *thī̃* (S_1 Y_e) or *thī* (B_1 V_1) reading of the rhymes of B51 *(sā̃ce karāra kare hamasõ, hama tāhū pai sā̃cī na mānatī thī̃.* etc.) present in the manuscripts that normally preserve the earliest forms becomes *tī̃* (D_2 E) or *tī* (S_2 S_7) in later texts. Three apparently later sources (C_e D_2 U_e) present the variant *jānata tī* at the beginning of Ś122 against the *jānata hī* of our main text drawn from five other sources.

In a few cases it was Bhagvandin himself who reworked the *Śatak*'s reading into a more markedly Bundeli form in the *Ṭhasak,* which in turn became an accepted reading in the *Granthāvalī*. Thus the *jānatī hī̃* in Ś$_e$ in the first line of B61 became the *jānatī tī̃* (G_e Ṭ$_e$). Similarly, the *jānata te* form of the *Śatak* in Ś70 allowing for Braj interpretation has again been refashioned to a distinctly Bundeli *jānatī tī̃* (G_e Ṭ$_e$).

Other shifts in dialect during transmission include the case of Ś120 *(choḍi pativrata . . .),* where V_1, C_e and O_e use the more standard Braj *chā̃ḍ-* verbal root against *choḍ-*, a version which though present in the earliest layer represented by B_1 and the *Sudhāsar* was probably perceived as more modern since it is shared with Khari Boli.

---

the superintendent of government printing, India, 1903 (vol. 9, part 1, p. 80), Cf. Varma, *Linguistic Survey of India*, p. 907.

[21] According to Grierson, *Linguistic Survey of India* (vol. 9, part 1, pp. 93-4, 69-70) the masculine perfective participle in Bundeli is formed by adding the suffix *-o,* and not the most frequent Braj *-yau*. This form, however, is also accepted as 'standard Braj merging into Kanaujī'. See Varma, *Linguistic Survey of India,* pp. 930, 904.

[22] E.g. Ś109 *ghaṭo* in the *Ṭhasak* and the *Granthāvalī* versus *ghaṭyau* in D_2; Ś109 *baḍho* in the *Ṭhasak* and the *Granthāvalī* versus *baḍhyau* in the D_2; Ś18 *jako* in the *Ṭhasak* and the *Granthāvalī* versus *jakyau* in the *Śatak* (!); Ś46 *haṭako* in the *Śatak, Ṭhasak* and the *Granthāvalī* versus, *haṭakyau* in the *Sudhāsar* manuscripts.

[23] Grierson, *Linguistic Survey of India,* vol. 9, part 1, pp. 93-4, 81. See Varma, *Linguistic Survey of India,* pp. 930, 908.

[24] For a list of sources for Ṭhākur's poetry and their abbreviations, see below pp. 69-78.

The morphological variation is, however, only one of the possibilities where transmission may vary. Poems show differences on a larger scale. The following version of a *savaiyā* can be found in the B_1 manuscript as well as in those of the *Sudhāsar* and of the Yajnik tradition (G_e, V_1),

vaha ghera kai ghāghare ghera ghiryau, phiri nībī-cunāina maĩ nadhi gau|
urajhyau surajhyau tribalī kī galī, gahi nābhi kī sundaratā sādhi gau|
kahi ṭhākura, choḍi calyau tita tẽ, girite giri kandara maĩ dhādhi gau|
chatiyā̃ maĩ chipyau mana choḍi dai rī, ā̃giyā-bāda bā̃dhata maĩ bādhi gau|| Ś28||

My mind was besieged and surrounded by her skirt in its fullness and was entangled in the drawstrings and rumples.
It got trapped in the lane of the three folds of her skin and perceiving the beauty of her navel joined it.
Ṭhākur says, leaving that place it went away, fell and sank into the caves of her hills.
Oh, give me back my mind that is hiding among your breasts. When you were binding the string of your bodice I myself became bound. (Ś28)

The only major variation within the three apparently early sources is that the scribe of the *Sudhāsar* manuscript omitted the initial *vaha* and thus produced a hypometrical line. The often eccentric J_1 manuscript and Baburamdin's *Sundarī-tilak* not only made up for the two lost syllables but also presented a more homogenous Bundeli (or Southern Braj) text with perfective endings in *-o* instead of *-yo*,

ghuri ghāgharo-ghera ghiro ugharo, puni nībī-cunāvana ke madha gau|
urajho surajho tribalī kī balī, puni nābhi kī sundaritā dhadha gau|
kavi ṭhākura, chūṭi calau una tẽ, kuca kī giri kandara maĩ phādhi gau|
chatiyā̃ maĩ chapyau mana chā̃ḍi dai rī, ā̃giyā-bāda bā̃dhata maĩ bādha gau||

This version repeats the word *puni* 'then' in the first and the second lines, while the other versions give the more fortunate 'pheri' or 'phiri' in the first line. The earlier versions repeated the word *choṛi* in the third and the fourth lines. Later transmission eliminates this repetition through the introduction of the intransitive form *chūṭi* in the third line. Moreover, it introduces the standard Braj word *chā̃ḍi*, instead of Khari Boli root *choṛ-*.

STYLE AND REFLECTION ON THE ART

With the powerful last line of the above poem, we reach the most marked peculiarity of Ṭhākur, the style of his quatrains. Although *lokokti*, the insertion of proverbs into the poem, has been classified as an *alaṅkāra* in the Sanskrit *Kuvalyānanda,* a sixteenth-century treatise on rhetoric, it was rarely used in poetry. Proverbs in the last line are a defining feature of Ṭhākur's poetry, setting him apart from most other Brajbhasha poets.[25] Proverbs render his relatively simple language even more down-to-earth and thus evoke the simplicity of the pastoral life and suggest the verbal superiority of its protagonists over other, more refined people.

The use of proverbs in a simple language and the occasional use of Bundeli features

[25]For a list of idioms and proverbs in Ṭhākur's last lines see Mathur, *Kavi ṭhākur aur unkā kāvya*, pp. 63-5, Ray, *Svacchand kāvyadhārā aur kavi ṭhākur*, p. 20, etc.

revitalises the centuries-old theme of the cowherd-girls' longing speech. Bundeli features also emphasise Bundela identity and create a situation reminiscent of the Rajput painting traditions. In miniature painting, the Rajput courts developed their own styles and the miniatures served almost like banners to a state. Similarly, the use of Bundeli features may have shown that the poem originated from Bundelkhand, increasing the prestige of the Bundela ruler. The fact that two of the best poets of the time, Ṭhākur and Padmākar worked mostly in Eastern Bundelkhand can also evince this pride in the region. According to the family lore Ṭhākur was born in Orcha but moved to Jaitpur in his childhood with his family. This move also parallels with a shift of Brajbhasha poetic activities towards the East at that time.

Ṭhākur's simplicity and (to a certain extent) regionalizing impulses should not be glossed over as a move towards more realistic pastoral tradition. It is rather a possible progression from the highly ornate poetry of his predecessors, such as Keśavdās, Dev and Ānandghan. Simplicity in *śṛṅgāra* poetry is a common feature of both Ṭhākur and Padmākar. While the love poetry of Padmākar combines this simplicity with overt classicism, Ṭhākur does it with *anyokti* and proverbs. Behind this move in Ṭhākur lies an increased poetic consciousness in searching for an individual style and ridiculing age-old conventions as is illustrated in the *sīkha līne* poem cited above (N37). However, in his own compositions Ṭhākur attacks not the conventions but rather second-rank imitative poetry. It is clear from the following quatrain that his poetic ideas were not as anti-classicst as twentieth-century scholarship presented them. The aim of his poetry was to 'earn greatness in the royal assembly' and to 'enchant the mind of the connoisseurs among the experts.'

> *The one who strings it like a charming necklace of pearls and produces it by joining rhymes and syllables;*
> *Forming the matter in an excellent way speaks of the path of love and of the story of God's name;*
> *Ṭhākur: I like that poet who earns greatness in a royal assembly—*
> *And the thing that enchants the mind of the connoisseurs among the scholars is called poetry.* (N36)

INTERTEXTUALITY

Ṭhākur's quatrains participated in the broader life of Brajbhasha poetry. Since the concepts of authorship and poetic originality in early modernity, just as before, was more fluid than perceptions of authorship in our times, poets were free to borrow phrases and imagery from earlier literature. This was not considered plagiarism but a way to improve on earlier verses and to enter into dialogue with each other. This could happen through *samasyāpūrti*, recycling an image or a set phrase, or by addressing a poetic theme for which there is a limited range of possible treatments. It could also express one's reverence for an earlier poet.

Some poems by Ṭhākur share parts of the last line with quatrains by others. These are instances of a poetic challenge called *samasyāpūrti*. In this practice one had to produce a new poem on a given phrase or line. Sometimes it is not difficult to recognise the earlier poem that contained a phrase that has become the *samasyā* for later poets, at other times the diachronic sequence is elusive. Below, I would like to draw the attention to three cases of *samasyāpūrti*.

Three *savaiyās*, given in the *Miscellanea* as M1, M2 and M3, were composed on the last line of R54, one of Ṭhākur's most popular poems present in twenty-two sources. The *samasyā* was as follows,

dhani ve dhani sāvana kī ratiyā̃ pati kī chatiyā̃ lagi sovatī haĩ|
Blessed are indeed the monsoon nights in which I sleep on the chest of my lord.

M2 and M3 are by a certain Rāmcaritra[26] while M1 may include the signature 'Sūrati'.[27]

The last line of the *savaiyā* M4 by an unknown author, found in a manuscript in Allahabad is similar to Ś133 and Ś134.

tuma sai iha bāta sai kāma kahā bunabe mai na bīna bajāibe mai|| 4||

What do you have to do with this matter in weaving or in playing the vina?

The second half of the line is an idiomatic phrase meaning "you do not have anything to do with it" parallel with the modern Hindi idiom *tum na tīn mẽ ho na terah mẽ* "you are neither in three nor in thirteen".

The *savaiyā* M5 by an unknown poet and found in an anthology called *Prayāgnārāyaṇ-vilās,*[28] presents a case bordering on plagiarism although it is not possible to determine which one was the earlier version. Here, it is not only the last line but also the first one that is similar to those of *jaba te, alī, lāla bidesa gayo . . .* (Ś84),

jā dina te paradesa gaye piya tā dina te tana chījatu hai|
nisivāsara bhauna suhāta nahī̃, sudha āye usāsana lījatu hai|
aba aura upāya banai na kachū anubhau itano sukha kījatu hai|
una pyāre piya kī unhārī, sakhī, nanadī mukha dekhikai jījatu hai|| M5||

My body has been wasting from the day my beloved went abroad.
My home pleases me neither during the day nor at night. I sigh whenever I remember.
There is no other way whatsoever to experience some bliss,
I live on looking at the face of my sister-in-law, my friend, which is like that of my dear lover.

Ṭhākur's version is as follows,

jaba te, alī, lāla bidesa gayo, china hī china yū̃ tana chījata hai|
kuca kā̃cukī prānapiāre binā asuvāna kī dhārana bhījata hai|
kaha ṭhākura, āpano hāla yahai, sajanī, tumahī sukha dījata hai|
vaha prānapiāre unhāra, sakhī, nanadī mukha dekha kai jījata hai|| Ś84||

[26]I was not able to find any information on Rāmcaritra in literary histories and manuscript catalogues.

[27]Sūrat or Sūratrām is the author of some stray quatrains and of the popular *Bārah Khaṛī* a poem on morals that is preserved in several nineteenth-century manuscripts (the earliest dating from 1823/4) as is attested in the different catalogues of the Rajasthan Oriental Research Institute. Sūrat is also the signature of Sūrati Miśra, a poet active in the first half of the seventeenth century. However, the fact that this poem is built on variations of Ṭhākur's well-known line makes it unlikely to predate Ṭhākur's version.

[28]B. Dikshit, ed. *Prayāganārāyaṇ-vilās,* Lucknow: Navalkiśor Press, 1906, p. 40.

Since my Dear Child went abroad, my companion, my body is continuously wasting.
Without the one who is as dear as my life, the breasts in my bodice are drenched with streams of tears.
Ṭhākur says, such is my condition, O my sister, that only you console me:
I live on looking at the face of my sister-in-law, my friend, which is like that of my lover.

In contrast with the rather conventional M5, Ṭhākur's treatment is more sensuous, emotional and poetically more sophisticated. For example, instead of the pedestrian *jā dina te... tā dina te* structure, Ṭhākur has the more intensive *jaba te... china hī china*. His third line, however, is problematic and its text may be corrupt. His version contains three vocatives, *alī*, *sajanī* and *sakhī*, all addressed to a confidante but the phrase "it is only you who console me" seems to address another person, the sister-in-law. It is possible, but unlikely that the first three lines are, in fact, addressed to the sister-in-law and the last one to a companion. A way around this may be the stretching of the meaning of the phrase to "I can confide only in you" or "only you give me happiness (by your advice to look at the sister-in-law)". It may have been the case that someone observing the third line as corrupt changed it entirely even getting rid of the poetic signature.

The following case of shared lines may not be a *samasyāpūrti* at all. The second line of M6 is shared with the first line of U14 (*Kūṭ kabitta* 8). The shared line provided a structure based on paradoxes in both poems.

mīna marai jala ke parase, kabahū̃ na marai vaha pāvaka pāye|

A fish dies by the touch of the water but it never dies receiving fire.

Sometimes the poet himself took his own lines or phrases as *samasyā*s recycling his own compositions, as happened in the following five cases,

udho jū, doṣa tumhaī̃ na unhaī̃, hama āpuhī pā̃va pai pāthara pāre|| B59
ūdho jū, doṣa tumhaī̃ na unhaī̃, hama līnhī hai āpane hātha hī bīchī|| B60

hamaī̃ ko ganai, kāsõ parojana hai bunibe mẽ na bīna bajāibe mẽ|| Ś133
hamaī̃ kā kahibe saũ parojana hai bunibe maī̃ na bīna bajāibe mẽ|| Ś134

jo biṣa khāya so prāna tajai, gura khāya so kāhe na kāna chedāvai||Ś45
nā biṣa khāū̃ na prāna tajaũ, gura khāū̃ na kāhū sõ kāna chidāū̃|| Ś60

cahaī̃ āśikī au ḍara mānana ko, kahau, dvai dvai kahā bani āvatī haī̃|| Ś53
yaha āsakī au ḍara pāvana kau, kahau, do do kahā̃ bani āvatī haī̃|| Ś155

aba kā kahiyai, apane urajhaī̃ sabahī kī khusāmadi kījatu hai||Ś83
apane urajhe surajhāyabe kaũ sabahī kī khuśāmada kījatu hai||N19

The closely similar beginning of N4 and N14, distantly evoking the *āndharo adhama...* opening words of Tulsīdās's *Kavitāvalī* 74, is also reminiscent of a *samasyā*.

aiso andha, adhama, abhāgo, abhimāna bharo| N4
andha, abibekīe, abhāge, abhimāna bhare| N14

The variant of N14 collected in the *Śatak* is almost identical with N4:

aise andha, adhama, abhāge, abhimāna bhare| N14 var

At another instance, Ṭhākur developed an idea emerging in a *dohā* by Bihārī,

kara sameṭa kaca bhuja ulaṭi khaẽ sīsa paṭu ṭāri|
kākau manu bā̃dhe na yaha jūrā-bā̃dhanahāri|| *Bihārī-ratnākar* 687||

Collecting her hair, she turns her arm upside down and casts her veil back to her shoulder.
Whose mind would she not bind—the girl who is binding her hair behind?

While Bihārī's treatment is a description of a moment of beauty Ṭhākur used the idea for an emotional effect in Ś28,

Oh, give me back my mind that is hiding among your breasts. When you were binding the string of your bodice, I myself became bound. (Ś28)

As has been seen, Ṭhākur did not only elaborate earlier textual treatments but may also have produced texts that served as examples for later poets. As noted by Surendra Mathur, the text of the quatrain *sukavi sipāhī hama . . .* (N25), for example, was closely reworked later by Bhāratendu Hariścandra in his poem *sevaka gunījana ke, cākara catura ke haĩ.*[29] Poems playing with another aspect of the same N25, namely the contrast of the words meaning "lord" (ṭhākura) and "servant" (cākara), were also in circulation as is illustrated in quatrain M7 by an unknown author.

Sometimes the limited range of possible treatments of a category almost determines poems to be similar to on each other. For example, the theme of meeting the lover in a dream (*svapna darśan)* and then waking up to a bleak reality regretting the loss of the dream in *sāpane haũ phulavāī gaī . . .* (Ś71) is particularly close to that of many other quatrains. Such poems include *jhahari jhahari jhīnī būnda hai parati māno . . .* attributed to Dev by Shivdatt Chaturvedi, *sapane mẽ gaī dekhana haũ . ..* attributed to Dev by Surendra Mathur (although none of them are present in the collected works of Dev) and *sovata āju sakhī sapane . . .* by Dvijdev.[30]

Similarly, intertextuality may also emerge from building up a poem on a set phrase. For example, the exploitation of the Hindi idiom designating a parochial person, *kūp-maṇḍūk*, "frog in a well", both in Ṭhākur (N16) and Vr̥nd (*Satsaī* [31] 93) results in contrasting it to a lake *(mānas)* or an ocean. Similarly, both Ṭhākur (Ś101) and Vr̥nd (*Satsaī* 254) use the idiom "Will the day not dawn, if there is no cockerel in a village?" to conclude a poem. Various poets exploited the possibilities of the idiom "fragrance in gold" to illustrate the impossibility of perfection. The last line of the poem N2 is as follows,

rūpavanta ādimī kasakavanta hoto, hutī̃ sone maĩ sugandha, tau sarāhibe kaũ ko hato|

If a beautiful man was sensitive to others' pain and if there was fragrance in gold, who could then praise them?

[29] Mathur, *Kavi ṭhākur aur unkā kāvya*, p. 22.

[30] For the three poems see S. Chaturvedi and V. Mishra, *Dev kī dīpśikhā*, 2nd edn., New Delhi: Vāṇī Prakāśan, 1988, p. 67; Mathur, *Kavi ṭhākur aur unkā kāvya*, p. 86 and Chaturvedi and Mishra, *Dev kī dīpśikhā*, p. 68, respectively. Dev's works are collected in L. Malviy, ed., *Dev sampūrṇ granthāvalī*, 3 vols., Delhi: Āditya Prakāśan, 2002.

[31] J.R. Cheler, ed. *Vr̥nd granthāvalī,* Agra: Vinod Pustak Mandir, 1971.

Padmākar rebuts this in his *Jagadvinod*,[32]

sone mẽ sugandha na sugandha mẽ sunyau ri sone,
sona aura sugandha tomẽ donõ basiyatu hai| 18

Neither fragrance in gold nor gold in fragrance have been heard of—gold and fragrance: both reside within you.

Both authors may be indebted to Vṛnd's *Satsaī* (1704),

jaisau guna dīnau daī taisau rūpa nibandha|
e doū kahā̃ pāiyai sonau aura sugandha|| 80||

When the Creator gave virtues, did he attach the same beauty to them?
Where are both gold and fragrance found together?

Vṛnd's *Nīti-satsaī* offers some more instances of intertextuality. The following couplet is similar to the concluding line of N12,

jāsoṁ rakṣā hota hai hvai tāhī soṁ ghāta|
kahā karai koū jatana bāri kakariyā khāta|| 54||

When your protector strikes you:
What can you do when your fence eats your cucumbers?

In spite of the shared rhetorical question and shared vocabulary there are striking differences between the two poems. The *kavitta* form has a larger scope to elaborate on the same image. In addition, Ṭhākur applies internal rhyming to reinforce the absurdity of situation. Moreover, the idea of being subordinate to a protector is absent from Ṭhākur,

rājā hvai kai tajai nyāya, saṅgī hvai kai karai ghāya|
bārī kheta khāya, tau upāya kahā kījiyai|| N12 ||

When your king abandons law, when your companion strikes you,
when your fence eats your field—what is then the way ahead?

The following *kavitta* elaborates the comparison of the clouds to an elephant driven by the Love God,

Its body is the dark cloud; its teeth are the white-footed herons
and the call of the eastern wind resounds.
It has beautiful head-ornaments, the lightning, and a cover of rainbow;
and the staff of its goad, the flash, is fair.
Ṭhākur says, mounted on it is the Intoxicating Love-god;
and venting its constant anger the wind urges it on.
When my beloved is abroad, this hostile companion of love,
the elephant-asterism-rain, falls and tramples my heart. (R63)

This imagery is shared with a song attributed to Sūrdās already in the early *Sūrsāgar*,

In all directions the thickening clouds,
Like strong, lustful elephants of the Love-god,

[32]V. Mishra, ed., *Padmākar: Jagadvinod* Varanasi: Vāṇī Vitān, 1965.

break the chains with which they are bound
And sprinkle passion from the temples of their fine
dark bodies—they sprinkle little raindrops.
They run: they refuse to be turned aside
by the goad of the wind, their mahout,
And all beyond control, they shatter the bounds of ponds
with tusks that are rows of airborne herons.
Our tears, too, without shores to restrain them,
overrun their bodice-banks, flood our breasts.
Once, in time long past, there came a moment
when the Lord of Airavat joined hands
to submit to the Lord of Braj.
Now all has changed. Kanh, Sur's dark lion,
is gone, and our bodies melt
like hail upon the ground.

(Translated by J.S. Hawley)[33]

Ṭhākur's deep respect for one of the first influential poets of quatrains, Tulsīdās, is explicit in N38 *(bedamata sumrata . . .)* as is his devotion to Rama in B8 *(dhanā aura sadanā . . .)* and B12 *(rāma mero paṇḍita . . .)*. He also expressed his indebtedness to Tulsīdās by using textual material evoking the devotee poet. For example, the last line of B18 is reminiscent of Tulsīdās's *Kavitāvalī,*

mana mõ na basyau asa bālaka jau tulasī jaga mẽ phala kauna jie|| 2||

If such a child has not settled in your heart, Tulsī, then what is the fruit of living in the world?

While Tulsīdās was speaking about devotion towards the child Rama, Ṭhākur applied the same idea to Krishna.

neka kiyo na saneha gopāla sõ deha dhare ko kahā phala pāyo|| B18||

If you did not have the least love for Krishna, then what fruit did you receive from living a human life?

Another instance of close reworking is Ś66 and *Rāmcaritmānas* 1,259 as well as Vrind's *Nīti satsaī* 60.

dila sā̃co lagyau jihi ko jihi pai, tihi kõ titahī pahũcāvata hai|
. . .
paramesura kī paratīti yahai, milyau cāhata tāhi milāvata hai|| Ś66||

When one's heart is truly set on something, it takes the person right there.
. . .
God is famed for the fact that he gives exactly what one wants.

jehi ke jehi para satya sanehū| so tehi milai na kachu sandehū||

[33]The Hindi original is nr 220 in J.S. Hawley, *Sur's Ocean,* Cambridge: Harvard University Press, (forthcoming). Its equivalent in the *Sūrsāgar* is 3303/3921 (vol. 2, p. 1380).

It is beyond any doubt that one receives what he truly loves.

(Translated by R.C. Prasad)[34]

jiya cāhai soī milai, jiyata bhalau hiya lāgi|
pyāsau cāhata nīra kauṁ, kahā karai lai āgi|| *Nīti satsaī* 60||

If one is absorbed in living properly and sets his heart on a thing, he will receive that very thing.
The thirsty one wants water; what would he do if one brings him fire?

The last line of the following *savaiyā* elaborates on an idiom also used by Tulsīdās in *Rāmcaritmānas* 2, 127,

aba, ūdho suno, yaha prīta kī rīta, ju kāchiye kācha suī naciye|| B57||

Now listen, Uddhav, this is the way of love: one has to dance according to one's clothes.

tumha jo kahahu karahu sabu sā̃cā| jasa kāchia tasa cāhia nā̃cā||

All that you do or say is fitting, for one should dance in keeping with the role one has assumed.

(Translated by R.C. Prasad)[35]

Interestingly both lines are parts of dialogues suggesting that the phrase has a strong colloquial tint. The *Mānas* presents the idiom as part of Vālmīki's praise when he meets Rama while Ṭhākur employs it as the nub in the cowherdesses' riposte to Uddhava.

In spite of the fact that Ṭhākur never seems to have produced any quatrain on the Ramayana theme, intertextuality demonstrsates that he kept the poetry of Tulsīdās. in high regard. For example his quatrains about "the strangeness of the Creator's *(vidhi)* work or simply of Fate *(bhāgi)* (N1, N2, N14, N17) develop the theme of "the Creator's doings are all perverse" *(bidhikaratаba ulaṭe saba ahahī)* addressed in the *Ayodhyākāṇḍa* of the *Rāmcaritmānas* (2,119). As has been mentioned, Ṭhākur's description of good and bad people is also reminiscent of the *sant-asant* verses in the *Rāmcaritmānas* (1, 4-6 and 7, 39-41). Other overlap in themes includes quatrains describing the *Kaliyuga*, a favourite theme of Tulsīdās (cf. *Rāmcaritmānas* 7, 96-103, *Kavitāvalī* 7, 79-88, etc.).

There must be many other instances of developing earlier imagery or poetic phraseology as well as of providing patterns for later poets as exemplified in some of the Ṭhākur monographs[36] and further research may show the great extent to which early modern Hindi poets were in dialogue with each other.

One can even find instances of straightforward plagiarism, when the same poem is

[34]R. C. Prasad, ed. *Tulasidasa's Shriramacharitamanasa: The Holy Lake of the Acts of Rama,* Delhi: Motilal Banarsidass, 1990; rpt. 1999, p. 147.

[35]Ibid., p. 275.

[36]Mathur, *Kavi ṭhākur aur unkā kāvya*, pp. 81-91, for example, presents closer or more distant similarity to Ṭhākur in quatrains attributed Tulsīdās, Raskhān, Ānandghan (Ghanānand), Ālam, Matirām, Bhikhārīdās, Dev, Padmākar, Hanumān, Dvijbaldev, and Hariścandra. While some of the parallels may not have arisen from direct influence, the closeness of some of Hariścanda's *savaiyās* is striking. Relying less on textual parallels, Ray, *Svacchand kāvyadhārā aur kavi ṭhākur*, pp. 211-36 compares Ṭhākur with other "*svacchand*" poets.

presented under a different signature, as was the case with Ś97 *(cārihū̃ ora udai…)*, which was attributed to Īśvar kavi in the *Śivsiṁh Saroj*.[37] Its third line reads as,

kavi īśvara bhūli gayo juga pāribo yā bigarī ko sudhāri le rī|

This version may have relied on a variant of Ś97,

kahi ṭhākura bhūli gayo jau gopāla, tau tū bigarī kõ sudhāri lai rī|

CONCLUSION

According to the preserved memory, Ṭhākur's poetry is deeply rooted in the political realities of his time through his application of the Krishna theme to express his opinion about the contemporary political setting. This must have been a widespread attitude among poets although the clues establishing context in many cases have been lost. In contrast with this general approach, Ṭhākur's early modern individualism, use of proverbs and of regional language are distinctive features of the poet. His sensual perception of nature, as well as his down-to-earth yet intensive language, which occasionally borders on the harsh and indecent, distinguish him from others.

Ṭhākur's quatrains appear in innumerable nineteenth-century anthologies, both handwritten and printed. His popularity at that time suggests that moving away from the ornamented Brajbhasha of Ānandghan and Dev towards simplicity, along with his poetic self-assertion, prepared the aesthetic sensibilities of Hindi audiences for a less ornate and more individualistic western literature.

Influential twentieth-century scholars considered Ṭhākur to be one of the major representatives of *rītimukta* or "convention-free" poetry. Since many Ṭhākur poems showed conventional features they had to split his poetic corpus in order to show in its major part a more marked *rītimukta* poet uninterested in or outright inimical to conventions. Since literary histories had known of several poets called Ṭhākur or Ṭhākurdās, scholars assigned to one of them the more conventional part of the Ṭhākur-corpus. As we are going to see in the next chapter, the earliest sources do not support this division of the poems but suggest that the innovative and the conventional were both present in Ṭhākur's oeuvre. His quatrains represent continuity rather than rupture with earlier poetic traditions.

The language of Ṭhākur's poems shows a moderate use of Bundeli features. In his time, this was a conscious expression of regional identity rather than ignorance of the standard form. Transmission, however, may have reworked such distinctive features into more standard literary Braj. Since twentieth-century scholarship was conscious of this tendency, it changed some of his word forms into Bundeli dialect.

Ṭhākur's quatrains were part of the lively literary circulation of his times. This is shown not only by the widespread distribution of his manuscripts over the western and central part of the Hindi belt but also by the fact that several of his lines are shared with other poets—often within the widespread poetic practice of *samasyāpūrti*. His poems build on stylistic features and imagery used by other poets, sometimes reflect upon the art of poetry and even pay tribute to one of the greatest early poets of quatrains, Tulsīdās (N31).

[37] P. 15, quoted on p. 84 in Gupta's *Sarvekṣaṇ*.

The Text

PROSODY

Since prosody and especially stress has played an important role in establishing the text of Ṭhākur's poems, I will briefly survey the basic prosodic elements used in his *kavitta*s and *savaiyā*s.

Traditional Hindi prosody relying on Apabhramsha handbooks on meter, called *piṅgala-śāstra,* was centred on moraic metres *(mātrika chanda)* but also acknowledged the role of syllabic metres *(vārṇika chanda).*

Moraic metres are based on the counting of metric units depending on the length of the syllables. A metric unit is called mora in Latin and *mātrā* in Sanskrit and other Indic languages. In *mātrika chanda*, short syllables count as one and long syllables as two. Short syllables are naturally short syllables not followed by a consonant cluster (as the syllable *bi* in *ambikā*). Long syllables are either naturally long (as the syllable *kā* in *ambikā*) or naturally short vowels followed by a consonant cluster (as the syllable *am[b]* in *ambikā*). The metrical value of the word *ambikā*, therefore, is 2+1+2. A moraic verse is organised around this principle. A *dohā*, for example, has 13+11 morae in a line. A line in the *savaiyā* quatrain has eight units of dactylic (*bhagaṇa* 2-1-1) or anapaestic (*sagaṇa* 1-1-2) metric sequences. The name of the first version is *kirīṭ savaiyā* and of the second *durmilā savaiyā.* The last sequence in a dactylic line can also be a spondee (2+2). Then the *savaiyā* is called *mattagayand savaiyā.*

Syllabic metres rely on counting the number of syllables. A line in the *ghanākṣarī kavitta* quatrain, for example, has 16+15 syllables.

Research started by the Canadian student Florence Fairbanks in the late eighties[1] and applied successfully to Sūrdās by Kenneth Bryant and to Harirām Vyās by Heidi Pauwels[2] has fundamentally changed the approach to Hindi prosody. Although merely counting morae or syllables does not necessarily give a rhythm, traditional prosody did not speak about the role of the stress. Most Braj metres rely heavily on sequences of stressed and unstressed or indifferent syllables. The distinctive role of stress was never theorised by Hindi poets. For example, the *ghanākṣarī kavitta*'s 16+15 line can be divided into seven units of four syllables and a final unit of three. There is stress on the first syllable of all these eight units while the rest is indifferent. The regular occurrence of the stress gives the *kavitta* particular energy and makes it especially fit for descriptions of battles or conflicting emotions.

Scholarly disagreement about the position of Hindi stress made the discovery of its poetic role difficult. Concerning prosody, the general rule is that stress does not fall on the last syllable but on the next long syllable counting from the back. This means that,

[1]F. Fairbanks, 'Hindi Stress: A New Approach thru Meter', paper presented at the Linguistics Club, University of Minnesota, 1987.

[2]K.E. Bryant, 'Three-three-two versus Four-by-four: Metrical Frames for the Padas of Surdas', in *Devotional Literature in South Asia: Current Research 1985-1988*, ed. R. Stuart McGregor, Cambridge: Cambridge University Press, 1992, pp. 209-24. H. Pauwels, *New Indo-Aryan Poetry in Performance*, pp. 311-38.

1. Stress is on the penultimate syllable of a word if it is long. (ba*nā*ya, dena*vā*re)
2. If the penultimate syllable is short, but the one before it is long, the stress is on that syllable. (a*khaṇ*dita, ka*hā*vata)
3. If the last three syllables are short, then the stress is on the fourth syllable from the back. (*gā*vatahĩ, *a*numati)

The above general rules are modified in the following four cases,

1. If the last syllable is the only long syllable among the last three syllables, then the stress is on the third syllable from the back. (*u*rajhī, ku*sa*maye)
2. Stress in a disyllabic word of the short-long type can be on either of its syllables. (ma*hī*, *ma*hī)
3. Stress in words containing only three short syllables can be either on its first or second syllable. (*ka*hata, ka*ha*ta)
4. Each component of a compound word may have its own stress. (*kā*madh*e*nu)

The application of these rules divides a *kavitta* line into eight units each starting with a stressed syllable,

*thā*kura ka|*ha*ta, hama |*bai*rī beva|*kū*phana ke|,
*jā*lima da|*mā*da haĩ a|*dā*niyā̃ sa|*su*ra ke|

The stress is clearly audible in traditional recitation but its role has not been theorised in early modern times. It was in the late nineteenth century that Jagannāthdās Ratnākar, one of the last poets and earliest philologists of Brajbhasha, recognised the importance of syllabic pattern for the stressed syllables of the *ghanākṣarī kavitta*s. Without being aware of the use of stress he applied the above rules to this poetic form in his booklet *Ghanākṣarī-niyam-ratnākar.*[3]

ORAL AND WRITTEN TRANSMISSION

An examination of the material from the nineteenth and early twentieth centuries shows that variation within the text attributed to Ṭhākur was more extensive and more substantial than published in the twentieth-century 'collected poems' books. Ṭhākur's text has variants due to the dynamics of oral transmission and conscious manipulation, shown in the removal of embarrassing words or the changing of unfamiliar Bundelkhandi features into standard Braj.

ORAL TRANSMISSION

Although the poems in this book have been collected from written sources many of them had a life in oral transmission before and possibly after being committed to writing. Oral performance could take place in various ways. People can simply recite or sing quatrains

[3] J. Ratnakar, *Ghanākṣarī-niyam-ratnākar,* Varanasi: Bhārat Jīvan Press, 1897.

to set melodies (*dhun*).[4] While *kavittas* could also be set to classical music, it was probably not the practice with *savaiyās*.[5]

Ṭhākur considered himself not simply a poet but also a soldier as well as a political counsellor as illustrated in quatrain N25 (*sukavi sipāhī* . . .). Although in two manuscripts this is considered to be a *bharauā*, a verse with lowly or indecent vocabulary, suggesting that it may not be taken at face value, this quatrain may give us a hint that Ṭhākur was not a poet *per se* but rather, as was the case with Rahīm, Sundar Kavirāy, Raslīn and others, a courtier who also had political or military roles. This is why unlike his more celebrated contemporary, Padmākar, Ṭhākur did not compose any longer work but limited himself to independent quatrains, which he never seemed to take the trouble to collect.

According to Ṭhākur real poetry was made to "earn greatness in the royal assembly", where expert connoisseurs were present. It is important to notice that although many poems praise the generous ruler, the ultimate judge for poetry is the learned assembly rather than the king (N36, N37). Notwithstanding the idealising tendency in *savaiyā* N36, one can assume that Ṭhākur composed most of his quatrains for presentation in a royal assembly. The anecdotes quoted above have preserved descriptions of how several quatrains were performed. The stories suggest that their author recited many of these poems blatantly to one or another ruler but they also propose contexts beyond public performance.

Courtly *kavittas* and *savaiyās* once presented to the public started to circulate probably orally although some of them may have made it into manuscript anthologies at an early stage. A picture of oral circulation in Ṭhākur's time can be gained from the writings of Thomas Duer Broughton (1778-1835), who in the years following 1802 was the commander of the British Resident's escort at the court of Daulat Rao Sindia, the leader of the strongest Maratha army. His two books, *Letters Written in a Mahratta Camp During the Year 1809: Descriptive of the character manners domestic habits and religious ceremonies of the Mahrattas* (1813) and *Selections from the popular poetry of the Hindoos* (1814), present a selection of the stock of poems collected "from the verbal communications of the Sipahees, and others not raised above them in the general scale of society". They also talk about the context in which the officer heard them. The poems, mostly courtly *kabittas*, were normally recited by Brahmin soldiers,

> I had remarked that in talking upon any subject, he frequently quoted the verses of some favourite poet . . . I expressed a wish for further information respecting the dialect in which they were written, and that he would make a collection for me of similar compositions. My new studies soon became known, and many individuals of the same rank in life contributed to increase my stores by voluntary offers of all the information they possessed upon the subject; evincing at the same time such evident symptoms of gratified pride at the distinction conferred upon their rustic lore, as led me to follow up my pursuit with increased satisfaction.[6]

[4]Two set melodies for *savaiyās* collected in Vrindaban are published in I. Bangha and B. Déri, *Ánandghan: A Jótudásúhoz: a nőhöz és istenhez*, New Delhi: Hungarian Information and Cultural Centre, 1996, pp. 51-2.

[5]In the late 1990s, I asked the young Ustad Vasifuddin Dagar, one of the most outstanding singers of dhrupad, to perform a *savaiyā* by Ānandghan in a cultural programme. He set the *savaiyā* to music and sang it but mentioned that elder singers had reminded him that *savaiyās* are not to be set to music.

[6]T.D. Broughton, *Selections from the popular poetry of the Hindoos*, London: Whittingham and Rowland, 1814, pp. 6-7, quoted in Bangha, *The First Published Anthology of Hindi Poets*, p. 38.

Broughton did not rely exclusively on his *sipahees*. In his *Letters Written in a Mahratta Camp* he gave an account of the circumstances in which certain poems were sung. Some *kabittas*—including one by Keśavdās—were sung in a *rāslīlā* performance at the festival of *Janmāṣṭamī*, some others were probably sung at Holi festivities. As an introduction to the translation of a *kavitta* on the spring *(basant)* by Dev, Broughton tells that a *basant* song is sung in spring, when

> [t]he general gladness diffuses itself even among the poor women who grind the corn, and who now always lighten their labour by a song… An industrious woman, when not inclined to sleep, will arise at any hour of the night and busy herself with the mill: and any person lying awake, would be sure to hear two or three women so employed, singing over their work in a strain which, if not positively beautiful, is far from being unpleasing, and accords well with the stillness of the hour. Some of these songs, those especially which allude to the *Busunt*, possess no inconsiderable share of merit.[7]

Some information is also given about the circumstances in which a couplet by Bihārī and a *kavitta* by Keśavdās, were performed.

> Another of our licensed Fuqeers sings his petitions, and dances, in a most ridiculous manner, to a pair of dry sticks, which he uses like castanets. Many go about in groups and earn a livelihood by singing old Hindoo songs in a manner that is far from being disagreeable.[8]

Broughton's sources were not the learned scholars or the professional scribes who bequeathed us extensive manuscript material, but a larger group of learned villagers or singers. Broughton's foreword to his selections also introduces the aesthetics of the poetry he collected, which in all probability rely on what the soldiers explained to their officer. Based on what Broughton writes, one can observe that knowledge of traditional aesthetics in India was not the monopoly of poets and scholars.

Broughton's poems acquired through oral transmission show slightly more eccentric variants than their corresponding versions in manuscripts. However, in spite of some confusing variants, his readings indicate that learned villagers were an appreciative audience for *rīti*-poetry and as can be judged from Broughton's notes they interpreted them more or less in the same way as their poet must have intended.

As has been mentioned by Broughton, and as was the case with the Persian couplet recited by Niẓām ul-Mulk to Nādīr Śāh, poems were frequently used to illustrate certain points in a conversation. The case of a *kavitta* by the poet Debendra quoted by Ānandrām Mukẖlis in his *Safar-nāma* (1745), shows that it was enough to contextualise a poem even on the basis of a short passage from it. When Ānandrām had difficulties in crossing the Ganges he quoted a quatrain in which the cowherdesses forsaken by Krishna express their plight to his messenger, Uddhav,

hā hā kari kari ūdho āvata hai hiyo rūndho
    syāma jū saũ kahyau jāe tanhā tana mere kī|
gokula tū taja dīnī mathurā saṅkalpa kīnī
    bindrābana saũha līnī bhūle sudhi khere kī|

[7] T.D. Broughton, *Letters Written in a Mahratta Camp During the Year 1809: Descriptive of the character manners domestic habits and religious ceremonies of the Mahrattas* London: Murray, 1813. A new edition with an Introduction by the right Honourable Sir M.E. Grant Duff G.C.S.I. F.R.S.); New Delhi and Madras: Asian Educational Services, 1995, p. 37.

[8] Ibid. p. 130.

kahai kabi debendhara rahata ucāṭa hama
    jaba sudhi āvata biraja ke basere kī|
prīti kī caḍhāe nāva kāṭi dīnī māñjha dhāra
    kīnī brajanātha kidhau thala kī na tīre kī||[9]

My heart is constricted imploring you, Uddhav,
    go and tell the Dark One the matter of my lonely body.
"You abandoned Gokula and fancied Mathura,
    I swear on Brindavan, you forgot this small village.
The poet Debendra says, we are bewildered
    when we remember of your stay in Braj.
You boarded us on the boat of love and drove it into the middle of the current,
    o Lord of Braj, did you make us of the deep or of the shore?

The fact that the backdrop for Ṭhākur's poems was oral performance is confirmed not only by the evidence of variants, such as longer phrases or entire lines, which cannot go back to written transmission but rather represent flaws and subsequent corrections of memory but also by the fact that in handwritten transmission there are only a few independent collections of Ṭhākur. The poet did not produce any longer composition but limited himself to independent quatrains, which he or his relatives or associates never bothered to collect. Apart from two closely related longer manuscripts now in Vrindaban and in Benares,[10] one in Chatarpur[11] and one in Patiala,[12] as well as three smaller ones with 10-20 poems each, Ṭhākur's poems are found only in anthologies along with those of other late classicist or *rīti* poets popular in the nineteenth century.[13] The *Sudhāsar*, a massive anthology of more than 250 poets, preserved more quatrains of Ṭhākur than any of the manuscripts exclusively devoted to him.

In the case of Ṭhākur, many variant readings emerged due either to the flaws of oral transmission or to conscious manipulation. Certain types of variations suggest that for a period, the poems were transmitted not in writing but orally, and thus they were exposed more to 'improvement' and corruption. The poem *sīkha līne mīna mṛga...* (N37) has been

[9] S. A. 'Ali, ed. *Safarnāma-i Mukhlis: The Diary of the travel of Anand Ram Mukhlis, d. 1164 A.H.*, Rampur: 1946, pp. 97-8. The quatrain is here quoted with some emendation. In footnote 2 on p. 97 the editor of the *Safarnāma* with the help of a pandit made a rather eccentric attempt at transcribing into Devanagari the occasionally corrupt text given originally in the Urdu script. A variant of the same poem without the signature of Debendra can be found on f. 53r of our Kasganj manuscript (N). The third line of the poem in the manuscript reads as *maĩ tau kuṭumba tyāgi lagī hõ tumhāre pāya, tuma tau taji dīnī jaise kāñcurī sapere kī.*

[10] The manuscript called Vrindaban1 (V_1) in this edition has 96 quatrains. The other one (K_3), which I was not able to consult directly, is in the Yajnik Collection at the Nāgarīpracāriṇī Sabhā. Its contents and readings, however, as published in the *Ṭhākur granthāvalī*, are usually identical with those of the Vrindaban manuscript. Bhavanishankar Yajnik was a priest at the Gokulnāth temple in Gokul, which suggests that the Benares manuscript also came from Braj.

[11] In 1905 an undated manuscript apparently with 98 poems was reported to be in the collection of Babu Jagannathprasad, Head Accountant, Chatarpur. See S. Das, *Annual Report on the Search for Hindi Manuscripts for the Year 1905*, Allahabad: United Provinces Government Press, 1908; reprint, Varanasi: Nāgarīpracāriṇī Sabhā, 1995, p. 92 (05-98).

[12] A Gurmukhi manuscript called *Ṭhākur-satsaī* containing 49 quatrains by Ṭhākur.

[13] See the list of handwritten and printed Ṭhākur-collections and anthologies on pages 69-78.

quoted above in a variant but it is recorded in a further less powerful variant version as well. It is easy to see that the *sīkha līnho* repetition in each of the first four lines is a kind of dramatic reinforcement of the uselessness of repeating tradition itself. The variant takes up exactly this point,

sīkhi līnaĩ dātā gyātā kali maĩ kalapataru
    sīkhi līnau prabala pratāpa adhikānau hai|
sīkhi lene khañjana capala mṛga aise naina
    sīkha līne sarasa sugandha sarasānau hai|
ṭhākura kahata yaha kāma sabahī ko nāhi
    jānata jihāna haĩ kaṭhini yaha bānau hai|
ḍela so banākaĩ āni melata sabhā kaĩ bīca
    logana kabitta kaibo khela kari jānau hai|[14]

In this example apart from the *sīkhi līne* phrases only the rhymes and the last line remind the reader of the probable original. Such drastic changes cannot occur in written transmission. The original of this *kavitta* must have been so popular that many people knew it by heart and by the time this variant was written down it has almost completely changed. A similar case can be observed with *savaiyā* N22, which is also present in a substantially different variant in the *Rasik-vinod* (N23). The *Rasik-vinod*'s version, while preserving the overall meaning, drastically changed the wording and the order of phrases and lines. Therefore, it is probably a variation on N22 that emerged over a period of oral transmission, rather than a conscious reworking of the same theme. A similarly considerable variation on Ś129 can be found in Ś130.

Which parts of a *kavitta* are the most liable to change? The *sīkhi līne* phrases and the last line are the most solid part of the quatrain, while the inventory of conventional similes and the morals of the third line are easily changed.[15]

The most powerful part of a quatrain is normally its last line, which intensified with the use of proverbs creates an instant impression on the audience. Ṭhākur stated that poetry should enchant the audience, the *sabhā*. It seems that court poets used every possible means to enhance this instant impression, including their appearance. The poet's clothes, like the final line of the quatrain, might linger in the mind of the audience. Family lore noted Ṭhākur's magnificent attire: his turban, short jacket *(mirzaī)*, tasselled Bundelkhandi shoes and a sword on one side and a copper inkwell on the other.[16]—This is typical courtly appearance, except for the unlikely inkwell, which evokes the world of iconic miniature paintings.

One can also detect cases when probably conscious manipulation changed the quatrains. Lala Bhagvandin[17] tells a story according to which *Ṭhākur* cured a lady called Sujān from an illness when he recited a *savaiyā* passing at the back of her house. *Savaiyā* Ś116 is one of the relatively rare Brajbhasha poems that present the words of a lover. The reading quoted with the contextualising story on p. 21 is found in the *Ṭhākur ṭhasak* and subsequently in the *Granthāvalī*. The first line of the poem is problematic with the confusing meaning *"my*

[14] *Kabitt saṅgrah*. Manuscript preserved at the Ras Bharati Sansthan, Vrindaban, nr. 548 f. 68v.

[15] The day after I wrote down the previous lines I tried to remember the original poem. The *sīkhi līnau* phrases and the last line were not a problem but I confused the rest.

[16] Bhagavandin, *Ṭhākur ṭhasak*, 'Ṭhākur kavi kā jīvancarit', p. 8.

[17] Ibid. 'Ṭhākur kavi kā jīvancarit' p. 15.

mind is to roam in your lane". Moreover, the word *cita* 'mind' is repeated in the second line producing *punarukti doṣa*. In two other collections, Baburamdin Singh's *Sundarī-tilak* (1892) and Bhairav Singh's *Rasik-vinod* (1910), however, the first and the last lines are as follows,

gati merī yahī nisavāsara hai, nita terī galīna ke gāhibo hai|

. . .

mana bhāvai tihāre soī kariyai, hamaī neha ko nāto nibāhibo hai||

Day and night my ways are such that I always have to wander in your lane.

. . .

Do what pleases your mind—I am to fulfil my love's commitment.

This more polished and probably later version has Braj forms of the rhyming infinitives (*gāhibo* etc.) rather than Bundeli (*gāhane* etc.). The context is also clearer. The hero *(nāyaka)*—and not his mind—passes repeatedly by the house of his beloved about whom people already started to gossip. There is nothing in the verses that could be linked to healing or even pleasing the heroine through praising her beauty. The poem is rather an exhortation to the heroine to meet the hero through enacting her desire.

Unlike most other *rītimukta* poets, Ṭhākur does not claim to have been inspired by personal love. The above *savaiyā*, however slightly, is contextualised as a love poem. The removal of the word Sujān from a poem to which a love context is attributed may reflect distantly the debates on the Hindu ascetic Ānandghan whose alleged personal love to a Muslim courtesan whom he called Sujān became the object of heated debates.[18]

It may not be a coincidence that another poem addressed to Sujān, the *rūpamāna sundarī sujāna, kāna daikai sunau* . . . (Ś100) is present in two versions, one underlining, and another downplaying the Persianate aspect. Apart from the *Ṭhasak,* which served as the basis for the text of the *Granthāvalī,* this *kavitta* is present in manuscript D_1. The readings of this Datiya manuscript are weaker and contain Persianate words. Was the Persianate layer in this poem subdued by a later editor? Alternatively, were the readings Islamicised in order to mock Ṭhākur? Whatever the case, it is clear that the use of the word *sujān* incited Persianate associations, which seems to have been embarrassing to some readers.

There are also instances of prudishness. For example in Ś25 and Ś26, twentieth-century editions have variant readings for the word for 'breasts' present in the other sources. Similarly, in the last line of N22 Bhagvandin emended a 'very harsh' (*kaṭu*) word into the milder *bāvare* 'crazy'.

AUTHORSHIP

This book collects Ṭhākur's quatrains from a range of handwritten and published anthologies. Most of them have a poetic signature *(chāp)* at the beginning of the third line clearly indicating the name of their author. Paratexts in anthologies may also present the name of the author before each poem quoted. In the few instances when a signature is missing, only the attribution of the anthologist affirms that Ṭhākur was the composer of the quatrain. In these cases, however, I also scrutinised the possible authorship on stylistic or historical

[18] I. Bangha, 'Lover and Saint: The Early Development of Anandghan's Reputation'. *Journal of the Royal Asiatic Society*, vol. 11, no. 2, 2001, pp. 175-90.

grounds. Since Ṭhākur has produced a few quatrains without signature it is also likely that his other unsigned poems still lie undiscovered in anthologies.

One cannot exclude the possibility that the author of some Ṭhākur quatrains was not the Bundelkhandi courtier Ṭhākur. Poems that contain the word Ṭhākur or a similar sounding one were sometimes catalogued under the authorship of Ṭhākur and poems by others were sometimes included into a collection or a sequence of Ṭhākur's quatrains, suggesting that he produced them. For example, M9 is the ninth in a sequence of twelve quatrains, where all other poems bear the signature *ṭhākura*. Similarly, a poem by Dev was included into the *Ṭhākur ṭhasak* (186), and subsequently into the *Granthāvalī* (183), one by Raskhān into the *Ṭhākur-satsaī* (6) and one by Sūrdās into our V_1 manuscript (64)—collections otherwise devoted exclusively to Ṭhākur.

While in some such cases the authorship is made clear by the presence of another signature, such as Harikeś (M10)[19] or Murlī (M9)[20] unnoticed by the cataloguers, in many other cases the reader is left to reject a quatrain on stylistic grounds (M9) or is left in ambiguity. Poems of which the authorship is still uncertain are marked with U and are presented in a separate section of the edition.

Three cases of uncertain authorship are worthy of special mention. A manuscript preserved at the Alwar branch of the Rajasthan Oriental Research Institute (Nr. 4832/4) has a colophon claiming that it was written in 1778 (*Saṁvat* 1835) in Ujjain, a date apparently too early for Ṭhākur although it may just allow the authorship of the young poet. This anthology, along with *pads*, couplets, quatrains etc. of Bihārī, Dev, Dayānidhi, Padmākar and others, contains two poems by Ṭhākur, *sāmila ho pīra maĩ . . .* (N31) numbered as 105 on folio 68v and *madamāte guvāla garūra bhare . . .* (R22) numbered as 124 on folios 73v-74r. Interestingly, the editors of the *Granthāvalī* accepted both of these poems as composed by the later '*rītimukta*' Bundelkhandi Ṭhākur. The cataloguer of the manuscript also seemed to have doubts about the early date of copying although the year given by him, 1878 (*Saṁvat* 1935), is apparently a misreading of the colophon on f. 82v. The presence of some later poets, such as Naṭnāgar (1808-63),[21] Dayānidhi (fl. 1801-18)[22] and Padmākar (1753-1833), however, casts a shade of doubt on the authenticity of the colophon.

The second border case is the *Kūṭ kabitta,* a description of which was published in the *Khoj* Report for 1923-5.[23] This is a tiny collection of nine coded quatrains, of which six are published in the *Khoj*. Its manuscript was copied in 1785 (*Saṁvat* 1842), which again would just allow the authorship of the young Ṭhākur, if one accepts Bhagvandin's dates. While almost all of the quatrains attributed to our Ṭhākur have a poetic signature, here the signature is present only in the last quatrain. It may be the case that a young Ṭhākur experimented

[19]Poem 170 on ff. 37v-38r in an unnumbered manuscript at Sūkar Kṣetra Śodh Sansthān, Kasganj is a *savaiyā* by Harikeś containing the word 'ṭhākur' as part of the epithet of Krishna.

[20]Poem numbered as 55 on ff. 36r-37r in our B_5 manuascript

[21]V. Sharma, ed. *Hindī sāhitya kā bṛhat itihās,* vol. 8: *Hindī sāhitya kā abhyutthān: bhāratendu yug saṁ 1900-1950*, Kāśī: Nāgarīpracāriṇī Sabhā, 1972, vol. 8, p. 128.

[22]Dayānidhi composed his *Varṇa-ekākṣarī* in 1801 and settled down permanently in Vrindaban sometime before 1818. He died sometime before 1843. U. Bansal, *Kavivar dayānidhi aur unkā kāvya,* Kasganj: Sūkarkṣetr Śodh Sansthān, 2001, pp. 186 and 141.

[23]Hiralal, ed., *The twelfth report on the search of Hindi manuscripts for the years 1923, 1924 and 1925* Kāśī: Nāgarīpracāriṇī Sabhā, 1944, pp. 1470-1, nr. 426.

with a different style. These coded quatrains may also belong to another, older Ṭhākur, maybe to the one that Navīn called the 'old' Ṭhākur.

The third example is a popular *savaiyā* that was part of the oral lore until recently and was recited to Ganga Prasad 'Barsaiya' around the turn of the millennium by an old Pandit in Jaitpur. Its text, which contained accidentally the word 'ṭhākura' reads as follows in the collection *Rasik-vinod,*

dhani haĩ una tāta je māta janī, jaba janma liyo so gharī dhani haĩ|
dhani haĩ jehi ṭhākura grāma basau, jāha ḍolo, lalī, so galī dhani hai|
dhani haĩ dṛga jeu tumai darasaĩ, parasaĩ kara teu baṛe dhani haĩ|
dhani hau, dhani tū, dhani tero hitū, jinakī dhana hau so dhanī dhani haĩ||

Blessed is the father for whom your mother gave birth to you. Blessed is the hour in which you were born.
Blessed is the lord in whose village you live. Blessed is, my dear, the lane in which you move about.
Blessed are the eyes that show you. The hands that touch you are very much blessed.
You are blessed, blessed you are, blessed is your friend. Blessed is the lord to whom you belong.

The poet, in fact, composed this *savaiyā* along the lines of *Rāmcaritmānas* II. 121,5-6,

te pitu mātu dhanya jinha jāe| dhanya sŏ nagaru tahāṁ tẽ āe||
dhanya sŏ desu sailu bana gāũ| jahā̃ jahā̃ jāhī dhanya sŏi ṭāũ||[24]

'Blessed are the parents who gave birth to these princes, and blessed that city from which they have come!
Blessed are the plains and hills and woods and villages, blessed every spot which they visit.' (Translated by R.C. Prasad)[25]

The *Rasik-vinod* is silent about the author of this popular *savaiyā* present in seven of my sources. In the six other sources, however, the words *jehi ṭhākura* are changed into *kabi ṭhākura* and the poem is explicitly introduced as one composed by Ṭhākur. This was clearly prompted first by the use of the word *ṭhākura* and secondly by a very well known *savaiyā* by Ṭhākur in which the last line starts as *dhani ve dhani pāvasa kī ratiyā̃*. The variant *kabi* may be a secondary reading introduced at a very early stage of circulation. The quatrain's style does not seem to resemble that of the other poems by Ṭhākur but taking into consideration that Ṭhākur wrote on a wide range of subjects it is not outright possible to deny his authorship.

To make the poem more in line with those of Ṭhākur four out of the seven sources (B_1, M_3, Ṭ and U) even changed the order of the second and the third lines so that the perceived poetic signature should come in the third line as usual.

The reading of the Udaipur and more or less of the *Ṭhākur-satsaī* manuscripts is as follows,

dhana tāta vahai jiha māta janī jiha deha dharī su gharī dhana hai|
dhana hai dṛga vai ju tuṁhī̃ darasaĩ, parasaĩ kara ve ju mahā dhana hai|

[24] V. Mishra, ed., *Rāmcaritmānas,* Varanasi: Kāśīrāj, [1962], p. 189.
[25] Prasad, ed., *Shriramacharitamanasa*, p. 272.

dhana hai kabi ṭhākura dhāma vahai, jahā̃ ḍolai lalī, su galī dhana hai|
dhana hai, dhana tū, dhani tero hitū, jiha kī dhana tū̃ su dhanī dhana hai||

The exuberance of variants in this *savaiyā* intrigued the scribes and one manuscript (M3) is nothing else than a folio containing two versions of this poem—an instance of early Indian textual criticism.

THE SOURCES

The study of early modern Indian literary culture is still seriously hindered by the fact that an immense part of this literature, still lies unexplored in manuscript collections. Although several texts have been published during the nineteenth and the twentieth centuries only a few are available in critical editions. The last few decades saw an upsurge of interest in the study of eighteenth- and early-nineteenth-century Indian history. No corresponding increase occurred in the study of the literary texts of this period, however.

As far as Ṭhākur is concerned, several monographs on him were produced in the past fifty years,[26] yet a thorough philological investigation still remains to be done. In the course of my research, I was not only able to find important variants to many quatrains published in the three earlier Ṭhākur-editions based on philological research, namely Kashiprasad's *Ṭhākur śatak* (1904), Lala Bhagvandin's *Ṭhākur ṭhasak* (1924) and Chandrashekhar Mishra's *Ṭhākur granthāvalī* (1973), but was also able to increase the so far largest *Ṭhākur* corpus of 270 *kabitta*s published in the *Granthāvalī* with sixty quatrains.

The material collected for this edition was available mostly in handwritten and lithographed anthologies from the nineteenth century and in printed books from the twentieth century. Most quatrains must have circulated orally before being committed to writing. Although book printing was well established in India already in Ṭhākur's lifetime, the overwhelming majority of his poems circulated in manuscripts in the nineteenth century. This was the time of transition from manuscript to print culture and literature circulated in both forms during this century.

Although written transmission is normally less liable to changes than oral communication, one can also perceive a distinction between handwritten and printed circulation. Manuscript transmission, for example, may present more readings that are eccentric. Printed books became influential vulgates, since their texts circulated more widely than manuscripts. They were also clearer in their script and allowed passages lost from one copy to be reconstructed from other copies. The *Śṛṅgār* section of this edition presents 255 eccentricities, or forms that differ from at least eighty percent of the readings. However, only three of these variations belongs to the twenty-three early printed anthologies of various poets examined. (In contrast with this, there were forty-two eccentricities in the *Śatak*, *Ṭhasak* and the *Granthāvalī*, which suggest a strong editorial hand in these publications.)

[26]Monographs on Ṭhākur include Mathur, *Kavi ṭhākur aur unkā kāvya*, A. Singh, *Rīti kavitā ke sandarbh mẽ ṭhākur kā kavittva-kṛtitva*, Amritsar: Guru Nanak Dev University, 1985, V. Avasthi, *Kavi ṭhākur: kavitt evaṁ racnākār,* Lucknow, 1990, G. Pandey, *Kavi ṭhākur,* Ranchi: College of Commerce, 1990, Varma, *Kavivar ṭhākur*, J. K. Sharma, *Rītimukt kavi ṭhākur aur unkā kāvya,* New Delhi: Sañjay Prakāśan, 2006 (with a Hindi commentary on some 165 quatrains), Ray, *Svacchand kāvyadhārā aur kavi ṭhākur*. The authors of these monographs draw heavily on Bhagvandin and Vishvanath Prasad and Chandrashekhar Mishra but do not always know about each other's work.

While no two sources give the same readings, in the case of the longer collections it is not difficult to recognise how they were dependent on each other. In this way, four major groups of longer sources can be established. The three twentieth-century *Ṭhākur* editions, for example, present a gradual development. Namely, the *Granthāvalī*'s principal source was the *Ṭhasak,* which in turn relied on the *Śatak.* In the critical apparatus the siglum E indicates that all three Ṭhākur editions agree on a given reading. It goes without saying that all *Sudhāsar* manuscripts are closely related to each other, although no two manuscripts present the same text with the same sequence of the poems. In the apparatus, the siglum S indicates that all *Sudhāsar* manuscripts agree on a given reading.

The *Granthāvalī*'s second most substantial source was our K_3 manuscript in the Yajnik-collection of the Nāgarīpracāriṇī Sabhā (referred to as Y_e in this edition). This now lost book is apparently an apograph of the V_1 manuscript. Although B_1 and V_1 show a difference of 30 poems, one part of B_1 presents close affinity with V_1. Ṭhākur's poems in B_1 can be found in four sections, each with its own numbering sequence. The longest string of Ṭhākur's poems in the manuscript (93 quatrains)[27] is in its second sequence, which I will call section *b*. With the exception of five (numbered as 20, 21, 22, 31, 96) all of its Ṭhākur quatrains are also present in V_1. Moreover, the order of poems in section *b* and in V_1 repeatedly shows shared sequences. For example, V_1's 1-8, 14-20, 39-51, 58-63, 66-81 figure in the same order in section *b* as 74-81, 45-51, 82-93 (with modification), 33-38, and 55-73 (with modification) respectively. In contrast with this, the other three (*a, c* and *d*) smaller sequences do not show any particular affinity. Out of the 22 *a-, c-* and *d*-series Ṭhākur-poems only 3 are shared with V_1: N31 (*a*7; 9), R22 (*a*11; 53) and Ś146 (*a*87; 13).

For the rest of the sources correspondences are less clear. Nevertheless, one cannot miss that the three anthologies published by the Navalkiśor Press in Lucknow, namely Bhāratendu's *Sundarī-tilak* (1883), Paramanand Suhane's *Ṣaṭ-ṛtu-hajārā* (1894) and his *Pāvas-kavitta-ratnākar* (1893) also form a group loosely connected both to Prabhudayal Mital's *Brajbhāṣā sāhitya kā ṛtu-saundarya* (1961) and to the *Sudhāsar.*

The complexity of sources relying on each other can be illustrated by the examination of the similarities between the Ṭhākur-poems in three late printed books, namely those of Bhagvandin (1924), Ramchand Shukla (1929) and Hariaudh (1934). One would expect that between three printed volumes divided in time by no more than ten years it would be easy to determine correspondences and it would seem that both Hariaudh and Shukla relied on the slightly earlier *Ṭhasak.* Indeed, the text of most poems quoted by Shukla (Ś8, Ś44, B32, N27, N33, N36, R45) and of three others (R54, Ś76, Ś97) quoted by both Shukla and Hariaudh is mostly shared with those of the *Ṭhasak* against those of the other sources. In the first part of *sukabi sipāhī hama una rajapūtana ke . . .* (N25) Shukla is also close to the *Ṭhasak.* There are, however, a few deviations already in some of these poems probably due to the interference of oral lore. In the second half of N25, for example, Shukla's text tends to be eccentric. Moreover, the fact that there are four poems (Ś108, B22, N29, N30) quoted by Hariaudh but missing from the *Ṭhasak* indicates that Hariaudh also relied on other sources. Apart from the above deviations, in Ś15 Hariaudh is either eccentric or follows the *Śatak* against the *Ṭhasak*; in Ś104 he presents his own, eccentric variants; in Ś140 he gives readings different from the *Ṭhasak* in about one third of the cases and in R7 both Hariaudh and Shukla give readings close to the *Ṭhasak* variants quoted in the introduction. In R2, R27

[27]Poems numbered in this sequence as 43, 94 and 95 are not by Ṭhākur.

and Ś139, Shukla again gives readings close to the *Ṭhasak* variants quoted in its introduction.

The lack of correspondence in three apparently closely related collections is even more striking. In 1892, Baburamdin mentioned in his introduction to his edition of the *Sundarī-tilak*[28] that Hariścandra had first prepared this compilation between 1869 and 1871 with the help of Hanumān kavi. This first version contained only 266 *savaiyā*s by 46 poets. Then Mannālāl 'Dvij' came out with a second, enlarged, anauthorised edition. Hariścandra also kept enlarging the book. (Śivsiṁh Seṅgar, for example, was familiar with a version containing 67 poets. A later edition had 427 poems by 69 poets and Baburamdin's 1892 version has 1455 poems.) The *Sundarī sarvasva* published by Mannālāl 'Dvij' in 1885 is a further enlarged, appropriated version of Hariścandra's collection. For this Ṭhākur edition, I consulted Hariścandra's 1883 version of the book (C_e) and Baburamdin's 1892 version (U_e) as well as the *Sundarī sarvasva* (1885). One would expect a substantial overlap of the Ṭhākur quatrains and an increase of the number of these quatrains with the growth of the collection. This is, however, not the case. The *Sundarī sarvasva* does not have any poem by Ṭhākur. In contrast with the 29 Ṭhākur quatrains of the 1883 edition, Baburamdin only had ten and out of these ten only six *kabitta*s are shared between the two editions. It appears that neither Baburamdin, nor 'Dvij' were as much impressed by Ṭhākur as was Hariścandra.

The Sudhāsar

With 136 poems by Ṭhākur, the massive anthology called *Sudhāsar* is the richest handwritten depository the Bundelkhandi author's poetry. Since modern scholars have not yet treated this anthology as a resource for Ṭhākur, it is worth presenting it in more detail. The *Sudhāsar* serves not simply as a source but also as a witness to the early reception history of Ṭhākur given that the distribution of the quatrains into various sections and subsections as well as the occasional introductory lines indicate the poems' reception in the early nineteenth century.

The compiler of this anthology, Gopālrāy 'Navīn' was a poet in his own right. According to the research of Mayashankar Yajnik, Gopāl Siṁh [*sic*!] 'Navīn' was a *kāyastha* from Vrindaban.[29] Relying on the doctoral research of Sureshdatt Mishra, Umarani Bansal[30] tells that Navīn's father, Khaḍgarāy, was also a Brajbhasha poet who composed under the pen name 'Pravīn' or 'Pravīnrāy'. 'Pravīn' mostly worked under the patronage of Ajīt Siṁh, the younger brother of Karam Siṁh, the ruler of Patiala (r. 1813-45). Gopālrāy was initiated into the Caitanya Sampradāya by Rāmbakhś Miśra and studied poetry first with Dayālāl Gosvāmī 'Dayānidhi' in Vrindaban, where he was a fellow disciple with the poet Gvāl.[31] Just like Gvāl, in his poetry, Navīn hardly ever addresses Dayānidhi as his guru.[32] Navīn

[28] B. Singh, ed., *Sundarītilak*, Bānkīpur (Patna): Khadgavilās Press, 1892, *Bhūmikā*, pp. 1-2.

[29] Khoj 35-69a based on Mayashankar Yajnik's article published in *Sāhitya Samālocak* in July 1925 [Śrāvan, *Saṁvat* 1982, p. 220].

[30] Bansal, *Kavivar dayānidhi*, pp. 102-4 relying on S. Mishra, 'Kavivar gopālrāy aur unkā kāvya', 1982.

[31] D.S. Vidyarthi, *Pañjāb ke darbārī kaviyõ ke paripekṣya mẽ kavi gvāl ke kavitva kā adhyayan*, Patiala: Bhāṣā Vibhāg, 1983, pp. 114 and 564; and B.S. Pachauri, *Mahākavi gvāl: vyaktitva evaṁ kṛtitva*, 2001 p. 147 quoted in Bansal, *Kavivar dayānidhi*, p. 103.

[32] Vidyarthi, *Kavi gvāl*, p. 139.

went on to Īś, the famous poet of Jaipur, and it was Īś whom he presented in his works as his guru.[33]

śrī gurū īśa pravīna kṛpā kari dīna ko chāpa navīna kī dīnī. (*Sudhāsar* 5)
My master, the expert Īś kindly gave the pen name 'navīn' to this humble person.

Oral lore remembers a rift between Navīn and his friend Gvāl over the disrespect of Īś. Navīn wanted Gvāl to refrain from giving a poem composed by his guru Īś as an example of a faulty composition in one of his works to be presented in Amritsar.[34]

Navīn went to the kingdom of Nabha in Panjab to seek patronage in the court of Maharaja Jasvant Siṁh (r. 1783-1840), where he composed the anthology *Sudhāsar.*

rasika sujāna kulabhānu jasavanta siṅgha
bhūpa mālavendu kī kripā te bana āyo hai|
lāgata suhāyo rasa-raṅga sarasāyo so
sudhāsara navīna grintha adbhuti banāyo hai|| 1 (S_1 f. 447r; S_3 f. 291[81]v, etc.)

It was composed by the grace of the sun of the family of expert connoisseurs, king Jasvant Singh, the moon of Malwa.
Since he is pleased when the colours of poetic emotions abound, Navīn prepared this extraordinary book, the Sudhāsar.

His son, Devendra Singh, succeeded Jasvant Singh but he was eventually deposed after the 1845 Anglo-Sikh wars.[35] His loss of kingship might have been the reason for Navīn's departure from Nabha to seek patronage in the royal court of Alwar in Rajasthan.[36] According to Kishorilal Gupta, Navīn's descendants in the 1960s were still under the patronage of the Alwar royal court.[37] Umarani Bansal does not mention Alwar but the Gwalior[38] and the Bharatpur courts that extended patronage to Navīn.[39] It is worth mentioning that two of the three Devanagari *Sudhāsar* manuscripts examined for this project come from Bharatpur and Alwar while the third one, a smaller selection, is now found in Vrindaban.

Navīn was a prolific author who apart from the *Sudhāsar* is credited with several works: *Sarasras, Nehnidān* (composed before 1860),[40] *Raṅgtaraṅg* (composed in 1842 and published in print in 1843),[41] *Dampati-vākya-vilās, Vṛndāvandhāmānurāgāvalī, Ras-sāgar* and *Gurucandroday-kaumudī.*[42]

* * *

[33] Gupta, *Saroj sarvekṣaṇ,* p. 383.

[34] Vidyarthi, *Kavi gvāl,* p. 161. Gvāl's work on faulty poems, the *Kavi-darpaṇ*, however, quotes an example from Dayānidhi and not from Īś. Kishorilal, ed., *Gvāl kavi kṛt kavi-darpaṇ,* Delhi: Anaṅg Prakāśan, 2007, p. 18.

[35] *The imperial gazetteer of India*, new edn., 26 vols. Oxford: Clarendon Press, 1907, vol. 18, p. 264.

[36] Vidyarthi, *Kavi gvāl,* p. 115.

[37] Gupta, *Saroj sarvekṣaṇ,* p. 383.

[38] Cf. Khoj 35-69a based on Mayashankar Yajnik.

[39] Bansal, *Kavivar dayānidhi,* p. 103.

[40] Khoj 05-39: mentions a *Neh nidān* manuscript copied in 1860 (*Saṁvat* 1907).

[41] *Raṅgtaraṅg.* India Literature Society, Muradabad, *Saṁvat* 1900.

[42] Bansal, *Kavivar dayānidhi,* p. 103. Manuscripts of the last four works can be found in the Vrindaban Research Institute and in the Sūkar Kṣetra Śodh Sansthān.

The *Sudhāsar* 'Pond of nectar' is organised into six uneven *taraṅgs* 'waves', namely *Śṛngār* "love", *Brajras-rīti* "ways of the emotions of Braj", *Rāj-samāj kā varṇan* "description of the royal court", *Nīti* "proper conduct", *Bhakti* "devotion" or *Devrati-nirved-vinay* "delight in God, disregard of worldly things and petition" and *Kavinām-dānlīlā* "Dānlīlā with the names of the poets". The *Sudhāsar* of the Yajnik collection, not inspected for my edition but described in Khoj (35-69a), presents the work of 257 poets.

Out of the seven manuscripts of this work that I was able to consult only three (S_1, S_6 and S_7) were complete. The last portion of S_5 is missing while S_2, S_3 and S_4 are selections. One can distribute the seven manuscripts into two recensions. The slightly shorter S_1 represents one recension and all the others another one. In a passing note Rampher Tripathi mentioned that Navīn compiled the anthology called *Prabodhras-Sudhāsar* twice, first in 1824 and then again in 1838.[43] Unfortunately, he did not give any further reason for this claim. It is, however, tempting to think that the first part of S_1 indeed represents a recension prepared earlier than the other one. There are occasional poems as well as long sequences of poems absent from this part of S_1. (Some of them were added to the manuscript at a later stage on the margin.) Among the absent sequences, the most conspicuous one is the sequence about the reason for the compilation of the book, the *granthakāran*. (Introduced into the S_1 manuscript as marginalia in a sequence numbered as 12-27 in the manuscript.) The sequence deeply roots the *Sudhāsar* in the court of Malwa under the patronage of Jasvant Singh. The poem praising Jasvant Singh of Malwa at the end of the compilation is, however, present in S_1 on f. 447r. This suggests that Navīn must have started the first recension before arriving in Malwa and when he obtained patronage, he reworked it into its extended form.

The reworking process can be illustrated by the sequential positioning of Ṭhākur's quatrain *gvārana ko yāra* . . . (B22). This quatrain was originally in the *aur nānābidhi ke brajkelī* subsection of the *Brajras-rīti* section (as in S_1). Later, the compiler introduced it into the *maṅgalācaraṇ* section of the second recension. Manuscripts S_6 and S_7 give the poem twice: in the *maṅgalācaraṇ* and in its original place, while S_2, S_3, and S_5 only give it in the *maṅgalācaraṇ*. (In S_1 it is reintroduced into the *maṅgalācaraṇ* as part of the marginalia.) This is indicative of a diachronic sequence of the *Sudhāsar* manuscripts. The oldest version is S_1, followed by S_6 and S_7. The latest versions are apparently S_2, S_3 and S_5, which eliminate the repetition of this poem.

A further difference between the two recensions is that the entire *uddīpan* subsection within *saṁyog* is missing from the first recension. The introduction of a new *uddīpan* subsection results in having two extended *ṣaḍṛtu* sequences in the anthology since the *pravās birah mai uddīpan* subsection already had one. At a later stage of transmission, S_3 introduced both *ṣaḍṛtu* sequences together towards the end of the book, in the place of the *nīti* section, which it omitted.

The compilation reflects the poetic preferences of Navīn's times. It presents relatively few quatrains by Keśavdās and other early *rīti* authors and a high number of eighteenth- and early nineteenth-century poets. Among the most frequently quoted authors are Navīn's father, Pravīn, and his guru, Īś. Ṭhākur is also well represented with 136 quatrains. The distribution of his 135 kabittas in the extended second edition is as follows, 1 poem is included into the *maṅgalācaraṇ*, 80 into the *śṛṅgār* section, 33 in the *Brajras-rīti*, none in

[43]R. Tripathi, 'Rītimukt śṛṅgār kāvya: Pramukh kavi', in *Hindī sāhitya kā bṛhat itihās (Rītikāl: rītimukt)*, ed. Bhagirath Mishra, Varanasi: Nāgarīpracāriṇī Sabhā, 1972, p. 67.

the *rāj-samāj*, 15 in the *nīti* section and 6 in the *bhaktapakṣa* section. Apart from these, two manuscripts (S_2 and S_7) in their paratexts erroneously attribute to Ṭhākur a poem without signature (U8, *rūsanhārī ghanerī hatī* . . . in the *śṛṅgār* section) while three others (S_1, S_5 and S_6) introduce it as *benisān* ('without signature'). The distribution of the poems indicates that Navīn perceived Ṭhākur to be primarily a love poet, who also composed quatrains on Krishna or bhakti themes as well as on *nīti*. It is interesting to note that the *rāj-samāj* 'royal court' section presents no quatrain of Ṭhākur in spite of his being a court poet.

The first recension includes only 93 quatrains by Ṭhākur, which with the exception of one in the *śṛṅgār* section, *vaha kañja so komala* . . . (Ś108), are also present in the extended later recension. This means that the later recension added 43 Ṭhākur quatrains. This recension positions many of these quatrains among the poems of three subsections in the first part of the compilation, in *ūḍhā parakīyā* followed by the *prema paripūran alajjā parakīyā* and in the *uddīpan ke bhed sakhī dūtī varnan*. This indicates that Navīn may have gained access to them at the time of his revision of the first half of the early recension. One can even speculate that they may represent the latest poetic output of Ṭhākur, which have not yet achieved wider circulation in 1824, the proposed time for the first recension. These poems are B44, R10, R13, R16, R24, R25, R26, R34, R47, R48, R50, R55, R65, R66, Ś4, Ś11, Ś20, Ś22, Ś23, Ś28, Ś33, Ś55, Ś77, Ś79, Ś80, Ś89, Ś93, Ś94, Ś95, Ś99, Ś102, Ś103, Ś105, Ś110, Ś113, Ś120, Ś126, Ś129, Ś133, Ś135, Ś141, Ś144, and Ś149. This suggest that while Ṭhākur's bhakti and *nīti* poems may belong to his earlier career, a substantial part of his *ṛtu-varṇan* and *śṛṅgār* poems may have been composed in the later part of his life.

As has been mentioned, the *Ṭhākur-satsaī*, parts of B_1 as well as the V_1 and the K_3 manuscripts attempted to collect Ṭhākur's poems. The contents of all four have a substantial overlap with that of the *Sudhāsar*. Although 44 out of the 49 Ṭhākur-poems in the *Ṭhākur-satsaī* are present in the *Sudhāsar* indicating its closeness to Navīn's anthology, it has also five additional quatrains (R29, Ś14, U4, B53, N36 numbered in the manuscript as 9, 10, 11b, 43 and 46 respectively). In a similar way, V_1 has nine (B3, B16, B64; Ś3, Ś81, Ś107, Ś134, R22, R27) and B_1 has 19 additional quatrains (B3, B16, B35, B64, Ś3, Ś10, Ś31, Ś81, Ś107, Ś134, R13, R22, R27, R35, N11, N18, N21, U4, U7). It is important to note that 37 out of the *Sudhāsar*'s 43 later Ṭhākur quatrains are included into B_1 and V_1 (B44, Ś4, Ś11, Ś20, Ś22, Ś23, Ś28, Ś33, Ś55, Ś77, Ś79, Ś80, Ś89, Ś93, Ś94, Ś95, Ś99, Ś103 [only in B1], Ś105, Ś110, Ś113, Ś120, Ś135, Ś141, Ś144, Ś149, R10, R14, R25, R26, R34, R47 R48, R50, R55, R65, R66). The sequence of quatrains in the Ṭhākur manuscripts and in the *Sudhāsar* does not show any similarity, which indicates that the Ṭhākur manuscripts are not collections of Ṭhākur's quatrains extracted from the *Sudhāsar*. Since the *Sudhāsar* had its own organising principle, the substantial overlap rather suggests a movement to the opposite direction: Navīn, especially in the second edition, relied on manuscripts close to V_1, B_1 and maybe the *Satsaī*.

Narayan and Nayar's Hindi bibliography mentions that Jagannāthdās Ratnākar published Navīn's *Sudhāsar* in 1875 in Varanasi.[44] In a different publication, Kishorilal Gupta says that, the Bhārat-Jīvan Press in Varanasi printed its section about *Nāyikā-bhed*.[45] However,

[44]P. Narayan and S.B. Nayar, *Hindī-sāhitya-sāriṇī: Hindī mẽ san 1964 ke ant tak prakāśit sabhī granthõ kā vaijñānik prakriyānusār vargīkṛt evaṁ kramabaddha vivaraṇ*, vol. 1, Hoshiarpur: Vishveshvaranand Institute, 1971, p. 74. This is listed as our source S_E.

[45]Gupta, *Saroj sarvekṣaṇ*, p. 383.

he does not give any further detail. The entire *Sudhāsar* has never been published in spite of the fact that fourteen documented manuscripts attest its popularity.[46] Out of them, eight are in the Gurmukhi script and six in Nagari. Out of the three Devanagari (S_1, S_2, S_5) and four Gurmukhi (S_3, S_4, S_6, S_7) manuscripts of this work inspected for this critical edition five are collated in their entirety and the readings of two others (S_5, S_6) are provided when there is a scarcity of other sources. Three manuscripts (S_2, S_3 and S_4) are selections from the *Sudhāsar*. S_2 is independent of S_3, while the still smaller S_4 relies on S_3. S_5 is an incomplete manuscript. Only S_6 and S_7 manuscripts give the full text of the final edition. Since they are closely related to each other, only the readings of the S_7 manuscript have been collated.

The following table shows the structure of the *Sudhāsar* and the position of Ṭhākur's poems.[47] (ṬK_e stands for the present edition. Major structural differences between manuscripts are highlighted.)

	S_1	S_2	S_3	S_4	S_5	S_6	S_7	ṬK_e
Maṅgalācaran								
	2v m12 (& 273rv 25)	1v 1	1v 2		2rv 11| 9	2rv 9 (& 279r)	1v 11 (& 196r)	B22
Granthakāran	(all mg)							
I. Śṛṅgār								
nakh-sikh								
	6r 30	3v 2			6r 45|2	7r 21	5r 47	Ś15
	25v m 4				26r 18	32v 164	20rv 179	Ś26
nāyikābhed								
svakīyā (1)								
	40v 5	7rv 3			40v 7b	45r 9|259	30r 7|271	Ś106
	——	8v 4			54rv 4	58v 9|349	39v 10|366	Ś89
parakīyā (2)								
	60r 4	10r 5			59v 4	63v 7|379	43r 5|407	Ś19
	——	10r 6			60v 10	64v 13|385	44r 11|413	Ś113
	63r 16	—			62r 19	65-66 22|394	45r 20|422	Ś136
	63v 19	11r 7			62v 22	66r 25|397	45r 23|425	Ś7
	63-4 21	11r 8			62-3 25	66v 28|400	45v 26|428	Ś83
		11r 9			63r 28	67r 31|403	45v 29|431	B44
		11v 10			63v 31	64v 34|406	46r 32|434	Ś110
		11v 11			63v 34	67-8 37|409	46rv 35|437	Ś120
		12r 12			64v 37	68r 40|412	46v 38|440	Ś135
		12r 13			64-5r 40	68v 43|415	46-7 41|443	Ś144
		12v 14			66r 48	69v 51|423	47v 49|451	Ś129
		12-13 15			67-8r 4	71rv 62|434	48-9 60|462	R66
		13r 16			68r 5	71v 63|435	49r 61|463	Ś55
	68v 2	13rv 17			68r 7	71-2 65|437	49r 63|465	Ś9
		13v 18(24)			68v 8	72r 66|438	49rv 64|466	Ś4
	69-70 7	13v 19			68-9 11	72rv 69|441	49v 67|469	Ś146

[46]The manuscripts are listed in Saheb Singh, 'Provincialisation of the Vernacular: Navīn's Sudhāsar in the Gurmukhi Script', M. Phil. dissertation, University of Oxford, 2009, p. 33.

[47]Information on the presence of Ṭhākur's poems in manuscript S_5 has not been entered systematiclally due to the poor quality of the copy available for consutation.

<table>
<tr><th></th><th>S_1</th><th>S_2</th><th>S_3</th><th>S_4</th><th>S_5</th><th>S_6</th><th>S_7</th><th>ṬK$_e$</th></tr>
<tr><td></td><td></td><td></td><td></td><td></td><td>68v 10</td><td>72r 68|440</td><td>49v 66|468</td><td>Ś11</td></tr>
<tr><td></td><td>70r 8</td><td>14r 20</td><td></td><td></td><td>69r 13</td><td>72v 71443</td><td>49v 69|471</td><td>Ś123</td></tr>
<tr><td></td><td>70r 9</td><td>14rv 21</td><td></td><td></td><td>69rv 15</td><td>73r 73|445</td><td>50r 71|473</td><td>Ś46</td></tr>
<tr><td></td><td>70rv 10</td><td>14v 22</td><td></td><td></td><td>69v 16</td><td>73r 74|446</td><td>50r 72|474</td><td>Ś140</td></tr>
<tr><td></td><td></td><td>16r 23(34)</td><td></td><td></td><td>72v 8</td><td>76r 98|470</td><td>52r 12|497</td><td>Ś149</td></tr>
<tr><td></td><td></td><td>17r 24</td><td></td><td></td><td></td><td>81v 133|505</td><td>56r 10|532</td><td>R34</td></tr>
<tr><td></td><td>273r 19</td><td></td><td>148r 130</td><td></td><td></td><td>278rv 30|153</td><td>195v 19</td><td>Ś32</td></tr>
<tr><td></td><td></td><td>17rv 25</td><td></td><td></td><td></td><td>81-2 134|506</td><td>56rv 11|533</td><td>Ś94</td></tr>
<tr><td></td><td></td><td>19r 26var</td><td></td><td></td><td>82v 9</td><td>87rv 175|547</td><td>60rv 10|604</td><td>Ś20</td></tr>
<tr><td>sāmānyā (3)</td><td></td><td></td><td></td><td></td><td></td><td></td><td></td><td></td></tr>
<tr><td></td><td>96v 29</td><td>21rv 27</td><td></td><td></td><td>93r 24</td><td>95-6 57|612</td><td>65rv 2|661</td><td>Ś97</td></tr>
<tr><td></td><td>97v 33</td><td></td><td></td><td></td><td></td><td></td><td></td><td>Ś108</td></tr>
<tr><td></td><td>98r 35</td><td>21v 28</td><td></td><td></td><td>94r 30</td><td>66v 63|618</td><td>67r 7|668</td><td>U7</td></tr>
<tr><td>das avasthā</td><td></td><td></td><td></td><td></td><td></td><td></td><td></td><td></td></tr>
<tr><td>proṣitapatikā (1)</td><td></td><td></td><td></td><td></td><td></td><td></td><td></td><td></td></tr>
<tr><td></td><td>108r 15</td><td>22v 29 (2)</td><td></td><td></td><td>102r 14</td><td>103v 110|665</td><td>72r 15|716</td><td>Ś64</td></tr>
<tr><td></td><td>106r 5</td><td>22v-23r
30var (3)</td><td></td><td></td><td>102v 17</td><td>104r 113|668</td><td>72r 18|719</td><td>Ś76</td></tr>
<tr><td>khaṇḍitā (2)</td><td></td><td></td><td></td><td></td><td></td><td></td><td></td><td></td></tr>
<tr><td>kalahāntaritā (3)</td><td></td><td></td><td></td><td></td><td></td><td></td><td></td><td></td></tr>
<tr><td></td><td>116v 1
195r 1</td><td>47v 47var</td><td>109v 114</td><td></td><td></td><td>218v 97|1424</td><td>154v 29|1464</td><td>Ś122</td></tr>
<tr><td></td><td></td><td>31</td><td></td><td></td><td>99r</td><td>110v 10|710</td><td>76v 1|761</td><td>Ś77</td></tr>
<tr><td>svādhīnpatikā (7)</td><td></td><td></td><td></td><td></td><td></td><td></td><td></td><td></td></tr>
<tr><td></td><td></td><td></td><td></td><td></td><td></td><td>120v 12|772</td><td>84r 9|823</td><td>Ś93</td></tr>
<tr><td>āgamapatikā (10)</td><td></td><td></td><td></td><td></td><td></td><td></td><td></td><td></td></tr>
<tr><td></td><td></td><td></td><td></td><td></td><td></td><td>133rv 13|850</td><td>93r 1|900</td><td>R50</td></tr>
<tr><td>nāyak bhed</td><td></td><td></td><td></td><td></td><td></td><td></td><td></td><td></td></tr>
<tr><td></td><td></td><td></td><td></td><td></td><td></td><td>139v 31|897</td><td>97v 1|947</td><td>Ś126</td></tr>
<tr><td></td><td></td><td>30v-1r
32(32)</td><td></td><td></td><td></td><td>140v 38|904</td><td>98r 3|954</td><td>R10</td></tr>
<tr><td></td><td>150v 1</td><td></td><td></td><td></td><td></td><td>143v 61|927</td><td>100v 1|977</td><td>Ś155</td></tr>
<tr><td>caturavidhi darśan</td><td></td><td></td><td></td><td></td><td></td><td></td><td></td><td></td></tr>
<tr><td></td><td></td><td></td><td>69-70r
72</td><td></td><td></td><td>149v 31|964</td><td>105r 9|1014</td><td>Ś28</td></tr>
<tr><td>uddīpan vibhāv</td><td></td><td></td><td></td><td></td><td></td><td></td><td></td><td></td></tr>
<tr><td>sakhī dūtī varnan</td><td></td><td></td><td></td><td></td><td></td><td></td><td></td><td></td></tr>
<tr><td></td><td></td><td></td><td>75v 100</td><td></td><td></td><td>155v 33|999</td><td>109r 10|1049</td><td>Ś133</td></tr>
<tr><td></td><td></td><td></td><td>75-6r
102</td><td></td><td></td><td>155-6 35|1001</td><td>109rv
12|1051</td><td>Ś141</td></tr>
<tr><td></td><td></td><td></td><td></td><td></td><td></td><td>156-7 41|1007</td><td>110r 6|1056</td><td>Ś95</td></tr>
<tr><td></td><td></td><td></td><td></td><td></td><td>158r 8</td><td>157v 46|1012</td><td>110v 11|1061</td><td>Ś23</td></tr>
<tr><td></td><td></td><td></td><td>81r 129</td><td></td><td></td><td>161v 20|1036</td><td>113v 20|1085</td><td>Ś22</td></tr>
<tr><td></td><td></td><td>34rv 33(43)</td><td>81v 132</td><td></td><td></td><td>162r 23|1039</td><td>113-4r
23|1088</td><td>Ś99</td></tr>
<tr><td></td><td></td><td>34v 34</td><td>82v 137</td><td></td><td></td><td>162-3 30|1046</td><td>114v 30|1094</td><td>Ś105</td></tr>
<tr><td></td><td></td><td></td><td></td><td></td><td></td><td>163r 32|1048</td><td>114v 32|1096</td><td>Ś102</td></tr>
<tr><td></td><td></td><td>35r 35(45)</td><td>84r 145</td><td></td><td>165rv 7</td><td>164v 41|1057</td><td>115v 9|1105</td><td>Ś79</td></tr>
<tr><td></td><td></td><td>35v 36(45!)</td><td>84v 148</td><td></td><td></td><td>165r 44|1060</td><td>116r 12|1108</td><td>Ś80</td></tr>
</table>

	S_1	S_2	S_3	S_4	S_5	S_6	S_7	ṬK$_e$
	180v 6		86r 158			166-7|1072	117v 4|1120	Ś36
ṣaḍṛtu								
pāvas								
		36rv 37([48])	211/2r 7		173rv 6	170v 7|1096	120rv 7|1143	R48
		36v 38(49)	211/2v 10		174r 9	171rv 11|1100	120v 11|1147	R65
		37r 39(42)	213/4r 18		175v 16	172v 18|1107	121v 4|1154	R55
		37rv 40([28/29])	214/5r 22		176v 21	173rv 23|1112	122r 9|1159	R47
phāg								
			221/12r 13		184r 14	179v 15|1146	127r 14|1202	R24
			222/13r 18			180v 21|1162	127v 20|1208	R16
			224/15r 31			183rv 39|1180	129rv 2|1224	R13
		39v 41([5b])				185rv 51|1192	129rv 13|1235	R26
		40rv 42([56])	227/18v 47			186v 59|1200	131v 21|1243	R25
basant								
grīṣma								
		42v 43(2)	231/22r 3			190v 3|1223	134rv 3|1266	Ś33
anubhāv								
biyog								
pūrvānurāg (1)								
		45v 44	98r 51			205r 8|1335	144v 8|1378	Ś103
	181v 3	45v-6r 45	99rv 58		187-8r 3	206v 17|1344	145v 5|1387	Ś40
	182v 6				188v 5	207r 20|1347	146rv 8|1390	Ś152
pravās (2)								
	186v 10		102v 76			211-2 56|1382	149v 6|1426	Ś67
	189rv 2	47r 46	105r 89			214r 69|1396	151rv 3|1438	Ś62
	116v 1 195r 1	47v 47v ar	109v 114			218v 97|1424	154v 29|1464	Ś122
pravās birah mai uddīpan ṣaṭṛtu								
pāvas								
	196r 1		224/25v 7			219r 105|1432	155r 7|1472	R51
	197r 6	48r 48	235/26v 12			220r 110|1437	155v 13|1477	R56
	210r 61	49r 49				229-30 165|1492	162r 61|1531	R60
	212v 75		249/40v 81			231v 179|1506	163v 75|1565	R59

<table>
<tr><th></th><th>S_1</th><th>S_2</th><th>S_3</th><th>S_4</th><th>S_5</th><th>S_6</th><th>S_7</th><th>ṬK$_e^*$</th></tr>
<tr><td></td><td>212v 76</td><td></td><td></td><td></td><td></td><td>231-2 180|1507</td><td>163v 76|1566</td><td>R54</td></tr>
<tr><td></td><td>213v 81</td><td>49v 50</td><td>250-1/ 41-</td><td></td><td></td><td>232v 185|1512</td><td>164r 81|1571</td><td>R52</td></tr>
<tr><td>phāg</td><td></td><td></td><td></td><td></td><td></td><td></td><td></td><td></td></tr>
<tr><td></td><td>217rv 1</td><td>50rv 51</td><td>45r 5</td><td></td><td></td><td>235v 203|1530</td><td>166r 2|1588</td><td>R8</td></tr>
<tr><td>vasant</td><td></td><td></td><td></td><td></td><td></td><td></td><td></td><td></td></tr>
<tr><td></td><td>223rv 17</td><td>51rv 52(1)</td><td>259/50v 3</td><td></td><td></td><td>240r 232|1559</td><td>169v 17|1616</td><td>R11</td></tr>
<tr><td></td><td>224r 20</td><td>51v 53(2)</td><td>260/51rv 3</td><td></td><td></td><td>240v 235|1562</td><td>170r 20|1619</td><td>R6</td></tr>
<tr><td>abhilāṣādi das dasā</td><td></td><td></td><td></td><td></td><td></td><td></td><td></td><td></td></tr>
<tr><td></td><td>227-8 1</td><td></td><td>110r 116</td><td></td><td></td><td>243r 243|1580</td><td>172r 5|1638</td><td>Ś50</td></tr>
<tr><td></td><td>231r 15</td><td></td><td>112v 129</td><td></td><td></td><td>246r 267|1594</td><td>173v 20|1652</td><td>Ś56</td></tr>
<tr><td></td><td>231-2 4</td><td>52-3 54</td><td>113rv 133</td><td></td><td></td><td>246r 272|1599</td><td>174r 4|1657</td><td>Ś137</td></tr>
<tr><td>II. Brajrasarīti</td><td></td><td></td><td></td><td></td><td></td><td></td><td></td><td></td></tr>
<tr><td>Braj mahimā</td><td></td><td></td><td></td><td></td><td></td><td></td><td></td><td></td></tr>
<tr><td></td><td>244r 4</td><td>55rv 55</td><td>122v 4</td><td>40rv 4</td><td></td><td>255r 4|14</td><td>180v-1r 14</td><td>B11</td></tr>
<tr><td></td><td>245-6 12</td><td>55v 56</td><td>124r 12</td><td>43rv 12</td><td></td><td>257r 12|22</td><td>181v 12</td><td>B6</td></tr>
<tr><td></td><td>250-1 13</td><td>57r 57(1)</td><td>128v 34</td><td>49v 34</td><td></td><td>261r 13|44</td><td>184r 13</td><td>B31</td></tr>
<tr><td></td><td>260r 1</td><td></td><td>136r 69</td><td>59rv 75</td><td></td><td>268r 1|86</td><td>188v 14</td><td>Ś49</td></tr>
<tr><td></td><td>260rv 1</td><td></td><td>136v 71</td><td>59v-60r 77</td><td></td><td>268rv 3|88</td><td>188v-9r 16</td><td>B42</td></tr>
<tr><td></td><td>263r 3</td><td>57v 58</td><td>138v 83</td><td>63r 90</td><td></td><td>270v 3|102</td><td>190rv 3</td><td>B28</td></tr>
<tr><td></td><td>263rv 4</td><td></td><td>139r 84</td><td>63r 91</td><td></td><td>270-1 4|103</td><td>190v 4</td><td>Ś127</td></tr>
<tr><td></td><td>263v 5</td><td></td><td>139r 85</td><td>63rv 92</td><td></td><td>271r 5|104</td><td>190v 5</td><td>B27</td></tr>
<tr><td></td><td>266v 1</td><td>57-8 59</td><td>141v 97</td><td>66rv 104</td><td></td><td>273r 1|120</td><td>192r 3</td><td>B30</td></tr>
<tr><td></td><td>269v- 270r 1</td><td></td><td>144-5r 112</td><td>69v 119</td><td></td><td>275v 12|135</td><td>193v 12</td><td>B40</td></tr>
<tr><td></td><td>270v 4</td><td>58rv 60</td><td>145v 115</td><td>70rv 122</td><td></td><td>276rv 15|138</td><td>194r 4</td><td>R53</td></tr>
<tr><td></td><td>270-1r 6</td><td>58v 61</td><td>145v 6r 117</td><td>70-1 124</td><td></td><td>276v 17|140</td><td>194rv 6</td><td>Ś47</td></tr>
<tr><td></td><td>271v 10</td><td>58-9 62(1)</td><td>146v 121</td><td>71v 127</td><td></td><td>277r 21|144</td><td>194v 10</td><td>Ś42</td></tr>
<tr><td></td><td>271v 11</td><td></td><td>146v 122</td><td>71-2 128</td><td></td><td>277r 22|145</td><td>194v-5r 11</td><td>Ś54</td></tr>
<tr><td></td><td>272r 13</td><td></td><td>147r 124</td><td>72rv 130</td><td></td><td>277v 24|147</td><td>195r 13</td><td>Ś48</td></tr>
<tr><td></td><td>272r 14</td><td></td><td>147r 125</td><td>72v 131</td><td></td><td>277v 25|148</td><td>195r 14</td><td>Ś26</td></tr>
<tr><td></td><td>272rv 15</td><td></td><td>147rv 126</td><td>72v 132h</td><td></td><td>277-8 26|149</td><td>195r 15</td><td>Ś118</td></tr>
<tr><td></td><td>273r 19</td><td></td><td>148r 130</td><td></td><td></td><td>278rv 30|153</td><td>195v 19</td><td>Ś32</td></tr>
<tr><td></td><td>273rv 25 (& 2v m 12)</td><td>1v 1</td><td>1v 2</td><td></td><td>2r (11)9</td><td>279r (& 2rv 9)</td><td>196r (& 1v 11)</td><td>B22</td></tr>
<tr><td>Braj vaibhav</td><td></td><td></td><td></td><td></td><td></td><td></td><td></td><td></td></tr>
<tr><td></td><td>275r 1</td><td></td><td>149rv 138</td><td>75rv 145</td><td></td><td>279v 38|161 •</td><td>196rv 1</td><td>B10</td></tr>
<tr><td></td><td>280v-1r 9</td><td>59r 63</td><td>154rv 161</td><td>81-2 171</td><td></td><td>284r 10|187</td><td>199rv 26</td><td>B45</td></tr>
</table>

	S_1	S_2	S_3	S_4	S_5	S_6	S_7	ṬK$_e$
Uddhav kau Braj mẽ āyabau								
	290r 10	59v 64	c163r 206	90r 219		291r 11|230	204r 53	B56
	293r 22		165rv 218	92v 3r 231	191v 12	293r 24|243	205v 66	B62
	295rv 22	60r 66	167v 229	95r 241	193v 20ā1	294v 35|254	206v 77	B65
	296v 26b	60r 67	168r 233	95v 245	194v 23b	295rv 39|258	207r 81	B61
	296v 27	60rv 68	168rv 234	95v 6r 245	195r 24b	295v 40|259	207r 82	Ś82
	301rv 46	60v 69		98r 257		297rv 51|271	208v 93	B51
	301v 48	60-1 70	170v-1r (246	98v 259		297v 53|273	208v 95	Ś68
	300rv 42		172v 254	100rv 267	198rv 37	268-9 61|280	209v 103	N35
	302rv 51	60-1 70b	173v	101v 272		299-300 66|285	210r 108	B55
	303rv 55	61rv 71	174v 263	102r 276	199v 44b	300v 70|289	210v 112	B63
	307rv 74	62r 72	177r 277		205r 7	303r 87|306	212v 128	B53
	308r 77	62r 73	178r 280		205-6r 1	304r 81|310	212-3 131	Ś66
saṁjog								
	308v 79	62v 74	178v 282		-	304r 93|312	213r 133	Ś57
III. dānsamāj /Rājsamāj								
IV. nīti								
	347v 5	66v-7r 75		26v-7r 156	235v 4	334v 8	234v 8	N28
	348r 8	67r 76		27rv 159	236r 6	334-5 11	234v 11	N32
	348rv 10	67rv 77		27v 8r 161	236v 8	335r 13	234-5 13	N2
	348v 11	67v 78		28r 162	236v 9	335rv 14	235r 14	N14
	351v 24			30-1 175	239v 21	337v 27	236rv 8	N8
	354r 35					339v 39	237v 28	N10
	356r 43	69v 79		36r 194		341r 47	238rv 36	N30
	358v 57	70v 80			243v 41	343r 61	239v 39	N4
	366r 93	71-2 81				349r 98	243r 74	N1
	366v 95	72r 82				349rv 100	243v 76	Ś112
	367r 98	72v 83				349-50 103	243v 79	N31
kavi aur kāvya								
	372v 127	74r 84			245v 48	354r 132	246v 104	N37
					End (246v)			
bhaḍauvā								
	377r 6	75rv 85				357v 6	248v 132	N16
	378v 13	75v 86				358-9 13	249v 139	N25
	380-1r 24	76r 87				360v 24	250v 150	N9

	S_1	S_2	S_3	S_4	S_5	S_6	S_7	ṬK$_e$
V. devstuti, bhaktapakṣa, nirveda, karunā-binay								
	389v 2b	77v 88	—			367v 2	254v-5r 7	B12
	412v 101	80r 89				385v 101	265v 106	B29
Bhaktipad								
	418rv 13	81v 90	275/66r 5			390r 13	269v 146	B8
	419-20 19	82r 91	275-6/66v-7r 8			391rv 19	270rv 152	B9
	420v 22	82v 92	—			391-2 22	270v 155	B21
	421r 24	83r 93	276/67r 10			392rv 24	270-1 157	N27
nirveda								
karunā-vinay								
VI. dānalīlā								

LIST OF SOURCES

MANUSCRIPTS

A—Rajasthan Oriental Research Institute, Alwar, 4832(4), ff. 68v and 73v-74r.—The extant manuscript has only folios 31-165. Folio 82v indicates a date and place: *Saṁvat* 1835 in Ujjain. This is, however, not a proper colophon and may simply indicate the time and place of composition of the work on the previous pages. On the following folio, there is a copy of a document issued by Maharāṇā Javān Siṁh of Udaipur (r. 1828-38) in 1837: *Saṁvat* 1894 bhādavā suda 15. This anthology contains *pads*, couplets, quatrains etc. of Bihārī, Dev, Dayānidhi, Padmākar and others. (There is a detailed description of the contents in Jatav, R., *Rājasthānī-hindī hastalikhit granth sūcī: Alvar-saṅgrah*. Rajasthan Oriental Research Institute, Jodhpur: Rajasthan Oriental Research Institute, 1989, pp. 247-50.) It also includes two poems by Ṭhākur, *sāmila ho pīra maī*. . . (N31) numbered as 105 on f68v and *madamāte guvāla garūra bhare* . . . (R22) numbered as 124 on ff. 73v-74r. According to the cataloguer, the manuscript was written in *Saṁvat* 1935. This seems to be a misreading of the colophon on f. 82v. The presence of later poets, such as Naṭnāgar (1808-63), Dayānidhi (fl. 1801-18) and Padmākar (1753-1833) indicate that the date 1778 (*Saṁvat* 1835) is not the date of the copying of the entire manuscript.

B_1—Rajasthan Oriental Research Institute, Bharatpur, 216, ff. 129-86 (the first 128 folios are missing). (The Institute received the book from the District Library, Bharatpur.) Folios 131r-149v (section *a*) contain 98 numbered quatrains out of which 17 are attributed to Ṭhākur on folios 131-3, 135, 142, 146. A new collection by the same hand introduced as *Ṭhākur ke kabitta* starts on f. 149v (section *b*). Up to folio 165v it includes 96 numbered poems by Ṭhākur interspersed with one by Amareś (43), Padmākar (94) and Dev (95) each. The numbering continues on folios 165v-168v and the collection includes 17 more quatrains by various authors, such as Nāgarīdās, Kiśor, Padmākar, Ras Ānand, Amareś and others numbered as 97-113. After *kabitta* 32 it contains the following couplet *vidhivata jagya karata sadā te dvija uttama gota; sādhu nikaṭa cali jāta hī so phala paga paga hota.* This section shows close similarities to manuscript V_1 in its sequence (see above p. 59). Folios 169r-172r contain a collection of Rahīm's 48 couplets introduced as *atha dohā navāb khānkhānān kr̥t likhyate.* After this, a new collection of quatrains starts, where folios 176rv and 185rv (section *c*) contain five more kabittas by Ṭhākur numbered in their respective sequences as 20-1 (section *c*) and 23-5 (section *d*). After the *Sudhāsar* manuscripts, this is the second richest handwritten source for Ṭhākur's poetry with its 115 quatrains. The readings of this manuscript tend to be the most reliable and whenever possible, the present edition follows it. The published catalogue gives a list of authors in this book.[48]

B_2—*Phuṭkar kabitta*—Rajasthan Oriental Research Institute, Bharatpur, 38-48. This anthology of 27 *kabitta*s on eight folios numbered as 4v-11v is catalogued under eleven numbers. Section 40 includes N2 on ff. 5v-6r (5), and section 46 has Ś15 on f. 9rv (17). The Institute received the book from the District Library, Bharatpur.

B_3—*Kabitta*—Rajasthan Oriental Research Institute, Bharatpur, 444, ff. 64-84. (The Institute received the book from the District Library, Bharatpur.) On f. 76v, it contains Ś111 (numbered as 1). An inscription on the inside cover reads, *faujdār nihālsiṁhjī sāh* (*faujdār*, in this context means, *jāṭ*) and in English *Holi book*. Before the *Kabitta* (catalogued as 444), the manuscript comprises Brajdūlah's *Pad-saṅgrah* on Holi (ff. 1-4; catalogued as 441), an anthology what the cataloguer called *Rādhā-kr̥ṣṇa kī līlāẽ ādī* containing *pad*s by Sūrdās, Dhīraj, Brajnidhi, Paramānand, Kabīr, Mīrā etc. (ff. 4-61; catalogued as 442) and Somnāth's *Prem-pacīsā* (ff. 61-3; catalogued as 443). The catalogue gives a list of authors in this book on p. 228.

B_4—*Nakhśikh varṇan va kabitta* (by Balibhadra)—Rajasthan Oriental Research Institute, Bharatpur, 297, 9ff. This manuscript is bound together with and follows B6. At the end, on a folio numbered as 15v, after two quatrains by Padmākar, is the poem *tere draga tīcchana haĩ . . .* (U3) copied by another hand. This *kabitta* includes the word *ṭhākura* in its last line but its authorship is unclear. The Institute received the book from the District Library, Bharatpur.

B_5—*Kabitt saṅgrah*—Rajasthan Oriental Research Institute, Bharatpur, 231, 148ff. The beginning of the manuscript is missing. It includes B56 on f. 10r-v (numbered as 16), Ś111 on f. 19r-v (33), Ś40 on ff. 25v-26r, R54 on ff. 24v-25r (35) and M8, a poem with the signature Bākūrāy (probably for Ṭhākurāy) with the same rhyme *(-ana de[va])* as Ś55 and N34. It was perceived as Ṭhākur's since the name Bākūrāy/Ṭhākurāy is missing from the index of the catalogue. The Institute received the book from the District Library, Bharatpur.

B_6—*Phuṭkar kabitta saṅgrah*—Rajasthan Oriental Research Institute, Bharatpur, 296, ff. 6-9. On f. 7rv this manuscript includes Ś123, R22, Ś122 and Ś36 written by various hands. The Institute received the book from the District Library, Bharatpur.

B_7—*Phuṭkar kabitta*—Rajasthan Oriental Research Institute, Bharatpur, 1219(3), 11ff. It includes Ś15 on f. 1r. The Institute received the book from the District Library, Bharatpur.

[48] R. Jatav, Devkumar, and Vinodkumar, *Rājasthānī-hindī hastalikhit granth-sūcī*, Jodhpur: Rajasthan Oriental Research Institute, 1995, pp. 226-7.

B_8—Rajasthan Oriental Research Institute, Bharatpur, 1359, ff. 3-23. This incomplete manuscript includes Ś99 on f. 8v (numbered as 24) and B35, Ś79, Ś118, Ś68, Ś57 on ff. 13r-16v (40-4), and N4 on f. 17v (50). The Institute received the book from the District Library, Bharatpur.

B_9—Rajasthan Oriental Research Institute, Bharatpur, 2488 ff. 4-38. It includes Ś123 on f. 17v-18r. The Institute received the book from the District Library, Bharatpur.

B_{10}—Rajasthan Oriental Research Institute, Bharatpur, 4461, 1f. It includes B56 on its verso. The Institute received the book from Dharmeshvar Shastri, Cauburja, Bharatpur.

B_{11}—Rajasthan Oriental Research Institute, Bharatpur, 25, ff. 4-7 (as indicated in the catalogue. According to the manuscript's own numbering: ff. 130-3). This short anthology includes two poems by Ṭhākur, Ś61 (10) and Ś146 (11), on f. 4rv (130rv). In spite of the fact that the numbering of the poems is continuous, the initial three folios of the manuscript are catalogued separately as nr. 24. It includes nine quatrains by Catur, Motīrām and others. The Institute received the book from the District Library, Bharatpur.

B_{12}—Rajasthan Oriental Research Institute, Bharatpur, 232, ff. 70-237. Its first 69 folios are missing. On ff. 118v-119r it includes R59 (numbered as 129). The Institute received the book from the District Library, Bharatpur. The catalogue gives a list of authors in this book on pp. 229-30.

B_{13}—Rajasthan Oriental Research Institute, Bikaner, 34756, ff. 2-48. It includes quatrains by Ṭhākur. This manuscript was not collated for this edition.

C—*Dohõ kī pustak*—Private Collection of Mr. Raghuvir Singh, Chatarpur (M.P.) (without Nr.). It includes Ś78 on p. 12 (numbered as 68), as well as Ś123 (108), R32 (113), R28 (114) on pp. 21-23, Ś150 on p. 32 (178) and Ś111 on p. 44 (246).

D_1—*Kabitta saṅgrah*—Private collection of Kamata Prasad Saraiya, Dhamtalpura, Datiya (M.P.) (without Nr.). The manuscript includes eighteen quatrains by Ṭhākur on ff. 42r-47r (numbered as 118, 122, 128, 129, 136), on f. 50r (151) and on ff. 103r-106v (333-44).

D_2—*Kavitta sār saṅgrah mẽ kabitta sphuṭ*—Private collection of Dr. Kishorilal, collected from Pt. Keshav Kishor Tivari, Dāntare kī Nariyā, Datiya (M.P.) (without Nr.) 10ff. It was written in 1876 (*Saṁvat* 1933) in Himmat Bahādur's town, Rajdhān (near Fatehpur, U.P.). Its colophon reads as *iti śrī kavitta sār saṅgrah tẽ kabitta sphuṭ śrī mahārāj śrī bābā rāmgiri jī kī ājñā pāy saṅkar lāl caraṇsevak likhyate saṁvat 1933 jyeṣṭha māse daśamyā kṛṣṇa pakṣe guru vāsare śubh sthān Rajdhān antaravede śrī Kṛṣṇāya namaḥ*. The manuscript contains 84 *kabittas* by Hulās, Ṭhākur, Kiśor, Padmākar, Rasrāj, Cain, Bhagavant, Raskhān, Gurudatt, Devakīnandan, Śrīpati, Lāl, Jasvant, Kavīndra, Haṭhī, Śāh, Nipaṭ, Kamlājan, (Kiśor,) Dūlah, Pajaneś, Kālikāprasād etc. The *kabittas* are collected from a bigger anthology called *Kavitta sār saṅgrah*. On f. 10v, there are seven poems by Keśav, Tulsīdās and Rahīm that do not form part of *Kabitta sphuṭ*. The collection includes 22 poems by Ṭhākur with readings close to those of the *Sudhāsar*.

F—*Kabitta*—Private collection of Udaya Shanker Dubey, Karerua (U.P.) (without Nr.). The folio contains three quatrains by various authors, one of which is Ṭhākur's Ś52. The manuscript was obtained from Tikamgarh (M.P.).

G—*Padmākar aur Ṭhākur ke savaiye*—Oriental Institute, Vadodara (Govind Gillābhāī Collection 24, 2ff. It includes Ś123, Ś142 and Ś13. The Institute received the book from Shankarlal Vajpeyi, Aurangabad, as indicated on its cover.

I_1—*Sphuṭ kabitta-savaiyā*—Hindī Sāhitya Sammelan, Allahabad, 4364/2030, ff. 53v-80r. A colophon on f. 53v states that the text was copied on *māh badī 5 saṁvat 1874* in Alwar by Hīṅgan Khān for Kuṁvar Rāmbakas. According to its catalogue card prepared in 1955, it has 52 pages, and was acquired from Shivnarayan Bohra. (Interestingly, the 1957 catalogue only indicates *Saṁvat* 1874 in brackets and mentions that the manuscript has 52 pages. The 1971 and 1987 catalogues do not list this book.) The manuscript contains poems by Padmākar, Dev, Sekh, Gopīnāth etc. It includes R14 on f. 54rv.

I_2—*Kabitta saṅgrah*—Hindī Sāhitya Sammelan, Allahabad, 7757/4347, 79ff. This incomplete book acquired from Datiya and written in the Muriya script contains 50 *kavitta*s from various authors such as Rāmpratāp, Bodhā etc. between ff. 39r (as numbered on the rectos, or 1 on the versos) and 56v (or [18] on the versos). This *kabitta* section is followed by some empty pages and then between ff. 64v and 75r there are 48 and 29 verses from the first and second *prakāśa*s of Keśavdās's *Rāmcandrikā* respectively. The manuscript has R30 on f. 39r (1r) (numbered as 1) and Ś150 on ff. 39v-40r (1v-2r) (numbered as 4) and it also contains poem M4 by an unknown poet on f. 40rv (2rv) (numbered as 5), in which the last line is similar to that of Ṭhākur's Ś133 and Ś134). The 1987 catalogue describes this manuscript on pp. 248-9.

I_3—Hindī Sāhitya Sammelan, Allahabad, 3-4/5587, 48ff. The manuscript contains poems by various poets including Ṭhākur and Padmākar. It is described on p. 189 in the 1971 catalogue. This manuscript was not collated for our edition.

I_4—Hindī Sāhitya Sammelan, Allahabad, 8207/4391, 23ff. This incomplete manuscript was acquired from Sitapur. On my visit to the Sammelan in August 2008, the keepers were not able to locate the manuscript. The 1987 catalogue on p. 282 gives the number as 8207/4641.

I_5—*Sphuṭ kavitta*—Hindī Sāhitya Sammelan, Allahabad, 8430/4783, 10ff. The manuscript includes poems by Ṭhākur, Rahīm, Bihārī and others. On my visit to the Sammelan in August 2008 the keepers were not able to locate the manuscript. The 1987 catalogue describes this manuscript on p. 154.

I_6—Hindī Sāhitya Sammelan, Allahabad, 3-15/1114, 174ff. The manuscript contains 605 *pad*s by various poets including Ṭhākur. The 1971 catalogue describes this manuscript on p. 47. On my visit to the Sammelan in August 2008, the keepers were not able to locate the book.

J_1—*Ṭhākur kā kabitta*—Khāsmohar Saṅgrah, Pothikhānā, Sawai Mansingh II Museum, Jaipur, 7683, 7ff. It contains 23 poems by Ṭhākur. Number 11 is applied to two poems while number 22 is missing. It is introduced as *śrī gaṇeśāya namaḥ. atha ṭhākur kā kabit likhyate*. It does not have a final colophon, which suggests that the collection is incomplete.

J_2—*Navras-saṅgrah*—Shree Sanjay Sharma Museum, Jaipur, 753/23, 140ff. It has N26 on ff. 12v-13r in the *Śṛṅgārras-barnan* section.

J_3—*Kabitta saṅgrah*—Shree Sanjay Sharma Museum, Jaipur, 190/224, 8ff. The manuscript has Ś108 (8) and Ś84 (9) on f. 2r.

J_4—*Dohā-kabitta saṅgrah*—Shree Sanjay Sharma Museum, Jaipur, 692/730, 15 ff. The manuscript has Ś36 on f. 14v.

J_5—*Kabitta saṅgrah*—Shree Sanjay Sharma Museum, Jaipur, 933/727. The manuscript has a *pad* by Ṭhākurdās on f. 8rv.

K_1—*Kabitta saṅgrah*—Nāgarīpracāriṇī Sabhā, Varanasi, 1543. The manuscript has Ś123 on f. 4v.

K_2—*Kabitta*—Nāgarīpracāriṇī Sabhā, Varanasi, 3104(2). The manuscript contains Ś153 on f. 17r.

K_3—*Kabitta*—Nāgarīpracāriṇī Sabhā, Varanasi, Yajnik Collection. This manuscript, described in the *Khoj* Report 32-216, was collated in the *Ṭhākur granthāvalī*. The manuscript is today unavailable since the interal Sabhā catalogues do not include this book. The readings of this manuscript as published in the *Granthāvalī* will be referred to as Y_e.

M_1—Rajasthan Oriental Research Institute, Jodhpur, 13515(2) ff. 11-16. The first ten folios and the end of this collection are missing. It includes two quatrains by Ṭhākur—Ś123 on f. 12v (37) and Ś145 on ff. 12v-13r (38). This incomplete collection is bound together with Devīdās's *Rājnīti rā kavitta* (ff. 3-10, with the first two folios missing) at the beginning and is followed by Pṛthvīrāj Sāndū's *Abhaivilās* on ff. 20-29, the first few folios of which are missing. Folios numbered as 17, 18 and 19 are unavailable. The colophon of the *Rājnīti rā kavitta* on f. 27v reads as *iti śrī devīdāskṛt rājnīti rā kabitta saṁpūraṇ subhaṁ bhūyāt lekhaka pāṭhakayauḥ* || *1860 rā mītī kātik bad 14 liṣataṁ sevag motīrāṁm bhagavāṁndāsona (pothī) motīrāṁm rī vās sojat madhe*. The colophon of the *Abhaivilās* on f. (29v) reads as *abhaivilās saṁpūraṇ*|| *liṣatuṁ sevag motīrām bhagavāṁdāsot rī pothī hai sahī*. Since all text was written by Sevag Motīrām, Ṭhākur's quatrains must also have been committed to writing around *Saṁvat* 1860 (1803 CE).

M_2—*Kavitta*—Rajasthani Research Institute, Chopasni, Jodhpur, 7249. It includes R20 on f. 86r (4).

M_3—*Sphuṭ kavitta*—Rajasthani Research Institute, Chopasni, Jodhpur, 6069, 1f. It includes two versions of *dhani haĩ tuva tāta au māta* . . . (U4), a *savaiyā* of uncertain authorship.

M_4—*Sphuṭ kavitta*—Rajasthan Oriental Research Institute, Jodhpur, 34756, ff. 2-48. Several folios are missing. It contains poems by Nāgarīdās, Mādhavdās, Padmākar, Tulsīdās, Ānandghan, Mīrā, etc. and includes some of the most popular quatrains of Ṭhākur, Ś74, Ś111, Ś13, Ś129, Ś86 and Ś120.

M_5—*Phuṭkar kavatta-savaiyā*—Rajasthan Oriental Research Institute, Jodhpur, 15052(3) ff. 22r-38. The anthology in a relatively recent, lined copy book contains quatrains by Ānandghan, Ālam, Bhūṣan, Nāgarīdās, Nāth, Matirām, Ṭhākur, etc. It includes Ś74, Ś111, Ś13, Ś129, Ś86, Ś120, B56, Ś123, Ś1, Ś121 and U4.

M_6—*Śṛṅgār kavitta*—Rajasthan Oriental Research Institute, Jodhpur, 13513(1), ff. 33-46. The anthology includes U4 on f. 34v.

N—*Kabitta saṅgrah*—Sūkar Kṣetra Śodh Saṁsthān, Kasganj (U.P.), without number. The manuscript includes Ś111 on f. 22v (97) and R54 on f. 37r (164) and a *savaiyā* by Harikeś containing the word *ṭhākura* as part of the epithet of Krishna on ff. 37v-38r (170).

O_1—*Kabitta*—Bundelā Śodh Saṁsthān, Seondha (M.P.), without number, 1f. It includes N13.

O_2—*Kabitta*—Bundelā Śodh Saṁsthān, Seondha (M.P.), without number, 1f. It includes B67 and Ś40.

P—*Kabitta saṅgrah*—DAV College, Chandigarh, 1580, 68ff. This incomplete manuscript contains poems by seventeenth- and eighteenth-century poets, such as Senāpati, Matirām, Gaṅg, Ālam, Tulsīdās, Brahma, Nandan etc. On f. 48r, the quatrain *rūsanahārī ghanerī hatī* . . . (U8) of uncertain authorship is present, which in the *pañcamottaraṅg* of some *Sudhāsar* manuscripts (S_2, S_7) was attributed to Ṭhākur. Since the manuscript contains no other poem by Ṭhākur and all the other poets included into it predate him, it is likely to represent a collection going back to a time when Ṭhākur was not yet popular. The attribution of the *savaiyā* to Ṭhākur in the *Sudhāsar* is erroneous (see above p. 63).

S_1—*Prabodh-ras-sudhāsar*—Rajasthan Oriental Research Institute, Bharatpur, 620 (vols. 1-2), 237+213=450ff. This 36.5x26.5 cm manuscript has 16 lines per page and 17 syllables per line, which equals to 7650 *anuṣṭup* strophes. It was copied in 1853 (*Saṁvat* 1910) by Tejā sipāhī as commissioned by Prohit Harsukh Singh. It includes 93 quatrains by Ṭhākur. About this manuscript see pp. 62-3.

S_2—*Sudhāsar pañcamottaraṅg*—Vrindaban Research Institute, Vrindaban, 6773, 88ff. This 17.2x26.5 cm manuscript has 18 lines per page and 22 syllables per line, which equals to 2178 *anuṣṭup* strophes. It was copied in 1878 (*Saṁvat* 1935). The text is introduced with the following words *śrī rādhāramaṇo jayati| atha prācīkavi samūha vānī rasasānīmaya navīna kṛti sudhāsara grantha liṣyat.* Its final colophon reads as *iti śrī navīna-viracitāyā sudhāsara nāṁma grantha kavi samūha vānī devastuti bhaktapakṣa nirveda karuṇā varnana pañcamottaraga saṁpūrṇam. saṁvat āśāḍ [kṛsna].* On f. 64r it contains the following paratext, *śrī rādhāramaṇo jayati namaḥ śrī gusāī soṁhanlāljī śrī hare hare hare*, which situates the manuscript in a Vaishnava milieu. This collection of 459 *kabitta*s includes 93 stanzas by Ṭhākur. Its numbering restarts repeatedly. Contrary to what its colophon states this is not the fifth *taraṅg* but a selection from the later edition of the *Sudhāsar*. The manuscript was donated to the VRI by Atulkrishna Goswami.

S_3—*Sudhāsar saṅgrah ke phuṭkal kabitta*—Panjabi University, Patiala, 115412 (366), 294ff (in its own numbering 209+1+84ff.). This manuscript in the Gurmukhi script has an average of 13 lines on each folio and 24 characters in a line, which equals to 5713 *anuṣṭup* strophes. The second *taraṅg* finishes on f. 209v. After this, there is a blank folio and then the folio numbering restarts with f. 1 continuing up to f. 84r. This new section starts with *uddīpan-nirūpana mai ṣaṭa-ritu-varnana*. After f. 294 (84), there are some 30 empty folios. It was written in a Sikh environment as is clear from phrases such as *srī vāh gurujī sadā sahāya* and *srī gurū nānaka deva* etc. inserted at the end of the sections. According to the colophon on f. 294r (84r), it was copied in 1862 (*Saṁvat* 1919) in Kālikāpurī, apparently the modern-day Kalka. The colophon reads as *sãta srī akāla purasa jī sadā sahāya| saraba sakti saṁyukti mahārājādhirāja pratāpadhārī srī gurū gobinda siṁghaya namo namaḥ| saṁvat 1919 vaiśākh sudī 5 sanī| kālikāpurī*. English and Panjabi stamps on f. 1r and 31r state that *This book belongs to Bhai Mohan Singh Vaid and sons, Tarn Taran (Punjab)*.

S_4—*Sudhāsar*—Government Language Department (Bhāṣā Vibhāg), Patiala, 13(a, b), 2-104ff. (f. 1 is missing) (in Gurmukhi). This 21.5x15 cm manuscript has an average of 22 lines on each folio and 20 characters in a line, which equals to 2860 *anuṣṭup* strophes. The Urdu-script title on the cover page identifies the text as *Braj-mahimā varnan* and *Braj-ras-rīt-barnan*. The first part of this manuscript (ff. 2-38), which includes 200 poems from the third and fourth *taraṅgs (Rājasamāj-nirūpan* and *Nīt, prastāv, bisar varnan)* of the *Sudhāsar*, is misidentified in the published catalogue as Ānandghan's *Iśklatā*. Its second part (13b) containing 289 poems is based on the *Braj-ras-rīt varnan* of the *Sudhāsar*. The numbering of the poems in this section restarts with 1. The manuscript does not have a colophon. An English stamp on the cover page states that the manuscript once belonged to the 'Panjabi Department, Patiala and East Punjab State University, Patiala'. Several spelling mistakes in this manuscript originate in erroneous readings of a Devanagari exemplar. For example, it misreads the character *na* for *ta* (Ś48, 1; B42, 1) and *va* for *ba* (not marked in the edition), *ya* for *pa* (Ś127, 1).

S_5—*Sudhāsāgar*—Rajasthan Oriental Research Institute, Alwar, 4817, 246ff. This 19x30.3 cm manuscript has an average of 19 lines per page and 20 syllables per line, which equals to 5842.5 *anuṣṭup* strophes. This manuscript is incomplete. It contains the *Sudhāsar* up to the *kavi-kāvya* section, which is about four fifths of the anthology. About fifty pages from the end have been lost. (Only nine quatrains were collated from this manuscript.)

S_6—*Sudhāsar*—Sikh History Department, Khalsa College, Amritsar, 2186, 416ff (in Gurmukhi). This 32x24 cm manuscript has an average of 15 lines per page and 24 syllables per line, which equals to 9360 *anuṣṭup* strophes. Its readings and structure are very close to S7. According to the catalogue, it was copied in AD 1908 but I was not able to find any date in the manuscript itself. (Only eleven quatrains have been collated from this manuscript.)

S_7—*Sudhāsar*—Sikh History Department, Khalsa College, Amritsar, 2187, 290ff (in Gurmukhi). This 32x17 cm manuscript has an average of 13 lines per page and 45 syllables per line, which equals to 10,603 *anuṣṭup* strophes. It was copied in *sāl* 1911 (? AD 1854) *bhādõ sudī* 11.

Ṭ—*Ṭhākur-satsaī*—Panjabi University, Patiala, 115412 (366) 5ff (in Gurmukhi). The manuscript is part of a larger book but its folios are numbered independently of the rest. It contains 49 quatrains by Ṭhākur and a famous *savaiyā* by Raskhān (*brahma mai ḍhūḍhyo . . .* numbered as 6). The quatrain *dhriga kāna jo . . .* (B56) is included twice as nr. 8 and 40. Number 11 is assigned to two different poems thus the number given to the last completed poem is 49. At the bottom of f. 5v, after poem 49 the scribe wanted to start a new stanza beginning as *ka[vitta:] kaha*. The text, however, stops at this point and on the next folio a new collection starts with the words *[dāṁne]sa jī ko*. This manuscript presents an effort independent of B_1 and V_1 to collect Ṭhākur's quatrains. Almost half of its poems (22 out of 49) are missing from both B_1 and V_1: B6, B40, B53, B54, Ś14, Ś58, Ś62, Ś130, Ś136var (present in V_1), Ś137 (present in B_1), Ś152, R14 (present in B_1), R16, R29, R54, N2, N14, N17, N20, N36, N37, U4 (present in B_1). While there are similarities between B_1 and V_1 in the sequence of quatrains, no such similarity can be observed between either B_1 or V_1 and the *Satsaī*. The high number of eccentric readings in the *Satsaī* suggests that its scribe (or the scribe of its exemplar) wrote many quatrains down from memory.

U—Rajasthan Oriental Research Institute, Udaipur, 4288 (10-15), ff. 71-145. This massive book mostly contains quatrains distributed into sections according to author. A work ending on f. 237r of the manuscript bears the following colophon: *iti śrīman mahārājedra śī svāī pratāpsiṁh jī dev viracitāṁ vairāgyamañjarī saṁpūrṇa|| Saṁvat 1888 kā jyeṣṭh sudī 7 bhairamadine|| liṣāvate ṭhākurāṁ rājyaśrī 8 ī raṇajīt siṁh jī ku cāmaṁnpati ciraṁjīvau| leṣak kāyastha māthur ṣamrāj || yodhnagare*. A seal in the manuscript indicates that at some time it belonged to 'R.S. Derashri, Banera'. The catalogue tells that its 21st section (ff. 172-219) was copied in 1831 (*Saṁvat* 1888) by Jatī Khūbcand, Pañcolī Khemrāj in Jodhpur. The *Ṭhākur ke kabitta* in section 14 on ff. 126r-7r includes 10 quatrains by Ṭhākur, Ś97, R18, Ś123, Ś36, Ś19, Ś38, U4, N11, B56, Ś122.

V_1—*Ṭhākur-kabitta*—Vrindaban Research Institute, Vrindaban, 9678, 16ff. It contains 95 *kabittas* by Ṭhākur and one *pad* (numbered as 64) with the signature Sūrdās.[49] There is neither introduction nor colophon in the manuscript. Its internal numbering restarts again and again dividing the manuscript into sections of 13, 13, 12, 14, 13, 27, 4 and 2 poems without section headings. Only poems 10 and 11 are announced to be 'parikriyā' (i.e. *parakīyā*) and 'parikriyā kalahataritā' respectively. As has been mentioned, this manuscript has close affinity to section *b* of B_1 and 86 of its poems are also present in the later *Sudhāsar* anthology. The manuscript was donated to the VRI by Madanlal Sharma (Beri).

V_2—*Kabitta saṅgrah*—Ras Bhāratī Saṁsthān, Vrindaban, 548. The manuscript includes 15 quatrains by Ṭhākur on ff. 68v-71v (R61, N37, Ś74, Ś136, Ś108, Ś111, R54, N31, B68, Ś137, Ś19, Ś76, R14, Ś97, B16). There are two *kavittas* on f. 68v. introduced with the word *Ṭhākur* and numbered separately. On f. 69r the words *Syām kavi* are crossed out and the section is introduced as *Ṭhākur kavi*. This section has 13 quatrains numbered consecutively.

V_3—*Kabitta saṅgrah*—Ras Bhāratī Saṁsthān, Vrindaban, 118, 74ff. The colophon on f. 75r states that this book was written in 1830 (*Saṁvat* 1887) in Vrindaban. On ff. 29v-30v, it includes a sequence of seven poems numbered 2-8 and introduced as *Kabi ṭhākur*. This sequence contains B64 (2), B67 (3), B55 (5), Ś9 (6), B55 (7) and Ś73 (8). (The quatrain numbered as 4, however, is by Kāsīrām and is introduced accordingly.)

V_4—*Phuṭkar kabitta*—Braj Cultural Research Institute, Vrindaban, unnumbered manuscript, 107 ff. It is written in black ink with deletions in yellow. The first six folios contain a prose *śakunāvalī*, which is followed by poems of Senāpati, Padmākar, Dev, Balavant, Bhūṣan, Ānandghan, Dayānidhi, Kāśināth, Tulsīdās, Sambhu, and others including ghazals as well as a *rekhtā* by Somnāth in the Nagari script. The last few folios include poetry in the Urdu script. Ṭhākur is represented with four *kabittas*, Ś76 and Ś56 on ff. 11v-12r (19, 20), Ś113 on f. 32v (17) and Ś123 on f. 45r (17). According to the colophon on f. 80r dated *Caitra badī 9, saṁvat 1905* (1848CE) this *Phuṭkar kabitta* was copied by Gaṅgāprasād Miśra for

[49] The poem is present in N. Vājpeyī, ed., *Sūrsāgar*, 2 vols., Varanasi: Nāgarīpracāriṇī Sabhā, 1950-2, vol. 2, pp. 1107-8 numbered as 2574/3162.

Lālā Rāmbakas. Another colophon on f. 107r dated *Vaisākh sudī, saṁvat 1906* (1849 CE) states the same.

Z_1—*Kabitta saṅgrah*—Private collection of I. Bangha, ff. 17-61. This incomplete manuscript originally had a collection of 111 *arillas* by the poet Cand on the rectos up to f. 58. Later a collection of quatrains by various poets was written on the versos, which includes 9 poems by Ṭhākur. N31 (19), Ś78 (21), R12 (24), B56 (25), Ś123 (28), Ś20 (29), Ś46 (30), Ś108 (31), Ś15 (32).

Z_2—*Kabitta saṅgrah*—Private collection of I. Bangha, f. 2 (f. 1, containing verses 1-5, is missing). The first nine verses of this loose folio in black ink may all be *samasyāpūrti* for "*. . . urajhīṁ akhiyāṁ surajhāvahī ko?*" Verses 8 and 9 contain the signature Nidhi. Then, after a *dohā* follow a *kavitta* by Padmākar and *savaiyā* Ś109 by Ṭhākur with its last words missing.

Printed Books

A_e—'Hariaudh ', Ayodhyasingh Upadhyay, *Hindī bhāṣā aur uske sāhitya kā vikās*. Bhagalpur: The United Press, 1934.

B_e—'Barsainya', Ganga Prasad. 'Bundelkhaṇḍī kavi ṭhākur (ṭhākurdās kāyastha) aur unkā kāvya'. *Bundelī basant*, 2002, pp. 25-9.

C_e—*Sundarī-tilak* (of Hariścandra). Lucknow: Navalkiśor Press, 1883.

D_e—Dvij, Mannalal, ed. *Śṛṅgār sudhākar*. Benares: Amar Yantrālay, 1887.

F_e—Khān, Hāfizullah, ed. *Ṣaṭ-ṛtu-kāvya-saṅgrah*. Lucknow: Navalkiśor, 1889.

G_e—Mishra, Chandrashekhar, ed. *Ṭhākur granthāvalī*. Benares: Nāgarīpracāriṇī Sabhā, 1973.

H_e—Gupta, Kishorilal. *Hazārā : Saroj-ullikhit tathākathit kālidās hazārā kā uplabdha aṁśa*. Allahabad: Smṛti Prakāśan, 1978.

I_e—Shukla, Ramchandra. 1929. *Hindī sāhitya kā itihās*. Allahabad: Indian Press.

J_e—Suhane, Paramanand, ed. *Ṣaṭ-ṛtu-hajārā*. Lucknow: Navalkiśor Press, 1894.

K_e—Sardār Kavi, ed. *Śṛṅgār saṅgrah*. Benares: Ānandvan Chāpekhānā, 1864.

L_e—Kishorilal ed. *Vidvanmod taraṅginī: Śivsiṁh Saroj kā adyāvadhi aprakāśit prasiddh ādhār granth: saṅkalankartā śrī subbāsiṁh 'śrīdhar'*. Allahabad: Hindī Sāhitya Sammelan, 1991.

M_e—Mital, Prabhudayal. *Brajbhāṣā sāhitya kā ṛtu-saundarya*. Mathura: Sāhitya Saṁsthān, 1961.

N_e—'Braj', Gokul Prasad, ed. *Digvijay bhūṣaṇ*. Balrampur: Jaṅgbahādurī Yantrālay 1868.

O_e—Singh, Bhairav, ed. *Rasik-vinod*. Prayāg: Indian Press, 1910.

P_e—Suhane, Paramanand, ed. *Pāvas-kavitta-ratnākar*. Lucknow: Navalkiśor Press, 1893.

Q_{e1}—Manuscript at Bābū Jagannāth Prasād (Chatarpur) as described in the *Khoj* Report of 1905.[50]

Q_{e2}—*Kūṭ kabitta*—Manuscript at Thakur Naunihal Singh, Kānthā, Unāo Distr (*Saṁvat* 1842) as described in the *Khoj* Report of 1923-5.[51]

Q_{e3}—*Satak*—Manuscript described in the *Khoj* Report of 1920-2, p. 462.[52]

R_e—Pratap Narayan, Maharaj. ed. *Raskusumākar.* Allahabad: Indian Press, 1894. (The editor is also called Daduā Sāhab.)

S_e—Ratnakar, Jagannathdas, ed. *Navīn: Sudhāsar.* Benares: Amar Prakāś Yantrālay, 1875.

Ś$_e$—Kashiprasad, ed. *Ṭhākur śatak.* Benares: Bhāratjīvan Press, 1904.

Ṭ$_e$—Lala Bhagvandin. ed. *Ṭhākur ṭhasak.* Benares: Sāhitya Sevak Kāryālay, 1924.

Ṭ^i_e—Poem quoted in the 'Ṭhākur kavi kā jīvancarit' section (pp. 1-23) of the *Ṭhākur ṭhasak* (Its variants are only mentioned when different from the main text of Ṭ$_e$.)

U_e—Singh, Maharajkumar Baburamdin, ed. *Sundarī-tilak* (of Hariścandra). Bāṅkīpur (Patna): Khaḍgavilās Press, 1892.

V_e—Mishrabandhu, *Miśrabandhu vinod 1-2.* Lucknow: Gaṅgā Pustakmālā, 1913 (new revised and enlarged edn. 1972).

X_e—Khān, Hāfizullah. *Sūkti-sudhā arthāt hāfizullah khā̃ kā hazārā.* Lucknow: Navalkiśor Press, 1932 (6th edn.) and Lucknow: Uttar Pradeś Hindī Sansthān, 2006 (new edn.)

Y_e—Yajnik Collection, Nāgarīpracāriṇī Sabhā, Kāśī. Quoted as variant readings in G_e.

Z_e—Suhane, Paramanand, ed. *Nakhśikh-hajārā.* Lucknow: Navalkiśor Press, 1893.

MANUSCRIPTS ERRONEOUSLY PERCEIVED TO CONTAIN *KABITTAS* BY *ṬHĀKUR*

Phuṭkar kavitta—Rajasthan Oriental Research Institute, Alwar, 6053(4), ff. 19v, 29v. (*Saṁvat* 1885)—(The catalogue mentions on p. 48 that it contains poems by Ṭhākur).

Rajasthan Oriental Research Institute, Bharatpur, 230, ff. 32v-33r. (Here the poem is not by Ṭhākur but by Mīrā although the catalogue attributed it to Ṭhākur.)

Kabitta—Nāgarīpracāriṇī Sabhā, Varanasi, 431, 5r (10). (In this collection, the cataloguer misread the word *kuṭhāra* as Ṭhākur).

[50]Shyamsundardas, *Hasatalikhit hindī granthõ kī khoj kā vivaraṇ san 1905 (Annual report for the search for Hindi manuscripts for the year 1905),* Allahabad: United Provinces Government Press, 1908; repr. Varanasi: Nāgarīpracāriṇī Sabhā 1995 [VS 2052], p. 92.

[51]Hiralal, ed., *The twelfth report on the search of Hindi manuscripts,* pp. 1470-1 (426).

[52]Referred to in J. Chaturvedi, *Brajbhāṣā rītiśāstra granth koś,* Prayag: Hindi Sahitya Sammelan, 1965, p. 23.

Early Anthologies without Poems by Ṭhākur

Dvij, Mannalal, ed. *Sundarī sarvasva.* Benares: Amar Yatrālay, 1885.

Giridharlal, Munshi, ed. *Nakhśikh saṅgrah.* Lucknow: Lucknow Printing Press, 1902.

Mishra, Matadin, ed. *Kavitta ratnākar,* 2 vols. Lucknow: Navalkiśor Press, 1876.

'Shankar', Gaurishankar Dvivedi. *Bundel-vaibhav, athavā bundelkhaṇḍ ke hindī kaviyõ kā sāṅgopāṅg itihās,* vols. 1-2. Agra: Śānti Press, *Saṁvat* 1992 (1935) (Bundel-vaibhav granthamālā 3, Ṭīkamgaṛh).

CONCORDANCE

Bhagavān—Bhakti aur Līlā

ṬK$_e$	G$_e$	Ṭ$_e$	Ś$_e$	B$_1$	S$_1$	S$_7$	S$_{2-6}$	D$_2$	J$_1$	Ṭ	U	V$_1$	Other
B1	1	1											
B2	200	10	29										
B3	207			163r b82								7r 39	
B4	215	6											
B5	214	19	38										
B6					245v/6r 12	181v 12	S$_2$ S$_3$ S$_4$			3v 26			
B7	216	5	35										
B8	B1			159-60 b61	418rv 13	269v 146	S$_2$ S$_3$ S$_6$					12rv 73	
B9	B2			157v b47	419v/20r 19	270rv 152	S$_2$ S$_3$	1r 2				3rv 16	
B10	B3			157v b46	275r 1	196rv 1	S$_3$ S$_4$					3r 15	
B11	B4			158v b52	244r 4	180v/1r 14	S$_2$ S$_3$ S$_4$			3v 25		4v 24	
B12	2	2, j		158r b49	389v 2b	254/5r 7		1r 3				3v 18	
B13	206	20	34										
B14	205	15	107										
B15	211	25											
B16	212	9	92	158r b50				7v/8r 67				3v/4r 19	V$_2$
B17	213	11	39										
B18	3	136	1										

ṬK$_e$	G$_e$	Ṭ$_e$	Ś$_e$	B$_1$	S$_1$	S$_7$	S$_{2-6}$	D$_2$	J$_1$	Ṭ	U	V$_1$	Other
B19	4	4											
B20	19	33	12										
B21	B9			151v/2r b15	420v 22	270v (155)	S$_2$					14v 87	
B22	9			154rv b28	273rv 25, 2v m12	1v 11	S$_2$ S$_3$ S$_5$ S$_6$			3r 23		5v 30	H
B23								7r 58					
B24								7r 59					
B25	8	3											
B26	28	126, j											
B27	B5			157r b44	263v 5	190v 5	S$_3$ S$_4$					9r 52	
B28	B10			152r b16	263r 3	190r 3	S$_2$ S$_3$ S$_4$			2r 13		14v 88	
B29	B7			161r b69	412v 101	265v 106	S$_2$					12v/13r 77	
B30	B6			159v b60	266v 1	192r 3	S$_2$ S$_3$ S$_4$			2v 17		12r 72	
B31	B8			161r b70	57r 57	184r 13	S$_2$ S$_3$ S$_4$			2r 12		13r 78	
B32	10	41											I$_e$
B33	11	89											
B34	12	67											
B35				153r b22									B$_8$
B36	13	44											
B37	14	62											
B38	16	34	23										
B39	18	40	95										
B40					269v/70r 1	193v 12	S$_3$ S$_4$			2v 18			D$_1$
B41													C$_e$
B42	B11			160r b64	260rv 1	188v/9r 16	S$_3$ S$_4$			2r 16		12v 75	
B43	17	65											
B44	26			158rv b51		45v 431	S$_2$					4r 20	

ṬK$_e$	G_e	Ṭ$_e$	Ś$_e$	B_1	S_1	S_7	$S_{2\text{-}6}$	D_2	J_1	Ṭ	U	V_1	Other
B45	27			163r b81	280r /1v 9	199rv 26	S_2 S_3 S_4			3rv 24		2r 8	
B46													D_e
B47	68	83	100										
B48	30	75	20										
B49	36	156, j											
B50	32	168	89										C_e, U_e, V_e
B51	69	166	83	163rv b 84	301rv 96	208v 93	S_2 S_4	2v 15				7v 41	Y_e
B52								3rv 26					
B53	38	184			307rv 74	212v 128	S_2 S_3 S_5	3v 29		5r 44			
B54	31	178								5r 43			
B55	39	153			302rv 51	210r 108	S_2 S_3 S_4	2v 18				8v 47	V_3, Y_2
B56	41	138	2		290rv 10	204v 53	S_2 S_4	3r 21	2v/3r 8	5v 40	127r 9	2v 12	B_5, B_{10}, U_e, V_3, Z_1, Y_e
B57	42	172	99										
B58	40	135	91										
B59	43	181	101										
B60	44	179	102										
B61	45			157rv b45	296v 26b	207r 81	S_2 S_3 S_4	2r 12		5v 41		3r 14	
B62	46			161rv b72	165rv 218	205v 66	S_3 S_4	2v 19				13rv 80	
B63	47			162v/3r b80	303r 55	210v 112	S_2 S_3 S_4	3r 24				1v/2r 7	
B64	48			150v b7								15v 93	V_3
B65					295rv 22	206v 77	S_2 S_3 S_4	2r 14					
B66													D_1
B67								2v 16					O_2
B68													H_e, V_2

Śṛṅgār

ṬK$_e$	G$_e$	Ṭ$_e$	Ś$_e$	B$_1$	S$_1$	S$_7$	S$_{2\text{-}6}$	D$_2$	J$_1$	Ṭ	U	V$_1$	Other
Ś1	70	173	56										C$_e$
Ś2	56	51	47										D$_1$
Ś3	138			155v b36								10v 61	
Ś4	59			158v b54		49rv 466	S$_2$					5r 26	
Ś5	64	171	67										
Ś6	52	169	43					2v 17					
Ś7	53	176			63v	45r 425	S$_2$						C$_e$, O$_e$
Ś8	85	158, j											I$_e$, O$_e$
Ś9					68v	49r 465	S$_2$						C$_e$, U$_e$, V$_3$
Ś10	128	21	69	132r a6									O$_e$, X$_e$
Ś11	B26			151r b10		49v 468	S$_5$					13v 82	
Ś12	73	35	81										
Ś13	72	187, j											C$_e$, O$_e$, G
Ś14										1v 10			
Ś15	B12	j	87		6r 30	5r 47	S$_2$ S$_5$ S$_6$		4v 14				A$_e$, B$_3$, B$_7$, H$_e$, N$_e$, X$_e$, Z$_1$
Ś16	74	27	16										
Ś17	75	28											
Ś18	76	39	33										
Ś19	77	38			60r 4	43r 407	S$_2$		15		5		H$_e$, V$_2$
Ś20	78	29		162r b76		60rv 604	S$_2$ S$_6$					1r 3	Y$_e$, Z$_1$
Ś21	79	30											
Ś22	80			154v b29		113v 1085	S$_3$					5v/6r 31	
Ś23	81			162r b77		110v 1061	S$_5$					1rv 4	
Ś24												11r 65	
Ś25	B13	j											D$_1$
Ś26	B17			160r b63	272r 14	195r 14	S$_3$ S$_4$			2v 3r 20b		12v 74	
Ś27	B23			155v/6r b37	25v ^{mg}	20rv 179	S$_6$					10v 62	

ṬK$_e$	G$_e$	Ṭ$_e$	Ś$_e$	B$_1$	S$_1$	S$_7$	S$_{2-6}$	D$_2$	J$_1$	Ṭ	U	V$_1$	Other
Ś28	B28			155v b35		104r 1014	S$_3$		3v/4r 11b			10rv 60	U$_e$
Ś29													Z$_e$
Ś30	B14		65										
Ś31	82	159, j		133r a12									
Ś32	B15			153v/4r b25	273r 19	195v 19	S$_3$					6v 35	
Ś33	B16			159r b57		134r 1266	S$_2$ S$_3$					11v 68	
Ś34	24	32	21										
Ś35	25	52	17										
Ś36	20	63			180v/1r 6	117v 1120	S$_3$				4		B$_6$, D$_1$, J$_4$
Ś37	21	64											
Ś38	22	191									6		
Ś39	23	192											
Ś40	57	31		156r b39	181v 3	145v/6r 1387	S$_2$ S$_3$		5r 16	3v/4r 30		9v 54	B$_5$, O$_2$, Y$_e$
Ś41	127	26	3										
Ś42	129	58	15	164rv b90	271v 10	194v 10	S$_2$ S$_3$ S$_4$			2v 19		8v 48	Y$_e$
Ś43	130	47	13										
Ś44	133	45, j							4r 12				C$_e$, I$_e$, R$_e$, Ve
Ś45	135	152											
Ś46	136	59	46		70r 9	50r 473	S$_2$						Z$_1$
Ś47	139			162rv b78	270v/1r 6	194rv 6	S$_2$ S$_3$ S$_4$					1v 5	
Ś48	144			159v b59	272r 13	195r 13	S$_3$ S$_4$			3r 21b		11v -12r 70	
Ś49	145			160r b62	260r 1	188v 14	S$_3$ S$_4$			2r 15		12r 71	
Ś50	146			162v b79	227v -8r	172r 1638	S$_3$					1v 6	
Ś51	158	85											
Ś52	170	61											F
Ś53													C$_e$
Ś54	134	81	82	164v b91	171v 11	194v/5r 11	S$_3$ S$_4$			2v 20		9r 51	C$_e$, Y$_e$

ṬK$_e$	G$_e$	Ṭ$_e$	Ś$_e$	B$_1$	S$_1$	S$_7$	S$_{2-6}$	D$_2$	J$_1$	Ṭ	U	V$_1$	Other
Ś55	B30			155r b33		49r 463	S$_2$					10r 58	
Ś56				185rv d23	231r	173v 1652	S$_3$			1r 5			V$_4$
Ś57	B34			161v/2r b74	308v 79	213r 133	S$_2$ S$_3$					1r 1	B$_8$
Ś58										5r 42			
Ś59	143	j											
Ś60	131	177											
Ś61													B$_{11}$
Ś62					189r	151rv 1438	S$_2$ S$_3$			3v 29			
Ś63	29	79	68										
Ś64	33	78	24		108r 15	72r 716	S$_2$						
Ś65	37	147, j	98										
Ś66	51	54		160v b67	308r 77	212v/3r 131	S$_2$ S$_3$					4v 23	C$_e$, O$_e$, Y$_e$
Ś67	54			150v b6	186v	149v 1426	S$_3$					15rv 92	
Ś68	62	73	8	161r b71	301v 48	208v 95	S$_2$ S$_3$ S$_4$					13r 79	B$_8$, Y$_e$
Ś69	66	82	96										
Ś70	71	151	88										
Ś71	137	87											
Ś72	157	72	11										
Ś73	159	165	64										V$_3$
Ś74	160	68	44						1rv 2				C$_e$; H$_e$, V$_2$
Ś75	161	76	10										
Ś76	162	69	9	185v d24	106r	72r 719	S$_2$ S$_6$						A$_e$, C$_e$, H$_e$, O$_e$, V$_2$, V$_4$
Ś77	163			158rv b 58		76v 761	S$_2$					11v 69	
Ś78	210	144	30										C, Z$_1$
Ś79	B32			154r b27		115v/6r 1105	S$_2$					6v/7r 37	B$_8$
Ś80	B33			155r b32		116r 1108	S$_2$					7r 38	
Ś81	B35			158v/9r b55								11r 66	

ṬK$_e$	G_e	Ṭ$_e$	Ś$_e$	B_1	S_1	S_7	S_{2-6}	D_2	J_1	Ṭ	U	V_1	Other
Ś82				151v b13	296v 27	207r 82	S_2 S_3 S_4					14r 85	
Ś83				132v a10	63v/4r 214	45v 428	S_2						C_e, U_e
Ś84													J_3
Ś85													D_1
Ś86													C_e, O_e
Ś87	34	71											
Ś88	35	84	85										
Ś89	B18			151rv b12		39v 10	S_2					14r 84	
Ś90													D_1
Ś91	196	150											
Ś92	197	180	103										
Ś93	B29			154v b30		84r 823						6r 32	
Ś94	B27			154r b26		56rv 533	S_2 S_6					6v 36	
Ś95	B31			151v b14		110r 1056						14rv 86	
Ś96	140	j											
Ś97	124	155	26	141v a61	96v	66rv 661	S_2		3r 9	1r 3	126r 1		A_e, C_e, I_e, V_2, V_e
Ś98	148	70	106										
Ś99	152	37		156r b38		113v/4r 1088	S_2					10v/1r 63	B_8, C_e, O_e, V_e, X_e, Y_e
Ś100	153	66											D_1
Ś101	151	167	84										
Ś102	149	86				114v 1096							U_e
Ś103	150	80, j	80	135v a27		144v 1378	S_2 S_3			4r 32			C_e, O_e
Ś104	193	22	70						5v 17				A_e, V_e
Ś105	B22			155rv b34		114v 1094	S_2					10r 59	
Ś106					40v 5	30r 271	S_2						
Ś107	154			163r b83								7rv 40	D_1

ṬK$_e$	G$_e$	Ṭ$_e$	Ś$_e$	B$_1$	S$_1$	S$_7$	S$_{2-6}$	D$_2$	J$_1$	Ṭ	U	V$_1$	Other
Ś108					97v				11a				A$_e$, C$_e$, H$_e$, J$_3$, R$_e$, Z$_1$, V$_2$
Ś109	174	148, j						2r 11					Z$_2$
Ś110	182			160v b66		46r 434	S$_2$					4rv 22	
Ś111		18	78						7				B$_3$, B$_5$, C, H$_e$, N, O$_e$, V$_2$ X$_e$
Ś112	58			161v b73	366v 95	243v 76	S$_2$					13r 81	
Ś113	60	56		163v b86		44r 413	S$_2$					7v/8r 43	V$_4$, Y$_e$
Ś114	61	77	66										
Ś115	67	133	105										
Ś116	65	55, j											C$_e$, O$_e$
Ś117	63	49	97										
Ś118	B21			156rv b40	172rv 15	195r 15	S$_3$ S$_4$			3r 22		9v 55	B$_8$
Ś119	55	50											
Ś120	84	175		162r b75		46r 437	S$_2$					1r 2	C$_e$, O$_e$, Y$_e$
Ś121	86	164	63										
Ś122	88	170	45		116v & 195r	154v 1464	S$_2$ S$_3$	2r 13	6v/7r 21		127r 10$^{v\ ar}$	2v 11	B$_6$, C$_e$, O$_e$, U$_e$
Ś123	89	60	42	131rv a1	70r 8	49v 471	S$_2$		2rv 6	1r 1	126rv 3		B$_6$, B$_9$, C, C$_e$, G, K$_1$, M$_1$, V$_4$, V$_e$, X$_e$, Z$_1$
Ś124	141	j											
Ś125	87	163											
Ś126						97v 947	S$_5$						
Ś127	B19			160v 1r b 68	263rv 4	190v 4	S$_3$ S$_4$			2r 14		12r 76	
Ś128	B20	j											C$_e$, R$_e$, U$_e$
Ś129	126	48	4			47v 451	S$_2$						C$_e$
Ś130										5rv 45			

ṬK$_e$	G$_e$	Ṭ$_e$	Ś$_e$	B$_1$	S$_1$	S$_7$	S$_{2-6}$	D$_2$	J$_1$	Ṭ	U	V$_1$	Other
Ś131	83	146	93										
Ś132	142	j											
Ś133	125	162											C$_e$, O$_e$
Ś134	165	183	41	160v b65				8r 68				4r 21	C$_e$, Y$_e$
Ś135	164	46		163v b85		46v 440	S$_2$					7v 42	Y$_e$
Ś136	166	17	25		63r 16	45r 422				1v 7^{var}		2rv 10	C$_e$, H$_e$, V$_2$, Y$_e$
Ś137	167	74	7	153r b21	231v/2r	174r 1657	S$_2$ S$_3$		1v 3	1r 4			H$_e$, V$_2$
Ś138	168	23	14										
Ś139	169	16, j	77										C$_e$, Q$_e$, I$_e$
Ś140	132	137			70rv 10	50r 474	S$_2$ S$_5$ S$_6$						A$_e$
Ś141	171	174	76			109rv 1051	S$_3$						
Ś142	172	42	51										C$_e$, U$_e$, G^{var}
Ś143	173	160, j											
Ś144	175	53		163-4 b87		46v/7r 443	S$_2$					8r 44	
Ś145	176	189	18										
Ś146	177	43	94	146v a87	69v/70r 7	49v 469	S$_2$		2r 5			2v 13	B$_{11}$, C$_e$, M$_1$, O$_e$, X$_e$, Y$_e$
Ś147	179	188	19										
Ś148	180	182	40										D$_1$
Ś149	181	190	6	164v b92		52rv 497	S$_2$					8v/9r 50	Y$_e$
Ś150													C, I$_2$
Ś151		j											
Ś152					182v	146rv 1390	S$_5$			4r 31			
Ś153													K$_2$
Ś154													D$_1$
Ś155					150v 1	100v 977							

R̥tu-Varṇan

ṬK$_e$	G$_e$	Ṭ$_e$	Ś$_e$	B$_1$	S$_1$	S$_7$	S$_{2\text{-}6}$	D$_2$	J$_1$	Ṭ	U	V1	Other
R1	15	90, j											
R2	B37	j											I_e
R3													D_e, J_e, M_e
R4	90	92	60										
R5	92	88	62										
R6	B38			150rv b5	224r	170r 1619	S_2 S_3						
R7	B40	91, j											A_e, C_e, I_e, J_e, M_e
R8	B41			151r b9	217rv	166r 1588	S_2 S_3					16r 96	
R9	91	93	61										
R10	B36			150r b4		98r 954	S_2					15v 94	
R11	B39			153rv b23	223rv	169v 1616	S_2 S_3					6r 33	
R12													Z_1
R13				133v a15									
R14				165rv b96		129rv 1224	S_3			4r 33			H_e, I_1, J_e, M_e, V_2
R15													J_e
R16	93	99	90			127v 1208	S_3			4rv 34			C_e, J_e, L_e, M_e
R17	94	98	57										
R18	95	97	71						7r 23		126r 2		
R19	96	95	58										
R20	97	94, j											L_e, M_2, U_e
R21	98	96	59										
R22	99			132v/3r a11								9rv 53	A, B_6
R23	100	100											
R24	101			151r b11	222r 13	127r 1202	S_2					13v/14r 83	
R25	B42			158v b53		131v 1243	S_2 S_3					4v/5r 25	
R26	B43			150v/1r b8		130v 1235	S_2					16r 95	

$\d{T}K_e$	G_e	$\d{T}_e$	$\acute{S}_e$	B_1	S_1	S_7	S_{2-6}	D_2	J_1	$\d{T}$	U	V1	Other
R27	B44	101, j		135v a28					3r 10				I_e, M_e, V_e
R28	102	104	48										C
R29	103	102, j								1v 9			
R30	104	105											I2
R31	105	106											
R32	106	103, j											C
R33	B50	108, j											
R34	B25			153v b24		56r 532	S_2 S_6					6rv 34	
R35	107	123	54	176r c20									D_1
R36	108	107	55					9r 79					D_1
R37	109	118											
R38	110	120											
R39	111	110	49										
R40	112	119											
R41	113	117											
R42	114	122	53										
R43	115	114											
R44	116	116											
R45	117	157, j											I_e
R46	118	113											
R47	119	111		149v b2		122r 1159	S_2 S_3					4rv 28	J_e
R48	120			149v/50r b3		120rv 1143	S_2 S_3					5v 29	
R49	121	112	22										
R50	B45			156v b41		93r 900						9v/10r 56	
R51	B46			156v/7r b42	196r	155r 1472						10r 57	
R52	B47			152v b19	213v	164r 1571	S_2 S_3					15r 91	
R53	B48			164r b88	270v 4	194r 4	S_2 S_3 S_4					8r 45	
R54	B49	115, j	79		212v	163v 1566	S_3		1v/2r 4	1v 11			A_e, B_5, C_e, D_1, H_e, I_e, J_e, M_e, N, O_e, P_e, V_2

$\d{T}K_e$	G_e	$\d{T}_e$	$\acute{S}_e$	B_1	S_1	S_7	$S_{2\text{-}6}$	D_2	J_1	Ṭ	U	V1	Other
R55	B51			152rv b17		121v 1154	S_2 S_3					14v/5r 89	J_e, M_e,
R56				131v a3	197r	155v 1477	S_2 S_3			3v 28			
R57													J_e, M_e, P_e
R58													J_e, M_e, P_e
R59	155	121	52	131v a2	212v	163v 1565	S_3		4rv 13	3v 27			B_{12}, C_e, M_e, P_e, R_e
R60	156	109	50	164r b89	210r	162r 1531	S_2 S_3					8rv 46	
R61													D_1, V_2
R62													D_1, M_e
R63													J_e
R64								8v/9r 82					
R65	147			149v b1		120v 1147	S_2 S_3					5r 27	
R66	B24			152v b18		48v/9r 462	S_2					15r 90	
R67	123	125											
R68	122	124, j											
R69													M_e

Saṁsār aur nīti

$\d{T}K_e$	G_e	$\d{T}_e$	$\acute{S}_e$	B_1	S_1	S_7	$S_{2\text{-}6}$	D_2	J_1	Ṭ	U	V_1	Other
N1	201	36	5		366r 93	243r 74	S_2		6v 20				
N2	202	142	27		348rv 10	214v/5r 13	S_2 S_4			5v 47			B_2
N3	186	127	32										
N4	188	128		132v a9	358v 57	239v 39	S_2			4v 39			B_8
N5	204	130	31										
N6	218	131	104										
N7	208	143											X_e
N8				185v d25	351v 24	236rv 18	S_4 S_5			4v 38			
N9	209	145	75		380v/1r 24	250v 150	S_2						

ṬK_e	**G_e**	**Ṭ$_e$**	**Ś$_e$**	**B_1**	**S_1**	**S_7**	**S_{2-6}**	**D_2**	**J_1**	**Ṭ**	**U**	**V_1**	**Other**
N10					354r 35	237v 28	S_6						
N11				176rv c21							127r 8		
N12	192	154											
N13	194	129	37					7v 66					O_1
N14	203	141	74		348v 11	235r 14	S_2 S_4			5v 48			
N15	195	161											
N16					377r 6	248v 132	S_2						
N17										4v 35			
N18				152v/3r b20									X_e
N19	190	57											C_e, O_e
N20										5v 49			
N21				131v/2r a4									
N22	49	8											
N23													O_e
N24	50	7											
N25	5	14, j	73		378v 13	249v 139	S_2 S_6	9v 84					I_e, V_e, Q_e
N26													J_2
N27	217			164v b 93	421r 24	270v/1r 157	S_2 S_3					8v 49	
N28	184	132, j			347v 5	234v 8	S_2 S_4						I_e
N29	185	140											
N30					356r 43	238rv 36	S_2 S_4						A_e, O_e, X_e
N31	187			132rv a7	367r 98	243v 79	S_2					2r 9	A, A_e, H_e, X_e, V_2, Z_1
N32	189	134	86	132v a8	348r 8	234v 11	S_2 S_4			4v 37			O_e
N33	191	139											
N34	198	24	36										I_e
N35	219			159r b56	300rv 42	209v 103	S_3 S_4					11rv 67	

$ṬK_e$	G_e	$Ṭ_e$	$Ś_e$	B_1	S_1	S_7	S_{2-6}	D_2	J_1	Ṭ	U	V_1	Other
N36	6	13, j	72							5v 46			
N37	7	12			372v 127	246v 104	S_2 S_5			4v 36			I_e V_2
N38	199	185		157v/8r b48								3v 17	Y_e

POEMS OF UNCERTAIN AUTHORSHIP ATTRIBUTED TO ṬHĀKUR

$ṬK_e$	G_e	$Ṭ_e$	B_1	S_1	S_7	S_{2-6}	J_1	Ṭ	U	
U1										B_e
U2										C_e
U3										B_4
U4			154v b31				1r 1	1v/2r 11b	126r 7	B_e, M_3^1, M_3^2, M_5, M_6, O_e, X_e
U5								1r 2		
U6				295r 20	206v 74	S_2 S_3 S_4				
U7			133r a13							
U8				98r 35	67r 668	S_2 S_5 S_6				P
U9	178	149								
U10-15										Q_e (Kūṭ kabitta)

EDITORIAL PROCEDURES

THE ORDER OF THE POEMS

Apart from a few short sequences, the order of the poems is different in each manuscript and edition. Since the poems lend themselves to various interpretations, they fit into various categories and to various groupings. *Rīti*-poets, such as Dev, often recycled their quatrains in various works under various labels.

In this edition, the arrangement of the quatrains neither follows any source nor is in alphabetical order. This would be as arbitrary as any other imposed order. I therefore, decided to structure the poems according to traditional categories used in various anthologies. In this way four major sections were assembled, *Devotion and God's sports in the world*, *Love*, *The seasons*, and *The world and proper conduct* broadly corresponding to the traditional categories of bhakti, *śṛṅgār, ṛtu-varṇan* and *nīti*. *Ṛtu-varṇan* can traditionally be considered as a subgroup of *nāyikā-bhed* and thus the collection could have reflected the three major themes of *rīti* poetry, namely bhakti, *śṛṅgār* and *nīti*. Since Ṭhākur was a particular prolific author of the description of seasons, I created a separate chapter for these poems. I also attempted to distribute the poems within one section into smaller traditional subgroups.

My distribution of the poems often corresponds to that of the *Sudhāsar* with the difference that I allocated its *Brajras-rīti* poems into the *Śṛṅgār* and Bhakti sections of this book.

Bhakti poems about divine love are normally in the worldly pastoral setting of Braj *(Braj līlā).* Moreover, worldly poems on love can also be interpreted as poems on the love of Krishna and Radha, the exemplary lovers, whose names or epithets normally stand for the heroes and heroines in the *Śṛṅgār* poems. There is, therefore, a substantial overlap between Bhakti and *Śṛṅgār* and any distinction between the two is, more often than not, arbitrary. In my distribution, I followed a relatively mechanical rule. If there is only one word, normally an epithet of the lovers, that refers to the world of Braj, I put the poem within the *Śṛṅgār* section. If, however, there is more than one reference to the world of Braj and thus a network of mythological meanings is established, then the poem is interpreted as *Braj līlā* within Bhakti.

Orthographic Variants not Marked in the Edition

While our printed sources also make an effort to standardise their readings, there is a proliferation of orthographic variants in the manuscripts. The orthography of this edition is normally standardised, if there is already a 'standard Braj' reading among the variants.

Most of the variants encountered in the manuscripts are merely orthographic and do not carry any distinction of meaning or metre. Marking all variants would produce an enormous critical apparatus where most of the variants hold little new information. In this editition, therefore, most orthographic variants are considered zero variants and are not listed. If, however, a variant generally perceived as orthographic for some reason carries a variation in meaning or metre, it ceases to be orthographic variant and will be marked. (E.g. *avasosa* vs. *aba soṣa*—Although *ba* and *va* are generally perceived as orthographic variants here they also indicate variation in the perceived meaning.) If there are several orthographic variations within the same word, they may be marked in the apparatus.

The following is a list of variations (zero variants) not marked in the edition. (C stands for any consonant, V for any vowel.)

CHARACTERS AND SIGNS

ṛ/ri/ra
e/ai (except in verbal endings: e.g. cale/calai)
o/au
kha/ṣa
ś/s
ḍ/ṛ
ḍh/ṛh
ba/va
anusvār/anunāsik

Nasalisation or omission of nasalisation is not indicated if it does not have metrical or lexical value. It is, however, marked in verbal endings, where it distinguishes singular from plural. It is also marked in a few other cases, where disambiguation is needed.

Initial characters

e-/ye-
o-/vo-

Final characters

-Ce/-Cye
-o/-au/-yo/-yau
-Vi/-Vya
-Vu/-Vva
-Vo/-Vvo

Medial characters

-a-/-i-/-u- (in unstressed syllables)
VmV/Vm̊vV
-Vi(-)/-Vya(-)
-Vu(-)/-Vva(-)
-Vo(-)/-Vvo(-)

Unmarked variations of monosyllabic words

kaĩ/ kai
tẽ/te
laĩ/lai
daĩ/dai

The following variations are, however, usually marked as meaningful,

kahā—kahā̃ (=H kyā—kahā̃)
kau—kaũ (=H kā—ko)
me—mẽ (=S -maya—H mẽ/maĩ)
hau—haũ (=H ho—hū̃/maĩ)
hū—hū̃ (=H bhī—hū̃)

THE APPARATUS AND THE NOTES

Testimonia: A list of sources in which a specific poem is available is given with each quatrain in the topmost register of the apparatus, where reference is made to the manuscript or the edition with page or folio numbers and with the serial number of the poem in brackets. In the case of the *Granthāvalī*, Hariścandra's *Sundarī-tilak,* Baburamdin's *Sundarī-tilak,* the *Kālidās-hazārā,* the *Rasik-vinod,* the *Śatak* and the *Ṭhasak* only the unbracketed serial number is given without page or folio numbers. The abbreviation used for the smaller sources may also be given in brackets.

This layer also presents notes relevant to the entire stanza. These general notes may refer to the context of the poem—normally as perceived in a specific source, they may indicate missing or inverted lines or any other information relevant to the entire quatrain.

Variants: The middle layer is the critical apparatus presenting all variant readings found in the sources indicated in the top layer with the exception of orthographic variants. This edition is a scholarly edition and, therefore, the variants are often metrically, linguistically or stylistically inferior to the readings established in the main text. Sometimes two or more variants can be equally valid. On such occasions, I prefer alternative readings to the vulgate text of the *Granthāvalī.*

Notes: The lower layer presents notes on certain words or phrases that the modern reader may find difficult to interpret. These notes are not definitive and often present only one or two interpretations from a wide range of possibilities. Although I have made every effort to interpret the poems in light of early modern Hindi literary culture, the text in some places remains obscure. It is only hoped that connoisseurs of Brajbhasha keep improving these interpretations.

In order to focus the attention on the poems, I tried to keep the notes as brief as possible using a wide range of abbreviations. Most readers will be familiar with most of these abbreviations since they are based on the abbreviation system of R.S. McGregor's *The Oxford Hindi-English Dictionary.*

If the lemma has a modern standard Hindi variant, it is usually given in brackets immediately after it and the etymological note will refer to this modern standard form. If the lemma refers to a variant reading, it is indicated as "var." If a variant reading is corrupt, the indication is "apa." (for *apapāṭha*). If the interpretation of the lemma is uncertain, it is indicated by "(?)". This is followed by the etymology in square brackets. If a word is found in its source language in the same form as the lemma, only an indication of the source language is given. When the word differs, then after the indication of the source language the original form is given. In the majority of such instances, the etymology goes back to a Sanskrit form and the indication of the source language (S) is omitted before the source word. If it goes back to a hypothetical Old or Middle Indo-Aryan form, it is indicated with asterisk (*).

The etymology is followed by dialectal or stylistic indications, by the lexical category, and then occasionally by grammatical qualities of tense, case etc. before presenting an English interpretation. If dialectal or stylistic indications refer to the indicated grammatical category but not to the root of the word, then they follow the grammatical indications.

Dictionaries do not always agree on labels. The *Bṛhat hindī koś‚* for example, normally classifies as poetic (in most of the cases, but not exclusively, referring to Braj or Avadhi poetry) what *The Oxford Hindi-English Dictionary* would classify as Braj or Avadhi. In spite of the fluid boundary between Braj and Bundelkhandi, based on information communicated by expert Indian scholars I use the label Bundelkhandi more frequently than do the dictionaries. If the dialectal provenance of a certain word is unclear, I label it as "reg." (regional usage). If a word is distorted in order to fit the metre or the rhyme, or to make some poetic effect, it is labelled as "poet."

Many entries are often taken directly from *The Oxford Hindi-English Dictionary,* which in etymology relies on R.L. Turner's *A Comparative Dictionary of the Indo-Aryan Languages.* For words with no etymology and for complex poetic phrases I drew on a variety of dictionaries and on my discussion with three leading Brajbhasha experts. In brackets an abbreviation of the name of the expert or of the dictionary consulted may be given.

Sometimes more than one interpretation is possible and sometimes other meanings of the same word lend an important shade of meaning. Various interpretations are separated by semicolons and numbers.

ABBREVIATIONS

In the Critical Apparatus

Σ	is used when at least four fifths of the sources agree. (If E or S present variants to the Σ sources, they are counted as one source.)

E	stands collectively for the three printed collections of Ṭhākur (G_e, $Ś_e$, $Ṭ_e$ including $Ṭ_e^j$) or for any two if the poem is not present in a third one.
S	stands collectively for all the *Sudhāsar* collections from which Ṭhākur's actual poem is presented or for at least eighty percent of them.
ac	before correction *(ante correctionem)*
conj.	conjecture
ditto.	dittography
emend.	emendation
haplo.	haplography
mg	marginalia
pc	after correction *(post correctionem)*
unm.	unmetrical
unrh.	unrhyming
vl	variant reading *(varia lectionis)*
*	illegible character
—	lacuna
<>	unclear reading
[/]	ambiguous reading
x x	crossed out in the manuscript

In the Notes on the Text

apa.	corrupt variant reading (*apapāṭh*)
var.	variant reading
(?)	uncertain interpretation

Etymology

When the lemma is followed by its modern standard Hindi equivalent in brackets then the etymology of the standard Hindi word is given.

A	Arabic
ad.	adapted from
cf.	compare
H	modern standard Hindi
P	Persian
S/unmarked	Sanskrit
T	Turkish

Stylistic and Dialectal Usage

Av.	Avadhi
Br.	Braj
Bund.	Bundeli
Dak.	Dakkani
East.	eastern Hindi
Guj.	Gujarati

kūṭ	coded
poet.	poetic
Punj.	Punjabi
Raj.	Rajasthani
reg.	regional
vulg.	vulgar

Grammar

abs.	absolutive
acc.	accusative case
adj.	adjective
adv.	adverb
ag.	agentive
conj.	conjunct
dir.	direct case
emph.	emphatic
encl.	enclitic
f.	feminine noun
fig.	figurative sense
fut.	future tense
imp.	imperative
imperf.	imperfective participle
interj.	interjection
interr.	interrogative
m.	masculine noun
obl.	oblique case
onom.	onomatopoetic
pass.	passive
perf.	perfective participle
pl.	plural
poss.	possessive
pres.	present tense
pron.	pronoun
rel. pron.	relative pronoun
subj.	subjunctive
suff.	suffix
v.caus.	causative verb
v.i.	intransitive verb
v.t.	transitive verb
voc.	vocative case

Provenance of Interpretation

(BHK)	Kalika Prasad, R. Sahay, M. Shrivastav: *Bṛhat hindī koś*. Varanasi: Jñānmaṇḍal Limiteḍ, 7th enlarged edn., 1992 (1st edn. 1952).

(BSK) D. Gupta, P. Tandan: *Brajbhāṣā sūr koś,* 3 vols., Lucknow: Lucknow University, 1962.

(DB) W.M. Callewaert, S. Sharma: *Dictionary of Bhakti: North-Indian Bhakti Texts Into Khaṛī Bolī Hindī and English,* 3 vols., New Delhi: D.K. Printworld, 2009.

(GSh) Professor Govind Sharma (personal communication).

(HSS) Shyamsundardas: *Hindī śabd-sāgar,* 11 vols., Varanasi: Nāgarīpracāriṇī Sabhā, *http://dsal.uchicago.edu/dictionaries/dasa-hindi/.*

(KL) Dr. Kishorilal (personal communication)

(MHK) R. Varmā: *Mānak hindī koś,* Allahabad: Hindi Sāhitya Sammelan, 1966.

(Platts) J. T. Platts: *A Dictionary of Urdu, Classical Hindi and English,* New Delhi: Munshiram Manoharlal, 1993. *http://dsal.uchicago.edu/dictionaries/platts/.*

(RHS) Badri Prasad Sakaria & Bhupatiram Sakaria: *Rājasthānī hindī śabdkoś,* 2 vols., Jaipur: Pañcaśīl Prakāśan, 1993.

(RKS) Kishorilal: *Rītikāvya śabdkoś.* Indore: Manasvī Prakāśan, 2010, 2nd edn; (1st edn. 1976).

(RSh) Professor Ramdeo Shukla (personal communication).

(RSK) S. Lalas, N. Dadhich: *Rājasthānī sabad kos: rājasthānī-hindī vr̥had koś,* 4 vols., Chopasni, Jodhpur: Rājasthānī Śodh Saṁsthān, 1962-78.

(SBK) D.P. Sharma: *Sāhityik brajbhāṣā koś,* 3 vols., Lucknow: Uttar Prades Hindī Saṁsthān, 1985-90.

(SSS) H. Bahri; R.K. Varma: *Sūr śabd-sāgar,* Allahabad: Smr̥ti Prakāśan, 1981.

Ṭhākur-kabittāvalī
Hindi Text with Critical Apparatus and Notes

भक्ति और लीला-वर्णन

गनेश-स्तुति

1 प्रनव प्रसिद्ध आदि-मंगल-महोदधि सो,
जोई उर ध्यावै तासु बेस रखवारो है।
2 बुद्धि को भँडार, अवतार करतार हू को,
बिद्या को सिँगार, सदा सुख देनवारो है।
3 ठाकुर कहत, महा छलियान छलिबे कों,
दुःख दल दलिबे कों दिग्गज दँतारो है।
4 संभु को दुलारो, गिरिजा को प्रान प्यारो, सदा
टेढ़ी सूँडवारो, सोई साहेब हमारो है॥ B1॥

भक्ति

जो सुख देइ तो देइ दई, दुख देइ न देख हिये डरने है।
2 होत न काहू की नेकी करी, अब यौं निरधारि हिये धरने है।
ठाकुर, भाँतिन भाँति अधीन ह्वै दीन ह्वै आइ पर्यौ सरने है।
4 को करि सोच वृथा ही मरै, हरि, होने वही जौ तुम्हैं करने है॥ B2॥

---

1 Granthāvalī 1, Ṭhasak 1 2 Granthāvalī 200, Śatak 29, Ṭhasak 10.

1.1 प्रसिद्ध] Ṭ$_e$, प्रसिध्ध G$_e$ **1.2** बुद्धि] Ṭ$_e$, बुध्धि G$_e$ • सिँगार] G$_e$, सिंगार (unm.) Ṭ$_e$ **1.3** कों] G$_e$, को Ṭ$_e$ • दुःख] Ṭ$_e$, दुख्ख G$_e$ • कों] G$_e$, को Ṭ$_e$ **1.4** संभु] G$_e$, शंभु Ṭ$_e$ • को] Ṭ$_e$, कौ G$_e$ **2.1** है] G$_e$Ṭ$_e$, हैं Ś$_e$ **2.2** है] G$_e$Ṭ$_e$, हैं Ś$_e$ **2.3** है] G$_e$Ṭ$_e$, हैं Ś$_e$ **2.4** होने] G$_e$Ṭ$_e$, ह्वैहै Ś$_e$ • है] G$_e$Ṭ$_e$, हैं Ś$_e$

1.1 प्रनव- [praṇamati] Br. v.t. Av. to bow down to, to salute; प्रणव 1. [cf. Br. pranavaũ] v.i. (poet. pres.) I bow to; 2. [S] m. the sound OM; आदि-मंगल-महोदधि [S] poet. the ocean of bliss at the beginning; सो adj. (who is) like; तासु (उसका) [tasya] pron. Av. of the one (who); बेस [P beś] adj. 1. more; 2. excellent; 3. [S veśa] m. house, dwelling. **1.2** करतार [kartṛ-] m. the Creator. **1.3** छलिया [cf. chala-] m. deceiver; दँतार (दन्तुर) [S] adj. having large teeth, tusked. **1.4** सूँड [śuṇḍā-] f. an elephant's trunk. **2.1** जो... दई Br. If the Creator gives happiness, then let him give it; डरने [II ḍarnā] v.i. (inf. Bund. Av.) (you should not) be afraid. **2.2** नेकी [P nīkī] f. goodness; होत न... करी 'good thing is not done by anyone' nobody does any good; निरधार (निर्धार) [S] m. 1. resolution; 2. conclusion. **2.3** भाँतिन भाँति Br. adv. in every way; आइ पर्यौ v.i. I have come. **2.4** वृथा [S] adv. in vain; होने वही reg. (that) is to be.

सद है, अबही हद है, कब लौं बद-नेक नहीं पहिचानि परै।
घर-बाहिर घाट-कुघाटन बाटन लाभ घनी किधौं हानि परै। 2
कहि ठाकुर, सूझत सूझै नहीं, नर बूझै जिही सिर आनि परै।
यह रंच निहारौ, कृपा के निधान, कछू परपंच न जानि परै॥ B3॥ 4

छोटे कों छोटो, बडे कों बडो, औ लटे कों लटो उपजाय दयो है।
सुद्ध कों सुद्ध, असुद्ध असुद्ध कों, आपुन सीख सिखाय दयो है। 2
ठाकुर, जासों लगो जगदातम आतम को बिसराय दयो है।
देखिये वाको बिचार अनूपम, एक कों एक लगाय दयो है॥ B4॥ 4

मेरी कही मान, मन, सपनो सो जान जग, 1
छोडि अभिमान, फेर ऐसो नहीं दाव रे।
दीन ह्वै दया कों सीख, संपति बिपति-भीख 2
एक सम दीख, नहीं बनैहै बनाव रे।

---

3 Bharatpur1 f. 163r (82), Granthāvalī 207, Vrindaban1 f. 7r (1/39). 4 Granthāvalī 215, Ṭhasak 6. 5 Granthāvalī 214, Śatak 38, Ṭhasak 19.

3.1 सद] B_1, बद G_e, सब V_1 • पहिचानि] B_1G_e, पहिचान V_1 **3.2** कुघाटन] B_1G_e, कुं घाटन V_1 **3.4** निहारौ] G_eV_1, तिहारौ B_1 • परपंच न] B_1G_e, परपंचनि V_1 **4.3** को] *em.* का E **5.1** मेरी] G_eŚ$_e$, मेरौ Ṭ$_e$ • **5.2** संपति] G_eṬ$_e$, संपति औ (unm.) Ś$_e$ •

3.1 सद [cf. sadyaḥ] Br. adj. fresh, new. (The variants 'saba' and 'bada' derive from this slightly obscure reading); सद [sadyaḥ] Br. adj. fresh, new (RKS); बद var. [P] adj. bad, forbidden (cf. harām); बद है var. it is bad for a man; सब है apa. all are; हद [A ḥadd] f. limit(s) (of knowing it); सद... हद है poet. (your creation) is fresh (and therefore) it still has its limits. कब लौं Br. (but) how long? **3.2** लाभ [S] m. (here f.) profit; लाभ घनी किधौं हानि 1. great profit or loss; 2. profit or great loss. **3.3** सूझत सूझै नहीं Br. one cannot even imagine it; जिही (जिसी) [cf. Br. jihi] pron. Br. obl. emph. whose; सिर आनि परै Br. it befalls (one's head); नर... परै Br. only the man understands it to whom it befalls. **3.4** यह pron. (look at) this; रंच Br. adv. a little, somewhat (cf. H zarā); परपंच (प्रपंच) [S] m. 1. the visible world; 2. trick, deceit; 3. riddle. **4.1** लटा [cf. H ulaṭā] adj. 1. Bund. bad; 2. Av. weak; उपजाय दयो Br. created. **4.2** आपुन reg. ag. you yourself (taught pure and impure teachings). **4.3** आतम Br. the (Supreme) Self; जासों लगो जगदातम Br. (has) the one who is connected to the Supreme Self (forgotten about his self)? का var. [H kyõ] reg. interr. why (would he)? **4.4** वाको बिचार Br. God's idea; एक कों एक लगाय दयो है idiom. connected one with (another similar) one. **5.1** सपनो (स्वप्न) [S] m. dream; फेर (फिर) Br. adv. again; दाँव [dātu-, dāman-] f. occasion. **5.2** दीख- (देखना) [*dṛkṣati, *drakṣati] reg. v.t. to look, to consider; बनैहै v.i. (Br. fut.) will arise (again); बनाव [cf. H banānā] m. opportunity.

3 ठाकुर कहत, ब्रजचंद चंदमुखी राधा
बृंदाबन बीथिन मैं हरि गुन गाव रे।
4 बीती जात उमर, भँडार तन रीति जात,
चीति, जात काल के हवाले होत बावरे॥ B5॥

*रस नाँही मिल्यौ है जिनैं ब्रज कौ तिनैं भागि लिख्यौ है कछ्छ जस ना।
2 जस ना मलिये कौ प्रभाव यहैं, तिसनांही सु तीरथ के बसना।
बस नाँही रह्यौ मन तौ अपने, कहि ठाकुर, मोह कसै कसना।
4 कस नाँही कियौ हरि के भजनैं, धिक है, धिक है तिन की रसना॥ B6॥

1 एकै खिन खिन माँझ पावै पद साहिबी को,

---

6 Sudhāsar [S$_1$ f. 245v-246r (12), S$_2$ f. 55v (-/56), S$_3$ f. 124r (12), S$_4$ 43rv (12), S$_7$ 181v (12)], Ṭhākur-satsaī (Ṭ) f. 3v (26). The Sudhāsar presents this siṃhāvalokan savaiyā in the subsection on 'Braj mahimā' within the 'Brajrasarīti' section.

5.3 बृंदाबन] G$_e$Ṭ$_e^{pc}$, बृंद्राबन Ś$_e$Ṭ$_e^{ac}$ • मैं] G$_e$Ṭ$_e$, में सु (unm.) Ś$_e$ **5.4 बीती**] Ś$_e$Ṭ$_e^{pc}$, चीति G$_e$Ṭ$_e^{ac}$ • रीति] G$_e$Ṭ$_e$, रीतौ Ś$_e$ • चीति] Ṭ$_e$, बीति G$_e$, बीतौ Ś$_e$ • **6.1 जिनैं**] **S**, जिन्हैं S$_1$Ṭ • तिनैं] **S**, तिन्हैं S$_1$Ṭ • भागि] S$_2$, भाग Σ • कछ्छ] Σ, कछु S$_3$ • जस] S$_1^{pc}$Σ, ज (unm.) S$_1^{ac}$ **6.2 मलिये**] **S**, मिलिये S$_7$, मलिवे Ṭ • तीरथ] Σ, नीरथ S$_4$ **6.3 रह्यौ**] **S**, रहै Ṭ • कहि] Ṭ, कबि **S** • मोह कसै] S$_1$Ṭ, मोहन कौं **S** **6.4 हरि**] **S**, हर Ṭ • धिक है धिक] **S**, धिग है धिग Ṭ • है तिन] **S**Ṭ, हौ तिन S$_2$

5.3 वीथी [S] f. lane; **5.4 भंडार** [S] m. storehouse, treasury; **रीतना** [rikta-] v.i. to become empty; **चीति** v.t. imp. Br. look! be careful! **के हवाले होत** Br. you are deposited at the hands of (time). **6.1 जिनैं... तिनैं** Br. for them who... **जस** (जैसे) [yādṛśa-] Br. adv. as if (nothing is written). **6.2 तिसनां ही** reg. they are thirsty even when; **तीरथ के बसना** poet. living in a sacred place (with water). (The form 'basanā' is used instead of 'basane' for the sake of rhyme.); **जस ना मलिये... बस ना** Br. The effect of not getting (Krishna's) fame is that they are thirsty even when living at a holy ford; (in this interpretation there is no sabhaṅga yamaka) **जस-नाम लिये... बसना** Br. The effect of taking the name of the fame (of Krishna) is that a person does not need to live in a holy place; (in this interpretation the otherwise plural subject is singular.) **6.3 बस नाँही रह्यौ** if the mind is not under one's control; **कसना** [kaṣati] v.t. to bind; to attract; **कस** var. m. 1. [cf. karṣati] a means of binding; fastening; 2. [kaṣāya-] test, proof; 3. labour toil; 4. tenacity, power; 5. [H kaise] interr. Av. Br. how? **कस करना** var. idiom. to make an effort; **मोह कसै कसना** reg. then how to control illusion? **मोहन कौं कसना** var. reg. do they then want to attract the Enchanter? **मोहन कौं कस ना** var. Br. they do not make an effort for the Enchanter;

एकै खिन खिन माँहि होत लटपट हैं।
एकै जीव जीवत हैं उमर अँदाज भरि, 2
एकै जीव होतै हिंसु होत चटपट हैं।
ठाकुर कहत, कोऊ हरि-हर दास जे हैं, 3
तिनकौं न ब्यापैं जे दुनी के खटपट हैं।
सटपट सारी देखी घट-पट-वारी चीज, 4
नटखट, रावरे अजब अटपट हैं॥ B7॥

धना और सदना, कबीर, पीपा, मीरा, ब्यास, 1
गीध, रयदास सुख-सोभनि सों सनि गौ।
फेरि अजामेल, स्योरी, सिला, अंबरीष, गज, 2

---

7 Granthāvalī 216, Śatak 35, Ṭhasak 5. 8 Bharatpur1 f. 159v-60r (61), Granthāvalī B1, Sudhāsar [S_1 f. 418rv (13), S_2 f. 81v (-/90), S_3 f. 275(66)rv (5), S_7 f. 269vv (146)], Vrindaban1 f. 12rv (8/73). The Sudhāsar presents this poem within the description of 'bhakti pantha'.

7.1 माँहि] $G_eṬ_e$, माह $Ś_e$ • **7.3** हैं] $G_eṬ_e$, वे $Ś_e$ • **8.1** सदना] Σ, सधना S_7 • कबीर] $S_1^{pc}Σ$, कबीरा $B_1S_1^{ac}$ • ब्यास] Σ, बाई S_7 • रयदास] $B_1S_1G_eV_1$, रैदास (unm.) S_2S_7, रविदास S_3 • सुख] Σ, मुख S_7 • सोभनि] $B_1G_eV_1$, सोभन S • सों] Σ, को S_7 • सनि] $B_1G_eS_2S_1V_1$, सन S_3, सुन S_7 • गौ] Σ, गों S_2

7.1 लटपट [H laṭ 'tangled hair'] adj. ruined; हैं v.i. pl. (are). (In this kavitta the word 'ekai' sometimes attracts singular, as in the first half line, and sometimes plural). **7.2** अँदाज [P] m. limit; होतै v.i. imperf. as soon as (is born); हिंसु [cf. hiṃsā] adj. killed; चटपट [caṭ 'cracking sound'] adv. quickly; suddenly (cf. caṭpaṭ ho jānā 'to die suddenly'). **7.3** कोऊ... हैं those who are the servants of Hari or Shiva; खटपट [H khaṭ 'the sound of knocking'] f. 1. wrangling, quarrel; 2. the suffering of the world. **7.4** सटपट f. confusion; घट-पट m. 1. body and clothes; 2. [ghaṭa- 'truth' + paṭṭa- 'tablet (for writing upon)'] m. Vedantic discourse; घट पट वारी चीज (all) things related to body and clothes; नटखट [?anartha- + H khaṭ] m. 1. (voc.) 'naughty child' Krishna; 2. (your) mischief; अजब [A] m. wonder; अटपट adj. incoherent; nonsensical. **8.1** धना [dhanya-] m. 'wealthy' Dhannādās; सदना m. N. of a butcher bhakta; गीध [gṛddha-] m. 'the vulture' Jaṭāyu; रयदास (रविदास) [S] m. Raidās; सनना [saṃdadhāti] v.i. to be mixed, to be soaked.

गनिका गरीबनी को पातक उतनि गौ।
3 ठाकुर कहत, देखौ धुअ, प्रहलाद आदि,
कहाँ लौं बखानौं बेद भेद करि भनि गौ।
4 धाम-धाम धाएं, कहौ, कौन को सुधार भयौ,
राम-राम गाऐं काम कौन को न बनि गौ॥ B8॥

1 बेदन को सार, निरधार धराधीसन को,
ईसन कौ जाप यौ, असीसन कौं लहिबो।
2 जोग को जलूस, करामात को खजानो, कर-

---

9 Bharatpur1 f. 157v (47), Datiya2 f. 1r (2), Granthāvalī B2, Sudhāsar [S_1 f. 419v420r (19), S_2 f. 90r (-/91), S_3 f. 275v-6r(66v-7r)v (8), S_7 f. 270rv (152)], Vrindaban1 f. 3rv (3/16). • The Sudhāsar presents this poem within the 'Bhaktapada' (S_1) or 'Bhaktipantha' (S_3) subsection of the 'Devstuti, bhaktapakṣa, nirveda, karunā, binaya' section.

8.2 फेरि] G_e, फेरी S_2, फेर $B_1S_3S_7S_1V_1$ • अजामेल] Σ, अजामेर S_1 • सीला] $B_1^{pc}G_e S_2S_3$, *om.* (unm.) B_1, सिल V_1 • अंबरीष] $B_1G_eS_2S_3V_1$, अंमरीष S_1S_7 • गज] $V_1^{pc}\Sigma$, ज V_1^{ac} • गरीबनी... गौ] $B_1^{pc}\Sigma$, *om.* (eyeskip) B_1^{ac} • गरीबनी को] Σ, गरीबि नीकौ S_2 • उतनि] B_1G_e, उतरि S_1, °हू तनि S_2, हूँ तिन S_3S_7, उत्तिनि V_1 **8.3** ठाकुर... देखौ] $B_1^{pc}\Sigma$, *om.* (eyeskip) B_1^{ac} • कहत] Σ, कहैत V_1 • धुअ] G_eS_2, ध्रुव $S_1S_3S_7$, धूअ B_1V_1 • प्रहलाद] $B_1G_eS_1S_2V_1$, प्रहलादि S_3S_7 • बखानौं] $B_1G_eS_1$, बषानौ $S_2S_3S_7V_1$ • भेद] $S_1^{pc}\Sigma$, भेदा S_1^{ac} • करि] $B_1^{pc}G_eS_2S_3S_1V_1$, किरि B_1^{ac}, कर S_3S_7 • भनि] $B_1G_eS_1S_2V_1$, भन S_3S_7 **8.4** धाऐं] B_1S_1, धाए $G_eS_2S_3S_1V_1$, धाम S_3 • गाऐं] B_1S_1, गाए $G_eS_2S_3S_1V_1$ • बनि] $B_1G_eS_1S_2V_1$, बन S_3S_7 **9.1** निरधार] $B_1D_2^{pc}G_eS_1S_7V_1$, निरधारा D_2^{ac}, निराधार S_2S_3 • कौ जाप यौ] Σ, कों जायबो G_e • लहिबो] D_2**S**, कहिबौ $B_1G_eV_1$

8.2 स्योरी (शवरी) [S] f. woman of the Śavara tribe; सिला (शीला) [S] Br. f. 'the stone' Ahalyā; अंबरीश[S] m. Ikshvaku king, a great devotee of Vishnu (Bhagavata Purana, 9,4); गरीबनी [cf. A garīb, with H nī] adj. (Br. f.) poor; पातक [S] m. sin; उतन- [uttanoti, H utarnā] v.i. to be removed, to be finished; तनना var. [H tānnā] 1. v.i. to be stretched; 2. (here:) v.t. to drag and destroy. **8.3** धुअ (ध्रुव) [S] reg. m. 'fixed' the ascetic Dhruva who became the pole star; भेद करि adv. 1. in various ways; 2. mysteriously; भन- [bhanati] reg. v.i. to speak. **8.4** धाम धाम धाए 1. running from one abode to another; 2. even if Rām ran from one abode to another... (but his name is greater than himself); काम बनना idiom. to succeed. **9.1** निरधार (निर्धार) [S] m. foundation; धराधीश [S] poet. m. 'lord of the land' king; ईसन कौ (japa) for the gods; जाप [jalpa-, japya-] m. repeating God's name (cf. japa); यौ (यों) reg. adv. thus; असीस (आशिष) [S] f. blessing.

तब्यता की सिद्धि, जो पै हौंसनि उमहिबो।
ठाकुर कहत, चारु चिंता को इलाज, दुबिधा 3
कों दूरि कीबो, दुख दारिद को दहिबो।
रसना-नवेली को सिंगार, मुख सुख सोऊ, 4
जीवन को लाभ सदा स्यामा-स्याम कहिबो॥ B9॥

कीरतिकुँवरि कहें कीरति बढति अति, 1
गोरी के कहे तें गरुवाई अधिकाती है।
लाडिली कहे तें लाल परम दयाल होत, 2
प्यारी के कहे तें सखी सुनत सिहाती है।
ठाकुर कहत, ठकुराइनि कहे तें ठकु- 3

---

10 Bharatpur1 f. 157v (46), Granthāvalī B3, Sudhāsar [S_1 f. 275r (1), S_3 f. 149rv (138), S_4 f. 75rv (145), S_7 f. 196rv (1)], Vrindaban1 f. 3r (2/15). • The Sudhāsar presents this poem in the 'baibhava braja kau' (the superhuman power of Braj) subsection of the 'Brajrasrīti' section.

9.2 करामात] Σ, करामाति S_2 • खजानो] Σ, षजांनैं S_2 • की] $D_2G_e\mathbf{S}$, कौ B_1, *om.* (unm.) V_1 • सिद्धि] $D_2S_1S_2$, सिद्ध $B_1S_3V_1$, सिध्ध G_e, सिध S_7 • जो पै] Σ, जोवै G_e • हौंसनि] G_eV_1, हौसन $B_1D_2\mathbf{S}$ **9.3** ठाकुर कहत] Σ, ठा° B_1 • चारु] Σ, चार S_7 • दूरि] $B_1G_eS_2V_1$, दूर $D_2S_1S_3S_7$ **9.4** रसना] $D_2G_e\mathbf{S}$, रसवा B_1V_1 • सिंगार] $B_1^{ac}D_2G_eS_1S_3S_7$, सिगम S_2, श्रिंगार $B_1^{pc}V_1$ • मुख सुख] $B_1D_2S_2S_7$, सुखमुख G_eV_1, मुष मुष S_1 • जीवन] Σ, जीवनि B_1 • को] D_2^{pc}Σ, *om.* (unm.) D_2^{ac} • लाभ] B_1^{pc}Σ, लाल B_1^{ac} • स्यामा] $S_1S_3V_1$, राम D_2, स्याम $G_eS_2S_7$ **10.1** °कुँवरि] $B_1G_eS_1V_1$, कुमर S_3S_4, कुमार S_7 • कहें] G_eS_1, कहै $B_1S_3S_4S_7V_1$ • कीरति] Σ, कीरत S_7 • बढति] $B_1G_eS_3V_1$, बढत S_1S_7 • गोरी] Σ, गौरी S_4 • कहे तें] Σ, कहते V_1 • गरुवाई] G_eS_1, गरुआई $S_3S_4S_7$, गरवाई B_1V_1 • अधिकाती] Σ, अधिकाति G_e • है] Σ, हैं B_1 **10.2** दयाल] Σ, दयालु S_3 • सुनत] Σ, सुनति S_3 • सिहाती] $B_1\mathbf{S}V_1$, सिहाति G_e • है] $G_eS_3S_7V_1$, हैं B_1S_1

9.2 जुलूस [A] 'accession to the throne' m. pomp; करामात [A] f. pl. marvellous deeds; कर्तव्यता [S] f. duty; सिद्धि [S] f. fulfilment; जो पै conj. if (there is enthusiasm for true desires then there is...); जोवें var. [dyotate, H johnā] Br. v.t. perf. obl. on seeing it; उमह- [unmathayati] Br. v.i. 1. to swell; 2. fig. to exalt. **9.3** चारु इलाज adj. m. fine remedy. **9.4** रसना [S] f. tongue; नवेली [cf. nava-] f. a beautiful young woman; सिगम apa. **10.1** कीर्तिकुमारि [S] f. 'Kīrti's daughter' Radha; गोरी [cf. gaura-, H gorā] f. fair-complexioned woman; गौरी apa. [S] f. Parvati; कहते (कहने से) [kathayati] v.t. imperf. obl. (used as verbal n. obl.) by the saying (of 'Gori'); गरुवाई [cf. guru-] Av. Br. f. 'weight' importance. **10.2** सखी सुनत Br. when a companion (of hers) hears it; सिहा- [? śikhā] Br. v.i. to be delighted.

राइस बढत, महा ममता बढाती है।
4 कहत किसोरी के न थोरी लाभ, मोर जीय,
राधा के कहे तें कोटि बाधा मिटि जाती है॥ B10॥

1 बेदन के भेदन तें, अज-ईस-जापन तें,
रिषि मुनि तापन तें कैयक बपुष की।
2 नारद तें, सारद तें, पुनि सनकादिक तें,
चाह भरी साधन तें, संतन के रुख की।
3 ठाकुर-सुहाई, इन सब तें पियारी लागै,

---

11 Bharatpur1 f. 158v (52), Sudhāsar [S_1 f. 244r (4), S_2 f. 55rv (-/55), S_3 f. 122v (4), S_4 f. 40r (4), S_7 f. 180v-1r (14)], Granthāvalī B4, Ṭhākur-satsaī (Ṭ) f. 3v (25), Vrindaban1 f. 4v (11/24). The Sudhāsar presents this poem in the subsection on 'Braj mahimā' within the 'Brajrasarīti' section. Cf. N38 on the literature of Tulsīdās.

10.3 ठाकुर कहत] Σ, ठा B_1 • ठकुराइनि] B_1V_1, ठकुराइन G_e**S** • कहे तें] G_e**S**, कहते B_1V_1 • ठकुराइस] B_1**S**, ठकुराई सी G_e, ठकुराइ सी V_1 • बढत] Σ, बढति S_3 • ममता] Σ, महमा S_4 • बढाती] Σ, बढाति G_e • है] Σ, हैं B_1 **10.4** थोरी] Σ, थोरो G_e • मोर] B_1V_1, मेरे G_e, मोरे S_1, मेरो S_3S_7, सोरे S_4 • जीय] $B_1G_eS_1V_1$, जिय S_3S_7, जिय॥ S_4 • कहे ते] B_1G_e**S**, कहते V_1 • कोटि] $B_1G_eS_1S_4V_1$, कोट S_3S_7 • मिटि] $B_1G_eS_1S_4$, मिट S_3V_1 • जाती] Σ, जाति G_e, जानी S_4 • है] $G_eS_1S_3S_7V_1$, हैं B_1S_4 **11.1** अज] Σ, अत S_4 • रिषि] $B_1G_eS_1S_3V_1$, रिष $S_1S_4S_7$, रि* Ṭ • मुनि] Σ, मुन Ṭ • तापन] Σ, ताप (unm.) Ṭ • कैयक] $B_1G_eV_1$, कैइक S_1S_2, कैईक $S_3S_4S_7$, कईयक (unm.) Ṭ • बपुष] $B_1G_eS_1S_2$ṬV_1, विपुष S_3S_7, वबपुख (unm.) S_4 **11.2** नारद तें] Σ, नारद जें S_4 • पुनि] B_1G_e**S**V_1, पुन S_3Ṭ • चाह] Σ, चाहि S_4 • साधन] Σ, सिध्धन G_e • रुख] Σ, हख (unrh.) S_4

10.3 ठकुरायस [cf. H ṭhākur] poet. f. lordship, power; ठकुराई var. [cf. H ṭhākur] f. authority; महा [S] 1. adj. (creates) great (attachment); 2. adv. greately (increases); ममता [S] f. 'the sentiment of being mine' attachement; महमा (महिमा) var. [S] f. greatness. **10.4** लाभ [S] m. (here f.) (cf. labdhi f.) gain, advantage; मोर जीय Br. 1. o my heart; 2. in my heart; मिटि जाति है Br. v.i. (singular for rhyming) disappear. **11.1** अज [S] adj. not-born; कैयक [H kaī] Br. adj. several; वपुष [S] m. body; बपुष की 1. (the asceticism of the rishis and munis) in various bodies; 2. (the stories) of (taking) a human body. **11.2** शारदा [S] f. Sarasvatī, the goddess of learning; सनक [S] m. Name of a son of Brahmā; सनकादिक [S] m. 'Sanaka and the others' collective name for the four sons of Brahmā; रुख [P] m. 'face' favour; (mental) attitude; संतन के रुख की poet. according to the liking of the saints.

मोहन कहत, मोहि देनहारी सुख की।
रूपभरी, रसभरी, जोसभरी, जसभरी, 4
मदभरी बातैं ब्रजबालनि के मुख की॥ B11॥

*राम मेरो पंडित अखंडित सुदिन सोधै, 1
राम मेरो गुरु, जप मेरो राम नाम है।
राम राम गावत हौं, राम राम ध्यावत हौं, 2
राम राम सुनत सुखद आठो जाम है।
ठाकुर कहत, साँचौ राम कौ भरोसौ मोहि, 3
राम ही सों काम, राम मेरौ धन धाम है।
राम मेरौ बैद, बिसराम मेरो राम, भैया, 4

---

12 Bharatpur1 f. 158r (49), Datiya2 f. 1r (3), Granthāvalī 2, Sudhāsar [S_1 f. 389v (2b), S_2 f. 77v (-/88), S_7 ff. 254v-5r (7)], Ṭhasak 2, Ṭhasak 'Jīvancarit' (Ṭ^j_e) pp. 18-9, Vrindaban1 f. 3v (5/18), Yājñik. • The Sudhāsar presents this poem within the 'Rām avatār varnan' subsection of the 'Devstuti, bhaktapakṣa, nirveda, karunā binaya' section.

11.3 सुहाई इन] $B_1G_eS_2S_3S_7$, **सुखद इन** S_1^{ac}, **सुखदाइन** (unm.) S_1^{pc}, **सहाइ इन** S_4, **सुहा*इन** Ṭ, **सुहाई ईन** V_1 • **पियारी**] $B_1G_eS_4S_7$ṬV$_1$, **सुहाई** S_1, ×**संतन के रु**×⟨**ष/पि**⟩**यारी** S_2, **प्यारी** (unm.) S_3 • **लागै**] Σ, **लागैं** S_1 • **कहत**] Σ, **कहति** S_4 • **मोहि**] Σ, **मोह** Ṭ **11.4 रूप**] Σ, **रुप** V_1 • **जोस**] Σ, **तोस** S_4 • **जस**] Σ, **र**×**स**× **जस** (eyeskip) V_1 • **मद॰**] Σ, **भेद॰** G_e • **॰बालनि**] $B_1^{pc}S_1$, **बालन** $B_1^{ac}G_eS_2S_3$ṬV$_1$, **बाला जू** S_7 • **के**] Σ, **की** V_1 **12.1 मेरो**] Σ, **मेरे E** • **सुदिन**] B_1D_2**E**$S_1S_7V_1$, **सदिन** S_2S_7 • **सोधै**] $B_1D_2S_2S_7V_1$, **सोधैं ES**$_1$ • **मेरो**] Σ, **मेरे E** • **गुरु**] B_1D_2**E**S_1S_7, **गुर** $S_2V_1Y_e$ • **जप**] Σ, **जय** S_2 • **मेरो**] Σ, **मेरे E** • **राम**] Σ, ⟨**ऐ/रा**⟩**म** V_1 • **है**] Σ, **हैं E** **12.2 राम गावत हौं**] $B_1^{pc}D_2^{pc}S_1S_2$, **राम गावत है** B_1^{ac}, **नाम गावतहिं E**, **गावत हौं** (unm.) D_2^{ac}, **राम गावतहिं** Ṭ^j_e, **राम गावत हौ** $S_7V_1Y_e$ • **राम**] Σ, **रोम** S_2 • **राम ध्यावत हौं**] D_2S_2, **राम** ⟨**धा**⟩**वत हौं** B_1, **नाम ध्यावतहिं** G_eṬ$_e$, **राम धावत हौं** S_1, **राम ध्यावतहिं** Ṭ^j_e, **राम धावत हौ** $S_7V_1Y_e$ • **राम राम**] D_2G_e**S**Ṭ$_e$, **राम नाम** $B_1V_1Y_e$ • **सुनत सुखद**] $B_1^{ac}S_1S_2V_1Y_e$, **सु**⟨**ष**⟩**त सुषद** B_1^{ac}, **सुनत सुखद सु** (unm.) D_2, **सोचत कटत E**, **सुखद सुनत** S_7 • **है**] $B_1D_2S_2S_7$, **हैं** G_eS_1, **हौ** V_1Y_e **12.3 ठाकुर कहत**] D_2**ES**V_1, **ठा॰** B_1, **ठाकुर कहैत** Y_e • **साँचौ**] Σ, **साँची E** • **राम... मोहि**] Σ, **आस मोहिं राम ही की E** • **सों**] Σ, **से** Ṭ$_e$ • **राम... धाम**] Σ, **धन धाम मेरे राम E** • **मेरे**] G_eṬ^j_e, **मेरो** Ṭ$_e$ • **धन**] Σ, **धनु** S_7 • **है**] Σ, **हैं E**

11.3 ठाकुर-सुहाई Br. 1. it pleases the poet Ṭhākur; 2. f. the praise of Krishna; **मोहन कहत** Br. so says Krishna; **देनहार-** (**देनेवाला**) Br. m. giver. **11.4 जोश** [P] m. passion, enthusiasm. **12.1 मेरे** (**मेरे लिए**) var. pron. obl. for me; **अखंडित** [S] adj. faultless, auspicious; **सुदिन** adj. appropriate day; **सोध-** [śodhayati] Av. Br. v.t. to determine. **12.2 गावतहिं** (**गाते ही**) apa. Br. v.t. imperf. as I sing.

राम मेरी औषद, जतन मेरौ राम है॥ B12॥

अद्धर को है अधार हरी, नर बंधक बंधन माँझ रस्यो है।
2 दोस लगावत दीनदयालहिं, हौंसु हिये हर भाँति नस्यो है।
ठाकुर, याको तु भेद न जानत, माया के गाँसन माँझ धँस्यो है।
4 घींच पै मीच न नीचहि सूझत, मोह के कीच के बीच फँस्यौ है॥ B13॥

*मन मेरो मतंग भयौ मदमत्त, सु माया-समुद्र मैं आन धस्यौ है।
2 ज्ञान-महावत लाज को आँकुस, संक की सांकर नाहिं गस्यौ है।
ठाकुर, मैं हूँ उपाय किये, वह आवै न हाथ, कुसंग बस्यौ है।
4 घींच पै मीच न नीचहि सूझत, मोह के कीच के बीच फँस्यौ है॥ B14॥

1 जाने जौन काज कों अरंभ कर दीन्हों, ताकों
तौन काज कहा बिन भये लटकत है।

---

13 Granthāvalī 206, Śatak 34, Ṭhasak 20. 14 Granthāvalī 205, Śatak 107, Ṭhasak 15. 15 Granthāvalī 211, Śatak 5, Ṭhasak 25.

12.4 राम मेरौ] Σ, राम मेरे **E** • बैद] Σ, बैद्य D$_2$ • बिसराम] Σ, बिलराम V$_1$ • मेरो] B$_1$D$_2$**S**Ṭ$_e$V$_1$, मेरे G$_e$Ṭ$_e^j$ • भैया B$_1$S$_1$S$_2$V$_1$Y$_e$, भिया D$_2$, साँचे G$_e$, भया S$_7$, सांचो Ṭ$_e$ • मेरी] B$_1$D$_2$**E**S$_1$, मेरौ S$_2$V$_1$Y$_e$ • औषद] **E**S$_2$V$_1$, औषदि B$_1$, औषधि D$_2$, औषध S$_1$S$_7$ • मेरौ] Σ, मेरे **E** • है] Σ, हैं **E** **13.1** अद्धर] Ṭ$_e$, अध्धर G$_e$, आँधारे Ś$_e$ • है] G$_e$Ṭ$_e$, *om.* (unm.) Ś$_e$ • हरी] G$_e$Ṭ$_e$, हरि (unm.) Ś$_e$ • नर] G$_e$Ṭ$_e$, इक Ś$_e$ • रस्यो] G$_e$Ṭ$_e$, हँस्यो Ś$_e$ **13.2** हर] G$_e$Ṭ$_e$, हरि Ś$_e$ **14.1** मन] (unm.) Σ **14.2** ज्ञान] Ś$_e$, अरु ज्ञान (unm.) G$_e$Ṭ$_e$ • **14.3** ठाकुर] Ś$_e$, कहि ठाकुर (unm.) G$_e$, कह ठाकुर (unm.) Ṭ$_e$ **14.4** घींच] Ś$_e$, नित घींच (unm.) G$_e$Ṭ$_e$ •

12.4 जतन (यत्न) [S] Br. m. 1. effort; 2. (here:) the goal of an effort. **13.1** अद्धर [a-dhara-] adj. helpless; अधार [ādhāra-] Br. m. basis, support; हरी [hari] m. (metri causae) Krishna, God; बंधक [S] m. 1. one who binds; 2. violator, ravisher; 3. bonds, fetters. (The word has a negative connotation. Its feminine form, 'bandhakī', means harlot.) रसना v.i. to feel delight, to be attracted; (cf. Yamalārjun); इक... हस्यो है apa. **13.2** दोष लगाना idiom. to blame; हौंस [A havas] Br. f. intense desire; enthusiasm; हौंसु हिये reg. with intense desire in the mind; **13.3** तु [H to] poet. adv. (then); गांस [? grāsa-] f. (here m.) 1. trap; 2. power; धँसना [dhvaṃsati] v.i. to sink. **13.4** घींच f. neck; मीच [mṛtyu-] Br. f. death. **14.1** धँसना [dhvaṃsati] v.i. to sink. **14.2** संक (शंका) [S] reg. f. fear, awe; सांकर [śṛnkhalā-] f. chain; गस- [grasati] Br. v.t. 1. to grasp; 2. (here:) to control. **14.3** मैं हूँ Br. (as many others) I also; कुसंग [S] m. bad company. **14.4** घींच f. neck; मीच [mṛtyu-] Br. f. death. **15.1** जाने (जिसने) rel. pron. ag. reg. the one who; जौन (जो) Bund. Av. 1. rel. pron. which; 2. conj. if; लटकना [cf. *laṭṭa-] v.i. 'to hang' 1. to be kept pending (a matter), 2. v.t. to close down; 3. v.t. to neglect.

कहा करौं कहाँ देखौं, घाबडो ह्वै जात मन, 2
        चिंता को प्रबाह जब आन झटकत है।
ठाकुर, यों मन समुझायो करैं बार बार 3
        मानत है नाहीं, या बृथा ही भटकत है।
ऐसो कहा कोऊ हीन बंधु अटकत, जैसो 4
        दीन के भए तें दीनबंधु अटकत है॥ B15॥

दौलत या दीजै कै न दीजै, कछु सोच नाहीं, 1
        लोच मन एतौ एक जनम सुधारियै।
संग परबीनन के, दीनन पै दया कछू, 2
        प्रेम में मगन, ऐसे दिनन निवारियै।
ठाकुर कहत, जो अधीन सब रावरे के 3
        जासों जैसौ नातो, तासों तैसौ ओर पारियै।
एहो ब्रजराज, तेरे पाइ परि हाथ जोरौं, 4

---

16 Bharatpur1 f. 158r (50), Datiya2 f. 7v-8r (67), Granthāvalī 212, Śatak 92, Ṭhasak 9, Vrindaban1 ff. 3v-4r (6/19), Vrindaban2 f. 71v. The order of lines in V_1 is adcb.

16.1 दौलत] D_2EV_1, दौलति B_1V_2 • या] Σ, जौ **E** • दीजै] $B_1D_2V_1V_2$, दीजौ **E** • कै] $B_1^{pc}D_2V_1$, *om.* (unm.) B_1^{ac}, तौ **E**, या V_2 • दीजै] Σ, दीजौ **E** • कछु] **E**V_1, कछू $B_1D_2V_2$ • नाही] $B_1D_2V_1$, नाहि V_2, फिर **E** • लोच मन] $B_1D_2V_1$, एतो वर **E**, एते पर V_2 • एतौ एक] $B_1D_2V_1$, दीजौ मेरो **E**, एक मेरौ V_2 • सुधारियै] Σ, सुधारियो **E** **16.2** के] $B_1D_2V_1$, को **E**, में V_2 • दीनन पै] B_1**E**V_1, दीनन पर (unm.) D_2, दया जैसें V_2 • दया कछू] V_1, दया कछू B_1D_2, दया नित **E**, दीननन में V_2 • प्रेम में मगन] Σ, ऐसें करि प्रभु V_2 • ऐसे] Σ, मेरे V_2 • दिनन] B_1V_2, दिन D_2, दिन जु **E**, दिन (unm.) V_1 • निवारियै] $B_1V_1V_2$, निरवारियै D_2, निवारियो **E** **16.3** ठाकुर कहत] Σ, ठा॰ B_1 • जो] **E**, या D_2, यौ B_1V_1, जू V_2 • सब] Σ, भयौ **E** • के] $B_1^{ac}D_2V_1$, की B_1^{pc}, तौ **E**, है V_2 • जासौं] B_1^{ac}Σ, जसौं B_1^{pc} • ओर] Σ, डोर V_2 • पारियै] $B_1D_2V_2$, पारियो **E**, पाइयै V_1

15.2 घाबड़ो ह्वै जात [cf. ghabrānā] Br. poet. v.i. becomes confused; झटकना [cf. *jhaṭṭ-] v.t. to jerk, to jolt. **15.3** या pron. this (soul). **15.4** हीन बंधु [S] obl. by (seeing) a friend in need; अटकना [*aṭṭakk-] v.i. 1. to be stopped, hindered; 2. to be attached to; कहा... अटकत Br. is anyone attached to a friend in need (in the same way as)? दीन के भए तें Br. 1. by one's being destitute; 2. since he is (called) 'dīn' (destitute). **16.1** लोच [cf. locyate, H locnā] m. desire. **16.2** निवारियो var. [nirvārayati] v.t. subj. let (me) pass. **16.3** जो Br. conj. since; रावरे के poet. (subject) to you; ओर [avarā-] f. (till the) end; पार- (पालना) [pālayati] Br. v.t. 1. to protect; 2. to keep (a promise); डोर पारियै apa. idiom. 'to stitch' to lay a snare.

प्रानहूँ नजर, पै न नियत बिगारियै॥ B16॥

हारि पर्यौ लरि ह्वै बलहीन, सो ग्राह तें लै गज तू जितयौ रे।
2 फेर सुन्यो प्रहलाद के साँकरे, आवन कौं न खिनौ बितयौ रे।
ठाकुर, हौं अजामेल तें आगरौ पापी उजागरौ यौं हितयौ रे।
4 रावरी ओर चितोत-चितोत किते दिन बीते, न तूँ चितयौ रे॥ B17॥

प्रानन प्रेम की गाँस नहीं, नहिं कानन बाँसुरी को सुर छायो।
2 बैनन सों न जप्यो नँदनंदन, नैनन सों ब्रजचंद लखायो।
ठाकुर, हाथ न माल लई, नहीं पाइन सों हरिमंदिर धायो।
4 नेक कियो न सनेह गोपाल सों देह धरे कौ कहा फल पायो॥ B18॥

राधा

1 मेंहदी लपेटे लाल, लाल बस कीन्हें निज,
छीगुनी अनौटा नगजटित सँवारे हैं।

---

17 Granthāvalī 213, Śatak 39, Ṭhasak 11. Cf. Vinay patrikā 242 'taba tuma mohū se saṭhani ko haṭhi gati na dete'. 18 Granthāvalī 3, Śatak 1, Ṭhasak 136. The last line is reminsicent of Tulsīdās's 'Kavitāvalī' v. 2. 19 Granthāvalī 4, Ṭhasak 4.

16.4 एहो] EV_2, एरे $B_1D_2V_1$ • तेरे] $D_2^{pc}\Sigma$, ते (unm.) D_2^{ac} • परि] $B_1V_1V_2$, पर D_2, *om.* **E** • हाथ] Σ, कर **E** • जोरौं] $D_2V_1V_2$, जोरूं B_1, जोरे गहौं **E** • नजर पै] **E**, पै नजर D_2, जजाइयै V_1, नजरि पै B_1V_2 • न नियत] EV_1V_2, न नीयत्ति B_1, एक नियत ना (unm.) D_2 • बिगारियै] Σ, बिगारियो **E** **17.1** लरि] $G_e\d{T}_e$, हरि $\acute{S}_e$ • ह्वै] $G_e\d{T}_e$, ज्यों $\acute{S}_e$ • **17.4** रावरी] $G_e\acute{S}_e$, रावरो $\d{T}_e$ • **18.2** सों] $\acute{S}_e$, ना $G_e\d{T}_e$ **18.3** पाइन] $\acute{S}_e\d{T}_e$, पायन G_e **18.4** गोपाल] $\acute{S}_e\d{T}_e$, गुपाल G_e

---

16.4 प्रानहूँ नजर idiom. 'I even offer you my life' I beg you; नज़र [A naẕr] f. an offering (to a superior); जजाइयै var. [H jīnā] v.caus. reg. imp. to make to live, to animate; नीयत [AP] f. intention, resolve. **17.1** ग्राह [S] m. crocodile; जितयौ [H jitānā] v.t. perf. Br. you made (him) win. **17.2** फेर Br. m. call; साँकरा [saṅkaṭa-] m. difficulty; खिनौ (क्षण भी) Br. m. not even a moment; बितयौ (बिताया) [cf. vṛtta-] v.t. perf. Br. to pass. **17.3** आगरौ [agra-] adv. more (advanced); उजागरौ adj. 'bright' 1. well-known; 2. notorious; हितव- [cf. hita-] reg. v.t. to be friendly, to favour; हितयौ v.t. perf. Br. favoured me (thus) (ironic; i.e. you make much effort to redeem any sinner). **17.4** चितोत (चितवत) [H citavnā] v.t. imperf. Br. looking; चित- [cf. citta-] v.i. to look (at). **18.1** गाँस m. arrowhead; सुर [śara-] m. arrow. **18.2** लखा- [lakṣayati] Av. Br. v.t. to show; नैनन ना ब्रजचंद लखायो Br. your eyes did not show you Krishna. **18.3** माल [mālā-] f. garland. **19.1** लपेटे v.t. perf. (Radha's feet) being covered with; छीगुनी f. the little finger or toe; अनवट [*anuvarta-] m. Av. toe-ring (esp. with little bells or a mirror attached); सँवारना [saṃvārayati] v.t. to adorn.

दीपति के दीप तरवान को बखानै कौन, 2
पाँचो अँगुरिन मैन-सर पाँचौ पारे हैं।
ठाकुर कहत, ठकुराई के निकेत, रस- 3
रूप के भँडार निरधार निरधारे है।
पंकज-बरन असरन के सरन, राधे, 4
रावरे चरन सुख करन हमारे हैं॥ B19॥

येई हैं वे बृषभानुसुता, जिनसों मनमोहन मोह करै हैं।
कामिन तौ उनसी नहिं दूसरि, दामिन की दुति कों निदरै हैं। 2
ठाकुर, कै हमहीं यह जानतीं, कै उनहूँ को जनाइ परै हैं।
छोटी नथूनी बडे मुतियान, बडी अँखियान बडी सुघरै हैं॥ B20॥ 4

श्याम

धनि धनि कहत दिगंतन के ईस, नेक 1
जाकी बकसीस दुख दारिद बितोति है।
देवन को देव, सेव करत सुरेस सेस, 2
भजत महेस काहे करी वाकी होति है।

---

20 Granthāvalī 19, Śatak 12, Ṭhasak 33. 21 Bharatpur1 f. 151v-2r (15), Granthāvalī B9, Sudhāsar [S_1 f. 420v (22), S_2 f. 82v (-/92), S_7 f. 270v (155)], Vrindaban1 f. 14v (23/87). The Sudhāsar presents this poem within the description of 'Braj mahimā'.

19.2 अँगुरिन] $Ṭ_e$, आँगुरिन G_e **19.4** असरन] G_e, अशरण $Ṭ_e$ • सरन] G_e, शरण $Ṭ_e$ • चरन] G_e, चरण $Ṭ_e$ **20.1** करै हैं] $G_eṬ_e$, करै है $Ś_e$ **20.2** हैं] $G_eṬ_e$, है $Ś_e$ **20.3** हमहीं] $G_eṬ_e$, हमहूँ $Ś_e$ • जानतीं] $G_eṬ_e$, जानती $Ś_e$ • हैं] $G_eṬ_e$, है $Ś_e$ **20.4** हैं] $G_eṬ_e$, है $Ś_e$ **21.1** धनि धनि] $B_1G_eS_1^{pc}S_2$, धन धन $S_1^{ac}S_7V_1$ • बितोति] S_1S_2, बितोत $B_1G_eS_7V_1$ **21.2** होति] S_1S_2, होत $B_1G_eS_7V_1$

19.2 दीपति के दीप Br. 'light even for brightness' brighter than brightness itself; तरवा [talapāda-] m. sole (of the foot); पारना [cf. H paṛnā] Br. v.t. to throw; (here:) to shoot; मैन-सर पाँचो पारे हैं (its five toes) shot Kāma's five arrows. **19.3** निरधार (निर्धार) [S] Br. adv. assuredly, certainly; निरधार- [nirdhārayati] Br. v.t. to ascertain. **20.2** कामिन [kāminī-] f. attractive woman; निदर- [nirdarati] Av. Br. v.t. to treat with disrespect; to surpass. **20.3** कै... कै either... or; यह this (i.e. Krishna's love); जान- [jñāpayati, H janānā] poet. v.t. tell; जनाइ परै है reg. (Krishna) has to tell. **20.4** मुतिया [H motī] m. pearl (in the small nose-ring). **21.1** दिगंत [S] m. 'end of a direction' the horison; बितो- [cf. H bitānā] Br. v.i. to cause to pass away, to end. **21.2** सुरेश [S] m. 'lord of the gods' Indra; काहे Br. interr. why? भजत महेस काहे Br. why does Shiva worship him? कड़ी [kaṭa-] f. chain, fetter; करी वाकी होति है Br. 1. his work is done (in the world); 2. his fetters are (in the world).

3 ठाकुर कहत, गोरी राधिका को कंत रूप-
रस को महंत है, सराहि सकै को तिहै।
4 मन को मनोरथ है, तन को अराम धाम,
स्याम अभिराम मेरी आँखिन की जोति है॥ B21॥

1 ग्वारन को यार है, सिँगार सुख-सोभनि को,
सांचो सरदार तीन लोक रजधानी को।
2 गाइन के संग देखि आपनो बखत लेखि,
आनँद बिसेखि रूप अकह कहानी को।
3 ठाकुर कहत, सांचो प्रेम को प्रसंग, वारो
जा लखि अनंग-अंग-रंग दधि-दानी को।

---

22 Bharatpur1 f. 154rv (28), Granthāvalī 9, Hariaudh p. 484 (4), Sudhāsar [S_1 f. 273rv (25) and f. 2v (mg12) (S_1^m), S_2 f. 1v (-/1), S_3 f. 1v (2), S_5 f. 1v (9), S_6 f. 2r (9), S_7 f. 1v (11)], Ṭhākur-satsaī (Ṭ) f. 3r (23), Vrindaban1 f. 5v (4/30). Most Sudhāsar manuscripts present this poem within the description of 'Kṛṣṇadhyān' within the 'maṅgalācaraṇ'. In S_1, however, the poem was originally included towards the end of the 'aur nānābidhi kī brijkelī barnan' (description of other various love sports in Braj) subsection of the 'Brajrasrīti' section. For more details see the Introduction.

21.3 कहत] Σ, कहैत V_1 • सराहि] S_1S_2, सराह $B_1G_eS_7V_1$ • तिहै] S_1S_2, तहै $B_1G_eS_7V_1$ **21.4** अराम] Σ, आराम V_1 • जोति] $S_1S_2V_1$, जोत $B_1G_eS_7$ **22.1** ग्वारन] Σ, ग्वारनि B_1, ग्वालन A_e • यार] Σ, पार G_e • सिँगार] Σ, श्रिंगार V_1 • सुख] S_7^{ac}Σ, सुभ $S_3S_7^{pc}$ • सोभनि] $B_1G_eV_1$, सोभन SṬ • को] Σ, कौं S_2 • सरदार] A_eSṬ, सिरदार $B_1G_eS_1V_1$ • तीन] Σ, तीनि B_1S_2 • रजधानी] Σ, रज⟨आ⟩नी S_5 • को] Σ, कौं S_2S_6 **22.2** गाइन] Σ, गाइनि B_1V_1 • के] Σ, को G_e • देखि] $B_1G_eS_1^mV_1$, देख SṬ • लेखि] $A_eG_eS_2$, लेष SṬV_1 • आनँद] $A_eG_eS_3S_5S_6S_7$ṬV_1, आनद B_1, आंनद $S_1S_1^mS_2$ • बिसेखि] $B_1G_eV_1$, बिसेस $S_1^mS_5$, बिसेख $A_eS_1S_2S_3S_6S_7$Ṭ • रूप] A_eSṬ, सुख $B_1G_eV_1$ • अकह] Σ, अकहि S_3 • को] Σ, कौं S_6 **22.3** ठाकुर कहत] Σ, ठा॰ B_1 • को] Σ, के B_1 • जा लखि] $B_1G_eS_1^{pc}S_2S_6V_1$, अंगन $S_1^mS_5$, जा लख $S_1^{ac}S_3S_7$Ṭ • अनंग] Σ, *om.* (eyeskip) S_5 • अंग रंग] B_1G_eSṬV_1, रंग दंग A_e, आं रंग (unm.) S_2 • दधि] $A_eB_1G_eS_1S_1^mS_2S_3$, दध S_5S_6ṬV_1 • को] Σ, कौं S_6

21.3 कंत [S] m. lover; को (कौन) Br. interr. who? तिहै var. pron. obl. Br. him. **21.4** अराम (आराम) Br. 1. [P] m. rest; 2. [S] m. pleasure-place, garden; जोति [jyoti-] f. light. **22.1** सिरदार तीन लोक रजधानी को [cf. trilokanātha] lord of the capitals of the three words; पार apa. [pāla-] m. protector. **22.2** बखत [A vaqt or P bak̲ht] reg. m. time of good luck; बिसेख- [viśeṣa-] Br. 1. adj. special; 2. v.i. to appear in a special way. **22.3** सांचो प्रेम को प्रसंग Br. it is the true subject of love; वारो v.t. imp. (let's) sacrifce (the colours of Kāmdev's body); जा लखि दधि-दानी को seeing this collector of curds.

पुन्य नंद जू को, अनुराग ब्रजबासिन कौं, 4
भाग जसुमति को, सुहाग राधारानी को॥ B22॥

ए री, सुन, चारु यौ चरित्र बृजमंडल को, 1
मोहि आइ आइ जात हरि भांति हासी है।
कोऊ कहै याही बनाये रबि चंद दोऊ, 2
कोऊ कहै याकी, सुनी, सिंधुसुता दासी है।
ठाकुर कहत, स्वामी रसिक, सुजान, सर्व- 3
ज्ञ, सिरमौर सो महेस उर बासी है।
धौरी गाइ पीछै स्याम गोप यह दौर्यौ जात, 4
तासौं कहत लोग कै जौ अलख अबिनासी है॥ B23॥

मैं हू सुन्यौ, मेरी बीर, चरित अपार यह 1
घाट पनघट गली गांउ की अथैया है।
कोऊ रीझ रीझ याकी मन मैं बलैया लेत, 2
कोऊ कहै परै याकी अज ईस पैंया है।
ठाकुर कहत, कोऊ पाली कहै विश्व याकी, 3
कोऊ कहै पाल्यौ याहि जसुमति मैंया है।
नारिन को यार कोऊ गोरुन को संगी कहै, 4
कोऊ कहत गोप, कोऊ कहत गुसैयां है॥ B24॥

---

23 Datiya2 f. 7r (58). The manuscript introduces the poem as 'gopina kī ukta' (the words of the cowherd women). 24 Datiya2 f. 7r (59).

22.4 पुन्य] $B_1G_eSV_1$, पुत्र A_e, पुन S_6, पुन्न Ṭ • जू] $B_1G_eS_1S_1^mS_2S_3$ṬV$_1$, जी $S_5S_6A_e$ • कौं] Σ, *om.* (unm.) S_1^{ac}, संग (unm.) S_1^{pc} • अनुराग…जसुमति को] Σ, *om.* (eyeskip) V_1 • ब्रजबासिन] Σ, ब्रजबासिनि B_1 • को] Σ, कौं S_2S_6 **23.1** हासी] *em.* हासि (unrh.) D_2 **23.3** °ज्ञ] (unm.) D_2 **24.4** कहत] D_2^{pc}, हत (unm.) D_2^{ac}

23.1 चारु [S] adj. lovely, charming (story); यौ (यह) pron. reg. this; मोहि आइ आइ जात हासी है idiom. Br. I cannot help laughing again and again. **23.2** सिंधुसुता [S] f. 'the daughter of the (milk-)ocean' Lakshmi. **23.3** सो (lives in Shiva's heart) as. **23.4** धौर- [dhavala-] Av. Br. adj. bright, white (cow); कै जौ (कि) conj. poet. that. **24.1** अथैया (अथाई) [āsthāyikā-] Av. Br. f. meeting place for villagers. **24.2** (की) बलैया लेना [A balā] idiom. to seek to take another's misfortunes on oneself (i.e. to express his or her attachment); पैया [H pā(ya)] f. dimin. Br. (falls at his) foot. **24.3** पाली [S] f. playground.

1 झूम देइ झूला में झुलावती जसोदा माय,
चूम चूम बदन बलैया लेत प्यारे की।
2 झीनी सोहै झँगुली औ झालर झडूली लसै,
अँखिया रसीली नीकी कंज सो सुखारे की।
3 ठाकुर कहत, चितचोर चितवन चारु,
रूप में मिलत त्यौं किलौलैं किलकारे की।
4 कंजहू तें कोंरीं जिन्हैं बंदत महेस अज,
लागै सबै पैंयाँ या गुबिंद गभुवारे की॥ B25॥

1 धम धम धौंसन की धुनि सुनि लाजैं घन,
फहरैं निसान आसमान अंग छैठे हैं।
2 केहरी, करिंद, मोर, हंस, मुसा, नादिया हू,
और सब बाहन उमाहन उमैठे हैं।
3 ठाकुर कहत, सुर-असुर समूह, नर-
नारिन के जूह नंद मंदिर मैं पैठे हैं।
4 आवौ, चलैं, लीजिये जू, कीजिये जनम धन्य,

25 Granthāvalī 8, Ṭhasak 3. 26 Granthāvalī 28, Ṭhasak 126, Ṭhasak 'Jīvancarit' ($Ṭ^j_e$) p. 22.

25.4 महेस] G_e, महेश $Ṭ_e$ • लागै] $Ṭ_e$, लागैं G_e • गुबिंद] G_e, गोबिंद $Ṭ_e$ **26.2** मोर] $G_eṬ_e$, हय $Ṭ^j_e$

25.1 झूम [cf. H jhūmnā] f. swaying, swinging; झूला [*jhulyati] m. hanging cradle. **25.2** झँगुली [? adhyaṅgaka-, H jhagā] f. a long loose garment, tunic, (esp. as worn by very young children); झालर [jhallarī-] Bund. f. infant's curly hair before the first shaving; झँडूला [*jhaṇṭa-] adj. before the first shaving. **25.3** मिलत Br. (thus waves of shouts of joy are mixed in... किलोल [kallola-] m. f. 1. wave; 2. joy; किलकार [kilikilā-] m. shouts in delight. **25.4** कोंवर- (कोमल) [S] Br. adj. soft, delicate; अज [S] m. 'not born' Brahma; पैया [pada-, H pā(ya)] f. dimin. Br. small foot; गबुवार [cf. garbha- + H vālā] adj. 'of birth' (hair); one who has not undergone the tonsuring ceremony yet, small (child). **26.1** धम धम f. repeated loud sound (as of a drum); धौंसा m. kettledrum; फहरना v.i. to wave, to fly (a flag); निसान m. sign; flag; छैठै [H reg. chaha ṭho] num. (East.) (of) six (parts, types) (i.e. 'of the six deities'); ठो encl. (East.) (a particle used with cardinal numerals preceding nouns). **26.2** केहरी [kesarin] Av. Br. m. (Durgā's) lion; करींद m. Airavata, Indra's elephant; मोर [mayūra-] m. (Kārtikeya's) peacock; हय var. [S] m. (Kalki's) horse; हंस [S] m. (Brahmā's) wild goose; मूसा [mūṣaka-] m. (Gaṇeśa's) rat; नादिया m. the bull Nandī; उमाह m. swelling; exultation; उमेठना [udveṣṭate] v.i. to hold oneself erect (in pride). **26.3** जूह [yūtha-] Av. Br. m. flock; troop.

करुनानिधान कान्ह पान देन बैठे हैं॥ B26॥

*आवत हैं देखे कैसी मुरली लगी है मुख, 1
जैसी ही गरैयाँ लीनें लाल हू के बेटे की।
याही कों सराहै सेस, याही कों बखानैं बेद, 2
याही की कहानी कंठ पूतना लपेटे की।
ठाकुर कहत, याकी आदि अज ईस दै कै 3
खबर न काहूवै समेटे या बडेटे की।
कैयक लपेटे गए, कैयक चपेटे, एक 4
पेटे की न पाई या करेटे अहरेटे की॥ B27॥

---

27 Bharatpur1 f. 157r (44), Granthāvalī B5, Sudhāsar [S_1f. 263v (5), S_3 f. 139r (85), S_4 f. 63rv (92), S_7 f. 190v (5)], Vrindaban1 f. 9r (14/52). The Sudhāsar presents this poem in the 'Brajrasrīti' section as part of the 'gocāraṇ-līlā' (the divine sport of grazing the cows) subsection.

26.4 आवौ चलैं] G_eṬ$_e$, आवो चलो Ṭ$_e^j$ **27.1** हैं] $B_1G_eV_1$, है **S** • देखे] G_eV_1, देख B_1**S** • जैसी ही] Σ, तैसी⟨है/ही⟩ S_4 • लीनें] B_1V_1, लियैं **S**, नीली G_e **27.2** सराहै] $B_1S_3S_4S_7$, सराहैं $G_eS_1V_1$ • सेस] Σ, सोस S_4 • बखानैं] $B_1G_eS_1V_1$, बखानै $S_3S_4S_7$ • कंठ] Σ, कथा S_7 • लपेटे] Σ, लषेटे B_1 **27.3** ठाकुर कहत] G_e**S**, ठा॰ B_1, ठाकुर कहैत V_1 • आदि] Σ, आद S_7 • दै] $B_1G_eV_1$, लै **S** • खबर] Σ, खबरि S_4 • काहूवै] B_1**S**V_1, काहुवै G_e • या] $B_1G_eS_1S_3V_1$, या की S_4, पा S_7 • बडेते] Σ, ढेटे (unm.) S_1 **27.4** कैयक] Σ, कैईक S_7 • गए कैयक] $B_1G_eS_1S_3$, गये कैईक S_4S_7, गयेकै (unm.) V_1 • एक पेटे] Σ, *om.* (eyeskip) S_7 • या] $B_1G_eS_1S_3V_1$, पाई (dittography) S_4, नही पार या S_7

26.4 लीजियै जू Br. let's take (his bliss); पान देना idiom. 'to distribute betel-leaf' to honour (cf. nyautā denā 'to invite for food'). **27.1** आवत हैं देखे Br. I saw him coming; गरैयाँ [*galādamana-] reg. f. neck-rope, halter (normally not applied to calves); जैसी ही adv. just like, the same as; नीली var. [nīla-] adj. blue, dark (cow); लाल हू के Br. (as he is) also (holding the neck-rope of) a red cow's (calf) (i.e. the neck-rope looks like the flute and the redness of the cow resembles the lips); नीली लाल हू के var. dark and also red cow's (calves); **27.2** लपेटना [*lapeṭṭ-] v.t. 1. to wrap; 2. to subjugate; 3. to trap; कंठ पूतना लपेटे की (the story) of being embraced by Pūtanā. **27.3** आदि अज [S] adj. 'the primordial unborn one' Brahma; ईश [S] m. Shiva; दै abs. Br. up to, even (KL); लै कै (से लेकर) var. postp. Br. beginning from; काहुवै (किसी को भी) pron. obl. Br. to anyone; समेटना [saṃveṣṭayati and saṃvṛtta-] v.t. to gather up, to wind up, to finish; बड़ेटना [H baṛā] v.t. to enlarge; समेटे या बडेटे की of the gathering up or of the creating (of the universe). **27.4** कैयक [H kaī + eka-] adj. some; चपेटना [cf. *lapeṭṭa-] v.t. to attack; पेटा (पेट) [*peṭṭa-] m. (here f.) 'belly' the inner thoughts; (के) पेट की थाह न पाना idiom. one cannot understand the mind (of); करेटे [kālā-] poet. adj. black, dark; अहरेट- [ābhīra-] reg. m. son of a herdsman; की 1. (the matter of his mind, the matter) of (Krishna).

1 जैसो मंजु माथे पै मुकट, तैसो, कंजमुख,
कंजदल-नैन मैन-सर तें उकाढे हैं।
2 कानन मैं कुंडल बिराजैं, पटपीत काँधे,
कर मैं मुरलि, ताके होत सुर गाढे हैं।
3 ठाकुर कहत, अंग ललित त्रिभंग किये,
अभरे लकुट सों सुराग रस बाढे हैं।
4 गौवन कौं टेरत हैं, बछ्रान हेरत हैं,
देखि री, गुपाल वे तमाल तर ठाढे हैं॥ B28॥

---

28 Bharatpur1 f. 152r (16), Granthāvalī B10, Sudhāsar [S_1 f. 263r (3), S_2 f. 57v (-/58), S_3 f. 138v (83), S_4 f. 63r (90), S_7 f. 190r (3)], Ṭhākur-satsaī (Ṭ) f. 2r (13), Vrindaban1 f. 14v (24/88). The Sudhāsar (S_6) presents this poem as 'gocāran-līlā' in the 'Brajrasrīti' section.

28.1 जैसो] $B_1G_eS_1V_1$Ṭ, जैसै **S** • मंजु] $B_1G_eS_1S_2S_7V_1$, मंज S_3Ṭ, मेंज S_4 • मुकट] $B_1G_eS_1S_2S_3V_1^{pc}$, मुकटे S_4, मुकटि S_7, मुकट तैसो पीत पट (unm.) Ṭ, मुक (unm.) V_1^{ac} • कंज°] B_1G_e**S**V_1, कंत S_4, कंज×∗× Ṭ • कंजदल] Σ, कंजल (unm.) Ṭ • तें] B_1G_e**S**V_1, जे S_4, *om.* Ṭ • उकाढे] लेम Σ, ⟨के/का⟩ढे (unm.) Ṭ • हैं] $G_eS_1S_4S_7$, है $B_1S_2S_3$ṬV_1 **28.2 बिराजैं**] $G_eS_2V_1$, बिराजै B_1**SṬ** • काँधे] Σ, ज कांधैं (unm.) S_4 • मुरलि] Σ, मुरल Ṭ • हैं] G_e**S**, है B_1S_3ṬV_1 **28.3 कहत**] G_e**SṬ**, *om.* (unm.) B_1, कहैत V_1 • ललित] Σ, ललति S_7 • त्रिभंग] V_1^{pc}Σ, त्रभ (unm.) V_1^{ac} • किये] Σ, कियो S_7 • अभरे] B_1V_1, उभरे **SṬ**, अभिरे G_e • लकुट] **SṬ**, मुकट B_1G_e, मुक (unm.) V_1 • रस] $B_1G_eS_1$ṬV_1, रंग **S** • हैं] $B_1G_eS_1S_4S_7$, *om.* (unrh.) S_2, है S_3ṬV_1 **28.4 गौवन**] G_e**S**V_1, गवन (unm.) B_1^{pc}, गोपन S_3, गउवन (unm.) B_1Ṭ • टेरत] Σ, हेरत G_e • हैं] $B_1G_eS_1S_4S_7$, है S_2S_3ṬV_1 • हेरत] B_1**SṬ**, टेरत G_eV_1 • हैं] $B_1G_eS_1$, हौ S_2, है $S_3S_7V_1$Ṭ, हौं S_4 • देखि] $B_1G_eS_2V_1$, देख **SṬ** • तमाल तर] $B_1^{ac}G_eS_1S_3S_7$ṬV_1, मुमाल तर B_1^{ac}, तमातर (unm.) S_2S_4 • हैं] $B_1G_eS_1S_4S_7$, है S_2S_3ṬV_1

28.1 उकाढ- [utkṛṣṭa-] Br. adj. excellent. **28.2 पटपीत** m. yellow throw-on (whisk), scarf on the neck; **काँधे** m. obl. on his shoulder. **28.3 अभर** [S] adj. 'difficult to hold' heavy; **उभरे** var. [udbharati] v.i. perf. 1. to be high; 2. to sway; **आभिरे** var. [cf. abhīra-] poet. adj. of cowherd-boys; **अभिरना** var. [cf. H bhirṇā] v.i. 'to join' to rely on (here:) to lean on; **मुकट** (**मुकुट**) apa. [S] m. crown; **सुराग** [S cf. anurāga-] poet. m. (the joy of) love.

जाउ न कुंजन मैं, छिपि कै करी जोर जमातैं घनी ब्रजबाल की।
भोग सँजोग की चाह अचाह की, प्रेम-प्रयोग बियोग के जाल की।
ठाकुर, या बिजिया सों कहैं ते विनोद चहैं, लहैं सोभा रसाल की।
आई भली, छबि छाई भली, समुझाई भली भली बातैं गुपाल की॥ B29

गोवर्धन-धारण

*गोपी-गोप-गाइन पै, बृज पै, बसैयन पै
कोप मघवा को, लोग अकबक जोहैं री।

---

29 Bharatpur1 f. 161r (69), Granthāvalī B7, Sudhāsar [S_1 f. 412v (101), S_2 f. 80r (-/89), S_7 f. 265v (106)], Vrindaban1 f. 12v-13r (12/77). • The Sudhāsar presents this poem within the 'Devstuti, bhaktapakṣa, nirveda, karunā, binaya' section. The first three lines mostly contain the words of a woman who knows Krishna and the last one is the reply of the other women.
30 Bharatpur1 f. 159v (60), Granthāvalī B6, Sudhāsar [S_1 f. 266v (1), S_2 ff. 57v -58r (-/59), S_3 f. 141v (97), S_4 f. 66rv (104),S_7 f. 192r (3)], Ṭhākur-satsaī (Ṭ) f. 2v (17), Vrindaban1 f. 12r (7/72). The Sudhāsar presents this poem in the 'Brajrasrīti' section and introduce it as 'girarāj-dhāran'.

29.1 जाउ] $B_1G_eV_1$, जेउ S • छिपि] $B_1G_eS_2$, छिप $S_1S_7V_1$ • जोर] $B_1G_eS_7V_1$, जोरि S_1S_2 **29.2** भोग] Σ, योग G_e • अचाह] Σ, *om.* (unm.) S_2 • प्रयोग] $B_1G_eS_1V_1$, बियोग S_2S_7 **29.3** बिजिया] $B_1S_1S_2V_1$, बिधिया G_e, बिजीया S_7 • कहैं] $G_eS_1S_2V_1$, कहै B_1S_7 • ते] SV_1, तैं B_1, वे G_e • चहैं] G_eS_1, चहै $B_1S_2S_7V_1$ • लहैं] G_eS_1, लहै $B_1S_2S_7V_1$ **29.4** छबि] Σ, छब S_7 **30.1** गाइन] Σ, गईयन Ṭ • बृज पै] B_1G_eṬV_1, ब्रिज के S • कोप] Σ, काप S_2 • लोग] $B_1G_eV_1$, लोक SṬ • जोहैं] $B_1G_eS_1$Ṭ, जोहै SV_1

29.1 जाउ न v.t. imp. Br. 1. do not go! 2. emph. do go! छिपि कै Br. adv. stealthily; करी जोरि var. [cf. H joṛnā] Br. why did you join? जमात [A] f. group; करी... ब्रजबाल की Br. he rounded up a huge group of Braj girls. **29.2** भोग सँयोग poet. 1. enjoyment of union; 2. combination of enjoyments (cf. Ś64); योग संजोग की var. reg. 1. of yoga (i.e. union with God) and of union (with the beloved); 2. realising union; भोग... अचाह की poet. his desire is for the enjoyment of union and then not to love; प्रेम-प्रयोग [S] m. love put into practice; जाल [S] m. network, multitude; प्रेम... की Br. of multitudes of the practice of love (i.e. union) and separation. **29.3** बिजिया (विजया) (?) [S] Br. f. 1. Krishna's garland (the girls got hold of it instead of Krishna and talk to it); 2. a girl's name; 3. hemp (a petty thing in contrast with the mango flower) (HSS); बिधिया var. [vidhi-] reg. f. way, kind; शोभा [S] f. 1. radiance; 2. fig. virtue; रसाल [S] m. 1. person full of emotion, joyful person; 2. mango tree. ते... रसाल की Br. he wants entertainment and takes on the radiance of a person full of emotion; या बिधिया... लहैं var. reg. to talk in this way one needs delight and to take on the virtues of a delightful connoisseur; **29.4** छबि छाई भली Br. his radiance has spread well in my mind (i.e. I now recognise who he is); समुझाई भली Br. you explained (Krishna's matters) well. **30.1** मघवा [S] m. Indra; अकबक adj. amazed, speechless.

2 खलभल देखि कह्यो आऔ उत इत सबै,
सबैही बचाए चाव अपने अनोहैं री।
3 ठाकुर कहत, प्यारीं साँवरे बदन पेखैं,
लेखैं धनि भाग, देखें कौ न मन मोहैं री।
4 छिगुनी पै गिरि सौहै, गिरि पर जलधार,
जलधार ऊपर सुहाए मेघ सोहैं री॥ B30॥

युगल प्रेम

हौ तुम यातैं भली हर भाँतिन, औ अघ-घात न या कलिकाल के।

---

31 Bharatpur1 f. 161r (70), Sudhāsar [S_1 f. 57r (57), S_2 f. 57r (1/57), S_3 f. 128v (34), S_4 f. 49v (34), S_7 f. 184r (13)], Granthāvalī B8, Ṭhākur-satsaī (Ṭ) ff. 2r (12), Vrindaban1 f. 13r (13/78). The Sudhāsar presents this poem as the description of the river Yamunā within the 'Brajrasrīti' section.

30.2 खलभल] $B_1G_eS_1S_3S_7$ṬV_1, षलभ (haplography) S_2S_4 • देखि] $B_1G_eS_1S_2S_3$, देख S_4 S_7ṬV_1 • आऔ... चाव] Σ, *om.* (eyeskip) S_2 • उत इत सबै] G_eV_1, छाऔ उत इत B_1, आवौ आवौ इतै **S**, आवौ दौर इतै S_7, आवो आवो इत Ṭ • सबैही] B_1ṬV_1, सबैई G_e, सबही **S** • बचाए] Σ, चाप (unm.) S_4 • अपने] G_e**S**, आपनैं B_1Ṭ, आपनौ V_1 • अनोहैं] Σ, आनोहे Ṭ, अनैहै V_1 **30.3** ठाकुर कहत] Σ, ठा° B_1 • प्यारीं] *conj.* प्यारी B_1G_e $S_1S_2S_7V_1$, पयारी (unm.) S_3Ṭ • साँवरे] G_eV_1, साँवरौ B_1**S**Ṭ • पेखैं] G_eS_1, पेषै $B_1S_2V_1$, देखैं S_3, देखौ S_7, ए पै Ṭ • लेखैं] $B_1S_3S_7$, लेषै S_2ṬV_1, लखैं G_e • धनि] $B_1G_eS_1S_3S_4V_1$, धन्य S_1S_7, धैन Ṭ • भाग] Σ, भागि B_1 • देखें] $B_1G_eS_1$, देषै S_2V_1, पेखै S_3, पेखैं S_7, देख Ṭ • मोहैं] B_1G_e, मोहै **S**ṬV_1 **30.4** गिरि] $B_1G_eS_2V_1$, गिर **S**Ṭ • सोहै] Σ, सोहैं S_2 • गिरि] B_1G_e, गीर S_2, गिर $S_1S_3S_4$ṬV_1, गिरहू S_7 • पर] $B_1G_eS_1S_2S_4$ṬV_1, पै सो S_3, पै S_7 • सुहाए] $B_1G_eS_1$ṬV_1, सुहायौ **S** • सोहैं] $B_1G_eS_1$, सोहै G_e**S**V_1Ṭ **31.1** भली] $B_1G_eS_2V_1$, बडी **S**Ṭ • हर] $G_eS_2S_3$Ṭ, हरि $B_1S_1S_4S_7V_1$ • भाँतिन] B_1^{pc}Σ, ⟨ब⟩तिन B_1^{ac} • अघ] Σ, अधि Ṭ • घात न] **S**, घाति न B_1, पाँति न G_eV_1, घाती न Ṭ • या] Σ, पा Ṭ • कलिकाल] Σ, कलिकालि V_1

30.2 खलभल (खलबल) [*khalabhala-] f. 1. confusion; 2. commotion; कह्यो [kathayati] v.t. perf. Br. (Krishna) said; उत इत Br. adv. (from) everywhere; चाव अपने obl. (through) his eagerness; अनोहैं (अनोखा) [anapekṣa-] reg. adj. uncommon, wonderful. **30.3** प्यारीं [S] Br. f. pl. the lovely girls (see); पेख- [prekṣate] v.t. 1. to see; 2. to desire; लेख- [cf. H likhnā] v.t. to consider; लख- var. [laksate] v.t. 'to see' to understand, consider; धनि [dhanya-] adj. fortunate, blessed. **30.4** छिगुनी f. the little finger; सुहाय- [śobhā-] Br. adj. pleasant, charming. **31.1** यातैं adv. because of it (the wonder of Radha and Krishna); औ (और) [apara-] adj. other (things); अघ [S] m. sin; घात [S] m. destruction; घातन [S] m. 'killing' destroyer; पातन var. [pātana-] m. 'overthrowing' overthrower.

पूजत मंजु मनोरथ दास के, कूजत हैं खग रूप रसाल के। 2
ठाकुर, यौ समौ तेरे प्रसाद, महेस-कृपा ते लखैं भले भाल के।
कालिंदी, रावरी कुंज-कछारनि पुंजन कौतिक लाडिली-लाल के॥ B31॥ 4

अपने अपने निज गेहन मैं चढ़े दोऊ सनेह की नाँव पै री।
अँगनान मैं भीजत प्रेम भरे समयो लखि मैं बलि जाँव पै री। 2
कह ठाकुर, दोउन की रुचि सों रँग द्वै उमड़े दोउ ठाँव पै री।
सखि, कारी घटा बरसै बरसाने पै, गोरी घटा नँदगाँव पै री॥ B32॥ 4

आऔ, चलौ, देखियै जू, लेखियै जनम धन्य, 1
 केसर गुलाल सों सरीर साधियतु है।
और मैं कहाँ लौं कहौं नाम नर-नारिन के, 2
 दुःख तैं निकासि सुःख भौन धाँधियतु है।
ठाकुर कहत, उन्हैं साँवरो दिखावनो है, 3

---

32 Granthāvalī 10, Rāmcandra Śukla (I_e) p. 443, Ṭhasak 41 33 Granthāvalī 11, Ṭhasak 89.

31.2 पूजत] Σ, पूज (unm.) V_1 • **मंजु**] $B_1G_eS_1S_2S_4V_1$, मंज S_3S_7Ṭ • **कूजत**] Σ, पूजत Ṭ • **हैं**] $B_1G_eS_1$, है **S**ṬV_1 • **खग**] $B_1G_eS_1S_2S_4$ṬV_1, कल S_3S_7 **31.3 यौ समौ तेरे प्रसाद**] Σ, तेरे वै समो तेरे प्रसादि (unm.) Ṭ • **समौ**] $B_1G_eS_1V_1$, समै **S** • **प्रसाद**] $B_1G_eS_1S_2S_4$ṬV_1, प्रसादि S_3S_7 • **महेस**] B_1G_e**S**Ṭ, महेम S_2, यो महेस (unm.) V_1 • **ते**] **S**, सों B_1G_eṬV_1 • **लखैं**] B_1S_1, लखै G_e**S**ṬV_1 • **भले**] Σ, भल Ṭ **31.4 कालिंदी**] Σ, कालिदी S_4 • **रावरी**] Σ, पबरी S_4 • **कछारनि**] $B_1G_eV_1$, कछारन **S**Ṭ • **लाल**] B_1G_e**S**S_3^{pc}Ṭ, ला (haplography) S_3^{ac}, *om.* (unm.) V_1 **32.1 निज**] **E**, सुठि I_e • **मैं**] G_e, में I_eṬ$_e$ • **नाँव**] G_e, नाव I_eṬ$_e$ **32.2 मैं**] G_e, में I_eṬ$_e$ • **जाँव**] G_e, जावँ I_eṬ$_e$ **32.3 ठाँव**] **E**, ठावँ I_e **32.4 सखि**] G_e, सखी I_eṬ$_e$ **33.2 दुःख**] Ṭ$_e$, दुख्ख G_e • **सुःख**] Ṭ$_e$, सुख्ख G_e

---

31.2 मनोरथ दास के the desires of your worshipper; **कूजना** [kūjati] v.i. to call, to cry; **रसाल** [S] adj. 'full of emotion' beautiful; **खग रूप रसाल के** birds of beautiful forms. **31.3 यौ समौ** [samaya-] reg. adv. at this time; **तेरे प्रसाद** m. obl. out of your grace; **महेश** [S] m. Shiva (who was also interested in watching the sports of the divine couple); **लख-** [lakṣaṇa-] Br. v.t. to see; **भले भाल का** 'of good forehead' fortunate. **31.4 कालिंदी** [S] f. voc. o Yamuna; **कछार** [kaccha-] m. riverbank; **कौतुक** [S] m. wonder; **लाडली** [lāḍya-] f. 'lovely woman' Radha. **32.1 गेह** [gṛha] m. house. **32.2 समयो (समय)** [S] m. emph. poet. (at the) time (of) (cf. H bhīgte samay); **पै** 1. postp. at (that time); 2. conj. but. **33.1 लेख-** [? cf. H lekhā 'account; reckoning'] Av. Br. v.t. to consider; **लेखियै जनम धन्य** idiom. let's consider our birth fortunate; **33.2 धाँधना (धंसना)** [dhvaṃsati] reg. v.t. to enter into.

तातैं हम बातन को ब्यौंत नाधियतु है।
4 प्रेम को न अंत है, महंत है मनोज आज,
राधिका के कंतहि बसंत बाँधियतु है॥ B33॥

1 आजु यहि कौतुक छको है नंदनंद, बीर,
बरनो न जात सो बिचित्र चित्र मोपै री।
2 चलु, बलि, तोहि यौं दिखाइ लाऊँ, बन घनो
पायो है निहार, बलिहार भयौ सो पै री।
3 ठाकुर कहत, कहाँ नीलमनि, सोनबेलि,
सुषमा सकेलि कै न उपमा अरोपै री।
4 घन को निहारै तब वारै होत आपुन पै,
बीजुरी निहारै तब वारै होत तोपै री॥ B34॥

1 *काहे को बिकल होती एती उर अंतर में,
हेरौ, हँसौ, बोलौ, काहे आनन बिहाल है।
2 देह दुबराई आवे, मेह असुवान छावे,
नेह के नगर कछू देखौ एक चाल है।

34 Granthāvalī 12, Ṭhasak 67. 35 Bharatpur1 f. 153r (22); Bharatapur8 ff. 13v-14r (40). The poem presents a companion's words to Radha. (KL)

33.3 दिखावनो] *em.* दिखावने **E** **35.2** छावे] B_1, छामे B_8 • एक] B_1, ए⟨का⟩ B_8 • है] B_1, में (unrh.) B_8

33.3 उन्हें pron. obl. to them (i.e. to the cowherd women); दिखावनो [cf. H dekhnā] v.caus. (Br. inf.) to show; ब्योंत [cf. H byoṃtnā] m.f. 'the cutting out of clothes' 1. style; 2. shrewdness; नाध- [naddha-] Br. v.t. 1. to yoke, to attach; 2. to turn to; हम बातन को ब्यौंत नाधियतु है Br. I resort to clever words. **33.4** महंत [S] m. priest (who places flower on the head when blessing); राधिका... है 1. idiom. decorates Radha's lover with spring. (On the occasion of Vasant Pañcamī yellow mustard flowers and mango flowers—both signs of Kāma—are placed on the ground, worshipped and then put on the head.); 2. the spring captivates Radha's lover. **34.1** छकना v.i. to be intoxicated, immersed; बीर [vīra-] m. f. voc. Br. o my companion; बरनो न जात मोपै I am not able to describe. **34.2** बलि idiom. Br. 'I sacrifice myself' I beg you; दिखाई लाऊँ बन घनो Br. let me show you the deep forest; पायो है निहार Br. I managed to glimpse. **34.3** न उपमा अरोपै Br. no simile fits. **35.1** विकल [S] adj. restless; आनन [S] m. face; बिहाल [P be-hāl] Br. adv. in a bad state. **35.2** दुबराई (दुबलाई) [durbala-, H dublā] f. 1. thinness; 2. weakness; मेह असुवान poet. clouds of tears; छामे (छाता है) var. v.i. (pres. reg.) spreads; कछू देखौ एक चाल है poet. look a bit, it is the same style (that both are in a plight); चाल f. practice, style.

ठाकुर कहत, हमें इतहू निहारौ, फेरि 3
उतहू निहारौ, भयौ एक ही सो हाल है।
जैसै बाँसुरी की धुनि धुनि के गई हौ तुम, 4
त्यौं ही घूँघरू की धुनि घाइल गुपाल है॥ B35॥

ऐसे, कहौ, कहा कारज होत है, जो मग माँझ कबौं दरसाने।
ये दिन ऐसे ही बीतत हैं, हमहूँ तरसीं, तुम हूँ तरसाने। 2
ठाकुर, और बिचार कछू नहिं, ये अभिलाष हिये सरसाने।
कै हमहीं बसियै नँदगाँव, की आपही आय बसौ बरसाने॥ B36॥ 4

*कैसे पीत-पटवारो छोर छहरत जात, 1
उलटी मुरलि खोंसे अंग अलसानो सो।
लटपटे पेचन की बाँधे अटपटी पाग, 2
नटखटी नंद को निकाइन निकानो सो।
ठाकुर कहत, हित हौंस अभिलाषन सौं 3
बित्त कौं बिसारि चित्त चारु चकवानो सो।
लेख धन्य भाग सोभा सुखन बिसेष देख, 4
गोरी कों गुविंद फिरै देखत दिवानो सो॥ B37॥

36 Granthāvalī 13, Ṭhasak 44. 37 Granthāvalī 14, Ṭhasak 62.

35.3 ठाकुर कहत] B_8, ठा॰ B_1 **36.1** कहौ] *em.* कहौं G_e, कबौं T_e **37.1** कैसे] G_e, कैसो T_e

35.3 हमें pron. obl. (look at) us (i.e. me and esp. you); हमें... निहारौ Br. look at us here and then look (at Krishna) there. **35.4** धुनि (ध्वनि) [S] Br. f. sound; धुनना [dhunoti] v.t. 'to card cotton' 1. to beat up; 2. (here:) to be wounded (KL); घायल [cf. ghāta-] poet. adj. wounded. **36.1** कबौं adv. sometimes; ऐसे... दरसाने Tell me what is it good for if you appear on the road every now and then. **36.2** तुम हूँ तरसाने reg. I also make you suffer. **36.3** सरसना v.i. to flourish, to become strong. **36.4** की conj. poet. or. **37.1** पटवारो छोर (पट का छोर) Br. the border of the garment; छहरना v.i. to be scattered, dispersed; खोंसना v.i. to tuck in. **37.2** लटपटा adj. tangled, hanging loose; पेच [P] m. 1. turn, twist; 2. coil (as of turban); अटपटा adj. 1. confused; 2. twisted; पाग f. turban; नंद को idiom. 'Nanda's son' Krishna; नटखटी f. naughtiness; निकाइन (निकाई) [cf. P nek] poet. m. beauty; निकाना adj. beautiful. **37.3** हौंस (हवस) [A] f. desire, lust; चकवानो [cf. H caknā] adj. bewildered, confused. **37.4** गोरी कों देखत Br. looking at Radha.

देखती ती ललितादि जहाँ तहाँ, हौं हू गई दबि पाँवन गाढे।
2 चाह भरे मुख-चंदन सों चितवैं चहुँ चित्र मनो लिखि काढे।
ठाकुर, को घट को बढ है, निरधार करैं अनुराग न बाढे।
4 कुंज के भौन में पुंज प्रभान किशोर किशोरी बराबर ठाढे॥ B38॥

राधिका स्याम लसे पलका पर, का पर जाति कही छबि हाल की।
2 आपने हाथ सों भावती लै कर प्रीति सों आँजुरी जोरी गोपाल की।
ठाकुर, तापै धरो मुख बाल नै, को बरनै उपमा वहि काल की।
4 पानन मैं तिय आनन यौं दिपै चंद चढो मनो कंज की नाल की॥ B39॥

1 एकै नंदगांव के झपट बरसानै जात,
  एकै बरसाने के सु पाथल थिरांनै है।
2 ब्रंद्राबंन हारन मैं, जमुना कछारन मैं

---

38 Granthāvalī 16, Śatak 23, Ṭasak 34. 39 Granthāvalī 18, Śatak 95, Ṭhasak 40. 40 Datiya1 ff. 50v-51r (151), Sudhāsar [S$_1$ f. 269v-270r (1), S$_3$ f. 144v-145r (112), S$_4$ f. 69v (119), S$_7$ f. 193v (12)], Ṭhākur-satsaī (Ṭ) f. 2v (18). The Sudhāsar presents this poem in the 'aur nānābidhi kī brijkelī barnan' (description of other various love sports in Braj) subsection of the 'Brajrasrīti' section. The poem contains the words of a cowherd woman to another one.

38.1 देखती ती] Ś$_e$, दीखती तो G$_e$Ṭ$_e$ • ललितादि] G$_e$Ṭ$_e$, ललिता जो Ś$_e$ **38.3** करैं] G$_e$Ṭ$_e$, करै Ś$_e$ **38.4** किशोर किशोरी] Ś$_e$Ṭ$_e$, किसोरी किसोरी G$_e$ **39.1** लसे] G$_e$Ṭ$_e$, लसैं Ś$_e$ **39.2** सों] G$_e$, से Ś$_e$Ṭ$_e$ • सों] G$_e$, से Ś$_e$Ṭ$_e$ • आँजुरी] G$_e$Ṭ$_e$, अंजुरी Ś$_e$ • गोपाल] Ś$_e$Ṭ$_e$, गुपाल G$_e$ **39.3** तापै] G$_e$Ṭ$_e$, तापैं Ś$_e$ **39.4** की नाल] G$_e$Ṭ$_e$, सनाल Ś$_e$ **40.1** एकै] Σ, पकै S$_4$ • सु पा] S$_3$S$_4$S$_7$, °ई (unm.) D$_1$, सु या S$_1$Ṭ • है] D$_1$S$_3$Ṭ, हैं S$_1$S$_4$S$_7$

38.1 ललितादि (my friend) Lalitā and other girls; गाढा adj. 1. intense; 2. bold, smart. **38.2** चितवैं चहुँ Br. they are looking all around; चित्र मनो लिखि काढे Br. as if painted on a picture. **38.3** को घट को बढ है Br. who is small? who is big? निरधार करैं Br. if we are to decide it (then love does not increase). **38.4** प्रभान [prabhā-] f. (Br. pl.) radiances. **39.1** पलका m. bed; का पर जाति कही Br. who can tell? **39.3** धरो मुख बाल नै the girl put her face (on it). **39.4** पानन [pāṇi] m. f. pl. hands; की postp. (rhyme) (here:) on (H par). **40.1** एकै... एकै... one... some other...; नंदगांव के reg. (one) from Nandagamv ; झपट adv. quickly; पाथल (पत्थर) [prastara-] m. (remain like a) stone; पा थल poet. the feet at one place; केई (के ही) var. reg. from (Barsana) itself; थिरांनै [cf. sthira-] reg. v.i. perf. remained.

एकन के दौर दौर पगहु पिरांनै है।
ठाकुर कहत, कहौ कौन कैसौ भेदु-भाउ, 3
कौन कुंज जाउँ, दोऊ सुख सौं सिरानै है।
बूझत कहा है, बीर, बावरी सी डोलत है, 4
लाडिली के संग लाल काल के हिरानै है॥ B40॥

कौन से केलि के मंदिर ते उत नींदभरे उठि जात प्रभाते।
हैं अदले-बदले पट-भूषण, दोऊ सराहत सौंह सिराते। 2
ठाकुर, ते हती ता खिन ता थल, मोहिं बताव, भटू, चरचाते।
गोकुल गैल में आनँद फैल में गोपी गोपाल बतात कहां ते॥ B41॥ 4

---

41 Sundarī-tilak (C_e) pp. 50–51 (298). This quatrain presents the words of one sakhī to another describing Radha and Krishna after a night together.

40.2 ब्रंद्राबंन] D_1, बंसीबट SṬ • हारन] D_1S_1Ṭ, छारन S_3S_4 • के] Σ, वै S_7 • दौर दौर] D_1, देख (haplography) S_4, देख देख S_1S_3Ṭ, देखि देखि S_7 • पगहु] D_1, सु पग SṬ • है] D_1S_3Ṭ, हैं $S_1S_4S_7$ **40.3** कहौ कौन कैसौ] D_1, कोऊ कहा जानै SṬ • भेदु] D_1, भेद SṬ • जाउँ] D_1, जाय $S_1S_3S_7$, जाप S_4, जा×⟨त⟩×इ Ṭ • सौं सिराने] S_1Ṭ, सौ हिरानै $S_3S_4S_7$, ⟨लौं सिहां⟩नै D_1 • है] D_1S_3Ṭ, हैं $S_1S_4S_7$ **40.4** बूझत] Σ, बूझति S_3S_7 • कहा] Σ, कहाँ S_1 • है] D_1Ṭ, हैं S_1, हौ $S_3S_4S_7$ • सी डोलत है] D_1, भई है आज SṬ • लाल] S, ⟨बा⟩ल D_1 • हिरानै] D_1S_1Ṭ, बिराने $S_3S_4S_7$ • है] D_1S_3Ṭ, हैं $S_1S_4S_7$ **41.1** उत] *conj.* उस C_e

---

40.2 बंसीबट var. Br. m. the banyan tree in Vrindaban under which Krishna played his flute; हार Bund. m. 'line of trees' forest; छार var. 1. [cf. H chārṇā] reg. f. 'leaving' land gained by the retreat of the river; 2. [kṣāra-] Br. m. dust; कछार [cf. kaccha-] m. bank; पिराना [H pīrā] v.t. to ache; **40.3** कौन कुंज जाउं reg. to which grove shall I go? सिरानै [cf. śītala-] v.i. perf. 1. cooled, assuaged; 2. pleased; हिरा- (हरना) var. [cf. hārayati] Br. v.i. to be lost; सिहाना (सिहरना) var. [cf. śikhara-] Br. v.i. to feel a thrill of emotion. **40.4** काल के [kalya-, H kal] reg. adv. since yesterday; हिराना (हेराना) [caus. of H hernā] v.i. 'to require searching' to be lost; बिरा- (बिला-) var. [vilīyate] reg. v.i. to vanish. **41.2** हैं... भूषण their clothes and ornaments are mixed up; दोऊ (दोनों) [cf. dva-] num. obl. Br. both (he and she); सौंह (सामने) Br. adv. (praising each other) in front; सिराना v.i. to be pleased. **41.3** ते हती reg. you were present (at that time); चरचाते [cf. carcā-] v.t. imperf. poet. you who were talking to them; 2. [carcā te] Br. those words (of the two). **41.4** गैल [gati-] reg. f. (obl.) on the way of; फैल m. 1. game, sport; 2. spread, extent; 3. [P] bad action, vice; बता- v.i. to talk to each other.

*ए कहैं ऐसी है, वे कहैं वैसी है, ऐसी न वैसी है, तो तनु बाँको।
हेरें हसै, बिलसैं गहै बाँह, पै चाहै चकोर लौं चंद उवा को।
ठाकुर, गौरी गिरीस सु होंस तमासो लखैं, सुनैं सोरहु वाको।
गोरी गुपाल सौं, री, बगरो, अगरो झगरो दुहूँ ओर जुवा को॥ B42॥

वंशी

यह को है, कहाँ को, न जानिये, चीन्हिये नित्तहि मो मग घेरत है।
ब्रज मैं यह रीति कुरीति चली, यह न्याउ न कोऊ निबेरत है।
नख ते सिख लौं तन ताकि रहै, एजू, ऐसे कहा कोऊ हेरत है।
मुरली में ह्वै नाम सुनाय, सखी, मोहिं राधिका राधिका टेरत है॥ B43॥

---

42 Bharatpur1 f. 160r (64), Granthāvalī B11, Sudhāsar [S_1 f. 260rv (1), S_3 f. 136v (71), S_4 f. 59v-60r (77), S_7 f. 188v-9r (16)], Ṭhākur-satsaī (Ṭ) f. 2r (16), Vrindaban1 f. 12v (10/75) The Sudhāsar presents this poem within the description of 'Braj mahimā' and introduces it as 'jūvā khel'. 43 Granthāvalī 17, Ṭhasak 65.

42.1 कहैं] $B_1G_eS_1S_3S_7$, कहै B_1S_4ṬV$_1$ • वे कहैं] $G_eS_1S_3$Ṭ, वे कहै $B_1S_4S_7V_1$ • है] Σ, हिं B_1 • न] Σ, त S_4 • तो तनु] $B_1G_eS_1V_1$, ता ततु S_3, तो ततु S_4, ता ततु S_7, तो तन Ṭ **42.2** हेरें] Σ, हरै S_4, हेरै S_7 • हसै] $G_eS_4V_1$, हसैं $B_1S_1S_3S_7$Ṭ • बिलसैं] $B_1S_1S_3$Ṭ, बिलसै $G_eS_4S_7V_1$ • गहै] $G_eS_7V_1$, गहैं B_1**S**, गह Ṭ • बाँह] B_1G_eṬV$_1$, बाहैं $S_1S_3S_7$, बाहै S_4 • चाहै] $G_eS_4S_7$ṬV$_1$, चाहैं $B_1S_1S_3$ • उवा] Σ, ऊवा B_1S_1 **42.3** गौरि] B_1, गोरी $G_eS_3S_4S_7V_1$, गोर Ṭ • गिरीस] Σ, गिरास S_4 • सु होंस] B_1, सुरेस $G_eS_1S_3S_7$Ṭ, सरेसु S_4, सुरोस V_1 • लखैं सुनैं] $B_1G_eS_1$, लषै सूनै $S_3S_4S_7$ṬV$_1$ • सोरहु] $B_1G_eS_1$, सोर है S_3S_7Ṭ, सोरहूं S_4V_1 **42.4** सौं] B_1G_eṬV$_1$, °हि **S** • दुहूँ] $B_1G_eS_4$ṬV$_1$, दुहुँ S_1, दुहि S_3S_7
43.4 है] G_e, हैं Ṭ$_e$

42.1 ऐसी न वैसी neither like this nor like that; तो [tava] poss. pron. reg. your; तनु [S] m. body; बांका [vaṅku-] adj. 'bent' beautiful; तो तनु बांका Br. (even) your body is crooked (i.e. how can then your mind be staright?) **42.2** बिलसना [vilasati] v.i. to enjoy oneself, to take delight (in); पै conj. but; उव- (उगना) [cf. udaya-, udgāti] reg. v.i. (heavenly body) to rise; चंदउवा [cf. candrodaya-, H candovā] reg. m. moonrise. **42.4** बिगड़ना [vighaṭate x vigraha-] v.i. 1. to deteriorate (the matter between Radha and Krishna); 2. (Radha) to grow angry with; (This secondary meaning cannot be missed by the reader but because of the masculine perfective ending it cannot be a primary one.) बगरना reg. v.i. to be spread; अगर- [agra-] reg. v.i. to go forward, to progress; झगरो जुवा को Br. the row over the gamble (played at wedding). **43.2** यह रीति कुरीति चली this custom has been on as a bad custom; निबेर- [cf. cf. nivṛta-] Br. v.t. to settle (this issue).

*चीन्हत नाहिनै, को है गुविंद, कहाँ को गुपाल, कहाँ को कन्हाई।
एक अहीर बजावत बाँसुरी, सो सुनि काल्हि हौं देखन धाई। 2
ठाकुर, तामैं अमारग कौन है, तौन कहौ हम सों समझाई।
चारहू ओर तें, काहे ब, रे, तुम मोहिं लुवाभुवा लै भई, माई॥ B44॥ 4

*देह मेरी छूटै, पै न छूटै मोह मोहन सौं, 1
खूटै गुर लोग, टूटै सब ही सौं रसु री।
चाहौ कहौ कुलटा, कलंकनी कुनारी कहौ, 2
चाहौ कहौ मानस है, चाहौ कहौ पसु री।
ठाकुर कहत, तेरो सुनह सिखायौ कौन, 3
तैं ही तौ बिचारि, कछ्छ मेरो रह्यौ बसु री।
नाम बस्यौ रसना मैं, अंतर सरूप बस्यौ, 4

---

44 Bharatpur1 f. 158rv (51), Granthāvalī 26, Sudhāsar [S_2 11r (9), S_7 45v (29/431)], Vrindaban1 f. 4r (7/20). 45 Bharatpur1 f. 163r (81), Granthāvalī 27, Sudhāsar [S_1 f. 280r-281v (9), S_2 f. 59r (-/63), S_3 f. 154rv (161), S_4 f. 81v (171), S_7 f. 199rv (26)], Ṭhākur-satsaī (Ṭ) f. 3rv (24), Vrindaban1 f. 2r (8/8). The Sudhāsar presents this poem within the description of 'Braj mahimā'.

44.1 गुविंद] Σ, गोबिंद S_7 • कहाँ] G_e**S**, कहा B_1V_1 • कहाँ] G_e**S**, कहा B_1V_1 **44.2** हौं] Σ, हौ V_1 **44.3** तामें] B_1**S**, यामैं G_e, यामै V_1 • अमारग] Σ, अमारघ V_1 • है] $G_e S_2 V_1$, हैं B_1 • तौन] $B_1 G_e V_1$, सोन **S** • सों] G_e**S**, सूँ B_1, सो V_1 **44.4** तें] $B_1 G_e$, ते **S**V_1 • ब रे] Σ, बुरौ S_7 • मोहिं] Σ, मान S_7 • लुवाँभुवाँ लै] $B_1 G_e V_1$, भया सै S_7, लुवाभुया लै S_2 • भई] $B_1 S_2 V_1$, भई मोरे S_7, भईं G_e **45.1** छूटै] $B_1 G_e S_1$ṬV_1, छूटौ $S_2 S_3 S_7$, खूट्यौ S_4 • पै] Σ, पैं S_2 • छूटै] $B_1 G_e S_1$ṬV_1, छूटौ **S** • खूटै] $B_1 G_e S_1 V_1$, छूटै $S_2 S_3 S_4$Ṭ, छूटौ S_7 • गुर] Σ, गुरु $B_1 S_3$ • टूटै] $B_1 G_e S_1 S_3$ṬV_1, टूटैं S_2, टटैं S_4, टूटौ S_7 • सब] Σ, सभ Ṭ • रसु] Σ, रस S_3Ṭ **45.2** चाहौ] Σ, चाहौं S_2 • कहौ] Σ, कहों S_4 • कुनारी] B_1**S**Ṭ, कुनारि $G_e V_1$, उतारी S_4 • कहौ] Σ, कहौं S_2 • चाहौ] G_e**S**Ṭ, चाहै B_1, ⟨च⟩ (unm.) V_1 **45.3** ठाकुर कहत] G_e**S**Ṭ, ठा॰ B_1, ठाकुर कहैत V_1 • तेरो] B_1^{pc}**S**ṬV_1, ⟨मे⟩रौ B_1^{ac}, तो सों G_e • सुनह] $B_1 S_2 S_7 V_1$, सिखहि G_e, सुनहि $S_1 S_3 S_4$Ṭ • सिखायौ] Σ, सिया⟨खो⟩ Ṭ • बिचारि] $S_2 S_4 V_1$, बिचार $B_1 G_e$**S**Ṭ • कछ्छ] $B_1 G_e S_1$Ṭ, कछु **S**V_1

44.3 तौन pron. Br. Bund. that. **44.4** बुरौ (बुराई) var. Br. m. disgrace; लुवाभुवा Bund. f. gossip, slander; लुवाभुवा लेना idiom. to gossip, to slander; भईं var. v.i. pl. Br. were; माई f. voc. my friend. **45.1** खूंटना [*khunṭati] v.i. to be over, to break up (relationship); गुर [guru-] reg. adj. elder. **45.2** कुलटा [S] f. a promiscuous woman. **45.3** तेरो pron. Br. your (teaching); सुनह (सुनेगा) [śṛṇoti] reg. v.t. fut. (who) will listen to; तैं (तू) pron. reg. you.

आँखिन मैं छबि बसी, कानन मैं बँसुरी॥ B45॥

1 जिन बलबीरहि बिलोक्यो है न, बीर, ते चहैं
सो कहैं, बाल-कुटिलाई मन माखैं ना।
2 ठाकुर बकै, न कुल-काज बाजि आडे, ब्रज-
राज साज मोही, काज लाजहूँ ते राखैं ना।
3 पीत पट, कुंडल, लकुट, बनमाल धरें
बाँसुरि बजावनि बनक बर नाखैं ना।
4 भाखैं साँच, संगम न राखैं, आवैं मरी, स्याम-
रंग-रस-चाखैं आन अब अभिलाखैं ना॥ B46॥

विरह

दिन बीसक तीसक तें यहि खोर ह्वै धेनु उबेरतु ही नहियाँ।
2 फिर कुंज के भौन बजाइकै बाँसुरि प्यारी कों टेरतु ही नहियाँ।
कबि ठाकुर, सोच इतो चित को, इत को पग फेरतु ही नहियाँ।

---

46 Śṛṅgār-sudhākar (D_e) p. 371 (Pūrvānurāg 13). 47 Granthāvalī 68, Śatak 100, Ṭhasak 83.

45.4 रसना] Σ, रसन S_2 • अंतर] B_1G_eSṬ, अंता (unm.) S_4, अंत (unm.) V_1 • सरूप बस्यौ] Σ, स्वरूप बस्यौ S_1, बस्यौ है कान्ह S_7 • आँखिन] B_1G_eṬV_1, नेंनन **S**, नैन (unm.) S_4 • छबि] $B_1G_eS_1S_7V_1$, छबी S_2S_4, छब S_1Ṭ • बँसुरी] B_1^{pc}Σ, ⟨च⟩सुरी B_1^{ac} **47.1** तें] G_e, ते $Ś_e$$Ṭ_e$

46.1 जिन … न Br. those who have not seen Krishna; बलवीर [S] m. 'Balarāma's brother' Krishna; बीर [vīra-] m. f. voc. Br. o my companion; ते… कहैं may say whatever they want; कुटिलाई f. crookedness; बाल-कुटिलाई children's mischief; माखना v.i. to be angry; माखैं न reg. people are not angry. **46.2** ठाकुर बकै Ṭhākur says; कुल-काज [kula-kārya-] m. the observance followed by the family; बाजि (बाधा) [S] f. obstacle; न आडे reg. hinders me; साज [sajya-, P sāz] m. decoration (for me); काज [kārya-] m. (would not he protect my) work (and honour); ते राखैं ना Br. will he not protect (my goal and good reputation)? **46.3** कुंडल [S] m. large earring; लकुट [S] m. staff, club; बनक [P] Br. f. attire, decoration; नाखैं ना [cf. naṣṭa-] Br. v.t. (pres./subj.) I am not going to throw away; (or: won't he throw them away in order to come)? **46.4** भाखैं साँच Br. I am telling the truth; संगम 1. [saṃgopana-] m. 'hiding completely' deceit 2. [S] m. companionship; संगम न राखैं Br. 1. I am not deceiving you; 2. won't he protect me of deceit?; 3. won't he protect our companionship? मरी [perf. of H marnā] adj. wretched (slanderers); आवैं मरी Br. 1. I am dying (for Krishna); 2. even if wretched slanderers come; अभिलाख- [cf. abhilāṣā-] poet. v.t. to desire. **47.1** खोर [*khora-] Br. f. lane, alley; उबेरना Bund. v.t. to lead to graze.

इहि ओर सनेह की आँखिन सों अब तौ हरि हेरतु ही नहियाँ॥ B47॥

जा दिन जान लगे परदेस कौं, रौंदि हियो छतिया पै गली करी।
औध की आस बताइ दगा करि, राखि गए फिर स्वाँस चली करी।
ठाकुर, आप महा सुख लूटत, बावरी सी बृषभानलली करी।
सोहत है तुमकों सबही सु भले जू भले, लला, आपु भली करी॥ B48॥

*बृंदा सी बृंद अनेक छलीं, तहँ गूजरी नेह सों को अँग टोहै।
भौंर की नाव भयो मन ज्यौं, अब जानि परी बल ही जग जोहै।
ठाकुर, वे ब्रज-ठाकुर हैं, सु बनी न बनी उनकों सब सोहै।
मीर बडे बडे जात बहे, तहँ ढोलिये पार लगावत को है॥ B49॥

कहिबे की कछू न, कहा कहिये, मग जोवत जोवत ज्वै गयो री।
उन तोरत बार न लाई कछू, तन तें बृथा जोवन ख्वै गयो री।
कहि ठाकुर, कूबरी के बस ह्वै रस मैं बिसासी बिस ब्वै गयो री।

---

48 Granthāvalī 30, Śatak 20, Ṭhasak 75. 49 Granthāvalī 36, Ṭhasak 156, Ṭhasak 'Jīvancarit' (Ṭ$_e^j$) p. 5. 50 Granthāvalī 32, Śatak 89, Sundarītilak (C$_e$) p. 44 (258), Bābūrāmdīn (U$_e$) 627, Ṭhasak 168, Miśrabandhu Vinod (V$_e$) pp. 731–2.

47.4 इहि] Ś$_e$, यहि G$_e$Ṭ$_e$ • हरि] Ś$_e$Ṭ$_e$, हेरि G$_e$ **48.2** करी] G$_e$Ś$_e$, कर Ṭ$_e$ **48.3** आप] G$_e$Ṭ$_e$, आइ Ś$_e$ **48.4** तुमकों] G$_e$, तुमको Ś$_e$Ṭ$_e$ • आपु] G$_e$Ṭ$_e$, आजु Ś$_e$ **50.1** कहिबे की कछू न] C$_e$U$_e$V$_e$, कहा कहिये (unm.) G$_e$, का कहिये (unm.) Ś$_e$Ṭ$_e$ • कहा कहिये] C$_e$U$_e$V$_e$, कहिबे की नहीं **E** • ज्वै] C$_e$U$_e$V$_e$, जो **E** • री] C$_e$U$_e$V$_e$, है **E** **50.2** तें] U$_e$**E**, ते C$_e$V$_e$ • जोवन] Σ, जीवन U$_e$ • ख्वै] C$_e$U$_e$V$_e$, खो **E** • री] C$_e$U$_e$V$_e$, है **E** **50.3** कहि] **E**, कबि C$_e$U$_e$V$_e$ • बिसासी बिष] C$_e$U$_e$, बिस बावरो **E**, बिसवासी बिसै V$_e$ • ब्वै] C$_e$U$_e$, बो **E**, *om.* V$_e$ • री] C$_e$U$_e$V$_e$, है **E**

48.1 रौंदना v.t. to crush; छतिया पै गली करी Br. you made your way over her chest. **48.2** दग़ा [P] f. deceit. **48.3** बावरी ... करी Br. you made Radha like a mad woman. **48.4** सु भले जू भले Br. so you are good indeed. **49.1** वृंदा [S] f. Radha; बृंद poet. m. (obl.) in Vrindaban; गूजरी [gurjarī-] f. cowherd-woman; टोहना [*ṭoh-] v.t. to grope; to search; अंग टोहै Br. 1. (can) touch his body; 2. (should) deliberate, ponder. **49.2** भौंर [bhramara-] m. whirlpool; बल ही जग जोहै Br. the world considers only the power. **49.3** बनी न बनी reg. be it a good matter or not; उनकों सब सोहै Br. everything goes well with Krishna. **49.4** मीर m. leader; ढोलिया m. drummer (insignificant man); पार लगाना idiom. to carry across. **50.1** कहिबे की कछू ना it is not something to tell; मग जोवत जोवत ज्वै गयो idiom. Br. I do not have the strength to wait for him any more (cf. H khāte khāte khā cukā). **50.2** उन (उन्होंने) pron. ag. Br. he (Krishna); तोरत [troṭayati] Br. v.t. imperf. (in) breaking it off (with me); बार न लाई कछू Br. did not delay at all. **50.3** बावरो var. adj. mad (Krishna); रस में विष बोना idiom. 'to throw venom in the juice' to spoil.

मनमोहन को हिलिबो-मिलिबो दिन चारि की चांदनी ह्वै गयो री॥ B50॥

*साँचे करार करे हमसों, हम ताहू पै साँची न मानती थीं।
अरु बावन ह्वै कै छल्यौ बलि कौं, तब ते मन मैं डर आनती थीं।
कहि ठाकुर, रीझ रहीं अखियाँ, उन सों मिलिकै सुख मानती थीं।
तुम रावरे राम के राज करो, हम तौ धरे बासन जानती थीं॥ B51॥

---

51 Bharatpur1 f. 163rv (84), Datiya2 f. 2v (15), Granthāvalī 69, Sudhāsar [S_1 f. 301rv (46), S_2 f. 60v (-/69), S_4 f. 98r (257), S_7 f. 208v (93)], Śatak 83, Ṭhasak 166, Vrindaban1 f. 7v (3/41), Yājñik. The Sudhāsar presents this poem within the 'uddhava kau braj mẽ āyabau' (Uddhava's coming to Braj) subsection of the 'Brajrasrīti' section.

50.4 दिन] Σ, दिना V_e • चारि की] V_e, चारिक **E**, चारि को U_e, चारि कै C_e • चांदनी] $C_eU_eV_e$, चैत सो **E** • ह्वै] $C_eU_eV_e$, हो **E** • री] $C_eU_eV_e$, है **E** **51.1** साँचे करार करे] Σ, साँची करारैं करीं **E** • ताहू पै] Σ, तौ तऊ **E** • साँची] $B_1D_2SY_e$, नेकु **E**, सीची V_1 • मानती] Σ, मानतती (dittography) S_4 • थीं] S_1Y_e, थी B_1V_1, तीं D_2**E**, ती S_2S_7 **51.2** अरु] $B_1D_2S_2S_4S_7V_1$, उन **E**, अर S_1 • बावन] $B_1D_2S_1$, बामन **E**$S_2S_4S_7V_1$, बाचन V_1 • ह्वै] Σ, हो D_2 • कै छल्यौ बलि कौं] Σ, बलि जाइ छले **E** • तब ते मन मैं डर आनती] Σ, हम सो बतियाँ पहिचानती **E** • मैं] B_1, मै Σ • डर] SY_e, उर $B_1D_2V_1$ • थीं] S_1Y_e, थी B_1V_1, तीं D_2**E**, ती S_2S_7 **51.3** कहि] Σ, कबि **E** • रीझि रहीं] S_1, रीझि रही $B_1S_2Y_e$, रीझ रहीं D_2, रीझ रही S_4S_7, बीधि गईं **E**, हाथ चलै गहियै यह जीभ चलै न बनै गरीकि रही (hyperm.) V_1 • उन] Σ, तिन **E** • मिल] **E**$S_1S_2S_7V_1$, मिलि $B_1D_2S_4$ • मानती] B_1**E**$S_1S_7V_1$, सानतीं D_2, सोनती S_2S_4 • थीं] S_1Y_e, थी B_1V_1, तीं D_2**E**, ती S_2S_7 **51.4** रावरे] Σ, तौ अब **E** • के] Σ, को S_2 • राज] Σ, काज S_7 • धरे] Σ, घरे $Ś_e$ • बासन] $B_1D_2S_1S_4S_7Ś_e$, बसन $G_eS_2V_1Y_e$ • थीं] S_1Y_e, थी B_1V_1, तीं D_2**E**, ती $S_2S_4S_7$

50.4 हिलना-मिलना v.i. to become intimate with; दिन चारिक चैत var. idiom. Br. the four days of the Chaitra month (short time that passes fast. Cf. 'cār din kī cāṃdnī' and 'cait kī cāṃdnī'); हो var. [cf. Br. hvai] v.i. (Khaṛī Bolī). **51.1** क़रार [A] m. agreement, engagement; करे [karoti] v.t. (Br. perf. used as past conditional) If he had made; तीं (थीं) var. Bund. v.i. were. **51.2** उर आन- idiom. Br. to clasp to the heart; to embrace. **51.2** बावन (वामन) [S] m. dwarf (avatar); **51.3** बीध- var. [*vibadhyate Br. bījh-] reg. v.i. to be entangled; गरीकि var. for a moment. **51.4** राम के राज करना 1. idiom. to live happily; 2. worship him as your king Rama; धरे बासन जानना 1. idiom. to know well; to be familiar with (cf. H rakhe bartan jānnā); 2. we know of his stealing of our clothes (or: pots i.e. of butter).

उद्धव प्रसंग

जौ चाहौ तौ मेल कै फुलेल डारौ चोटिन मैं, 1
चाहौ तौ बनावो जटा कुटिल लटन के।
चाहौ तजौ भूषन, बिभूति कों लगावो अंग, 2
ओढौ मृगचर्म, त्यागो ओढवो पटन के।
ठाकुर कहत, तुम काहे कौं झुकौ, री बाम, 3
हम तौ करत काम स्याम के रटन के।
जैसी उन कही तैसी तुम सैं कही है आन, 4
नातर कहावैं कहा चाकर भटन के॥ B52॥

आनि जुरीं बिजुरी सी, कितेक कितेकहू प्रेम-कथा रस बाँची।
ऊधो सुनो तुम, ऊधो सुनो तुम, ऊधो सुनो तुम, या धुनि माँची। 2

52 Datiya2 f. 3rv (26). The manuscript introduces the poem as 'ūdhau bacana gopina prati' (Uddhava's words towards the cowherd women). 53 Datiya2 f. 3v (29), Granthāvalī 38, Sudhāsar [S_1 f. 307rv (74), S_2 f. 62r (-/72), S_3 f. 177r (277), S_5 f. 205r (7), S_7 f. 212v (128)], Ṭhākur-satsaī (Ṭ) f. 5r (44), Ṭhasak 184. • The Sudhāsar ($S_1S_5S_7$) presents this poem within the 'uddhava kī ukti ukti lāl prati' (Uddhava's words to Krishna) subsection of the 'Brajrasrīti' section. D_2 introduces the poem as 'ūdhau bacana śrīkṛsṇa prati. gopina kī kathā.' (Uddhava reports to Krishna the words of the Gopis.)

52.1 जौ चाहौ] *em.* चाहौ (unm.) D_2 • तौ बनावो] *em.* बनावो (unm.) D_2 • **52.2** ओ-ढौ] *conj.* औडौ D_2 • ओढवो] *conj.* वोढवो D_2 **52.3** तुम] D_2^{pc}, तु (unm.) D_2^{ac} • **53.1** आंनि] $S_1S_2S_5$, आन $D_2S_3S_7$, आइ G_eṬ, आय $Ṭ_e$ • जुरीं] D_2**E**S_1, जुरी **SṬ** • कि-तेक कितेकहू] $D_2S_1S_3S_5$, कितेकउ **E**, कितेकहूं S_2, कितीक कितीकन S_7Ṭ • प्रेम] D_2**SṬ**, प्रेम प्रवाह **E**S_2 • रस] D_2**S**, तिन **E**, उन Ṭ **53.2** सुनो] D_2**E**S_3S_7Ṭ, सुनौं $S_1S_2S_5$ • सुनो तुम या] Σ, सुनौ तुनौ तुम या (dittography) S_2 • धुनि] Σ, धुन Ṭ

52.1 जौ चाहौ Br. if you want (I don't mind if you); फुलेल [*phullataila-] m. scented oil; बनावो जटा reg. make your hair matted, put your hair in dreadlocks; लट [cf. laṭṭa-] m. lock of hair; tangled hair. **52.2** ओढना [oḍh-] v.t. to wrap. **52.3** झुकना [*jhukkati] v.i. to bend down; to feel compelled; रटना [*raṭyati] v.i. to repeat. **52.4** नातर (नहीं तो) [cf. na tarhi] Br. conj. otherwise; कहावैं (कहलाते हैं) Br. v.i. pres. pl. (used as sing.) I am called; भटन के चाकर Br. servant of the lords. **53.1** जुड़ना v.i. to assemble; आनि जुरीं Br. They (i.e. the cowherd-women) have assembled; बिजुरी सी Br. (beautifully and fast) like lightning; कितेकहूं (कितना भी) Br. adj. 'no matter how many' many; कितेक कितेकहू Br. adj. (?) very many; बाँची Br. 1. v.t. perf. (the gopīs) read through; 2. v.t. perf. opted for, choose; 3. v.i. perf. remained (in them); तिन var. Br. pron. obl. they (the gopīs) ; कथा तिन बाँची var. Br. they read through (etc.). **53.2** या धुनि माँची Br. they stirred up this noise.

ठाकुर, कौन सकै कहि कै जो बियोग-कथा गिरा बांचिकै नाँची।
फेरि हमैं इतनी कहितै बनी, साँची है, साँची है, साँची है, साँची॥ B53॥

*जैसई लाल बडे रिझवार हैं, वैसई संग मिलो अनमोलो।
चंदमुखी तजि राधे सी बामहिं कूबरी सों हित मानि कै बोलो।
ठाकुर, तो सों कहा कहियै, चुपकै रहियै गहि कै अनबोलो।
आँधरे साहब के घर में दमरी को हिसाब हजारा को जोलो॥ B54॥

*खेत-कुटुंब तें लीन्ही उखारि, निबेरि निबेरि कै स्वाद नवीनी।

---

54 Granthāvalī 31, Ṭhākur-satsaī (Ṭ) f. 5r (43), Ṭhasak 178. 55 Datiya2 f. 2v (18), Granthāvalī 39, Sudhāsar [S_1 f. 302rv (51), S_2 ff. 60v-61r (-/70b), S_3 f. 173v (259), S_4 f. 101v (272), S_7 f. 210r (108)], Ṭhasak 153, Vrindaban1 f. 8v (9/47), Vrindaban3 f. 30r, Yājñik. • The Sudhāsar presents this poem within the 'uddhava kau braj mẽ āyabau' (Uddhava's coming to Braj) subsection of the 'Brajrasrīti' section.

53.3 कौन] Σ, कासो Ṭ • सकै] **S**, सों का D_2**E**, कहा Ṭ • कहि कै] **S**, कहिये D_2**E**Ṭ • जो] $D_2S_1S_3S_5$, गति **E**, जे S_2S_7, *om.* (unm.) Ṭ • बियोग] D_2**S**, देखिकै **E**, प्रेम (unm.) Ṭ • कथा] D_2Ṭ, मेरी **E**, बिथा **S** • गिरा] D_2**S**, गीरा S_2, गर Ṭ • बांचिकै] D_2**S**, तहँ **E**, नांधके Ṭ **53.4** फेरि हमैं] S_2, फेर हमैं D_2**S**Ṭ^{pc}, प्रेर* हमै Ṭ^{ac}, हाँ **E** • इतनी] Σ, इतनो Ṭ • कहितै बनी] D_2**S**, कहनेई परी हमैं **E**, *om.* (unm.) S_2, कहनो पर्‌यो Ṭ • साँची है] S_7^{pc}Σ, *om.* (unm.) S_7^{ac} • है] D_2**E**$S_2S_3S_7$, हौ S_1, हौं S_5, तू Ṭ • है] D_2**E**$S_2S_3S_7$, हौ S_1, हौं S_5, तू Ṭ • है] D_2**E**$S_2S_3S_7$, हौ S_1, हौं S_5, तू Ṭ **54.1** जैसई] **E**, *om.* Ṭ • लाल] **E**, कांन्ह Ṭ • बडे] **E**, भले Ṭ • हैं] **E**, है जू और Ṭ • वैसई] **E**, तैसोई Ṭ • संग] **E**, साथ Ṭ • मिलो] **E**, जुरो Ṭ **54.2** तजि] **E**, तजी Ṭ • °हिं] **E**, और (unm.) Ṭ • मानि कै बोलो] **E**, कीनो अडोलो Ṭ **54.3** तो] **E**, का Ṭ • कहियै] **E**, कहीए Ṭ • चुपकै रहियै गहि कै] **E**, मन मै यह आवत ह्वै Ṭ **54.4** हजारा] **E**, हजार Ṭ • जोलो] G_e, भोलो Ṭ, जो लौं Ṭ$_e$ **55.1** कुटुंब] Σ, कुटम V_3 • तें] D_2**E**S_1, तै **S**V_1V_3 • लीन्ही] D_2**E**, लीनी **S**$V_1V_3Y_e$ • उखारि] **E**S_1, उषार $D_2S_3S_7$, उषारी S_2, दुषारि S_4, उघारि V_1Y_e, ऊषारि V_3 • निबेरि निबेरि] $V_1V_3Y_e$, निबेर निबेर D_2**S**, नबेर नबेर **E**, निबेरि निबेरी S_2 • नवीनी] Σ, °नि भीनी V_3

53.3 कौन सकै कहि कै Br. emph. (?) who can tell; गिरा [S] f. 'Sarasvatī' speech, voice; नाँची v.i. perf. 'danced around' turned around (in dizziness and fell); **54.1** रिझवार Br. adj. m. 'delighted' lover; संग अनमोलो Br. valuable company. **54.2** राधे f. voc. (used as dir., poet.) Radha; बाम [vāmā-] Br. f. woman; हित [S] 1. adj. proper; 2. m. love; बोलो v.t. perf. Br. Bund. (he) spoke. **54.3** अनबोलो Br. m. silence. **54.4** दमड़ी [dramma- (fr. Gr)] f. a coin of 1/8 Paisa, a farthing; जोलो reg. m. difference; भोलो (भूल) var. reg. (?) m. mistake; दमरी...जोलो idiom. Br. (there is) a difference of thousands in an account of farthings. **55.1** उघाड़ना apa. [udghāṭayati] v.t. to uncover, to reveal; निबेड़ना [cf. nirvartate] v.t. to sort, select; नबीन- (नवीन) 1. [S] Br. adj. new (in taste); निबेरि...नवीनीं Br. selecting the ones that are new in taste.

फेरि दुरे दुरे चाखीं अघाय, रुचे न रुचे की जनार न दीनी। 2
ठाकुर, ऊधौ, सुनौ सुख पाय कै गोपिन की या कथा रस भीनी।
खाईं कछू, बगराईं कछू, हरि, हाइ, गुलाम की गाजरैं कीनी॥ B55॥ 4

*धिक कान जे आन की बात सुनैं, इहाँ एकही रंग रह्यो रँगि डोरो।

---

56 Bharatpur5 f. 10r-v, Bharatpur10 f. 1v, Datiya2 f. 3r (21), Granthāvalī 41, Jaipur1 ff. 2v-3r (8), Marwar5 f. 31r (1), Śatak 2, Sudhāsar [S_1 f. 290rv (10), S_2 f. 59v (-/64), S_4 f. 90r (219), S_7 f. 204r (53)], Ṭhākur-satsaī (Ṭ) f. 5r (40), Ṭhasak 138, Udaipur 127r (9), Bābūrāmdīn (U_e) 187, Vrindaban1 f. 2v (12/12), Vrindaban3 f. 30rv (7), Z_1 ff. 31v, 32v (25), Yājñik. • The Sudhāsar presents this poem within the 'uddhava kau braj mẽ āyabau' (Uddhava's coming to Braj) subsection of the 'Brajrasrīti' section.

55.2 फेरि $S_4V_1V_3$, फेर D_2**E**$S_1S_3S_7$, फेरी S_2 • दुरे दुरे] **E**$S_2S_3V_3$, दुरैं दुरैं D_2, दुरैं दुरै S_1V_1, दुरै डरै S_4, दुरै दूरै S_7 • चाखीं] D_2S_1, खाईं **E**, चाषी $S_2S_4S_7V_1$, चाखि S_3, चषीं V_3, चाबी Y_e • रुचे न रुचे] D_2**S**V_1Y_e, रुचीं न रुचीं **E**, रुची न रुची V_3 • की] Σ, कि G_e • जनार] D_2**S**V_1, जनाय **E**, जनाव S_3, जनावनि V_3, जनाइ Y_e • न] Σ, *om.* V_3 **55.3** ऊधौ] D_2**S**V_1Y_e, यों **E**, यौ V_3 • सुनौ] $D_2S_3S_4S_7V_1Y_e$, कहतीं **E**V_3, सुनौं S_1S_2 • सुख पाय] D_2**S**V_1Y_e, ब्रजबाल **E**, ब्रिजबालि V_3 • कै] D_2**S**V_1Y_e, सो **E**, सु V_3 • गोपिन की] D_2**S**V_1Y_e, ऊधो सुनो **E**V_3 • या] Σ, य (unm.) V_3 **55.4** खाईं] **E**S_1, षांई D_2, खाई **S**V_1V_3 • बगराईं] **E**S_1V_3, बगरांई D_2, बगराई **S**V_1• कछू] Σ, कछु V_1• हाइ] Σ, गोपी **E** • गुलाम] Σ, गुलान S_2 • की] Σ, कीं D_2 • गाजरैं] D_2**E**S_1V_1, गाजरै **S**, गजरै V_3 **56.1** धिक] (unm.) B_5**E**$J_1M_5S_7$, --- B_{10}, धृक (unm.) $D_2S_1S_2$, धुक (unm.) S_4, ध्रिग (unm.) ṬV_1Y_e, *om.* UU_eZ_1, धकि (unm.) V_3 • कान] Σ, तान D_2, वे कान्ह (unm.) V_3 • जे] $B_5D_2S_1V_1Y_e$, --- B_{10}, जो **E**$J_1M_5S_2$Ṭ, जि S_7, °न UU_eZ_1, ते V_3 • आन की] $B_5B_{10}D_2J_1M_5$**S**V_1Y_e, दूसरी **E**ṬV_3, दूसरौ UU_eZ_1 • बात] D_2^{pc}**ES**V_1Y_e, तान B_5B_{10}Ṭ, बातु D_2^{ac}, बांनि J_1V_3, बान M_5, नाम UU_eZ_1 • सुनैं] B_5B_{10}**E**$J_1S_1S_2UY_e$, सुनै $D_2M_5S_4S_7$Ṭ$U_eV_1V_3$, सुनौ Z_1 • इहां] J_1, रचि B_5, उर B_{10}, अरु D_2, अब **E**, ईह M_5, यहाँ **S**, और Ṭ, नही UU_e, ह्या (unm.) V_1Y_e, औरु V_3, नहि Z_1 • एकही] Σ, ये कहीं J_1, येकहि Z_1 • रंग] Σ, रँगा (unm.) B_{10} • रह्यौ] J_1**S**$UV_1V_3Y_e$, रँग्यौ $B_5B_{10}D_2U_e$, रहो **E**Z_1, रयो M_5, रहे Ṭ • रँगि] $J_1S_4V_3$, रुचि B_5B_{10}, रंग $D_2M_5S_1S_7U$, मिलि **E**, रगी S_2, यह U_e, रग V_1Y_e, रस Z_1Ṭ • डोरो] Σ, डोरौं B_{10}

55.2 दुरना v.i. to lie hidden; रुचे न रुचे की (बात) (the matter of) whether he liked them or not; जनार (जानकारी) [cf. H jānnā] reg. f. news, notice; जनाय न दीनी var. he did not tell anyone; **55.3** सुख पाय कै Br. with delight (ironic!); ब्रजबाल सो var. that woman of Braj. **55.4** गाजर [gārjara-] f. carrot (Vaishnavas do not eat it); गुलाम की गाजर 1. slave's carrot (i.e. something insignificant; passers-by tend to steal carrot from a low-caste man's field); 2. a carrot stolen by a slave (and eaten in haste); बगराना v.t. to scatter. **56.1** डोरा m. thread, string (cf. H ḍorā milanā 'to become similar').

दूसरो नाम कदाचि कढै तौ हलाहल मैं रसना गहि बोरो।
ठाकुर, एक ही टेक पढी, ब्रजबालन को जु सुभाव है भोरो।
ऊधो जू, वे अँखियाँ जरि जाहु जे साँवरो छाँडि तकैं कोऊ गोरो॥ B56॥

बन जाइ बने, बिगरे बिगरे, भरमाए न काहू कहे लचिये।

---

57 Granthāvalī 42, Śatak 99, Ṭhasak 172.

56.2 दूसरो] D_2**E**$J_1S_1S_2S_4$ṬV_1Y_e, और कौं $B_5B_{10}M_5V_3$, दूसरे S_7, कजात (unm.) U, धो-खेहु दूसरो U_e, जौ कहु दूसरौ Z_1 • नाम] $B_{10}D_2$**ES**Ṭ$U_eV_1V_3Y_eZ_1$, नाउ B_5, आंकं J_1, नाव M_5, बाम S_1, क⟨इ/दू⟩स U • कदाचि] $B_5B_{10}S_1S_2S_4V_3$, कदाच $D_2M_5S_7$Ṭ, कजात G_eṬ$_e$, कदात J_1, कुजात Ś$_e$, नांम UV_1Y_e, *om.* U_eZ_1 • कढै] $B_5B_{10}D_2$**E**$J_1M_5S_1S_2S_7$Ṭ$UU_eV_1V_3$, कढैं B_5B_{10}, कटै S_4, सुनौ Z_1 • तौ हलाहल] $B_5B_{10}J_1M_5S_1S_2S_7V_1V_3Y_e$, रसना $D_2UU_eZ_1$, रसना जो **E**, जौ हलाहल S_4, तु हलाहल Ṭ • मैं] J_1**S**Y_e, में B_5B_{10}, गहि कै $D_2Z_1^{pc}$, कहूँ G_eṬ$_e$, कहै Ś$_e$, गहिये U, मुख U_e, मे M_5ṬV_1V_3, गहि कौ Z_1^{ac} • रसना गहि] J_1M_5**S**V_1V_3, रसना यह B_5B_{10}Ṭ, तौ हलाह (unm.) D_2, तो हलाहल **E**, जु हलाहल UZ_1, काढि हलाहल U_e, रसना नहि Y_e • बोरो] Σ, बोरौं B_5B_{10} **56.3** ठाकुर] Σ, कहि ठाकुर, (unm.) $B_{10}Z_1$, कबि ठाकुर, (unm.) V_3 • एक ही टेक] D_2J_1**S**, दूसरी टेक B_5B_{10}, यों कहतीं **E**, प्रेम को नेम M_5, दूसरो नाम Ṭ, टेक न टारत U, चित्त की वृत्ति U_e, एक ही बानि V_1Y_e, कर जोरि V_3, ⟨टे⟩क न छूटत Z_1 • पढी] $J_1S_1S_2S_7V_1Y_e$, रही B_5^{ac}, नही B_5^{pc}, न⟨ही⟩ B_{10}, परी D_2, ब्रज° **E**, यही M_5U_e, पटी S_4, न जानती (unm.) Ṭ, कैसैंहु U, कह्यौ V_3, कैसहू Z_1 • ब्रज°] $B_5B_{10}D_2J_1M_5$**S**Ṭ$V_1V_3Y_e$, °बाल **E**, ऐसो U, हम U_e, एक Z_1 • °बालन कौं] $B_5B_{10}D_2$**S**Ṭ, सो ह्याँ बनिता° G_eṬ$_e$, °बासिन को J_1, नारीन को M_5, सु ह्याँ बनिता° Ś$_e$, सुभाव UZ_1, कैसे हूं टेक U_e, °नारन कौ V_1Y_e, °भांमिंनि कौ V_3 • जु] $B_5B_{10}J_1M_5S_1S_7$Ś$_e V_1V_3Y_e$, यो D_2, °न G_eṬ$_e$, जो S_2S_4, यह (unm.) Ṭ, पर्‌यौ U, तजैं U_e, परौ Z_1 • सुभाव] $B_5B_{10}J_1M_5$ **S**Ś$_e$Ṭ$V_1V_3Y_e$, सुभाइ D_2, को भाव G_eṬ$_e$, कछु U, नहीं U_e, जिय Z_1 • है] Σ, हैं B_{10}, *om.* U_eZ_1 • भोरो] D_2**E**J_1M_5**S**Ṭ$U_eV_1V_3Y_e$, भोरौं B_5B_{10}, ⟨भो/ओ⟩रौ U, मौरौ Z_1 **56.4** ऊधो जू] B_5D_2**ES**UV_3, उधौ जू (unm.) $B_{10}V_1$, ऊधव J_1, उधो जु (unm.) M_5, बावरी U_e, ऊधौ (unm.) Z_1Ṭ • वे] Σ, ये B_{10}, उवे (unm.) M_5, वै U • अँखियाँ] Σ, अषीयां M_5 • जरि] B_5B_{10}**E**$S_1S_2UV_1V_3$, जर $D_2M_5S_4S_7$Ṭ, ऊधव J_1, बावरी U_e, बर Z_1 • जाहु] $B_{10}M_5S_1U$, जाउ $B_5S_2S_4S_7$, जायँ **E**, जावु J_1, जाहिं U_eṬ, जाव $V_1V_3Y_e$, जांइ D_2Z_1 • जे] D_2S_7U, जो B_5**E**J_1S_1ṬU_e, रे M_5, वे S_2S_4, सो V_1Y_e, सु V_3, ते Z_1 • साँवरो] Σ, सोवरो J_1, स्याम कौ S_7 • छाँडि] B_5B_{10}**E**J_1**S**V_3, छोड $S_7M_5UZ_1$, छांड D_2Ṭ, छोड़ि U_e, ताकि V_1Y_e • तकैं] **E**S_7V_1, तकै $B_5J_1M_5S_1S_2S_4V_3$, ⟨त⟩कैं B_{10}, निहारतीं $D_2U_eZ_1$, निहारति U, लखै Ṭ • कोऊ] $B_5B_{10}J_1$**S**Ṭ$V_1V_3Y_e$, *om.* $D_2UU_eZ_1$, तन **E**, कोउं M_5 • गोरो] Σ, गोरौं B_5B_{10} **57.1** बिगरे बिगरे] G_eŚ$_e$, बिगरै बिगरे Ṭ$_e$ •

56.2 कदाचि (कदाचित) [S] adv. (if) ever. **56.3** टेक पढी they have learnt (only) one obstinate habit. **56.4** गोरो Br. (cf. Shiva is fair-complexioned). **57.1** बन जाइ बने Br. if something has [or: has to] become, let it become; बिगरे बिगरे if something has gone [or: has to go] wrong, let it go wrong; भरमा- Br. v.i. to be confused; काहू कहे Br. (to) what is said by anyone; लचना v.i. to bend, to yield.

जग आपनो रंग पसार, बिसार न औरन के रँग में रचिये। 2
कहि ठाकुर, या भवसागर में परि नेह कलंकन सों बचिये।
अब, ऊधो सुनो, यह प्रीत की रीत, जु काछिये काछ सुई नचिये॥ B57॥ 4

थिगरी न लगै, ऊधो, चित्त के चँदोवा फटे, 1
बिगरी न सुधरै सनेह-सरदन को।
आपनेई हाथ लै कै करत हवाल ऐसो, 2
कापै होनहार यों हलाल गरदन को।
ठाकुर कहत, हौं बिचार यौं बिचार देख्यौ, 3
बिरलो मिलै है जो सहाय दरदन को।
बैर प्रीति रीति जासौ जैसी जहाँ मानि लियो, 4
एक सी निबाहिबो है काम मरदन को॥ B58॥

*यों हीं लुभानी, पत्यानी लखे छबि, देखि डरानी नहीं रँग कारे।
ऐसी रँगी रति के रँग में, घर-बाहिर लोग सिखै सब हारे। 2

---

58 Granthāvalī 40, Śatak 91, Ṭhasak 135. 59 Granthāvalī 43, Śatak 101, Ṭhasak 181.

57.4 ऊधो] Ś$_e$Ṭ$_e$, उधो (unm.) G$_e$ **58.1** चित्त] Ś$_e$Ṭ$_e$, *om.* (unm.) G$_e$ • न सुधरै] G$_e$Ṭ$_e$, नहीं सुधरै (unm.) Ś$_e$ **58.2** होनहार] G$_e$Ṭ$_e$, होनिहार Ś$_e$ • यों] G$_e$Ṭ$_e$, यौं Ś$_e$ **58.4** लियो] G$_e$Ṭ$_e$, लिया Ś$_e$ • को] G$_e$Ṭ$_e$, का Ś$_e$ **59.1** हीं] Ś$_e$Ṭ$_e$, ही G$_e$ • लुभानी] Ś$_e$, लुभानो G$_e$Ṭ$_e$ • पत्यानी] Ś$_e$, पत्यानो G$_e$Ṭ$_e$ • डरानी] Ś$_e$, डरानो] G$_e$Ṭ$_e$

57.2 पसार [prasārayati] v.t. imp. spread! बिसार न (v.i. abs.) adv. not even by mistake. **57.3** नेह-कलंक Br. stain on one's love. **57.4** काछ [kakṣyā-, kakṣa-] m. dhoti; the end of a dhoti tucked in at the waist behind; काछ काछना idiom. 'to wear a dhoti' to play a role. सुई (वही) Br. pron. emph. that very, the same. **58.1** थिगरी (थिगली) Br. Bund. f. patch; चित्त के (the canopy) of mind; चंदवा [candrodaya-] m. 1. tester, canopy; 2. cloth; सर्द [P] adj. 1. cold (insensitive); 2. impotent. **58.2** लै कै Br. (you) taking (our neck); हवाल [A aḥvāl, pl. of ḥāl] poet. m. state, condition; कापै होनहार (किसपर होनेवाला है) Br. who is to suffer? हलाल [A, cf. H halālnā 'to cut'] m. 1. cutting; 2. fig. ill-treatment. **58.3** हौं यौं देख्यौ Br. I have come to see it in this way; बिचार बिचार having reflected on this idea; बिरला [virala-] adj. (a) rare (one). **58.4** बैर प्रीति रीति Br. the custom of enmity and love; काम मरदन को Br. it is a man's duty. **59.1** यों हीं adv. without any reason; ही var. [hṛdaya-] m. heart; पत्या- [pratyāyayati] Av. Br. v.t. to trust; ही लुभानो पत्यानो var. reg. my heart became infatuated and trusted; लखें Br. v.t. having seen; छबि रंग कारे Br. the beauty of the black colour (the colour of the poisonos snake and of the large black bee). **59.2** सिखें v.t. perf. obl. Br. having taught.

ठाकुर, ताको इहै फल पैयत, बासर-रैन अनंद बिसारे।
उधो जू, दोष तुम्हैं न उन्हैं, हम आपुही पांव पै पाथर पारे॥ B59॥

*वे सब जानती हीं उनकों, पर मोपै परी यह डीठ तिरीछी।
घैर सहो घरहाइन कौ, अरु बानी सही कछु तीर तें तीछी।
ठाकुर, वे हरि छाँडि गये अब, योंही बकैं बकबादिन छी छी।
ऊधो जू, दोष तुम्हैं न उन्हैं, हम लीन्ही है आपने हाथ ही बीछी॥ B60॥

*ऊधौ जू, भाग हमारे लटे, उनकी तौ घनी सुघरी उघरी है।
बाँह हमारे ही कंध तै खैंचि कै कूबरी कंध पै जाइ धरी है।
ठाकुर, या कहनावति और की साँचियै आजहू आनि परी है।
मारै चिरी कौं चिरी कहा, बीर, पै मीर सिकार की कारीगरी है॥ B61॥

60 Granthāvalī 44, Śatak 102, Ṭhasak 179. 61 Bharatpur1 f. 157rv (45), Datiya2 f. 2r (12), Granthāvalī 45, Sudhāsar [S_1 f. 296v (26b), S_2 f. 60r (-/67), S_3 f. 168r (233), S_4 f. 95v (244b), S_7 f. 207r (81)], Ṭhākur-satsaī (Ṭ) f. 5r (41), Vrindaban1 f. 3r (1/14). The Sudhāsar presents the poem within the description of 'Braj mahimā'.

59.4 उधो] G_e, ऊधो Ś$_e$Ṭ$_e$ **60.1** हीं] Ś$_e$, तीं G_eṬ$_e$ **60.2** कौ] G_eṬ$_e$, की Ś$_e$ • **60.3** बकैं] Ś$_e$Ṭ$_e$, बकै G_e **61.1** ऊधौ] B_1D_2**S**Ṭ, उधौ (unm.) G_eV_1 • जू] Σ, जी Ṭ • भाग] $B_1D_2S_1S_3S_7V_1$Ṭ, भागि G_eS_4, भागी S_2 • उनकी] Σ, उनकौ Ṭ • तौ] Σ, तै S_2 • घनी] Σ, घरी Ṭ • उघरी] Σ, दुघरी S_4 • है] $B_1D_2G_eS_1S_3S_7V_1$, हैं S_2S_4 **61.2** बाँह] Σ, कंध Ṭ • ही] Σ, °ई D_2, तें Ṭ • कंध तै] Σ, खैंच के Ṭ • खैंचि] $B_1G_eS_1V_1$, ऐंच D_2, खैच $S_3S_4S_7$, बांहि सु Ṭ • जाइ] Σ, जाई V_1 • है] Σ, हैं S_4 **61.3** या] Σ, जो Ṭ • कहनावति] $S_1S_2S_3$, कहनावत $B_1D_2G_eS_7$ṬV_1, कहना बलि S_4 • साँचियै... आनि] Σ, उर हमारी सो आंन Ṭ • साँचियै] Σ, सांची सु D_2 • °हू] Σ, हीं D_2 • आनि] $G_eS_2S_4V_1$, जान D_2, आन $B_1S_1S_3S_7$ • है] Σ, हैं S_4 **61.4** चिरी] Σ, चीरी Ṭ • कौं] B_1D_2**S**, कूँ G_eV_1, कौ Ṭ • चिरी कहा] $B_1S_1S_7$Ṭ, कहा चिरी $D_2G_eS_2S_3S_4V_1$ • पै] Σ, पह (unm.) D_2, ⟨एय⟩ Ṭ • कारीगरी] Σ, गारीगरी S_3

59.3 बिसारना [vismārayati] v.t. to forget. **59.4** पार- [pātayati and H parṇā] v.t. to cause to fall, to let to fall. **60.1** जानती तीं var. Bund. v.t. imperf. (all others) knew (Krishna); डीठ [dṛṣti-] f. glance; तिरीछ- (तीक्ष्ण) [S] reg. adj. sharp, censuring. **60.2** घैर m. insult; घरहाई f. slanderer. **60.3** बकवादिन f. garrulous woman. **60.4** बीछी [vṛkṣika-] f. scorpion. **61.1** लट- reg. adj. bad; उनकी pron. of them; सुघरी [su + H ghaḍī] f. auspicious time; उघड़ना v.i. to be exposed, revealed. **61.2** बाँह [bāhu-] f. (the upper) arm. खैंचना (खींचना) [*khinc-] Br. v.t. to draw away. **61.3** कहनावत f. saying, proverb; और की of someone else; साँचियै आनि परी है Br. has turned out to be true. उर हमारी सो आंन परी है var. Br. has become relevant with regards to my heart. **61.4** चिड़ी f. bird; मारै चिरी कौं कहा चिरी Br. why would a bird pounce on (another) bird? मीर [P] m. chief (i.e. Krishna) (has); कारिगरी [P] f. expertise.

*आवते जौ आप, तौ सिखावते हमैहू जोग, 1
        भोग बिसरावते बताय धोती नेती है।
तुमहि पठायो, तुम डेल सो चलायो आनि, 2
        जानी न परत कौन बैरी, कौन हेती है।
ठाकुर कहत, तुम सगुन बिसारि निज, 3
        त्रिगुन कौं ध्यावौ, तौनि महनति केती है।
ए तो दोऊ काज निज कर के करे तें होत, 4
        परहथ बंजन, सँदेसैं होत खेती है॥ B62॥

वे तो हुते गोप, हम गोपीं हुतीं, हो चुकी वा, 1

62 Bharatpur1 f. 161rv (72), Datiya2 f. 2r (19), Granthāvalī 46, Sudhāsar [S_1 f. 165rv (218), S_3 f. 293r (22), S_4 f. 92v-93r (231), S_7 f. 205v (66)], Vrindaban1 f. 13rv (15/80). • The Sudhāsar presents this poem within the 'uddhava kau braj mẽ āyabau' (Uddhava's coming to Braj) subsection of the 'Brajrasrīti' section.

62.1 हमैहू] G_eV_1, हमहूं B_1, हमै (unm.) D_2, वे हमै S_3, हमैंवे S_1S_7, हमै घे S_4 • बताय] $B_1D_2G_eS_1S_7V_1$, बनाय S_3, बजाय S_4 • है] Σ, हैं B_1^{ac} **62.2** तुमहि] $B_1D_2S_1S_4V_1$, तुमही G_e, तुम है S_3S_7 • आनि] $B_1G_eV_1$, आन D_2**S** • जानि] B_1, जान $D_2S_1S_3S_7$, जानि G_eV_1, *om.* S_4 • न] Σ, ना S_7 • परत] Σ, परति S_4 • है] $B_1^{pc}\Sigma$, हैं B_1^{ac} **62.3** ठाकुर कहत] Σ, ठा° B_1, ठाकुर कहैत V_1 • तुम] Σ, हम D_2 • सगुन] Σ, सगन S_3 • बिसारि] B_1G_e**S**, बिसार $D_2S_7V_1$ • त्रिगुन] *conj.* निगुन G_e, निर्गुन D_2, त्रिगुन $B_1S_1S_3S_7V_1$, त्रिगन S_4 • ध्यावौ] B_1G_e, ध्यावैं D_2, धावौ S_1, धावै $S_3S_4S_7$, ध्यावै V_1 • तौनि] $B_1G_eV_1$, तौन D_2, तामैं **S** • महनति] $B_1G_eS_3S_4S_7$, महिनत D_2S_1, महनती V_1 • है] Σ, हैं B_1, *om.* (unm.) V_1 **62.4** निज] $D_2^{pc}\Sigma$, *om.* (unm.) D_2^{ac}, नित S_1 • कर] Σ, हाथ S_7 • तें] G_e, ते $B_1D_2V_1$, ही **S** • °हथ] $B_1D_2G_eS_1V_1$, °हाथ S_3S_7, हेरथ (unm.) S_4 • बंजन] $B_1D_2S_1S_3S_4V_1$, बनज S_7G_e • सदेसैं] Σ, संदेसौ S_3 • है] Σ, हैं B_1

62.1 धोती-(नेती) f. the yogic exercise of cleaning the entrails by swallowing a string; नेती f. the yogic exercise of cleaning the synus by introducing a string through the nose and taking it out through the mouth; भोग बिसरावते Br. would he discard pleasure? बताय v.t. (Br. abs.) telling. **62.2** तुमहि पठायो Br. he sent you; डेल m. lump, stone, pebble; डेल सो चलायो poet. throw in (arguments) like pebbles (i.e. useless things), you churn out (your arguments). **62.3** तौन pron. Br. Bund. that; त्रिगुन var. [S] 1. m. (meditate on) the three guṇas; 2. apa. adj. having three guṇas (i.e. saguna); महनति (मेहनत) [AP] reg. f. effort. **62.4** कर [S] m. hand; बंजन [vy-añjana-] m. 1. vegetables (as eaten with rice, lentils etc.); 2. seasoning, relish; बनिज var. [vānijya-] m. commerce; संदेस (संदेश) [S] Br. m. (obl.) by order.

अब वे महीप, रानी कैसे हूजियत है।
2 उनहीं दयो तौ भोग, उनहीं बियोग दीन्हो,
उनहीं पठायो जोग, मान लीजियत है।
3 ठाकुर कहत, अवसर न सवाद कछू,
ऊधो सौं वृथा ही बकवाद कीजियत है।
4 ऐसी सुनौ, इतै कितै हेरती हौ, मेरी बीर,
जैसी चलै बात तैसी पीठ दीजियत है॥ B63॥

---

63 Bharatpur1 f. 162v-3r (80), Datiya2 f. 3r (24), Granthāvalī 47, Sudhāsar [S_1 f. 303r (55), S_2 f. 61rv (-/71), S_3 f. 174v (263), S_4 f. 102r (276), S_7 f. 210v (112)], Vrindaban1 f. 1v-2r (7/7). • The Sudhāsar presents this poem within the 'uddhava kau braj mẽ āyabau' (Uddhava's coming to Braj) subsection of the 'Brajrasrīti' section. Cf. Vṛnd: 'jaisī calai bayāra taisī dījai oṭa' (23 Nīti-satsaī) and Dīndayāl Girī: 'jaisī bahai bayāra pīṭha taba taisī kījai.'

63.1 गोप] Σ, गोय S_4 • हम गोपी] Σ, गोपी हम G_e • हुतीं] G_eS_1, हुती Σ • हो] Σ, ही S_1 • वा] Σ, सो D_2, व S_7 • हूजियत] $B_1S_1S_2$, हूजिय (unm.) D_2^{ac}, हूजियतु $D_2^{pc}G_eV_1$, कै जियति S_3, कै जियत S_7, हूंजियत S_4 • है] Σ, हैं S_7 **63.2** दीन्हो] Σ, दीनौं S_1S_7 • जोग] Σ, ग (haplography) D_2 • लीजियत] B_1**S**, लीजियतु D_2G_e, लीजियति S_3, लीजियतू V_1 **63.3** ठाकुर कहत] Σ, ठा° B_1 • अवसर न] Σ, अबर ना (unm.) S_2 • कछू] Σ, कछु S_3 • ऊधौ] Σ, उधो G_e • सौं] $D_2S_1S_2$, सूं B_1, सो $G_eS_3S_4S_7V_1$ • ही] S_3^{pc}Σ, *om.* (unm.) S_3^{ac} • बकवाद] Σ, बकवादि V_1 • कीजियत] B_1**S**, कीजियतु D_2G_e, कीजियति S_3, कीजियैतु (unrh.) V_1 **63.4** सुनौ] $B_1D_2S_3S_4S_7$, सुने G_e, सुनौं S_1S_2, सुनै V_1 • इतै] $B_1D_2G_eS_1V_1$, इतौ $S_2S_4S_7$, एतौ S_3 • हेरती] Σ, हरती S_2, हेरते S_7 • हौ] Σ, है S_7 • बात] $B_1G_eV_1$, ब्यार **S**D_2, ब्यारि S_2S_4 • तैसी] Σ, तैमी S_2 • पीठ] $D_2G_eS_3S_7V_1$, पीठि $B_1S_1S_2S_4$ • दीजियत] B_1**S**, दीजियतु $D_2G_eV_1$, दीजियति S_3

63.1 वा (वह) pron. that (matter). **63.3** सवाद (स्वाद) [S] m. taste; delight; अवसर न स्वाद कछू Br. it is neither the occasion for nor there is delight in (telling it). **63.4** ऐसी सुनें Br. having heard such talk; इतै कितै हेरती हौ Br. why are you looking here (at me)? बात 1. [vāta-] m. wind; 2. [vārtā-] f. talk; जैसी... है Br. turn your back to where the wind blows from.

*कूबरी कान्हर का इकलास किया, सबही बिधि खूब है अल्ला।
क्या करिये, रिस लागती है, चुप ह्वै रहिये बसि प्रेम के तल्ला।
ऊधो सँदेस पठाय पठाया है, पै न डरैं हम जोग के हल्ला।
जैसे को तैसो ही जाइ मिलै, उतै फूटी मसीत को आँधरो मुल्ला॥ B64॥

*रस रीति की प्रीति कौं चीनौ नही, कपटी-चटसार की पाटी पढे।

---

64 Bharatpur1 f. 150v (7), Granthāvalī 48, Vrindaban1 f. 15v (2/93), Vrindaban3 f. 29v(2). Lines c and d are in the reverse order in V_3. Ṭhākur's signature is missing from the texts of G_e and V_1. V_3 introduces the poem as 'kabi ṭhākur'. The inclusion of the poem into V_1, a selection of Ṭhākur's quatrains, clearly indicates that even without the signature this poem was perceived as one written by him. While there does not seem to be any doubt about the authorship in any of the sources Ṭhākur's signature in V_3 is a secondary reading, where even the line order needed to be changed to include it. The lack of explicit attribution with a signature is a sign of unease about the syncretism of this savaiyā. 65 Datiya2 f. 2r (14), Sudhāsar [S_1 f. 295rv (22), S_2 f. 60r (-/66), S_3 f. 167v (229), S_4 f. 95r (240), S_7 f. 206v (77)]. • This poem does not bear Ṭhākur's signature but both collections introduce it as a poem by Ṭhākur. (Datiya2 has it in a sequence of poems by Ṭhākur connected with the phrase anya ca 'and another one'.) The style with the sharp words of the cowherd women and the use of a strong idiom at the end confirms this attribution. • The Sudhāsar presents this poem within the 'uddhava kau braj mẽ āyabau' (Uddhava's coming to Braj) subsection of the 'Brajrasrīti' section.

64.1 कूबरी] $B_1G_eV_1$, कांन्हर V_3 • कान्हर] $B_1G_eV_1$, कूबरी V_3 • का] B_1V_1, कों G_e, सौंई V_3 • इकलास] $B_1G_eV_1$, षलास V_3 • किया] $B_1V_1V_3$, कियो G_e • बिधि] $B_1G_eV_1$, मिलि V_3 **64.2** क्या] $B_1V_1V_3$, का G_e • करिये] B_1G_e, करिऐ V_1, कहियै V_3 • रिस] $B_1G_eV_3$, रस V_1 • लागती] B_1V_1, लागति G_eV_3 • ह्वै $B_1G_eV_1$, कै V_3 • बसि] B_1G_e, बचि V_1, बलि V_3 • प्रेम] $B_1G_eV_1$, प्रीति V_3 • तल्ला] $B_1G_eV_1$, भल्ला V_3 **64.3** ऊधो] B_1G_e, उधौ V_1, ठाकुर ऊधौ V_3 • सँदेस] $B_1G_eV_1$, *om.* V_3 • पठाय] B_1V_1, पठायो G_e, पढाइ V_3 • पठाया है] (unm.) $B_1V_1V_3$, पठायहै G_e • पै न] $B_1G_eV_1$, नांही V_3 • डरैं] B_1G_e, डरै V_1V_3 **64.4** को] G_eV_1, कौं B_1V_3 • ही] $B_1G_eV_1$, हू॰ V_3 • उतै] $B_1G_eV_1$, बिडौं V_3 • मसीत] $B_1G_eV_1$, मसीति V_3 • को] $B_1G_eV_1$, कौं V_3 **65.1** रीति] $S_1S_3S_4$, रीत D_2S_7, रीनि S_2 • प्रीति] Σ, प्रीत S_7 • चीनौ] S_3S_7, जानो D_2, चीनौं $S_1S_2S_4$

64.1 इकलास (इख़लास) [A] m. Br. pure affection, love; ख़लास var. [A] adj. 1. freed, released; 2. poor; अल्ला (अल्लाह) [A] m. God. **64.2** रिस [riṣ-; x īrṣyā-] f. anger; तल्ला [talẽ] poet. adv. at the foot of, under; भल्ला apa. 1. [bhalā-] adj. good; 2. [bhālā] m. spear. **64.3** पठाय पठाया है reg. he sent to give (a message); पठायो पठायहै var. Br. he sent and will be sending; हल्ला m. 1. noise, shout; 2. assault. **64.4** जैसे को तैसो ही जाइ मिलै Br. one meets such people as he is; उतै Br. adv. thither (i.e. in Mathura). **65.1** चीनौ Br. v.t. perf. he recognised; चटसार Br. f. (primary) school.

2 हम कौं प्रभु छोडि कै जात रहे उत कूबरी के सँगवाती बढे।
तब चौरे मैं चौरी बखानत ते, अब काम परै बहु घाती गढे।
4 हम जानी कछू पिय मोह मढे, नकटे हरि चैतूवा मीत कढे॥ B65॥

1 *जानिऐ न जाति रघुनाथै कहा करनौ है,
औरै दोस यौंही बिन काज दीजियतु है।
2 तब तौ पियूष से पिऐ, री, बैन मोहन के,
अब बैठी बिसु सौ बियोग पीजियतु है।
3 ठाकुर कहत, उधौ, हम पै बनी है कौन,
झुठी बेसरम होकै पैज कीजियतु है।
4 तब हम जानती ती औध लौ जिऐगौ कौन,
अब देखौ औधि के बितीतैं जीजियतु है॥ B66॥

---

66 Datiya1 ff. 104v-105r (338). The poem contains the words of a cowherd woman towards another girl in the first two lines and towards Uddhava in the last two lines.

65.2 कौं] D_2**S**, वै त (unm.) S_2 • प्रभु] $S_1S_2S_4$, हरि D_2, प्रभ S_3S_7 • छोडि] S_4, छोड $D_2S_1S_3S_7$, छो⟨टि⟩ S_2 • संगवाती] Σ, सगवानी S_2 • बढे] Σ, चढे S_2 **65.3** तब] *conj.* जब Σ • चौरे] Σ, चोर S_3 • चौरी] Σ, चौ (unm.) S_1 • बखानत] Σ, बखानति S_3 • काम] **S**, गाढ D_2 • बहु घाती गढे] **S**, गुन औरै बढे D_2 **65.4** हम] Σ, हम। S_1 • जानी... मढे] **S**, जानतीं तीं हरि मीत कढे D_2 • नकटे] S_2, न कढे $D_2S_1S_3S_7$, नकठे S_4 • चैतुवा] S_2S_7, चैतूवा $D_2S_1S_4$, चैतबा S_3 **66.2** पियूष] *conj.* पयुष D_1

65.2 जात रहे perf. reg. goes away; (here:) as soon as he went away (cf. H jāte hī, KL); वै 1. [H ve] pron. (pl. resp.) he, that, 2. [vai] poet. adv. indeed, truly; सगवाती [cf. sa-gotra-] f. relationship, fondness; के सगवाती बढ़े Br. he went forward (entered) into relationship with; सगवाती चढ़े var. reg. entered into a relationship. (or saṅga bātī caṛhe 'lit lamps together'.) **65.3** चौड़े में idiom. openly, publicly; चोरी f. the stealing (of butter); घाती [H ghāt 'trickery'] f. deception; गढ़ना [*gaṭhati] v.t. to forge, to create. **65.4** मोह मढ़े he is coated with infatuation; नकटे [H nāk-kaṭā] adj. shameless, barefaced; न कढे (न निकले) apa. चैतुवा मीत idiom. friend (only) in the Chaitra month (when there is work and salary; or: the supposed mating season for humans) (cf. H mausamī mitra); कढ़ना [*kaḍḍhati] Br. v.i. to turn out to be (cf. H nikalnā). **66.1** रघुनाथै Br. emph. obl. it is not known to Krishna himself; औरै Br. others (blame God). **66.2** बैन (वचन) [S] m. (pl.) words; विसु (विश) [S] Br. m. poison. **66.3** हम पै (हम से) Br. by us; बनी [vanati] v.i. perf. work was done; कौन (क्या) [S] poet. interr. what; पैज (प्रतिज्ञा) [S] Br. f. vow; कीजियतु है (की जाती है) [karoti] v.t. pass. imperf. Br. (false vow) is made (by Krishna). **66.4** औधि के बितीतैं Br. after passing the promised time (of his coming).

कूबरौ नीकौ मिलौ है त्रिभंगमै, कोऊ न काऊ कौं देख हसैया।
रानी भई तज चेरपनौ अरु भूप भये, बलि, गाइ-चरैया।
ठाकुर, साथ सुहायौ मिलौ जग-पावन की सुधि को बिसरैया।
जैसिही कूबरी तैसेई कान्ह, ऐसे गुनी हर बंस रिझैया॥ B67॥

*परभात भयैं सुधि आवै, भटू, लिखि प्रीतम कौं पठई पतिया।
अब ब्यौरे कहै समझावन कौं, मुख तें निकसैं मधुरी बतिया।
कवि ठाकुर, प्रीति की रीति यहै, ऊधौ, ब्यारि चले तें फटै छतिया।
दिन द्वै मैं चलै ब्रज द्वारिका तैं भई बैरिनि गोपिन कौं रतिया॥ B68॥

---

67 Datiya2 f. 2v (16), Seondha2 (O_2). 68 Kālidās-Hajārā (H_e) 329, Vrindaban2 f. 70v.

67.1 नीकौ] O_2, आछौ D_2 • कोऊ... देख] O_2, देष न काहुवै कोऊ D_2 • हसैया] D_2, हसईआ (unm.) O_2 **67.2** चेरपनौ] D_2, दासीपन O_2 • अरु] D_2, अर O_2 • बलि] D_2, बल O_2 • चरैया] D_2, चरईआ (unm.) O_2 **67.3** ठाकुर] D_2, कहि ठाकुर (unm.) O_2 • जग-पावन] D_2, बृजबालन O_2 • सुधि] D_2, सुद O_2 • बिसरैया] D_2, बिसरईआ (unm.) O_2 **67.4** जैसिही... कान्ह] D_2, कांन जू तैसिय कूबरी O_2 • ऐसे] *conj.* आसे D_2, आ ⟨पै⟩ O_2 • रिझैया] D_2, रिझईआ (unm.) O_2 **68.2** समझावन] H_e, समझा मन V_2 • तें] H_e, ते V_2 • निकसैं] V_2, निकसै H_e **68.3** यहै] H_e, इहै V_2 **68.4** दिन] H_e, दिनन (unm.) V_2 • मैं] H_e, में V_2 • चलै] H_e, चलैं V_2 • तैं] H_e, तें V_2

67.1 कूबड़ा [*kubba-] adj. m. (here used for a female) hunchbacked; काऊ (किसी) pron. any, either (of the two). **67.2** बलि idiom. Br. 'I sacrifice myself' I beg you. **67.3** साथ [sārtha-] m. company; सुहायौ (सुहावना) [śubhāna-] adj. pleasant, attractive; जग-पावन Br. purifying the world. **67.4** गुणी [S] m. 'virtuous or skilled person' 1. fig. rascal; 2. musician; बंस [vaṃśa-] m. 1. lineage, family; 2. flute. **68.1** सुधि आवें Br. remembering him; पठई v.t. perf. Br. I sent; पतिया [patra-] reg. f. letter. **68.2** ब्यौरा [vivaraṇa-] Br. m. details; कहै v.t. pres. Br. you say; समझाना [sambuddhyate] v.t. to convince; समझा मन apa. **68.3** ब्यारि (बयार) [*vātāra-] Br. m. cool wind. **68.4** ब्रज द्वारिका poet. from Braj to Dvārakā; चलै तैं Br. since he went.

शृंगार

प्रेम

*सुनिकै धुनि चाह बढी चित में, उत जैयै घने सुख पावने री।
ढिग आन लख्यो, उनकी उलटी कहूँ ताल कहूँ सुर गावने री।
कहि ठाकुर, भूल सु नैनन की, तिन सों कहा नेह बढावने री।
चलु दूर, भटू, हौं बृथा भटकी, लगैं दूर के ढोल सुहावने री॥ Ś1॥

हौं करिहौं हित फूलौ फिरै मन, जानत नाहीं, अजान है एतौ।
या पथ पाँव धरै पहिचान अहै इहि में दुख औ सुख केतौ।
ठाकुर, जो या कथा सुनि पावतौ, तौ सुनिबे कहँ कान न देतौ।

---

1 Sundarītilak (C$_e$) 303, Granthāvalī 70, Marwar5 f. 31v (7), Śatak 56, Ṭhasak 173. Although C$_e$ and M$_5$ present important variants their readings may be secondary to the ones recorded in the Śatak (cf. 'kabi' vs. the usual 'kahi' of B$_1$ and **S**). 2 Datiyāl f. 105rv (340), Granthāvalī 56, Śatak 47, Ṭhasak 51.

1.1 धुनि] **E**, *om.* (unm.) M$_5^{ac}$, धुन M$_5^{pc}$ • चाह बढी चित में] *conj.* चाह उठी जिय में C$_e$, यौं चित मैं हुलसी **E**, चाह * M$_5^{ac}$, चाह बडी चित मे M$_5^{pc}$ • उत] **E**, तहां C$_e$, बित M$_5$ • घने] Ś$_e$Ṭ$_e$, कछु C$_e$, *om.* (unm.) G$_e$, घनो M$_5$ • पावने] **E**, पावनो C$_e$M$_5$ **1.2** आन लख्यौ] **E**, जाय सबै समझी C$_e$M$_5$ • उनकी] Σ, उन (unm.) M$_5$ • उलटी] **E**, *om.* M$_5$C$_e$ • कहूँ ताल कहूँ] Σ, कहु ताल कहु M$_5$ • गावने] **E**, गावनो C$_e$M$_5$ **1.3** कहि] **E**, कबि C$_e$M$_5$ • भूल सु नैनन की] **E**, कूर समाज जहां C$_e$M$_5$ • कूर C$_e$, कुर M$_5$ • तिन सों कहा] Σ, हे तहा कीत M$_5$ • सों] **E**, ते C$_e$ • कहा] **E**, कह C$_e$ • बढावने] **E**, लगावनो C$_e$M$_5$ **1.4** चलु दूर] **E**, भलि देखि C$_e$, भई भुल (unm.) M$_5$ • भटू] Σ, भटु (unm.) M$_5$ • हौं] Σ, में ×*× M$_5$ • बृथा] Σ, बृथ (unm.) M$_5$ • भटकी] **E**, अटकी C$_e$, भठकी M$_5$ • लगै] **E**, सुने C$_e$, सुन्यो M$_5$ • दूर] Σ, दुर M$_5$ • के] Σ, को M$_5$ • ढोल] **E**, बोल C$_e$, ढाल M$_5$ • सुहावने] **E**, सुहावनो C$_e$M$_5$ **2.1** हौं] G$_e$Ṭ$_e$, मै D$_1$, हौ Ś$_e$ • करिहौं] **E**, करिहौ D$_1$ • हित] **E**, हितु मै करिहौ हितु D$_1$ • मन... है] **E**, सहसां जग D$_1$ • एतौ] **E**, जेतौ D$_1$ **2.2** पाँव] **E**, पाइ D$_1$ • पहिचान] **E**, पहिचानि D$_1$ • अहै] **E**, ऐ⟨है⟩ D$_1$ • इहि] G$_e$, यह D$_1$, इह Ś$_e$Ṭ$_e$ • में] **E**, मै D$_1$ **2.3** पावतो] **E**, पाउतौ D$_1$ • कहँ] **E**, मह D$_1$ • कान] Ś$_e$Ṭ$_e$, काम G$_e$, कांनु D$_1$

1.1 पावने (पाने) [prāpayati] reg. v.t. inf. m. pl. to receive; री Br. interj. (addressing females, expressing affection). **1.2** ताल [S] m.f. rhythm; सुर गावने Bund. the tone of his singing. **1.3** तिन सों Br. with him (Krishna) (who is attractive only to the eyes); बढावने v.t. inf. Bund. to promote, to develop. **1.4** दूर का ढोल सुहावना लगता है idiom. 'distant drums are felt pleasant'. **2.1** फूलौ फिरै मन Br. my mind goes around swelling (with the idea that). **2.2** पाँव धरै Br. having put the feet on; अहै (है) reg. v.i. is; इहि में Br. in it (i.e. in the love). **2.3** कहँ (को) Av. Bund. postp. for, to.

जानतौ जौ इतनी परतीति, तौ प्रीति की रीति को नाम न लेतौ॥ Ś2॥ 4

*चाह देखी चोजवारी, आस देखी आनँद की, 1
रस देख्यो रसवारो, जानी बडे रसिया।
तौन सब झूठी भई, एक ही अनूठी भई, 2
साँची भई एक मानी, फासी लिये फसिया।
ठाकुर कहत, उपखानो यो प्रमान्यो गयो, 3
मान्यो गयो मंत्र सो न कैसहूँ उमसिया।
स्वाद तें न छोड्यो जाइ, टेढे तें न लीलि सकै 4
प्रीति भई मोहन की गुर भर्‌यौ हसिया॥ Ś3॥

समुझाइ सिखाइयै कासु, भलै अब नाँव न कोऊ तुमैं धरिहै।

---

3 Bharatpur1 f. 155v (36), Granthāvalī 138, Vrindaban1 f. 10v (9/61). 4 Bharatpur1 f. 158v (54), Granthāvalī 59, Sudhāsar [S_2 f. 13v (24/18), S_7 f. 49rv (64/466)], Vrindaban1 f. 5r (13/26). The Sudhāsar introduces the poem as praśnottar 'question-answer'. The poem starts with the words of a companion towards a woman in love.

2.4 इतनी परतीति] Ś$_e$, कोऊ प्रीत की रीत D_1, इतनी परतीत G_eṬ$_e$ • प्रीति] Ś$_e$Ṭ$_e$, प्रीत D_1G_e • रीति] D_1Ś$_e$Ṭ$_e$, रीत G_e • नाम] **E**, नाउ D_1 • न] D_1Ś$_e$Ṭ$_e$, *om.* (unm.) G_e **3.2** फासी] B_1G_e, फासा V_1 • लिये] G_e, लये B_1, लय V_1 **3.3** ठाकुर कहत] G_e, ठा° B_1, ठाकुर कहैत V_1 • मान्यो गयो] $B_1^{pc}G_eV_1$, *om.* (unm.) B_1^{ac} • कैसहूँ] G_eV_1, कैसैहूँ B_1 **3.4** छोड्यौ] B_1V_1, छाँड्यौ G_e • लीलि] G_eV_1, लील B_1 • गुर] G_eV_1, गुरु B_1 • भर्‌यौ] B_1V_1, भरी G_e **4.1** समुझाइ] G_e, समुझाई B_1V_1, समझाय **S** • सिखाइयै] G_e**S**, सिषाईयै B_1V_1 • कासु] Σ, कासौं S_7 • न कोऊ] $B_1G_eS_7$, कोऊ (unm.) S_2, न कोउ V_1

2.4 जौ [yadi] conj. reg. if; परतीति (प्रतीति) [S] poet. f. credibility; इतनी परतीति poet. (that) credibility (in love) is so little. **3.1** चाह [*cāh-] f. 1. desire; 2. love; चोजवार [codya-] Br. adj. (full) of merriment; रसवार- (रसवाला) Br. adj. 1. savorous; 2. joyful; जानी v.t. perf. I realised (the matter that he...) रसिया [rasika-] m. 1. a man of feeling or passion; 2. a pleasure-seeker. **3.2** तौन pron. Br. Bund. that; अनूठा [*anna-uṭha-] adj. wonderful; साँची भई एक मानी Br. I accepted only one of them to be true; फँसिया [cf. spāśa-] reg. m. pl. those who were to be trapped. **3.3** उपखानो [upākhyāna-] Br. m. saying, idiom; उमसना (उबसना) [udvāsyate 'to rot'] v.i. to be changed. **3.4** टेढ- [*treḍḍha-] Br. m. 1. slant; 2. crookedness; लीलना [nigilati] reg. v.t. to swallow; हँसिया f. (here m.) reg. 1. [aṃs(i)ya-?] sickle; 2. [hāsī] smile. **4.1** कासु [kasya] Av. Bund. interr. to whom; भलै (भला) [cf. bhalla-] interj. is it at all possible that; तुमै (तुम्हें) pron. acc.-dat. Bund. you; नाम धरना idiom. to slander.

गृहकाज औ लाज तजी जिहिनें फँदी नेहफँदा सु कहे डरिहै।
कहि ठाकुर, त्यौं हित नीकैं अरी कत, याहि तौ मोहन की अरि है।
तुम्हें काहे परे तपने कपने, अपने कोऊ जानि कुवा परिहै॥ Ś4॥

*को उनसों परबीन बडो, अपकीरति कत आपनी औरै सुनावै।
आजु बनी जौ बनी, सु बनी, अब का कहिकै कोउ बाद बढावै।
ठाकुर, एक विचार हिये, अब नीर उलीचि को कीच मचावै।
ऐसे हीं सोच के सोचै परे, अब ऊमर फोरि को जीव उडावै॥ Ś5॥

---

5 Granthāvalī 64, Śatak 67, Ṭhasak 171. • (GSh: The figure is 'anyokti', a general statement with an 'aprastut' without a 'prastut'.)

4.2 जिहि॰] B_1G_e, तह S_2, तुह S_7, जिह V_1 • ॰नें] $B_1^{pc}V_1$, नेह (unm.) B_1^{ac}, सो G_e, नै **S** • फदी] Σ, फँदि G_e • सु कहै] **S**, सु किहै B_1, किहि कों G_e, किहै (unm.) V_1 **4.3** त्यौं] Σ, तौं G_e • कत] $B_1G_eV_1$, कित ×नीकै× S_2, कित S_7 • याहि] Σ, याही V_1 **4.4** तुम्हैं] $B_1G_eV_1$, तुमैं **S** • परे] Σ, परैं S_2 • तपने] Σ, तपनैं B_1 • कपने] $G_eS_7V_1$, कपनैं B_1, *om.* (unm.) S_2 • कोऊ] Σ, कोउ G_e • जानि] $G_eS_2V_1$, जानैं B_1, जान S_7 • कुवा] G_eV_1, कुआ B_1S_2, कूआ S_7 **5.2** कहिकै] G_eṬ$_e$, कहियै Ś$_e$ **5.4** ऐसे] G_eṬ$_e$, हम ऐसे (hyperm.) Ś$_e$ •

4.2 जिहिनें (जिसने) rel. pron. reg. ag. the one who; सो pron. Br. that (person); कहै [cf. Br. kāhe] reg. interr. obl. of what (is she afraid)? **4.3** नीकैं poet. adv. excellently; (here:) intensely; अड़ना [*aḍ-] v.i. (perf.) 1. to be obstinate, to jibe; 2. to be determined; कत reg. interr. why (were you so intensely obstinate in love)? याहि (यही) pron. Br. emph. it; अरि (अड़) [cf. H aṛnā] f. obstinacy; (here:) obstinate question. **4.4** काहे reg. interr. why? तपना v.i. to suffer from heat, to burn; काँपना v.i. to tremble (from cold); तुम्हें... कपने Br. why did you have to burn and tremble (if I suffer)? अपने जानि Br. of one's own accord. **5.1** उनसों Br. 1. as him; 2. than him; अपकीर्ति [S] f. disrepute; औरै सुनावै Br. tells to others (i.e. he is not afraid). **5.2** आजु बनी जौ बनी Br. today happened what happened; सु बनी Br. it happened well; बाद [vāda-] m. dispute. **5.3** एक विचार हिये Br. there is a thought in my mind (why to reveal it?) उलीचना [udricyate] v.t. to sprinkle; to pour off; कीच (कीचड़) [cikka-] Br. m. mud; मचाना [*macyate] v.t. to produce; कीचड़ मचाना idiom. to make mud. **5.4** सोचै परे Br. I fell into a dilemma, ऊमर [udumbara-] reg. m. wild fig (ficus glomerata) (often with worms in it that fly away when the fruit is broken.); फोड़ना [sphoṭayati] v.t. to burst open; ऊमर फोड़ना idiom. a hidden thing to be revealed; जीव [S] m. 1. living creature; 2. (here:) worm; उड़ाना [uḍḍāpayati] v.t. 1. to let fly; 2. to efface; जीव उड़ जाना idiom. to be confused; to loose (one's) head.

यहि प्रीति-अजार के औरै तबीब, परंतु कछू सुन लीजतु है।
तुम भेद न जानती, बेद्य बनीं फिरौ, सोचन सों तनु छीजतु है।
कहि ठाकुर, एक से रोगन कौं, री, इलाज न एक सो कीजतु है।
जग एकन को भँटे बायरे, बीर, सु एकन कों पथ दीजतु है॥ Ś6॥

यह प्रेमकथा कहियै किह सौं, सो कहे सौं कहा कोऊ मानत है।
पुनि ऊपरी धीर धरायो चहै, तन रोग नहीं पहचानत है।
कहि ठाकुर, जाहि लगी कसकैं सु तौ को कस के उर आनत है।

---

6 Datiya2 f. 2r (17), Granthāvalī 52, Śatak 43, Ṭhasak 169 7 Sundarītilak (C_e) 295, Granthāvalī 53, Rasikvinod (O_e) 696, Sudhāsar [S_1 f. 63v, S_2 f. 11r (11/42), S_7 f. 45r (23/425)], Ṭhasak 176. The Sudhāsar presents this poem within the 'ūḍhā parakiyā' section and introduces it as 'sakhī prata ukta'.

6.1 यहि] **E**, यह D_2 • प्रीति] **E**, प्रीत D_2 • के] D_2, को **E** • परंतु] **E**, जरंत D_2 • सुन] **E**, सिख D_2 • लीजतु] **E**, लीजत D_2 **6.2** भेद न जानती] D_2, बेद भई फिरौ **E** • बेद्य बनीं फिरौ] D_2, भेद न जानती **E** • सोचन] D_2, रोगन **E** • तनु] **E**, तन D_2 • छीजतु] **E**, छीजत D_2 **6.3** कहि] D_2, कबि **E** • एक से रोगन कौं] D_2, रोगन के **E** • एक] D_2, एक से एक **E** • सो] D_1, तैं G_eṬ$_e$, ते Ś$_e$ • कीजतु] **E**, कीजत D_2 **6.4** भँटे] G_eṬ$_e$, भटा D_2, भट Ś$_e$ • सु] D_2, सो **E** • कों] G_e, को Ṭ$_e$$D_2$, का Ś$_e$ • दीजतु] **E**, दीजत D_2 **7.1** कहियै] **S**, कहिबे C_e**E**O_eṬ$_e$ • किह सौं] S_1, की नहीं C_e**E**, कि नहीं O_e, कह सौं S_2S_7 • सो कहे सौं] S_1, कहिबे ही C_e, कहबोई **E**, कहबोहि O_e, सो कहै सो S_2S_7 • कहा] **S**, करौ C_e**E**O_e • कोऊ] **S**, कोउ C_e**E**O_e • है] Σ, हैं O_e **7.2** पुनि] C_e**E**O_e, परि S_2S_7, पर S_1 • धरायौ] C_e**E**O_e, बधायौ **S** • नहीं] C_e**E**O_e, न वा **S** • रोग] Σ, राग C_e • पहचानत] Σ, पहिचानत O_e • है] Σ, हैं O_e **7.3** कहि] **E**S_1S_7, कबि $C_eO_eS_2$ • जाहि] Σ, ताहि S_1 • सु तौ] **S**, नहीं C_eO_e, नहिं **E** • को] **S**, सो C_e**E**O_e • के] O_e**S**, कैं **E**, कै C_e • है] Σ, हैं O_e

---

6.1 अजार [P āzār] Br. m. disease; के [H. ke lie] postp. reg. for; तबीब [A] m. doctor; कछू सुन लीजतु है Br. I listen to some words. **6.2** छीजना [chidyate] v.i. to waste away, to dwindle. **6.3** एक से रोगन कौं Br. for similar diseases; एक से एक var. idiom. one better than another; superbly; तैं var. pron. obl. Br. (done) by you. **6.4** भंटा (भटा) m. unripe aubergine; बायला [vātāla] adj. causing wind; पथ [pathya] Br. m. proper food. **7.1** सो कहे सौं (वह कहने से) Br. by telling it (i.e. if one speaks of it); कहबोई करौ var. Br. if you keep telling; कोऊ मानत है Br. will anyone believe it? **7.2** ऊपरी from above (i.e. from outside). **7.3** जाहि (जिस) pron. obl. Br. for whom; कसक f. 1. ache, pang; 2. compassion; को (क्यौं) Br. interr. why? कस के 1. (abs.) forcibly; 2. Br. interr. how? उर आनत idiom. Br. experience within.

बिन आपने पायँ बिवाई गए कोउ पीर पराई न जानत है॥ Ś7॥

पिय प्यार करैं जेहि पै, सजनी, तेहि की सब भाँतिन सैयत है।
मन मान करौं तौ परौं भ्रम मैं, फिर पाछे परे पछतैयत है।
कवि ठाकुर, कौन की कासौं कहौं, दिन देखि दसा बिसरैयत है।
अपने अटके, सुनि एरी भटू, निज सौत के मायके जैयत है॥ Ś8॥

हम एक कुराह चली तौ चली, हटकौ इन्हैं ये न कुराह चलैं।
यह तौ, बलि, आपनौ सूझ तौ है, प्रन पालियै सोई जो पालेंइ पलैं।
कहि ठाकुर, प्रीति करी है गोपाल सौं, टेरि कहौं, सुनो, ऊँचे गलैं।

---

8 Granthāvalī 85, Rāmcandra Śukla (I_e) p. 444, Hariaudh pp. 486-7, Ṭhasak 158, Ṭhasak 'Jīvancarit' (Ṭ^j_e) pp. 4-5 . A 'svakīyā nāyikā' is speaking. 9 Sundarītilak (C_e) p. 23 (134), Sudhāsar [S_1 f. 68v, S_2 f. 13rv (23/17), S_7 f. 49r (63/465)], Bābūrāmdīn (U_e) 202, Vrindaban3 f. 30r(6). The Sudhāsar presents this poem within the 'Alajja parakiyā' subsection of the 'Ūḍhā parakiyā' heroine.

7.4 पायँ] $G_eS_2O_e$, पीर C_e, पाइ S_1S_7, पायें Ṭ$_e$ • बिवाई] G_e**S**Ṭ$_e$, बेवाई C_e, बेवाय O_e • गए] G_eO_e, गये C_eṬ$_e$, गयैं **S** • कोउ] $G_eO_eS_1$, कोऊ $C_eS_2S_7$Ṭ$_e$ • न] **ES**, को C_e, का O_e • है] C_e**E**S_1S_7, हैं O_eS_2 **8.1** भांतिन सैयत] $A_eG_eI_e$, सइयत (unm.) Ṭ$_e$, भाँति निभइयत (unm.) Ṭ^j_e **8.2** पाछे] A_eI_e, पीछे **E** • पछतैयत] $A_eG_eI_e$, पछतइयत (unm.) Ṭ$_e$ **8.3** बिसरैयत] $A_eG_eI_e$, बिसरइयत (unm.) Ṭ$_e$ **8.4** सुनि] **E**, सुन A_eI_e • जैयत] $A_eG_eI_e$, जइयत (unm.) Ṭ$_e$ **9.1** चली तौ चली] C_e**S**, चलीं तौ चलीं U_e, चीलीं तौ चली V_3^{ac}, चलीं तौ चली V_3^{pc} • तौ] Σ, तु S_7 • हटकौ] Σ, बरजौ V_3 • इन्हैं ये] $C_eS_1U_e$, इनें ए S_2S_7, सब ये V_3 • चलैं] $C_eS_1S_2U_e$, चलै S_7V_3 **9.2** बलि] Σ, *om.* V_3 • सूझ तौ] **S**U_e, सूझनो C_e, जग सूझतौ V_3 • है] Σ, हैं S_2 • प्रन] Σ, पनु V_3 • सोई जो] **S**U_e, सोइ जो C_e, जेई (unm.) V_3 • पालें] S_1U_e, पालै $C_eS_2S_7$ • पलैं] $C_eS_2U_e$, पलै S_1S_7 **9.3** प्रीति] $C_eS_1S_7U_e$, प्रति S_2, चूक V_3 • करी है] Σ, परी मैं V_3 • गोपाल] C_eU_e, गुपाल **S**V_3 • सौं] S_1S_7, सौ $S_2U_eV_3$, सों C_e • टेरि] $S_2S_7V_3$, टेरे C_eU_e, टेर S_1 • कहौं सुनो] U_e, कहौ सुनो C_e, कह्यौ सुनौं S_1, कह्यौ सुनि S_2S_7, कहौ जब V_3 • गलैं] $C_eS_1U_eV_3$, गलै S_2S_7

7.4 बिवाई [vipādikā-] f. crack on the heel; पराया [cf. para-] adj. of someone else. **8.1** पिय... पै (from) the one whom my lover loves. **8.2** पाछे परे Br. adv. afterwards. **8.3** दिन देखि Br. seeing how (bad) the times are; दसा बिसरैयत Br. one forgets her own (previously good) condition. **8.4** अपने अटके Br. when one's desires are balked. **9.1** एक adv. alone; हटकना v.t. to forbid, to drive away; इन्हैं them (i.e. my slanderers);. **9.2** सूझ f. (here m.) perception, understanding; यह... है this is after all a matter of her own perception to everyone; प्रन... पलैं Br. only that vow should be followed which can be followed. **9.3** ऊँचे गले idiom. 'in a high voice' loudly, openly.

हमैं नीकी लगी, सो करी हमनै, तुम्हैं नीकी लगै न लगै तौ भलैं॥ Ś9॥

गुनगाहक सों बिनती इतनी, हक-नाहक नाहिं ठगावनो है।
यह प्रेम-बजार को चातुर लोग सुनैन-दलाल अँकावनो है।
कहि ठाकुर, यौं गुन गौंहन ही परबीनन सौं परखावनो है।
फिरि देखु बिचारि निहारि कै, री, सु जमा पर दाम लगावनो है॥ Ś10॥

जीव को जीव है, पीव को पीव है, प्यार ते प्यारो, प्रतीति निबाहौ।

---

10 Bharatpur1 f. 132r (6), Granthāvalī 128, Hāfizullah Khān: Hazārā (X_e) p. 299 (Śṛṅgār ādi ras 180), Rasikvinod (O_e) p. 105 (489), Śatak 69, Ṭhasak 21. The poem contains the words of a young heroine to her companion. 11 Bharatpur1 f. 151r (10), Granthāvalī B26, Sudhāsar [S_5 f. 68v (10), S_7 f. 49v (66/468)], Vrindaban1 f. 13v (18/82).

9.4 ॰नै तुम्हैं] S_1U_e, तुम्हैं (unm.) C_e, नैं तुमैं S_2, ॰नै तुमै S_7V_3 • नीकी] Σ, नीको U_e • लगै न लगै] $\mathbf{S}V_3$, लगो ना लगो C_eU_e • भलैं] $C_eS_1U_e$, भलै $S_2S_7V_3$ **10.1** ॰गाहक] $B_1O_eX_e$, ॰ग्राहक **E** • बिनती इतनी] Σ, इतनी बिनती O_e • नाहिं] Σ, नाहि B_1 • ठ-गांवनो] $B_1O_eX_e$, ठगावने $G_eṬ_e$, हठ गावने (unm.) $Ś_e$ • है] Σ, हैं B_1 **10.2** को] B_1, के **E**, की O_eX_e • चातुर लोग सु] B_1, अंतर सो पर॰ **E**, चांदनी चौक में O_eX_e • लैरी] B_1, नैन Σ • अकावनो] $B_1O_eX_e$, अँकावने **E** **10.3** कहि] B_1**E**, गुण O_eX_e • यौं गुन गौंहन ही] B_1, औगुन छोडि सबै **E**, रूप ये जौहर है O_eX_e • सौं] B_1, लै Σ • परखावनो] $B_1O_eX_e$, परखावने **E** • है] Σ, हैं B_1 **10.4** फिरि] B_1, अब Σ • देखि] B_1**E**, देखु O_eX_e • बिचारि] $B_1O_eŚ_eX_e$, बिचार $G_eṬ_e$ • निहारि] B_1**E**, संभारि O_eX_e • री सु] B_1, माल Σ • लगावनो] $B_1O_eX_e$, लगावने **E** • है] Σ, हैं B_1 **11.1** पीव को] Σ, ⟨मी⟩व V_1 • प्यारे ते प्यारो] Σ, प्यार तें प्यो G_e • प्रतीति] Σ, परतीति G_e

---

9.4 तुम्हैं नीकि लगै न लगै Br. whether you like it or not. **10.1** गुणग्राहक [S] m. 'the buyer of virtue' lover; हक़-नाहक़ adv. without cause or reason. **10.2** यह pron. this (jewel of beauty); लोग m. pl. (here: coll. sing.) person; यह... अँकावनो है Br. the clever one in the bazar of love, the expert eye, who is the middleman, will have to have to assess it; चांदनी चौक var. m. the main bazar (where expensive jewellery is sold); के अंतर var. postp. (with)in; नैन-दलाल m. (obl.) (by) the eyes, the (expert) middleman; सो var. pron. Br. that (jewel); परनैन var. m. the eyes of the other; लै (लेकर) var. v.t. abs. Br. taking (a middleman); लोग Br. m. sing. (?) man; अँका- [aṅka-] v.caus. (their eyes are) to estimate (its price). **10.3** गुन ठाकुर var. poet. Ṭhākur calculates that..; गुण [S] m. your virtues (and your beauty); गौंह [gama-] f. occasion; गौंहन ही Br. when occasion arises; परबीनन लै var. Br. with experts. **10.4** माल जमा var. Br. the merchandise is gathered (i.e. you are ready for love); दाम लगाना idiom. 1. to make an offer; 2. to set the price; **11.1** जीव को जीव है Br. you are the soul of my soul; पीव को पीव Br. the dearest person; प्यो var. [priya-] Br. m. (voc.) lover; प्रतीति [S] f. trust; निबाह- [nirvāhayati] v.t. to accomplish, to fulfil.

देह की देह, सरूप सुहाग को, भागि तें पायौ है जो कछु चाहौ।
ठाकुर, राधे कहै सजनीन सौ, नेह के नाते अथाह न थाहौ।
सूझती हौ ततौ बूझती कहा हौ, बूझती हौ ततौ सूझती का हौ॥ Ś11॥

रूप

सुरझी नहीं केतो उपाय कियौ, उरझी हुती घूँघट खोलन पै।
अधरान पै नेक खगी ही हुती, अटकी हुती माधुरी बोलन पै।
कबि ठाकुर, लोचन नासिका पै, मडराइ रही हुती डोलन पै।
ठहरै नहिं, डीठि फिरै ठठकी इन गोरे कपोलन गोलन पै॥ Ś12॥

लहरैं उठैं अंग अनंगहु की, मद जोबन के बहराति फिरै।
बडरी अँखियान तिरीछें चितै, सखियान लखैं लहराति फिरै।

---

12 Granthāvalī 73, Śatak 81, Ṭhasak 35. 13 Gujarat (G), Granthāvalī 72, Marwar5 f. 25r (32); Rasikvinod (O_e) 692, Sundarītilak (C_e) 13, Ṭhasak 187, Ṭhasak 'Jīvancarit' (Ṭ^j_e) p. 20. (The poem can be a description of mugdhā navayauvanā.)

11.2 भागि] $B_1G_eV_1$, भाग **S** • तैं] Σ, ते S_7 **11.3** सौं] Σ, कों G_e **11.4** हौ] Σ, हौं S_7 • ततौ] G_eS_5, तौ तौ $B_1S_7V_1$ • कहा हौ] S_5, काहे हौ G_e, काहे हौं S_7, काहौ हो B_1V_1 • बूझती] Σ, बुझति V_1 • हौ] Σ, हौं S_7 • ततौ] G_eS_5, तौ तौ $B_1S_7V_1$ • हौ] Σ, हौं S_7 **12.4** डीठि] G_eṬ$_e$, डीठ Ś$_e$ **13.1** लहरैं] Σ, लहरे M_5 • उठैं] C_e**E**G, उठे M_5, जो उठैं (unm.) O_e • अनंगहु] $C_eM_5O_e$, उमंगन **E**, अनंगहू G• भहराति] C_eG, भहराती **E**, भहराती O_e, भेरात (unm.) M_5 • फिरै] Σ, फीरे M_5 **13.2** बडरी] **E**O_e, बड़िही C_eM_5, बडडी G • अँखियान] Σ, अषीयांन M_5 • तिरीछें] Σ, चितै **E** • चितै] $C_eGM_5O_e$, तिरछी G_eṬ$_e$, तिरछे Ṭ^j_e • सखियान लखैं] C_eO_e, चित लोगन के **E**, सखि×∗×यांन लखें G, सषीयांन लषे M_5 • लहराति] C_eG, लहराती **E**O_e, लहरात M_5 • फिरै] Σ, फीरे M_5

11.2 देह की देह f. the body of my body; सुहाग [saubhāgya-] m. married happiness; चाहौ [H cāhnā] v.t. perf. Br. I wanted. **11.3** राधे poet. f. Radha; थाहना [stāgha-] v.t. to fathom. **11.4** सूझना [śudhyati] v.i. (here: v.t.) to understand; ततौ conj. poet. then; का Br. intcrr. what? **12.1** (The poem talks about the glance of the hero.) **12.2** खगना v.i. 1. to plunge into; 2. to be attached to. **12.3** मँडराना [cf. maṇḍala] v.i. to hover or wander around. **12.4** ठठक- (ठिठकना) reg. v.i. to stand still; गोलन [gola-] adj. (Br. pl.) round. **13.1** बहरा- [cf. viharati] Br. v.t. to amuse, to please (the people). **13.2** चितै v.t. perf. Br. she looks.

कहि ठाकुर, पानि खरी पखरी थिर सी न रहै, थहराति फिरै।
सिर ओढनी डारें कसे छतिया, फरिया पहिरें फहराति फिरै॥ Ś13॥

झूलत पाट की डोरी गहे, पटली पर बैठन त्यो ऊकरू की।
पाइन दै दुमदी मचकै लचकै करहां कर गोल उरू की।
सीखन को बिपरीत रतै, कव ठाकुर जू, चटसाल सुरू की।
खोटी पड़ें उचकै तीया, चोटी-चमोटी लगै जनु काम-गुरू की॥ Ś14॥

*कोमलता कंज तें, गुलाब तें सुगंध लै कै,

---

14 Ṭhākur-satsaī f. 1v (10) (Ṭ).

13.3 कहि] C$_e$G$_e$M$_5$Ṭ$_e$, कवि GO$_e$, कह Ṭ^j_e • पानि खरी पखरी] C$_e$GM$_5$, है तन ओप खरी G$_e$Ṭ$_e$, आन खरी निखरी O$_e$, है अति ओप खरी Ṭ^j_e • पानि] Σ, पानी M$_5$ • थिर सी न रहै] C$_e$GM$_5$, छिनहू न थिरै G$_e$Ṭ$_e$, थिर सी रहै (unm.) O$_e$, निरखे न थिरै Ṭ^j_e • थहराति] C$_e$G, थहराती EO$_e$, थेरात (unm.) M$_5$ • फिरै] Σ, फीरे M$_5$ **13.4** ओढनी डारें] C$_e$GO$_e$, ओढे उढोनी E • छतिया] Σ, छतीया M$_5$ • फरिया पहिरें] Σ, पहीरे फरिया M$_5$, फरिया पहरे Ṭ^j_e • फहराति] C$_e$G, फहराती EO$_e$, फेहरात M$_5$ • फिरै] Σ, फीरे M$_5$ **14.2** दुमची] *conj.* दुंम⟨ची/दी⟩ Ṭ **14.4** पड़ें उचकै] पड़े --- उचकै Ṭ

13.3 खरा [khara-] adj. pure; fair; excellent; पखरी (पखुवा) [cf. pakṣa-] reg. f. the upper arm; पानि खरी पखरी 1. her hands and her beautiful upper arms; 2. water in a stagnant pond (pokhaṛī); थहराना (थरथराना) v.i. 1. to tremble, to shake; 2. to sway (BHK). **13.4** ओढे var. v.t. perf. having wrapped; उढोनी var. [cf. H oṛhnā] f. woman's shawl; कसे छतिया her (growing) breasts are tight (in her bodice); फरिया Bund. f. a small shawl worn together with the skirt; फहराना v.i. to wave, to flap. **14.1** पाट [paṭṭa-] m. silk cloth. डोरी [cf. davara-] f. string, cord; पटली [S] f. 1. tree, stalk; 2. poet. stool, platform; 3. (here:) the seat of a swing; उकड़ूँ [utkuṭaka-] adj. squatting (with the feet flat on the ground). **14.2** दुमची [? cf. H ṭhumkā] (?) f. jerk; मचकना [*macc-] v.i. to move the hand to and fro (to power a swing); लचकना [cf. *lacc-] v.i. to bend, to sag; to be elastic; करिहाँ poet. f. waist (BHK); गोल [gola-] v. the roundness (of her thigh). **14.3** सीखन को बिपरीत रतै Br. in order to learn the 'viparīta rati'. **14.4** खोटी [*khoṭṭa-] f. fault, mistake; उचकना [cf. uuca-] v.i. to be jerked up; to spring up; चोटी [S] f. the hair plaited and hung down behind, a cue; चमोटी [cf. carmapaṭṭa-] f. dimin. reg. small leather strap; whip.

चंद तै प्रकास कीनौ उदित उजेरो है।
2 रूप रति आनन तें, चातुरी सुजानन तें,
नीर लै निवानन तें, कौतुक निबेरो है।
3 ठाकुर कहत, आ मसालौ बिधि-कारीगर
लोचन निहारि को न होय चित्त चेरो है।
4 कंचन को रंग लै, सवाद लै सुधा को,
बसुधा को सुख लूटि कै बनायो मुख तेरो है॥ Ś15॥

नेत्र

---

15 Hariaudh (A_e) pp. 484-5, Bharatpur2 f. 9vr (17), Bharatpur7 f. 1r (7), Granthāvalī B12, Kālidās-Hajārā p. 113 (H_e), Jaipur1 f. 4v (14), Nakh-śikh-hajārā (N_e) p. 95 (6), Sudhāsar [S_1 f. 6r (30), S_2 f. 3v (11/2), S_5 f. 6r (2), S_6 f. 7rv (21), S_7 f. 5r (47)], Śatak 87, Ṭhasak 'Jīvancarit' (Ṭ^j_e) p. 2, Z_1 ff. 37v, 38v (32), Hāfizullah Khān: Hazārā (X_e) (pp. 131-2, Rādhikā aur Rukminī kī stuti 155 [mukhmaṇḍal-varṇan] in Dikshit's edn). B_2, N_e and the Sudhāsar present this poem as 'Mukha varnana'. (In the latter it is a subsection of the 'Sikh-nakh' section.)

15.1 कंज] Σ, ⟨केंज⟩ B_2, कज्ज X_e • सुगंध] Σ, सुगंधि S_5 • लै कै] Σ, लीनौ Z_1 • तै] Σ, सों X_e • कीनौ] $B_2J_1\mathbf{S}$, गहि A_e, लैकें $B_7N_eX_e$, कियो G_eŚ$_e$, कीन्हों Ṭ^j_e, लीनौ Z_1 • उदित] Σ, उदति Ś$_e$ • है] Σ, हैं S_2 **15.2** रति] Σ, रस Z_1 • तें] Σ, सों $B_7N_eX_e$ • तें] Σ, सों $B_7N_eX_e$ • नीर] Σ, रीत S_7 • लै निवानन] $A_eB_2B_7G_eJ_1S_1S_5$Ś$_e$, लै निवाजन N_e, नीरवानन Ṭ$^j_e X_e$, लै निमानन $S_2S_6S_7$, लै नीमानन Z_1 • तें] Σ, सों $B_7N_eX_e$ • निबेरो] Σ, निबेर्‌यौ S_2 • है] Σ, हौ (unrh.) Z_1 **15.3** कहत] Σ, बिचार B_7N_e, बिचारि X_e • आ] S_1S_2Ṭ^j_e, यौं $A_eG_eJ_1$Ś$_eZ_1$, यहै B_2, के $B_7N_eX_e$, या $S_5S_6S_7$ • मसालौ] $\mathbf{E}J_1S_1Z_1$, सँवार्‌यो A_e, सामां B_2, बनायौ $B_7N_eX_e$, मसाले $S_2S_5S_6S_7$ • बिधि] Σ, बिध Z_1 • लोचन] $B_2J_1\mathbf{S}$, रचना $A_eB_7N_e\mathbf{E}Z_1X_e$ • निहारि] Σ, बिलोकि Ṭ^j_e, निहर Z_1 • को न] $B_2J_1N_e\mathbf{S}$Ṭ^j_e, जन A_eG_eŚ$_e$, कान्ह B_7, करै Z_1, होत X_e • होय] $J_1S_1S_5$, होत $B_2B_7\mathbf{E}S_2S_6S_7N_e$, चित A_e, को न Z_1, कान्ह X_e • चित] $B_2B_7J_1\mathbf{S}N_e$Ś$_eX_e$, होत A_e, चित्त G_eṬ^j_e, भयै Z_1 • है] Σ, हैं S_2 **15.4** कंचन] Σ, सोंने सों $B_7N_eX_e$ • को] $A_eB_2\mathbf{E}J_1S_2S_6Z_1$, सु° B_7X_e, सों N_e, कौं S_1 • लै] Σ, लैं S_1 • सवाद] Σ, सवा (unm.) Z_1 • लै] Σ, लैं S_1 • को] $A_eB_2B_7\mathbf{E}J_1N_eS_2S_7Z_1X_e$, कौं $S_1S_5S_6$ • को] Σ, कौं S_1S_6 • लूटि] $A_eB_2B_7\mathbf{E}N_eS_1S_2S_5X_e$, लुटि (unm.) J_1, लूट $S_6S_7Z_1$ • है] Σ, हैं S_1

15.1 उदित [S] adj. 'risen (as the moon)' evident; उजेरो [*ujjvālaka-] Br. 1. m. light; 2. adj. bright. **15.2** रति [S] f. 'enjoyment, passion' Kāma's wife; आनन [S] m. face; निवान [cf. nīpa-] poet. m. lake, reservoir; नीरवान var. [S] adj. 'having water or brightness' bright; निबेड़ना [cf. nivṛta-] v.t. to fulfil. **15.3** मसाला [A pl.] m. raw materials; को reg. interr. who? आ (यह) reg. this; चेरा [ceṭa-] m. servant. **15.4** कंचन [S] m. gold.

डीलदार, सीलदार, लाज को अहार जिन्हें, 1
          तीछन, मृगा से, देख देख रहियत है।
मीन और खंजन से, अलसे, अनोखे देखे, 2
          कंजदलहू तें ये बिसेष चहियत है।
ललित ललौहैं कसकौहैं चसकौहैं जान, 3
          ठाकुर कहत, सुख पाइ रहियत है।
औरन के नैन कहा नैनन के लेखे आवैं, 4
          ऐसे नैन होइँ तब नैन कहियत है॥ Ś16॥

तान लगे, तरवार लगे, बरछीहु लगे, लगे तीर अन्यारो।
बज्र को घाव लगे तें जियै, औ जियै बिष बाउ पिये मतवारो। 2
ठाकुर, जीवत सर्प डसो, अरु जीवत है नर सिंह बिदारो।
काल ग्रसे पै जियै जू जियै, न जियै इक नैन कटाक्ष को मारो॥ Ś17॥ 4

*मोहीं में रहत, रहै मोहीं सों उदास सदा, 1
          सीखत न सीखत, न सीख निरधारो है।
चौंको सो, चको सो, कहूँ जक सों जको सो, कहूँ 2
          पाइन थको सो, भाँति भाँतिन निहारो है।
ठाकुर, अचेत चित चोजवारी बातन मैं, 3

---

16 Granthāvalī 74, Śatak 16, Ṭhasak 27. 17 Granthāvalī 75, Ṭhasak 28. 18 Granthāvalī 76, Śatak 33, Ṭhasak 39. (GS: ullekha alaṅkāra in the first two lines.)

17.2 तें] G_e, ते Ṭ_e **18.1** रहै] $\mathrm{G}_e\text{Ś}_e$, रहैं Ṭ_e **18.2** जको] $\mathrm{G}_e\text{Ṭ}_e$, जक्यौ Ś_e • भाँति भाँतिन] $\mathrm{G}_e\text{Ṭ}_e$, भाँत भाँतन Ś_e

---

16.1 डीलदार [cf. ḍīl 'bulk, size'] adj. voluminous; सीलदार [śīla-] adj. humble; अहार [āhāra-] m. food; लाज को अहार जिन्हें idiom. those who who live on (i.e. like) modesty. **16.2** चहिय- [cāh-] Br. v.t. pass. 'are wished or liked' are superior to. **16.3** ललौहैं [cf. H lāl] Br. adj. (pl.) slightly red; कसकौहैं [cf. H kasaknā 'to feel pain'] Br. adj. (pl.) torturing; चसकौहैं [cf. H caskā] Br. adj. (pl.) inflaming desire; exciting; जान v.t. imp. consider! रहियत Br. v.i. (imperf.) stay (in delight). **17.1** तान poet. m. wound; अन्यार- [anī-] Br. adj. pointed, sharp. **17.2** बाउ 1. (?) [vāyu] m.f. (poisonous) wind, air; 2. [cf. H pyālā] reg. (?) cup. **17.4** जियै जू जियै Br. if one survives, then let it be (i.e. one may survive). **18.1** मोहीं में रहत Br. (my mind) stays in me; निरधार- [nirdhāra-] Br. v.t. to decide. **18.2** पाइन थको सो Br. tired in his legs. निहारो v.t. perf. (here: pres.) Br. Bund. look.

जानत न हरि सों कहा धौं बोलहारो है।
4 ऐसो चित चतुर, सयानो, सावधान मेरो,
एरी, इन आँखिन अजान करि डारो है॥ Ś18॥

1 *येही हिय द्वार के कदीम दरबान दोऊ,
इनहिं छिपाय काहू ऊपरी लयो है री।
2 हौं तौ इन दोहिन के पहरैं रही ती हाय,
बारी खेत खायौ, ऐसौ ऊलट भयौ है री।
3 ठाकुर कहत, बूझें आँसू भरि भरि लेत,

---

19 Granthāvalī 77, Kālidās-Hajārā (H$_e$) 321, Jaipur1 ff. 4r-5v (15), Sudhāsar [S$_1$ f. 60r (4), S$_2$ f. 10r (6/37), S$_7$ f. 43r (5/407)], Ṭhasak 38, Udaipur f. 126v (5), Vrindaban2 f. 71r. The Sudhāsar (S$_1$) presents this poem within the ūḍhā parakiyā section and introduces it as 'nāyaka kī ukti sakhī prata'.

18.3 अचेत] G$_e$Ṭ$_e$, कहत Ś$_e$ • जानत] G$_e$Ṭ$_e$, जानतु Ś$_e$ **18.4** ए री] Ś$_e$, ये री G$_e$Ṭ$_e$ **19.1** येही] J$_1$SU, येई **E**H$_e$V$_2$ • द्वार] **E**J$_1$SU, चारु H$_e$V$_2$ • कदीम] Σ, कदिम U • दरबान] **E**J$_1$UV$_2$, दरमान H$_e$**S** • दोऊ] Σ, दोय J$_1$ • इनहिं] **E**H$_e$V$_2$, इनकौं J$_1$, इनह S$_1$, यनहि S$_2$, यिनहि S$_7$, इहनै U • काहू] J$_1$S$_2$S$_7$U, कैसे **E**, कहि H$_e$V$_2$, कोऊ S$_1$ • ऊपरी] **ES**, उपरी J$_1$, कौनै धौं H$_e$V$_2$, हस रै U • लयो] Σ, ललयो (dittography) S$_2$ **19.2** हौं... हाय] **E**J$_1$S$_1$U, इह मोपै अकथ कथा न कछ्रू कही जाइ H$_e$V$_2$, यह कछ्रू अकथ कथा न मोपै कही जाति S$_2$S$_7$ • हौं] **E**S$_1$, मैं J$_1$U • दोहिन] S$_1$, दोइन **E**, द्रोहिन J$_1$, दोहन U • के] **E**U, कैं S$_1$ • पहरैं] S$_1$, रहत **E**, पहिरै J$_1$U • रही ती] J$_1$S$_1$, भरोसे **E**, हुती (unm.) U • हाय] Σ, सोघ J$_1$ • बारी] Σ, बारि S$_7$ • खेत] Σ, बे⟨ठ⟩ U • खायौ] Σ, षाषा J$_1$ • ऐसौ] H$_e$S$_2$S$_7$V$_2$, बडो **E**J$_1$, यह S$_1$, ऐसै U • ऊलट] H$_e$S$_1$S$_2$V$_2$, उलट **E**J$_1$S$_7$U

18.3 जानत न (न जाने) idiom. Br. who knows; बोलहारो है (बोलनेवाला है) Br. v.t. (what) it says. **18.4** ये var. pron. [pl. for sing.] this (mind); चित चतुर Br. (originally) clever mind; इन आँखिन (Br. pl. ag.) these (i.e. my) eyes. **19.1** क़दीम [A] adj. old (and therefore reliable); दरबान [P] m. guardian; दरमान var. reg. m. guardian; छिपाय [*chipp-] v.t. abs. Br. hiding, (here:) eluding; ऊपरी [cf. ūpara-] m. success; इनहिं... है Br. has anyone reached his aim by eluding or bypassing them? कहि कौनै धौं var. Br. tell me who; हस रै apa. laughingly, oh. **19.2** बारी 1. [cf. vāṭikā- x pālin-] m. gardener; बैठ खायौ apa. Br. did not do any work.

नेकहू न सोध देत, कौन कों दयो है री।
मेरो मन, मेरी आली, मोहिं यह जानी जात, 4
दृग-बटपारन के भेद मैं गयौ है री॥ Ś19॥

बाँके बनैत पटैत दमानकी औ कमनैत भले सुथरे ये।

---

20 Bharatpur1 f. 162r (76), Granthāvalī 78, Sudhāsar [S_2 f. 19r (-/26), S_6 ff. 87rv (175/547), S_7 f. 60rv (10/604)], Ṭhasak 29, Vrindaban1 f. 1r (3/3), Yājñik, Z_1 f. 36v (29). The Sudhāsar (S_7) includes this savaiyā into the 'kulṭā' (promiscuous woman) subsection of the parakiyā section.

19.3 बूझें] $H_eJ_1S_1V_2$, बूझे $\mathbf{E}S_2$, बूझै S_7U • आँसू] Σ, आंशु U • भरि भरि] Σ, भर भर U • लेत] H_e**S**V_2, देत **E**J_1U • नेकहू... दयो] **ESU**, बात के कहें ते ऐसो ऊठग ठयो H_eV_2 • नेकहू] **E**S_1, तनक J_1, यतनों S_2, यितनौ S_7, इतनोउ (unm.) U • सोध] **E**J_1**S**, भेद U • कौन] **E**J_1**S**, कोऊ U • कों] $G_eJ_1S_1$, कौ $S_2S_7Ṭ_e$U **19.4** मोहिं] Σ, मोह U • यह] **E**S_2S_7U, इमि J_1, इह H_eV_2, यहै S_1 • जानी] **E**$H_eS_2S_7V_2$, जांनि J_1S_1, जान U • जात] **E**, जाति S_2S_7, जोहि H_e, परी J_1S_1U, जाइ V_2 • दृग] H_eJ_1**S**UV_2, नैन **E** • बटपारन] **E**H_eJ_1U, बटबारन **S**V_2 • मैं] **E**$H_eS_1S_2V_2$, कौं J_1, मै S_7U **20.1** बाके] B_1**S**V_1Y_e, बाँकी **E**, ⟨ऐ⟩छे Z_1 • बनैत पटैत] B_1**E**S_2V_1, पठैत बनैट S_6, पटैत बनैट S_7, बनै है पटैत Z_1 • दमांनकी औ] $B_1S_2S_6S_7^{pc}V_1$, दिवानिन है **E**, मैदान के औ S_7, दया न कीयौ Y_e, दमानिकी है Z_1 • भले] Σ, Y_e, बडी **E** • सुथरे ये] B_1**S**V_1Y_e, सुघरे री **E**Z_1

19.3 शोध [S] m. information; सोध देना idiom. Br. to tell; भेद देना var. idiom. to confess; कौन कौ दयौ है Br. to whom they have given (my mind); कोऊ कौ दयौ है var. Br. 1. who has given them what? 2. who has given (anything) to anyone? ऊठग var. m. pretext; **19.4** मोहिं यह जानी जात Br. it seems to me; बटपार [H bāṭ + mār] m. highwayman, robber; भेद [S] m. 1. revolt; 2. plot; भेद में गयौ है Br. (my mind) is gone because of the treachery (or: joined the revolt). **20.1** बाँकी var. [vaṅku-] adj. f. (they are) flirtatious; बनैत [cf. bāṇa-] reg. m. spearman; पटैत [cf. paṭā 'cudgel'] m. one who fights with a cudgel; दमानकी [H damānaka 'shower of arrows in a battle'] poet. m. one who showers arrows; दिवानिन var. [P dīvānā] f. mad woman; कमनैत [cf. H kamān] Br. m. bowman; सुथरा [susthira-] adj. elegant; सुघड़ var. [cf. H gharṇā] adj. f. expert.

2 देत न पीठ बसीठनि, चाहत ईठ ह्वै, जान ते डीठ करे ये।
ठाकुर, चोट न चूकत कैसहू कै, इक मारे सु मारे डरे ये।
4 रोक, री, रोक, करैंयाँ कहा, कजरारे कटाछि कजाकी भरे ये॥ Ś20॥

1 मरद मुछारे, गभुवारे जौन होनहार,
तेऊ झूमि झूमि मतवारे से परे रहैं।
2 कोऊ घाट बाट, कोऊ चौहट अथाइन में,
कोऊ पौर खोरिन मैं ऊसई धरे रहैं।
3 लागत ना दारू, उपचार करि हारे बैद,
ठाकुर कहत, ऐसे हिय मैं अरे रहैं।

---

21 Granthāvalī 79, Ṭhasak 30.

20.2 देत न] B_1**ES**, देत (unm.) V_1, ईठन Z_1 • पीठ] **ES**V_1, पीठि B_1, देत Z_1 • बसीठनि] V_1Y_e, बसीठ बसीठिन **E**, बसीठन $B_1S_2S_7Z_1$, नसीठन S_6 • चाहत] B_1**E**$S_7V_1Z_1$, चाह (unm.) S_2, चाहति S_6 • ईठ ह्वै] B_1**S**V_1, देन सु **E**, ई ह्वै (unm.) Y_e, दीठ भऐ Z_1 • जान ते] $S_2V_1Y_e$, जात तें B_1S_7, जाति ते S_6, *om.* **E**, ⟨जम⟩ Z_1 • डीठ] Σ, दीठि **E** • करे ये] B_1**S**V_1Y_e, करेरी **E**Z_1 **20.3** कैसहू] B_1**S**, कैसहु **E**Z_1, कैसैहू V_1Y_e • कै इक] $B_1S_6V_1Y_eZ_1$, ऐसहु **E**, कै यक S_2S_7 • मारे सु मारे] $B_1S_2S_6V_1Y_e$, होत हैं ढीठ **E**, मारे सु मार S_7, मार सु मार Z_1 • डरे ये] B_1**S**V_1Y_e, करेरी **E**, घरेरी Z_1 **20.4** रोक री रोक] Σ, रोकि री रोकि B_1 • कहा] B_1**E**$S_2V_1Y_eZ_1$, कहां S_6S_7 • कजरारे] B_1**E**S_2, काजरारे V_1, कजरा जे Z_1 • कटाछि] B_1, कटाक्ष **ES**, कटाच्छि V_1Y_e, कजाक Z_1 • कजाकी] B_1**S**V_1Y_e, कटा सों **E**, कटाछ Z_1 • ये] B_1**S**V_1Y_e, री **E**Z_1

20.2 देत न पीठ Br. they do not turn their back (on messengers) (i.e. they keep sending or examining agents); कड़ेरा var. [cf. kaḍḍati] adj. (East.) 1. hard, firm; 2. harsh; ईठ [iṣṭa-] 'desired' m. friend; चाहत ईठ ह्वै Br. they look at them as friends; जान (जान-बूझकर) v.t. abs. (used as adv.) on purpose, intentionally; डीठ (ढीठ) [dhṛṣṭa-] reg. 1. adj. audacious; brash; stubborn; 2. f. audacity; insolence; obstinacy; ते डीठ करे ये you made them (i.e. the messengers or glances) brash; डीठ करैये (डीठ करनेवाले) Br. they are brash; चाहत देन var. Br. want to give. **20.3** डीठ करे var. Br. (glances) made bold; डर- (पड़ना) [H ḍālnā] v.i. to fall; मारे डरे Br. 1. the ones who are struck fall; 2. they kill; मारे डरैये Br. 1. the ones who are struck are to fall; 2. they are murderous. **20.4** रोक री रोक imp. stop them, oh, stop them! करैया कहा Bund. what are they doing? कटाक्ष [S] m. sidelong glance; कजरार- [cf. H kājal] Br. adj. painted with lampblack; कटा var. [S] f. murder, slaughter; कजाकी [P] Br. f. robbery. **21.1** मुछार- (मूँछवाला) reg. adj. with mustache; गभुवार- [garbha- + H vālā] reg. adj. small (child whose head has not yet been shaven); जौन Br. Bund. rel. pron. (the one) who; जौन होनहार Bund. those who have (great) future. **21.2** अथाई [āsthāyikā-] f. place for conversation; ऊसई (वैसे ही) Bund. adv. same as they were. **21.3** दारू [P] f. medicine; उपचार [S] m. cure, treatment; अड़ना [*aḍ-] v.i. 1. to come to a stop; 2. to be firm.

एक, दस, सौ लौं, औ सहस्र लौं, कहाँ लौं कहौं,
　　　　आँखन के मारे कैयो लाखन डरे रहैं॥ Ś21॥

*मानि कही, चलि बेगि, गुसाइनि, लेत कहा इत झेल किये मैं।
तैंही हने हैं, निकासिहै तैंही, न या चतुराई है और बिये मैं।
ठाकुर, मैन-लुहार सुधारि धरे खरसान, निहारि लिये मैं।
भौंह-कमानन तें दृग-बान चले, ते भले घले लाल हिये मैं॥ Ś22॥

काम के तीर सी, प्रेम गभीर सी, दाहन भीर सी जोति जगै है।
पानिप बूडी सी, जालिम जूडी सी, कौन की देखे न देह डगै है।

---

22 Bharatpur1 f. 154v (29), Granthāvalī 80, Sudhāsar [S_3 81r (129), S_7 113v (20/1085)], Vrindaban1 f. 5v-6r (5/31). The Sudhāsar (S_7) includes this poem into the 'madhyam dūtī' ('middle messenger') subsection of the 'dūtī' (messenger) section. It is explained in a dohā [S_7 f. 113r (16/1081)] that the madhyam dūtī uses both soft and harsh words in her message. The Sudhāsar (S_7) introduces it as 'dūtī kī ukti nāyikā prati' (the words of the messenger towards the beloved girl). 23 Bharatpur1 f. 162r (77), Granthāvalī 81, Sudhāsar [S_5 f. 158r (8), S_7 110v (11/1061)], Vrindaban1 f. 1rv (4/4). The Sudhāsar (S_7) includes this poem into the 'upālambha' (complaint) subsection of the 'caturkarma sakhīn ke' (the four activities of a companion) section and introduces it as 'sakhī kī ukti nāyakā prati' (the words of the beloved girl's friend to the lover).

22.1 मानि] B_1G_e, मान S_3V_1, मानु S_7 • चलि] Σ, चल S_3 • बेगि] $B_1G_eV_1$, बेग **S** • गुसाइनि] $B_1G_eS_3$, गुसाईनि V_1, गुसाइन S_7 • कहा] Σ, कहां S_3 • झेल] Σ, ⟨झे/के⟩ल V_1 **22.2** तैंही] $B_1G_eV_1$, तोही **S** • हैं] $B_1S_7G_e$, है S_3V_1 • निकासिहै] G_e, निकसिहैं B_1, निकासेहै S_3, निकासेहैं S_7, निकाशहै V_1 • तैंही] $B_1G_eV_1$, तोही **S** • न] $B_1G_eV_1$, नै **S** • या] Σ, यौं G_e **22.3** मैन] Σ, में (unm.) V_1 • लुहार] S_3^{pc}Σ, *om.* (unm.) S_3^{ac} • सुधारि] Σ, सुधार S_3 • खरसान] Σ, बरसान S_7 • निहारि] Σ, निहार S_3 **22.4** भले घले] $B_1G_eV_1$, घले भले **S** **23.1** दाहन] Σ, दाहैन S_5 **23.2** पानिप] Σ, पानि (unm.) V_1 • बूडी] Σ, बूड S_5 • जूडी] Σ, जूड S_5 • देखे न] G_eV_1, देषि न B_1, देख न S_5, देखत S_7

21.4 कैयो [cf. *kiyatta-] reg. 1. interr. how many? 2. adj. several (SBK); डर- [cf. H ḍālnā] Br. v.i. to be thrown down, dashed. **22.1** मानि कही Br. believe me what I said! गुसाइनि [gosvāminī-] f. voc. o lady! लेही कहा (क्या पाओगी) reg. what do you gain? झेल poet. f. delay. **22.2** तैं pron. (Br. ag.) you; हन- [han-] v.t. to strike (with an arrow); निकासिहै तैंही reg. you yourself will remove it; या Br. adj. this (skill); यौं var. adv. (here adj.) such; बिय- [dvitiya-] Br. adj. other; न... बिये मैं Br. no one else has this skill; **22.3** लुहार [lohākāra-] m. blacksmith; खरसान [khara- + śāna-] Br. m. whetstone. **22.4** घलना [*ghalyati] v.i. to penetrate. **23.1** गभीर (गंभीर) [gambhīra-] adj. deep (love). **23.2** जूडी [*jūḍa-] f. shivering fit; fever; malaria; डगना [cf. H ḍag] v.i. to tremble.

ठाकुर, धन्य वा मोहन, माई री, कंज से कोमल अंग अँगै है।
4 तीछी तिरीछी बिलोकनि रावरी, बीछी के डंक ते बंक लगै है॥ Ś23॥

लाख हजार चुबाइन कै झर द्वै दस पांचक अच्छर भाखै।
2 रूप सरूप अनूपनि कौ लखि दूरि करी मनु रंभा सु लाखै।
कोटि उपाय करो न करौ कोउ, लागी है प्रानन सौ, सुधि नाखै।
4 तोहि दई करतार कृपा कर ही सब अंग मैं ऊधमि आँखै॥ Ś24॥

वयःसंधि

1 भूलि गई खेल जो खेलौननि सौं खेलतीं तीं,
भूली गई बोलनि बतानि चंचलाई की।
2 आवन लगी है मिलिबे की लाज मोहन जू सों,
भावन लगी है रस रीत कविताई की।

24 Vrindaban1 f. 11r (13/65). Ṭhākur's signature is missing from this savaiyā. 25 Datiya1 f. 103v (335), Granthāvalī B13, Ṭhasak 'Jīvancarit' ($Ṭ^j_e$) pp. 2-3. cf. 'āi gaye abatālī doū kuca, chāpa laye sira syāma suhāī' Ālam-keli 328,3.

23.3 अंग] Σ, आंग S_5 • अँगै] Σ, अग (unm.) S_5 **23.4** तीछी] Σ, तीखी S_7 • रावरी] Σ, रावडी V_1 • है] Σ, हैं S_5 **24.1** अच्छर] *em.* अछर (unm.) V_1 **24.2** रूप] *em.* रुप (unm.) V_1 • दूरि] *em.* दुरि (unm.) V_1 • रंभा सु] *em.* रंभा (unm.) V_1 **24.4** दई] *em.* दइ (unm.) V_1 • ही] *em.* हि (unm.) V_1 • मैं] *conj.* मै V_1 • ऊधमि] *em.* उधम (unm.) V_1 **25.1** भूलि] G_e, भूल $D_1Ṭ^j_e$ • गई] G_e, गए D_1, गईं $Ṭ^j_e$ • जो] D_1, जो जो **E** • खेलौननि सौं खेलतीं] D_1, खेलती खेलौनन **E** • तीं] D_1, तें **E** • भूलि गई बोलनि] **E**, बिस --- D_1 • गई] G_e, गईं $Ṭ^j_e$ • बतानि] **E**, बतान D_1 **25.2** मिलिबे की] D_1, *om.* **E** • मोहन जू] D_1, देखि मनभावन **E** • सों] *conj.* *om.* (unm.) D_1, कों **E** • भावन] **E**, चा⟨हन⟩ D_1 • रस रीत] D_1, रीति भाँति **E**

23.3 अँग- [? cf. aṅgīkṛt] v.t. to hold. **23.4** डंक [cf. *ḍank-] m. sting; बाँका [vaṅku-] adj. 'crooked, bent' difficult. **24.1** चवाई Br. m. slanderer; झर Av. Bund. m. 1. flame, burning; 2. hatred; कै झर Br. on (i.e. as response to) the hatred; पांचक [pañca- + eka-] nuBr. m. some five; द्वै दस पांचक nuBr. m. a few (as opposed to lākh hajār; cf. H mere do akṣar sun lo!). **24.2** रूप सरूप Br. the beauty of their form; मनु Br. conj. as if; लाखै num. hundreds of thousands. **24.3** नाख- [cf. naṣṭa-] poet. v.t. to throw away, to destroy; सुधि नाखै Br. destroys my sense. **24.4** सब अंग मैं… आँखै among all your parts only your eyes (are mischievous); ऊधम [uddhama-] m. 1. commotion; 2. mischief; ऊधमी adj. mischievous. **25.1** खेल [*khel(l)-] m. play, amusement; जो जो var. rel. pron. all the... (that); खेलतीं तीं (खेलती थी) Bund. v.i. (pl. for sing.); बता- [vārtā-] reg. v.i. to converse; चंचलाई [cañcala-] Br. f. playfulness, childishness. **25.2** मनभावन var. [S] m. 'delight of the mind' Krishna, the lover; भावन लगी reg. v.t. started to please; रीति भाँति var. poet. custom and manners.

ठाकुर कहत, दोऊ उरज नकीब मानौ 3
अदल बदल दई ठौर ठकुराई की।
जोबन-महीप की अवाई कौ अदब जान 4
अगल बगल भई भीर लरिकाई की॥ Ś25॥

उरोज

हैं मृदु बैनन, नैनन, स्रोनन, अंगन-अंगन कोमल सो रहै।
मोहन कों जिन तू सकुचाव, री, यौं इक अंग प्रसंग को जोर है। 2
ठाकुर, तैं यह भेद न जानति, मैं इह खेद को कीनौ निचोर है।
बीर, कठोर उरोजनि सौं दिन-राति लग्यो उर यातें कठोर है॥ Ś26॥ 4

---

26 Bharatpur1 f. 160r (63), Granthāvalī B17, Sudhāsar [S$_1$ f. 272r (14), S$_3$ f. 147r (125), S$_4$ f. 72v (131), S$_7$ f. 195r (14)], Ṭhākur-satsaī (Ṭ) ff. 2v-3r (20b), Vrindaban1 f. 12v (9/74). • The Sudhāsar presents this poem in the 'aur nānābidhi kī brijkelī barnan' (description of other various love sports in Braj) subsection of the 'Brajrasrīti' section.

25.3 दोऊ उरज] D$_1$, जोर जोबन **E** • मानौ] D$_1$, आय **E** • अदल बदल दई] **E**, *दल करौ है ठौर D$_1$ **25.4** जोबन] D$_1$, मदन **E** • कौ अदब जान] D$_1$, लखि होन लागी **E** • भई भीर] D$_1$, सब फौज **E** **26.1** हैं] G$_e$, है B$_1$SṬV$_1$ • मृदु] B$_1$G$_e$S$_1$S$_4$V$_1$, म्रिद S$_3$S$_7$Ṭ • स्रोनन] B$_1$G$_e$S$_3$S$_7$V$_1$, ⟨स्रो/ओ⟩नन S$_1$, औनन S$_4$, सैनन Ṭ • अंगन अंगन] G$_e$**S**, अंग अंगन (unm.) Ṭ, अंगनि अंगन B$_1$V$_1$ • रहै] Σ, रहैं S$_4$ **26.2** तू] Σ, तुह (unm.) Ṭ • यौं इक] Σ, इओ इ Ṭ • है] Σ, हैं S$_4$ **26.3** यह] B$_1$G$_e$S$_1$V$_1$, यहि S$_3$S$_4$S$_7$, इह Ṭ • जानति] G$_e$V$_1$, जानत B$_1$SṬ • इह] ṬS$_1$V$_1$, इहि B$_1$G$_e$, यहि S$_3$S$_4$S$_7$ • को] B$_1$G$_e$S$_1$S$_7$ṬV$_1$, की S$_3$S$_4$ • निचोर] B$_1$G$_e$S$_1$ṬV$_1$, निबौर S$_3$S$_7$, निबेर S$_4$ • है] G$_e$S$_1$S$_3$ṬV$_1$, हैं B$_1$S$_4$ **26.4** कठोर] Σ, उरोज S$_1$ • उरोजनि] B$_1$V$_1$, सरोजनि G$_e$, कठोरनि S$_1$, उरोजन S$_3$S$_4$S$_7$Ṭ • राति] G$_e$S$_3$S$_4$, रात B$_1$S$_1$S$_7$ṬV$_1$ • यातें] Σ, ⟨आ⟩रते (unm.) Ṭ • है] Σ, हैं S$_4$

25.3 **जोर आना** var. idiom. to acquire strength; **नक़ीब** [A] m. adjutant, aid; **अदल-बदल** m. complete change; **ठकुराई** [ṭhakkura-] f. supremacy, authority (of childhood). **25.4** **मदन** var. [S] m. 'intoxicator', Kāma, the god of love; **महीप** [S] poet. m. king; **अवाई** [H ānā] f. coming; **अदब** [A] m. good manners; **अगल बगल** adv. (moved) aside; **लरिकाई** [H laṛkā] Br. f. childhood. **26.1** **सो रहै** Br. let it be; let's leave it apart. **26.2** **जिन तू सकुचाव** Br. do not cause embarrassment; **इक अंग** Br. (only) one part of your body (i.e. your breasts); **प्रसंग** [S] m. 1. attachment, relationship; 2. sexual intercourse; **ज़ोर** [P] m. 'strength' importance; **इक प्रसंग को जोर है** Br. the matter of only one part of the body is important. **26.3** **तैं** pron. reg. dir. you; **निचोड़** [*niścoṭayati] m. 'juice' essence; **निबोर-** apa. [? H nibeṛnā] v.t. to abandon; **इह खेद को कीनौ निचोर है** Br. I have fathomed this pain. **26.4** **यातें** Br. conj. therefore; **कठोर सरोजनि... कठोर है** var. Br. your heart wearing (a garland of) unfeeling lotuses is, therefore, unfeeling.

बनक

डारत कै पग-पाँवडे रीझि कै, कै कै खुसामद मानि खुस्याली।
झारत कै पिय प्यारे की गैल, निहारत कै गति की चलि चाली।
ठाकुर, या घघरा के घने ढिग को बरनै, सुनि लै, मेरी आली।
घेर कै घूम कै भूम कै झूमत, चूमत कै तरवान की लाली॥ Ś27॥
*वह घेर कै घाघरे घेर घिर्यौ, फिरि नीबी-चुनाइन मैं नधि गौ।

---

27 Bharatpur1 f. 155v-6r (37), Granthāvalī B23, Sudhāsar [S_1 f. 25v(mg) (131,4), S_6 f. 32v (164), S_7 f. 20rv (179)], Vrindaban1 f. 10v (10/62). The Sudhāsar (S_1) presents this poem as 'prasaṅg kari ghāghare kau varṇan' (a description of the skirt in this context). 28 Bharatpur1 f. 155v (35), Granthāvalī B28, Jaipur1 f. 3v-4r (11), Sudhāsar [S_3 f. 69-70r (72), S_7 f. 104r (9/1014)], Bābūrāmdīn: Sundarī-tilak (U_e) 22, Vrindaban1 f. 10rv. (8/60). S_3 does not indicate any specific context to this poem.

27.1 पाँवडे] Σ, या बडे G_e • रीझि] B_1G_e, रीझ **S**, रीझे V_1 • खुसामद] Σ, खुसामदि S_7 • मानि] Σ, खांन S_6 **27.2** पिय] $B_1G_eS_1S_6S_7^{ac}$, पग S_7^{pc}, पीय V_1 • प्यारे] $B_1G_eS_1S_7^{ac}V_1$, प्यारी $S_6S_7^{pc}$ • चलि] $B_1G_eV_1$, चल **S** • चाली] Σ, चाली ×या× V_1 **27.3** ढिग] B_1G_e S_6S_7, ढगं S_1, ⟨ढि/ठि⟩ (unm.) V_1 • बरनै] Σ, बरनैं S_7 • सुनि] Σ, सुन S_6 **27.4** घेर] $B_1G_eV_1$, घेरि **S** • घूम कै] $B_1G_eV_1$, घूमत कैं S_1S_7, घूमति कै S_6 • भूम कै] G_e, भूम अ B_1, भुव **S**, भूअ (unm.) V_1 • चूमत] Σ, भूमत S_6 **28.1** वह घेर कै] B_1, घेर कै (unm.) **S**, वह घिर कै G_eV_1, घुरि J_1U_e • घाघरैं] B_1G_e**S**V_1, घाघरो J_1U_e • घिर्यौ] B_1G_e**S**V_1, घिरो उघरो J_1U_e • फिरि] $B_1G_eS_7V_1$, पुनि J_1U_e, फेर S_3 • चुनाइन] B_1G_e**S**V_1, चुनावन J_1U_e • मैं नधि] B_1G_e**S**V_1, के मध J_1U_e

---

27.1 डारत Br. v.t. imperf. it spreads; कै... कै Br. conj. either...or..; पग-पाँवडा [*pādapaṭa-] m. doormat; या var. pron. reg. it; बडे रीझि कै var. with great deligth; कै खुसामद v.t. abs. Br. flattering (him); खुस्याली [P k͟huś-ḥālī] reg. f. happiness. **27.2** झारना [*jhārayati] v.t. to sweep; चाली [*calyā-] reg. f. motion, gait; गति की चाली f. (with) swiftness of movement; चलि (चंचल) poet. adj. restless, fickle; **27.3** घाघरा [gharghari-] m. an ample ankle-length skirt; ढिग [*ḍhigga-] reg. m. the edge of a garment. **27.4** घेर [*gher-] m. fullness (as of a skirt); घूम [cf. *ghummati-] m. going or turning round; भूम [bhūmi-] f. earth; भुव var. [bhūmi-] reg. f. earth; भूम कै घूम कै var. reg. going round the earth; तरवा [*talapāda-] Br. m. the sole of the foot. **28.1** घेर [*gher-] m. 1. the act of surrounding, siege; 2. fullness (as of a skirt); घुर- (घुलना) var. [cf. H gholnā] v.i. 1. to be dissolved in; 2. fig. to be intimate with; वह var. pron. that (i.e. my soul); घाघरा [ghargharī-] m. an ample ankle-length skirt; घेर कै घाघरे var. [cf. ghervālā] poet. (obl.) a skirt in its fullness; घिरो उघरो var. Br. (my mind) was surrounded and (then) it emerged; घेरना [*gher-] v.i. 1. to besige, to surround; 2. to importune; घेरे घिर्यौ var. was surrounded in the siege; नीवि [S] f. drawstring for a woman's dhoti; चुनाव [cf. H cunnā] f. 1. tuck, frill (in cloth); 2. crease, rumple; नधना [naddha-] v.i. 1. to be attached; 2. to be entangled.

उरझ्यो सुरझ्यो त्रिबली की गली, गहि नाभि की सुंदरता सँधि गौ। 2
कहि ठाकुर, छोडि चल्यो उत तें, गिरते गिरि-कंदर मैं धँधि गौ।
छतियाँ मैं छिप्यौ मन छोडि दै री, अँगिया-बँद बाँधत मैं बँधि गौ॥ Ś28 4

जगर मगर जरबाफिये बसन साजे, 1
जेवर जड़ाऊ भक्क झलक प्रमान की।
अंग अंग रंग रंग अमल तरंगमयी 2
अमित उमंग, है न ऐसी ओप आन की।
ठाकुर, निहारी बर बनक बिनोदवारी 3
भारी भीर सोहै संग सुंदरी तियान की।
भली भाँति करति प्रकाशित गली है यह, 4
आवति चली है, सो लली है वृषभान की॥ Ś29॥

संयोग

---

29 Nakhśikh-hajārā (Z_e) p. 237 (71). The poem is an illustration to the 'lāvanya hāva' (charming flirtation).

28.2 उरझ्यो] B_1SV_1, उरग्यौ G_e, उरझो J_1U_e • सुरझ्यो] B_1SV_1, सुरग्यौ G_e, सुरझो $J_1^{ac}U_e$, *** J_1^{pc} • गली] $B_1G_eSV_1$, बली J_1U_e • गहि] $B_1G_eSV_1$, पुनि J_1U_e • नाभि] $B_1G_eS_7U_eV_1$, नामि J_1, नाभ S_3 • सधि] $B_1G_eSV_1$, धध J_1U_e **28.3** कहि] $B_1G_eSV_1$, कवि J_1U_e • छोडि] $B_1G_eS_7V_1$, छूटि J_1U_e, छोड S_3 • चल्यौ] Σ, चलौ U_e • उत] B_1S, तित G_e, उन J_1U_e, त V_1 • तें] Σ, ते S_7 • गिरते] SV_1, गिरि तें B_1G_e, कुच की J_1U_e • गिरि] $B_1G_eJ_1U_e$, गिर SV_1 • धधि] $B_1G_eSV_1$, फंधि (unrh.) J_1U_e **28.4** छिप्यौ] Σ, छिपौ S_7 • छोडि] $B_1G_eV_1$, छांडि J_1U_e, छोड S_3, छाड S_7 • बंद] J_1U_eS, बंध $B_1G_eV_1$ • बँधि] Σ, बँध U_e

---

28.2 उरग- var. [ullagna-] Br. v.i. to be detached; सुरग- var. [sulagna-] Br. v.i. to be attached; संध- [saṃdadhāti] poet. v.i. to be joined, mixed. **28.3** तित var. Br. adv. there; गिरि [S] f. hill; कंदर [S] Av. Br. m. cave, cavern; धँध- (धँसना) [dhvaṃsati] poet. v.i. to sink into, to penetrate. **28.4** अंगिया [aṅgikā-] f. bodice; अंगियाबंद m. the string of the bodice; बांधत v.t. imperf. Br. when she was binding. **29.1** जगर मगर (जगमग) [*jag-] Br. adj. dazzling; जरबाफिये [P zarvāfta] reg. adj. made of golden and silver thread; साज- (सजाना) [sajjati] Av. Br. v.t. (perf.) 1. to adorn; 2. to wear; भक्क reg. adj. snow-white; झलक f. brightness, reflection, glimpse; झलक प्रमान की 1. evidenced or showed brightness, 2. brightness of (long) measure. **29.2** ओप [*opp-] f. lustre; न आन की Br. of nobody else. **29.3** निहारी [nibhālayati] Br. v.t. perf. I saw; बनक [P] Br. f. attire, decoration; संग adv. together (with her). **29.4** गली यह poet. this lane; आवति चली है (चली आ रही है) Br. v.i. the one who is coming; सो (वह) Br. it is; वृषभान 1. Vṛṣabhānu, Rādhā's father, 2. the sun in the Taurus, summer sun; (parikarāṅkura alaṅkāra).

1 *नाहर सी ननदी निगोडी फिरै आहट कों,
हटको कहीं के तुम्हैं आए जौ न हटकै।
2 पासऊ परोस दिबरानी औ जिठानी, तेऊ
जगतीं, जहाँ की तहाँ गैल लोग भटकै।
3 ठाकुर कहत, करै बिनती हजार जौ लौं,
तौ लौं उर लाई लाल बाल बरबट कै।
4 चटकै न पाटी पाँव धरिये पलंग ऐसें,
हे हरि, हरा कै मेरी जेहर न खटकै॥ Ś30॥

*दिवरानी जिठानी सबै जगतीं, घर के सुनिहैं, न गहौ बहियाँ।
2 हमैं सोवन देहु, जरूर कहा, इतनी सुनि लीजियै, मो सइयां।
कहि ठाकुर, काहे परे अकुलात हौ, धीर धरौ हियरा महियां।

---

30 Granthāvalī B14, Śatak 65. 31 Bharatpur1 f. 133r (12), Granthāvalī 82, Ṭhasak 159, Ṭhasak 'Jīvancarit' (Ṭ^j_e) p. 4. 'svakīyā nāyikā'

30.1 कहीं] *em.* कही **E** **30.2** °ऊ] G$_e$, यौं Ś$_e$ • परोस] G$_e$, परोसिन (unm.) Ś$_e$ **31.1** दिवरानी B$_1$Ṭ^j_e, देवरानी G$_e$Ṭ$_e$ • जिठानी B$_1$Ṭ^j_e, जेठानी G$_e$Ṭ$_e$ • जगतीं] G$_e$Ṭ$_e$, जगती B$_1$ • घर के] B$_1$, खडको G$_e$Ṭ$_e$ **31.2** देहु] B$_1$, देउ G$_e$Ṭ$_e$ • जरूर कहा] B$_1$, उलाइत का G$_e$Ṭ$_e$ • इतनी… सइयां] B$_1$, हरि धीर धरो हिरदै महियाँ G$_e$Ṭ$_e$ **31.3** कहि] B$_1$G$_e$, कह Ṭ$_e$ • काहे… महियां B$_1$, क्यों उकताव लला इतनी सुनि राखिय मो पहियाँ G$_e$Ṭ$_e$

30.1 नाहर [nakṣadhara-] m. lion; आहट [āghaṭṭayati] f. noise; हटकना [cf. H haṭnā] v.i. to go away; हटको कहीं के (people will say) 'move away, you rascal'; जौ न हटकै poet. if I don't forbid you; **30.2** पासऊ परोस (पास-पड़ोस में ही) adv. around, in the neighbourhood; जगना [cf. jāgṛta-] v.i. to be awake; जहाँ की तहाँ Br. adv. here and there; गैल [gati-] reg. f. road, path. **30.3** जौ लौं Br. adv. while (she); उर लाई लाल बाल poet. the Dear One embraced the girl; बरबट (के) [? bala- + varta-] adv. by force. **30.4** चटकना [cf. *caṭa-] v.i. to crack; पाटी [paṭṭa-] f. side pieces of a bedstead; हरा [hāra-] m. necklace; कै Br. conj. or; जेहरि Br. f. chain with small bells worn on the ankles; खटकना [H khaṭ] v.i. to sound, to rattle. **31.1** घर के (घर के लोग) the people of the house; खडको (खटका) var. [cf. H khaṭ] Br. m. sound (of footsteps). **31.2** जरूर (ज़रूरत) [A] (here:) poet. (? f.) pressing need (cf. H muśkil f.). उलाहित var. [cf. Br. ulāha 'to spring up'] Bund. m. hurry. सइयां [cf. svāmī-] reg. m. lord; **31.3** परे (लेटे हुए) v.i. perf. lying flat (cf. H idiom. 'paṛe paṛe akulānā' to loose heart) अकुलाना [cf. ākula-] v.i. to be agitated; उकताना var. v.i. 1. to be irritated; 2. to be restless; क्यों उकताव var. reg. why are you in a hurry? पहियाँ var. [pakṣa-] Av. postp. adv. near, (here:) from.

सब रैनि धरी, न बकावो हमैं, अबै सेर में पोनी कती नहियाँ॥ Ś31॥

छबि देखत ही बनि आवति है, उपमान अनेक ते वारि धरे।
सखि, वा बतरानि-जम्हानि समै मुसिकानि भँडा सुख के उखरे।
कहि ठाकुर, चाहनि सों उमगे, अलसान सने, आँखियान अरे।
सुखसेज कौं आवत दोऊ चले सु मनोज मजेज के तेज भरे॥ Ś32॥

कौंल को महल, तामैं खस कौ बितान तन्यौ,
चंदन चहल राखी सखिन मँचाके हैं।

---

32 Bharatpur1 f. 153v-4r (25), Granthāvalī B15, Sudhāsar [S_1 f. 273r (19), S_3 f. 148r (130), S_7 f. 195v (19)], Vrindaban1 f. 6v (9/35). • The Sudhāsar presents this poem in the 'aur nānābidhi kī brijkelī barnan' (description of other various love sports in Braj) subsection of the 'Brajrasrīti' section. 33 Bharatpur1 f. 159r (57), Granthāvalī B16, Sudhāsar [S_2 f. 42v (2/43), S_3 f. 231/22r (grīṣma 3), S_7 134r (3/1266)] Vrindaban1 f. 11v (3/68).

31.4 रैनि] B_1, रैन G_eṬ$_e$ • धरी] B_1Ṭ^j_e, परी G_eṬ$_e$ • बकावो] B_1, खिजावो G_eṬ$_e$, बकाओ Ṭ^j_e • अबै] G_eṬ$_e$, अबी B_1 **32.1** छबि] Σ, छब V_1 • बनि] B_1G_e, बन **S**V_1 • उपमान] Σ, उपमानि V_1 • वारि] $B_1G_eV_1$, बार **S** **32.2** बतरानि] $B_1G_eV_1$, बतरान **S** • जम्हानि] $B_1G_eV_1^{pc}$, जम्हाँन S_1, जभ्यान S_3, जमान S_7, जम्हा V_1^{ac} • मुसिकानि] B_1 $G_eS_7V_1$, मुसक्यान S_1S_3 • भँडा] $B_1G_eS_1V_1$, भया S_3S_7 • सुख] Σ, मुख S_1 **32.3** कहि] Σ, कवि S_3 • चाहनि] $B_1G_eV_1$, चाहन **S** • सने] Σ, समैं S_1 **32.4** सु] $B_1G_eS_1V_1$, सौ S_3S_7 **33.1** कौ] Σ, कै S_3 • चंदन] B_1**S**, चंद की G_e, चंद (unm.) V_1 • सखिन] Σ, सखन S_3 • मँचाके] Σ, मैचाक (unrh.) V_1 • हैं] B_1G_e, है **S**V_1

31.4 सब रैन परी var. Br. the whole night is still ahead us; **बकाओ** [? cf. H baknā] v.caus. to cause to shriek; **खिजाना** var. [kṣīyate + krudhyati] v.t. to irritate; **पोनी** f. a bundle of wool (which is cut to extract the yarn from); **कतना** [*kartati] v.i. to be spun; **सेर... नहियाँ** idiom. reg. we have to spin a seer and not even a handful of wool has been spun. **32.1 देखत ही बनि आवति है (देखते ही बनती है)** idiom. Br. worth seeing; **ते** pron. Br. (obl.) (on) it; **वारि धरे** Br. sacrificed. **32.2 भंडा** [bhāṇḍāra-] m. multitude; **उखड़ना** [cf. *utskṛta-] v.i. 1. to be rooted; 2. to become useless. **32.3 चाह** [*cāh-] f. 1. desire, eagerness; 2. fondness; **चाहों से** adv. eagerly, lovingly; **उमग-** [unmagna-] Av. Br. v.i. 1. to be elated; 2. to swell; **अलसा** [ālasya-] reg. m. drowsiness; **आँखियान** Br. f. (pl. obl.) 1. with each other's eyes; 2. with our eyes; **अड़ना** [*aḍ-] v.i. 1. to stop; 2. to be wedged, locked. **32.4 कौं** postp. Br. to; **सु** 1. poet. (expletive particle); 2. [so] pron. Br. those (two who...); 3. adv. well; **मजेज** [A mizāj] m. 1. nature; 2. haughtiness. **33.1 कौंल** [kamala-] poet. m. lotus; **खस** [P k̲has] m. the fragrant grass Andropogon muraticum (used in thatching); **चहल** [*cakhalla-] 1. m. (here: f.) reg. mud (of sandalwood mixed with water); 2. f. merriment, festivity; **चंद की चहल** apa. merriment at moonlight; **सखिन राखी** Br. the companions made; **माचाना** [*macyate] v.t. to produce.

2 छूटत फुहारे खगे सुमन सुगंधवारे
बीजन बहल राखी ललित बनाके हैं।
3 ठाकुर कहत, गोरी सहित गुपाल सोभा
सुखनि रसाल केलि-कौतिकन याके हैं।
4 हम जाय जोए दुहूं दुहुनि मैं गोए सेज
सौरभ भिजोए सोए बसन बिछाके हैं॥ Ś33॥

पूर्वराग

देखत ही चित लेइ चुराइ, सु या ब्रज माँझ सुनी चरचा इक।
2 तातें गई चलि नंद के मंदिर देखन नैनन को सुखदाइक।
ठाकुर, को सुषमा बरनै, अरे, काम लगै जिनको छबि पाइक।

34 Granthāvalī 24, Śatak 21, Ṭhasak 32.

33.2 खगे] Σ, खरे S_7 • राखी] $B_1G_eV_1$, छोरी **S** • ललित] Σ, ललीत (unm.) V_1 • ब-नाके] Σ, बनाक (unrh.) V_1 • हैं] B_1G_e, है **S**V_1 **33.3** ठाकुर कहत] G_e**S**, ठा° B_1, ठाकुर कहैत V_1 • सुखनि] $B_1G_eV_1$, सुखन **S** • कौतिकन] B_1**S**, कोक नय G_e, कौ न (unm.) V_1 • याके] $G_eS_3S_7V_1$, पाकें B_1, ⟨या/पा⟩के S_2 • हैं] $B_1G_eS_2$, है $S_3S_7V_1$ **33.4** जोए] Σ, जोवे S_7 • दुहूं दुहुनि] B_1, दुहुँ दुहुँन G_e, दोऊ दुहुन S_2S_7, दोऊ दुरन S_3, दुहूं दुहुन V_1 • गोए] Σ, गोवे S_7 • बसन] $B_1S_2S_7$, बिछन G_e, बसत S_3, बछन V_1 • हैं] B_1G_e, है **S**V_1

33.2 फुहारा [H favvārā x H phuhār] m. 1. fountain; 2. watering can; खगना v.i. 1. to be set, to stick; 2. to be mixed in (flowers in the fountain); वीजन [S] m. (here f.) fan; बहल [cf. vāhana-] m. vehicle; बीजन बहल poet. vehicle with fan; छोरी var. (?) Br. v.t. perf. abandoned (i.e. kept for subsequent use). **33.3** शोभा [S] f. radiance, beauty; रसाल [rasa-] adj. impassioned; केलि-कौतिकन Br. m. pl. amorous sports; कोक var. [S] m. sexual pleasure; केलि-कोक var. [S] f. amorous play; नय var. [S] m. custom (of sexual treatises); गोरी... याके हैं Br. Krishna is together with Radha, whose radiance and impassioned amorous sports are pleasures (for us) (RSh) (alternative interpretations: 1. Krishna is together with Radha, whose radiance and amorous sports are impassioned with pleasures; 2. Krishna together with Radha is radiant and their amorous sports are impassioned with pleasures; 3. Krishna together with Radha, who play amorous sports, is impassioned with the joys of radiance; 4. The radiance of Krishna together with Radha, who plays amorous sports, is impassioned with pleasures. etc.) **33.4** जोहना [dyotate] v.t. to see; गोय- [gopayati] Br. v.i. to be hidden; दुहुँ दुहुँन मैं गोए Br. hidden in each other; भिजो- [H bhigonā x H bhījnā] reg. v.t. to soak; बसन [S] m. clothes; बिछन var. [*vicchādana-] m. bedding. **34.1** चित लेइ चुराइ Br. steals the mind; चरचा इक Br. the matter (that he steals the mind). **34.3** काम लगै Br. Kāma appears to be (only); पाइक [H pāyak 'footman, armed attendant'] Br. m. slave (of his beauty).

काहे न जाइ सबै ब्रज देखन, सांचहूँ साँवरो देखबे लाइक॥ Ś34 24॥

कािल्ह कहूँ हँसि बोली गोपाल सों, जानि न जाइ कहा कहो कौनैं।
ता छिन तें कछु बावरी सी भई, ए सखी, साध रही गहि मौनैं।
ठाकुर, तैं फिरि आईं बुलावन कै तुहि हेरत स्याम सलौनैं।
जाइ इते पर जौ मिलि बैठिये, तौ फिर पैठियै कौन के भौनैं॥ Ś35॥

*कौन हौ जू, जोतिसी हैं, आगम बखानत हैं,
धाम धाम नाम जग जाहिर हमारौ तौ।
आवौ, बैठि जावौ, पान खावौ, पाइ छ्ववावौ, फेरि,

---

35 Granthāvalī 25, Śatak 17, Ṭhasak 52. 36 Bharatpur6 f. 7v, Datiyal f. 105r (339), Granthāvalī 20, Jaipur4 f. 14v, Sudhāsar [S_1 f. 180v-1r (6), S_3 f. 86r (158), S_7 f. 117v (4/1120)], Ṭhasak 63, Udaipur f. 126v (4). The Sudhāsar presents this poem within the svayaṃdūtikā section. S_1 introduces it as 'nāyak hī āpa jotasī kau rūpa palaṭyau' i.e. 'the lover himself took the appearance of an astrologer'. S_1 adds 'vyaṅga hai' i.e. 'it is ironical' (Since Radha recognised him). This interpretation, however, seems overcomplicated. S_3 and S_7 simply mention that it is in 'prasnottar' i.e. 'question-answer' form.)

35.1 जानि] G_eṬ$_e$, जानी $Ś_e$ • कहा कहो] G_eṬ$_e$, कहीं घर $Ś_e$ **35.3** तैं] G_eṬ$_e$, ते $Ś_e$ • आई] G_e, आईं $Ś_e$Ṭ$_e$ • तुहि] G_e, तुहिं $Ś_e$Ṭ$_e$ **36.1** कोन हौ जू] B_6, को हौ (unm.) **E**D_1U, कोंन हो जू J_4, को हौ जू (unm.) S_1, को है (unm.) S_3, को हैं (unm.) S_7 • जोतिसी] $B_6G_eJ_4$**S**, जोतिकी D_1U, जोतिषी T_e • हैं] S_1, हौं कछु D_1, है B_6J_4, हैं कछु **E**, है जू (unm.) S_3, हैं जू तू (unm.) S_7, हां कछु (unm.) U • आगम] B_6J_4**S**, आगमु D_1, जोतिसै G_e, जोतिषै Ṭ$_e$, जोतिष U • बखानत] D_1**S**, बिचारत **E**U, बिचारति B_6J_4 • हैं] S_1S_7, है $B_6J_4S_3$, हौ D_1**E**U • धाम धाम] B_6J_4**S**, ऐहूं ⟨ना/धा⟩म D_1, येही सुभ **E**, इ काम U • नाम जग] $B_6J_4S_1S_3$, धाम कामु D_1, काम धाम G_e, काम जग S_7, धाम काम Ṭ$_e$, धाम धाम U

34.4 सांचहूँ Br. adv. truly. **35.1** कहूँ Br. adv. somewhere; कहा कहो कौनैं Br. Bund. who said what; कही घर कौनैं var. 1. what was told at home? 2. whom did she tell it at home? **35.2** साध [śraddhā-] f. desire; मौन साधना idiom. to observe silence; रही v.i. perf. (your desire) remained (as it was) (i.e. was not fulfilled); गहि v.t abs. Br. having taken to, since you took to (silence). **35.3** तैं pron. reg. 1. dir. you; 2. they (her companions); बुलावन कै Br. (then you came back) to call me (saying that); तुहि हेरत स्याम Br. Krishna is looking for you. **35.4** जाइ जौ मिलि बैठिये Br. if you meet Krishna and sit down with him; पैठियै कौन के भनैं idiom. Br. 'whose house will you (be able to) enter?' who will respect your honour? **36.1** बिचारना var. v.t. 1. to think; 2. to know; जाहिर [A] adj. well-known.

सुचिते, सुचित ह्वै कै गनित निकारौ तौ।
3 ठाकुर कहत, इह प्रेम की परिच्च्छा निज
इच्छा के प्रमान कछु मंत्र उर धारौ तौ।
4 मेरो मन मोहन सों लाग्यौ लाख लाख भाँति,
मोहन को मन मो सों लागिहै बिचारौ तौ॥ Ś36॥

1 जोतिषी बिचार कहै, राधिका जू, सुनौ बात,
मोकों गति जानि परै तेरे निज स्याम की।
2 डोलत ही खोर खोर, हेरत तिहारी ओर,
तेरो बोल सुने गैल भूलि जात धाम की।
3 ठाकुर कहत, काम काज ना सोहात कछू,
बाढो रस प्रेम भूली बात सबै जाम की।

37 Granthāvalī 21, Ṭhasak 64.

36.2 आवौ] B_6G_eSU, अऔ D_1, आयौ J_4, आओ $Ṭ_e$ • बैठि] $D_1\mathbf{E}S_1$, बेंठि B_6J_4, बैठ S_3S_7U • जावौ] Σ, जाउ D_1 • पाँन खावौ] **S**, पांउ छुऔं D_1, पानी पियौ **E**, पाव धावौ ×क× B_6, पाव⟨ण⟩ ⟨छुवा⟩यौ J_4, पाय छुवावौ U • पाइ छुवावौ] **S**, पान खावौ B_6**E**, पांन षाउ D_1, पान षायौ J_4, पांन पांन षांवो (dittography) U • फेरि] $B_6D_1S_7^{ac}$, फेर $\mathbf{E}J_4S_1S_3$, छोरि S_7^{pc}, तुम U • सुचिते] $B_6D_1J_4$**S**, हौय कै **E**, बुझु U • सुचित] $B_6D_1\mathbf{E}J_4S_3S_7$, स्वचित S_1, रस चित U • ह्वै कै] $B_6J_4S_3S_7$, हो कै D_1, नेक **E**, हवै कैं S_1, गन U • गनित] Σ, गणति S_7 • निकारौ] Σ, निहारौ U **36.3** कहत] D_1**ESU**, कहति B_6J_4 • इह प्रेम] $B_6J_4S_3$, बूझौ प्रैंम D_1, प्रेम नेम **E**, प्रेंम (unm.) S_1, एक प्रेम ही S_7, पूछौं पेम U • की] $S_3^{pc}\Sigma$, को **E**, *om.* (unm.) S_3^{ac} • परिच्च्छा] J_4, परिछ्या (unm.) B_6, परिछ्या D_1S_1, परेखो **E**, प्रीछा (unm.) S_3, प्रीछा S_7, परिक्षा U • निज] B_6J_4**S**, निजु D_1, देखि **E**, निजं U • इच्छा] D_1S_1, सिछा (unm.) B_6, इछ्छा $\mathbf{E}S_3S_7$, सिच्छा J_4, छा (unm.) U • के प्रमान] **S**, के बिचार B_6J_4, की प्रतीत D_1, की परिछ्छा **E**, कै बिलासन U • कछू मंत्र] $B_6J_4S_1$, रीत नीकै D_1, भली भाँति **E**, करूं मंत्र S_3, कहूं मंत्र S_7, की बात U • उर धारौ] B_6J_4**S**, निरधारौ D_1**EU** **36.4** मोहन] Σ, मोहनि U • सों] $B_6\mathbf{E}S_1S_7U$, सौ $D_1J_4S_3$ • लाग्यौ] $B_6J_4S_1S_3^{pc}S_7$, लागौ D_1, लागत **E**, *om.* (eyeskip) S_3^{ac}, लाग U • लाख लाख] B_6J_4**S**, है भाँति **E**, हर भां∗ D_1, चुक्यौ भांति (unm.) U • भाँति] Σ, भांत D_1 • मोहन को] Σ, मेरौ मन° S_1 • मन] $B_6\mathbf{E}J_4S_3S_7U$, मो सौ D_1, °मोंहन S_1 • मो सों] $B_6\mathbf{E}S_7$, मन D_1, मो सौ J_4U, सौं S_1 • लागिहै] $B_6D_1\mathbf{E}J_4$, लाग है **SU** • बिचारौ] Σ, बिचार B_6 **37.1** जोतिषी] $Ṭ_e$, जोतिसी G_e • मोकों] G_e, मोको $Ṭ_e$ •

36.2 सुचिते [su-citta-] poet. m. obl. 'in your good mind' concentrated; सुचित poet. adj. unoccupied, at leisure. **36.3** परेखो var. Br. m. test, verification; इछ्छ के बिचार var. poet. 1. considering your opinion; 2. considering my desire; मंत्र [S] m. advice; उर धारौ idiom. Br. 1. let me put (dhārõ) in my heart; 2. find in your heart; निरधार- var. [nirdhārayati] Br. v.t. to determine;

जैसी रट तोहि लगी, राधे, स्यामसुंदर की,
तैसी रट वाहि लगी, राधे, तेरे नाम की॥ Ś37॥

बैठे पटा पर बिप्र बखाने, लगी पलका सों सुनै सियरा सों।
जोतिष, देख ले, ऐसी कहै गठियाय ले आँचर के छियरा सों।
ठाकुर, वा दिन देहौ कहा निज बूझि ले बात सबै जियरा सों।
मोहन को मन तो सों लगै, जब तै लगै मोहन के हियरा सों॥ Ś38॥

बिप्र की बानी सुने सकुची कही, वा दिन तेरे बिषाद नसैहौं।
रंक तें ह्वैहौ निसंक महा, मनमोहन कों जब अंक लगैहौं।
ठाकुर, मीठो करौं मुख रावरो, पावँ परौं, जग कीरति गैहौं।
हाथन चूरा, गरे मनिमाल, सु कानन कौं मुकताहल देहौं॥ Ś39॥

वे तौ नैन बान मारि घायल कै जात रहे,

---

38 Granthāvalī 22, Ṭhasak 191, Udaipur f. 126v (6). 39 Granthāvalī 23, Ṭhasak 192.

38.1 बैठे] **E**, बैठो U • लगी] **E**, सुनै U • सों] **E**, के U • सुनै] **E**, लगी U **38.2** जोतिष] **E**, जोतिक U • ले] **E**, कै U • गठियाय] **E**, गंठियाय U • आँचर] **E**, अंचर U **38.3** ठाकुर] **E**, कह ठाकुर, (unm.) U • निज] U, यह **E** • बूझि ले] **E**, पूछहूं U **38.4** तो सों] G_e, तों सो $Ṭ_e$, तौ सौ U • जब तै] U, तैं **E** • मोहन] U, मनमोहन **E** **39.3** परौं] G_e, परौ $Ṭ_e$

38.1 पटा m. a board on which to sit to eat, or while taking part in religious ceremonies; लगी पलका सों Br. sitting on the bed; सियरा सों Br. coolly, quietly. **38.2** जोतिष ऐसी कहै Br. the almanac says; देख ले imp. have a look! गठियाना [grantha-] v.t. 1. to wrap up; 2. to make a knot; छियरा reg. m. edge, border; आंचल के छोर पर गांठना idiom. to learn by heart. **38.3** देहौ कहा Br. what will you give me (as a reward); बूझि... सों Br. ask all this from your heart. **39.1** नसैहौं Br. v.t. fut. I will demolish. **39.3** मीठौ करौं मुख रावरो idiom. Br. 'I will feed you with sweets' I will offer you my best hospitality.

दायल दगा के देनहार, तिनैं गाइयै।

2 हाइ दई, नेह कौ तबीब है न कोऊ और

जाकै पास धाय जाय दरद सुनाइयै।

3 ठाकुर कहत, यह प्रेम की बिथा है दीह,

चोट को न चिन्ह कल पलहू न पाइयै।

4 एक ठोर पीर होय, औषदि लगावै कोऊ,

---

40 Bharatpur1 f. 156r (39), Bharatpur5 ff. 25v-26r, Granthāvalī 57, Jaipur1 f. 5r, Seondha (O_2), Sudhāsar [S_1 f. 181v (3), S_2 ff. 45v-46r (-/45), S_3 f. 99rv (58), S_7 f. 145v-6r (5/1387)], Ṭhākur-satsaī (Ṭ) ff. 3v-4r (30), Ṭhasak 31, Vrindaban1 f. 9v (2/54), Yājñik. The Sudhāsar (S_1) presents this poem within the 'pūrvā anurāga' section.

40.1 वे तौ] $Y_e\Sigma$, बाँके **E**, आप J_1 • बान] Σ, मारि B_5 • मारि] B_1B_5**E**$J_1S_2S_7V_1$, मार $O_2S_1S_3$Ṭ • कै जात] $Y_e\Sigma$, कियो री **E**, कर जात (unm.) O_2 • रहै] $B_1B_5J_1O_2$**SṬ**V_1, मोहिं **E**, रहैं S_7, है हे Y_e • देनहार] $B_5G_eS_7O_2$, मनिहार J_1, दांनहार S_2S_3, देनहारे S_1Ṭ, देत हाय $Ṭ_e$, दैनहारि V_1 • तिनैं] $B_5O_2S_2S_7$Ṭ, जिन्हैं G_eJ_1, तिन्हैं $B_1S_1Ṭ_eV_1$, तने S_3 • गाइयै] Σ, गाईऐ Ṭ **40.2** हाइ] Σ, एरी **E** • दई] Σ, बीर **E** • नेह कौ] $B_1B_5S_1S_2V_1Y_eO_2$, प्रीति कौ **E**, *om.* J_1, नेहु कौ S_3S_7Ṭ • तबीब है] B_1B_5**SṬ**V_1Y_e, न दूसरो **E**O_2, दूसरो न नेह को J_1 • न कोऊ] B_1B_5**SṬ**V_1Y_e, तबीब **E**J_1O_2 • और] B_1**SṬ**V_1Y_e, औ (unm.) B_5, कोऊ **E**, मिलै J_1, आह O_2 • जाकै] Σ, ताकै O_2 • पास] $B_1B_5^{pc}O_2$**SṬ**V_1Y_e, द्वार **E**, पा (unm.) B_5, घर J_1 • धाय] B_1B_5**ESṬ**V_1, जाय $J_1O_2Y_e$ • जाय] B_1B_5**ESṬ**V_1, धाय $J_1O_2Y_e$ • दरद] **E**$O_2S_1S_3S_7$Ṭ, दर दरद (dittography) B_5, बचन J_1, दरस S_2, दरध V_1 • सुनाइयै] Σ, सुनाईऐ Ṭ **40.3** ठाकुर] Σ, ×ठाकुर कहत, यह प्रेम की बिथा है देह चोट को न चिन्ह कल पलहू न पाइयै× ठाकुर, B_5 • ठाकुर कहत] Σ, ठा° B_1, ठाकुर कहैत V_1 • यह] $B_1B_5S_2S_7$ṬV_1Y_e, कहूँ **E**, करै J_1, कीजे O_2, इह S_1, यहि S_3 • प्रेम] B_1B_5**SṬ**V_1Y_e, चोट **E**, आपनो J_1, *om.* O_2 • की] B_1B_5**SṬ**V_1Y_e, को **E**O_2, *om.* J_1 • बिथा है] $B_1B_5S_1S_2$ṬV_1Y_e, न चिन्ह **E**, उपाय J_1, कथा S_3S_7, न सौ O_2 • दीह] B_1**S**V_1Y_e, देह B_5, कछू **E**, होय J_1, जतन O_2 • चोट को न] $B_1B_5O_2$**SṬ**, बिन देखे **E**, रोग कौं न J_1, सु चोट कौ न (unm.) V_1 • न] $S_1S_2S_3S_7^{pc}$, *om.* (unm.) S_7^{ac} • चिन्ह] B_1B_5**SṬ**V_1, चैन G_e, चिन्हैं J_1, चिंन O_2, नैन $Ṭ_e$ • कल] $B_1B_5O_2$**SṬ**V_1Y_e, नैन G_e, कहा J_1, चैन $Ṭ_e$ • पलहू] B_1B_5**ESṬ**, ⟨प⟩तन J_1^{ac}, ⟨अ/ज⟩तन J_1^{pc}, पलकहू (unm.) O_2, पलहु V_1 • न पाइयै] Σ, कराइयै J_1, न पाईऐ Ṭ

40.1 घायल [ghāta-] adj. wounded; घायल कै जात रहै Br. keeps wounding me; दायल [cf. H dāṃv] m. 'one who takes his chance' revenger; दगा [P] m. deceit, fraud; तिनैं गाइयै Br. he should be considered in this way. **40.2** तबीब [A] m. doctor. **40.3** दीह [dīrgha-] adj. long, big.

रोम रोम पीर कहाँ औषदि लगाइयै॥ Ś40॥

आइ अगीत पछीत गई, निसि टेरत मोहिं सनेह के कूकन।
जानत हैं कि न जानत हैं, कोई यौं न जरै नर-नारि सरूकन।
ठाकुर, ह्वै न सकी कहि कै, अब का कहिये हरि सों यह चूकन।
देखि उन्हें न दिखाइ कछू, ब्रज पूरि रह्यौ चहुँ ओर चुहूकन॥ Ś41॥

*ठाढे रहे घनस्याम उतै, इत आनि अटा चढि हौं पुनि झाँकी।
जानत हौ तुमहू ब्रजरीति, न प्रीति रहै पलहूँ भरि ढाँकी।

---

41 Granthāvalī 127, Śatak 3, Ṭhasak 26. 42 Bharatpur1 f. 164rv (90), Granthāvalī 129, Śatak 15, Sudhāsar [S_1 f. 271v (10), S_2 f. 58v59r (1/62), S_3 f. 146v (121), S_4 f. 71v (127), S_7 f. 194v (10)], Thākur-satsaī (Ṭ) f. 2v (19), Ṭhasak 58, Vrindaban1 f. 8v (10/48), Yājñik. • The Sudhāsar presents this poem in the 'aur nānābidhi kī brijkelī barnan' (description of other various love sports in Braj) subsection of the 'Brajrasrīti' section. S_4 introduces it as 'nainana kī' (sports of the eyes). • The end of the second line evokes Rahīm: 'khaira, khūna, khāṃsī, khusī, baira, prīti, mada-pāna; rahimana dābe̞ na dabaiṃ, jānata sakala jahāna.' Dohāvalī 44

40.4 ठोर] $B_1B_5G_eJ_1$**S**ṬV_1, जांगा O_2Ṭ$_e$ • पीर] Σ, होय Ṭ$_e$, *om.* (unm.) Ṭ • होय] $B_1B_5G_eO_2V_1$, कोऊ J_1, जहाँ **S**Ṭ, तहां Ṭ$_e$ • औषदि] $B_1B_5J_1V_1O_2$, औषद G_e, औषध $S_1S_2S_7$Ṭ, औषधि S_3Ṭ$_e$ • लगावै] $B_1B_5G_eJ_1$**S**V_1, ल×∗×गावै O_2, लगाऊं Ṭ$_e$ • कोऊ] B_1 $B_5G_eO_2$**S**Ṭ, वीर J_1Ṭ$_e$, कोउ V_1 • रोम रोम] Σ, ठौर ठौर J_1 • कहाँ] B_1**E**$O_2S_1S_3S_7$ṬV_1, कहा B_5S_2, कितै J_1 • औषदि] $B_1B_5J_1V_1$, औषद G_e, वोषद O_2, औषध S_1S_7Ṭ, औषधि S_3Ṭ$_e$ • लगाइयै] $S_1^{pc}\Sigma$, लगाइहै S_1^{ac}, लगाईऐ Ṭ **41.1** गई] Ś$_e$, दई G_eṬ$_e$ • निसि] G_eṬ$_e$, निस Ś$_e$ **41.2** यौं] G_eṬ$_e$, ये Ś$_e$ **41.3** ह्वै] Ś$_e$, हौं G_eṬ$_e$ • सकी] Ś$_e$, सकौं G_eṬ$_e$ **42.1** रहे] Σ, रहैं B_1 • इत] $B_1S_1S_3S_7V_1$, इत मैं पुनि **E**, यत S_2, पत S_4, इन G_e^{vl}, उतै Ṭ, इति Y_e • आनि] B_1**E**V_1, आन **S**Ṭ • चढि] B_1**E**$S_1S_2S_4V_1$, चढ S_3S_7Ṭ • हौं पुनि] B_1S_1, हौ पुनि $S_2S_3S_4V_1$, *om.* **E**, हौ पुन S_7Ṭ **42.2** जानत B_1**S**ṬV_1, जानति **E** • हौ] Σ, हौं S_7 • ब्रजरीति] B_1**E**S_2S_3, ब्रजकीत S_4^{ac}, ब्रजरीत $S_1S_4^{pc}S_7V_1$, ब्रजरीत रीत (dittography) Ṭ • न प्रीति] B_1**E**S_3S_4, *om.* (unm.) S_2, न प्रीत S_1S_7ṬV_1 • पलहू भरि] B_1**S**V_1, कबहूँ पल **E**, पलहूँ भर S_7Ṭ

40.4 ठोर [sthāvara-] m. place, spot. **41.1** अगीत (आगे) [agratas] reg. adv. 1. in front (of the house); 2. first; पछीत (पीछे) [paścāt] reg. adv. 1. behind; 2. then; आइ अगीत पछीत गई reg. 1. she came forward then withdrew; 2. first she came, then she left; निशि [S] adv. at night; कूक [*krukna-, krukta-] f. shrill cry, call (of birds). **41.2** जानत हैं v.t. imperf. Br. people know; कि conj. or; सलूक [A sulūk] m. treatment. **41.3** ह्वै न सकी Br. I could not be his; कहि कै Br. (even if I have) given my word; का Br. interr. how? चूकन [*cukk-] f. (Br. pl.) (about my) mistakes. **41.4** उन्हें pron. pl. him (i.e. Krishna); चुहूक (चहक) reg. f. 'warbling' slander. **42.2** ढाँकना [*ḍhaṅk-] v.i. to be concealed.

ठाकुर, भूलत कैसैंहूँ नाहिनै, ऐसी अरी वा बिलोकनि बाँकी ।
भावत ना छिन बैठिबो भौन को, घूँघट कौन को, लाज कहाँ की॥ Ś42॥

भावती, रूप महाछ्छवि छाजती आवती, आनँद सों झिलती हौ।
बूझति यातें सनेह कथा कछ्छू, प्रेम के पंथन मैं पिलती हौ।
ठाकुर, एक दिना हित-हौंसन काहे न आन हिये हिलती हौ।
चंद से आनन, को हौ, कहौ, नितही हमकों इतही मिलती हौ॥ Ś43॥

वा निरमोहिनि रूप की रासि जो ऊपर के उर आनति ह्वैहै।
बारहूँ बार बिलोकि घरी-घरी सूरत तौ पहिचानति ह्वैहै।
ठाकुर, या मन की परतीति है जो पै सनेह न मानति ह्वैहै।

---

43 Granthāvalī 130, Śatak 13, Ṭhasak 47. 44 Sundarī-tilak (C_e) 296, Granthāvalī 133, Ramchandra Shukla (I_e) p. 444 (I_e), Jaipur1 f. 4r (12), Raskusumākar (R_e) p. 159 (433), Ṭhasak 45, Ṭhasak 'Jīvancarit' ($Ṭ^j_e$) p. 19, Miśrabandhu Vinod (V_e) p. 731.

42.3 भूलत] B_1, कैसहुँ **EṬ**, कैसहूँ S_1, कैसैंहू **S**, कहैत भूलत (unm.) V_1, भूलत Y_e • कैसैंहू] $B_1V_1Y_e$, भूलत **ESṬ** • नाहिनै] Σ, नाहिन S_4 • बिलोकनि] B_1**E**V_1, बिलोकन $S_1S_2S_4$, बिलोकत S_3S_7, बिलोक Ṭ • बाँकी] Σ, वाकी S_4 **42.4** छिन] Σ, छन V_1 • बैठिबो भौन को] Σ, भौन को बैठिबो **E** • भौन] $Ṭ^{pc}$Σ, भवन (unm.) $Ṭ^{ac}$ • घूंघट] S_4^{pc}Σ, यूं घट S_4^{ac}, घूंघन Ṭ • कौन को] B_1**E**S_1S_3ṬV_1, कौंन की $S_2S_4S_7$ **44.1** निरमोहिनि] $I_eJ_1Ṭ^j_eV_e$, निरमोहीनि C_e, निरमोहिन $G_eṬ_e$, निरमोहिनी R_e • की] Σ, कि V_e • जो ऊपर] $C_eṬ^j_e$, जऊ उर G_eI_e, जू ऊपरि J_1, जौ उपर R_e, जोऊ उर $Ṭ_e$, न ऊपर V_e • के] $C_eJ_1R_eV_e$, हेत $G_eṬ_e$, हेतु I_e, ते $Ṭ^j_e$ • उर आनति] $C_eR_eṬ^j_e$, न ठानति $G_eI_eṬ_e$, उर आंनत J_1, मन आनति V_e • ह्वैहै] Σ, हूहै J_1 **44.2** बारहूँ] **E**J_1, बारइ C_e, बार हु R_e, बारहि I_eV_e • सूरत] Σ, सूरति C_e • पहिचानति] Σ, पहिचांनत J_1 • ह्वैहै] Σ, हूहै J_1 **44.3** की] Σ, को I_e • परतीति] Σ, परतीत **E** • मानति] Σ, मांनत J_1 • ह्वैहै] Σ, हूहै J_1

42.3 नाहिनै adv. (reg. emph.) no; अड़ना [*aḍ-] v.i. 1. to come to a stop; 2. to stick; to be jammed. **42.4** भौन को postp. Br. at home. **43.1** भावती pron. Br. f. you; छाज- [*chadyati] Br. v.i. to grace (a scene); झिल- (झिलमिलाना) [*jhil-] reg. v.i. to be radiant. **43.2** बूझति Br. v.t. imperf. you ask (the people something about love); यातें Br. conj. for this reason; पिलना [cf. H pelnā] v.i. to enter. **43.3** हित हौंसन Br. out of the enthusiasm of love; काहे न Br. why not? आन Br. v.i. abs. coming; हिये [hṛdaya-] Br. m. obl. in my heart; हिलना [*hillati] v.i. to become familiar or intimate with. **43.4** को हौ Br. who are you? **44.1** निरमोहिनि (निर्मोहिनी) [S] f. girl without love; ऊपर के उर (से) Br. superficially; जऊ var. conj. although; आनती ह्वैहै v.i. (Br. presum.) 'must bring (my matter)' probably thinks (about me); जऊ उर हेत न ठानति ह्वैहै var. although she is probably not intent (on love) in her heart. **44.2** बारहूँ बार बिलोकि घरी घरी Br. looking at me again and again in every moment; सूरत तौ पहिचानति ह्वैहै Br. at least she must recognise my face. **44.3** प्रतीति [S] f. trust; जो पै Br. conj. if.

आवत हैं नित मेरे लिये, इतनो तौ बिसेषहू जानति ह्वैहै॥ Ś44 133॥

हौं बरजी बर बीसक लौं, दुलही, यहि मारग स्यामरो आवै।
ढीठ भई चितवै चहुँ ओर, अमंद हँसै, हँसि हार हलावै।
हौं तौ कही न बिलोकु गोपालहिं, यौं उरझी, अब को सुरझावै।
जो बिष खाय सो प्रान तजै, गुर खाय सो काहे न कान छेदावै॥ Ś45॥

काहु के होइ तौ कैसी करौ किन, जैसे मनै लगे तैसे सिखाए।
ज्यौं ज्यौं, अरी, हटको इन लोगन, त्यौं त्यौं खरे बिगरैं ये सवाए।
ठाकुर, काह्वै रुचे न तौ का करौं, मोहिं तौ ऐसे लटे भले भाए।

---

45 Granthāvalī 135, Ṭhasak 152. This poem does not contain Ṭhākur's poetic signature. It's last line is similar to that of Ś60. 46 Granthāvalī 136, Sudhāsar [S_1 70r (9), S_2 f. 14rv (30/21), S_7 50r (71/473)], Śatak 46, Ṭhasak 59, Z_1 ff. 36v, 38v (30).

44.4 हैं] Σ, है $Ṭ_e^j$ • लिये] Σ, लए G_e • °हू] $C_eJ_1R_e$, कै **E**I_e • जानति] I_e**E**R_eV_e, जानत C_eJ_1 • ह्वैहै] Σ, हूहै J_1 **46.1** काहु] ES_2, काहू $S_1S_7Z_1$ • कैसी करौ] $S_1S_2^{pc}S_7$, कोऊ कहै **E**, कैसी कैरौ, S_2^{ac}, कहौ ⟨कि/का⟩नि Z_1 • किन] S_1, जिनैं S_2S_7, निज $G_eṬ_e$, जिन $Ś_e$, कोऊ Z_1 • लगे] **S**, लगी **E**, ल⟨गे⟩ Z_1 **46.2** अरी] **S**, खरो $G_eṬ_e$, खरी $Ś_e$, हरे Z_1 • हटको] **E**, हटक्यौ **S**, हटके Z_1 • इन] ES_1, यन S_2, यिन S_7, इनि Z_1 • बिगरैं] Σ, बिगरे S_7 • सवाए] Σ, सबए (unm.) S_2 **46.3** ठाकुर] Σ, कहि ठाकुर (unm.) Z_1 • काह्वै रुचे न तौ] ES_7, का करौ Z_1 • काह्वै] **S**, काहु **E** • का करौं] Σ, काहुयै न रुचे Z_1 • मोहिं] Σ, मेरे Z_1 • ऐसे लटे] **S**, ऐसे लगे **E**, अतिही (unm.) Z_1 • भले] Σ, मन Z_1

44.4 बिसेषहू Br. adv. especially; बिसेष कै var. abs. (used as adv.) Br. especially; जानति ह्वैहै v.t. (Br. fut. presumptive) must know. **45.1** बर [bala-] adv. vehemently; बीसक [H bīs + H ek] num. reg. some twenty times; लौं postp. Br. up to; दुलही (दुल्हन) [durlabha-] f. bride. **45.2** अमंद हँसै Br. laughs loudly; हँसि v.i. abs. Br. laughingly; हला- (हिलाना) [*hillati] v.caus. Br. to shake. **45.3** यौं adv. in this way. **45.4** गुड़ खाना to eat raw sugar (as offered to children to distract them before their ears are pierced); गुर... छेदावै idiom. Br. when one has taken the jaggery why shouldn't she let her ears be pierced (i.e. one should accept the consequences of love). **46.1** काहु के होइ Br. they belong to someone; कैसी करौ किन Br. why shouldn't one do as she wishes? कोऊ var. pron. Br. someone (else); जिनैं var. rel. pron. (Br. obl.) to whom, to whoever; निज मनै लगी var. idiom. Br. it occurs in their own mind. **46.2** खरा var. [khara-] adj. genuine, true, right; खरे [khara-] adv. well, a lot; हटक- (हटाना) [*haṭṭ-] reg. v.t. 'to drive away (animals)' to forbid; ज्यौं ज्यौं हटको Br. (perf. for pres.) as I forbid; सवा(या) [sapāda-] adv. 1. a quarter more; 2. much larger; 3. great. **46.3** काह्वै रुचे न Br. if it does not please someone; भाए [bhāti] v.i. 1. perf. I liked; 2. reg. pres. I like (cf. Br. bhāvai) लटे भले भाए reg. I like good and bad; लगे भले भाए (भले और भाए लगे) var. Br. I liked (cf. H acchā lagnā).

नैन हमारे, हमारे मनैं, लगे चाहैं जहाँ ही तहाँ ही लगाए॥ Ś46॥

राधा, न नोहरिया लगै, कान्ह की काल्हि की मैं गति या अवलोको।
बावरो सो बिन मोल बिकानो, सन्यो सो सनेह, न मानत रोकों।
ठाकुर, है कहा रूप अतूल सी, मोहनै फूल सी बूझत मोकों।
देखत है दिखवाई लगी फिरै, द्वारन द्वारन देखत तोकों॥ Ś47॥

ठाढे हूजै, यामैं कछू टेढकी न मारी जात,

---

47 Bharatpur1 f. 162rv (78), Granthāvalī 139, Sudhāsar [S_1 f. 270v1r (6), S_2 f. 58v (-/61), S_3 f. 145v-6r (117), S_4 70v-1r (124), S_7 f. 194rv (6)], Vrindaban1 f. 1v (5/5). • The Sudhāsar presents this poem in the 'aur nānābidhi kī brijkelī barnan' (description of other various love sports in Braj) subsection of the 'Brajrasrīti' section. • S_4 omits the last line.

46.4 मनै] ES_1S_2, लगे S_7, मेनै Z_1 • लगे] $S_1S_2Z_1$, लग्यौ **E**, मनै S_7 • चाहैं] **E**, चाहे SZ_1 • जहाँ ही तहाँ ही] **S**, जहाँई तहाँई EZ_1 **47.1** न नोहरीया] Σ, मनोहरिया G_e • कान्ह] Σ, कान S_3 • की] Σ, कों G_e • काल्हि] $B_1G_eS_1S_2V_1$, काल S_3S_7, काल्ह S_4 • अवलोको] Σ, अवलोकों G_e **47.2** बिन] Σ, बिनि B_1 • बिकानो] $B_1G_eS_1S_2S_4V_1$, बिकान्यो S_3S_7 • सन्यो] Σ, सुन्यो S_7 • रोकौ] $B_1G_eS_1V_1$, रोक्यौं S_2, रोक्यौ $S_3S_4S_7$ **47.3** फूल] Σ, फल S_2 • बूझत] B_1G_e**S**, बूझति S_3, बूझन V_1 **47.4** देखत... तोकों] Σ, *om.* S_4 • दिखवाई] G_e, दिखवाय B_1SV_1

46.4 **नैन हमारे हमारे मनै** Br. the eyes are mine and the mind is also mine; **हमारे मनैं** idiom. Br. to my mind; **लगे चाहैं** Br. 'want to be fixed' want to be in love; **जहाँ ही तहाँ ही** Br. exactly there where (they want). **47.1** **नोहर** poet. adj. unattainable; **न नोहरिया लगै** Br. (Krishna) does not seem unattainable; **मनोहरिया लगै** var. Br. you look enchanting (to Krishna); **कान्ह की या गति (को) अवलोको** Br. I saw this behaviour of Krishna; **अवलोको** v.t. (Br. perf. m.) I saw (given in m. for the sake of rhyme); **47.2** **सनना** [H sānnā] v.i. 1. to be mixed with; 2. fig. to be imbued with; **रोकों** Br. 1. f. (does not even consider) any prohibition (H rok bhī); 2. v.t. (when) I stop him; . **47.3** **है कहा रूप अतूल सी** Br. what is this incomparable beauty? **मोहनै** adj. emph. Br. very charming (flower); **बूझ-** [budhyate] Br. v.i. to consider. **47.4** **देखत है** v.t. imperf. Br. it seems; **दिखवाई** f. desire to see.

स्वात लौं, अघैहैं पिकबैनी पल कौ थिरैं।
चाहवारी चोजन सों, रसभरी मोजन सों 2
हादिल भई हैं घनस्याम स्याम सुमिरैं।
ठाकुर कहत, देखौ रसवारे ग्रंथन मैं, 3
प्रेमवारे पंथन मैं, एही ठहरी सिरैं।
साँवरे सरोज से बदन के गुपाल, तौ पै 4
गोपिन की ललनीं, ते अलनी भई फिरैं॥ Ś48॥

---

48 Bharatpur1 f. 159v (59), Granthāvalī 144, Sudhāsar [S_1 f. 272r (13), S_3 f. 147r (124), S_4 f. 72rv (130), S_7 f. 195r (13)], Ṭhākur-satsaī (Ṭ) f. 3r (21b), Vrindaban ff. 11v-12r (70). • The Sudhāsar presents this poem in the 'aur nānābidhi kī brijkelī barnan' (description of other various love sports in Braj) subsection of the 'Brajrasrīti' section.

48.1 ठाढे] Σ, ठाडे V_1 • टेढकी न] Σ, येंडकी×नकी× न (dittography) Ṭ • स्वात] B_1, स्यान $G_eS_4V_1$, स्यात $S_1S_3S_7$Ṭ • अघैहैं] $G_eS_1S_4$ṬV_1, अपैहै B_1, अघैये S_3, अघय्यै S_7 • पि-क॰] Σ, ×⟨पि⟩×क Ṭ • कौ] $B_1G_eS_1V_1$, कै $S_3S_4S_7$Ṭ **48.2** चाहवारी] $B_1G_eS_1S_3S_4V_1$, चाहेवारी Ṭ, चारबारी S_7 • रसभरी] $B_1G_eV_1$, हितवारी $S_1S_3S_7$Ṭ, हनिवारी S_4 • हादिल] $B_1S_1S_3V_1$, हायिल G_eS_7, हाटल S_4, हसदिल (unm.) Ṭ • हैं] $B_1G_eV_1$, है **S**, है॥ Ṭ • घनस्याम स्याम] Σ, स्याम घनस्याम S_7 • सुमिरैं] $B_1G_eS_1V_1$, सिमरै S_3Ṭ, समरै S_4, सुमरै S_7 **48.3** ठाकुर कहत] G_e**S**Ṭ, ठा॰ B_1, ठाकुर कहैत V_1 • ग्रंथन] Σ, ग्रंथ न S_1 • एही] G_e**S**V_1, येई B_1, इही T • ठहरी] B_1S_1, ठहरीं G_eṬV_1, ठहरै $S_3S_4S_7$ • सिरैं] $B_1G_eV_1$, सिरै $S_3S_4S_7$Ṭ **48.4** सरोज] Σ, सरोजन (unm.) Ṭ • गुपाल] Σ, गोपाल Ṭ • गोपिन] B_1G_e, गोपन **S**Ṭ, गोपीन (unm.) V_1 • फिरैं] $B_1G_eS_1V_1$, फिरै $S_3S_4S_7$Ṭ

48.1 **ठाढे हूजै** Br. v.i. imp. stand erect (as clever ones do)! **यामैं** Br. in it (i.e. in standing); **टेढकी** [*treddha-] Bund. f. 1. crookedness; 2. slant; **टेढकी मारना** idiom. 'to bend' to make a trick; **स्यान** var. [sajñāna-] adj. cunning, clever; **स्यान लौं** var. Br. adv. like (a clever person); **अघैहैं** [āghrāpayati] Br. v.i. fut. 1. will be satisfied; 2. will be delighted; **पिकबैनी** [pika-, vacana-] adj. f. woman with the voice of a cuckoo; **पलकौ थिरैं** Br. (she will be satisfied when she can look) with unblinking eyes. **48.2** **चोज** [codya-] m. (here f.) wonderful words; **मौज** [A] f. 1. wave; 2. surge of emotion; **हादिल** (?) 1. [cf. H hāyal dil] adj. wounded in the heart; 2. [cf. PA ḥādiṣa 'misfortune', ? with H -la] poet. adj. destroyed. **हायल** (**घायल**) var. [cf. ghāta-] poet. adj. wounded; **48.3** **एही** (**यही**) pron. emph. reg. it is it (love) that; **सिरैं** [śiras-] adj. (Br. obl.) 'at the head' as the most important. **48.4** **ललनी** [S] poet. f. daughter; **अलिनी** [cf. alī] poet. f. black bee.

आवहु, लाल, दिखाय लियावहुँ भूषन मंजु मँजीर से बोलैं।
2 झूमै झुकै लचकै औ लफै सु अदान करै बहु भाँति अमौलैं।
ठाकुर, राजैं जराव के जेवर, ते वै प्रभानि की खानि सी खोलैं।
4 चंग चढावत बाँहैं चलैं, मनि-मोतिन हेमलता फरी डोलैं॥ Ś49॥

1 घैरवारी, बैरवारी, चौचँद-चबाववारी —
नारी दुखिहाई ते निहारि हियैं माखैंगी।
2 गाँव, घर, गलिन, सखी री, घाट, पनघट

---

49 Bharatpur1 f. 160r (62), Granthāvalī 145, Sudhāsar [S_1 260r (1), S_3 136r (69), S_4 f. 59r (75), S_7 f. 188v (14)], Ṭhākur-satsaī (Ṭ) f. 2r (15), Vrindaban1 f. 12r (71). The Sudhāsar includes this poem in the 'Brajrasrīti' section and introduces it as 'pataṅg khel'. 50 Bharatpur1 f. 162v (79), Granthāvalī 146, Sudhāsar [S_1 f. 227v-8r, S_3 f. 110r (116), S_7 f. 172r (5/1638)], Vrindaban1 f. 1v (6). The Sudhāsar introduces this poem as 'abhilāṣ' (longing) in the 'abhilāṣādi 10 dasānirūpan' (The ten conditions such as longing etc.) section.

49.1 दिखाय] Σ, दिखाप S_4 • लियावहु] G_eṬV_1, लिवावहु B_1S_7, लिवांवहुँ S_1S_3, लवा-बहु S_4 • मंजु] $G_eS_1V_1$, मंज $S_3S_4S_7$Ṭ • मँजीर] Σ, मतीर S_4 • से] $B_1S_1S_4S_7$ṬV_1, *om.* (unm.) G_e, सो S_3 • बोलैं] $B_1G_eS_1S_3S_7V_1$, बोलै S_4Ṭ **49.2** झूमै] Σ, झूमैं S_1 • झुकै] $G_eS_3S_4S_7V_1$, झुकैं B_1S_1Ṭ • लचकै] $G_eS_3S_4S_7V_1$, लचकैं B_1S_1Ṭ • लफै] Σ, लफैं B_1Ṭ • सु अदानि] B_1, सो अदान $S_3S_4S_7$, सुख दान G_e, सु अदान S_1V_1Ṭ • करै] Σ, करैं Ṭ • बहु] Σ, बद Ṭ • भंति] Σ, भांत Ṭ • अमौलैं] Σ, अमौलै Ṭ **49.3** राजैं] $B_1G_eS_1S_4V_1$, राजै S_3S_7Ṭ • जराव] Σ, जरा (unm.) S_4 • वै] Σ, ब्रि Ṭ^{ac}, बौ Ṭ^{pc} • प्रभानि] G_e, प्रभान Σ • खानि] $B_1G_eS_4V_1$, खान $S_1S_3S_7$Ṭ • खोलैं] $B_1G_eS_1S_3S_7V_1$, खोलै S_4Ṭ **49.4** चढावत] $B_1G_eS_1S_4S_7V_1$, चढावति S_3, चड़ावत Ṭ • बाहैं चलैं] $B_1G_eS_1V_1$, बाहै चलै $S_3S_4S_7$, बांह चलै Ṭ • चलैं] $G_eS_1S_3V_1$, चलै S_4S_7 • मनि] $B_1G_eV_1$, मनो **S**Ṭ • फरी] B_1G_e**S**, फरि V_1, फल Ṭ • डोलैं] $B_1G_eS_1S_3S_7V_1$, डोलै S_4Ṭ **50.1** चबाव°] $B_1G_eS_1V_1$, चबाय° S_3S_7 • नारी] Σ, नारि G_e • निहारि] $B_1G_eS_1$, निहार $S_3S_7V_1$ • माखैंगी] $B_1G_eS_1V_1$, माखैगी S_3S_7

49.1 लियावहुँ [H lānā] v.caus. (Br. fut.) I'll bring (and show); मंजीर [S] m. anklet. **49.2** झूमना [*kṣumbhati] v.i. 1. to sway; 2. to move imposingly; लचकना [*lacc-] v.i. to bend, to be elastic ; लफना v.i. 1. to bend; 2. to twist the hips; अदा [A] m. 1. elegance, charm; 2. flirtatious gesture. **49.3** ते pron. they; वै [S] emph. Br. encl. indeed. **49.4** चंग [Γ] f. paper kite with a lamp or small cymbals attached to it; फर- (फलना) [phalati] Br. v.i. to bear fruit; मनि-मोतिन हेमलता फरी Br. a golden creeper bearing fruits of jewels and pearls. **50.1** घैरवारी f. sladerer; चौचंद m. slight, defamation; चवाव [caturavāda-] f. libel, insult; दुखिहाय- [duḥkha- + hata-] Br. adj. suffering; ते pron. Br. they; माखना [cf. amarṣa- 'anger'] v.i to be angry.

घातैं जोर-जोर कै, अनेक बातैं भाखैंगी।
ठाकुर कहत, हमैं जा दिन मिलैंगे कान्ह, 3
करि सनमान, लाज रंचहू न राखैंगी।
खोलि खोलि पलकनि, नैनन की ललकनि, 4
छवि छलकनि कौ, छवीलो रस चाखैंगी॥ Ś50॥

जब तें बिलोकि गई रावरो बदन, बाल, 1
तब तें अचेत सी बियोग झार झुरई।
हेम की लता सी, चपला सी, चारु चाँदनी सी 2
मदन सताई पै न मैं जनाई भुरई।
ठाकुर कहत, भूमि बिकल बिहाल परी, 3
देखियै गोपाल, ताहि उपमा न जुरई।
रति के भँडार तें दुराइ कै चोराइ मानो 4
काहू आनि मंदिर मैं रूप-रासि कुरई॥ Ś51॥

घर-बाहर, पास-परोस के बैर, अकेले कबै कर पैयत है।

---

51 Granthāvalī 158, Ṭhasak 85. 52 Granthāvalī 170, Karerua (F), Ṭhasak 61.

50.2 गाँव] Σ, गांम S_7 • गलिन] Σ, गली मै S_7 • जोर-जोर] Σ, जोरि जोरि S_7 • भाखैंगी] $B_1G_eS_1V_1$, भाखैगी S_3S_7 **50.3 ठाकुर कहत**] Σ, ठा° B_1 • मिलैंगे कान्ह] $B_1G_eS_1S_7^{pc}V_1$, मिलैगे कान S_3, मिलैं कान्ह (unm.) S_7 • करि] $B_1G_eS_1V_1$, कर S_3S_7 • सनमान] $B_1G_eS_1V_1$, अभिमान S_3S_7 • राखैंगी] $B_1G_eS_1V_1$, राखैगी S_3, भाखैगी S_7 **50.4 खोलि खोलि**] $B_1G_eS_1S_7$, खोल खोल S_3, षोल षोलि V_1 • पलकनि] $B_1G_eS_1V_1$, पलकिन S_3S_7 • नैनन] Σ, नैननि B_1 • की] B_1^{pc}Σ, *om.* (unm.) B_1 • ललकनि] $B_1G_eV_1$, ललकन **S** • छलकनि] $B_1G_eV_1$, छलकन **S** • चाखैंगी] B_1S_1, राखैंगी G_e, चाखैगी $S_3S_7V_1$ **52.1 पास**] **E**, बैर F • बैर] **E**, बास भयो F • कबै] **E**, *om.* F • पैयत] **E**, आइयतु (unm.) F

50.2 घात 1. [S] m. (here: f.) blow; 2. [cf. Pk. ghatta-; ? x ghāta-] f. treachery; trickery; 3. (?) here: v.t. to strike down; **भाख-** [cf. bhāṣate] Br. v.t. to say. **50.4 ललक** [cf. lalati] f. 1. desire; 2. zeal; 3. sudden gush (of any liquid); **छलक** [cf. *chalakka-] f. 1. overflowing; 2. splash; **राखैंगी** var. [rakṣā-] v.t. to protect, to accomplish. **51.1 झार** [*jhāla-] Av. Br. m. heat, burning; **झुरना** [*jhurati] v.i. 1. to dry up; 2. to pine, to wither. **51.2 जनाना** [H jānnā] v.caus. to show, to tell; **भुरई (भूल ही से)** Br. f. emph. (obl.) (even) by mistake. **51.3 भूमि** [S] f. (obl.) on the earth (she became); **विकल** [S] adj. restless; **बिहाल** [P behāl] reg. adj. in a bad state; **उपमा न जुरई** poet. no simile can be made. **51.4 दुराइ कै** Br. adv. secretly; **मानो** conj. as if (somebody poured all beauty into that house; **कुर-** Br. v.t. to pour, to throw. **52.1 बैर** Br. m. (pl.) enmity; **अकेले कबै कर पैयत है** Br. when can it be done alone? (i.e. you will need help; or, at least two pepole are needed for enmity.)

2 मग माँझ कजात मिले, सजनी, तौ बिलोकत चित्त डरैयत है।
कहि ठाकुर, भेंटबे के उपचार बिचारत द्यौस बितैयत है।
4 बतियाँ न बनैं जिनसों कबहूँ, छतियाँ तिन्हें कैसे लगैयत है॥ Ś52॥

*इतै राखी चहैं कुल की कुलकानि, उतै नँदनंदनै ध्यावती हैं।
2 निज गैल में आनि कढ़ै जो कहूं, न झरोखन झांकन पावती हैं।
कवि ठाकुर, है न बनाव कछू, दुबिधा मिलि सांच सचावती हैं।
4 चहैं आशिकी औ डर मानन को, कहौ, द्वै द्वै कहा बनि आवती हैं॥ Ś53॥

---

53 Sundarī-tilak (C_e) pp. 51–52 (304). The quatrain contains the words of a companion to the heroine. The last line is similar to that of Ś155.

52.2 माँझ] E, माही F • कजात] E, कदाच F • बिलोकत] E, बिलोक कैं F • चित्त] E, चित्तु F • डरैयत] E, चुरैयतु F **52.3** भेंटबे] E, देखबे F • के] E, ⟨कै/कौ⟩ F • उपचार] E, ⟨उ⟩पचार F • बिचारत] E, बिचार न F • द्यौस] E, दुजौ F • बितैयत] E, पइयतु (unm.) F **52.4** न] E, कहैबौ ना F • कबहूँ] E, *om.* F • तिन्हें कैसे] E, कहौ कौनै F • लगैयत] E, लगैयतु F **53.4** बनि] *conj.* बति C_e

---

52.2 कजात [kadācit] reg. adv. at some time, hardly ever; डरैयत [darati] v.i. (Br. pass. imperf.) is frightened. **52.3** भेंटना [*bheṭṭ-] v.t. to meet; 2. to embrace; उपचार [S] m. pretext; द्यौस [S] poet. m. day. **53.2** निज... कहूं Br. if somehow he appeared on his usual way, (then you...); झरोखा m. small window; झांकन पावती है Br. (?) (you are not) able to glimpse him in the window. **53.3** बनाव [cf. H banānā] m. 1. remedy; 2. falsity; है न बनाव कछू m. there is no falseness (in what I say); truely I say; दुविधा [dvi-vidha-] Br. f. dilemma; 2. (here:) suspicion, apprehension; सांच सचावती हैं Br. (becoming suspicious) you try to make (your suspicion) true. **53.4** आशिक़ी [A] f. love; मानन [māna-] m. (Br. pl. obl.) prestige, reputation; द्वै द्वै... हैं idiom. can the two things be at the same time?;

*सुनती कहा ठाढी भई चुप हौ, उत देखहु कौन सै गोहन गो।
वह बैन बजाय रिझाय हमैं, अरी, धेनु कहूँ बन दोहन गो।
कहि ठाकुर, ऐसियै जानि परै, अरी, गुंज की मालन पोहन गो।
कोऊ दौरियो टेरियौ फेरियो, री, यौ अहीर कों मोहन मोहन गो॥ Ś54॥

54 Bharatpur1 f. 164v (91), Sundarī-tilak (C_e) p. 20 (119), Granthāvalī 134, Sudhāsar [S_1 f. 171v (11), S_3 f. 146v (122), S_4 f. 71r-72v (128), S_7 f. 194v-5r (11)], Śatak 82, Thākur-satsaī (Ṭ) f. 2v (20), Ṭhasak 81, VrindabanA f. 9r (51), Yājñik. • The Sudhāsar presents this poem in the 'aur nānābidhi kī brijkelī barnan' (description of other various love sports in Braj) subsection of the 'Brajrasrīti' section. • The editors of the Granthāvalī seem to have confused the readings of the Yājñik manuscript in their footnotes. The readings of this manuscript normally correspond to those in V_1.

54.1 सुनती] B_1**S**Ṭ, *om.* (unm.) C_e, सजनी G_eṬ$_e$, सुनतीं Ś$_e V_1 Y_e$ • कहा ठाढी भईं] Σ, ठाढ़ी कहा दुचिती (unm.) C_e • ठढी] Σ, डाढी Ṭ • भई] B_1**S**, भईं **E**V_1, *om.* Ṭ • चुप हौ] B_1S_1ṬV_1Y_e, सुचिती C_e**E**, चुप कै S_3S_7, चुप हौं S_4 • उत] B_1**S**Ś$_e$ṬV_1Y_e, चल G_eṬ$_e$, चलु C_e • देखहु] $B_1S_1S_3S_7$ṬV_1Y_e, देखु री C_e, देखियै **E**, देखह S_4 • सै] B_1**S**ṬV_1Y_e, सी C_e, के G_eṬ$_e$, सु Ś$_e$ **54.2** वह] B_1C_e**E**S_1Ṭ, वहि S_3S_4, बहु S_7, वहै V_1 • बैन] B_1**S**ṬV_1Y_e, बेनु C_e**E** • बजाय] Σ, बजाई V_1 • हमैं] Σ, है⟨से⟩ Ṭ • अरी] B_1S_1ṬV_1Y_e, अब **E**, री सु C_e, अर S_3S_7, अह S_4 • धेनु] $B_1C_eS_4$**E**, धेन $S_1S_3S_7$ṬV_1Y_e **54.3** कहि] B_1**S**V_1, कबि C_e**E**, कह Ṭ • ठाकुर] Σ, ठाकु (unm.) V_1 • ऐसियै जानि] $B_1S_1S_4$ṬV_1Y_e, ऐस ही जानि C_e**E**, ऐसी अजान S_3S_7 • परै] B_1**S**ṬV_1Y_e, परी C_e**E** • गुंज] Σ, गुज S_4 • की] B_1**S**ṬV_1Y_e, के C_e**E** • मालन] B_1**S**ṬV_1Y_e, हारन C_e**E** • पोहन] C_e**E**$S_1S_3S_7$, योहन S_4, गोहन B_1ṬV_1Y_e **54.4** दौरियो] Σ, दौरिखो S_4, टैरियो (?) Y_e • टेरियौ फेरियौ] $B_1C_eS_1S_3S_4$ṬV_1, फेरियौ G_eṬ$_e$, टेरयौ फेरीयौ S_7, फेरियौ टेरियौ Ś$_e$ • यौ] $B_1S_1S_4V_1Y_e$, वा **E**, ये S_3, वो S_7, इओ (unm.) Ṭ • अहीर] Σ, अहरे S_4 • कों मोहन] B_1C_e**S**Ś$_e$ṬV_1, कों मोहन मो मन G_eṬ$_e$, कों मोहन मोहनि (?) Y_e • मोहन] Σ, मोहनि V_1

54.1 सुनती (सुन रही हो) v.t. imperf. (used as cont.) you are hearing (it); सुचिती var. [cf. sucitta-] Av. Br. adj. 1. at leisure; 2. untroubled in mind; 3. [śuci strī] f. faultless woman; ठाढी भई चुप हो reg. standing silently; गोहन [? godhana-] Br. 'associate' postp. together with; कौन सै गोहन Br. together with whom; कौन सु गोहन var. Br. together with whom. **54.2** बैन बजाय Br. playing on his flute (i.e. openly); बैन (वेनु) [S] reg. m. flute (the conventional meaning 'vacana' speech cannot stand with the verb bajānā); कहूँ 1. somewhere, 2. I say; वन दोहन गो (वन में दोहने गया) Br. went somewhere to the grove to milk them (saṅketasthala: suggestion for a place to meet). **54.3** माल [mālā-] f. garland; पोह- [parivayati] poet. v.t. to string, to thread; गुंज... गो he went to thread a garland of 'guñja'-berries; गोहन var. postp. Br. with (a garland). **54.4** कोऊ pron. Br. somebody please; दौरियो टेरियो फेरियो Br. run, stop him, turn him back! अहीर [ābhira-] m. the shepherd, Nanda; मोहन मोहन गो 1. that charming Krishna went; 2. Mohan went to charm (the people), 3. that Mohan, that Mohan went (vīpsā alaṅkāra); मो मन मोहन गो var. Br. went to enchant my soul.

1 अब न अटोकि मोहि, तोहि सौंह साँवरे की,
छोडी कुलकानि, लोक-लीकन नकन दै।
2 मोहन सों मोह करिबे के समै का ह्वै मद,
मैं हूँ जकि जाऊँ, तौन, हेली, तू जकन दै।
3 ठाकुर कहत, जो ब कबितान गाई रीति
मुनि-मन भाई, ताई छबि सौं छकन दै।
4 रूप रस माधुरी के सुख न सकन दै री,
हरि कौं तकन दै री, बैरिन बकन दै॥ Ś55॥

का करियै पराधीन भई गुरु लोगन मैं निस-बासर जीजै।

---

55 Bharatpur1 f. 155r (33), Granthāvalī B30, Sudhāsar [S_2 f. 13r (22/16), S_7 f. 49r (61/463)], Vrindaban1 f. 10r (6/58). The Sudhāsar introduces the poem as 'nāyakā kī ukti sakhī sau'.
56 Bharatpur1 f. 185rv (23), Sudhāsar [S_1 f. 231r, S_3 f. 112v (129), S_7 f. 173v (20/1652)], Ṭhākur-satsaī (Ṭ) f. 1r (5), Vrindaban4 ff. 11v-12r (20). The Sudhāsar presents this poem within the 'abhilāṣ' (longing desire) section.

55.1 अब न] B_1**S**, आवनि G_e, अवरन V_1 • अटौकि] B_1V_1, अटकि G_e, अटोक S_2, अटक S_7 • मोहि तोहि] Σ, मोही तोही G_e • छोडी] $B_1G_eV_1$, छोडि **S** • लीकन] Σ, लोकन G_e • नकन] Σ, लकन S_7 **55.2** मोह] Σ, मोहि S_7 • जकि] $B_1G_eV_1$, जक **S** • जाऊँ] G_e, जांउ B_1, जाव **S**, जाउं V_1 • तू] $B_1G_eS_7$, तू जक जाव तौ न हेली तू (dittography) S_2, तु V_1 **55.3** ठाकुर कहत] G_e**S**, ठा° B_1, ठाकुर कहैत V_1 • गाई] Σ, गाइ V_1 • ताई] B_1G_e, तौन **S**, ताइ V_1 **55.4** न सकन] B_1**S**, निकसन G_e, निसकन V_1 • कौं] Σ, कौ S_7 • तकन] $B_1G_eS_2$, तनक V_1 • बैरिन] G_e, लोगन **S**, बैरीन B_1V_1 **56.1** का] Σ, कहा (unm.) Ṭ • करियै] B_1**S**, कहीए Ṭ, कहियै V_4 • पराधीन] Σ, परधीन Ṭ • भई] B_1**S**, भए ṬV_4 • गुरु] S_3, गुर Σ • लोगन] **S**V_4, लोगनि B_1, लोकन Ṭ • मैं] $B_1S_1V_4$, मै S_3S_7, सौ Ṭ • निस] Σ, बिस S_1 •

55.1 अवन poet. m. 1. coming; way; 2. [S] delight; love; desire; आवनि var. Br. m. coming; अटोक- [*ṭokk-] poet. adj. (imper.) not to obstruct, to allow; अटकना var. v.i. to be stopped; मोहि [mohayati] v.i. abs. Br. to be charmed; तोहि सौंह साँवरे की Br. I swear you on Krishna; नक- (नकारना) 1. [na + kāra-] poet. v.t. to deny, to reject; 2. [? naṣṭa-] poet. v.t. to throw away; 3. to jump or cross over. **55.2** ह्वै (हो) Br. v.i. subj. let there be; मद [S] m. intoxication, (here:) pride; का ह्वै मद 1. will I become proud? 2. if I become proud (at the time) of; 3. let me be intoxicated (at the time) of; हेली (सहेली) Br. f. female companion; जकना [H jak 'obsession, fascination'] v.i. 1. to be astonished; 2. to be stubborn; 3. to talk nonsense; तौन 1. [H to] Br. conj. Bund. then; 2 [to na] then wouldn't you...? **55.3** छकना [conn. *chakka-] v.i. 1. to be satiated; 2. to be astonished. **55.4** सक (शक) [A śakk] m. 1. doubt; 2. (here:) reluctance; faltering (KL); निकस- var. [niṣkasati, H nikalnā] v.i. to manifest; निसकन apa; तकना [tarkayati] v.i. to look, to stare. **56.1** बिस apa.

नाँ तर लाख बनै बिगरै निरसंक भुजा भरि कैं मिल लीजै। 2
ठाकुर, ऐसी उठै जिय मैं, कुल कानि की आजु बिदा करि दीजै।
जौ अपनौ बस होय, भट्ू, तौ गुपालहि आँखिन ओट न कीजै॥ Ś56॥ 4

ऐसी इह चाह की हिये में गुमराह होत, 1
लोकलाज कुलकानि हारिबोई करियै।
चाहै कोऊ नाम धरै, चाहै सो बडाई करै, 2
रूप यौ अनूप हियै धारिबोई करियै।
ठाकुर कहत, तुम ऐसे नौने लागौ स्याम, 3

---

57 Bharatpur1 f. 161v-2r (74), Bharatpur8 f. 15rv (44), Granthāvalī B34, Sudhāsar [S_1 f. 308v (79), S_2 f. 62v (-/74), S_3 f. 178v (282), S_7 f. 213r (133)], Vrindaban1 f. 1r (1/1). The Sudhāsar includes this quatrain into the 'bhari saṃjog mẽ gopina kī prārthanā' (the cowherd girls' request in full union) subsection of the 'Brajrasrīti' section.

56.2 बनै] S_3S_7, बनौं B_1V_4, बनैं S_1, बनी Ṭ • बिगरै] Σ, बिगरौ B_1V_4 • निरसंक] $B_1S_1S_7V_4$, निहसंक S_3, भर अंग Ṭ • भरि] $B_1S_1V_4^{pc}$, भर S_3S_7, गर Ṭ, बरि V_4^{ac} • कैं] S_1, CHECK B_1, *om.* (unm.) S_3, ⟨सु⟩ S_3^{pc}, के S_7, सो Ṭ, अंक V_4 • मिल] SṬ, मिलि (unrh.) B_1, मै V_4 **56.3** ऐसी उठै जिय मैं] Σ, यो मन मै उपजै Ṭ, नैंक अछूवनि मैं V_4 • उठै] **S**, उठैं B_1 • मैं] B_1S_1Ṭ, मै S_3S_7 • कानि] B_1V_4, काम S_1, कान S_3S_7Ṭ • की] Σ, को Ṭ • आजु] B_1, आज **S**Ṭ, आनि V_4 • करि] $B_1S_1V_4$, कर S_3S_7Ṭ **56.4** जौ] Σ, *om.* V_4 • अपनौ] B_1**S**, अपने Ṭ, आपनौ सौ V_4 • भटू] Σ, सषी V_4 • तौ] Σ, तू Ṭ • गुपालहि] $S_1S_3V_4^{ac}$, गुपालै (unm.) B_1, गुपालह S_7, गोपालहि Ṭ, पियारिय V_4^{pc} • आँखिन] **S**Ṭ, आंषि ते B_1, आंष की V_4 • कीजै] Σ, दीजै Ṭ **57.1** इह] S_1V_1, इहिं B_1B_8, यह G_eS_2, यहि S_3, ऐह S_7 • चाह] Σ, चाहि S_7 • गुमराह] B_8^{pc}Σ, ⟨बु/छ⟩मराह B_8^{ac} • कानि] Σ, कान $S_1S_3S_7$ • हारिबोई] S_2S_3, हरिबोई (unrh.) $B_1B_8G_e$, हारिबौई (unrh.) S_1S_7, हरबौई (unrh.) V_1 **57.2** कोऊ] $B_1B_8G_eS_1$, कोई $S_2S_3S_7V_1$ • नाम] Σ, नाउ B_1 • यौ] $B_8S_1S_2V_1$, औ $G_eS_3S_7$ • अनूप] $B_8S_1S_2S_7V_1$, अरूप G_eS_3

56.2 नातर [na tarhi] conj. reg. or else, otherwise; लाख बनैं बिगरै Br. myriads of things may be good or go wrong; निरसंक [niḥśaṅka-] Br. adv. without fear. **56.4** जौ अपनौ बस होय idiom. Br. if I can help it; ओट करना idiom. to hide (from my eyes). **57.1** इह pron. (Br. ag.) she; ऐसी इह चाह की reg. she loved in a way that...; गुमराह [P] adj. lost; हारिबोई करियै v.t. emph. subj. Br. she may indeed loose (cf. H hārte rahiye). **57.2** नाम धरना idiom. to defame; यौ (यौं) adv. so; रूप औ अरूप var. both beauty and ugliness.

अति अभिराम काम बारिबोई करियै।
4 बरसन जुग अँखियान लगौ, प्यारे लाल,
दरसन रावरो निहारिबोई करियै॥ Ś57॥

घेर करै सगरै घर के और नेह नया तुम सौ प्रगटो है।
2 लाज तजी कुल कांन तजी और स्वाद बिस्वाद सभे बिलटो है।
जो चुपके चुप मैं रहीए, मन मेरो, लला, तुम सौ अटिक्यो है।
4 औरन ने पगिया पलटी, हमने तुम सौ हियरा पलटो है॥ Ś58॥

1 काजर की रेख नैन, बेंदाहू लिलार सोहै,
नैनन की कोर तें झकोर खूब दै गई।
2 करे ज्यों सिंगार सब, भूषन अनेक रँग
काम की उमंग मैं चोराय चित्त लै गई।
3 ठाकुर कहत, प्रीति रीति ना बिचारी कछू,
जोबन के मान मैं गुमान कछु कै गई।
4 चट छल छाय कै, लटक मुसुकाय कै,

58 Ṭhākur-satsaī f. 5r (42) (Ṭ). 59 Granthāvalī 143, Ṭhasak 'Jīvancarit' ($Ṭ^{j}_{e}$) p. 20.

57.3 ठाकुर कहत] $B_8S_1S_3S_7G_eV_1$, ठा° B_1, ठाकुर कहात S_2 • तुम] B_1B_8**S**, तुमै G_eV_1 • नौंनैं] $B_1S_1S_2V_1$, लौंनें $B_8S_3S_7$, नौन G_e • लागौ] $B_1B_8S_1S_2V_1$, लागै $G_eS_3S_7$ • काम] Σ, धाम S_3 • बारिबोई] $B_1B_8G_eS_3V_1$, वरिबो ही (unrh.) S_1S_2, धारबोई S_7 **57.4** बरसन] Σ, बार मन S_3 • जुग] Σ, जु (unm.) B_8 • अँखियान] Σ, अँखियन (unm.) G_e • लगौ] $B_1B_8S_1$, जुग लगौ G_e, लागौ $S_2S_3S_7$, जुग लगौ (unm.) V_1 **58.2** तजी और] *conj.* तज और Ṭ

57.3 नौने [cf. P namak x H laun] Br. adj. 'salty' charming (saltiness increases thirst); तुमै (तुमही) var. pron. (reg. eph.) it is you who; नौन var. Br. adj. charming; वारिबोई करियै Br. we should definitely sacrifice (Kāma) (i.e. you are superior to Kāma). **57.4** जुग (युग) [S] m. obl. for ages, ages ago; जुग var. [yugala-] Br. m. pair; बरसन जुग अँखियन-जुग लगौ var. my two eyes started to shed tears ages ago; दर्शण [S] m. 'sight' beauty; निहारना [nibhālayati] v.t. 1. to keep looking at; 2. to look at expectantly; to wait for (your appearance). **58.2** बिलटना [vinaṣṭa-, cf. H ulaṭnā] v.i. to be destroyed. **58.3** जो चुपके चुप मैं रहीए Br. even if I remain silent. **58.4** पगिया (पगड़ी) [cf. *paggā-] Br. f. turban; पगड़ी बदलना idiom. 'to exchange turbans' to be close friends; पलटना [*pallaṭṭa-] v.t. to exchange. **59.1** बेंदा [cf. H bindī] m. big dot ornamenting the forehead; लिलाड़ [lalāṭa-] m. forehead; झकोरा देना to swing. **59.2** करे v.t. perf. Br. (are) made; ज्यों Br. conj. as (she); चोरा- (चोरना) [corayati] reg. v.t. to steal.

चटाक चित्त चोरिकै झटाक पट दै गई॥ Ś59॥

भूलि न प्रीति करौं तुमसौं, कबहूँ नहिं नैन सों नैन मिलाऊँ।
बात करौं न सुनौं तुम्हरी, अपने चित की कबहूँ न चिताऊँ।
मोहिं कहा परी, प्यारे गुपाल जू, लाज मरौं कुल कानि घटाऊँ।
ना बिष खाऊँ न प्रान तजौं, गुर खाऊँ न काहू सों कान छिदाऊँ॥ Ś60॥

नलिनी बिधु बीच कू ओट करै जुग फोर जुराव उडावहि कों।
बिबि चुंबक लोह कौ अंग मिलै फिरि दूसरौ अंग दिखावहि को।
कवि ठाकुर नेह की रीति यही बिछुरै जल मीन जिवावहि को।
गुनवारे गुपाल की आंखिन तै उरझी अखियां सुरझावहि को॥ Ś61॥

*कोटि कला करिकैं समझायौ, सिखापन कौपन जानत नाँही।

---

60 Granthāvalī 131, Ṭhasak 177. This poem does not contain Ṭhākur's poetic signature. Its last line is similar to that of Ś45. 61 Bharatpur11 f. 4r [130r] (10). 62 Sudhāsar [S_1 f. 189r, S_2 f. 47r (-/46), S_3 f. 105r (89), S_7 f. 151rv (3/1438)], Ṭhākur-satsaī (Ṭ) f. 3v (29). The Sudhāsar (S_1 and S_7) presents this poem within the 'Upālambha' (complaint) subsection of 'Pravāsa' (separation by distance) and introduces it as an example of 'Manopālambha' (complaint against one's mind).

59.4 लटक] G$_e$, लटकि Ṭ$_e^j$ • **60.3 गुपाल**] G$_e$, गोपाल Ṭ$_e$ • **61.1 नलिनी**] *conj.* निलनी B$_{11}$ • बिधु] *conj.* बुघ B$_{11}$ • जुग] *conj.* जग B$_{11}$ **62.1 कोटि**] $S_1S_2S_7$, कोट S_3Ṭ

59.4 चट [caṭa-] adv. quickly; **छल छाय कै** Br. making a trick (such as touching him under some pretext); **लटकना** [cf. *laṭṭa-] v.i. to bend; **चटाक** [caṭakka-] adv. 'with a crackling sound' quickly; **झटाक** (**झटका**) [*jhaṭṭ-] adv. with a jerk; with a dashing sound; **पट** [paṭṭa-] m. leaf of the door; **पट देना** idiom. to close the door. **60.1 नयन से नयन मिलाना** idiom. to be in love. **60.2 चिताना** [cf. H cetnā] v.caus. to expose. **60.3 मोहिं कहा परी** idiom. Br. what am I concerned with it? **लाज मरौं** Br. shall I die of shame. **60.4 गुर खाना** to eat raw sugar (as offered to children to distract them before their ears are pierced); **कान छिदाना** to let the ears be pierced; **ना गुर... छिदाऊँ** Br. I do not want to take the jaggery and thus I do not want to let my ears be pierced (i.e. I do not wan't any connection with it). **61.1 कू** (**कौन**) reg. interr. who? **ओट** [*oṭṭā-] f. screen; separation; **जुग** (**युगल**) [S] m. pair; **फोड़ना** [sphoṭayati] v.t. to separate (from a group); **जुराव** (**जिराफ़ा**) [A] f. giraffe (thought here to be a bird) (it was conceived to die, when separated from its mate). **61.2 बिबि** (**दो**) [conn. dva-] Br. adj. two (magnets on both sides of the iron). **62.1 सिखापन** poet. m. teaching; **कोपन** [kopa-] m. (Br. pl.) out of anger (my mind does not understand).

रूप-सुधारस के चसके, सो बनी-बिगरी पहचानत नाँही।
ठाकुर, ये बदनाम के बैर कै घैर, कछू उर आनत नाँही।
देखैं बिनां मनमोहन कौ मुख, का करियै, मन मानत नाँही॥ Ś62॥

प्रवास

दहने परी देह बियोग बिथा अब, आज लौं काहू दही नइयाँ।
कहने परी लाजहि छाड़ इती, जिती कौनहूँ ठाँव कही नइयाँ।
कवि ठाकुर, लाल अचाहि करी, तिहि तैं सहियै जु सही नइयाँ।
मनमोहन को हिलिबौ मिलिबौ सपने लौं भयो, हमरी गुइयाँ॥ Ś63॥

अब का कहियै, किहि सों कहियै, तन छीजतु है, पै न छीजतु है।
मन कौं बिसराम अराम घनो करि दीजतु है, पै न दीजतु है।
कहि ठाकुर, भोग सँयोग सबै सुख कीजतु है, पै न कीजतु है।

---

63 Granthāvalī 29, Śatak 68, Ṭhasak 79. 64 Granthāvalī 33, Sudhāsar [S_1 f. 108r (15), S_2 f. 22v (2/29), S_7 f. 72r (15/716)], Śatak 24, Ṭhasak 78. The Sudhāsar (S_1S_7) presents this poem within the 'parakiyā proṣitapatikā' section.

62.2 रूप] Σ, ×ठाकुर, ये बदनाँम के× रूप S_1 • चसके] Σ, चसकैं S_2 • सो] Σ, सौं S_1 • पहचानत] Σ, पहचातत S_2 **62.3** ये] Σ, ऐ S_3 • उर] **S**, घर Ṭ **62.4** देखैं] S_1, देष S_2Ṭ, देखे S_3S_7 • मनमोहन] $S_1S_3S_7$, मुख मोहन S_2Ṭ • मुख] $S_1S_3S_7$, हम S_2Ṭ **63.1** दही] G_eṬ$_e$, कही Ś$_e$ • नइयाँ] G_eṬ$_e$, नहियाँ Ś$_e$ **63.2** इती जिती] G_eṬ$_e$, इतौ जिते Ś$_e$ • कही] G_eṬ$_e$, रही Ś$_e$ • नइयाँ] G_eṬ$_e$, नहियाँ Ś$_e$ **63.3** जु सही] G_eṬ$_e$, जसही Ś$_e$ • नइयाँ] G_eṬ$_e$, नहियाँ Ś$_e$ **63.4** को] G_eṬ$_e$, कौं Ś$_e$ **64.1** अब का] **S**, का (unm.) **E** • किहि] **E**, किह S_1, कह S_2S_7 • छीजतु] G_e, छीजत Σ • छीजतु] **E**, छीजत **S** **64.2** मन] **S**, तन **E** • करि] Σ, कर S_7 • घनो] Σ, घनौं S_1 • दीजतु] **E**, दीजत **S** • दीजतु] **E**, दीजत **S** **64.3** कहि] **S**, कबि **E** • कीजतु] **E**, कीजत **S** • कीजतु] **E**, कीजत **S**

62.2 चसकना [*cassakk-] v.t. to acquire a taste for; बनी-बिगरी Br. adj. (f.) good and bad. **62.3** के [? kim, or H ki, + H (hī)] Br. conj. or; बदनाम [PH] m. disgrace; बैर 1. [vaira-] Br. m. enmity; 2. [velā-] f. (here m.) reg. time; उर आनत idiom. Br. 'brings into mind' cares. **63.1** दहने परी Bund. started to burn; देह [S] f. body ; काहू (किसी ने) pron. Br. obl. no one; कही var. v.t. perf. (no one has so far) said; नइयाँ [cf. Br. nāṃy] Br. Bund. adv. not. **63.2** कहने परी v.t. had to say (H bāt kahnī paṛī); इती... नइयाँ reg. so much as nowhere has been said; इतौ जिते var. so much as **63.3** अचाही करी [cf. H cāh 'love'] Br. acted contrary to love. **63.4** हिलना-मिलना v.i. to become intimate with; गुइयाँ [? P gū] poet. f. (woman's female) friend, companion. **64.1** तन छीजतु है पै न छीजतु है Br. my body is wasting away though does not waste away. **64.2** अराम (आराम) [P] Br. m. comfort. **64.3** भोग सँयोग combination of enjoyments (cf. Ś53).

मनमोहन प्यारे गुपाल बिना जग जीजतु है, पै न जीजतु है॥ Ś64॥

वे परबीन बिचच्छन लोग बने, सब पै कछु आन भये, री।
चीखे सवाद महा अति मीठे, सु सीखे सुभाइ नये ही नये, री।
ठाकुर, कौन सों का कहिये, अब वे चित चाहिबो, वे समये, री।
वे दिन, वे सुख, वैसे उछाह सु, वे सब, बीर, हिराय गये, री॥ Ś65॥

*दिल साँचो लग्यौ जिहि को जिहि पै, तिहि कों तितही पहुँचावत है।
बलि, हंस चुनै मुकताहल कों, अरु चातक स्वाति कों पावत है।

---

65 Granthāvalī 37, Śatak 98, Ṭhasak 147, Ṭhasak 'Jīvancarit' (Ṭ^j_e) p. 13. 66 Bharatpur1 f. 160v (67), Sundarītilak (C$_e$) 302, Granthāvalī 51, Rasikvinod (O$_e$) 443, Sudhāsar [S$_1$ f. 308r (77), S$_2$ f. 62r (-/73), S$_3$ f. 178r (280), S$_7$ f. 212v-3r (131)], Ṭhasak 54, Vrindaban1 f. 4v (10/23), Yājñik. • The Sudhāsar (S$_1$S$_3$S$_7$) presents this poem within the 'nahacaiṃ saṃjogāgam' subsection of the 'Brajrasrīti' section.

64.4 मनमोहन] **S**, मनभावन **E** • गुपाल] **S**, गोपाल **E** • जीजतु] **E**, जीजत **S** • जीजतु] **E**, कीजत **S** **65.1** बिचच्छन Ś$_e$Ṭ$_e$Ṭ^j_e, बिचक्षन G$_e$ • सब पै] **E**, पै समै Ṭ^j_e • भये] **E**, भयो (unrh.) Ṭ^j_e • री] **E**, ही G$^{vl}_e$ **65.2** चीखे] G$_e$Ṭ$_e$Ṭ^j_e, चीखें Ś$_e$ • महा] G$_e$Ś$_e$Ṭ$_e$, जहां Ṭ^j_e • सु] G$_e$Ś$_e$Ṭ$_e$, सो Ṭ^j_e • सुभाइ] G$_e$Ś$_e$Ṭ$_e$, स्वभाव Ṭ^j_e • नये ही नये] G$_e$Ṭ$_e$, °न एरी नए Ś$_e$, नयेई नये Ṭ^j_e **65.3** अब वे] G$_e$Ś$_e$Ṭ$_e$, अब ओ Ṭ^j_e • चाहिबो] G$_e$Ś$_e$Ṭ$_e$, चाहवे Ṭ^j_e • **65.4** सु वे] G$_e$Ś$_e$Ṭ$_e$, सो वे Ṭ^j_e • हिराय] G$_e$Ś$_e$Ṭ$_e$, हेराय Ṭ^j_e **66.1** लग्यौ] B$_1$S$_1$S$_2$Y$_e$, लगै C$_e$**E**O$_e$, लगौ S$_3$S$_7$V$_1$ • जिहि को] B$_1$C$_e$V$_1$Y$_e$, जेहि को **E**O$_e$, जिंह कौ **S** • जिहि पै] B$_1$, जिहि सों C$_e$, जेहि सों **E**O$_e$, जिंह पै **S**, जिहि सौ V$_1$Y$_e$ • तिहि कों] B$_1$O$_e$S$_2$, तिहि को C$_e$V$_1$, तेहि कों **E**, तिंह कौं S$_1$S$_7$, *om.* (unm.) Y$_e$ • तितही] B$_1$**ES**, तित को C$_e$, तित कों O$_e$, तिहि पै V$_1$Y$_e$ • पहुँचावत] C$_e$**E**S$_1$S$_2$S$_7$, पहुंचावति B$_1$, पहुँचावतु O$_e$S$_3$, पौहचावत V$_1$, पौंचावति (unm.) Y$_e$ • है] B$^{pc}_1$Σ, हौ B$^{ac}_1$ **66.2** बलि] Σ, बल S$_3$S$_7$ • चुनै] C$_e$**E**S$_2$V$_1$, चुगें O$_e$, चुनैं B$_1$S$_1$, चुगै S$_3$S$_7$ • मुकताहल] Σ, मुक्ताहल (unm.) C$_e$ • स्वाति] Σ, स्वात S$_3$S$_7$ • पावत] B$_1$C$_e$**E**S$_1$S$_7$, पावतु O$_e$, पावति S$_2$S$_3$V$_1$ • है] Σ, हैं S$_2$

65.1 वे pron. he (Krishna); विचक्षण [S] adj. clear-seeing; sagacious; लोग poet. m. man, folk; आन [anya-] Br. adj. different. **65.2** चीखें v.t. perf. Br. on tasting; सीखे सुभाइ नये ही नये Br. he has learnt new and new natures (i.e. his nature keeps changing). **65.4** उछाह [utsāha] Br. m. enthusiasm. **66.2** मुकताहल (मुक्ताफल) [S] Br. m. pearl.

कहि ठाकुर, यौं निजु भेव सुनौ, उरझावत सो सुरझावत है।
4 परमेसुर की परतीति यहै, मिल्यौ चाहत ताहि मिलावत है॥ Ś66॥

1 तुमही बिचारौ निरधारौ प्रेमपंथिन मैं
फेरि भारी ग्रंथन मैं कैसी निसरत है।
2 कहूँ आवै, कहूँ जाय, कहूँ रहै, कहूँ बसै
मनसा बिकल वाही माँझ बिसरत है।
3 ठाकुर कहत, मन-छलन ललन प्यारे,

---

67 Bharatpur1 f. 150v (6), Granthāvalī 54, Sudhāsar [S_1 f. 186v, S_3 f. 102v (76), S_7 f. 149v (6/1426)], Vrindaban1 f. 15rv (12/92). The Sudhāsar (S_1 and S_7) presents this poem within the 'pātī varnana', the section about love letters, and introduces it as 'parakīyā kī pātī' (letter of an adulterous woman).

66.3 कहि] $B_1\mathbf{S}V_1Y_e$, कबि $C_e\mathbf{E}O_e$ • यौं] $B_1C_e\mathbf{E}O_e$, या **S**, यौ V_1 • निजु] $\mathbf{E}V_1$, निज $B_1O_eC_e\mathbf{S}$ • भेव] $B_1\mathbf{S}V_1Y_e$, भेद $C_e\mathbf{E}O_e$ • सुनो] $C_e\mathbf{E}S_2S_3S_7V_1$, हुवौ B_1, सुनों S_1O_e • उरझावत] $B_1\mathbf{S}$, अरुझावत $C_e\mathbf{E}$, अरुझावतु O_e, उरझावति $S_3V_1Y_e$ • सुरझावत] $B_1\mathbf{E}O_e\mathbf{S}$, सरुझावत C_e, सुरझावति S_3V_1 **66.4** परमेसुर] $B_1\mathbf{E}S_1S_3V_1$, परमेश्वर $O_eS_2S_7C_e$ • परतीति] $B_1C_eS_1S_3V_1$, परतीत $\mathbf{E}O_eS_2S_7$ • यहै] $C_eS_1S_3S_7V_1$, यही $B_1\mathbf{E}O_eS_2$ • मिल्यौ] Σ, मिलौ C_eS_7 • चाहत] $B_1\mathbf{E}S_1S_2S_7V_1$, चाहिये O_eC_e, चाहति S_3 • मिलावत] Σ, मिलावतु O_e, मिलावति S_3 **67.1** बिचारौ] Σ, बिचार G_e • °पंथिन] Σ, पंछन V_1 • फेरि] $B_1G_eV_1$, फेर **S** • मैं] $B_1G_eS_1$, मै $S_3S_7^{pc}V_1$, *om.* (unm.) S_7^{ac} • कैसी] Σ, कैसे S_7 • निसरत] (unm.) Σ, निसरते (unm.) V_1 • है] Σ, ह V_1 **67.2** कहूँ] Σ, कहु* V_1 • कहूँ] $B_1\mathbf{S}$, रहै G_e, कहुं V_1 • रहै] $\mathbf{S}V_1$, कहूँ G_e • बिसरत] (unm.) $B_1G_eV_1$, मिसरत (unm.) **S**

66.3 भेद [S] m. secret, mystery; निज 1. [S] adj. special; true; 2. adv. with certainty (H niścay hī; अरुझाव- (उलझाना) [cf. uparudhyate] v.t. to entangle; सो pron. he (i.e. Krishna); सुरझाव- [cf. su + H ulajhnā] Br. v.t. to disentangle; उरझावत... है Br. he (both) entangles and disentangles. **66.4** परतीत (प्रतीति) [S] Br. f. 1. conviction, faith; 2. fame, notoriety. **67.1** निरधारना [nirdhārayati] v.t. to imagine; बिचारौ (विचार करो) [vicāra-] Br. v.t. imp. consider it (and decide); बिचार var. [vicāra-] Br. v.t. abs. considering it; प्रेमपंथी m. one who is on the way of love; फेरि [*phera-] poet. adv. then; भारी [bhārika-] adj. heavy, big; निसर- [niḥsarati, cf. H nikalnā] reg. v.i. to emerge, to prove to be. **67.2** रहै v.i. pres. Br. stops; बसै v.i. pres. Br. settles; मनसा 1. [S] f. mind; desire; 2. [S] adv. in the mind; बिकल [S] adj. inquiet; बिसरना 1. [vismārayati] v.t. to forget; 2. [vismarati] v.i. to be forgotten; मिसर- var. [cf. miśrita-] poet. v.i. to mix, to be united with.

न्यारे नेह बीरी वा निरास सरसत है।
जासों मन लाग्यौ, नैन लागे, लगी प्रीति पूरी,
ताकी कहूँ सूरति बिसारी बिसरत है॥ Ś67॥

*अरे लाल सनेही, सनेह तज्यौ, सज्यौ बैर, तऊ सुधि लीजत है।
हम आनन आन न जानैं कछू, जपि नाम तिहारौई जीजत है।
कहि ठाकुर, चूक सबै अपनी, तिहि तें तुम्हें दोस न दीजत है।

---

68 Bharatpur1 f. 161r (71), Bharatpur8 ff. 14v-15r (43), Granthāvalī 62, Sudhāsar [S_1 f. 301v (48), S_2 f. 60v (-/70), S_3 ff. 170v-1r (246), S_4 f. 98v (259), S_7 f. 208v (95)], Śatak 8, Ṭhasak 73, Vrindaban1 f. 13r (14/79), Yājñik. • The Sudhāsar presents this poem within the 'uddhava kau braj mẽ āyabau' (Uddhava's coming to Braj) subsection of the 'Brajrasrīti' section. • S_2 omits the third line.

67.3 न्यारे] $B_1G_eS_1V_1$, न्यारी S_3S_7 • नेह] Σ, कहु* V_1 • बीरी] B_1, बारी **S**, बारि G_e, ⟨बा/बी⟩री V_1 • वा निरास] $B_1G_eV_1$, वा निरारी S_1, बानि वकी S_3, बानि कैसे S_7 • सरसत] (unm.) $B_1G_eV_1$, की सरत (unm.) S_1, CHECK S_3, खिसरत (unm.) S_7 **67.4** ताकी] Σ, जाकी S_1 • कहूँ] Σ, कहुं V_1 • सूरति] $B_1G_eS_7$, सुरति S_1, सुरत S_3, सुरराति (unm.) V_1 • बिसारी] $B_1G_eV_1$, बिसारै **S** • बिसरत] (unm.) Σ **68.1** सनेह] B_8^{pc}Σ, *om.* (unm.) B_8^{ac} • तज्यौ] Σ, तजो **E** • सज्यौ] Σ, सजो **E** • सुधि] Σ, सुध S_4 • लीजत] B_1**S**, लीजतु B_8**E**V_1, लीजति S_3 • है] Σ, हैं S_4 **68.2** न जानैं] $B_1B_8S_1$, निहारोई **E**, न जानै **S**V_1Y_e • कछू] B_1B_8**S**, ना **E**, कछु V_1Y_e • जपि] Σ, जप S_3S_7 • तिहारौई] B_1B_8**E**V_1, तिहारौ ही **S** • जीजत] $B_1B_8S_1S_2S_7$, जीजतु **E**V_1, जीजति S_3, जीतत S_4 • है] Σ, हैं S_4 **68.3** कहि... है] Σ, *om.* S_2 • कहि] Σ, कवि **E** • चूक सबै] Σ, भूल कछू **E** • तिहि] $B_1B_8G_eṬ_eV_1$, तिंह **SŚ**$_e$ • तुम्हें] Σ, तुमै **S**, तुझै S_3 • दोस] Σ, दोष **E** • दीजत] $B_1B_8S_1S_2S_7$, दीजतु **E**V_1, दीजति S_3, हीजत S_4 • है] Σ, हैं S_4

67.3 मन-छलन Br. m. deceiver of the mind; ललन [S] Br. m. 'dear one' 1. child; 2. lover; न्यारा [*anyakāra-] adj. removed, distant; बीरी Br. f. plant, tree (of love prospers in hopelessness); बीरिवा Br. f. small plant, tree; न्यारे... सरसत है Br. 1. when the lovers are separated the tree of love prospers in their hopelessness (i.e. love increases in the torments of separation); 2. hopelessness prospers when one is separated from the tree of love (i.e. the beloved); बाड़ी var. [vāṭikā-] Br. f. orchard, garden; बार- var. Br. v.t. to burn; निरास [nirāśā-] Br. f. hopelessness, disappointment; सरस- Br. v.i. 1. to be luxuriant, to prosper; 2. to be overcome by emotion (BHK); की सरत है var. Br. does it go away? **67.4** बिसारी [vismārayati] v.t. (poet. abs.) having forgotten, effaced from memory; बिसरना [vismarati] v.i. to be forgotten; बिसारी बिसरत Br. can it be forgotten by force? **68.1** सज्यौ बैर Br. you made enmity. **68.2** आनन [S] m. face; आन [anya-] adj. other. **68.3** चूक [*cukk-] f. mistake.

चित आन की आन कह्यौ चहै, पै हित जानि अई-गई कीजत है॥ Ś68॥

जिहि भाँति निहारत आनि हते, तिहि भाँति निहारत ही नहियाँ।
फिरि का तिन सों चित दै मिलियै, हित कै अवगाहत ही नहियाँ।
कबि ठाकुर, का तिनसों कहियै, करि नेह निबाहत ही नहियाँ।
अब जान परी इनकी हमकौं, हमकौं हरि चाहत ही नहियाँ॥ Ś69॥

हरि लाँबी औ चौरी बखानत ते, अब गाढे परे गुन और कढे।
गुन का कहिये, सजनी, उनके, कपटीहिन की चटसार पढे।
कबि ठाकुर, चूक या नैनन की, हमसों नित नेह सनेह बढे।
हम जानती तीं हरि मीत ह्वैहैं न, कढे हरि चैतुवा मीत कढे॥ Ś70॥

*सापने हौं फुलवाई गई, हरि अंक भरी भुज कंठन मेली।

---

69 Granthāvalī 66, Śatak 96, Ṭhasak 82. 70 Granthāvalī 71, Śatak 88, Ṭhasak 151. The ending of the last line is shared with B64. 71 Granthāvalī 137, Ṭhasak 87. Cf. the popular kavitt on svapna darśaṇa 'jhahari jhahari jhīnī būṃda hai parati māno...' attributed to Dev by Hariścandra in his 'Sundarī-sindūr'.

68.4 कह्यौ] B_1B_8**S**V_1, कही G$_e$Ṭ$_e$, कहौ Ś$_e$ • चहै] Σ, चहैं B_1 • पै] Σ, यै S_4 • जानि] $B_8S_2V_1$, जान **ES** • अई] Σ, आइ S_4 • कीजत] B_1B_8**S**, कीजतु **E**V_1, कीजति S_3 • है] Σ, हैं S_4 **69.4** इनकी] G$_e$Ṭ$_e$, इनकौ Ś$_e$ **70.1** हरि लाँबी औ] G$_e$Ṭ$_e$, चोर मैं (unm.) Ś$_e$ • गाढे] G$_e$Ṭ$_e$, गाढ Ś$_e$ • और] G$_e$Ṭ$_e$, औरै Ś$_e$ • कढे] Ś$_e$, कढे जू (unm.) G$_e$Ṭ$_e$ **70.2** का कहिये] Ś$_e$, और सुनो G$_e$Ṭ$_e$ • हिन की] Ś$_e$, गुरु के G$_e$Ṭ$_e$ • पढे] Ś$_e$, पढे जू (unm.) G$_e$Ṭ$_e$ **70.3** भूल सु] Ś$_e$, चूक या G$_e$Ṭ$_e$ • हमसों नित] Ś$_e$, हमसों उनसों G$_e$, हमसे उनसे Ṭ$_e$ • नेह सनेह] Ś$_e$, नव नेह G$_e$Ṭ$_e$ • बढे] Ś$_e$, बढे जू (unm.) G$_e$Ṭ$_e$ **70.4** जानती तीं] G$_e$Ṭ$_e$, जानत ते Ś$_e$ • ह्वैहै] G$_e$Ṭ$_e$, बडे Ś$_e$ • चैतुवा मीत] G$_e$Ṭ$_e$, चैतु अमीत Ś$_e$ • कढे] Ś$_e$, कढे जू (unm.) G$_e$Ṭ$_e$

68.4 **आन की आन** idiom. Br. false (matters); **हित जानि** idiom. Br. 1. considering my love; 2. considering it of my interest; **आई-गई करना** idiom. to pay no heed. **69.2** **अवगाहना** [avagāhate] v.t. to inquire about, to care for. **69.4** **इनकौ** apa. **70.1** **लंबी-चौड़ी हाँकना** idiom. to talk boastfully; **ते** 1. [H the] v.f. (past tense of honā); 2. [H ve] pron. (polite) he; **गाढे परे** Br. when he got into trouble; **गुन और कढे** Br. his other qualities appeared. **70.2** **चटसाल** [caṭṭā- + śālā-] f. (here m.) Br. school for small children; **कपटीहिन** var. [H kapaṭīpan] reg. m. shrewdness. **70.3** **नेह-सनेह** m. love (the Ṭhasak seems to have changed the text to avoid this awkward twinning); **हमसों उनसों नेह बढे** var. Br. my love towards him increased. **70.4** **जानती तीं** v.t. (reg. imperf.) I knew; **ते** apa. Br. that; **बडे** var. great (friend); **चैतुवा मीत** idiom. friend (only) in the Chaitra month (when there is work and salary; or: the supposed mating season for humans) (cf. H mausamī mitra); **कढ-** 1. v.t. to prove to be (H nikalnā); 2. Br. adj. shrewd. **71.1** **फुलवाई (फुलवाड़ी)** [phulavāṭikā-] f. flower garden; **हरि अंक भरी** idiom. poet. Hari embraced me.

हौं सकुची कोउ सुंदरी देखत लै जिनि, बाँह सो बाँह पछेली।
ठाकुर, भोर भए, गए नींद के देखहुँ, तौ घर माँझ अकेली।
आँख खुली तब पास न साँवरो, बाग न बावरो, बृक्ष न बेली॥ Ś71॥

काहे, अरे मन, साहस छाँडत, काहे उदास ह्वै देह तजै है।
वे सुख वे दुख आए चले गए, एक सी रीति रही नहि रैहै।
ठाकुर, काको भरोस करैं हम, या जग-जालन भूल न ऐहै।
जानै सँजोग मैं दीन्हो बियोग, बियोग मैं सो का सँजोग न दैहै॥ Ś72॥

*परि गे किधौं काहु के पाले, अरी, गुरु लोगन के डर सों डरि गे।
दिया बारत ही तें किवारे लगे मग हेरो, न मेरी बिथा हरि गे।
कहि ठाकुर, औधि हती दिन बूडत, आवन की, री, घरी धरि गे।
अधिरात भई, हरि आए नहीं, हमैं ऊमर को सहिया करिगे॥ Ś73॥

---

72 Granthāvalī 157, Śatak 11, Ṭhasak 72. 73 Granthāvalī 159, Śatak 64, Ṭhasak 165, Vrindaban3 f. 30v (8).

72.2 वे दुख] G$_e$Ṭ$_e$, ये दुख Ś$_e$ • **73.1** किधौं] **E**, कियौ V$_3$ • गुरु] G$_e$Ś$_e$, गुरू Ṭ$_e$, गुर V$_3$ • लोगन] **E**, लोगनि V$_3$ • सों] **E**, कौं V$_3$ **73.2** दिया बारत] V$_3$, दिन बूडत **E** • किवारे लगे] **E**, किवार दीय V$_3$ • मग] **E**, मघु V$_3$ **73.3** औधि] G$_e$Ṭ$_e$, औध Ś$_e$, औ⟨धि/धा⟩ V$_3$ • की] G$_e$Ṭ$_e$, के Ś$_e$, सु V$_3$ • **73.4** अधिरात] **E**, अधराति V$_3$ • ऊमर] **E**, ऊमरि V$_3$

71.2 पछेल- [paśca-] Br. v.t. to remove. **71.3** गए नींद के poet. when sleep was over. **71.4** बावर- (बावला) [cf. vātula-, vyākula-] Br. adj. wretched. **72.2** रही नहि रहै v.i. (Br. perf. and fut.) did not remain and will not remain. **72.3** ऐहै (आएँगी) Br. fut. I will come; भूलि न idiom. Br. not even by mistake; या जग-जालन ऐहै Br. will I be entangled in the meshes of this world. **72.4** जानैं rel. pron. Br. ag. (the one) who; का (क्या) Br. interr. won't he...? **73.1** किधौं (या) Br. conj. either; पाला [cf. H pālan] m. 1. protection; 2. power, clutches; (के) पाले पड़ना idiom. to fall into the clutches of; डर सों डरि गे reg. (or) became afraid of; डर कौं डरिगे var. who will be afraid of? **73.2** दिया बारत Br. '(the time of) lighting the lamps' evening; बूड- var. v.t. to sink (the sun); to end (the day); किवार दीय var. reg. closing the door (RSh); through the door; मघु apa. [? mārga-] reg. m. road; हरि गे v.i. perf. Br. were lost, removed. **73.3** धर- [dharati] v.t. to determine (time). **73.4** अधिरात [ardha-rātri] Br. f. midnight; ऊमर [udumbara-] m. the wild fig; सहिया Bund. m. worm; हमैं... करि गे idiom. Br. 'he made me a worm in a fig' confined me (into the house).

बरुनीन में नैन झुकैं उझकैं, मनौ खंजन मीन के जाले परे।
दिन औधि के कैसे गनौं, सजनी, अंगुरीन के पोरन छाले परे।
कहि ठाकुर, कौन सौं का कहिये, हमैं प्रीति किये के कसाले परे।
जिन लालन चाह करी इतनी, तिन्हैं देखिबे के अब लाले परे॥ Ś74॥

मेरी कही कर मो जिय, रावरे तोसों कहौं हौं सनेह के नातैं।
एक दिना मनभावन आइहैं, को कहिहै सुख सों मुख बातैं।
ठाकुर, फेरि जुदे जुदे होयँगे, देखु बिचार, कहाँ मैं कहाँ तैं।
झेलो बियोग के ये उझिला, निकसै जिन, रे जियरा, हियरा तैं॥ Ś75॥

---

74 Sundarī-tilak (C_e) p. (249), Granthāvalī 160, Kālidās-hajārā (H_e) 330, Jaipur1 ff. 1rv (2), Marwar4 ff. 21v-22r (13), Marwar5 f. 25r (30), Śatak 44, Ṭhasak 68, Vrindaban2 f. 69r.
75 Granthāvalī 161, Śatak 10, Ṭhasak 76.

74.1 में] Σ, है C_e • झुकैं] $\mathbf{E}H_eJ_1M_4V_2$, झिकैं C_e, झूके M_5 • उझकैं] $\mathbf{E}H_eJ_1V_2$, झिझिकैं C_e, *om.* (haplography) M_4, उझके M_5 • मनौ] Σ, द्रिग J_1 • खंजन] Σ, षंनज M_5 • मीन] Σ, प्रेम **E** **74.2** दिन] $\mathbf{E}H_eV_2$, अब J_1M_4, दीन M_5 • औधि] $\mathbf{E}H_eJ_1V_2$, औध M_4, आधि M_5 • कैसे] $\mathbf{E}H_eM_5V_2$, ध्यौस J_1, द्यौस M_4 • गनौं सजनी] $C_e\mathbf{E}H_eV_2$, न जात गनें J_1M_4, गिनो सजनी M_5 • पोरन] $\mathbf{E}H_eJ_1V_2$, पोरवै M_4, पोर पे M_5 **74.3** कहि] $C_eH_eV_2$, कवि $\mathbf{E}J_1$, कहैं M_4, कही M_5 • कौन] $H_eJ_1M_4M_5V_2$, ऐसी **E**, का सों C_e • सौं का] $H_eJ_1M_4V_2$, कहा $C_e\mathbf{E}$, सों कहा (unm.) M_5 • कहिये] Σ, कहीये M_5 • हमैं] $C_eH_eJ_1M_4M_5V_2$, निज **E** • प्रीति] $C_eH_eŚ_eV_2$, प्रीत $G_eJ_1M_4Ṭ_e$, पीत M_5 • किये] $H_eM_4V_2$, करे $C_e\mathbf{E}$, कीये J_1M_5 **74.4** जिन] $C_e\mathbf{E}J_1M_4$, जिनि H_eV_2, जीन M_5 • इतनी] Σ, ईतनी M_5 • तिन्हैं] $C_e\mathbf{E}M_4$, तिनैं $H_eJ_1V_2$, तिन M_5 • देखिबे] $C_e\mathbf{E}M_4$, देखन $H_eM_5V_2$, देषिब J_1 • के] $C_e\mathbf{E}J_1M_4$, कौं $H_eM_5V_2$ **75.1** कहौं] $G_eṬ_e$, कही $Ś_e$ **75.2** मनभावन] $Ś_e$, भगवान सु $G_eṬ_e$ • **75.3** फेरि] $G_eṬ_e$, फेर $Ś_e$ **75.4** झेलो] $G_eṬ_e$, बीर $Ś_e$ • उझिला] $G_eṬ_e$, उलझा $Ś_e$ • जियरा] $G_eŚ_e$, जिअरा $Ṭ_e$ • हियरा] $G_eŚ_e$, हिअरा $Ṭ_e$

74.1 झुकना v.i. to become irritated; to be trapped; उझकना [? H ucaknā x H jhāṃknā] v.i. to spring up; जाला [jālaka-] m. 1. web; 2. trap; मनौ ... परे as if (the eyebrows) were traps for wagtails and fishes; झिक- var. Br. v.t. to look; झिझकना var. v.i. 1. to shrink; 2. to hesitate; प्रेम के जाले var. into the net of love. **74.2** पोर [*pora, ?parva] f. joint (of the body); छाला [challi-] m. blister. **74.3** कसाला [? kaṣṭa-] m. pain; **74.4** जिन rel. pron. (Br. obl.) 1. of whom; 2. ag. who; लालन [S] 'caressing' m. 1. dear child; 2. bringing up with love (cf. H lālan-pālan); लाले [? H lālac] m. pl. strong desire; (के) लाले पड़ना idiom. 1. intense or hopeless desire to be felt; 2. to be unattainable. **75.1** रावरे ... नातैं Br. I am telling it to you because of my affection for you. **75.2** भगवान var. [S] m. lord, husband; को (कौन) Br. interr. who (will say)? सुख सों Br. happily; मुख [S] m. (obl.) (from his) mouth. **75.3** फेरि Br. conj. if again; कहाँ मैं कहाँ तैं Br. where will I be and where will you be? **75.4** उझिला var. [*ujjhalati] reg. f. 'pouring out' outburst.

लगी अंदर की, करै जाहिर का, बिन माहिर को कही मानत है।
सुख औ दुख, हानि या लाभ जिती, घर की कोऊ बाहर रानत है।
कहि ठाकुर, आपनी चातुरी सों सबही सब भाँति बखानत है।
पर, बीर, मिले बिछुरे की बिथा मिलिकै बिछुरै सोई जानत है॥ Ś76॥

सोक को समुद्र, बिरहागि को भँडार

---

76 Hariaudh (A_e) p. 485, Bharatpur1 f. 185 (24), Sundarī-tilak (C_e) 297, Granthāvalī 162, Kālidās-hajārā (H_e) 327, Rasikvinod (O_e) 305, Sudhāsar [S_1 f. 106r, S_2 ff. 22v-23r (3/30), S_6 f. 104r (113/668), S_7 f. 72r (18/719)], Śatak 9, Ṭhasak 69, Vrindaban2 f. 71rv, Vrindaban4 f. 11r (19). The Sudhāsar (S_1) presents this poem as an example of 'parakīyā proṣitapatikā' (an adulterous woman whose lover is going away).

76.1 लगी] Σ, लहि V_4 • अंदर] $B_1C_eO_e\mathbf{S}$, अंतर $A_e\mathbf{E}H_eV_2V_4$ • की] $B_1C_eH_eO_e\mathbf{S}V_2V_4$, मैं $A_e\mathbf{E}$ • करै] $A_eC_e\mathbf{E}H_eO_eV_2V_4$, करौ B_1S_2, करौं $S_1S_6S_7$ • जाहिर] $B_1H_e\mathbf{S}V_2V_4$, बाहिर $A_eC_e\mathbf{E}O_e$ • का] $\mathbf{S}V_2$, CHECK B_1, को $A_eC_e\mathbf{E}H_eO_eV_4$ • बिन] Σ, बिनु S_7, चित V_4 • माहिर] $B_1H_e\mathbf{S}V_2V_4$, जाहिर $A_eC_e\mathbf{E}O_e$ • को कही] $B_1H_e\mathbf{S}$, कोउ न $A_eG_eT_e$, कोऊ न $C_eŚ_e$, का कोउ O_e, को कहि V_2, सो V_4 • मानत] $B_1C_eO_eS_1S_2S_6V_2$, मानतु $A_e\mathbf{E}H_e$, मानति S_7, पहिचानतु V_4 • है] Σ, हैं S_6 **76.2** सुख] $C_eH_eO_eS_2S_6S_7V_2$, दुख $A_eB_1\mathbf{E}S_1V_4$ • औ] Σ, हू V_4 • दुख] $C_eO_eS_2S_6S_7V_2$, सुख $A_eB_1\mathbf{E}H_eS_1V_4$ • हानि] $A_eB_1C_e\mathbf{E}H_eO_eS_2S_6V_2$, हाँन S_1S_7, संपति V_4 • या] $B_1O_e\mathbf{S}$, औ $A_e\mathbf{E}H_eV_2$, यों C_e, *om.* V_4 • लाभ] Σ, लोभ H_e^{vl}, हानि V_4 • जिती] $B_1C_eO_e\mathbf{S}V_2V_4$, सबै $A_e\mathbf{E}$ • कोऊ] $B_1C_e\mathbf{S}Ś_e$, कोउ $A_eG_eO_eT_e V_2V_4$ • रानत] $B_1S_1S_2V_2$, भानतु $A_e\mathbf{E}H_e$, मानत C_e, रानतु H_e^{vl}, भानत O_e, ठानत S_6S_7, आनतु V_4 • है] Σ, हैं S_6 **76.3** कहि] $B_1H_e\mathbf{S}V_2V_4$, कवि $A_eC_e\mathbf{E}O_e$ • सों] Σ, की V_4 • सबही] Σ, सबहू V_2, सबसौं V_4 • सब] Σ, सभ S_6 • भाँति] Σ, कोऊ V_4 • बषानत] $B_1C_eO_e\mathbf{S}V_2^{pc}$, बखानतु $A_e\mathbf{E}H_eV_2^{ac}V_4$ • है] Σ, हैं S_6, हों V_4 **76.4** पर बीर] $A_e\mathbf{E}H_eS_1S_6$, परि बीर B_1S_2, परिवार C_e, परबीन $H_e^{vl}S_7V_2V_4$, पर यार O_e • मिले] Σ, मिले मिले (dittography) H_e^{vl} • की बिथा] Σ, की ब्यथा C_e, कि ब्यथा O_e • मिलिकै] Σ, जौ मिलै V_4 • बिछुरै] $A_eC_e\mathbf{E}O_eS_2S_6S_7V_2^{pc}V_4$, बिछुर्यौ $B_1H_eS_1V_2^{ac}$ • जानत] $B_1C_eO_eS_1S_2S_6V_2^{pc}$, जानतु $A_e\mathbf{E}H_eV_2^{ac}V_4$, जानति S_7 • है] Σ, हैं S_6

76.1 लगी अंतर मैं Br. what has affected one inside; जाहिर [A] adj. evident; करै जाहिर का reg. why should I expose it? माहिर [A] adj. expert (capable of interpreting it). **76.2** रान- [cf. H rannā 'to sound'] poet. v.t. to tell aloud; घर... है Br. would anyone speak of the matters of the house publicly? ठानना var. [cf. sthānya-] v.t. 1. to resolve, to determine; to be intent on; 2. to tell, to express (KL); भानना var. [bhanati] v.t. to tell.

निरधार मैं असार, यो बिचार सो मनायो है।
2 रस मैं बिरस महा, होत बस परबस,
होत जस अपजस, जानिनि जनायो है।
3 ठाकुर, सँजोग मैं बियोग बनि जात, फेरि
महिमा निपुन गुन जात न गनायो है।
4 बिधि की खुसामद बरामद कै, मेरी बीर,
बाजौ बाजौ दिन काहू अधम बनायो है॥ Ś77॥

1 रूप है न, रस है न, गुन है न ज्ञान कहूँ,
सील है न सत्य, भाई निरस जमानो है।
2 रीति है न, प्रीति है न, नीति है न न्याव कहूँ,
घर-घर देखियत हरष हिरानो है।

---

77 Bharatpur1 f. 158rv (58), Granthāvalī 163, Sudhāsar [S_2 f. 24r (1/31), S_7 f. 76v (1/761)], Vrindaban1 f. 11v (4/69). The Sudhāsar introduces this quatrain as a description of a 'parakiyā' in the 'prastāv aṅg'. Cf. 'sudhā tẽ sravata biṣa... Śujānhit 224; Ghan-Ānand-kabitt 55.
78 Chatarpur (C) p. 12 (68), Granthāvalī 210, Śatak 30, Ṭhasak 144, Z_1 ff. 28v, 48v(29v) (21).

77.1 बिरहागि] G_e, बिरहागी S_2, बिरहाग $B_1S_7V_1$ • मनायौ] $B_1^{pc}\Sigma$, ⟨ब⟩नायौ B_1^{ac} **77.2** परबस] $B_1^{pc}G_eS_7V_1$, ⟨ब⟩रबस B_1^{ac}, परिबस S_2 • जाननि] Σ, जानिन S_7 • जनायो] G_eS_7, जनाय (unrh.) S_2, जनौयो (unrh.) V_1 **77.3** बनि] Σ, बन S_7 • फेरि] G_eS_2, फेर $B_1S_7V_1$ • निपुन] Σ, निपुनि S_7 • गनायो] $B_1^{pc}G_e$**S**, ⟨न⟩नायौ (dittography) B_1^{ac}, गनो (unrh.) V_1 **77.4** बिधि] Σ, बिध S_7 • खुसामद बरामद] $B_1G_eV_1$, षुसामदि बरामदि S_2, कुसामद बरामद S_7 • मेरी] Σ, मरी V_1 **78.1** रूप] $C^{ac}\Sigma$, दो दफे रूप C^{pc} • न] Σ, ना C • न] Σ, ना C • न] Σ, ना C • न] Σ, ना C • सत्य] **E**, सत्त CZ_1 • भाई] C^{pc}**E**, भा C^{ac}, भाव Z_1 • **78.2** रीति] $Ś_eṬ_e$, रीत CG_e, प्रीत Z_1 • न] Σ, ना C • प्रीति] $Ś_eṬ_e$, प्रीत CG_e, रीत Z_1 • न] Σ, ना C • नीति] $Ś_eṬ_e$, नीत G_eZ_1, नाति C • न] $Ś_eṬ_eZ_1$, *om.* (unm.) G_e, ना C • न्याव] Σ, न्याह Z_1 • घर घर] Σ, पूर घर Z_1 • देखियत] **E**, घेर ताते C, हेर देषौ Z_1 • हरष] **E**, हर्ष (unm.) C, हरक Z_1

77.1 निरधार [nirdhārayati] v.t. (poet. perf.) I determined; असार [S] adj. empty, vain; बिचार सो Br. with consideration; यो... है Br. I accepted this with consideration. **77.2** जाननि जनायो है Br. experts made it known to me. **77.3** फेरि Br. adv. after that; महिमा [S] f. importance; निपुन गुन Br. the virtues of the experts; जात न गनायो Br. is not taken into account. **77.4** बरागद [P] m. coming, appearance; सुशामद [P] m. flattery; खुशामद-बरामद m. flattery; बाजौ बाजौ [P bāz] adj. some, certain; काहू (किसीने) pron./adj. (Br. ag.) some(body). **78.1** भाई [bhāva-] poet. m. feeling. **78.2** घेर ताते var. Br. therefore there is gossip; हरष (हर्ष) [S] Br. m. joy; हिराना (हराना) [hārayati] v.t. 1. to worst, to foil; 2. to lose.

ठाकुर कहत, भूलो सकल सँजोग भोग, 3
कठिन कुजोग लोग सबही बिरानो है।
कौन कौं जतैये, कहाँ जैये, कहाँ पैये, बीर, 4
मन बहराइबे कौं ठौर न ठिकानो है॥ Ś78॥

*जानी जात रावरे सँजोगनि के, साँवरे जू, 1
सुख के समाजन समोइबो करति है।
देखिबे की आँखैं ते न खोलति, खुलाइ हारी, 2
हिय अँखियान मग जोइबो करति है।
ठाकुर कहत, जागै जोगी लौं समाधि साधे, 3
संग की अजानैं जानैं सोइबो करति है।
रोइबो करति निस-बासर बिकल भई, 4
आँसुन कि धार देह धोइबो करति है॥ Ś79॥

---

79 Bharatpur1 f. 154r (27), Bharatpur8 f. 14rv (41), Granthāvalī B32, Sudhāsar [S_2 f. 35r (45/35), S_7 f. 115v-6r (9/1105)], Vrindaban1 ff. 6v-7r (11/37). The Sudhāsar (S_7) includes this poem into the 'virah nivedan' (request in separation) subsection of the 'dūtī karma' (activities of a messenger) section.

78.3 भूलो] Σ, भूले Z_1 • भोग] C^{ac}Σ, योग C^{pc} • कठिन... है] **E**, अतही कुजोगन मै मन लिपटा⟨रौ/नौ⟩ है Z_1 • कुजोग] **E**, कुरोग C **78.4** कौं] Σ, सौ Z_1 • जैये] Σ, जईये (unm.) C • पैये] Σ, पईये (unm.) C **79.1** जात] Σ, जाति S_2 • सँजोगिनि] B_1G_e, ⟨रसे भो⟩गिन B_8^{ac}, संजोगिन $B_8^{pc}S_7V_1$, सजोगीन S_2 • सुख] Σ, सष S_2 • समाजन] Σ, समाजनि G_e • करति] G_e**S**, करत $B_1B_8V_1$ • है] $G_eS_2V_1$, हैं $B_1B_8S_7$ **79.2** खोलति] G_e, षोलत B_1B_8**S**, षोलैत V_1 • हिय] Σ, हीय V_1 • करति] G_e**S**, करत $B_1B_8V_1$ • है] $G_eS_2V_1$, हैं $B_1B_8S_7$ **79.3** ठाकुर कहत] Σ, ठा° B_1 • जागै] Σ, जागैं S_7 • साधै] Σ, साधैं S_7 • जानैं] Σ, जानै S_7 • करति] G_e**S**, करत $B_1B_8V_1$ • है] Σ, हैं B_8 **79.4** रोइबो... करति है] B_1^{mg}Σ, ×आंसुन की धाराइं जे वे चीर भीजै डारै ते तिहारैं मनहाइ कै निचोरिबौ करत हैं× B_1 • करति] G_e**S**, करत $B_1^{mg}B_8V_1$ • निस] Σ,भ्हरत्पुराम्ग, निसि G_e • करति] G_eS_7, करत $B_1^{mg}B_8S_2V_1$ • है] $B_8G_eS_2V_1$, हैं $B_1^{mg}S_7$

78.3 कुजोग [kuyoga-] Br. m. 'an inauspicious conjunction (of planets)' bad luck; बिरान- adj. (pl., the ending is distorted for the sake of rhyme) 'of someone else' alien (cf. H parānā). **78.4** जताना [jñāpayati] v.t. to tell; बहरा- [viharati] Br. v.t. to amuse. **79.1** जानी जात Br. it is obvious that; संयोग [S] m. (moments of) union (with you); संयोगिन apa. [S] f. pl. (of) the people in union (with you); समोना [saṃvapati] v.t. to mix closely; समोइबो करति है (समायी रहती है) reg. remains immersed. **79.2** देखिबे की आँखैं Br. the eyes to see you; खुलाई हारी reg. she became tired of opening them. **79.3** जागै [jāgarti] v.i. (Br. perf. obl. for adv.) when she is awake; संग की अजानैं Br. her ignorant companions. **79.4** विकल भई Br. (having become) distressed.

1 *चलिये, छबीले छैल, दलिये बिरह वाको,
जाकी छबि रति रूप खोइबो करति है।
2 रावरे चलन चरचान सुनि, साँवरे जू,
बावरी लौं बासर बितोइबो करति है।
3 ठाकुर कहत, लागै पल सों न पल कैंहू,
चौंधियानी चकित चितोइबो करति है।
4 आंसुनि की धारैं जे वै चीर भिजै डारै ते
तिहारे मन हाइ कै निचोइबो करति है॥ Ś80॥

1 होत कहा काहू चाहवरिन को चाह्यो चोज,

---

80 Bharatpur1 f. 155r (32), Granthāvalī B33, Sudhāsar [S_2 f. 35v (45/36), S_7 f. 116r (12/1108)], Vrindaban1 f. 7r (12/38). The Sudhāsar (S_7) includes this poem into the 'virah nivedan' (request in separation) subsection of the 'dūtī karma' (activities of a messenger) section. Ś79 and Ś80 are grouped together in V_1. In S_2 a poem by Navīn with an 'anyokti' is inserted between the two.

80.1 छबीले] Σ, ⟨छ/छा⟩बीले V_1 • रूप] Σ, रुप V_1 • करति] G_e**S**, करत B_1V_1 **80.2** चरचान] Σ, बरचांन S_2 • जू] Σ, जु V_1 • बावरी] G_e**S**, बावरे B_1V_1 • कर-ति] G_e**S**, करत B_1V_1 **80.3** ठाकुर कहत] Σ, ठा° B_1 • लागै] $B_1S_2V_1$, लगै G_e, लागो S_7 • सों] Σ, सो S_7 • कैहू] $B_1G_eV_1$, क्यौहू S_2S_7 • करति] G_eS_7, करत $B_1S_2V_1$ **80.4** आंसुन] Σ, आसुनि G_e • की धारैं] $B_1G_eV_1$, के धौरै S_2, के फोरै S_7 • वे] B_1G_e**S**, वी V_1^{ac}, ⟨वे/वो⟩ V_1^{pc} • भिजै] B_1**S**, भीजै G_eV_1 • डारै] Σ, डोरे S_7 • ते] $B_1G_eV_1$, तो S_2 • मन] Σ, मैन S_7 • हाइ] Σ, न्हाइ G_e • निचोइबो] G_e**S**, निचोरिबो B_1, निचोरबों (unrh.) V_1 • करति] G_eS_7, करत $B_1S_2V_1$

80.1 छैल [chavilla-] m. (handsome) boy; जाकी छबि Br. in front of whose beauty; खोइबो करति है Br. Rati (again and again) looses her own beautiful form. **80.2** बासर बितोइबो करति है Br. keeps passing her days. **80.3** लगै... कैंहू Br. her eyes do not close by any means; चौंधियानी [H caumdhnā x andha-] v.i. perf. Br. dazzled (woman). **80.4** जे rel. pron. Br. pl. (the streams of tears) which; वै [S] emph. Br. encl. indeed; भिज- (भिजाना) [bhiyañjati] poet. v.t. to drench; ते pron. Br. those (streams); हाय करना idiom. to say 'alas', to be distressed; निचो- (निचोड़ना) [*niṣcoṭayati] poet. v.t. to squeeze; तिहारे... करति है poet. keep distressing and squeezing your heart;

होत जाको चाह्यो ताको हुकम जरूर भौ।
तौन रंक राव कूर साहब सहूर मानि 2
सीस धरि चलिबौ सभी कौं मनजूर भौ।
ठाकुर, समीप जो सुभाय बोल बोल्यो, सोऊ 3
दाह के मिटाइबे कौं सुखद कपूर भौ।
एक दिन बीच दै नगीच देखि लीजत तौ, 4
दूर परौ देखत हौं, देखिबौऊ दूर भौ॥ Ś81॥

वे तौ छबि धाम, हम अबला अहीरन की, 1
हिलमिल कीनौ यौं सनेहवारौ सोत है।

81 Bharatpur1 f. 158v-9r (55), Granthāvalī B35, Vrindaban1 f. 11r (1/66). 82 Bharatpur1 f. 151v (13), Sudhāsar [S_1 f. 296v (27), S_2 f. 60rv (-/68), S_3 f. 168rv (234), S_4 f. 95v-96r (245), S_7 f. 207r (82)], Vrindaban1 f. 14r (21/85). • The Sudhāsar presents this poem within the 'uddhava kau braj mẽ āyabau' (Uddhava's coming to Braj) subsection of the 'Brajrasrīti' section.

81.1 काहू] G_e, काऊ B_1, काहु V_1 • चाहवारिन] B_1, चाहवारेन G_eV_1 • चोज] $B_1G_eV_1^{pc}$, *om.* (unm.) V_1^{ac} **81.2** सहूर] B_1G_e, सुर (unm.) V_1 • मानि] B_1G_e, मान V_1 • धरि] B_1G_e, धिर V_1 • सभी] B_1V_1, सबी G_e • मनजूर] G_e, मंजूर (unm.) B_1V_1 **81.3** दाह के] B_1G_e, दाहि कै V_1 **81.4** बीच] B_1G_e, बेच V_1 • दूर परौ] B_1G_e, दूरौ (unm.) V_1^{ac}, दू परौ (unm.) V_1^{pc} • हौं] V_1, हौ B_1G_e **82.1** अहीरन] $B_1\mathbf{S}$, अहिरनि V_1, अ×होरन की×हिरन S_2 • हिलमिल] $B_1S_1S_3S_7^{pc}V_1$, हिलिमिलि S_2S_4, हिल (unm.) S_7^{ac} • कीनौ] $B_1\mathbf{S}$, काम V_1 • सनेहवारौ] Σ, सनेहबारे S_7

81.1 कहा Br. interr. is ever (acquired)? काहू (कहीं) adv. somehow; चाहवरेन (चाहवालों) var. m. pl. obl. Bund. of those who wish; चाह्यो v.t. perf. Br. desired; चोज [codya-] m. 1. wonderful saying; 2. wonderful sentiment (SBK); delight (RKS); 3. (here:) object of desire; होत... चोज reg. do those people who love acquire their object of desire? होत जाको चाह्यो (जिसको चाहा जाता है) Br. the one who is loved; भौ (हुआ) [bhavati] v.i. (reg. perf.) became, was; ताको हुकम जरूर भौ reg. his or her orders have definitely been obeyed. **81.2** सहूर [A śu'ūr] Br. m. 1. knowledge, wisdom; 2. good management, order; तौन... मानि the lowly, the king, the wretched, the lord (all) accept its order (or: consider it wisdom); सीस धर- idiom. 'to put on one's head' to accept respectfully; सबी (शबीह) apa. [A] f. picture. **81.3** समीप [S] adv. (coming) near; सुभाय [svabhāva] Br. m. (obl.) in a natural way. **81.4** एक दिन बीच दै poet. every second day; नगीच [P nazdīk] Av. adv. (from) near; तौ (था) reg. v.i. imperf. (he used to see me); दूर परौ Br. he is far away; देखत हौं Br. I reckon (since). **82.1** हिलना-मिलना v.i. to become intimate with; हिलमिल काम var. the act(s) of becoming intimate; सोत [srotra-] m. spring, source; सनेहवारौ सोत Br. 1. the source of love (i.e. Krishna) (became intimate with us in this way); 2. (in this way his intimacy) is the source of love.

2 तौन अब अदलौ सौ बदलौ दिखात, बीर,
धीरज रहत बाढ्यौ अजस उदोत है।
3 ठाकुर कहत, देखौ प्रेमवारे ग्रंथनि मैं,
प्रीतिवारे पंथन मैं, काकौ काढ्यौ पोत है।
4 घैरवारौ तौ तरस-रीति न, बितोत तातैं
होन होत होत कहा जानैं कहा होत है॥ Ś82॥

*पिय मोहन कौ वह मोहनौं रूप निहारे बिना नहिं जीजतु है।
2 तिहि ते जु लटी-भली या जग मैं सिख मानि सबै सुनि लीजतु है।

83 Bharatpur1 f. 132v (10), Sundarītilak (C_e) p. 51 (301), Sudhāsar [S_1 ff. 63v-64r (21), S_2 f. 11r (12/8), S_7 f. 45v (26/428)], Bābūrāmdīn: Sundarītilak (U_e) 182. The Sudhāsar (S_1) presents this poem within the 'ūḍhā parakiyā' (self-asserting, explicit adulterous woman) section. The last line is similar to that of N19.

82.2 तौन] $B_1S_7V_1$, तौ S_3^{ac}, तौउ S_3^{pc}, तौनि $S_1S_2S_4$ • अब] B_1^{pc}**S**, *om.* (unm.) $B_1^{ac}V_1$ • अदलौ] Σ, दलौ (unm.) S_1 • दिखात] **S**V_1, ×सो ब× दिषात B_1, दिषत S_2 • रहत] $S_1S_3S_7V_1$, रह न S_2, रहति S_4 • अजस] B_1**S**, अजहुँ V_1 **82.3** कहत] B_1**S**, कहैत V_1 • देषौ] B_1**S**, देख्यौ V_1 • प्रेमवारे] $B_1S_1S_3S_7V_1$, प्रैमवारों S_2S_4 • ग्रंथनि B_1, ग्रंथन **S**V_1, गथन S_2 • काढ्यौ] B_1V_1, गढ्यौ S_1, कढ्यौ **S** • पोत] $B_1S_1S_3S_7V_1$, प्रोत S_2S_4 **82.4** र-स] $B_1S_1S_3S_7V_1$, रस्स S_2, र⟨र⟩स (dittography) S_4^{ac}, र⟨स⟩स S_4^{pc} • रीति] $B_1S_1S_2S_4$, रीत $S_3S_7V_1$ • बितोत] Σ, बिनोत S_4 • होन होत] S_1S_2, होत होत $B_1S_3S_4S_7$, होत (unm.) V_1 • जानैं] B_1S_1, जानै $S_2S_3S_7V_1$, तांने S_4 **83.1** मौंहनौं] **S**, मोहनी C_eU_e • नहिं] $C_eS_2S_7U_e$, नही B_1S_1 • जीजतु] $B_1C_eU_e$, जीजत **S** **83.2** ते] $C_eS_2S_7$, तें $B_1S_1U_e$ • जु लटी] Σ, जु जुटी (dittography) C_e • मानि] $B_1C_eS_2U_e$, मान S_1S_7 • सुनि] $B_1C_eS_1S_2S_7^{ac}$, सुख U_e, सुखि S_7^{pc} • लीजतु] $B_1C_eU_e$, लीजत S_1S_7, लीजव S_2

82.2 तौन pron. Br. Bund. he; अदला-बदला adj. changed; उदोत [uddyota-] Br. m. light, radiance; धीरज रहत बाढ्यौ उदोत है var. Br. since we have forbearance our (ascetic) brightness grows. **82.3** पोत [S] m. vessel, ship; काढ्यौ पोत Br. v.t. perf. saved the vessel; प्रोत apa. m. 1. woof; 2. [S] clothes. **82.4** घैर m. slander; घैरवारौ Br. Bund. m. slanderer; त [Br. tā-] pron. (obl.) poet. he (has no); तरस रीति न poet. it is not their custom to have compassion (empathy); बितो-, बितव- (बिताना) [cf. vyatīta-] reg. v.t. to spend (time); होन (होनहार) f. 'what is to be' 1. future; destiny; 2. (?) time; बितोत तातैं होन reg. (?) therefore I spend my time; होत होत (होते होते) Br. 1. as (the future) unfolds; 2. idiom. occasionally; होत होत होत कहा (होते होते का होता है) var. Br. (?) what occasionally happens (as time passes by); कहा जानैं कहा होत है Br. how do the slanderers know what happens? **83.2** तिहि ते Br. conj. therefore; लटा Bund. adj. bad; लटी-भली idiom. Bund. all kinds of (words); जुटी apa; सिख (सीख) [śikṣā-] Br. f. 1. lesson; 2. advice; सिख मानि Br. taking as an advice.

कहि ठाकुर, लाल के देखिबे कै लियै ज्वाब न काहूवे दीजतु है।
अब का कहियै, अपने उरझैं सबही की खुसामदि कीजतु है॥ Ś83॥

*जब ते, अली, लाल बिदेस गयो, छिन ही छिन यूँ तन छीजत है।
कुच कँचुकी प्रानपिआरै बिना असुवान की धारन भीजत है।
कह ठाकुर, आपना यंतर की, सजनी, तुमही सुख दीजत है।
वह प्रानपिआरे उन्हार, सखी, ननदी मुख देख कै जीजत है॥ Ś84॥

*साहस कै कस कै अब लौ जिय, भारी भयौ अब एक खिना है।
जानत ह्वैहै वही दुष जो सो रही तिय प्रीतम प्यारे बिना है।
ठाकुर, कौन सौ बुझिऐ जाइ सु दूर बसेरौ दियौ बिधिना है।
जानी न जाति वियोग गुपाल कौ और धौं, आली, कितेक दिना है॥ Ś85॥

---

84 Jaipur3 f. 2r (9). The manuscript does not differentiate between short and long i; therefore any short i in the text is the result of editorial intervention. The last line seems to be a samasyāpūrti. Another poem of smaraṇa alaṅkāra with similar first and last lines is quoted in the Introduction p. CHECK. 85 Datiya1 f. 106r (343).

83.3 लाल] C_eS, कांन्ह B_1, ला⟨ल/ख⟩ U_e • कै] $S_7^{pc}\Sigma$, *om.* (unm.) S_7^{ac} • काहुवे] S_2U_e, काउऐ B_1, काहुऐं S_1, काहूवे S_7, काहुहि C_e • दीजतु] $B_1C_eU_e$, दीजत S **83.4** अब] SU_e, परि B_1, सखि C_e • कहियै] Σ, करियै B_1 • उरझैं] $B_1S_1S_2$, अरुझे U_e, उरझे S_7C_e • षुसामदि] $B_1S_2S_7$, खुसामद C_eU_e, षुसामदी S_1 • कीजतु] $B_1C_eU_e$, कीजत S **84.1** ते] *conj.* त J_3 • यूँ] *em.* यु (unm.) J_3 • है] *conj.* ह J_3 **84.2** कँचुकी] *conj.* कैचुकी J_3 • भीजत] *conj.* बीजत J_3 • है] *conj.* ह J_3 **84.3** आपना] *em.* अपना (unm.) J_3 • °ही सुख] *em.* सुषही (unm.) J_3 • है] *conj.* ह J_3 **84.4** पिआरे] *conj.* ⟨पी⟩रे (unm.) J_3 • उन्हार] *conj.* पुनीआर J_3 • है] *conj.* ह J_3 **85.2** ह्वैहै] *conj.* ⟨ह्वै⟩है D_1

83.3 ज्वाब (जवाब) [A] reg. m. answer; काहुवे pron. Br. obl. to anyone. **83.4** अपने उरझैं Br. since I got entangled; खुशामद [P] m. flattery. **84.1** छीन [kṣaṇa-] poet. m. minute, moment; छीजना [chidyate] v.i. to wear away, to dwindle. **84.2** कँचुकी [S] f. bodice; धार [dhārā-] f. stream, current; भीज- (भीगना) [*bhiyajyate] Br. v.i. to be wet, to get drenched. **84.3** आपना यंत्र की reg. with your (words of a) plot (to look at the sister-in-law); दीजत Br. v.t. imperf. you give. **84.4** उन्हार [anuhāra-] poet. 1. m. resemblance, 2. adj. resembling; ननदी [nanandṛ-] f. husband's sister. **85.1** साहस कै idiom. Br. taking courage; with resolution; कस कै idiom. Br. 'keeping under control' well, a lot; जिय v.i. perf. poet. I lived; अबलौ जिय भारी भयौ है var. Br. (?) this weak life has become heavy (to live); खिना [kṣaṇa-] reg. m. moment. **85.2** जानत ह्वैहै वही (वही जानता होगा) (Br. fut. as presumptive) that person must know; जो सो रही तिय Br. the woman who sleeps. **85.3** कौन interr. who (should be asked)? दूर बसेरौ दियौ Br. he granted me separation.

*छल छोडि कै दौरि मिले तब, तौ अब और नहीं चित लावनो है।
रस लोभ अधीन भये, अब तौ कछु लालच दै बिरमावनो है।
कवि ठाकुर, बाँह गही, सो गही, पुनि मुद्दत लों पहुंचावनो है।
यह नेह की नाव चलाई, सो तो पर खेय के पार लगावनो है॥ Ś86॥

का कहियै, परी नेह अधीन, रिसान दै, लोग रिसानोई सोहै।
और कहा कहियै, कहि लेन दै नाम बुरो, तौ बखानोई सो है।
ठाकुर, याकी है मोहिं प्रतीत, सो बैर सबै रिस मानो ईसो है।
वा घनस्याम अकेले बिना सिगरो ब्रज, बीर, बिरानोई सो है॥ Ś87॥

काठ तें एतो कठोर भयो जोइ वा दिन कोरे हुते मधु माखन।
बातैं बनाइ कहैं डरकै, मिलकै बिछुरे उडिगे बिन पाँखन।

---

86 Sundarī-tilak (C_e) p. 15 (86), Marwar5 f. 25v (34); Rasikvinod (O_e) p. 71 (330).
87 Granthāvalī 34, Ṭhasak 71. 88 Granthāvalī 35, Śatak 85, Ṭhasak 84.

86.1 छोडि] C_eO_e, छोडी M_5 • दौरि] C_eO_e, दौरी M_5 **86.2** बिरमावनो] C_eM_5, बिलमावनों O_e **86.3** कवि] C_eO_e, कवी M_5 • गही सो गही] C_eO_e, गई सो गई M_5 • पुनि] C_eO_e, पुनी M_5 • मुद्दत] C_eO_e, मुदत (unm.) M_5 **86.4** यह] C_eO_e, यहे M_5 • खेय] C_eO_e, खेई M_5 **87.2** कहियै] G_e, कहिहैं Ṭ$_e$ **88.1** एतो] G_eṬ$_e$, एहो Ś$_e$ • जोइ] G_e, जाइ Ṭ$_e$, जो Ś$_e$ • वा दिन] G_eṬ$_e$, वा दिना Ś$_e$ • हुते] G_eṬ$_e$, हतै Ś$_e$ **88.2** उडिगे] Ś$_e$, उडिकै G_eṬ$_e$

86.1 छोड़ि कै postp. reg. without; और नहीं चित लावनो है Br. 1. you ought not bring anyone else in your mind, 2. you ought not bring your mind elsewhere. **86.2** रस लोभ अधीन भये Br. now I became subject to the desire of that emotion; लालच दै Br. having tempted, decoyed; बिलमाना [vilamba-] v.t. 1. to keep one waiting, 2. to trap in love. **86.3** बाँह गह- idiom. Br. to help; मुद्दत लों idiom. Br. 'for a long time' till the end. **86.4** सो तो पर Br. but he; पर 1. but; 2. the other (shore); खेना [kṣepayati] v.t. 1. to row, to punt (2. to pass through, to endure). **87.1** रिसान दै Br. let them fume; लोग रिसानोई सोहै reg. it is proper for the people to fume. **87.2** कहि लेन दै (कहने दो) Br. v.t. let them say; सो emph. poet. indeed (they did pronounce the bad name). **87.3** याकी है मोहिं प्रतीत Br. (?) I trust it; रिस मानोई सो है reg. they are indeed angry; ईसो है (ऐसा ही है) Bund. (for me) it is just like this; it is without foundation; बैर सबै रिस मानो ईसो है reg. all may cherish enmity and hatred. **87.4** सिगरो [sakala-] Br. adj. entire; वीराना [P] m. a desolate place; बिराना adj. belonging to someone else (cf. parāyā). **88.1** एहो var. interj. reg. o, look! जोइ 1. pron. (Br. emph.) the one who; 2. v.t. imp. Br. look; कोरा adj. plain; कोरे हुते मधु माखन Br. he was true honey and butter. **88.2** डरकै v.i. abs. Br. having fear, cautiously (not to say something improper); उडिकै बिन पाँखन var. Br. (he abandoned me) flying away though he does not have wings.

ठाकुर, वे न सँदेसो लिखैं, चलि आवत हैं उत तैं नर लाखन।
यों जु कियो बदनाम सबै ब्रज मैं अब, आँखैं लगाइ दिखात न आँखन॥ Ś88॥

मान

सोभा सुहात बिलोकत भावती, जानी कहानी न सोवन पाए।
मान्यौ न जात कछू नखरा, रिस के अखरा हिय तें बिसराए।
ठाकुर, रंगन रंग अनंग के अंगन अंग घनी छबि छाए।
कौन भली सों मिले भली भाँति सों, लाल भले जू, भले बनि आए॥ Ś89॥

*एक समै सुख की सदन सुकुमार बैठी,
अनख सौ भरी खरी सोभा तौन छावै है।
मान के मनावत मै ललित हलायौ सीस,
दूसरी मनाइबे की बतियां बनावै है।

---

89 Bharatpur1 f. 151rv (12), Granthāvalī B18, Sudhāsar [S_2 ff. 8v-9r (1/4), S_7 f. 39v (10)], Vrindaban1 f. 14r (20/84). This poem is about a 'dhīrā khaṇḍitā' a woman who is ironical in her wounded pride. The Sudhāsar (S_7) presents this savaiyā as an example of the 'dhīrādhīrā' (both firm and infirm) heroine.) 90 Datiya1 f. 106rv (344).

88.3 वे] $G_eṬ_e$, तैं $Ś_e$ **88.4 यों जु**] *em.* जु (unm.) **E** **89.1 सोवन**] $B_1G_eV_1$, मो मन S_2, सोवत S_7 **89.2 कछू**] $B_1G_eS_7$, की (unm.) S_2, कछु (unm.) V_1 • रिस] $B_1S_2S_7V_1$, रस G_e • हिय] Σ, जिय S_7 **89.3 रंगन**] $G_eS_2S_7$, रंगानि B_1V_1 • अनंग] Σ, *om.* (unm.) S_2 • अंगन] Σ, अंगनि B_1 **89.4 भली भाँति**] $B_1^{pc}G_eS_2S_7$, भांति (unm.) B_1^{ac}, भगति (unm.) V_1 • सों] $B_1G_eV_1$, सु S_2S_7

88.4 आँख लगना idiom. to be in love; **आँख दिखाना** idiom. 1. to be angry; 2. to look (with love). **89.1 सुहाना** [śubhāyate] v.i. to be attractive; to grace; **सोभा... भावती** Br. it pleases me to see your attractive radiance; **न सोवन पाए** Br. (that) you did not get any sleep. **89.2 नखरा** 1. [P nak͟harā] m. pretence; 2. [H na-kharā] adj. false, dishonest, bad; **मान्यौ न जात कछू नखरा** Br. I am not able to think of anything bad; **रिस** [riṣ- x īrṣyā-] f. anger, offence; **अखरा (अक्षर)** [S] reg. m. letter; **बिसराना** [vismarati] v.t. to efface (from memory). **89.3 रंगन रंग अनंग के** Br. died in the colours of Kāma; **अंगन अंग** Br. your every limb (is covered with). **89.4 भली** [cf. bhalla-] adj. (f.) good, kindly (woman); **भली भाँति सों** Br. adv. well; **भले बनि आए** Br. you are welcome! **90.1 सदन** [S] m. (here: f.) abode; **सुख की सदन** poet. a woman who is the abode of happiness; **अनख** [? anakṣa-] m. f. anger; **खरी** [khara-] adv. a lot, abundantly; **सोभा... है** Br. 1. her radiance has spread; 2. she spread (with) her radiance. **90.2 मान के मनावत मैं** Br. while one argued with her pride; **ललित हलायौ सीस** Br. she swayed her beautiful head; **दूसरी** [*dviḥsara-] adv. f. another (companion).

3 ठाकुर कहत, मुख, आँखिन की, नासा केर,
बेसर बिचित्र चार उपमा बतावै है।
4 बारिज पै खंजन है, खंजन दु बीचै कीर,
कीर मानौ मौतिन की मंजरी डुलावै है॥ Ś90॥

राखे हते हम रावरे को बल मान गुमान बडी गरुवाई।
2 काम परे बडे कामन में कहुँ ह्वैहें बिसेष कै आनि सहाई।
ठाकुर, गौर करौ, केहि कारन बैठि रहे मन मैं अरगाई।
4 थोरिहि बात मैं धोखो मिटो, बढियाई भई, कलई कढि आई॥ Ś91॥

रोजही आनि हरावत बातन, या ढिठई तुम्हैं कौनै सिखाई।
2 देखि लई तुमरी करतूत, सु बैठ रहो न करौ चतुराई।
ठाकुर, धोखो हतो अब लौं, अब रावरे देख लई या बडाई।
4 चोरी छिपाए कहाँ सों छिपै, बढियाई भई, कलई कढि आई॥ Ś92॥

1 *काम कर तेज, किधौं साहिबी मजेज, किधौं

---

91 Granthāvalī 196, Ṭhasak 150. 92 Granthāvalī 197, Śatak 103, Ṭhasak 180.

91.1 हम] $G_e Ṭ_e^{pc}$, मह $Ṭ_e^{ac}$ • **92.1** ढिठई] $G_e Ṭ_e$, ठिठई $Ś_e$ • **92.2** देखि] $Ṭ_e$, देथि G_e, देख $Ś_e$ • **92.4** बढियाई] G_e, बडपाई $Ś_e$, बडयाई $Ṭ_e$ • कढि] $G_e Ṭ_e$, कर $Ś_e$ •

90.3 आँखिन की Br. (simile) of the eyes; नासा केर (?केरी) Av. of the nose; बेसर m. small heavy nose-ring. **90.4** वारिज [S] m. (face like a) lotus; खंजन [S] m. (eyes like a) wagtail; बीचै postp. Br. between; कीर [S] Br. m. (nose like a) parrot. **91.1** रावरे को (आपके लिए) poet. for your sake; गरुवाई [cf. guru-] f. 1. weight; 2. fig. importance. **91.2** काम परे Br. 1. when needed; 2. when there is an opportunity; कामन [karma-] m. pl. obl. Br. works; कहुँ (कहीं) Br. adv. somewhere; somehow; काम... कहुँ Br. (thinking that) if ever there is any big need for work; आनि v.i. abs. Br. coming; बिसेष कै abs. (used as adv.) Br. especially. **91.3** ग़ौर [A] m. deep thought; रहे v.i. pres.-subj. Br. you remain; अरग- (अलग होना) Br. v.i. to be aloof. **91.4** बढियाई भई Br. 1. it is in fact good; 2. you became great (RS); क़लई [A] f. 1. veneer; 2. whitewashing; क़लई उखड़ना idiom. the real qualities to be exposed. **92.1** हराना [hārayati] v.t. 'to defeat' to tire out; कौनै (किसने) pron. (Br. ag.) who? **92.2** सु Br. conj. therefore. **92.4** चोरी [caurikā-] f. 1. stealing; 2. fig. hidden act; कहाँ सों Br. by what? how? बडयाई var. [cf. H baḍā] adj. supreme, best.

प्रेम की छकनि, ताकी तकनि अमोलै है।
कैधौं रस रीति, कैधौं प्रेम की परिक्षा कीन, 2
किधौं हित गाँठि हियैं लगी, तौन खोलै है।
ठाकुर कहत, ऐसौ चौंधियानो चकवानो 3
चतुर सुजान मन याही भ्रम डौलै है।
मेरे धोखें औरन के घूँघटनि खोलै, लाल, 4
औरन के धोखैं मोसूँ बोलैंहू न बोलै है॥ Ś93॥

मन-धन बिससे से, मोह सों भरे से, कान्ह, 1

---

93 Bharatpur1 f. 154v (30), Granthāvalī B29, Sudhāsar [S_7 f. 84r (9/823)], Vrindaban1 f. 6r (6/32).

93.1 छकनि] B_1G_e, छकन S_7V_1 • तकनि] G_eV_1, तकन S_7B_1 **93.2** कैधौ रस] $B_1S_7V_1$, किधौं रस G_e • कैधौ प्रेम] S_7, किधौं प्रेम B_1G_e, कीधौ प्रेम V_1 • परिक्षा] G_e, परिछा $B_1^{ac}V_1$, परिच्छा $B_1^{pc}S_7$ • गाँठि] B_1G_e, गाठ S_7V_1 • हियैं] $B_1S_7G_e$, हीयै V_1 • लगि] $B_1G_eV_1$, लागि S_7 **93.3** ठाकुर कहत] G_eS_7, ठा० B_1, ठाकुर कहैत V_1 • चौंधियानो] $B_1G_eV_1$, चौधआनौ S_7 **93.4** घूंघटनि] B_1G_e, घूंघट न S_7, घुंघटनि V_1 • लाल] $B_1G_eV_1$, कान्ह S_7 • मोसूँ] $B_1G_eV_1$, मोसों S_7 • बोलैं] $B_1G_eS_7^{pc}V_1$, बोलौ S_7^{ac}

93.1 कर Av. poss. part. (Love)'s; मजेज (मिज़ाज) [A] m. 1. nature; 2. haughtiness; छकन m. (here: f.) satisfaction; तकन [tarkayati] m. (here: f.) looking (at others); अमोल- [amūlya-] adj. priceless. **93.2** रस रीति [S] f. the proper usage of emotion; कीन (किया) v.t. perf. Br. made (either used here in the f. or, rather awkwardly, the marker of a definite direct object 'ko' is understood after 'parīkṣā'.); हित [S] m. love; गाँठ [granthi-] f. knot; तौन pron. Br. Bund. that, it. **93.3** चौंधियान- [H caumdhnā x andha-] Br. adj. dazzling; चक्वान- [cf. cakita-] Br. adj. astonishing; याही भ्रम डौलै है (Krishna's mind) wanders around in this perplexity. **93.4** मेरे धोखें Br. mistaking them for me; औरन के धोखैं Br. mistaking me for others.

हौ तौ बनमाली पर काली लौं कलोलौ हौ।
2 बोल काहू बनिता के, साँची तौन क्यौं न कहौ
किधौं चित चाहि काहू धन ताहि बोलौ हौ।
3 ठाकुर कहत, जैसौ चाँदनी-उजास तैसो
चंद को प्रकास, गाँठि हित की न खोलौ हौ।
4 रस के निधान बसकरन बिधान कहौ,
आज इडियान-छिडियान कैसे डोलौ हौ॥ Ś94॥

1 *आप सूनो सदन बिलोकि कै उसरि आए,

---

94 Bharatpur1 f. 154r (26), Granthāvalī B27, Sudhāsar [S_2 f. 17rv (-/25), S_6 ff. 81v-82r (134/506), S_7 f. 56rv (11/533)], Vrindaban1 f. 6v (10/36). The Sudhāsar introduces this poem as the words of a messenger to a man. (S_2 'sakhī kī ukti kiyaũ tā nāyaka prati' S_6 'sakhī kī ukti lacchata kiyauṃ tāṃ nāyaka prati'. S_7 'sakhī lachitā kī ukti nāyaka prati'.)

94.1 मन] Σ, मनि G_e • बिससे] Σ, बिसरे S_7G_e • सों] $B_1G_eV_1$, मैं S • बनमाली] Σ, बनवारी V_1 • कान्ह] Σ, कान S_6 • हौ] Σ, हौं S_6S_7 • काली] Σ, काला V_1 • लौं कलोलौ] $B_1G_eS_2$, लौं कलोलौं S_6S_7, लाकलाला V_1 • हौ] $B_1G_eS_2$, हौं S_6S_7, हा (unrh.) V_1 **94.2** बोल काहू] B_1G_e, बोले काहू S_2S_7, बोलो काहू S_6, बालकाहु V_1 • के] Σ, की S_7 • कहौ] Σ, कहौं S_6 • चाहि] Σ, चाह B_1 • काहू धन ताहि] Σ, काहू धन ताहि काहू धन ताहि (dittography) S_2 • बोलौ] Σ, बोलौं S_7 • हौ] $B_1G_eS_2V_1$, हैं (unrh.) S_2, हौं S_6S_7 **94.3** ठाकुर कहत] Σ, ठा° B_1 • जैसौ] Σ, जैसी G_e • गांठि] Σ, गांठ S_6 • खोलौ] $B_1G_eV_1$, खोलौं S_7 • हौ] Σ, हौं S_6S_7 **94.4** बिधान] Σ, बिघान V_1 • इडियान] Σ, इडियाने G_e • छिडियान] Σ, छिडियाने G_e • डोलौ हौ] $B_1G_eS_2V_1$, डोलौं हौं S_6S_7

94.1 मन [manas] m. 1. soul; 2. [maṇi-] m.f. precious stone; मनि-धन var. 1. f. jewel, who is a woman; 2. m. treasure of the jewel (if a snake looses its jewel, it becomes dejected); बिसस- [cf. vinaṣṭa-] poet. v.t. to destroy; (With its hissing sounds this is a superior reading to the more straightforward 'bisare'.) वनमाली [S] f. 'wearing a forest-garland' 1. Krishna; 2. peacock; काली [S] f. black snake (esp. Kāliyā, Krishna's enemy); कलोल- [kallola-] Br. v.i. 1. to wave; 2. to frolic, to gambol. **94.2** बोल [*bolla-] f. (here: m.) (some other woman's) speech; साँची तौन Br. Bund. that true (matter); चित (चित्त में) [citta-] Br. m. obl. in your mind; काहू (किसी) pron. obl. Br. some (other); धन [S] m. 1. wealth; 2. woman; ताहि (उससे) pron. Br. obl. (with) her. **94.3** उजास [? ujjvala-] m. light, gleam; गाँठि [granthi-] f. knot (of love) (i.e. being so inseparable as moon and moonlight). **94.4** निधान [S] m. treasury; बशीकरण [S] m. subjugation; बिधान [S] m. 1. arrangement; 2. method; इड़िया- (अड़ियाना) [H aṛnā] Br. v.i. 1. to be obstinate, to jib; 2. (here:) to be restless, to be out of oneself; छिड़िया- [cf. H cheṛnā] reg. v.i. to be headstrong.

वह चढ़ी छाजै पर लीबे कौं बयार है।
जानी सकुचानी, बोल मौहौं सौं बखानी नाहि, 2
फिकौ सौं लगत, बीर, प्यारे को पियार है।
ठाकुर कहत, मनमोहन सुजान सुनौ, 3
रावरे रिझैबे कौं न कोऊ हुसियार है।
राजी करिबे कौं तौ न कोऊ भेद जाने, 4
इतराजी करिबे कौं सब सब पै तयार है॥ Ś95॥

उपदेश

*आँखिन देखत ध्यान मैं बोलत, नेह बढाए नितै आ, नितै जा।

---

95 Bharatpur1 f. 151v (14), Granthāvalī B31, Sudhāsar [S_7 110r (6/1056)], Vrindaban1 f. 14rv (22/86). The Sudhāsar (S_7) includes this poem into the 'upālambha' (complaint) subsection of the 'caturkarma sakhīn ke' (the four activities of a companion) section. The Sudhāsar (S_7) introduces it as 'nāyikā kī sakhī kī ukti nāyak prati' (the words of the beloved girl's friend to the lover). (The context can be Krishna's wounded pride.) 96 Granthāvalī 140, Ṭhasak 'Jīvancarit' ($Ṭ^j_e$) p. 17. The poem contains the words of a messenger but it can be interpreted in various ways. The first line may be taken either as a statement about the heroine or as citing the words of the girl, referred to as 'yaha soca'. The apparently imperative or absolutive Khari Boli forms 'ā' and 'jā', rather awkwardly, stand for indicatives in the first and second lines.

95.1 सूनो] $B_1G_eS_7$, सुनो V_1 • बिलोकि] B_1, बिलोक $G_eS_7V_1$ • उसरि] $B_1G_eV_1$, उसर S_7 • वह] $B_1G_eV_1$, वहि S_7 • छाजै] $G_eS_7V_1$, छाजैं B_1 • पर] $B_1G_eV_1$, परि S_7 • बयार] S_7, बयारि (unrh.) $B_1G_eV_1$ **95.2** मौंहौं] B_1V_1, मोह G_e, मुह S_7 • प्यारे] $B_1G_eV_1$, प्यारी S_7 **95.3** कहत] $B_1G_eS_7$, कहैत V_1 • सुनौ] $G_eS_7V_1$, सुनौं B_1 **95.4** भेद] $B_1G_eV_1$, भेदु S_7 • जानै] $G_eS_7V_1$, जानैं B_1 • इतराजी] $B_1G_eV_1$, ईतराजी S_7 • है] $G_eS_7V_1$, हैं B_1

95.1 आप pron. 1. you yourself; 2. he; उसरना [utsarati] reg. v.i. to retreat; छाज [chādya-, H chajjā] m. balcony; roof; बयार [*vātāra-] m. cool wind. लीबे कौं बयार Bund. to take some fresh air; **95.2** जानी [jānāti] v.t. perf. knowing (that it was you) (she became embarrassed); मोहौ सौं Br. 1. (she didn't say these words) to me either; 2. (the lord talked) only to me; 3. (o my lord, did she say these words) right to me? नाहि [nātha-] m. he, her lover; फीकौ... पियार है Br. (then I asked her:) 'o my companion, does the love of your lover seem tasteless' **95.3** हुसियार [P hośyār] reg. adj. clever; रावरे... है Br. no one is clever enough to please you. **95.4** भेद [S] m. secret; एतराज [A i'tirāẓ] m. 1. objection, opposition; 2. criticism; तैयार [AP] adv. ready; इतराजी... है but all are ready to oppose all. **96.1** आँखिन देखत Br. 1. 'in front of the eyes', publicly; 2. as soon as you see him; 3. as soon as he sees me; ध्यान में in the mind; नेह बढाए Br. with increased love; नितै आ नितै जा 1. Br. you always come and go; 2. poet. he always comes and goes.

चंदमुखी, यह सोच बिहाइ कै मानी खुसी, अभिमानी कितै जा।
ठाकुर, छैल छ्वीले छिपे कहुँ सौतिन माहिं, सुहाग जितै जा।
दै जा दिखाई री, कै जा निहाल, बितै जा बियोग, चितै जा, चितै जा॥ Ś96॥

*चारहूँ ओर उदै मुखचंद सौं चाँदनी चारु निहारि लै री।
धन जोबन चारि दिना महिमान तौ एतौ बिचार बिचारि लै री।

---

97 Hariaudh (A$_e$) p. 486, Bharatpur1 f. 141v (61), Sundarītilak (C$_e$) 203, Granthāvalī 124, Ramchand Shukla (I$_e$) p. 444, Jaipur1 f. 3r (9), Sudhāsar [S$_1$ f. 96v, S$_2$ f. 21rv (2/27), S$_7$ f. 66rv (2/661)], Śatak 26, Ṭhākur-satsai (Ṭ) f. 1r (3), Ṭhasak 155, Udaipur f. 126r (1), Vrindaban2 f. 71v. The Miśrabandhu Vinod (V$_e$) p. 730 also quotes the second half of the last line. The Sudhāsar (S$_1$) presents this poem within the 'Premagarvitā' section. The reading 'pāṃv' popular in the edited books is a secondary reading introduced for the sake of alliteration. This change has taken place already in the phase of written transmission as S$_1$ attests it.

97.1 चारहूँ... निहार] Σ, धन जोबन चारि दिना महमान सु एतौ बिचार बिचारि V$_2$ • चारहूँ] (unm.) B$_1$J$_1$**S**Ś$_e$, यह चारोऊ Ṭ, यह चारहूँ A$_e$C$_e$G$_e$I$_e$Ṭ$_e$, इहै चांदनी U • ओर] Σ, चारु U • उदै] B$_1$**S**Ṭ, उदौ A$_e$C$_e$G$_e$I$_e$J$_1$Ś$_e$Ṭ$_e$U • सौं] B$_1$S$_1$, की A$_e$G$_e$I$_e$S$_2$S$_7$Ś$_e$, कौ C$_e$G$_e^{vl}$J$_1$TṬ$_e$U • चाँदनी] Σ, चांदिनी J$_1$ • चारु] Σ, चार Ṭ • निहारि] A$_e$B$_1$C$_e$I$_e$J$_1$S$_2$, निहार **E**S$_1$S$_7$ṬU **97.2** धन...महिमांन] B$_1$**S**, बलि तौ पै अधीन भयो पिय प्यारो तौ A$_e$C$_e$**E**I$_e$J$_1$V$_2$, धन योबन है दिन च्यार नयो U • चारि] S$_2$, चार S$_1$S$_7$ • महिमांन] B$_1$S$_2$S$_7$, मैंहमाँन S$_1$ • बलि A$_e$C$_e$**E**I$_e$, *om.* (unm.) J$_1$Ṭ, अब V$_2$ • तौ C$_e$J$_1$V$_2$, जौ A$_e$**E**I$_e$, तेरे Ṭ • पै A$_e$C$_e$**E**I$_e$J$_1$V$_2$, *om.* Ṭ • भयो A$_e$C$_e$**E**I$_e$J$_1$V$_2$, भए Ṭ • पिय A$_e$C$_e$**E**I$_e$J$_1$V$_2$, पीय Ṭ • प्यारो C$_e$J$_1$Ś$_e$V$_2$, प्यारी A$_e$G$_e$I$_e$Ṭ$_e$, पिआरे Ṭ • तौ एतौ बिचार बिचार] Σ, सु तू हू मनोरथ सारि V$_2$ • तौ] A$_e$C$_e$**E**I$_e$S$_1$S$_2$U, *om.* B$_1$S$_7$, तू J$_1$, सु Ṭ • एतौ] A$_e$C$_e$**E**I$_e$J$_1$Ṭ, अन्केक B$_1$, इतेक **S**, इतनोइ U • बिचार] Σ, बिचारि I$_e$ • बिचारि लै] A$_e$B$_1$C$_e$I$_e$J$_1$, बिचार लै **E**S$_1$S$_7$UṬ, बिचारी (unm.) S$_2^{ac}$, बिचा ⟨ले⟩ (unm.) S$_2^{pc}$

96.2 बिहा- [vijahāti] Br. v.t. to abandon; मानी [manyate] v.t. imp. poet. accept (happiness). **96.3** छैल [chavila-] m. boy; छिपे v.i. (Br. subj.) (that boy) may be hiding (somewhere); जितै जा (जीत जा) v.t. (poet. imp.) win back (your happiness). **96.4** कै जा (कर जा) reg. make (him); निहाल adj. happy; बितै जा बियोग poet. let separation be over; चित- Br. v.t. to look. **97.1** उदौ (उदय) var. [S] Br. 1. m. rise; 2. (here: adj.) risen; चार दिन का मेहमान idiom. remains only for a short time. **97.2** बलि idiom. Br. 'I sacrifice myself' I beg you; जौ पै Br. conj. if.

कहि ठाकुर, भूलि गयो वह कान्ह, तौ तू बिगरी कों सुधारि लै री।
बहुर्‌यौं न रहै न रहै समयौ, बहती नदी हाथ पखारि लै री॥ Ś97॥ 4

आगी बीच दैकै कहूँ दारूगंज दाबे जात, 1
पानी बीच दैकै कहूँ मीन जीजियतु हौ।
काम बीच दैकै कहूँ बाम सों बियोग होत, 2
कोक बीच दैकै कहूँ जोग लीजियतु हौ।
ठाकुर कहत, प्यारी, तुमही बिचारि देखौ, 3
ऐसो रूप पाइ कहूँ मान कीजियतु हौ।
पीठ दैकै बैठती हौ, पीठऊ पै बेनी परी, 4
बेनी बीच दैकै कहूँ पीठ दीजियतु हौ॥ Ś98॥

---

98 Granthāvalī 148, Śatak 106, Ṭhasak 70.

97.3 कहि] $B_1C_eJ_1\mathbf{S}$, कबि $A_e\mathbf{E}I_eV_2$, कह Ṭ, कहै U • भूलि] B_1S_2, चूकि $A_e\mathbf{E}I_eJ_1V_2$, चूक C_e, भूल S_1S_7Ṭ, कांन जो U • गयो] $A_eB_1^{pc}\mathbf{E}I_eJ_1\mathbf{S}V_2$, परी C_e, गए B_1^{ac}Ṭ, चूक U • वह कान्ह] B_1, जौ गोपाल $A_eC_e\mathbf{E}I_eJ_1$, वह लाल S_1S_2, वहु लाल S_7, है गुपाल Ṭ, गयें U, जो गुपाल V_2 • तौ] Σ, सु Ṭ • तू] $A_eB_1C_eJ_1\mathbf{S}V_2$, तैं $\mathbf{E}I_e$, तुही U • बिगरी] Σ, बिगरे C_e • सुधारि] $B_1C_eJ_1S_2V_2$, संहारि $A_e\mathbf{E}$, संभारि S_1I_e, सवार S_7, सुधार ṬU
97.4 बहुर्‌यौं] $B_1S_2S_7V_2$, अब $A_e\mathbf{E}I_e$, फिरि C_eJ_1, बहुरौं S_1, फेर Ṭ, बहुर्‌यां U • न रहै न रहै] B_1, रैहै न रहै $A_eC_e\mathbf{E}I_eJ_1$, समयौ जौ S_1S_2, समयौ यौं S_7, स⟨मियो/म्यो⟩ र⟨मियो/म्यो⟩ Ṭ, इहरै न रहै U, समयौ जु V_2 • समयौ] B_1U, यहौ समयौ $A_e\mathbf{E}J_1$, यही समयौ C_e, यहै समयौ I_e, रहै न रहै **S**, न हरे Ṭ, बनें न बनें V_2 • नदी] Σ, नपी U • हाथ] $B_1J_1S_2$ṬUV_2, पाँव $A_e\mathbf{E}V_e$, पाय C_eI_e, पाइ S_1, पान S_7 • पखारि] $A_eB_1C_eI_eJ_1S_2V_eV_2$, पखार $\mathbf{E}S_1S_7$ṬU

97.3 चूकना [*cukk-] v.i. to make a mistake; तैं pron. Br. you; बिगड़ी को संभालना idiom. to fix what has gone wrong. **97.4** न रहै न रहै Br. does not remain (vīpsā alaṅkār); बहुरौं समयौ जौ रहै न रहै var. Br. whether such time will come again or not; रैहै var. remains; यहौ समयो var. emph. such time (cf. H yahī samay); पखारना [prakṣālayati] v.t. to wash. **98.1** बीच [*vīcya-] 1. adv. in the middle (H bīc mẽ); 2. postp. in (cf. Panj. vicc); 3. (in the second half of the first line) m. 'intervening space' separation; बीच देना idiom. to separate; दारू [P] f. gunpowder; दारु [S] Av. Br. m. timber; गंज [P] m. heap, pile; दाब- (दबाना) v.t. to oppress; पानी बीच दैकै Br. 1. separating from water; 2. putting into the water (i.e. it has already been separated); 3. being put into the water (as if one had been a fish). **98.2** बाम [vāmā-] f. lovely woman; कोक [S] m. erotic love. **98.4** पीठ देना idiom. to reject; वेणी [S] f. braided hair (which enhances the beauty of the back);

रूप अनूप दई दयौ तोहि, सु मान किये न सयान कहावै।
2 और सुनो, यह रूप-जवाहर भागि बडौ, बिरलो कोऊ पावै।
ठाकुर, सूम के जात न कोऊ, उदार सुनें सबही उठि धावै।
4 दीजियै ताहि दिखाय दया करि, जौ चलि दूरि तें देखन आवै॥ Ś99॥

1 रूपमान सुंदरी सुजान, कान दैकै सुनौ,
मानवारे लोगन मैं महिमा वजन की।
2 बेदन पुरानन प्रमानन सुनी है बात,
सुख की सुहाती कीजै सबही के मन की।
3 ठाकुर कहत, जात आवत न जानी जात,

---

99 Bharatpur1 f. 156r (38), Bharatpur8 f. 8v (24), Sundarī-tilak (C_e) p. 35 (204), Granthāvalī 152, Rasikvinod (O_e) pp. 81-82 (383), Sudhāsar [S_2 f. 34rv (43/33), S_7 f. 113v-4r (23/1088)], Ṭhasak 37, Hāfizullah Khān: Hazārā (X_e) (p. 353, Śṛṅgār ādi ras 173 in Dikshit's edn.), Vrindaban1 ff. 10v-11r (11/63), Yājñik. The Sudhāsar (S_7) includes this poem into the 'madhyam dūtī' ('middle messenger') subsection of the 'dūtī' (messenger) section. It is explained in a dohā [S_7 f. 113r (16/1081)] that the madhyam dūtī uses both soft and harsh words in her message. The text of O_e follows that of C_e. Ṭhākur's signature is missing from the version of X_e. 100 Datiya1 f. 104rv (336), Granthāvalī 153, Ṭhasak 66.

99.1 दई दयो तोहि] $B_1C_eX_eV_1Y_e$, दयौ दई तोहि B_8**S**, दियो करतार **E** • सु] B_1B_8**S**V_1 Y_e, तो C_e**E**O_eX_e • किये] Σ, कियौ **S** **99.2** सुनो] B_8C_e**E**$O_eS_7X_e$, सुनौं B_1, सुनैं S_2, सूनो V_1 • रूप] Σ, रुप (unm.) V_1 • जवाहर] Σ, जवाहरि V_1 • भागि] B_1B_8**E**$S_2X_eV_1$, भाग C_eS_7, भाग्य O_e • बडौ] $B_1B_8S_7V_1$, बडे C_e**E**$O_eS_2X_e$ • बिरलो] $B_1B_8G_eS_7V_1$, बिरले $C_eO_eṬ_eX_e$, बिर भागी बडे बिरलौ (dittography) S_2 • कोऊ] $B_1B_8C_eO_e$**S**, कोउ **E**X_eV_1 **99.3** ठाकुर] Σ, होत न X_e • सूम] Σ, सुम (unm.) V_1 • के] Σ, की X_e • जात न] Σ, जाचन O_e, जाति X_e • कोऊ] $B_1B_8C_eO_e$**S**, कोउ **E**V_1, कोऊ जो X_e • सुनें] Σ, सुनै S_7X_e • उठि] Σ, उठ V_1 **99.4** दिखाय] Σ, दिषाई S_2, देखाय X_e • दया] Y_eΣ, कृपा **E**X_e • करि] $B_1B_8C_eG_eO_eS_2X_e$, कर $S_7Ṭ_eV_1$ • चलि] Y_eΣ, कोउ **E** • देखन] Σ, देखिबे C_eO_e **100.1** रूपमान] **E**, रूपवारी D_1 • सुंदरी] **E**, सुंदरै D_1 • कान] **E**, कान्ह D_1 • सुनौ] **E**, सुनौं सु⟨रै⟩ D_1 • मान॰] **E**, माल D_1 • लोगन मैं] **E**, नर D_1 • महिमा] **E**, उपमा D_1 • वजन] **E**, उजन D_1 **100.2** प्रमानन] **E**, कुरानन D_1 • सुनी है] **E**, तलासी D_1 • बात] **E**, हम D_1 • की] **E**, के D_1 • सुहाती] **E**, सुधा सी D_1 • कीजै] **E**, बात D_1 • सब॰] **E**, जग D_1 • ॰ही के मन] **E**, के जियन D_1

99.2 भागि बडे var. reg. with a great luck. **99.3** सूम [? A śu'm] adj. miser; सूम के (no one goes) to a miser (to ask); सुनें v.t. perf. Br. when they hear of it. **100.1** मान॰ [S] m. 1. measure; 2. pride, standing; वजन [P] m. 1. weight; 2. authority. **100.2** तलाशना var. [cf. P talāś] v.t. 1. to search; 2. to find; सुहाती [śubhāyate] v.i. imperf. attractive (matter).

एकही सी रीति निरधारी तन धन की।
हेर लीजै, हँस लीजै, हिल लीजै, मिल लीजै,
कुरस न कीजै, कीजै चाहते मे मन की॥ Ś100॥

*नाथ नथो है तिहारे पिया, सतरातीं कहा, कोउ स्यान सिखैहै।
पानिप नै कै चलै, सजनी, यहि भाँति न प्रीत सदा निरबैहै।
ठाकुर, जौ पै यही करने, तौ कहा मनमोहन को थकरै है।
ह्वैहै नहीं मुरगा जिह गाँव, भटू, तिहि गाँव का भोर ना ह्वैहै॥ Ś101॥

का कहि, बाल, गोपालहि बोधहिं, तो दृग-बान अमान लगे री।
तो हित, प्यारी, भए बदनाम, अराम बिसारि दिये घर के री।

---

101 Granthāvalī 151, Śatak 84, Ṭhasak 167. 102 Granthāvalī 149, Sudhāsar [S_7 f. 114v (32/1096)], Ṭhasak 86, Bābūrāmdīn: Sundarī-tilak (U_e) 1049. The Sudhāsar (S_7) includes this poem into the 'adhamā dūtī' ('middle messenger') subsection of the 'dūtī' (messenger) section. It is explained in a dohā [S_7 f. 114r (27/1092)] that the adhamā dūtī uses harsh words in her message.

100.3 जात] **E**, देषौ D_1 • न] **E**, ना D_1 • जानी] **E**, जानौ D_1 • रीति] **E**, रीत D_1 • निरधारी] **E**, सो निहारी D_1 • तन] **E**, ⟨मन⟩ D_1 **100.4** हेर] **E**, हिल D_1 • हँस] G_e, मिल D_1, हँसि $Ṭ_e$ • हिल] **E**, ⟨टेर⟩ D_1 • मिल] **E**, हंसि D_1 • कुरस न] **E**, रार भट्ट D_1 • मे] **E**, के D_1 **101.1** नाथ नथो] $Ś_e$, नाध नधो $G_eṬ_e$ **101.2** यहि] G_e, यह $Ś_eṬ_e$ • भाँति न] $G_eṬ_e$, भातिन $Ś_e$ • निरबैहै] $G_eṬ_e$, न निबैहै $Ś_e$ **101.3** मनमोहन] $Ś_e$, मनमोहनी $G_eṬ_e$ • को थकरै है] $Ś_e$, क्रोध करैहै $G_eṬ_e$ **101.4** जिह] $Ś_e$, जेहि $G_eṬ_e$ **102.1** का] **E**, को S_7U_e • कहि] **E**U_e, किहि S_7 • गोपाल] **E**U_e, गुपाल S_7 • बोधहिं] **E**U_e, बोधहि S_7 **102.2** बिसारि] S_7, बिसार **E**U_e

---

100.3 निरधार- [nirdhārayati] Br. v.t. to assume. **100.4** राड़ var. [rāṭi-] f. fight, quarrel; चाहत [cāhnā] f. desire; मे (मेरे) [S] poss. pron. obl. poet. my. **101.1** नाध (नाथ) [nastā-] f. (here m.) nose-rope (of a bullock); नधना var. [naddha-] v.i. to be yoked; नथना [cf. H nāth] v.i. 1. to have the nose bored and a string passed through it (a bullock); 2. to be under control; तिहारे poss. pron. Br. obl. (by) your (nose-rope); नाध नधो है तिहारे var. it is your nose-rope that he is bound by; पिया [priya-] m. (your) lover; सतरा- [śatru-] v.i. to show anger ; सिखैहै v.t. fut. Br. will you learn? **101.2** नै कै [nam-] v.i. abs. Br. (used as adv.) downwards; यहि भाँति Br. in this way (as you have been acting); निरबा- [nirvāhayati] v.t. to carry on, to maintain. **101.3** करने v.t. inf. Bund. (if you are) to do (this); थकरा- (थकना) v.caus. reg. to harass. **101.4** मुरगा [P murg] m. cock; भोर ना ह्वैहै Br. won't there be dawn? **102.1** का कहि Br. saying what? बोधहिं [bodhayati] Br. v.t. fut. pl. shall I explain (to Krishna); अमान [S] adj. immeasurable. **102.2** भए बदनाम Br. (Krishna) achieved bad fame.

ठाकुर, तूँ न तऊ पिघली, पग पारे हैं लालन बार घनेरी।
4 प्रीतम की सु भई गति, या छतिया कसकी न, कसाइन, तेरी॥ Ś102॥

तन को तरसाइबो कौने बद्यौ, मन तौ मिलि गो पय में जल जैसो।
2 कौन दुराव रह्यौ उनसों जिनसौ हित मानि लियौ चित ऐसो।
ठाकुर की बिनती या बिचारिबी, कौन सुभाव तें बोल अनैसो ।
4 प्रानपियारी प्रवीन पिया घट मैं बसि घूँघट घालिबो कैसो॥ Ś103॥

1 हिलिमिलि लीजिये प्रबीनन सों आठो जाम,

---

103 Bharatpur1 f. 135v (27), Sundarī-tilak (C_e) p. 34 (202), Granthāvalī 150, Rasikvinod (O_e) pp. 81-82 (382), Sudhāsar [S_2 f. 45v (-/44), S_3 f. 98r (51), S_7 f. 144v (8/1378)], Śatak 80, Ṭhākur-satsaī (Ṭ) f. 4r (32), Ṭhasak 80, Ṭhasak 'Jīvancarit' (Ṭ^j_e) p. 14. The Rasikvinod follows the text of the Sundarī-tilak.

102.3 पग पारे हैं] **E**U_e, यितने पर S_7 **102.4** गति] **E**$S_7^{pc}U_e$, *om.* (unm.) S_7^{ac} **103.1** तन को] (unm.) Σ, यों Ṭ^j_e • तरसाइबो] Ṭ^{pc}Σ, तरसायबे C_e, नरसाइबो Ṭ^{ac} • बद्यो] Σ, बदो Ṭ^j_e • मिलि गो] B_1**E**S_2S_7, मिलयो C_eO_e, मिल गो ṬS_3 • पय में] B_1C_e O_e**S**, पै मिलै **E**, पै मै (unm.) Ṭ • जैसो] Σ, जैसें **S** **103.2** कौन दुराव] $B_1C_eO_e$**S**ṬṬ^j_e, उनसों अब (unm.) G_e, उनसैं अब (unm.) $Ś_e$Ṭ$_e$ • रह्यौ उनसों] B_1O_eṬ, रह्यौ उतसों C_e, कौन दुराव **E**, रह्यौ तुमसौ **S**, रहो उनसौं Ṭ^j_e • जिनसौ] B_1**S**Ṭ, जिनके **E**O_e, जिनको C_e • हित मानि लियौ चित] B_1, तन में मिलयो मन C_eO_e, उर मध्य करो सुख **E**, चित मानि लियौ हित S_2S_3, हित मान लीयो मन Ṭ, संग साथ करौ सुख Ṭ^j_e • मानि] S_2S_7, मान S_3 • ऐसो] Σ, ऐसै **S** **103.3** की बिनती] Σ, या निरधार **E** • या बिचारिबी] B_1**S**Ṭ, सुनौ तुम्हैं **E**, सुनि लीजिये C_e, सुन लीजियै O_e • सुभाव] B_1O_e**S**ṬṬ^j_e, स्वभाव C_e**E** • तें बोल] B_1**S**Ṭ, या सीख्यो C_eO_e, पर्यो है **E**, परो है Ṭ^j_e • अनैसो] Σ, अनैसें **S** **103.4** प्रानपियारी] $B_1C_eG_eO_eŚ_e$, प्रानन प्यारी **S**Ṭ, प्रानपिआरी Ṭ$_e$, प्रानपिया Ṭ^j_e • प्रबीन प्रिया] $B_1C_eS_3S_7$Ṭ, सुनौ चित दै **E**, प्रवीन तिया O_e, प्रवीन पिया S_2, घट में बसि कै Ṭ^j_e • घट मैं] B_1**S**Ṭ, चित में C_eO_e, हिरदै **E**, हसि कै Ṭ^j_e • बसि] Σ, बस S_3, फिर Ṭ^j_e • घालिबो] Σ, काढिबो O_e • कैसो] Σ, कैसै S_2S_3

102.3 पग पार- idiom. Br. 'to throw at one's feet' to allow access to; बार घनेरी 1. adv. on many occasions; 2. his thick hair (H bāl ghane, rī). **102.4** गति [S] f. (miserable) condition; कसकना [cf. kaṣati] v.i. to feel a pang (as of the heart); कसाइन [A qaṣṣāb] f. butcher woman. **103.1** कौने (किसने) reg. interr. ag. who? बदना [vadati] v.t. 1. to vow; 2. to bet; पै (पय) var. [S] reg. m. milk; मिलै जल जैसो var. Br. as (milk) dissolves in water. **103.2** करो var. v.t. perf. Br. (you) made. **103.3** निरधार (निर्धार) var. Br. 1. v.i. abs. to think; 2. [S] m. decision; बिचारिबी (विचार करनी है) [cf. vicāra-] v.t. inf. (f.) Bund. should think, should consider; अनैस- [aniṣṭa-] Br. adj. 'undesired' bad. **103.4** हसि कै var. v.i. abs. Br. smiling (i.e. coquettishly)); घालना [*ghalyati] v.t. to put on.

कीजियै अराम जासों जिय कों अराम है।
दीजिये दरस जाकों देखिबे की साध होइ, 2
कीजिये न नीच संग नाम बदनाम है।
ठाकुर कहत, कछु मन में बिचारि देखौ, 3
गरब गरूरी को रखैया एक राम है।
रूप सो रतन पाइ, जोबन सो धन पाइ 4
नाहक गँवाइबो गँवारन को काम है॥ Ś104॥

जाकी लगी हुती रावरे कें जक, मोसों कही वाके पारन ही की।
सो मोहि जाति मिली हुती कुंजन जीति लई जिहिं जोति रती की। 2

---

104 Hariaudh (A_e) p. 484, Granthāvalī 193, Jaipur1 f. 5v (17), Śatak 70, Ṭhasak 22, Miśrabandhu Vinod (V_e) p. 730 quotes the last line. 105 Bharatpur1 f. 155rv (34), Granthāvalī B22, Sudhāsar [S_2 f. 34v (-/34), S_7 f. 114v (30/1094)], Vrindaban1 f. 10r (7/59). The Sudhāsar (S_7) includes this poem into the 'adhamā dūtī' ('inferior messenger') subsection of the 'dūtī' (messenger) section. It is explained in a dohā [S_7 f. 114r (27/1092)] that the adhamā dūtī uses harsh words in her message.

104.1 हिलिमिलि] A_eJ_1, हिलमिल **E** • सों] Σ, ते A_e • कीजियै अराम] A_eJ_1, कीजै वह काम **E** • जासों] Σ, जामैं $Ś_e$ **104.2** की साध] Σ, को हौस A_e • नीच] **E**, काम A_e, बीन J_1 • संग] $Ś_eJ_1$, साथ $G_eṬ_e$, जासों A_e **104.3** कछु] **E**, यह A_e, ठीक J_1 • मन] A_eJ_1, चित **E** • गरब गरूरी] **E**, जस अपजस A_e, मन औ ग्रमोन J_1 • रखैया] Σ, करैया A_e **104.4** सो] Σ, से A_e • जोबन] Σ, चातुरी A_e • सो] Σ, से A_e **105.1** जाकी] $B_1G_eV_1$, जाकै **S** • लगी] $B_1G_eV_1$, जकी **S** • रावरे कें जक] G_eV_1, जके रावरे कें B_1^{ac}, जक रावरे कें B_1^{pc}, रावरे कें जबक (unm.) S_2, रावरे को जक S_7 **105.2** मोहि] $B_1G_eV_1$, मुहि **S** • जाति] SV_1, जात B_1G_e • जिहिं] $B_1G_eV_1$, जह S_2, जिह S_7

104.1 हिलना-मिलना v.i. to meet; to come together; अराम (आराम) [P] Br. 1. m. well-being; 2. adj. healthy. **104.2** साध [śraddhā-] f. desire; कीजिये न नीच संग Br. do not associate with the lowly (whose name is disreputable); नबीन apa. **104.3** गरब... राम है Br. the protector of the proud is only God; ग्रमोन apa. **104.4** गँवाना [gamayati] v.t. to waste. **105.1** जाकै जकी var. going there she became fascinated; रावरे कें (आपके लिए) poet. for you (i.e. with you) (cf. Ś 91 'rāvare ko bala'); जक (झक) [*jhakk-] Br. f. obsession, fascination; जबक var. m. Raj. wound (RSK); कही v.t. (perf.) you asked (me to express it to her); पार- (पाड़ना) Av. Br. v.t. to place; (here:) to express (RSh); (See also pālana 'keeping, fulfilment'). **105.2** सो... कुंजन Br. I met her as she was going to the grove; जाति मिली Br. as she was going; जीति लई Br. v.t. vanquished; was more prominent than; जिहि rel. pron. (Br. ag.) who; जह var. rel. pron. reg. where.

ठाकुर, जौ ब रुचै सु करौ किन, जानि परै बहु भाँतिन नीकी।
4 वा गई टेरि गई कहि मैं, अब जाउ न जाउ या रावरे जी की॥ Ś105॥

*लाई ही हौं फुसलाय कैं, मोहन, सो तुम तौ वह रीझि खिझाई।
2 वा तौ गई खुनसाय, खिस्याय कैं, यातौ कहा तुम तैं बनि आई।
ठाकुर, प्रीति की रीति यहै, नित ही नित मोद बढ़ै है सवाई।
4 राखिबौ तौ कठिनाई नही, रस राखि बिदा करिबौ कठिनाई॥ Ś106॥

1 तन देखि, बन देखि, भूषन बसन देखि,
पिय देखि, प्यारो देखि बचन सहेली के।
2 रितु देखि, राति देखि, रोस देखि, रस देखि,

106 Sudhāsar [S_1 f. 40v5, S_2 f. 7rv (24/3), S_7 f. 30r (7/271)]. S_1 and S_7present this poem within the 'viśrabdha navoḍhā' subsection of his 'nāyikābheda' section. S_2 and S_7 introduce it as 'saṣī kau upālambha nāyaka prati' Complaint by the beloved woman's companion towards the lover. (cf. S_1: 'saṣī kī ukti nāika prata. upālambha deta hai.') 107 Bharatpur1 f. 163r (83), Datiya1 f. 103rv (334), Granthāvalī 154, Vrindaban1 ff. 7rv (2/40).

105.3 जौ] Σ, *om.* (unm.) V_1 • सु] Σ, सो S_2 • किन] G_e**S**, किनि B_1V_1 • जानि] Σ, जान S_7 **105.4** टेरि] $B_1G_eS_2$, टेर S_7V_1 • गई] $B_1G_eV_1$, दई **S** • कहि] $G_eS_2V_1$, कही B_1 • मैं] Σ, यौं G_e • रावरे] B_1G_e, आपने **S**, रोवरे V_1 **106.1** हौं] S_2S_7, वाहि S_1 • फुसलाय] S_2S_7, मनाइ S_1 • रीझि] S_7, रीझ S_1, रिझि (unm.) S_2 • खिझाई] S_1S_7, खिजाई S_2 **106.2** खिस्याय] S_1, षिसाय S_2S_7 • तैं] S_1, ते S_2S_7 **106.3** प्रीति] S_7, प्रीत S_1, ⟨प्रो⟩ति S_2 • यहैं] S_2S_7, इहै S_1 • है] S_1, जु S_2S_7 **107.1** देखि बन देखि भूषन] $B_1G_eV_1$, देषु बनु देषु भुषन D_1 • देखि] $B_1G_eV_1$, देषु D_1 • देखि प्यारो देखि] $B_1G_eV_1$, देषु प्यार देषु D_1

105.3 जौ ब रुचै Br. what pleases you; **करौ किन** Br. why don't you do? **जानि परै** Br. what prooves to be; **बहु भाँतिन** Br. in every way; **नीका** [nikta-] adj. attractive (here:) well-disposed. **105.4 वा गई** she has gone there; **टेरि गई कहि मैं** Br. I told it to you shouting (i.e. explicitly); **टेरि दई** var. Br. shouting 'O my god!' **106.1 लाई ही हौं** Br. I brought her along (i.e. I have done what I can); **फुसलाना** [cf. *phuss-] v.t. to inveigle, to coax; **तुम ...खिजाई** Br. you pleased her then irritated her. **106.2 खुनसाना** [cf. H khuns 'dislike'] Br. v.i. to feel dislike, to be spiteful; **खिसियाना** [*khiss-] v.i. to be embarrassed, abashed; **यातौ** poet. adv. in this way (cf. Br. etau 'so much'); **कहा... आई** Br. what did you do? **106.3 नित ही नित** Br. always, continuously, **मोद** [S] m. pleasure, delight; **सवाई** [sapāda-] adj. increased by a quarter. **106.4 राख-** [rakṣati] Br. v.t. to call, to engage; **रस राखि** Br. with love. **107.1 देखि** v.t. imp. Br. look, consider; **प्यारो** [priyakāra-] m. (with Br. encl.) (consider) also his love; **बचन सहेली के** Br. (consider) the words of your companion.

रीझ-खीझ देखि कै ये समय सु केली के।
ठाकुर कहत, कैसो मौन धरि बैठी आजु 3
छोडि कै सुभाय ये सकल अलबेली के।
चंद देखि, चांदौ देखि, चांदिनी बिछौना देखि 4
चांदनीहू देखि, देखि चौसर चमेली के॥ Ś107॥

आँख

*यह कोमल कंज सौ अंग गुपाल को, सो सबही पुनि जानती हौ।

---

108 Hariaudh (A_e) pp. 485-6, Sundarī-tilak (C_e) p. 34 (201), Kālidās-Hajārā (H_e) 324, Jaipur1 f. 3r (11a), Jaipur3 f. 2r (8), Raskusumākar (R_e) p. 57 (132), Sudhāsar [S_1 f. 97v], Vrindaban2 f. 69v (3), Z_1(31). In the Raskusumākar this poem is an illustration of 'śikṣā' (instruction), within the chapter about friends, companions and messengers (sakhā sakhī dūtī), In the Sudhāsar (S_1) it is within the 'Māninī' (woman with wounded pride) section. The variants of the C_e and R_e editions in the second half of the second line are more powerful. Yet the simpler wording of the main text is attested in manuscripts S_1 and V_2.

107.2 देखि] B_1G_e, देषु D_1, देष V_1 • राति] D_1G_e, रानि B_1, रात V_1 • देखि] B_1G_e, देषु D_1, देष V_1 • देखि रस देखि] B_1G_e, देषु रसु देषु D_1, देष रस देषि V_1 • रीझ खीझ] D_1, रीझि रीझ B_1^{ac}, रीझ रीझि B_1^{pc}, रीझि रीझि G_eV_1 • देखि] $B_1G_eV_1$, देषु D_1 • कै ये] $B_1G_eV_1$, कैजे D_1 • सु हेली] B_1, अकेली D_1, सहेली G_eV_1 **107.3** ठाकुर कहत] D_1G_e, ठा॰ B_1, ठाकुर कहैत V_1 • धरि] B_1G_e, धर D_1V_1 • आजु] D_1, आज $B_1G_eV_1$ • छोडि] $B_1G_eV_1$, छोड D_1 • ए] $B_1G_eV_1$, वे D_1 **107.4** देखि चांदौ देखि] $B_1G_eV_1$, देषु चादौ देषु D_1 • बिछौना देखि] $B_1G_eV_1$, बिछौना देषु D_1 • देखि देखि] $B_1G_eV_1$, देषु देषु D_1 • चौसर] $B_1G_eV_1$, चौसरा D_1 **108.1** यह] S_1, वह A_e, बलि $C_eJ_1R_e$, उह H_eV_2, अत J_3, *om.* Z_1 • कोमल] J_3S_1, कंज सौ $H_eJ_1R_eV_2Z_1$, कंज सों A_eC_e • कंज सौ S_1, कोमल $A_eC_eH_eJ_1R_eV_2Z_1$, कंज त J_3 • अंग] Σ, यं (haplography) J_3 • गुपाल] $A_eH_eJ_1S_1V_2Z_1$, गोपाल C_eR_e, गो** J_3 • सो] S_1, सोऊ $A_eC_eR_eV_2$, सोऊ J_1, सो ता J_3, सोउ H_e, सो तुमह (unm.) Z_1 • सबही] S_1, सबै $A_eH_eJ_1C_eR_eV_2$, सभ J_3, सब Z_1 • पुनि] $J_1S_1V_2$, तुम $A_eJ_3C_eR_e$, सुनि H_e, *om.* Z_1

107.2 रोष [S] m. 1. anger; 2. enthusiasm; रीझि रीझि देखि var. be very happy seeing; कै ये Br. is this...? कैजे var. Br. why would you make it...? अकेली var. [*ekkalla-] adj. f. (here used as a noun) solitude; (cf. a-kelī 'being without love-sports'); समय अकेली के var. poet. time for loneliness. **107.3** अलबेली [S] adj. (used as a noun) attractive woman; छोडि... के abandoning all the characteristics of an attractive woman. **107.4** चांदौ [candrātapa-] m. white canopy; चांदनी [cāndraṇa-] f. 'moonlight' a white cloth spread over a carpet; बिछौना [*vicchādana-] m. bedding; चौसर m. a necklace or garland of four strings (which is also an uddīpana). **108.1** सबही adj. emph. Br. 1. all this matter; 2. all (of you).

बलि, नेक रुखाई धरे कुम्हिलात, इतौहू नहीं पहचानती हौ।
कहि ठाकुर, यौं कर जोरि कह्यौ, इतने पै बिनै नहि मानती हौ।
दृग बान औ भौंहैं कमान, अजू, कहौ, कान लौं कौन पै तानती हौ॥ Ś108॥

*चाल न वा, चरचा न वा चातुरी वा, रस रीति न प्रीति को ढौर है।
साँच घटो, बढो झूँठ जहान मैं, लोभ के लाने जहाँ तहाँ दौर है।
ठाकुर, वे ही गुपाल, वही हम, कै या बयार वही सब ठौर है।

---

109 Datiya2 f. 2r (11), Granthāvalī 174, Ṭhasak 148, Ṭhasak 'Jīvancarit' (Ṭ^j_e) p. 13, Z_2 f. 2v (11). D_2 introduces the poem as 'saṣī bacana gopī prata' the words of of a companion towards a cowherd woman. The end of the last line is missing from Z_2.

108.2 बलि] $A_eH_eJ_1S_1V_2$, वह C_eR_e, पन J_3, बल Z_1 • नेक] Σ, नेकु A_e • रुखाई] $A_eC_eH_eJ_1R_eS_1V_2$, रुषा×**×ये J_3, दिषाई Z_1 • धरे] $A_eC_eJ_3R_eV_2$, धरैं H_eS_1, धरें J_1, दियै Z_1 • कुम्हलात] $A_eC_eH_eJ_1S_1V_2$, कुम्मलात J_3, कुँभिलात R_e, कुमल्यात Z_1 • इतौहू] S_1, इतौऊ $A_eH_eV_2$, इतौ हठ $C_eJ_1R_e$, ईतो हट J_3, इतौ हट Z_1 • नहीं] $A_eS_1V_2$, कौन पैं $C_eJ_1R_e$, नाहक J_3Z_1, नाहीं H_e • पहचानती] $A_eH_eS_1V_2$, ठानती $C_eJ_1J_3R_eZ_1$ **108.3** कहि] $C_eS_1Z_1$, कबि $A_eH_eJ_1R_eV_2$, कह J_3 • यौं... नहि] $A_eC_eH_eJ_1R_eS_1V_2$, होर इती बीनती सो मनाई न काहु की J_3, और सुना इतनी इतनै पै विनै नहि (unm.) Z_1 • यौं] Σ, या A_e • जोरि] Σ, जोर S_1 • कह्यौ] $A_eH_eS_1V_2$, कहै C_eR_e, कहौं J_1 • बिनै] Σ, बिनय (unm.) C_e • नहि] $C_eJ_1S_1$, नहीं $A_eH_eR_eV_2$ • हौ] Σ, ह J_3 **108.4** औ] $A_eC_eR_e$, जे H_e, सो J_3, ये J_1S_1, ए V_2, पे Z_1 • भौंहैं] $C_eH_eJ_1R_eS_1$, भौंह A_eJ_3, भौंहै V_2, भीहै Z_1 • कमान] Σ, कमोन J_1 • अजू] S_1, सुनी C_e, सो तो J_3, कहौ $A_eH_eV_2$, सु तौ J_1R_e, अज्यौ Z_1 • कहौ] S_1Z_1, अब A_eJ_3, तुम $C_eJ_1R_e$, अजु H_e, अजू V_2 • लौं] $C_eH_eJ_1R_eS_1V_2Z_1$, लै A_e, लु J_3 • पै] Σ, प J_3 **109.1** चाल] **E**, चाह D_2, *om.* (unm.) Z_2 • न वा] Σ, ना (unm.) Z_2 • न वा] Σ, वह ना वह Z_2 • वा] Σ, ना Z_2 • रीति] Σ, रीत D_2 • धौर है] **E**, वौर है D_2, डोरौ Z_2 **109.2** साँच] Σ, सांचु Z_2 • घटो] Σ, घट्यौ D_2 • बढो] **E**, बढ्यौ D_2, जूंठ Z_2 • झूँठ] Σ, ⟨ख/ब⟩डौ ठौ Z_2 • के लाने] **E**, कौं लोग D_2, सौ (unm.) Z_2 • जहाँ तहाँ] Σ, चहं दिस Z_2 • दौर है] Σ, डोरौ Z_2 **109.3** वे ही] D_2Z_2, वेई **E** • गुपाल] D_2Z_2, गोपाल **E** • वही हम] Σ, *om.* (unm.) Z_2 • कै... ठौर] D_2, वोही चबाउ बनो इकठौर **E**, वही बयार वही कद⟨रु⟩ और की औरौ • बनो] $G_eṬ_e$, रहो Ṭ^j_e

---

108.2 वह var. that (i.e. 'Gopāla's body). **108.3** कह्यौ I (the messenger) said; बिनै [vinaya x vinatī] Br. m. request. **108.4** भौंहैं तानती हौ 1. you stretch (the bow of) your eyebrows; 2. idiom. you are angry (with). **109.1** चाल [calyā-] f. conduct, behaviour; वा pron. reg. that, the same; चातुरी [S] f. accomplishment, skill; ढौर [? H *ḍholnā, cf. Br. ḍhaurī 'way, style'] Bund. m. 'flow' way, style. **109.2** के लाने (के लिए) postp. Br. for (the sake of). **109.3** कैया (कैसा) reg. interr. what kind of? कै या... ठौर Is this breeze the same everywhere? चबाउ var. [*caturvāda-] Br. f. slander; (here:) slanderer; इकठौर var. [eka-, sthāvara-] adv. gathered, in the same place; वोही चबाउ बनौ इकठौर है var. there is still the same slander going on;

मेरेई देखत, मेरी भटू, सिगरो ब्रज ह्वै गयौ और को और है॥ Ś109॥

बिन बूझें ही ऊतर कों करतीं, सो कबूतर की सी कला तुम को हौ।
हम आपनी चूक संहारि लैहैं, तुम औगुन और के नाहक टोहौ।
कहि ठाकुर, यामैं भलाई कहा, हम नीक हैं, बूझती एक कै दो हौ।
जु पराये नयाउ मैं बोलती हौ, सु तौ देबी कै सौति, कहौ तुम को हौ॥ Ś110॥

प्रतीति

---

110 Bharatpur1 f. 160v (66), Granthāvalī 182, Sudhāsar [S_2 f. 11v (15/10), S_7 f. 46r (32/434)], Vrindaban1 f. 4rv (9/22). S_2 introduces the poem with the following—apparently corrupt—sentence: 'kaunā ke uttara te bihaṃga kī sī [ka]lā pra⟨sna⟩ jāni paraiṃ hai'. (From someone's answer the sport of the pigeon is evident. [?]) There is no introduction in S_7.

109.4 मेरेई] Z_2, मेरेइ **E**, मेरे ही D_2 **110.1 ही**] Σ, °ई B_1 • ऊतर] $B_1G_eS_2$, उत्तर S_7V_1 • सो] Σ, हौं S_7 • तुम] B_1^{pc}Σ, ** B_1^{ac} • हौ] Σ, हौं S_7 **110.2 चूक**] Σ, चुक V_1 • संहारि] $B_1G_eV_1$, सभारि **S** • औगुन] Σ, ओगन V_1 • टोहौ] Σ, टोहौं S_7 **110.3 ठाकुर यामैं**] Σ, यामै ठाकुर (unm.) V_1 • कहा] Σ, कहां S_7 • नीक] Σ, नीके G_e • हैं] $G_eS_2V_1$, है B_1S_7 • बूझती] Σ, बूझत V_1 • हौ] Σ, हौं S_7 **110.4 जु**] Σ, जौं B_1 • नयाउ] B_1, °न ऐब G_e, नियाव **S**, नयब (unm.) V_1 • हौ] Σ, हौं S_7 • कै] Σ, की S_7 • सौति] B_1S_2, सौत G_eV_1, सौंह S_7 • कहौ] Σ, कहौं S_7 • हौ] Σ, हौं S_7

109.4 ह्वै गयौ और को और है Br. has been changed for the worse. **110.1 बिन बूझें** Br. without being asked; कों (क्यों) Br. interr. why? ऊतर कों करतीं Br. how come you (my companion) ask me to give an answer (without being asked?) कबूतर की सी कला idiom. the sport of a pigeon (who dances for its beloved without being asked [KL], or who does not understand the message it carries [KL], or who talks indistinctly [RSh]); तुम को हौ Br. who are you (to make me to dance like a pigeon)? **110.2 टोहना** [*ṭoh-] v.t. 'to grope' to search for. **110.3 बूझती** [budhyate] v.t. imperf. (still) you ask; बूझति एक कै दो हौ 1. you ask whether we are together or not; 2. you ask one and say two (you distort my words) (KL); 3. 'you consider one as two' you understand it wrongly (KL, RSh); 4. you ask twice instead of once (i.e. you do not trust me) (RSh). **110.4 नयाउ (न्याय)** [S] poet. m. justice; परायेन var. [H parāyā] m. (reg. pl. obl.) (about) others; ऐब var. [A 'aib] m. fault; ऐब मैं var. postp. reg. harmfully; बोलती हो v.i. pres. you speak; सु तौ Br. then; देवी [S] f. 1. Parvati; 2. wife; 3. virtuous woman; सौत [sapatnī-] f. 1. Parvati's co-wife, Ganga; 2. co-wife; 3. woman of base character; देवी की सौंह var. Br. I swear on the goddess.

एक ही सों चित चाहिये ओर लौं, बीच दगा को परै नहिं डाँको।
मानिक सो मन बेचि कै, जू, अब फेरि कहा परखाइबौ ताको।
ठाकुर, काम नहीं सब को, कोऊ लाखन में परबीन है जाको।
प्रीति किये में कछू न लगै, करि कै एक ओर निबाहिबो बाँको॥ Ś111॥

रूपवारी, जोबन-अनूप-, हय-गय-वारी,

---

111 Bharatpur3 f. 76v, Bharatpur5 f. 19rv (33), Chatarpur (C) f. 44 (246), Kālidās-Hajārā (H_e) 322, Jaipur1 f. 2v (7), Marwar5 f. 25r (31); Kasgañj (N) f. 22v (97), Rasikvinod (O_e) 306, Śatak 78, Ṭhasak 18, Vrindaban2 ff. 69v-70r (4), Hāfizullah Khān: Hazārā (X_e) p. 260 (Śṛṅgār ādi ras 15 [17 on p. 310 in Dikshit's edn.]). The Bundeli form 'parakhāvane' in the second line is an eccentric reading peculiar to C. Cf. 'rākhibau tau kaṭhināī nahī, rasa rākhi bidā karibau kaṭhināī' (Ś 106).

111.1 एक] Σ, ओर B_5B_3 • सों] $EH_eM_5NO_eX_e$, ते B_5, से B_3, सो CJ_1V_2 • चित] $EH_eJ_1O_eX_e$, मन B_5B_3C, चीत M_5, चित्त (unm.) NV_2 • चाहिये] $CEH_eJ_1O_eV_2X_e$, राषियै B_5B_3N, चाहीये M_5 • ओर] $EH_eJ_1M_5NO_eV_2X_e$, एक B_5B_3, छोर C • लौं] Σ, सौं B_5, सो B_3 • दगा को परे नहिं] Σ, बिचारन दगान कौ B_3, परे न दगा को N • परै] Σ, परैं X_e • डाँको] B_5B_3CNE, टांको $H_eM_5V_2X_e$, डोको (unrh.) J_1, दाको O_e **111.2** सो] Σ, सों J_1X_e • मन] Σ, मनु B_3, चित M_5 • बेचि] Σ, बेंच C, बेची M_5 • कै जू अब] $H_eM_5NV_2X_e$, दयौ तब B_5, कैं सुंदरि B_3, के सुंदर C, मोहन E, कै जू फिरि J_1, दियो अब O_e • फेरि… ताको] Σ, को सुरझै सुरझायबों काकों N • फेरि] $B_5B_3H_eJ_1O_eV_2X_e$, फेर CE, फेरी M_5 • कहा] Σ, पै ना J_1 • परषाइबौ] B_5B_3E, परखावने C, परखामनौ H_eV_2, परषांन जु J_1, परखावनो M_5X_e, परखाइये O_e • ताको] $B_3EH_eM_5O_eV_2X_e$, ताकौं B_5, वाको CJ_1 **111.3** ठाकुर] Σ, कहि ठाकुर (unm.) N • नहीं] $B_5B_3H_eJ_1M_5O_eV_2X_e$, नहिं CN, नयो $Ś_e$, न या $Ṭ_e$ • सब] Σ, उन O_e • को] Σ, ही B_3, कौं B_5 • कोऊ] B_5C, कौ (unm.) B_3, अब E, इक $H_eM_5V_2X_e$, यह J_1, ओंर N, यहां O_e • लाखन में] $C^{pc}Σ$, लाखन (unm.) C^{ac} • परवीन] Σ, प्रबीन (unm.) B_3CM_5 • है] Σ, हें N • जाको $EH_eM_5O_eV_2X_e$, ताको B_3CJ_1, जाकौं B_5, ताकों N **111.4** प्रीति] $B_5B_3H_eJ_1O_eV_2X_e$, प्रीत CM_5, प्रीरित (unm.) N • किये में कछू] B_5O_e, करे मैं कहा B_3, करें सो कहा C, करे मैं लगै E, कहा करिबे में $H_eJ_1M_5V_2X_e$, करे कों कछू N • न लगै] NO_e, जु लगै B_3, न लगैं B_5, लग है C, है कहा E, लगै $H_eJ_1M_5V_2X_e$ • करि कै] Σ, कर कें C, करी के M_5 • एक] B_3CNO_e, फिरि B_5J_1, इक $EH_eV_2X_e$, * ईक M_5 • ओर] Σ, नेह B_3 • निबाहिबौ] $B_5B_3CEJ_1NO_eV_2$, निबाहनो H_eX_e, नीबाहनो M_5 • बाँको] $B_5B_3CH_eNO_eṬ_e$, वाको $J_1M_5Ś_eV_2X_e$

111.1 ओर [avarā-] f. end; एक सौं var. only with one, exclusively; डांक Br. m. sting (of deceit). **111.2** अब फेरि Br. now after this; कहा परखाइबौ Br. what is the use of examining?. **111.4** में कछू न लगै idiom. 'it does not take much to' it is easy to; बांका [vaṅku-] adj. 'complicated' difficult.

फेरि हथियार-वारी न्यारियै अटत है।
ताही के उपायन कों करत अनेग नेग, 2
सारत गरज जाकी जा बिधि सटत है।
ठाकुर कहत, कूर चतुर गरीब गनी 3
जानै दोऊ दीन बात ऐसियै पटत है।
चाह करिबे को तौ उमाह सबही कै, पै 4
निबाह करिबे की बेर सब की फटत है॥ Ś112॥

ए तो ब्रजमंडल-बसत, तासों काज कहा, 1

---

112 Bharatpur1 f. 161v (73), Granthāvalī 58, Sudhāsar [S_1 f. 366v (95), S_2 f. 72r (-/82), S_7 f. 243v (76)], Vrindaban1 f. 13r (16/81). • The Sudhāsar presents this poem within the 'Nīti' section.

112.1 फेरि] B_1S_2, फेर $G_eS_1S_7V_1$ • न्यारियै] Σ, न्यारीयै B_1 **112.2** उपायन] B_1**S**, उपाय G_eV_1 • कों] B_1G_e, को **S**, कू V_1 • करत] B_1**S**, करत है G_eV_1 • अनेग] $B_1G_eS_1V_1$, अनेक S_2S_7 • सारत] Σ, सारज S_1 • जाकी] $B_1G_eS_1V_1$, ताकी S_2S_7 • बिधि] $B_1G_eS_2$, बिध $S_1S_7V_1$ **112.3** ठकुर कहत] G_e**S**, ठा° B_1, ठाकुर कहैत V_1 • जानै] $G_eS_7V_1$, जानैं $B_1S_1S_2$ • ऐसियै] Σ, ऐसीयै B_1 • पटत] Σ, रटत S_7 **112.4** को] $G_eS_1V_1$, कौं B_1, की S_2S_7 • तौ] Σ, बेर (unm.) S_7 • कैं] $B_1S_1S_2$, कौ $G_eS_7V_1$ • निबाह करिबे] $B_1G_eV_1$, निबाहिबे **S** • बेर] $B_1G_eV_1$, बेर देखौ S_1S_2, बेर देख S_7 • की] Σ, कौ S_2 • फटत] Σ, फटति S_2

112.1 -वारी (-वाली) suff. Br. (women) possessing (all kinds of attractiveness); हय [S] m. horse; गय [gaja-] m. elephant; फेरि Br. conj. and then; हथियार [*hastakāra-] m. weapon (esp. the ten 'hāvas' or flirtatious gestures); न्यारियै adj. (Br. emph.) separate(ly); अटना [aṭati] Av. Br. v.i. to go about. **112.2** ताही के उपायन कों Br. to find a means for that (i.e. to fulfill his/her desire); अनेग [aneka-] Bund. adj. 'not one' many; नेग 1. [cf. Br. nek] Bund. adj. some, a little; 2. gift; 3. poet. effort (KL, RSh); सारना [sārayati] v.t. to achieve, to complete; ग़र्ज [P] f. 1. aim, wish; 2. need; सटना v.t. 1. to join together, to unite; 2. to be done successfully. **112.3** कूर [krūra-] adj. dull; ग़नी [P] adj. rich; दोऊ दीन idiom. Br. 'the two religions' the two worlds; पटना [*paṭyati] v.i. to go well, to suit. **112.4** उमाह [cf. unmathayati] m. swelling, enthusiasm; निबाह [nirvāha-] m. carrying through, completion; बेर [vāra-] f. time; फटना [cf. *sphāṭyate] v.i. to be torn; to burst सब की फटत है idiom. vulg. everyone's anuses burst (i.e. they are unable to do the work).

आनँद के भौन, तुमैं देखि जीजियत है।
2 सोई तुम इत उत अलटि पलटि हेरो,
याही दुख दाहन करेजौ छीजियत है।
3 ठाकुर कहत, अनचाहते की चाह कहा,
चाहते की चाह कौं निबाहि लीजियत है।
4 बिना प्रीति, प्रीतम, परेषौ कौन काकौ करै,
प्रीति ही कौ, प्रीतम, परेखौ कीजियत है॥ Ś113॥

---

113 Bharatpur1 f. 163v (86), Granthāvalī 60, Sudhāsar [S_2 f. 10r (7/6), S_7 f. 44r (11/413)], Ṭhasak 56, Vrindaban1 f. 7v-8r (5/43), Vrindaban4 f. 32v (17), Yājñik. S_2 omits the last line. The reading of the last line in the Granthāvalī and the Ṭhasak is a secondary reading invented to eliminate the repetition of the word 'prītama' considered to be a poetic fault.

113.1 बसत] Σ, बसंत V_1 • काज] $Y_e\Sigma$, काम **E** • कहा] $B_1S_2V_1Y_e$, कहां S_7V_4, कौन **E** • के] $B_1^{pc}\Sigma$, *om.* (unm.) B_1^{pc} • तुमैं] $Y_e\Sigma$, तुम्हैं **E** • जीजियत] $B_1S_7V_1$, जीजियतु $\mathbf{E}V_4$, जीयत (unm.) S_2 • है] Σ, हैं S_2 **113.2** सोई] B_1V_4, सोऊ **E**, CHECK S_7, सो ही S_2V_1 • इत] $B_1V_1V_4Y_e$, इतै **E**, यत S_2, यित S_7 • उत] $Y_e\Sigma$, उतै **E** • अलटि पलटि] B_1V_4, उलटि पलटि Y_e, अनत पनत **E**, अलट पलट **S**, अल पलटि (unm.) V_1 • हेरो] Σ, हैं रों V_4 • दुष] $B_1\mathbf{S}V_1V_4$, दुख्ख G_e, दुःख $Ṭ_e$ • दाहन] $B_1^{ac}\Sigma$, दाह त्रासन (unm.) B_1^{pc} • करेजौ] $Y_e\Sigma$, सरीर **E** • छीजियत] $B_1\mathbf{S}V_1$, छीजियतु $\mathbf{E}V_4$ **113.3** ठाकुर कहत] $\mathbf{ES}V_4$, ठा० B_1, ठाकुर कहैत V_1 • अनचाहते की चाह कहा] $Y_e\Sigma$, मेरी चाह की अचाह करौ **E** • कहा] Σ, कहां S_7 • चाहते] Σ, ते (unm.) S_2 • कौं] $B_1\mathbf{S}V_1$, की **E**, कूं V_4 • निबाहि] $S_2V_1V_4$, निबाह $B_1\mathbf{E}S_7$ • लीजियत] $B_1S_7V_1$, कीजियतु **E**, लोजियत S_2, लीजियतु Y_eV_4 **113.4** बिना... करै] $B_1V_1V_4Y_e$, प्रीति बिनु प्यारे कोऊ काहे कौं परेखो देइ **E**, *om.* S_2, रूप दीप रावरो निहार प्रान वारै कोऊ S_7 • प्रीति] B_1V_4, प्रित V_1Y_e • करै] $B_1^{pc}V_1Y_e$, *om.* उन्म B_1^{ac}, करैं V_4 • प्रीति... है] $V_1V_4Y_e$, CHECK B_1, प्रीति की प्रतीति को परेखो दीजियतु है **E**, *om.* S_2, कहा पतंग की ज्यौं छार कीजियत है S_7 • कौं G_e, को $Ṭ_e$ • प्रतीति G_e, प्रतीत $Ṭ_e$ • कीजियत] B_1V_1, कीजियतु V_4Y_e

---

113.1 एतौ (इतने) Br. adj. (there are) so many; ब्रजमंडल-बसत Br. inhabitant of Braj; तासों with it (i.e. with living in Braj); भौन [bhavana-] Br. m. abode; जीजियतु है v.i. imperf. Br. one lives (on). **113.2** सोई तुम reg. 'that very same you' you yourself; अलटि पलटि (उलट-पलट) Br. adj. 1. changed; 2. confused; अनत पनत var. [anyatra- (twinned)] reg. adv. everywhere else; छीजना [chidyate] v.i. to waste away, to dwindle. **113.3** अनचाहत- Br. m. a person who is not in love; चाह f. 1. desire; 2. affection; अचाह करौ var. Br. you do not want; चाहत- Br. m. the beloved; निबाह [nirvāha-] Br. m. carrying through, completion. **113.4** परेखो [parīkṣā-] Br. m. anger.

कौन गुनाह परो हम सों अब लौं, घनस्याम, निहोरियतु है।
जो अपनी हितकारी महा, तिन सों कहूँ डीठि मरोरियतु है।
ठाकुर, आप सयानै बडे, मन-मानिक पाय न फोरियतु है।
यह प्रीति की रीत सुनौ 'हमपै करि प्रीत नहीं फिर तोरियतु है' ॥ Ś114॥

जो छबिता कछू देखियै नैन, सु वा छबि देखि सराहियतु है।
जासों लगी सुख आस कछू, तिहि के दुख दीरघ दाहियतु है।
ठाकुर, जौ वे अचाही भए, हम तौ उनको भलैं चाहियतु है।
या कुल रीत बडेन की, प्रीत जो बाँहि गहे की निबाहियतु है॥ Ś115॥

*गति मेरी यही निसवासर है, चित तेरी गलीन के गाहने है।
चित कीन्हो कठोर कहा इतनो, अरी, तोहि नहीं यह चाहने है।

---

114 Granthāvalī 61, Śatak 66, Ṭhasak 77. These are the words of a messenger to Krishna.
115 Granthāvalī 67, Śatak 105, Ṭhasak 133 116 Sundarītilak (C$_e$) 294, Granthāvalī 65, Rasikvinod (O$_e$) 693, Ṭhasak 55, Ṭhasak 'Jīvancarit' (Ṭ$^{j}_{e}$) p. 15.

114.1 कौन] (unm.) **E** • निहोरियतु] (unm.) Ś$_e$, निहोरितु G$_e$Ṭ$_e$ **114.2** जो] (unm.) **E** • डीठि] G$_e$Ṭ$_e$, डीठ Ś$_e$ • मरोरियतु] (unm.) Ś$_e$, मरोरितु G$_e$Ṭ$_e$ **114.3** कबि ठाकुर] Ś$_e$, ठाकुर, (unm.) G$_e$Ṭ$_e$ • फोरियतु] (unm.) Ś$_e$, कोरितु G$_e$Ṭ$_e$ **114.4** यह] (unm.) **E** • तोरियतु] (unm.) Ś$_e$, तोरितु G$_e$Ṭ$_e$ **115.1** देखि] G$_e$, देख Ś$_e$Ṭ$_e$ • सराहियतु] (unm.) Ś$_e$, सराहितु G$_e$Ṭ$_e$ **115.2** दाहियतु] (unm.) Ś$_e$, दाहितु] G$_e$Ṭ$_e$ **115.3** वे] G$_e$Ṭ$_e$, पै Ś$_e$ • हम तौ उनको] G$_e$Ṭ$_e$, हमसैं उनसैं Ś$_e$ • चाहियतु] (unm.) Ś$_e$, चाहितु G$_e$Ṭ$_e$ **115.4** निबाहियतु] (unm.) Ś$_e$, निबाहितु G$_e$Ṭ$_e$ **116.1** निस॰] Σ, निशि C$_e$ • चित] **E**, नित O$_e$C$_e$ • के गाहने] **E**, को गाहिबो O$_e$C$_e$ **116.2** कीन्हो] G$_e$, कीनो O$_e$, कीन्हों C$_e$Ṭ$_e$Ṭ$^{j}_{e}$ • अरी] G$_e$Ṭ$_e$, अब C$_e$Ṭ$^{j}_{e}$, अस O$_e$ • चाहने] **E**, चाहिबो C$_e$O$_e$

114.1 परो v.i. (Br. Bund. perf.) happened; घनस्याम Br. m. (voc.) O Krishna; निहोर- [niṣṭhura-] v.t. 1. to be harsh or insensitive (KL); 2. to reproach by alluding to past favours; to entreat; -इतु var. reg. suff. (sing. 3rd person.) निहोरियतु v.t. pass. imperf. Br. 1. that you are insensitive; 2. I entreat you. **114.2** डीठि मरोड़ना idiom. to turn the eyes away. **114.3** सयाना [sajñāna-] adj. clever; फोड़ना [sphoṭayati] v.t. to burst, to break into pieces; कोड़ना var. [koṭayate] v.t. to scratch; to cut. **114.4** सुनौ हमपै Br. listen to us. **115.1** छबिता (छवि) [S] poet. f. beauty; सु 1. poet. adv. well; 2. pron. Br. it. **115.3** अचाही Br. adj. without love; भलैं (भलाइयाँ) [cf. bhalla-] Br. f. pl. good things; चाहितु है (चाहती हैं) var. v.t. (reg. imperf. f. pl.) poet. I wish. **115.4** बाँही (बाँह) [bāhu-] poet. f. arm; बाँह गह- idiom. Br. to give shelter, to protect; प्रीत... है reg. love extended in support should be carried through. **116.1** गाह- [gāhate] Br. v.i. to wander, to roam; के गाहने है Bund. is to roam in. **116.2** चाहने var. 1. [cāhanīya-] reg. adj. proper; 2. [H cāhnā] v.t. (inf. Bund.) to want, to wish; तोहि... है Br. it is not what you want to wish.

कहि ठाकुर, नेक नहीं दरसी, कपटीन कों काह सराहने है।
4 मन भावै सुजान सोई करियौ, हमैं नेह को नातो निबाहने है॥ Ś116॥

का करियै तुम्हरे मन को, जिहि को अब लौं न मिटो दगा दीबो।
2 पै हम दूसरो रूप न देखिहैं, आनन आन को नाम न लीबो।
ठाकुर, एक सो भाव है तौ लगि जौ लगि देह धरे जग जीबो।
4 प्यारे सनेह निबाहिबे कौं हम तौ अपनो सो कियो अरु कीबो॥ Ś117॥

1 दूरि है बतात कहा, आव इतै मेरे पास,
आनँद-निवास, रस रास के निबाहू सौं।
2 चाह चाहौं अंतर की, अंतर न राख्यौ कछू,
ऐहौ कै बुलैहौ, पै न कैहौ जाहू ताहू सौं।
3 ठाकुर कहत, हे किसोर दिलजान मेरे,

---

117 Granthāvalī 63, Śatak 97, Ṭhasak 49. 118 Bharatpur1 f. 156rv (40), Bharatpur8 f. 14v (42), Granthāvalī B21, Sudhāsar [S_1 f. 172rv (15), S_3 f. 147rv (126), S_4 f. 72v (132), S_7 f. 195r (15)], Ṭhākur-satsaī (Ṭ) f. 3r (22), Vrindaban1 f. 9v (3/55). • The Sudhāsar presents this poem in the 'aur nānābidhi kī brijkelī barnan' (description of other various love sports in Braj) subsection of the 'Brajrasrīti' section.

116.3 कहि] G_e, कह Ṭ$_e$, कबि C_eO_eṬ$_e^j$ • दरसी] G_eṬ$_e^j$, दरसै C_eO_e, दरसीं Ṭ$_e$ • कों] G_e, को Σ • सराहने] **E**, सराहिबो C_eO_e **116.4** सुजान] **E**, तिहारे C_eO_e • करियौ] **E**, करियै C_eO_e • निबाहने] **E**, निबाहिबो C_eO_e **117.1** को] G_eṬ$_e$, कों Ś$_e$ **117.3** यौ लगि जौ लगि] *conj.* जौ लगि, तौ लगि **E** **117.4** कौं] G_e, को Ś$_e$Ṭ$_e$ **118.1** दूरि] $B_1B_8G_eS_4V_1$, दूर $S_1S_3S_7$Ṭ • है] B_1B_8**S**V_1, ह्वै G_e, ते Ṭ • बतात] B_1G_e**S**Ṭ, बसाति B_8, बातत (unm.) V_1 • कहा] Σ, कहां S_7 • आव इतै] Σ, आवत है G_e • निबाहू] $B_1B_8G_eS_1V_1$, उमाहू $S_3S_4S_7$Ṭ **118.2** चाह] $B_1B_8G_eS_1S_3$ṬV_1, चाहि S_4S_7 • चाहौं] $B_8G_eS_1V_1$, चाहौ $B_1S_3S_4S_7$Ṭ • राख्यौ] B_1B_8**S**V_1, राखौ G_eṬ • कछू] Σ, कछु Ṭ • कैहौ] $B_1S_1S_4S_7$, कैहौं $B_8G_eV_1$, कैयौ S_3 • जाहू] Σ, जाहु G_e

---

116.3 काह (क्या) reg. interr. what? (cf. Br. kahā) कपटीन... है Br. why do you want to be praised by hypocrites? **117.1** जिहि 1. [jīva-] m. (Br. obl.) (of) the mind, heart; 2. rel. pron. Br. (obl.) the one (for whom). **117.3** एक सो भाव है जौ लगि var. Br. as long as the same feeling remains; देह धरे Br. (I live) in this body. **117.4** अपनो सो idiom. Br. my best; कियो अरु कीबो Br. I did and will do. **118.1** है बतात [cf. H bāt] v.i. imperf. Br. you speak; आवत है var. Br. v.i. imperf. (but) you come; रास (राशि) [S] Br. f. abundance (of love); निबाहू सौं (निर्वाह से) Br. with the aim of fulfilling. **118.2** चाह [*cāh-] f. (obl.) (with) desire, eagerly; अंतर [S] m. 1. 'the inside' heart; 2. distance; कै Br. conj. or; जाहू ताहू सौं Br. (you shouldn't say it) to this or that person (i.e. we do not need an intermediator).

तेरे बस भई हौं मनोज के उमाहू सौं।
लिखि लैजा, लिखि दैजा, कै जा एकरार मोसों
तोही सों मिलूँगौं, न मिलूँगौं और काहू सौं॥ Ś118॥

परकीया

*जारहीं जात लखो कुँवना, तब धीरज नेक नहीं धरती है।
आपनी देखि घिनोची भरी मिस ठानि परायो कहो करती है।
ठाकुर, मानती नाहीं कहो, घर जात पराए नहीं डरती है।
रीति की रोसन, आपनी होंसन पानी परोसन को भरती है॥ Ś119॥

*छोडि पतिव्रत प्रीति निबाही, निभी नहि तौनि, हस्यौ सब कोऊ।

---

119 Granthāvalī 55, Ṭhasak 50. This poem can be an example of the guptā nāyikā.
120 Bharatpur1 f. 162r (75), Sundarī-tilak (C_e) 94, Granthāvalī 84, Marwar5 f. 25v (35), Rasikvinod (O_e) 248, Sudhāsar [S_2 f. 11v (16/11), S_7 f. 46r (35/437)], Ṭhasak 175, Vrindaban1 f. 1r (2/2), Yājñik. S_2 omits the second line.

118.3 ठाकुर कहत] $B_8G_eS_1^{pc}S_3S_4S_7$, ठा॰ B_1, ठाकुर कहित Ṭ, ठाकुर कहैत $S_1^{ac}V_1$ • हे] Σ, हौ **S** • किसोर] Σ, किसोरि S_4 • दिलजान] Σ, दिलजानि **S** • तेरे] Σ, तर Ṭ • भई] Σ, भइ V_1 • हौं] $G_eS_1S_7V_1$, हूं B_1, हू B_8, हौ S_3S_4Ṭ • उमाहू] $B_1B_8G_eS_1S_3S_7V_1$, उमाहे (unrh.) S_4, डछाहू Ṭ **118.4** लिखि] G_e, लिष Σ • लैजा] Σ, लै (unm.) B_8 • लिखि दैजा] $B_1B_8G_e$, लिख दैजा **S**Ṭ, लषि दजा V_1 • कैजा] Σ, कजा V_1 • एकरार] $B_1B_8G_e S_3$Ṭ, पेकरार S_4, इकरार S_7V_1 • तोही] Σ, तोई B_8 • मिलूंगौं] $B_1B_8G_eV_1$, मिलौंगौ S_1, मिलैगो S_4S_7, मिलौगौ S_3Ṭ • मिलूंगौं] $B_1B_8G_eV_1$, मिलौंगौ S_1, मिलौगौ S_3Ṭ, मिलैगो S_4S_7 **119.1** जारहीं] G_e, यारही $Ṭ_e$ **119.4** होंसन] G_e, हौंसनि $Ṭ_e$ **120.1** छोडि] B_1**ES**, छांडि C_eO_e, छाड M_5, छोड V_1 • पतिव्रत] C_e**E**$M_5O_eS_7V_1$, पतीव्रत B_1S_2 • प्रीत] Σ, पित (unm.) M_5 • निबाही निभी] B_1**S**Y_e, करी निबाही **E**, करी निबही $C_eM_5O_e$, निबाहनी निभी (unm.) V_1 • नही] $B_1M_5O_e$**S**V_1Y_e, नहि **E**C_e • तौनि] $B_1V_1Y_e$, स्रौन **E**, तौन $C_eM_5O_e$**S** • हस्यौ सब कोऊ] B_1**S**V_1Y_e, सुनी हम सोऊ C_e**E**M_5O_e •

118.3 दिलजान [P] m. lover; हे किसोर voc. Br. o Krishna; उमाह [cf. unmathayati] poet. m. desire. **118.4** लिखि लैजा लिखि दैजा Br. take (it from me) written and give (it to me) written; कै जा (कर जा) v.t. imp. Br. make; इकरार [A] m. contract (cf. ikrārnāmā). **119.1** जार [S] m. paramour; कुँवना [kūpa-] reg. m. (obl.) (towards) the well. **119.2** घिनोची (घड़ौंची) [*ghaṭamañcikā-] poet. f. a stand for pots; कहो v.t. perf. Br. Bund. (used as m.) 'what is said' words (by others). **119.4** रोस [P raviś] f. motion, way, conduct; रीति कि रोसन Br. (obl.) (?) according to the accepted conduct; होंस [A havis] f. lust, delight. **120.1** निभना (निबहना) [nirvahati] v.i. to be carried through, to be fulfilled; तौनि (वह) pron. Bund. it; स्रौन (श्रवण) var. [S] Br. m. (obl.) (with my) ear; सोऊ (वह भी) apa. pron. Br. (with encl.) that, too.

2 मौन भए रहनेंही पर्‌यो, कहनें ही पर्‌यो, सुनिहैं सब सोऊ।
साँची भई कहनावति वा, कहि ठाकुर, कान सुनी हुती जोऊ।
4 माया मिली नहिं राम मिले, दुबिधा मैं गए, सजनी सुनि, दोऊ॥ Ś120॥

हम तौ परनारी भईं, सो भईं, तुम तौ सुधरौ सखियाँ सिगरीं।
2 यह रीत चलै, जग नाम धरै तिहि ते न कढो मग मो ढिग रीं।
कवि ठाकुर, फाट्यो उलंक को चादर, देत कहाँ लौं बने थिगरीं।
4 नँदलाल गोपाल सो प्रीत करी, हम तौ बनिकै बिगरीं बिगरीं॥ Ś121॥

---

121 Granthāvalī 86, Marwar5 f. 32v (4), Ṭhasak 164, Śatak 63.

120.2 मौन... कोऊ] Σ, *om.* S_2 • भए] Σ, भऐं B_1 • रहनें ही] B_1S_7, रहनेई **E**, हरनो ही C_eM_5, रहनो ही O_e, रहैनैई V_1 • पर्‌यो] $B_1C_eO_e$**S**V_1, परो **E**, पसो M_5 • कहनें ही] B_1S_7, सहनेई **E**V_1, सहनों ही C_eO_e, सेहनो ही M_5 • पर्‌यो] Σ, परी M_5 • सुनिहैं सब] B_1, जो कह्यौ कछु $C_eM_5O_e$, जो कहै कछु **E**, सुनहै सब $S_7V_1Y_e$ • सोऊ] $B_1V_1Y_e$, कोऊ C_e**E**$M_5O_eS_7$ **120.3** कहनावति] Σ, केनावत (unm.) M_5 • वा] Σ, या O_e • कहि] B_1**S**V_1Y_e, कवि C_e**E**O_e, कवी M_5 • सुनी हुती] $B_1C_eM_5O_e$**S**, सुनी हती **E**, सुनि हूती V_1 **120.4** मिली] Σ, मीली M_5 • मिले] C_e**E**O_e**S**, मिल्यौ B_1V_1, मीले M_5 • दुबिधा] Σ, दुबध्या M_5 • मैं] B_1**E**O_eS_2, मे $M_5S_7V_1$ • सुनि] $B_1G_eS_2V_1$, सुनो $C_eM_5O_e$, सुनु $Ṭ_e$ **121.1** परनारी] **E**, परनार M_5 • भईं सो भईं] **E**, भई सो भई M_5 • सुधरौ सखियाँ] **E**, सषीयां सुधरो M_5 • सिगरीं] $G_eṬ_e$, सगरी $M_5Ś_e$ **121.2** यह] **E**, जहै M_5 • जग] **E**, कुल M_5 • ते] $M_5Ś_eṬ_e$, तँ G_e • न कढो मो मग] **E**, जीन ब⟨डो⟩ न मो (unm.) M_5 • रीं] $G_eṬ_e$, री $M_5Ś_e$ **121.3** फाट्यो] $M_5Ś_e$, फाटी $G_eṬ_e$ • उलंक] **E**, कलंक M_5 • को] $M_5Ś_e$, की $G_eṬ_e$ • चादर] **E**, बादर M_5 • देत कहाँ लौं बने] M_5, देऊँ कहाँ कहँ लौं **E** • थिगरीं] $G_eṬ_e$, थिगरी $M_5Ś_e$ **121.4** नँद०... करी] M_5, तुम आपनी और बचाव करौ **E** • बनिकै] G_e, बृज के M_5, बनकै $Ś_eṬ_e$ • बिगरीं बिगरीं] $G_eṬ_e$, बिगरी बिगरी $M_5Ś_e$

120.2 कहनेंही पर्‌यो 1. I had to tell that I had to remain silent; 2. (though I was originally silent about it) I had to tell it; 3. I could not help telling it (through my silence); **सुनिहै सब सोऊ** Br. all will listen to the same thing. **120.4 माया** [S] f. affection, love; **सुनि** [H sunnā] v.t. imp. Br. listen! **दुबिधा** [cf. dvi-vidhā-] Br. f. dilemma (of whether to love or to keep my honour); **गए दोऊ** Br. both (love and Rām) were lost. **121.2 तिहि ते** Br. for this reason; **ढिग** [*ḍhigga-] postp. near. **121.3 उलंक** (**निष्कलंक**) adj. (used as m.) Bund. blamelessness, honour; **चादर** [P] f. m. sheet, shawl; **कहाँ कहँ लौं** var. poet. in what places and for how long? **थिगरी** (**थिगली**) [cf. *thigga-] Br. Bund. f. patch. **121.4 हम... बिगरीं** Br. if I am thoroughly corrupted, then I am corrupted.

*जानत ही अपने नहीं होत, पराए पिया, यह बेदन गाई।
सो परहेलि कै प्रीति करी, गुरु लोगन की कुलकानि गँवाई।
ठाकुर, ते न भए अपने, अब कौन को दोस लगाइयै, माई।
दूध की माखी उजागर, बीर, सो, हाइ, मैं आँखिन देखत खाई॥ Ś122॥

---

122 Bharatpur6 f. 7r, Sundarītilak (C_e) 95, Datiya2 f. 2r (13), Granthāvalī 88, Jaipur1 ff. 6v-7r (21), Rasikvinod (O_e) 249, Śatak 45, Sudhāsar [S_1 f. 116v and 195r (ŚudhaAvl), S_2 f. 47v (-/47), S_3 f. 109v-110r (114), S_7 f. 154v (29/1464)], Ṭhasak 170, Udaipur f. 127r (10), Bābūrāmdīn: Sundarītilak (U_e) 138, Vrindaban1 f. 2v (11/11). Vrindaban1 and the Sudhāsar (S_1) introduce the poem as an example to the 'parakīyā kalahāntaritā' (an adulterous woman after a quarrel). It is repeated in the Sudhāsar (S_1^{vl} S_3 and S_7) as an example to 'prītopālambha' (complaint against love).

122.1 जानत ही अपने] B_6O_e**S**, जानत ती अपने $C_eD_2U_e$, अपने (unm.) **E**, आपनें J_1, जानत ही U, जानते ही अपने V_1 • नहीं] C_eO_e**S**V_1, नहिं B_6D_2**E**U_e, *om.* J_1U • होत] Σ, जो U • यह] $C_eD_2O_e$**S**V_1U_e, इह B_6, यह जानत मैं अरु $G_eṬ_e$, यह रीति सबै कुल J_1, यह जानत में अरु $Ś_e$, न हित है आपनै U • बेदन] D_2**E**J_1O_e**S**U_e, बेदनि B_6V_1, देवन C_e **122.2** सो परहेलि] $B_6O_eS_2V_1U_e$, से न सहेलि C_e, सो परिहेल D_2, सो अवहेलि $G_eṬ_e$, लाज को छोडि कै J_1, सो परिहेलि S_1, सो सब हेलि $Ś_e$, सो परहेल S_3S_7U • प्रीति] B_6C_e**EJ**$_1$ $O_eS_2S_3V_1U_e$, प्रीत $D_2S_1S_7$, पीत U • गुरु] C_e**E**$J_1O_eS_3U_e$, गुर $B_6D_2S_1S_2S_7UV_1$ • लोगन] C_eD_2**EO**$_e$**S**U_e, लोगनि $B_6J_1V_1$, लोकन U • की] B_6**ES**V_1, में $C_eO_eU_e$, मैं D_2J_1U • कानि] C_e**E**$J_1O_eS_2V_1U_e$, कान $B_6D_2S_1S_3S_7U$ **122.3** ते न] **E**$J_1O_eC_eU_e$, वे न **S**, जान D_2U, सो न B_6V_1 • भए अपने] Σ, अजान भई D_2U • को] $B_6C_eS_2S_3Ś_eṬ_eV_1$, कों $D_2G_eJ_1O_eS_1$, कुं U • दोस] D_2**ES**UU_eV_1, दोष $C_eB_6J_1O_e$ • लगाइयै] B_6C_e**E**$J_1O_eS_2S_3S_7V_1U_e$, लगाईये $D_2S_1S_1^{vl}$, लगाउ री U **122.4** माखी] Σ, माछी D_2 • उजागर] Σ, उजागरै U • बीर] $C_eD_2J_1O_e$**S**$Ś_eṬ_eU_e$, बीच $B_6G_eUV_1$ • सो] $B_6J_1O_eS_3S_7UU_e$, सों C_e, सु D_2**E**S_1, से S_2V_1 • खाई] Σ, माई S_1

122.1 पराया [para-] adj. of someone else. **122.2** परहेल- poet. v.t. to disregard. **122.3** कौन कौ दोस लगाइयै Br. who should be blamed? **122.4** उजागर adv. bright, clearly visible.

*अब का समझावती को समझै, बदनामी के बीजन बो चुकी री।
2 इतनौंही बिचार करो जिय मैं, इहि जाल परें, कहौ, को चुकी री।

---

123 Bharatpur1 f. 131rv (1), Bharatpur6 f. 7r, Bharatpur9 ff. 17v-18r, Chatarpur f. 21 (108), Gujarat f. 1r, Granthāvalī 89, Jaipur1 f. 2rv (6), Kashi1 f. 4v-5r (K_1), Marwar1 f. 12v (37), Marwar4 f. 22v (24), Marwar5 f. 31v (2), Sudhāsar [S_1 f. 70r (8), S_2 f. 14r ((28b)/20), S_7 f. 49v (69/471)], Śatak 42, Ṭhākur-satsaī f. 1r (1) (Ṭ), Ṭhasak 60, Udaipur f. 126rv (3), Vrindaban4 f. 45r (17), Miśrabandhu Vinod (V_e) p. 731, Hāfizullah Khān: Hajārā (X_e) p. 297 (Śṛṅgār ādi ras 172), Z_1 f. 34v (28). The Sudhāsar (S_1) presents this poem within the 'ūḍhā parakiyā' section and introduces it as an example of the 'alajja parakiyā'. G omits the second line. The second and third lines are in the reverse order in K_1. (K_1 does not differentiate between the short and the long u.)

123.1 अब] $B_1B_9CGEM_4UV_eX_eZ_1$, *om.* (unm.) $B_6M_1M_5$ṬV_4, निति J_1, आब K_1, यह S • का] Σ, को B_6M_4, काहा M_1, कहा (unm.) M_5 • समझावती] $B_1CES_1V_e$, समझावत $B_6M_1M_4S_7$ṬUZ_1X_e, समझावति $B_9GJ_1S_2V_4$, समुझै K_1, समजावत M_5 • समझै] Σ, समझावती K_1, समझैं U • बदनामी] $B_1B_6CEG^{pc}J_1M_4M_5S_1S_7Ś_e$ṬṬ$_eV_eX_e$, बदनाम $B_9K_1M_1S_2UV_4$, ब-दनामि G^{ac}, बजनाम Z_1 • के] Σ, कि M_1, को X_eṬ • बीजन] $B_1GEM_1S_1S_2UV_4Z_1$, बीजनि $B_6J_1X_e$, बीज तौ $B_9CK_1M_5S_7$Ṭ, बीज मैं M_4, बीज त V_e • बो] $B_1B_6CGJ_1M_1M_4M_5S$ṬṬ$_e$ $UV_4V_eX_eZ_1$, बै B_9K_1, बोइ G_e, बोय $Ś_e$ • चुकी] Σ, चुक Ṭ, चुकि U • री] Σ, जू B_9
123.2 इतनौंहीं... री] Σ, *om.* G • इतनौंही] $B_1J_1M_1M_5S_1$, इतनोइ B_6U, तब तो इतनों न $B_9CV_eX_e$Ṭ, इतनोहूँ **E**, तब तो आतना K_1, इतनों न M_4, यतनौंही S_2, यितनौही S_7, करि कोटि V_4, इतनोई Z_1 • बिचार] Σ, बीचार M_5, ⟨चि/चु⟩पाव Ṭ, उपाय V_4 • करो... कोचु की] Σ, को हो जब प्रित फदै कै छदै चुकी K_1, कियो जब तो केहिं काज परें कम कोचु M_4, कीयो जब ला⟨ग/ज⟩ परे पर को चुक Ṭ • करो] Σ, कियौ $B_9V_eX_e$ • जिय मैं] B_1S_2U, *om.* $B_9CV_eX_e$, जिय मै B_6M_1, तौ सखी **E**, चित मैं J_1, जीय मे M_5, जिइ मैं S_1, जि मै S_7^{ac}, जिय मै S_7^{pc}, सजनी V_4, मन मै Z_1 • इहि] B_1C, इह B_6S_1, यह $B_9ES_2S_7$, उहिं J_1, अप॰ M_1U, अपना M_5, अब V_4V_e, यहि X_e, कहु Z_1 • जाल] Σ, लाज EM_1V_4, *om.* M_5 • परें कहौ] B_1J_1, परे कहु B_6CZ_1, परै कहौ $B_9S_2S_7M_1V_4X_e$, की साज तौ G_eṬ$_e$, जकरे कहा M_5, परैं कहि S_1, की साज को $Ś_e$, परै नह U, परे कहौ V_e • कोचु की] $B_1B_6B_9CJ_1M_1S_1V_4V_eZ_1$, धोइ चुकी G_e, हो चुकी M_5, को सुषी S_2S_7, धोय चुकी $Ś_e$, धो चुकी Ṭ$_e$, को चुक U, कै चुकी X_e • री] Σ, जू B_9

123.2 कोचु var. [koca-] m. 1. shyness; 2. fear; को चुकी Br. (tell me, having been trapped) who made a mistake? कहु कोचु की var. tell me what modesty (is there)? चुकना [*cukk-] v.i. 1. to be adjusted (as a dispute); 2. (here:) to be released (from the trap).

कहि ठाकुर, सो रस रीति रंगी, करि प्रीति पतिव्रत खो चुकी री।
अब नेकी-बदी, जो बदी हुती भाल मैं, होनी हुती सु तौ हो चुकी री॥ Ś123॥

*बाहर लौं न कढै कबहूँ, कढि देहरी लौं बिछिया झमकावै।
आंचल ओट दै चोट करै, अरु ओट अटारी के चंचल गावै।
एक पलौ बिसरै न कबौं, अरु कोटि कला करि जी ललचावै।
आँखिन आवै, हियै लगि जावै, पै प्यारी परोसिन हाथ न आवै॥ Ś124॥

हौं ही समै लखि कै उत आई, कहौ करिहौं सब रावरे जी को।

---

124 Granthāvalī 141, Ṭhasak 'Jīvancarit' ($Ṭ_e^j$) pp. 20-21. Ṭhākur's poetic signature is missing from this quatrain. In $Ṭ_e^j$ it is presented as a poem by the 'rītimukt' Ṭhākur. 125 Granthāvalī 87, Ṭhasak 163.

123.3 कहि] $B_1^{pc}B_6B_9J_1SV_4Z_1$, *om.* B_1^{ac}, कबि $GEM_5V_eX_e$, कह CK_1, कहै M_1, कहैं M_4, कब Ṭ, ⟨का⟩हि U • सो रस] K_1**S**, या रस $CG^{pc}V_e$, काम न **E**, मै इह B_6, या सबरे B_9, गाय कहा कहियै B_1, या रस * G^{ac}, को कुल J_1, को अब M_1U, सों यह M_4, की अप॰ M_5, के संग Ṭ, तौ यह V_4, यों रस X_e, को सुभ Z_1 • रीति] $B_6J_1V_eX_e$, *om.* B_1, ब्रज B_9, रीत $CK_1M_1M_5$**S**UZ_1, या **E**, रीती G, प्रीत M_4Ṭ, रंग V_4 • रंगी] B_6M_4**S**V_eX_e, *om.* B_1, मै B_9, रंगे CGJ_1K_1, सबको **E**, चलै $M_1M_5UZ_1$, करी Ṭ, ग्यौ (unm.) V_4^{ac}, रग्यौ V_4^{pc} • करि प्रीति] $B_1B_6B_9$**E**J_1**S**, करि प्रीत CM_4, कर प्रीत $M_1ṬZ_1$, सब भाति×न× G, पत प्रित K_1, परपीर M_5, कर प्रा (unm.) U, मै प्रेम (unm.) V_4, परतीति V_e, सब भांति X_e • पतिव्रत] B_1B_6C**E**$J_1M_1V_4V_eX_eZ_1$, पतीवृत $B_9M_5S_2$Ṭ, पतवतां K_1, पति×**×ब्रत M_4, पति⟨वृ⟩ (unm.) S_1^{ac}, पत⟨वृ⟩ (unm.) S_1^{pc}, पतीब्रिति S_7, पतवृत U • खो] Σ, खोइ $G_eŚ_e$, होइ K_1 • चुकी] Σ, चुक ṬU • री] Σ, जू B_9 **123.4** अब] J_1M_5**S**U, यह B_1B_6, सखी C, अरी GV_eX_e, *om.* (unm.) B_9**E**$K_1M_1ṬV_4Z_1^{ac}$, अली M_4, --- Z_1^{pc} • नेकी-बदी] Σ, होनी हुती K_1, नीकी बदी V_4 • जो बदी हुती] B_6CGJ_1**S**V_eX_e, जु बदी ⟨हु/फु⟩ती B_1, जो लिखी हुती $B_9G_eM_4ṬṬ_eZ_1$, जो ⟨ली⟩षी रही K_1, लिषी हुंती (unm.) M_1, सु लिषी जुलि×षी× M_5, हुती जो लिखी $Ś_e$, जु लेखा सब भाल U, सो लिषी हुती V_4 • भाल मैं होनी हुती] V_4^{pc}Σ, *om.* (unm.) V_4^{ac} • भाल] Σ, भाग B_9, पाट M_5 • मैं] B_1**E**$J_1M_1M_4S_1S_2ṬUV_eX_e$, मै $B_6B_9GK_1M_5S_7Z_1$, पै C • होनी हुती] B_1B_6C**E**$J_1M_4M_5S_1S_7ṬUV_eX_e$, हौनी हती B_9S_2, होनि हूति G, होनी र⟨ई/ही⟩ K_1, हुनी हुती M_1, जो हौनै हती Z_1 • सु] B_1B_9CG**E**$J_1S_1S_2S_7^{pc}V_4V_e$, जौ B_6, सौ $K_1M_1M_4M_5S_7^{ac}ṬUX_eZ_1$ • हो] $B_1B_6CGJ_1M_1M_4M_5S_1S_2S_7ṬV_4V_eZ_1$, है B_9, होइ G_eK_1, होय $Ś_eṬ_e$, ह्वै X_e • चुकी] Σ, चुक ṬU • री] Σ, जू B_9

123.3 रंगे var. [raṅga-] v.i. perf. obl. Br. (used as an adv.) coloured. **123.4** नेकी [P] f. goodness, virtue; बदी [P] f. evil; misfortune; बद- [cf. vadati] reg. v.t. to write. **124.1** कढना [cf. *kaḍḍhati] v.i. to come out; बिछिया [vṛścika-] 'scorpion' f. a ring worn on the big toe by married women; झमकावै v.caus. pres. Br. makes it glitter (i.e. gives a sign). **124.2** ओट दै Br. hiding behind. **124.3** बिसर- [vismarati] reg. v.t. forget. **124.4** हियै लगि Br. up to the heart; हाथ में आना idiom. to be acquired.

बारही बार न ऐये इतै, यह मेरौ कछू है परोस न नीको।
ठाकुर, चाह भरे नितही तुम हार लै आवत मौलसिरी को।
कोऊ कहूँ लखि लेय जौ याहि, तौ होय, लला, मोहिं लील को टीको॥ Ś125॥

आपने रूप गुमान छकी अपने रँग के रँग मैं रँगती है।
देखि प्रबीनता रीझत नाहिन, दीनता देख हिंयै डगती है।
ठाकुर ताको बिचार यहै अपने हिंय की उकतैं जकती है।
जे बतिया न कहै मन की ते, कहौ, वै कबै छतियां लगती है॥ Ś126॥

*कैइक बेर कह्यो नित ऐहै, पै आए नहीं, तिहि त्रास भरैये।

---

126 Sudhāsar [S_6 f. 139v (39/897), S_7 f. 97v (1/947)]. The Sudhāsar presents this poem within the description of the 'upapati' S_6 introduces this poem as 'nāikā kī ukti man sau' a heroine's words to herself. S_7 introduces the savaiyā as 'nāik kī ukti man sau' a lover's words to himself. Since this is a description of a heroine, it is more natural to take the poem as the words of a man. 127 Bharatpur1 f. 160v-1r (68), Granthāvalī B19, Sudhāsar [S_1 f. 263rv (4), S_3 f. 139r (84), S_4 f. 63r (91), S_7 f. 190v (4)], Ṭhākur-satsaī (Ṭ) f. 2r (14), Vrindaban1 f. 12r (11/76). The Sudhāsar presents this poem in the 'Brajrasrīti' section as part of the 'gocāraṇ-līlā' (the divine sport of grazing the cows) subsection.

126.1 है] S_7, हैं S_6 **126.2** देखि] S_6, देख S_7 • दीनता] S_6, दीनन S_7 • देखि] S_6, देख S_7 • है] S_7, हैं S_6 **126.3** ताको] S_7, तांकै S_6 • जकती] S_6, जगती S_7 • है] S_7, हैं S_6 **126.4** ते] $S_6S_7^{ac}$, ने S_7^{pc} • है] *conj.* हैं S_6, *om.* (unm.) S_7 **127.1** कैइक] $B_1G_e S_1S_3S_7V_1$, कैईक S_4, कईयक (unm.) Ṭ • बेर] B_1G_eṬV_1, बार **S** • नित] $B_1^{pc}G_eS_1S_3S_7V_1$, नि (unm.) B_1^{ac}, तित S_4Ṭ • ऐहै पै] $B_1^{ac}S_3S_4S_7$, आहौ पै B_1^{pc}, आँहैं पै S_1, आइये पै G_e, आइहै Ṭ, आहैयै V_1 • तिहि] $B_1G_eV_1$, तिह S_1, तह $S_3S_4S_7$, निह Ṭ • त्रास] B_1SṬ, बास V_1, बासु G_e • भरैये] S_3, दुरैयै G_eV_1, भरै पैं S_4, डरेंयै $B_1S_1S_7$Ṭ

125.3 **मौलसिरी** [cf. bakula-] f. bullet wood (mimusops elengi) (a large evergreen tree whose cream-coloured flower is used in making perfumes). **125.4** **लील** [cf. nīla-] reg. adj. blue, dark; **काले रंग का टीका** idiom. bad repute. **126.2** **डगना** [cf. H ḍag] v.i. 1. to move; 2. fig. to be moved. **126.3** **उकत** (**उक्ति**) [S] reg. f. matter(s); **जकना** 1. v.i. to chatter, to talk nonsense; 2. v.t. to say. **126.4** **वै** [S] emph. Br. encl. indeed. **127.1** **कैयक बेर** interr. how many times? **नित** [nitya-] Br. adv. every day; **बास** var. [vāsa-] Br. m. house; **त्रास** [S] m. suffering; **भरैयै** var. [bharati] v.t. (either Br. pass. used for active or perf. reg. emph.) I am filled (with that pain); **दुरैयै** apa. [dūra-] reg. v.i. you lie hidden.

भागिन भेंट भई, मनमोहन, तातें कुबीध सुबीध जनैये।
ठाकुर, गायैं फिरैं बिडरी, सुनियै बिनती, ए समेटि चरैये।
बाँधन छोरन दोहन आहैं दुहूँ बिरियाँ किरिया करि जैये॥ Ś127॥

*न्यौते गए घर के सिगरे, सो बेरामि को ब्याज कै आजु रही मैं।
ठाकुर, है बहिरी इक दासी, सो राखी बरोठे बिचारि कै जी मैं।
आए भले खिरकी मग ह्वै, अस आइबो चाहत ही हुती ही मैं।
आजु निसा भरि, प्यारे, निसा भरि कीजिये, लालन, केलि खुसी मैं॥ Ś128॥

---

128 Sundarītilak (C_e) 182, Granthāvalī B20, Raskusumākar (R_e) 301, Ṭhasak 'Jīvancarit' (Ṭ$_e^j$) p. 3, Bābūramdīn: Sundarītilak (U_e) 369. The Raskusumākar takes the poem as an example of the 'muditā' (delighted) heroine explaining that a heroine is 'delighted' when her desire for another man is suddenly fulfilled.

127.2 भागिन] $B_1^{pc}\Sigma$, भागि⟨न⟩ B_1^{ac} • भेंट] Σ, भेंटि S_4 • मनमोहन] $B_1^{pc}\Sigma$, मनमोह (unm.) B_1^{ac} • तातें] $B_1G_eV_1$, याते **S**Ṭ • कुबीध सुबीध] $B_1S_1S_4S_7$, कुबुध्ध सुबुध्ध G_e, कुबीधि सुबीधि S_3, कुबीध सु तीज Ṭ, कुबुध (unm.) V_1 • जनैयै] B_1, जतैयै G_eV_1, सुनैये] $S_1S_3S_7$, सुनै पै S_4, जितईए Ṭ **127.3** गायैं] $B_1G_eS_1S_4V_1$, गायो S_3S_7, गाइ Ṭ • फिरैं] $B_1G_eS_1V_1$, फिरै $S_3S_4S_7$Ṭ • सुनियै] Σ, सुनीए Ṭ • समेटि] $B_1G_eS_4$, समेट $S_1S_3S_7$ṬV_1 **127.4** आँहैं] B_1**S**ṬV_1, आइ G_e • किरियां] B_1**S**Ṭ, किरपा G_e, किपा (unm.) V_1 • करि] $B_1G_eS_1V_1$, कर $S_3S_4S_7$Ṭ **128.1** सो] C_e**E**U_e, सु R_e • बेरामी] **E**R_e, बिरामी C_e, बीरामी U_e • आजु] **E**R_eU_e, आज C_e • मैं] **E**C_eU_e, मै R_e **128.2** इक] **E**, एक $C_eR_eU_e$ • बरोठे] **E**R_eU_e, बरोठ C_e • मैं] **E**C_eU_e, मै R_e **128.3** अस] **E**, यह $C_eR_eU_e$ • आइबो] **E**R_eU_e, आइबी C_e • चाहत ही] **E**, चहति ही C_eU_e, चाहतैइ R_e • मैं] **E**C_eU_e, मै R_e **128.4** आजु निसा भरि] C_eG_e, आजु निसा भर Ṭ$_e^j$ • लालन] C_e**E**U_e, कान्हर R_e • मैं] **E**C_eU_e, मै R_e

---

127.2 भागन [bhāgya-] Br. m. pl. obl. (used as an adv.) by chance; तातें कुबुध्ध सुबुध्ध जतैयै var. Br. then for this reason present your dullness as intelligence; बीधना (बिंधना) [*vindhati] v.i. to be engrossed, caught; बीध [cf. H bīdhnā] poet. f. entanglement (KL, RSh); सु तीज apa. ? good Tīj festival; जताना var. [jñapta-, jānāti] v.t. to tell. **127.3** बिडर- [vidārayati] Br. v.i. to scatter; गायैं फिरैं बिडरी Br. my cows go around scattered. **127.4** बाँधन छोरन दोहन Br. to bind, to release and to milk (the cows); आहैं (हैं) Bund. v.i. should be (bound, released and milked); आइ जैयै (आ जाइये) var. v.i. imp. Br. come; बिरियाँ [velā-, H bār] reg. f. (pl.) times; किरिया (क्रिया) [S] reg. f. activity. **128.1** न्योता [nimantra-] m. invitation, feast; सो conj. therefore; बेरामी [H bīmārī x P be-ārāmī] f. sickness; ब्याज [vyāja-] m. pretext. **128.2** बहरा [badhira-] adj. deaf; बरोठा [dvārakoṣṭhaka-] Br. m. porchway. **128.4** निशा [P niśān] m. assurance; निसा भरि adv. assuredly, without anxiety.

रोज न आइयै जू, मनमोहन, तौ यह निज मतौ सुनि लीजै।
प्रान हमारे तुम्हारे अधीन, तुम्हैं बिन देखें न कैसे हूँ जीजै।
ठाकुर, लाल पियारे, सुनौ, इतनी बिनती, सुनि चित्त मैं दीजै।
आतरैं, तीसरे, पाँचएँ, सातएँ, आठएँ, पाखऐ आइबो कीजै॥ Ś129॥

रोज न आईऐ जू, मनमोहन, इतनी बिनती हमरी सुन लीजै।
तूमरे तो कुल कान नही, हमरी कुल कांनहि लोक पतीजै।
ठाकुर ऐ घर चौचंद के डर यांते घर बाहर पांवन दीजै।
आंतरे, दूसरे, तीसरे, सांतै, पांचै आवन कीजै॥ Ś130॥

*एरी मेरी बीर, कंत कौन पै कमान जाइ,
राजन की मतिऊ पै चलै ना उपाव री।
तन धन छीन भयौ, मनुआ मलीन भयौ,
मनसा बिकल, कल पावत न बावरी।

---

129 Sundarī-tilak (C_e) 85, Granthāvalī 126, Marwar5 f. 25rv (33); Śatak 4, Sudhāsar [S_2 12v (14), S_7 47v (49/451)], Ṭ f. 5rv (45), Ṭhasak 48. The variants of C_e, **E** and M_5 try to eliminate the repetition of 'sun-' in the third line. 130 Ṭhākur-satsaī (Ṭ) f. 5rv (45). This savaiya is a variant on the previous one. 131 Granthāvalī 83, Ṭhasak 146, Śatak 93.

129.1 रोज] Σ, राज M_5 • आइयै] C_e**E**S_2, आये M_5^{ac}, आईये $M_5^{pc}S_7$ • जू] **S**, जौ Σ • निज] **S**, नेक Σ • सुनि] **S**, सुन Σ • लीजै] Σ, लीजिये **E** **129.2** प्रान] **ES**, नैन C_eM_5 • तुम्हारे] **E**, तिहारे C_e, तीयारे M_5, तुमै S_2, तुमारे S_7 • अधीन] Σ, बसै C_eM_5 • तुम्हैं] **E**S_2, सो कहौ C_eM_5, तुमै S_7 • न] **S**, सु Σ • हूं] **S**, कै Σ • जीजै] Σ, जीजिये **E** **129.3** ठाकुर] Σ, ठा⟨म्कु⟩र M_5 • लाल पियारे] C_e**S**, लालन प्यारे **E**, बाल पि⟨या⟩रे M_5 • सुनौ] C_e**E**S_2, सुनौं M_5S_7 • इतनी] *conj.*, बिनती C_e**E**M_5, यतनी S_2, यितनी S_7 • बिनती] **S**, इतनी C_e**E**, ईतनी M_5 • सुनि] **S**, पै अहो C_e**E**M_5 • चित्त मैं] **S**, चित C_e**E**, चीत M_5 • दीजै] C_eM_5**S**, दीजिये **E** **129.4** आतरैं] **S**, दूसरे C_e**E**, दुसरे (unm.) M_5 • तीसरे] C_e**E**, तिसरे (unm.) M_5, दूसरैं **S** • पाखऐ] S_7, तौ भलो **E**, तो भला C_eM_5, षांषए S_2 • कीजै] Σ, कीजिये **E** **130.1** इतनी] *em.*, इती (unm.) Ṭ **130.2** हमरी] *em.* ह हमरी (dittography) Ṭ **130.3** यांते] (unm.) Ṭ **130.4** सांतै पांचै] (unm.) Ṭ **131.1** मतिऊ पै] G_eṬ$_e$, मति ऊपै Ś$_e$

129.1 रोज न आइयै जौ Br. if you do not come every day; नेक 1. [? naika-] Br. adv. just; 2. [P] adj. good; मतौ [mati-] Br. m. (to this) advice. **129.2** न कैसे हूं जीजै Br. I cannot live at all. **129.4** आतरैं [antara-] reg. adj. second; पाखए [pakṣa] reg. m. obl. within a fortnight; षांषए apa. **130.2** तूमरे (तुम्हारे लिए) reg. for you; लोक पतीजै Br. people trust (in my family honour); **131.1** कंत [S] m. husband; कौन पै कमान जाइ Br. to whom should he go to earn money? राजन... उपाव Br. not even the kings' intelligence can find a solution.

ठाकुर कहत, या जहान मैं जबुर फैली, 3
मैली भई मति, कछु जतन बताव री।
खैबे कौं जु सौंह राखी, कैबे कौं सु पाप राख्यौ, 4
लैबे कौं अजस अरु दैबे कौं सु लावरी॥ Ś131॥

सामान्या

*आवै चली गजचाल सों बाल, बिसाल सरूप की रासि तुखी सी।
ओज-मनोज की मोज भरो तन, जानि परै सब भाँति पुखी सी। 2
ठाकुर, को उपमा बरनै, सब ओर निहारत एक रुखी सी।
राखै खुसी मन यारन के जजमानिनी बानिनी चंदमुखी सी॥ Ś132॥ 4

परकीया चेतावनी

बुरो मानती जो सिख देत, भटू, दुख पायती बात सुनाइबे में।
कही जात है, देखि, कुरीति, कछू समझैगी न जो समुझाइबे में। 2

---

132 Granthāvalī 142, Ṭhasak 'Jīvancarit' ($Ṭ_e^j$) p. 21. 133 Sundarī-tilak (C_e) 163, Granthāvalī 125, Rasikvinod (O_e) 366, Sudhāsar [S_3 75v (100), S_7 109r (10/1049)], Ṭhasak 162. The Sudhāsar (S_7) includes this poem into the 'śikṣā' (advice) subsection of the 'caturkarma sakhīn ke' (the four activities of a companion) section.

131.3 जबुर] $G_eṬ_e$, जबर $Ś_e$ **131.4** खैबे कौं] $G_eŚ_e$, खैबे कौ $Ṭ_e$ • सौंह] G_e, सौंहि $Ś_eṬ_e$ • कैबे कौं] $G_eŚ_e$, कैबे कौ $Ṭ_e$ • दैबे कौं] G_e, दैबे को $Ś_eṬ_e$ **133.1** मानती] **S**, मानतीं Σ • पायती] **S**, पावतीं Σ • बात सुनाइबे] Σ, जो समुझाइबे **E** • **133.2** जात है] **S**, जायगी Σ • देखि] Σ, देख **S** • कुरीति] C_e**E**, कुरीत O_e**S** • समझैगी] **S**, समझौगी Σ • जो समुझाइबे] Σ, बात बुझाइबे **E**

131.3 जबुर [A jabr] m. (here f.) 1. injustice; 2. compulsion. **131.4** सौंह f. [śapatha-] oath; शपथ खाना idiom. to take an oath; राख- [rakṣ-] v.t. to keep; to possess; लावरी (लबाड़ी) [cf. *labha-] f. lie, falsehood (cf. H 'labṛe ke ghar lobhī kā upavās'); लाव [lagana-] m. love. **132.1** तुख- [tuṣṭa-] Br. adj. 1. (?) proud (of her beauty); 2. satisfied (with me); सरूप [surūpa-] adj. attractiveness. **132.2** ओज [S] m. brilliance (of love); मोज [A] f. wave; पुख- [puṣṭa-] adj. nourished, healthy. **132.3** एक-रुखी सी (when she looks at every one) with the same emotion. **132.4** जजमानिनी [yajamāna-] reg. adj. offering donation (to the the priests) (and also to her lovers by showing her face); बानिन [cf. H baniyā-] f. merchant's wife. **133.1** बुरो... देत Br. if I teach you, you take it bad. **133.2** कुरीति [S] f. (your) bad ways ; बुझा- var. [budhyate] Br. v.t. to explain.

कहा लेउगी हाथ पराये बिके, कहि ठाकुर, लोग हँसाइबे में।
हमैं को गनै, कासों परोजन है बुनिबे में न बीन बजाइबे में॥ Ś133॥

चबाव

कहि आई इहाँ की कुरीति लखें, नित कौ सुख बात चलाइबे मैं।
अब पाँच की सात मिलाइबौ जू, इत लैहो कहा खिसियाइबे मैं।
कहि ठाकुर, राम के राज करौ, दुख पवती हौ समझाइबे मैं।
हमैं का कहिबे सौं परोजन है बुनिबे मैं न बीन बजाइबे में॥ Ś134॥

---

134 Bharatpur1 f. 160v (65), Sundarītilak (C_e) 164, Datiya2 f. 8r (68), Granthāvalī 165, Śatak 41, Ṭhasak 183, Vrindaban1 f. 4r (8/21), Yājñik.

133.3 कहा] Σ, कहां S_7 • लेउगी] Σ, पाओगी **E** • पराये बिके] Σ, परायवे कौ S_3 • कहि] $C_eO_eS_7$, कह $\mathbf{E}S_3$ **133.4** गनै] $\mathbf{E}O_eS_3$, गनौ C_e • परोजन] Σ, प्रयोजन C_e • बुनिबे] Σ, बनिबे G_e • न बीन] $\mathbf{E}O_eS_3$, न बीज C_e, नहीन S_7 • बजाइबे] $\mathbf{E}O_e$, बनाइबे C_eS_3, बुनाय (unrh.) S_7 **134.1** आई] Σ, आवत **E** • इहाँ] Σ, ह्याँ **E** • की] Σ, ×की× की D_2 • कुरीति] $B_1C_eV_1$, कुरीत $D_2\mathbf{E}$ • लखें] Σ, ⟨ले⟩खें $Ṭ_e$ • नित] $B_1D_2V_1Y_e$, न तौ **E**, सो C_e • कौ] $B_1V_1Y_e$, कहा C_e, का $D_2\mathbf{E}$ • सुख] Σ, इती **E** **134.2** अब] $B_1D_2V_1Y_e$, तुम C_eG_e, हम $Ṭ_e$ • की] Σ, कि C_e • मिलाइबौ जू] V_1Y_e, लगाइबौ जू B_1, लगावौ भले G_e, मिलाबहु जू D_2, मिलाइ कहौ C_e, सुनाइहैं जू $Ṭ_e$ • इत] $B_1D_2C_eV_1Y_e$, भला G_e, हहा $Ṭ_e$ • लैहौ] $B_1^{pc}D_2C_eṬ_eV_1$, लै⟨बो⟩ B_1^{ac}, पैहो G_e **134.3** कहि] Σ, कवि **E** • राम के राज करौ] Σ, कौन सों का कहिये C_e • हौ] Σ, जौ **E** • समझाइबे] Σ, समुझाइबे C_e **134.4** हमैं का] B_1, हमैं **E**, हम से D_2, परो C_e, हम सो V_1, हम कौ Y_e • कहिबे] $B_1D_2V_1Y_e$, बात कहे **E**, कौन C_e • सौं] $B_1D_2V_1Y_e$, को **E**, *om.* C_e • परोजन] $B_1D_2^{pc}V_1G_e$, परोज (unm.) D_2, प्रयोजन $C_eṬ_e$ • है] $B_1V_1Y_e$, का $D_2\mathbf{E}$, है जू हमैं C_e • बुनिबे] $B_1C_e\mathbf{E}$, बुनबे D_2V_1 • मैं] Σ, *om.* (unm.) B_1V_1 • बीन] $D_2\mathbf{E}V_1Y_e$, हीन B_1, बीज C_e • बजाइबे] $B_1D_2\mathbf{E}V_1$, बनाइबे C_e

---

133.3 हाथ पराये बिके (making people laugh) by being sold into another man's hand; परा- var. [palāyana-] Av. Br. v.i. to run away, to escape; परायवे कौ var. Br. (what comes to your hand) by running away? **133.4** हमैं को गनै Br. idiom. who takes me into account; परोजन [prayojana-] m. need, use; कासों परोजन है Br. am I useful for anyone? बुनिबे [*vunāti] v.t. inf. obl. Br. (I am neither in) weaving (nor in playing the vina) (i.e. I am useful neither in gross nor in delicate activities); बीन बनाय apa. making a Vina; **134.1** कहि आई reg. I have told; न तौ var. conj. otherwise; नित का ... मैं var. Br. what is continuous talking good for? **134.2** पाँच-सात करना idiom. to blame; भले var. adv. it's alright (if you blame me); खिसियाना [*khiss-] v.i. to grind the teeth in anger. **134.3** राम के राज करो idiom. enjoy yourself; समझाइबे मैं Br. by my teaching. **134.4** परोजन [prayojana-] m. 1. need, use; 2. purpose; कासों परोजन है Br. am I useful for anyone (in weaving or in music)? बुनिबे [*vunāti] Br. v.t. inf. to weave.

कहते न बनै कछु एकहूँ घाँ सब की सब तैहू बनै सहते।
घर बाहर घैर उठ्यो, री भटू, मनमोहन लालन के चहते।
कहि ठाकुर, हाथ चलै गहियै, यह जीभ चलै न बनै गहते।
सखि, या नँदगाँव को चौचँद, री, दिखते ही बनै, न बनै कहते॥ Ś135॥

*कहिबे सुनिबे की कछु न इहां, न लटी भली को दुख पावने है।
इनकी मरजी मैं सदां रहियै अपने जिय कौ समझावने है।

---

135 Bharatpur1 f. 163v (85), Granthāvalī 164, Sudhāsar [S$_2$ f. 12r (16/12), S$_7$ f. 46v (38/440)], Ṭhasak 46, Vrindaban1 f. 7v (42), Yājñik. 136 Sundarītilak (C$_e$) 306, Granthāvalī 166, Kālidās-Hajārā (H$_e$) 323, Sudhāsar [S$_1$ f. 63r (16), S$_7$ f. 45r (20/422)], Śatak 25, Ṭhākur-satsaī (Ṭ) f. 1v (7), Ṭhasak 17, Vrindaban1 f. 2rv (10/10), Vrindaban2 f. 69r, Yājñik. Vrindaban1 writes 'parikrayā' (parakiyā, adulterous woman) at the heading of this quatrain. The Sudhāsar (S$_1$) presents this poem within the 'ūḍhā parakiyā' section and introduces it as 'nāikā kī ukti sakhī prata' (the heroine's words towards a friend).

135.1 कहते] **ES**, कहि तें B$_1$, कहैते V$_1$ • बनै] Σ, बनैं B$_1$S$_7$ • कछु] **S**V$_1$Y$_e$, कछू B$_1$, कछुवे **E** • एकहू घां] B$_1$V$_1$Y$_e$, चहुँघाँ **E**, एकहीं घां **S** • तैंहूं] B$_1$V$_1$Y$_e$, भाँति **E**, हू ते **S** • बनै] Σ, बनैं B$_1$ • सहते] **ES**$_2$, सहतैं B$_1$, सहैते V$_1$ **135.2** बाहिर] B$_1$**ES**, बाहरि V$_1$ • घैर] B$_1$**S**, घैरु **E**, घेरि V$_1$ • उठ्यौ] B$_1$**S**, उठो **E**, रह्यौ V$_1$ • चहते] Σ, चहतैं B$_1$ **135.3** कहि] B$_1$G$_e$**S**V$_1$, कह Ṭ$_e$V$_1$ • यह] S$_2$V$_1$Y$_e$, इह B$_1$, अरी **E** • जीभ] Σ, जीव **S** • गहते] Σ, गहतैं B$_1$ **135.4** नँदगाँव] **E**, नंदगाउ B$_1$, नंदगाम **S**V$_1$ • चौचद] B$_1$V$_1$Y$_e$, कौतुक **ES** • दिखते] **S**V$_1$Y$_e$, दिषतैं B$_1$, लखते **E** • कहते] Σ, कहतैं B$_1$ **136.1** कहिबे... इहां] C$_e$**ES**, कहियै जु कहा कहिबे की नहीं H$_e$V$_2$, कहा कहीए परधीन की बात Ṭ • न इहां] C$_e$S$_1$V$_1$Y$_e$, नहियाँ G$_e$Ṭ$_e$, न यिहां S$_7$, नहीं आन Ś$_e$ • न] C$_e$S$_1$V$_1$Y$_e$, *om.* **E**, सु Ṭ • लटी] C$_e$H$_e$**S**Ś$_e$V$_1$, लटी औ G$_e$Ṭ$_e$, बुरी Ṭ, टी (unm.) V$_2$, लही Y$_e$ • पावने] **ES**$_1$, पावनौ C$_e$H$_e$S$_7$V$_1$V$_2$Y$_e$ • है] Σ, हैं V$_2$ **136.2** इनकी] G$_e$H$_e$**S**Ṭ$_e$V$_1$V$_2$, उनकी तो सबै C$_e$, उनकी Ś$_e$Ṭ • मरजी] Σ, सब की **S** • मै सदां रहियै] V$_1$Y$_e$, करिकै C$_e$, की सबै करने **E**, की सबै करनी H$_e$V$_2$, की सभै करनी Ṭ, मरजी करिकैं **S** • जिय] H$_e$V$_1$V$_2$Y$_e$, मन C$_e$**ES**, जीय Ṭ • समझावने] **ES**$_1$, समझावनौ C$_e$S$_7$ṬV$_1$Y$_e$, समझामनौ H$_e$V$_2$ • है] Σ, हैं V$_2$

135.1 एकहूँ घां Br. (I cannot defend myself) in one direction; तैहू (तेह) [tejas] m. (here f.) reg. anger; vehemence; सब... सहते Br. I suffer all the anger of all people; चहुँघाँ सब की सब भाँति var. Br. all kinds of censure from everyone and from everywhere. **135.2** घैर m. slander; के चहते (चाहने पर) Br. because I love. **135.3** हाथ चलें गहियै when hands move, they can be stopped. **135.4** लख- [lakṣyate] Br. v.t. to see. **136.1** लट- [cf. H ulṭā] adj. bad; पावने v.t. inf. Bund. to get. **136.2** मरजी [A marẓī] f. 1. pleasure, wish; choice; 2. (here:) rule, control (KL); की सबै करनी var. one should do all (she wishes) (H karnī hai).

कहि ठाकुर, लाल के देखिबे के लियै मंत्र यही उर ल्यावने है।
इन चौचँदहाइन में बसिकै समयौ यह, बीर, बरावने है॥ Ś136॥

का कहियै, कोऊ पीरकौ नाहिनै, यातैं हिये की जनैयतु नाहीं।
भागन भेंट जो होइ, भटू, तौ घरीक बिलोकैं अघैयतु नाहीं।

---

137 Bharatpur1 f. 153r (21), Granthāvalī 167, Kālidās-Hajārā (H$_e$) 326, Jaipur1 f. 1v (3), Marwar4 f. 48v (62/13), Sudhāsar [S$_1$ f. 231v-2r, S$_2$ ff. 52v-53r (-/54), S$_3$ f. 113rv (133), S$_7$ f. 174r (4/1657)], Ṭhākur-satsaī (Ṭ) f. 1r (4), Śatak 7, Ṭhasak 74, Vrindaban2 ff. 70v-71r. The Sudhāsar (S$_1$ and S$_7$) presents this poem as an example of 'cintā daśā varṇan' (description of the state of anxiety).

136.3 कहि] H$_e$SV$_1$V$_2$Y$_e$, कबि C$_e$E, कह Ṭ • लाल... ठहरावनौ] Σ, चार चवैयन के डर नीची कर नार निवाहनौ Ṭ • लाल] EH$_e$SV$_2$, काम C$_e$, कान्ह V$_1$Y$_e$ • के देखिबे] Σ, निकासिबे C$_e$ • के लियै] H$_e$S$_7$V$_1$V$_2$Y$_e$, कौं अब C$_e$E, के लयैं S$_1$ • यही] C$_e$SV$_1$Y$_e$, कोई E, इही H$_e$V$_2$ • उर ल्यावने] ES$_1$, ठहरावनौ C$_e$S$_7$V$_1$Y$_e$, ठहरामनौ H$_e$V$_2$ • है] Σ, हैं V$_2$ **136.4** इन... बसिकै] Σ, --- Ṭ • इन] Σ, इनि H$_e$V$_2$ • चौचंदहाइन] Σ, चौंचदआइन V$_2$ • में] Σ, सौं S$_7$ • बसिकै] H$_e$V$_1$V$_2^{pc}$Y$_e$, परिकै C$_e$E, मिलकैं S$_1$S$_7$V$_2^{ac}$ • यह] EH$_e$C$_e$SṬV$_2$, बर V$_1$Y$_e$ • बरावने] ES$_1$, बरावनौ C$_e$S$_7$, बिरावनो Ṭ, बितावनौ V$_1$Y$_e$, बितामनौ H$_e$V$_2$ • है] Σ, हैं V$_2$ **137.1** का] B$_1$EJ$_1$M$_4$S, कहा (unm.) H$_e$ṬV$_2$ • कोऊ] Σ, कोई E, कोउ M$_4$ • पीरकौ B$_1$SṬ, पीरक EJ$_1$M$_4$V$_2$, पीर कूं H$_e$ • नाहिनै] B$_1$EH$_e$J$_1$M$_4$S$_1$Ṭ, नाहि है S$_2$, नाह है S$_3$S$_7$, नाहिन V$_2$ • यातैं] B$_1$M$_4$S$_1$S$_3$S$_7$ṬV$_2$, तातें EJ$_1$, जानैं H$_e$, ⟨या/पा⟩ते S$_2$ • हिये] Σ, हिले S$_2$ • जनैयतु] B$_1$, जतैयत E, सुनैयतु H$_e$, जतैयतु J$_1$, सुनैयति M$_4$, सुनैयत S$_1$S$_3$S$_7$, सुनैयति S$_2$, बतईयत (unm.) Ṭ, सनैयति V$_2$ **137.2** भागन] B$_1$EH$_e$J$_1$S$_1$S$_3$S$_7$V$_2$, भागिनि M$_4$, भागीन S$_2$, भागै (unm.) Ṭ • जो होइ] B$_1$, भई EṬ, ह्वै जाति H$_e$M$_4$S$_2$V$_2$, ⟨सु/×ग×⟩जौ J$_1$, जौ हो S$_1$, ह्वै जात S$_3$S$_7$ • भटू] H$_e$M$_4$S$_2$S$_3$S$_7$V$_2$, कहू B$_1$, कबहूँ E, होय कबूं J$_1$, इकहूँ S$_1$, जौ कहू Ṭ • तौ] B$_1$H$_e$J$_1$S$_1$ṬV$_2$, सु E, तौ×*× M$_4$, सौ S$_2$S$_3$S$_7$ • घरीक] B$_1$J$_1$M$_4$S$_1$S$_2$Ṭ, घरीकु EH$_e$V$_2$, घरी को S$_3$ • बिलोकैं] B$_1$EH$_e$M$_4$V$_2$, बिलोकि J$_1$S$_1$S$_2$, बिलोक S$_3$S$_7$Ṭ • अघैयतु] B$_1$H$_e$J$_1$S$_2$S$_7$V$_2$, अघैयत EM$_4$S$_1$, अघैयति S$_3$, अघईयत (unm.) Ṭ

136.3 मंत्र [S] m. counsel; ठहराना [H ṭhaharnā] v.t. 1. to establish; 2. (advice) to be followed; चार var. [S] m. spy; नार var. f. neck (BHK); चार... निवाहनौ है var. Br. fearing spies and slanderers we have to bow our necks and manage somehow. **136.4** चौचंद m. 1. slander; 2. wrangle; चौचंदहाई 1. gossiper, 2. troublemaker; समयौ [samaya-] m. (acc.) reg. time; बर (बल) [S] Br. m. 'force' 1. obl. by force (cf. H balāt); 2. acc. (the time and the) tyranny; बरा- [cf. Av. Br. bār- 'to forbid'] Av. Br. v.t. 1. to hold oneself aloof from; 2. to avoid. **137.1** पीरकौ (पीरक भी) Br. (there is not) even (any) sympathiser; पीरक var. [cf. S pīḍā-] m. sympathiser (cf. Sūrsāgar 1-112); जता- var. [jñāpta-, jānāti] Av. Br. v.t. to tell. **137.2** भागन [bhāgya-] m. (pl. Br. obl.) by chance; अघाना [āghrāpayati] v.i. to be satisfied.

ठाकुर, वा घर चौचँद के डर, यातें घरी घरी जैयतु नाहीं।
भेंटन पैयत कैसे तिन्हें, जिन्हें आँखिन देखन पैयतु नाहीं॥ Ś137॥ 4

कैसी करौं, कासों कहौं, जानत न कोऊ भेद, 1
भेद जानिबे की करी कोटि चतुराई मैं।
साँची ह्वै कै, सौंह दैकै, निज परतीत कै कै 2
उनहीं सिखाई सीख, सोई ठहराई मैं।
ठाकुर कहत, प्रीति रीति सरसाइ हिये 3
मोद उपजाइ महा ममता बढाई मैं।
हिलि मिलि भाँति भाँति हेत करि देख्यौ, तऊ 4
चेटकी चवाइन के पेट की न पाई मैं॥ Ś138॥

*कैसे सुचित्त भए निकसौ, नहिं दैबो करौ सब के गलबाहीं।

---

138 Granthāvalī 168, Śatak 14, Ṭhasak 23. 139 Sundarītilak (C_e) 305, Granthāvalī 169, Rāmcandra Śukla (I_e) 439, Jagannāth Prasād, Chatarpur as in Khoj (Q_e) (1), Śatak 77, Ṭhasak 16, Ṭhasak 'Jīvancarit' ($Ṭ_e^j$) p. 11.

137.3 वा] Σ, या **E**, ए Ṭ • के] $B_1J_1M_4\mathbf{S}V_2$, को $\mathbf{E}H_eṬ$ • यातें] $B_1H_eM_4S_3S_7ṬV_2$, तातें $\mathbf{E}J_1$, घातें S_1, ⟨या/पा⟩ते S_2 • जैयतु] $B_1H_eJ_1M_4S_7V_2$, जैयत] S_1S_2, ऐयत **E**, जैयति S_3, देखने जईयत (eyeskip) (unm.) Ṭ **137.4** भेंटन... तिन्हें] Σ, कैसे मिलै उनके उर सै Ṭ • भेंटन] Σ, भेंटत S_7 • पैयत] $\mathbf{E}M_4S_2S_7$, कैसैं कै B_1S_1, पैयतु H_eV_2, क्योंकर पैयतु J_1, पैयति S_3 • कैसे] $\mathbf{E}H_eM_4S_2V_2$, पैयै B_1S_1, *om.* J_1, कैसी S_3S_7 • तिन्हें] **E**, उनैं B_1, तिनैं H_e, है J_1, जिनैं $M_4S_1V_2$, बनै $S_2S_3S_7$ • जिन्हें] $\mathbf{E}J_1$, जिनैं $B_1H_eṬ$, तिनैं $M_4\mathbf{S}V_2$ • आँखिन] Σ, आँषिनि M_4 • देखन] $B_1\mathbf{E}H_eJ_1M_4S_1V_2$, देखत $S_2S_3S_7$ *om.* (eyeskip) Ṭ • पैयतु] $B_1H_eJ_1V_2$, पैयत $\mathbf{E}M_4S_1S_2S_7$, पैयति S_3, पईयत (unm.) Ṭ **138.2** सांची] $Ś_e$, सांचौ $G_eṬ_e$ **139.1** सुचित्त] Σ, सुचित (unm.) Q_e • निकसौ] Σ, तिक सो C_e • नहिं...के] **E**, दै हँसो बिलसो सब सों C_e, बिहँसो बिलसौ हरि दै $I_eṬ_e^j$, बिहसौ न हसौ सब से Q_e

---

137.3 घरी घरी Br. in every moment; frequently; जैयत नाहीं Br. v.i. pass. I cannot go. **138.1** भेद [S] m. the secret (that nobody knows). **138.2** सौंह [śapaṭha-] f. oath; प्रतीति [S] f. trust; उनहीं pron. emph. they (the slanderers); सिखाई सीख Br. the teaching that they taught; ठहराना [H ṭhaharnā] v.t. (here:) to accept. **138.3** सरसाना [sarasa-] v.t. to increase; मोद उपजाइ Br. joyfully. **138.4** हिलना-मिलना v.i. to be intimate with; हेत [hetu-] m. affection; चेटकी m. magician; पेट की बात idiom. close secret. **139.1** सुचित्त [S] adj. careless; निकसौ [niṣkasati] v.i. (Br. pres.-subj.) you set forth; गलबाहीं [cf. H galā + H bāṃh] f. embrace.

जे छल-छिद्रन की छलिता छलती छिन एक घरी पल माहीं।
ठाकुर, वे जुरि एक भईं, रचिहैं परपंच कछू ब्रज माहीं।
हाल चवाइन कौ दहुचाल, सो लाल तुम्हैं या दिखात कै नाहीं॥ Ś139॥

ये जे कहैं, ते भले कहिबो करैं, मानस हाँसौं सबै सहि लीजै।
ते बकि आपुहि तें चुप होंइगी, काहे कौं काहुवै ऊतर दीजै।
ठाकुर, मेरे मते की यहै, धनि मानि कै जोवन-रूप पतीजै।

---

140 Hariaudh (A$_e$) p. 485, Granthāvalī 132, Sudhāsar [S$_1$ f. 70rv (alajja parakiyā 10), S$_2$ f. 14v (31/22), S$_5$ f. 69v (16), S$_6$ f. 73r (74/446), S$_7$ f. 50r (72/474)], Ṭhasak 137. The last line distantly evokes Tulsīdās's 'Kavitāvalī' 2 and 6 (mana mo na basyo asa bālaka jo tulasī jaga mẽ phala kauna jiye).

139.2 जे] G$_e$I$_e$Ś$_e$Ṭ$_e$, वै C$_e$, व (unm.) Q$_e$, ये Ṭ^j_e • छल] Σ, *om.* (unm.) Q$_e$ • छिद्रन] **E**I$_e$, छिद्रम C$_e$, छदम (unm.) Q$_e$ • की... माही] Q$_e$, कै छल ता छलि ताकती हैं सब की परछाहीं C$_e$, के छल ताकती हैं कपटी हित की अवगाहीं G$_e$Ś$_e$Ṭ$_e$, की बतियां छलती छिन एक घरी पल मांहीं I$_e$Ṭ^j_e • हित] G$_e$Ṭ$_e$, हिन Ś$_e$ **139.3** ठाकुर] C$_e$I$_e$Q$_e$Ṭ^j_e, ते जुरि **E** • वे] Ṭ^j_e, कै G$_e$Ṭ$_e$, ते Q$_e$, कैं Ś$_e$, वै I$_e$, सों C$_e$ • जुरि] I$_e$Ś$_e$Ṭ^j_e, मिलि C$_e$, सब G$_e$Ṭ$_e$, जुर Q$_e$ • भईं] Σ, भई C$_e$Q$_e$ • रचिहैं] I$_e$C$_e$Ṭ^j_e, परपंच G$_e$Ś$_e$Ṭ$_e$, ---हैं Q$_e$ • परपंच कछू] C$_e$I$_e$Q$_e$Ṭ^j_e, कछू रचिहैं G$_e$Ś$_e$Ṭ$_e$ **139.4** कौ] Σ, की I$_e$ • दहुचाल] G$_e$Ṭ$_e$, दहचाल C$_e$, दुहचाल I$_e$Ṭ^j_e, दुहुचाल Q$_e$, यह चाल Ś$_e$ • सो] C$_e$Q$_e$Ṭ^j_e, सु G$_e$Ś$_e$Ṭ$_e$, को I$_e$ • या] **E**, है I$_e$C$_e$, ⟨यौ⟩ Q$_e$ • दिखात] Σ, पात Q$_e$ • कै] Q$_e$Ś$_e$, कि C$_e$G$_e$I$_e$Ṭ$_e$Ṭ^j_e **140.1** ये] **E**S$_1$S$_6$, ए A$_e$, यो S$_2$, जे S$_5$, यौं S$_7$ • जे] Σ, जौ **E** • कहैं] Σ, कहै S$_5$ • ते] A$_e$**S**, तौ **E**, तैं S$_5$ • करैं] A$_e$**E**S$_1$S$_2$S$_6$, करौ S$_5$S$_7$ • हासौं] **S**, °ही सो A$_e$S$_7$, हाँसी **E** • सहि] Σ, सह S$_6$ **140.2** आपुहि] Σ, आपु (unm.) S$_5$ • तें] Σ, ते S$_6$S$_7$ • चुप] Σ, चुपु S$_2$ • हौंइगी] S$_1$S$_5$, होंयगी A$_e$, होहिंगी **E**, होइगी S$_2$S$_6$S$_7$ • कौं] Σ, *om.* (unm.) S$^{ac}_7$, कौ S$^{pc}_7$ • काहुवै] A$_e$**E**S$_1$, काहू कौं S$_2$S$_6$, काहूवौं S$_5$, काहू कौ S$_7$ • ऊतर] A$_e$**E**S$_1$S$_2$, उत्तर S$_5$S$_6$S$_7$ **140.3** धनि] Σ, धन S$_6$S$_7$ • मानि कै] **E**S$_2$S$_5$, मान कै A$_e$S$_1$S$_6$S$_7$

139.2 जे Br. rel. pron. (the women) who; छल-छिद्र [S] m. dissembling, trickery; छलिता [cf. chala-] poet. f. 1. deceitfulness; 2. deceitful woman; छलती छिन एक घरी पल माहीं Br. deceives you within a moment, hour or a minute; के छल var. (obl.) under the pretext of; हैं कपटी var. (though they are) malicious; हित var. [S] m. love. **139.3** प्रपंच [S] m. conspiracy. **139.4** हाल (हाल में) (?) [A ḥāl] adv. recently; दहुचाल [duścāla-] m. wicked conduct; दहु reg. adv. whether; perhaps (Br. dhaũ); हाल...दहु चाल their state and perhaps their conduct, too. **140.1** ये जौ कहैं Br. if they speak (badly); भले interj. good, let it be! मानस-हाँसौं Br. even the people's derision; मान सही सो var. if his measure is true. **140.2** काहे कौं Br. for what purpose? why? काहुवै (किसी को भी) pron. Br. obl. emph. to anyone. **140.3** मतौ [mati-] reg. m. opinion; मेरे मते की यहै Br. my opinion is this; धनि [dhanya-] adj. fortunate; पतिया- [pratyāyayati] Av. Br. v.t. to believe; जोवन-रूप पतीजै Br. you should trust in the beauty of youth.

या जग में जनमे को जिये को यहै फल है हरि सों हित कीजै॥ Ś140॥

घर बाहर लोग लुगाइन मैं परपंच बन्यौ, सो बिचारनो है।
फिर जानत राम दुहू दिसि को हित सौ चित्त तैं न बिसारनो है।
कहि ठाकुर, स्याम सुजान सिरोमनि एक दुओ निरधारनो है।
करि मंत्र जरूरो, गरूरो भलो बगरूरो उठ्यौ, सो संभारनो है॥ Ś141॥

घर पास परोसिनि घैर करो अरु नावँ धरो ब्रज-गावँरी री।

---

141 Granthāvalī 171, Sudhāsar [S_3 75v-76r (102), S_7 109rv (12/1051)], Śatak 76, Ṭhasak 174. The Sudhāsar (S_7) includes this poem into the 'śikṣā' (advice) subsection of the 'caturkarma sakhīn ke' (the four activities of a companion) section. The Sudhāsar (S_7) introduces it as 'sakhī kī ukti nāyak prati' (the words of the beloved girl's friend to the lover). 142 Sundarī-tilak (C_e) 129, Orinetal Institute, Baroda Nr. 24 f. (G), Granthāvalī 172, Śatak 51, Ṭhasak 42, Bābūrāmdīn: Sundarī-tilak (U_e) 189. The last two lines are in the reverse order in G. Hariścandra and Babūrām tends to share the readings of the Gujarat manuscript.

140.4 में] Σ, मै S_6S_7 • जिये को] Σ, *om.* S_7 • सों] Σ, कौ हिय ते S_7 **141.1** मै] **S**, नै **E** • बन्यौ] **S**, रचे **E** • बिचारनो] **S**, बिचारने **E** • है] Σ, हैं $Ś_e$ **141.2** दुहू] **S**, दुओ $Ś_e$, दोऊ $G_eṬ_e$ • दिसि] **E**, दिस **S** • को] **S**, की **E** • हित... विसारनो] **S**, अस चित्त तैं नाहिं बिचारने $Ś_eṬ_e$, आस चित्त तैं नाहिं बिचारने G_e • चित्त तैं] **E**, चितने **S** • है] Σ, हैं $Ś_e$ **141.3** कहि] **S**, कवि **E** • सिरोमनि] *conj.* सुनौ करि **E**, सिरोमन **S** • दुओ] *em.* दोऊ $G_eṬ_e$, दुवो $S_3Ś_e$, दुहौ S_7 • निरधारनो] **S**, निरधारने **E** • है] Σ, हैं $Ś_e$ **141.4** करि] Σ, कर S_3 • मंत्र] **S**, मंतर (unm.) **E** • भलो] **S**$Ś_eṬ_e^{ac}$, भरो $G_eṬ_e^{pc}$ • उठ्यौ] **S**, उठो $G_eṬ_e$, उठा $Ś_e$ • संभारनो] **S**, संहारने **E** • है] $G_eṬ_e$, हैं $Ś_e$ **142.1** पास परोसिनि] C_eGU_e, °हीं घर **E** • घैर] $C_eGŚ_eU_e$, घैरु $G_eṬ_e$ • करो] C_eGU_e, करैं **E** • अरु] C_eGU_e, घरहाइनैं G_e, घरिहां इन $Ś_e$, घरिहाइनै $Ṭ_e$ • धरो] C_eGU_e, धरैं **E** • ब्रज] C_eGU_e, सब **E**

141.1 नै ag. postp. reg.; प्रपंच [S] m. pl. conspiracies; सो बिचारने है Bund. I have to think of it. **141.2** दुहू दिसि को Br. (?) (God knows) the thoughts (of love) of both sides (i.e. of mine and of the slanderers); दोऊ दिसि की var. Br. the thoughts (of love) of both sides; अस var. reg. adv. (but they do not think) in this way; चित- [cf. citta-] Av. Br. v.i. to look, to gaze. **141.3** करि एक var. Br. putting all things together; एक दुओ निरधारनो है Br. (Krishna) alone is to decide about the two. **141.4** मंतर (मंत्र) [S] m. consideration, deliberation; जरूरो (जरूर) [A] 1. poet. adv. definitely (KL); 2. poet. adj. necessary; गरूरो [A gurūr] poet. m. pride; भलो [bhalla-] reg. adj. good; (here:) intense; बगरूरो (बगूला) poet. m. whirlwind (of pride). **142.1** घरहाइनैं var. [cf. H ghaira] reg. f. emph. slanderer; नाम धर- idiom. Br. to defame; गाँवरी [cf. grāma-] Br. f. (pl.) village-woman.

जब ढोल दियौ बदनाम भई, तब कौन को लाज लजावँरी री।
कवि ठाकुर, प्रेम के फंद परी ब्रजखोरी फिरौं भई बावरी री।
अब होन दे, बीर, हँसी सो हँसी, हिरदै बसी मूरति सावँरी री॥ Ś142॥

घेर भयौ सिगरी नगरी, हठि बैर भयौ हमरी बखरी मैं।
बात उजागर, सोच कहा, जो घटैगी जफा, सो कढै तखरी मैं।
ठाकुर, कीरति का बरनौं, सो अचानक भेंट गली सँकरी मैं।
मूसर चोट की भीति कहा, बदिकै जब मूंड दियो ओखरी मैं॥ Ś143॥

चौचँदहाई जरैं ब्रज की, जे परायो बन्यो हर भाँति बिगारैं।

---

143 Granthāvalī 173, Ṭhasak 160, Ṭhasak 'Jīvancarit' ($Ṭ^{j}_{e}$) p. 4. 144 Bharatpur1 f. 163v-4r (87), Granthāvalī 175, Sudhāsar [S_2 f. 12r (17/13), S_7 ff. 46v-47r (41/443)], Ṭhasak 53, Vrindaban1 f. 8r (6/44).

142.2 जब] C_eGU_e, तब **E** • दियौ] C_e, दै दै **E**, दयो G, दई U_e • भई] C_eGU_e, कियौ **E** • तब] C_eGU_e, अब **E** • को] Σ, की G **142.3** प्रेम...बावरी री] C_eGU_e, नैन सों नैन लगे अब प्रेम सों क्यों न अघावँ री री **E** • °खोरी] C_e, खोरि GU_e • री] Σ, *om.* (unrh.) G **142.4** होन दे] EU_e, हौंन द C_e, हौ दे G • बीर हँसी सो] C_eGU_e, बीस बिसै री **E** **143.4** बदिकै] $Ṭ^{pc}_{e}Ṭ^{j}_{e}$, बजिकै $G_eṬ^{ac}_{e}$ **144.1** चौचंद°] B_1EV_1, चौचदि **S** • जे] $B_1S_2Ṭ_eV_1$, जजे (unm.) G_e, जो S_7 • बन्यो] Σ, बनो **E** • हर] $\mathbf{EV_1}$, सब B^{ac}_{1}, हरि B^{pc}_{1}**S** • बिगारैं] $B_1\mathbf{E}S_2$, बिगारै S_7V_1

142.2 ढोल दियौ idiom. 'beating a drum' publicly; लजावँरी (लज्जा करनेवाली) [cf. lajjā-] adj. (f.) Br. am I ashamed. **142.3** नैन सों नैन लगे var. idiom. Br. 'our eyes met' we have fallen in love; अघाना var. [āghrāpayati] v.i. to be sated, satisfied. **142.4** बीस बिसै (बीसों बीसवें) var. 'twenty twentieths' adv. completely. **143.1** सिगर- [sakala-] Br. adj. all, the whole; हठि [haṭha-] Br. adv. 1. stubbornly; 2. by force; बैर [S] m. enmity; बखरी [vāskara-] reg. f. house, mansion. **143.2** उजागर adj. 'bright' manifest, clear; जफ़ा [A] f. injustice; कढना [cf. *kaḍḍhati] v.i. to become prominent; तखड़ी [? Panj. takkṛī] f. (a pair of small) scales; सो कढै तखरी मैं idiom. Br. that will be known. **143.3** कीर्ति [S] f. fame, praise; रति [S] f. pleasure (of the Lord, of Krishna); सो reg. adv. as, when; सँकड़ा [saṃkaṭa-] adj. narrow. **143.4** मूसर (मूसल) [musula-] m. 1. pestle; 2. club; भीति [S] f. fear; बदिकै Br. abs. (used as adv.) Br. resolutely; बजिकै var. abs. (used as adv.) Br. openly; मूड [muṇḍa-] m. head; ओखली [cf. H ūkhal] f. small mortar. मूसर... मैंCf. H okhlī mẽ sir diyā to muslo se kyā ḍar? **144.1** -हाई reg. suff. 'way, style' (expresses abstraction); चौचंदहाई f. 1. slander; 2. slanderer; जजे (जो) var. reg. rel. pron. pl. those who; परायो बन्यो Br. a matter that has come out well for others.

काहू की बेटी-बहून के घैर, कि के घर जाइ कमंध से पारैं।
ठाकुर, या बिसबास की हौंस न आठहूँ गाँठि रही है हमारैं।
वे करे पै ये करैं, करनी करि आवैं कहूँ तौ कहा करि डारैं॥ Ś144॥

चौहट को मिलिबो तौ रह्यौ, मिलिबो रह्यौ औचक साँझ-सवेरो।
और इती बिनती तुमसों, हरि, आइ अगीत-पछीत न घेरो।
ठाकुर, जौ मिलि जैयै कहूँ मग, तौ जहँ लौं इकही टक हेरो।
या ब्रज के ब्रजबासी सबै बदनाम करैं तुम्हरो अरु मेरो॥ Ś145॥

---

145 Granthāvalī 176, Śatak 18, Ṭhasak 189.

144.2 काहू] Σ, काहून V_1 • के] $B_1S_2V_1$, को **E**S_7 • घैर] **S**V_1, घैरु B_1**E** • कि के] B_1S_2, किते **E**, कर S_7, की के V_1 • कमंध] **E**S_2V_1, कबंध B_1, प्रबंध S_7 • से पारैं] B_1**E**, से पारै S_2V_1, सवारै S_7 **144.3** या बिसबास] **E**S_7V_1, या बसबास B_1, पावस बास S_2 • हौंस न] **ES**, हौंसनि B_1V_1 • गांठि] $B_1S_7V_1$, गांठ **E**, गांठहूं गांठि (dittography) S_2 • हमारैं] B_1**E**, हमारै **S**V_1 **144.4** करे] Σ, करैं B_1 • ये] B_1V_1, या **E**, ए **S** • करैं] Σ, करै S_7 • करि] Σ, कर V_1 • आवैं] *conj.* आवै Σ • कहा] Σ, कहां S_7 • डारैं] **E**, पारै **S**, डारै B_1V_1

144.2 घैर m. slander; काहू... घैरु Br. they slander the daughters and daughter-in-laws of some people (cf. H unhẽ ghair hai); किते Br. adj. many; कि के (किसके) Bund. pron. poss. whose (house shall I go when they...)? कमंध m. quarrel; कमंद [P] f. rope, noose; पार- [H parṇā] v.t. to throw; कमन्ध से पारैं Br. they seem to cast the noose of discord in many houses. **144.3** हौंस [A havas] f. 1. desire; 2. intention; गाँठ [granthi-] f. 'knot' 1. joint; 2. ill-feeling, guile; आठहूँ गाँठ adv. 'in all the eight joints of the body' in every possible way, completely (cf. Rasikpriyā 2-16-2) **144.4** पै conj. reg. or; वे करे पै या करैं reg. they may do this or that (i.e. no matter what they do); करनी [karaṇīya-] f. 1. action, deed; 2. misdemeanour; करनी करि आवैं कहूँ if they manage to do their bad actions; तौ कहा करि डारैं Br. then who knows what (mischief) they do. **145.1** चौहट को [H cau+hāṭ] 'at the market square' adv. publicly; तौ रह्यौ idiom. Br. did not happen; मिलिबो रह्यौ 'a meeting can happen' we can meet; औचक 1. adv. unexpectedly; 2. m. difficulty (BHK). **145.2** अगीत [agrataḥ] poet. adv. in front; पछीत (पीछे) [paścāt] poet. adv. behind; अगीत-पछीत poet. adv. on all sides. **145.3** जहाँ लौं adv. as much as you can, at least; इकही टक Br. adv. fixedly (i.e. you should look at me without hiding it since slander is already going on). **145.4** बदनाम करना idiom. to destroy one's reputation.

जब तें निरखे मनमोहन जू, तब तें अँखियाँ ए लगीं सु लगीं।
कुलकानि गई, भटू, वाही घरी, जब प्रेम के पुंज पगीं सु पगीं।
कहि ठाकुर, नेह के नेजन की उर मैं अनी आनि खगीं सु खगीं।
अब नाँवरे गाँवरे कोऊ धरौ, हम साँवरे रंग रँगीं सु रँगीं॥ Ś146॥

146 Bharatpur1 f. 146v (87), Bharatpur11 f. 4rv (10), Sundarī-tilak (C_e) 130, Granthāvalī 177, Jaipur1 f. 2r (5), Marwar1 f. 12rv (38), Marwar4 f. 48v (62/7), Rasikvinod (O_e) 476, Sudhāsar [S_1 f. 69v-70r (7), S_2 f. 13v (25/19), S_7 f. 49v (67/469)], Śatak 94, Ṭhasak 43, Vrindaban1 f. 2v (13/13), Hafizullah Khan: Hazara (X_e) p. 400 (Dohre kāfiye ke chand 18), Yājñik. The Sudhāsar (S_1) presents this poem as an example of 'alajjā parakīyā' (adulterous woman without modesty) and introduces it as the words of the heroine towards her companion.

146.1 जब तें] Σ, जा दिन सौं (unm.) B_{11}, जब त S_2 • निरषे] $B_1B_{11}V_1Y_e$, दरसे $C_e\mathbf{E}J_1M_1M_4O_e\mathbf{S}X_e$ • जू तब] Σ, जा दिन B_{11}, जु तब M_1 • ए] $B_1B_{11}M_4S_1V_1$, ये $C_e\mathbf{E}J_1O_e\mathbf{S}X_e$, न M_1 • लगीं] $\mathbf{E}M_4S_1X_e$, लगी $B_1B_{11}C_eJ_1O_eS_2S_7V_1$, जगी M_1 • सु] $B_1M_1M_4S_1$, जु B_{11}, सो $C_e\mathbf{E}J_1S_2S_7V_1X_e$ • लगीं] $\mathbf{E}M_4O_eS_1X_e$, लगी $B_1B_{11}C_eJ_1S_2S_7V_1$, जगी M_1 **146.2** °कानि] Σ, कांन $M_1S_1S_7$ • गई] $B_1C_e\mathbf{E}J_1O_eV_1X_e$, गटी B_{11}, तजी $M_1\mathbf{S}$, सबै M_4 • भटू] $B_1B_{11}J_1\mathbf{S}Y_e$, सखी $C_eO_eX_e$, भगि $\mathbf{E}$, ⟨च⟩ल M_1, मिटी M_4, भटु V_1 • वाही] Σ, वाई B_1, ताही M_4, वाहि O_e • जब प्रेम के] $B_1C_eJ_1O_e\mathbf{S}V_1X_eY_e$, निजु प्रीतम B_{11}, ब्रजराज के $\mathbf{E}$, हम कुंज के M_1, हम प्रेम के M_4 • पुंज] $B_1J_1\mathbf{S}V_1Y_e$, रंग B_{11}, प्रेम $\mathbf{E}$, फंद $C_eO_eX_e$, मग M_1, पंथ M_4 • पगीं] $\mathbf{E}S_1S_2X_e$, रंगी B_{11}, परी C_e, पगी $B_1J_1M_1M_4O_eS_2S_7V_1$ • सु] $B_1M_1M_4S_1$, जु B_{11}, सो $C_e\mathbf{E}J_1S_2S_7V_1X_e$ • पगीं] $\mathbf{E}S_1X_e$, रंगी B_{11}, पगी $B_1C_eJ_1M_1M_4O_eS_2S_7V_1$ **146.3** कहि] $B_1^{pc}C_eJ_1M_4S_1S_7V_1Y_e$, *om.* (unm.) B_1^{ac}, कबि $B_{11}M_4S_2X_e\mathbf{E}$, कहै M_1O_e • नेह... सु खगीं] Σ, कोऊ लाष कहौ यह देह तौ नेह दगी सु दगी B_{11} • अनी] $B_1B_{11}C_e\mathbf{E}J_1^{pc}M_1^{ac}M_4\mathbf{S}$, आनी J_1^{ac}, अनि $M_1^{pc}O_eV_1X_e$ • आनि] $B_1C_eJ_1M_4O_eS_1V_1X_e$, आन $B_{11}\mathbf{E}S_2S_7$, °यांन M_1 • खगीं] $\mathbf{E}O_eS_1X_e$, षगी $B_1B_{11}C_eM_1S_2S_7V_1$, पगी J_1, षं⟨नी⟩ M_4^{ac}, षंगी M_4 • सु] $B_1M_1M_4S_1$, सो $B_1B_{11}C_e\mathbf{E}J_1M_1O_eS_2S_7V_1X_e$ • खगीं] $\mathbf{E}O_eS_1X_e$, षागी B_1 B_{11}, खगी $C_eJ_1M_1M_4S_2S_7V_1$ **146.4** अब] $B_1B_{11}\mathbf{E}J_1M_4S_1V_1$, सब S_2S_7, कोऊ M_1, तुम $C_eO_eX_e$ • नाव] $B_1B_{11}V_1$, गाँव Σ • रे] Σ, °र V_1 • गाव] $B_1B_{11}V_1$, नाँव Σ • रे] Σ, र V_1 • कोऊ] $B_1C_eG_eJ_1M_4O_eS_1$Ś$_eV_1X_e$, केहू B_{11}, क्यों न $M_1S_2S_7$, कोई Ṭ$_e$ • धरौ] Σ, कहौ B_{11}, धरौं S_2 • साँवरे] Σ, भामरे M_4 • रँगीं] $G_eM_4O_eS_1$Ś$_e$Ṭ$_e$, रंगी $B_1B_{11}C_eJ_1S_2S_7V_1X_e$, लगी M_1 • सु] $B_1B_{11}M_1M_4S_1$, सो $C_e\mathbf{E}J_1S_2S_7V_1X_e$ • रँगीं] $\mathbf{E}S_1X_e$, रंगी $B_1B_{11}C_eJ_1M_4S_2S_7V_1$, लगी M_1, रंगा O_e

146.1 आंख लगना idiom. 'the eyes to be fixed on' to fall in love; लगीं सु लगीं emph. poet. the eyes that were fixed (on him) were indeed fixed. **146.2** भग- (भागना) [cf. bhagna-] Br. v.i. to run away; पगना v.i. 'to be soaked in' to be infatuated. **146.3** नेज [P] m. spear; अनी [anīka-] f. tip (of a spear); सो (वह) var. खग- [? *khacc-] poet. v.i. to penetrate; खगी सु खगी Br. (the tip) that penetrated penetrated thoroughly. **146.4** गाँवर (गँवार) [cf. grāma-] Br. adj. villager; नाँवरा (नाम) [nāman-] reg. m. name; नाम धरना idiom. to defame.

देखे अकेले किते दिन ह्वै गए, चाह गई चित सों कढि सोऊ।
आपनी सूझ तौ ह्वै रहौ आपनी, मेरी सुनौ, तौ कहै किन कोऊ। 2
ठाकुर, या ब्रज गाँव के लोग चवाई कहैं, तुम एक हौ दोऊ।
प्रीत हमैं तुमैं टूटि गए की अबे लौं प्रतीत न मानत कोऊ॥ Ś147॥ 4

*देखें घनस्याम मैं कही कै मोहि भाई छवि, 1
या सुनि लगाइ कै गोपाल सों अरझतीं।
ता दिन तें ननँद जिठानीं ठानी रार मोसौ, 2
पास औ परोस बसैं तेऊ आन खिझतीं।
ठाकुर कहत, कैसे बसिये, री, ऐसे बास 3
ऐसी नित नई जहाँ चरिचा सिरजतीं।
देखति हौं ब्रज की लुगांई भई कैसी, हम 4

---

147 Granthāvalī 179, Śatak 19, Ṭhasak 188. 148 Datiya 333, Granthāvalī 180, Śatak 40, Ṭhasak 182.

147.1 देखे] G$_e$Ṭ$_e$, अदेखे (unm.) Ś$_e$ **147.3** एक हौ] G$_e$Ṭ$_e$, ए कहौ Ś$_e$ **148.1** देखें] **E**, देष D$_1$ • मोहि भाई छवि] D$_1$, छवि भाई मोहिं **E** • या सुनि] **E**, इनकी D$_1$ • गोपाल] **E**, गुपाल D$_1$ • अरझतीं] **E**, उरझतीं D$_1$ **148.2** ठानी रार मोसौ] D$_1$, मोसों ठानी रार **E** • खिजतीं] **E**, षिजती D$_1$ **148.3** ऐसी नित] D$_1$, ऐसी ऐसी **E** • नई] D$_1$, बात G$_e$Ṭ$_e$, चर्चा Ś$_e$ • चरिचा] D$_1$, नित नौ G$_e$Ṭ$_e$, नित नई Ś$_e$ • सिरजतीं] G$_e$Ṭ$_e$, सिरजती D$_1$, सिर्जतीं (unm.) Ś$_e$

147.1 देखे v.t. perf. (since) I saw you, Krishna; अकेले adj. obl. alone (i.e. in private); चाह... सोऊ Br. has the very desire (to see me) left your mind? **147.2** सूझ [cf. śudhyati] f. perception, understanding; आपनी... आपनी Br. 'your own perception may be your own' (i.e. you have your own perception of it); मेरी सुनौ listen to my words; तौ कहे किन कोऊ Br. and no matter what others say. **147.3** चवाई [caturavāda-] f. (as a) libel, insult; तुम एक हौ दोऊ Br. (they say) 'the two of you are one'; **147.4** प्रीत... की Br. (the matter) of the breaking of our mutual love; प्रतीति मानना idiom. to believe. **148.1** मैं कही कै छवि Br. I said (to my companions) that his beauty; इनकी var. pron. poss. his (i.e. Krishna's matter); लगाइ कै v.t. Br. abs. putting me together (i.e. imagining my relationship with Krishna); अरुझ- (उलझना) [uparudhyate] Av. Br. v.i. 1. to interfere; 2. to wrangle (BHK). **148.2** जेठानी [jyeṣṭhājāni-] f. wife of the husband's eldest brother; राड़ [rāṭi-] f. quarrel, strife; ठानना [cf. sthānya-] v.i. to plunge (into an activity). **148.3** वास [S] m. 'residence' 1. house; 2. village; सिरज- [sṛj-] Br. v.t. to create; नौ var. [nava-] adj. new.

खेत की कहत खरियान की समझतीं॥ Ś148॥

1 हरिजू की गैल मेरी पौरि कौ दुवारो उतै,
वेऊ कढ्यौ चाहौं, मोहिं काम घनौ घर कौ।
2 ता पै घरहाई दुखहाईं घैर बांधती हैं,
बास छोडि दीजै कैसे कढिबो डगर कौ।
3 ठाकुर कहत, उकराहन भई हौं सुनि
सकल उराहन, जी है रह्यौ अधर कौ।

---

149 Bharatpur1 f. 164v (92), Granthāvalī 181, Sudhāsar [S_2 f. 16r (34/23), S_7 f. 52rv (12/497)], Śatak 6, Ṭhasak 190, Vrindaban1 ff. 8v-9r (12/50), Yājñik.

148.4 देखति] **E**, देखती D_1 • लुगांई] D_1, लुगाइन **E** • भई] D_1, भयौ **E** • कैसी हम] D_1, धौं कहा **E** • कहत] D_1, कहे तें (unm.) **E** • खरियान] **E**, खरियन (unm.) D_1 • समझतीं] **E**, समझती D_1 **149.1** हरिजू] **E**, यह हरिजू **S**, या हरिजू (unm.) $B_1^{ac}V_1$, ⟨य⟩ हरिजू (unm.) B_1^{pc} • हरिजू] Σ, हरिजु (unm.) V_1 • गैल] Σ, गैल यह **E** • पौरि] $B_1S_7V_1Y_e$, पौर **E**, पौरी S_2 • कौ दुवारो उतै] $B_1V_1Y_e$, अगवासो **E**, कौ दुवारु **S** • वेऊ] $B_1S_7V_1Y_e$, ह्याँ ह्वै **E**, वेहू S_2 • कढ्यौ] $B_1\mathbf{S}V_1Y_e$, कढौ $G_eṬ_e$, कढै $Ś_e$ • चाहै] $\mathbf{S}V_1Y_e$, चाहैं B_1, चाहौं **E** **149.2** पै] Σ, को $Ś_e$ • घर°] $\mathbf{E}S_7^{ac}$, घैरि B_1, घरि $S_2S_7^{pc}V_1$ • घैर] Y_eΣ, सोर **E** • बांधती] **S**, परती **E**, करती $B_1V_1Y_e$ • हैं] Σ, है S_7 • छोडि] $B_1S_7V_1$, छोड $\mathbf{E}S_2$ • दीजै] Σ, हीजै B_1 • कैसे] $B_1V_1Y_e$, कै **ES** • कढिबो] $B_1V_1Y_e$, निकसिबो **E**, निकरिबो **S** **149.3** ठाकुर कहत] Σ, ठ° B_1, ठाकुर कहैत कैहैत (dittography) V_1 • उकराहन] Σ, उकराइन $G_e^{vl}Ṭ_e$, ⟨उ/ड⟩कराहन S_2, डकराइन G_e, हौं कराहिन $Ś_e$ • सुनि] $B_1\mathbf{E}$, सन S_2, सुन S_7V_1 • सकल] $B_1\mathbf{S}Ś_eV_1Y_e$, सुनि कै $G_eṬ_e$ • उराहन] $B_1S_2V_1Y_e$, उराहनो **E**, डराहन S_7 • जी] $B_1G_eṬ_eV_1Y_e$, ज्यौं **S**, जु $Ś_e$ • है] $B_1V_1Y_e$, हो **E**, ह्वै **S** • रह्यौ] Y_eΣ, रहौ **E**

148.4 देखति हौं v.t. I see (how the people of Braj are nowadays); खलियान [khaledhānī-] m. granary; खेत... समझतीं idiom. I talk of the field but they think of the granary (i.e. they think of something different) (cf. ām kahat, sunai imalī). **149.1** गैल [cf. gati-] Br. f. path, way; पौर [pradura-] f. 1. threshold; 2. gate; उतै [cf. H ut] Br. adv. thither (whither); अगवास var. [agravāsa-] m. the front of a house; पौरि अगवासो var. Br. (this path of Krishna) is in front of my gate and house; चाहौं v.t. (Br. pres.) I want (to go out); चाहै var. v.t. (Br. pres. pl.) I want; मोहिं... कौ Br. but I have a lot of work at home. **149.2** घरहाई reg. adj. f. destroyer of the family; दुखहाई reg. adj. f. cruel; पार- [cf. H paṛnā] Br. v.t. to throw, (here:) to make (noise); छोडि दीजै v.t. pass. subj. Br. shall I abandon? कै Br. conj. or; कैसै var. interr. how (can I)? बास... कै Br. Shall I abandon the house or (the going out on the road; e.g. for water)? डगर [cf. *ḍag-] f. road, path; **149.3** उकराहन [cf. H akulānā)] Bund. adj. perplexed; उकराइन var. Bund. adj. perplexed; डकराना var. v.i. to bellow, to roar; अधर [S] m. lip; जी ह्वै रहौ अधर कौ 'my life went to my lips' (i.e. in order to depart).

एक घरी होइ तौ बराव कीजै, मेरी भट्टू,
देहरी के द्वार दुख आठहू पहर कौ॥ Ś149॥

*हम से मनमोहन से हित है, चुगली कर कोऊ कहा करहै।
अब तो बदनाम भई बृज में, गुरु लोगन जान कहा डर है।
कह ठाकुर, लाल के देखबे को बृज भूलो सबे, बिसरो घर है।
तुम आपने काम से काम करो, कोऊ आपुन जान कुंवा गिरहै॥ Ś150॥

*निज मंत्र न औरन सों कहने, अपने चित-चोज बिचारने है।
पुनि नेक को नेक, लटो को लटो, यह रीति सदा उर धारने है।
कह ठाकुर, प्यारे सुजान सुनौ, मन की उरझी निरबारने है।
चहुँ ओर से चौचंद चार उठो, सो बिचार के, यार, सँभारने है॥ Ś151॥

*जान-पहचान मुसक्यान नाहि काहू सौं,

---

150 Chatarpur (C) p. 32 (178), Allahabad2 (I_2) f. 39v-40r (4). 151 Ṭhasak, Jīvancarit ($Ṭ^j_e$) p. 11. (Lālā Bhagavāndīn accepted this poem as written by Ṭhākur but did not include it into the main body of his text.)

149.4 एक घरी] B_1SV_1, घरी पार $G_eṬ_e$, घरी पहर $Ś_e$, एक घरो Y_e • बराव] $B_1V_1Y_e$, बचाए **E**, दुराव **S** • कीजै] $Y_e\Sigma$, रहौं **E** • भट्टू] B_1V_1, बीर **ES**, भट्ट Y_e • के द्वार] $B_1V_1Y_e$, दुवार G_e**S**, दुआर $Ś_eṬ_e$ **150.2** में] C, मै I_2 • गुरु] C, गुर I_2 **150.3** भूलो] C, फूलौ I_2 **150.4** से] C, सौ I_2 • काम करो] $C^{pc}I_2$, *om.* (unm.) C^{ac} • आपुन] C, आपनै I_2 **151.3** निरबारने] *conj.* निनबारने $Ṭ^j_e$

149.4 **घड़ी** [ghaṭikā] f. short period of time, a period of 24 minutes; **बराव** [cf. vārayati] Br. m. avoidance, escape; **एक... कीजै** Br. I can avoid it, if it is only a few moments; **दुवार** [dvāra-] Br. m. gate. **150.1** **चुग़ली** [P] f. slander; **चुगली... करहै** Br. what will people achieve by slander? **150.2** **जान (के जानने से)** poet. obl. if they know about it. **150.4** **कुंवा गिरहै** Br. would (anyone) harm him or herself (on purpose)? (i.e. I am not causing harm to myself with my love.) **151.1** **चित** [citta-] m. mind; **चोज** [codya-] m. 1. 'wonder' beautiful feeling; **अपने चित-चोज बिचारने है** Br. think of the beautiful sentiments of your mind (KL). **151.2** **नेक को नेक** reg. (you should say) good for good; **लटा** poet. adj. bad. **151.3** **उरझी (उलझन)** [cf. H ulajhnā] Br. f. entanglement, confusion; **निरबारने** [nivārayati] reg. v.t. to remove. **151.4** **चौचंद** m. slur, insult; **चार** Br. m. 1. slander (KL); 2. [H cāl] scheme, trick; **सँभारना** [sambhārayati] v.t. to avoid, to be careful.

सु ताहू पर एतनैं चबाब कीजियतु है।
2 सास गनैं सास, नंद करत बिसास, पास
बैरिन कौ बास, दुख दूनौं पीजियतु है।
3 ठाकुर कहत, यह मन मैं बिचार देखौ,
कैसैं मन-मानक मरोरि लीजियतु है।
4 जारो वह देस जामैं देखवे की चोरी लागै,
और कहा आँखिन कीवार दीजियतु है॥ Ś152॥

1 कढौ जिन बाहिर, बढौ न अगैया, सेतौ,
बँधौ कुल-रीत जो हमेस चल आई है।

---

152 Sudhāsar [S_1 f. 182v, S_5 f. 188v (5), S_7 f. 146rv (8/1390)], Ṭhākur-satsaī (Ṭ) f. 4r (31). The poem is presented within the 'Parakiyā pūrvā anurāga' (the uncommunicated love of an adulterous woman) subsection of the 'Pūrvā anurāga' section and is introduced as 'bahiraṅga sakhī prīti lachchit kari nāikā saum̩ prasna karat hai. tākau uttara nāikā naim̩ dīnaum̩. prasnottara kari antaraṅga bhayau cāhi hai' (A non-confidential companion hinting at her love asks the heroine. The heroine answered her. Through the answer to her question she wants to become confidential). 153 Kashi2 (K_2) f. 17r.

152.1 मुसक्यान] S_1S_5, मुसकांन S_7Ṭ • नाहि] S_1S_7, चाहि S_5, नाह Ṭ • एतनैं] S_1S_5, एतनो S_7Ṭ • कीजियतु] S_1, कीजीयत S_5S_7Ṭ **152.2** गनैं] S_1S_5, गऐ S_7, गनै Ṭ • बि-सास] Σ, बिलस S_7 • बैरिन] S_1S_7Ṭ, बरिन S_3 • पीजियतु] S_1, पीजियतू S_3, पीजियत S_7, पीजीयत Ṭ **152.3** यह] S_1S_5, यहि S_7, यहै Ṭ • देखौ] **S**, पेखो Ṭ • मानक] **S**, मानस Ṭ • मरोरि] S_1S_5, मरोर S_7, करोर Ṭ • लीजियतु] S_1, तीजियतु S_3, लीजीयत S_7Ṭ **152.4** जारो] S_3S_7Ṭ, जारौं S_1 • वह] S_1Ṭ, यह S_3, वेई S_7 • लागै] Ṭ, लागी S_1, लगै S_3S_7 • कहा] S_1S_5Ṭ, कहां S_7 • किवार] S_7Ṭ, कीवरा S_1, किवारि S_3 • दीजियतु] S_1S_5, दीजियत S_7, दीजीयत Ṭ **153.1** कढौ] *conj.* कडौ K_2 • बढौ] *conj.* बडौ K_2 • न] *conj.* नै K_2 • अगैया] *conj.* (unm.) अगै⟨या/पा⟩ से (unm.) K_2 • बँधौ] *conj.* ब⟨धौ⟩ K_2 • कुल] *conj.* कु⟨ल⟩ K_2 • आई] *conj.* आवि K_2

152.1 नाही... Br. I did not (recognise or smiled at anyone); चाहि apa. if I you want; सु ताहू पर Br. in spite of this; चबाब [cf. *caturvāda-] Br. m. slander. **152.2** सास [śvaśrū-] f. mother-in-law; साँस [śvāsa-] f. sigh; साँस गनना idiom. 'keeps account of each sigh of mine' keeps a strict control; नंद (ननद) [nanandṛ-] f. sister-in-law; बिसास [viśvāsghāta-] Br. m. treachery; पास [pārśve] adv. nearby. **152.3** मानिक [māṇikya-] m. ruby, jewel; मरोड़ना [*muroṭati] v.t. to gripo; to dostroy; मरोरि लीजियतु है Br. v.t. pass. imperf. why would one destroy. **152.4** जार- (जलाना) [cf. jvālayati] Br. v.t. to burn down; fig. to be cursed; देखावे की चोरी लगी var. Br. (the matter of) looking is considered theft; किवाड़ [kavāṭa-] f. door; (में) कीवार देना idiom. to shut. **153.1** अगैया reg. adv. ahead (H āge); सैंत- Av. Br. v.t. to keep carefully; बँधौ v.t. imp. be tied.

जोबन कौ अहं मद बैठाव मन मँझ न, 2
कोविदनि कीज्यौ मतो लागति भलाई है।
ठाकुर कहत, प्रीति रीत कौ जु पैंडौ लटौ, 3
जालम जो जीउ गसौ लोग रु लुगाई है।
तैं तौ रूप रासि इतै, वीर रजीवारौ वहौ, 4
ब्रज कै चबाई तातैं मोहि कहि आई है॥ Ś153॥

*ऐ सुंगहा कछु सोधु न पावै, दहूँ दिस की रिस की भय भागै।
ऐसहू जो न संजोगु सुहायौ बियोग-सरागन यौ तन दागै। 2
ठाकुर, कोऊ न वैरु करै, घरहाइन कै घर घैरु न जागै।
ऐसौ उपाइ बताउ, भटू, हरि अंक भरौं पै कलंक न लागै॥ Ś154॥ 4

---

154 Datiyal ff. 105v-106r (342).

153.2 जोबन... है] (unm.) K_2 • मद] *conj.* म⟨द⟩ K_2 • बैठाव] *conj.* बठाव K_2 • मँझन] *conj.* म⟨यन⟩ K_2 • कोविदनि] *conj.* कौ दिनीनि K_2 • मतो] *conj.* मतोदि K_2 • लागति] *conj.* लागनि K_2 • भलाई] *conj.* भालाई K_2 **153.3** जु पैंडौ] *conj.* पेडौ (unm.) K_2 • जो] *conj.* ज K_2 • लोग] *conj.* ⟨लु/लि⟩अ K_2 • रु] *em.* र K_2 • लुगाई] *em.* लोगाई K_2 **153.4** तैं] *conj.* तै K_2 • रासि] *conj.* रास K_2 • कै] *conj.* ठै K_2 • आई] *em.* आवि (unrh.) K_2 **154.1** दहूं] *conj.* दुहूं D_1 **154.2** न] *conj.* नु D_1 • सराग] *conj.* ⟨त⟩रोगुं D_1 • तन] *conj.* त⟨न/नु⟩ D_1 **154.4** भरौं] *conj.* भरौ D_1 • पै] *conj.* ⟨पै/नै⟩ D_1

153.2 जोबन को अहं मद Br. (retain) the selfishness and intoxication of youth; कोविद-नि कीज्यौ मतो Br. consult the experts; लागति भलाई है Br. (this) is beneficial for you. **153.3** पैंडौ [padadaṇḍa-] Br. m. path, way; लट- [cf. H laṭnā, H ulaṭnā] Br. adj. weak, thin; जालम...है Br. it is cruel as it snatches the life of the men and women. **153.4** तैं] reg. you; रजीवारौ Br. adj. 1. inclined; 2. royal (KL); तातैं...है Br. therefore I have to tell. **154.1** ऐ (ये) pron. reg. these; सुंगहा [cf. H sugānā 'to doubt'] reg. m. person full of doubts, one who suspects; (here:) slanderer; शोध [S] m. ascertainment (of facts); रिस [riṣ-x īrṣyā-] f. anger, offence; भय [S] m. (here f.) fear; दहूँ... भागै Br. the fear of anger from all around should disappear. **154.2** जो न संजोगु सुहायौ Br. if he does not like this union; सराग (शलाका) [S] poet. m. long thin metal rod (used as an instrument of punishment); (Cf. 'viyoga-sarāgani bhūṃjai māṃsū' Padmāvat); दागना [cf. H dāg] v.t. to burn (esp. with an iron). **154.3** घरहाइन [cf. H ghair] reg. f. slanderer. घैर m. slander;

हम सौं हसि बोले, सुनैं हमनैं घर कोऊ कछू समझावती हैं।
यह मानि न हानि करौ हित की चित, का नघनी उर लावती हैं।
कहि ठाकुर, लाल पियारे सुनौ, कहनावत एक सुनावती हैं।
यह आसकी औ डर पावन कौ, कहौ, दो दो कहाँ बनि आवती हैं॥ Ś155॥

155 Sudhāsar [S_1 f. 150v (1), S_7 f. 100v (1/977)]. The anthologist introduces the poem as the words of a 'parakīyā nāyikā' (adulterous woman) towards an 'anabhigga nāyaka' (unaware lover). It is, however, easier to conceive the poem as presenting the words of a messanger. The last line is similar to that of Ś53.

155.0 हसि] S_1, हस S_7 • सुनैं] S_1, सने S_7 • हैं] S_1, है S_7 **155.1** मानि] S_1, बानि S_7 • हानि] S_7, हाँन S_1 • की] S_7, फौ S_1 • हैं] S_1, है S_7 **155.2** कहि] S_1, कह S_7 • पियारे] S_7, पयारे S_1 • सुनौ] S_7, सुनौं S_1 • हैं] S_1, है S_7 **155.3** पावन] S_1, माँमनि S_1 • हैं] S_1, है S_7

155.0 बोले v.i. pres. Br. she speaks; हमनैं सुनैं Br. I heard; कोऊ कछू Br. something else. **155.1** हानि [S] f. loss (in love); चित [citta-] reg. m. (obl.) in your mind; नघनी [cf. H naghnā 'to cross, to transgress'] Br. f. transgression, sin. **155.3** आशिक़ी [A] f. love; माननि m. (Br. pl.) prestige, reputation; दो दो... हैं idiom. can the two things be at the same time?.

ऋतु-वर्णन

वसंत

गावैं पिकबैनी, मृगनैनी हू बजावैं बीन, 1
नाचैं चंदमुखी चारु चाउ की चटक पै।
कीरतिकुमारी, बृषभान की दुलारी, राधे, 2
अटकी बिलोकि लोक-लाज की अटक पै।
ठाकुर कहत, चीर केसर के रंग रँगो, 3
अतर पगो सो मन मोहै पीत पट पै।
देख तौ देखात कैसौ राजत रसीलो आज, 4
आली री, बसंत बनमाली के मुकट पै॥ R1॥

कारे लाल करहे पलासन के पुंज, तिन्हैं 1
आपने झकोरन झुलावन लगी है री।
ताही की ससेटी त्रन-पत्रन लपेटी धरा- 2
धाम तें अकास धूरि धावन लगी है री।
ठाकुर कहत, सुचि सौरभ प्रकासन भो, 3

---

1 Granthāvalī 15, Ṭhasak 90, Ṭhasak 'Jīvancarit' ($Ṭ_e^j$) p. 22. 2 Granthāvalī B37, Rāmcandra Śukla (I_e) p. 437, Ṭhasak 'Jīvancarit' ($Ṭ_e^j$) pp. 3-4.

1.1 चंद॰] $G_eṬ_e$, चंद्र॰ $Ṭ_e^j$ • चाउ] $G_eṬ_e$, चौर $Ṭ_e^j$ **1.4** रसीलो] $G_eṬ_e$, रसीली $Ṭ_e^j$
2.1 आपने] **E**, अपने I_e **2.2** धूरि] I_e, धूर **E**

1.1 पिक [S] m. Indian cuckoo; चौर var. (?) apa.) चटक [cf. H caṭ] m.f. 'snap, smack' swiftness. **1.2** राधे [S] poet. f. voc. 1. o Radha! 2. (used as dir.) Radha (was caught); अटकी बिलोकि Br. seeing him you were caught; अटक f. obstacle; पै postp. (here:) by; **1.3** अतर [A] m. attar, perfume; मन मोहै पीत पट पै Br. the mind is enchanted by his yellow garment. **1.4** देखात कैसौ reg. how (lovely) it looks; राजत रसीलो बसंत Br. the beautiful spring is shining (on Krishna's crown). **2.1** कार- Br. adj. black; करह [cf. kali-] poet. m. bud; कारे... पुंज Br. 1. multitudes of black and red palash buds; 2. black and red buds and multitudes of palash flowers; (The palash, also called 'flame of the forest', has dark stalks and red petals.) तिन्हैं... लगी है (the wind) started to swing them through its own gusts. **2.2** ससेट (सरसेट) [cf. saṃtrasta-] Br. m. fear (RKS, SBK); ताही की ससेटी poet. fearing the same (i.e. the wind) (the dust ran away to the sky); त्रन (तृण) [S] Br. m. grass; लपेटी [*lappeṭṭ-] v.t. abs. reg. to enfold, to surround; धरा [S] f. earth, surface; धरा-धाम तें Br. from its dwelling place, the earth.

आछी भाँति रुचि उपजावन लगी है री।
4 ताती सीरी बैहर बियोग- वा सँयोग-बारी
आवनि बसंत की जनावन लगी है री॥ R2॥

1 *बौर मौर, किंसुक सु कंकन, कलिन सौन
भूषन, सु फूल कै पराग पट भायौ है।
2 ठाकुर, पताके पता, लाल कंज सिंहासन,
कुंज भेद पालकी, गयंद, रथ छायौ है।
3 पौन है सुदौर बने बिरिछ बराती तौर,
भौंर-चोपकादि बोल बाजने बनायौ है।
4 जोहन से मोहन बहार-बनरी है संग
सोहत बसंत बनरा सौ बनि आयौ है॥ R3॥

1 आम-मौर झौरैं, मौर-मौरन पै झूमैं अली,

---

3 Dvij: Śṛṅgār-sudhākar (D_e) (Vasant 27), Ṣaṭṛtu-hajārā (J_e) p. 17, Mītal (M_e) p. 41 (Vasant 141).

2.3 भो] G_e, मों I_eṬ$_e^j$ **3.1** कलिन] *conj.* कलित $D_eJ_eM_e$ • सौन] M_e, सौंर D_eJ_e **3.3** बिरिछ] D_eJ_e, बृच्छन M_e **3.4** सोहत] M_e, सोहन D_eJ_e

---

2.3 सौरभ [S] m. fragrance; प्रकासन भो reg. manifested itself, appeared (in the wind); मों (में) apa. [madhye] postp. reg. in; रुचि [S] f. desire. **2.4** तात- [tapta-] Br. adj. hot; सीर- [sītala-] Br. adj. cold; बैहर [cf. vāyu-, vātāra- and P bahār] f. wind; -बार- (-वाला) suff. (here:) with, bringing. **3.1** बौर मौर Br. mango flowers are his crown; कलिन सौन भूषन Br. the buds are golden ornaments; कलित var. 1. adj. having buds; 2. beautiful; सौंर var. (?) 1. m. blanket (BHK); 2. tumburu tree ('toothache tree', Zanthoxylum armatum); 3. [śyāmala-, H saumṛā] poet. adj. dark; 4. [H solah] poet. num. sixteen; फूल कै (the pollen) of flower (redundant here). **3.2** पताका [S] m. flag; पता (पत्र) [S] Br. m. leave; कंज [S] m. lotus; कुंज... रथ Br. the variety of groves (became) palanquins, elephants and chariots. **3.3** सुदौर Br. f. 'running well' walking wedding procession (cf. H paidal barātī); बिरिछ (वृक्ष) [S] reg. m. tree; बराती [varayātrā-] m. member of a marriage procession; तौर [A] adv. 'in the manner of' as; चोपक [cobadāra-] m. mace-bearer, orderly; बोल... है Br. the buzz (of the bees) became the music. **3.4** जोहन से मोहन Br. (spring) that enchants by being seen; बहार 1. [P bahār] m. the splendour of spring (KL); 2. [P bahār f. x H bayār m.] poet. f. spring breeze (the poet meant 'bayār' but kept the form 'bahār', which is f. in gender); बनरी [cf. Raj. bānaṛī, H banī] reg. f. bride; बनरा [cf. Raj. bānaṛo] reg. m. bridegroom; सोहन var. [śobhana-] Br. adj. pleasant, charming.

बिकल बियोगिन की तापन-तवाई मैं।
बरनी न जाति, बन महिमा कहाँ लौं कहौं, 2
करनी बिचारि भई सोचत सवाई मैं।
ठाकुर कहत, होती ता छिन पठाई पाती, 3
छाती मैं उमंग, करौं कौन चतुराई मैं।
धन्य बनिता हैं, सुरवनिता सराहैं ते, जे 4
कंत घर पाइहैं बसंत की अवाई मैं॥ R4॥

मौरन लगे हैं आम, द्रुमन पलास पुनि, 1
बहत बयार आठौ जाम निरदई है।
धाम धाम धकधक परति बियोगिनी जे 2
बिरह-बियोग अंग अंग निरसई है।
ठाकुर कहत, बसि बालम बिदेस रहे, 3
लिखत सँदेसो यह रीत नई लई है।
लीजिये खबर, प्यारे, कीजिये गहर जिन, 4
अब रितुराज की अवाई आन भई है॥ R5॥

भवन तें कढि, बढि द्वारिही लौं आय देख, 1

---

4 Granthāvalī 90, Ṭhasak 92, Śatak 60. 5 Granthāvalī 92, Ṭhasak 88, Śatak 62.

4.1 झौरैं] G$_e$Ṭ$_e$, मौरै Ś$_e$ • मौरन] Ś$_e$, झौरन G$_e$Ṭ$_e$ • अली] G$_e$Ṭ$_e$, अलि Ś$_e$ • बियोगिन] G$_e$Ś$_e$, बियोगन Ṭ$_e$ • तापन तपाई] G$_e$Ṭ$_e$, तप तपवाई Ś$_e$ **4.2** बिचारि] G$_e$, बिचार Ś$_e$Ṭ$_e$ • सोचत] Ś$_e$, सोकित G$_e$Ṭ$_e$ **4.3** होती] G$_e$Ṭ$_e$, होत Ś$_e$ **5.4** जिन] G$_e$Ś$_e$, निज Ṭ$_e$

4.1 मौर [mukura-] m. bud, blossom; झौंरना [cf. H jhomṭā 'swaying'] v.i. to move, to shake; झौंर var. [cf H jhomṭā 'coil, bunch'] Br. m. bunch, cluster; झूमना [? kṣubh- 'to be unsteady' x *jhaṭ- or *jhamp-] v.i 1. to sway; 2. to move imposingly; 3. to be delighted; तवाई [cf. tapta-] Br. f. 1. burning; 2. suffering; तापन-तवाई poet. f. 'suffering of pains'; मैं pron. I (became restless). **4.2** करनी [karaṇīya-] f. (Krishna's) bad behaviour; सोचत [H socnā] v.t. imperf. Br. worrying; सवाई [sapāda-] adj. increased by a fourth. **4.3** होती पठाई पाती Br. I would send a letter; ता छिन (तत्क्षण) Br. obl. 'at that moment' immediately; छाती मैं उमंग Br. when there is strong desire in my heart; करौं कौन चतुराई मैं Br. can I do anything clever? **5.1** मौर- (मौलना) [mukulāyate] Br. v.i. to blossom; पुनि [punaḥ] adv. then, furthermore; निरदयी [S] adj. merciless. **5.2** धकधक [*dhakk-] 1. f.m. beating; perturbation; 2. adv. a-tremble; धक-धक करना to beat fast (the heart); 2. to be perturbed; निरसई [nīrasa-] poet. adj. emph. dry. **5.4** गहर poet. f. delay.

अवनि-अकास धूम-धूँधर मढी है री।
2 कोकिला की कूकैं सुनैं हूकैं उठैं उर मांझ,
भौंरन की गुंज बिपरीत सी कढी है री।
3 ठाकुर कहत, काम आम चढ्यौ मौर बाँधि,
आगन की ऊक सो पलासन चढी है री।
4 कै हरि मिलाव, कै या बैहरि मिटाव, बीर,
कै हरि लै पीर जो सरीर में बढी है री॥ R6॥

*बौरे रसालन की चढि डारन कूकत क्वैलिया मौन गहै ना।
2 ठाकुर, कुंजन पुंजन गुंजत भौंरन को चै चुपैबो चहै ना।

---

6 Bharatpur1 f. 150rv (5), Granthāvalī B38, Sudhāsar [S_1 f. 224r, S_2 f. 51v (2/53), S_3 f. 51rv (35), S_7 f. 170r (20/1619)]. The Sudhāsar presents this poem as a description of Spring.
7 Hariaudh (A_e) pp. 482–3, Sundarī-tilak (C_e) 375, Granthāvalī B40, Rāmcandra Śukla (I_e) p. 436, Ṣaṭṛtu-hajārā (J_e) pp. 17-18, Mītal (M_e) p. 32 (Vasant 105), Ṭhasak 91, Ṭhasak 'Jīvancarit' ($Ṭ^j_e$) p. 3 . In G_e and $Ṭ_e$ the second and third lines are in the reverse order.

6.1 कढि] $B_1G_eS_1S_2$, **कढ** S_3S_7 • **बढि**] $B_1G_eS_2$, **चढि** S_1, **बढ** S_3S_7 • **आय**] Σ, **आई** S_3 • **देख**] $G_eS_1S_3S_7$, **देषि** S_2 • **अवनि**] $G_eS_2S_3$, **अवन** S_1S_7 • **धूम**] B_1G_e, **धूँर** $S_1S_3S_7$, **धूरि** S_2 • **धूँधर**] $G_eS_1S_3S_7$, **धूंधरि** B_1S_2 **6.2 कूकैं**] **S**, **कूक** B_1G_e • **सुनैं**] S_1S_2, **सुनि** B_1G_e, **सुनै** S_3S_7 • **हूकैं**] **S**, **हूक** B_1G_e • **उठैं** S_1S_2, **⟨ठी⟩** B_1^{ac}, **उ⟨ठी⟩** B_1^{pc}, **उठि** G_e, **उठै** S_3S_7 • **उर**] Σ, **र** (unm.) S_2 • **गुंज**] Σ, **गुंजैं** S_1 • **बिपरीत**] Σ, **बिपरीति** B_1S_3 • **कढी**] **S**, **बढी** B_1^{ac}, **⟨क⟩ढी** B_1^{pc}, **बढी** G_e **6.3 आम**] Σ, **⟨आ⟩प** S_2 • **बाँधि**] Σ, **बांध** S_3S_7 • **आगन**] $S_1S_2S_7$, **आंगन** S_3, **आमन** G_e • **पलासन**] Σ, **पलासना** S_2 **6.4 बैहरि**] Σ, **बैहर** S_1 • **जो**] $B_1G_eS_1$, **या** $S_2S_3S_7$ • **बढी**] B_1^{pc}**S**, **मढ़ी** $B_1^{ac}G_e$ **7.1 बौरे**] $C_eG_e^{vl}I_eJ_eM_eṬ_eṬ^j_e$, **बौर** A_e, **बीर** G_e • **कूकत**] A_e**E**I_eM_e, **कूकति** C_eJ_e **7.2 पुंजन**] $C_eG_eJ_eM_eṬ_e$, **कुंजन** $A_eI_eṬ^j_e$ • **को चै**] $C_eG_eṬ_e$, **भीर** $A_eI_eṬ^j_e$, **को वै** J_e, **को दल** M_e • **चुपैबो**] Σ, **चुप्प** M_e

---

6.1 अवनी [S] f. earth; **धूम** m. 1. [S] smoke; 2. [? *dhunman-] noise, uproar; **धुँधर** [cf. H dhuṃdha- 'haze, mist, gloom'] m. dust in the air; darkness; **मढ़ना** [*maḍh-] v.t. to coat. **6.2 हूक** [*hūkkā-] f. shooting pain; **विपरीत** [S] adj. 'against my nature' inimical. **6.3 आम** [āmra-] m. mango tree; **मौर** 1. [mukura-] Br. m. bud, blossom; 2. [mukuṭa-] m. crown; **बाँधि** [cf. bandhana-] v.t. abs. Br. having put on; **चढना** [*caḍhati] v.t. 1. to rise up; 2. to march against, to attack; **काम आम चढ्यौ मौर बाँधि** Br. 1. Kama climbed on the mango tree putting on a crown (of mango flowers); 2. Kama attacked mounting a mango-flower (arrow on his bow); **आमन** apa. m. field (bearing only one crop); **ऊक** [ulkā-] poet. f. 1. burning; 2. swiftness (KL). **6.4 बैहर** 1. [P bahār x vāyu-, vātāra-] poet. f. (hot) wind at spring; **हरि लै** [harati] v.t. imp. Br. remove. **7.1 बौर-** [cf. mukura-] Br. v.i. to flower (the mango tree); **रसाल** [S] m. mango tree; **डाल** [ḍāla-] f. branch; **क्वैलिया** [kokila-] reg. m. the Indian cuckoo. **7.2 चै** [caya-] m. group (does not want to hide).

सीतल मंद सुगंधित, बीर, समीर लगे तन धीर धरै ना।
ब्याकुल कीन्हो बसंत बनाय कै, जाय कै कंत सों कोऊ कहै ना॥ R7॥ 4

पौन के पुंज धरा तें ब रौर कै धूर ललै उडि जान लगे।
तिनही मैं मिले तिनपत्र दिखात बियोगी बिथा अकुलान लगे। 2
कहि ठाकुर, भागि सँजोगिन के उनही के हिये सगुनान लगे।
दिन पाँचक-सातक तें, सजनी, दिन फागुन के फगुनान लगे॥ R8॥ 4

*पत्र बन-बेलिन के किसलै कुसुम देख, 1
बन बन बाग ये छबीले छबि-छावने।
कोकिला की कूक सुनि हूक होत कैसी देख, 2
ऐसे निसि-बासर सु कैसे कै गँवावने।
ठाकुर कहत, हिये बिसद बिचारु देख, 3
ऐसे समै स्याम हू को नाहीं तरसावने।

---

8 Bharatpur1 f. 151r (9), Granthāvalī B41, Sudhāsar [S_1 f. 217rv, S_2 f. 50rv (-/51), S_3 f. 45r (phāg 5), S_7 f. 166r (2/1588)], Vrindaban1 f. 16r (17/97). The Sudhāsar presents this poem as 'vasant ritu mẽ phāg varṇan'. 9 Granthāvalī 91, Ṭhasak 93, Śatak 61. The kavitt contains the words of a messenger to a heroine with wounded pride.

7.3 सीतल] Σ, सौतल G_e • धरै] J_eM_e, रहै A_eC_e**E**I_e **7.4** कीन्हो] Σ, कीनो C_e • सों] Σ, से A_e **8.1** पौन] (unm.) Σ • धरा] B_1^{pc}Σ, ⟨के⟩रा B_1^{ac} • रौर] Σ, रौरि B_1S_2 • धूर] **S**, धूरि B_1G_e, धुर V_1 • ललै] $B_1S_1S_2S_7V_1$, लै लै G_eS_3 • उडि] Σ, उड S_7 **8.2** तिन°] Σ, तिन तिन (dittography) S_2 • मैं] Σ, मो V_1 • बियोगी] $B_1G_eS_1S_2V_1$, बियोग S_3S_7 • लगे] Σ, लये (unrh.) S_1 **8.3** कहि] $B_1G_eS_1S_7V_1$, कबि S_2S_3 • भागि] $B_1G_eV_1$, भागी S_2, भाग S_1S_3, भान S_7 • सँजोगिन के] $S_1S_2S_7$, सजोगिनि कौ B_1, सँजोगिन की G_e, संजोगनि के S_3, सँजोगिन कौं V_1 • सगुनान] $B_1S_2S_3S_7V_1$, सुगुनान G_eS_1 **8.4** फगुनान] $B_1G_eS_1V_1$, फगुवान $S_2S_3S_7$ **9.1** देख] G_e, देखु $Ś_eṬ_e$ **9.2** देख] G_e, देखु $Ś_eṬ_e$ **9.3** देख] $G_eŚ_e$, देखु $Ṭ_e$ • को] G_e, कौं $Ś_eṬ_e$ •

7.4 कीन्हो (किया) [karoti] v.t. perf. Br. made me (i.e. mujhe); बनाय कै Br. completely, well. **8.1** धरा [S] poet. f. earth; ब Br. adv. now; रौर [rava-] Br. f. outcry, noise; ललै (ले ले कर) v.t. abs. reg. taking. **8.2** तिनपत्र [tṛṇapatra-] m. grass-leaves; दिखात reg. v.t. imperf. (as soon as) she sees; **8.3** भागि सँजोगिन के Br. the good fortune of women who are with their lovers; सगुनाना v.i. 1. [śakuna-] to guess, to foretell; 2. to be aroused. **8.4** पाँचक-सातक num. five or six; फगुनान [phālguna-] 1. v.i. to be exciting; 2. v.t. to throw colour at Holi. **9.1** किशलय [S] m. bud; छावने (छाना) [chādayati] Bund. m. spread(ing). **9.2** हूक [*hūkkā-] f. 1. pain; 2. Br. pang (of remorse). **9.3** विशद [S] adj. clear; evident; तरसाना [cf. tarṣayati] v.caus. to cause to desire, to torture.

4 आम पर मौर देख, मौर पर झौंर देख,
झौंरन पै भौंर देख गुंजत सुहावने॥ R9॥

1 *दिन दिन, जाम जाम, घरी घरी, पल पल,
झल झल होत आवै छावै दोऊ दीन पै।
2 कूकि कूकि कोकिल हँकारै, ललकारै मोर,
मान जिनि करियो, हरावै मानिनीन पै।
3 ठाकुर कहत, गोरी कहत गुपाल जी सों,
देखौ बन बाग छबि आम-अमलीन पै।
4 घुमड्यौ फिरत घाम, झुमड्यौ फिरत काम,
उमड्यौ फिरत रितुराज विरहीन पै॥ R10॥

1 *फूलन फुलावन है, द्रुमन डुलावन है,

---

10 Bharatpur1 f. 150r (4), Granthāvalī B36, Sudhāsar [S_2 f. 30v (32/32), S_7 f. 98r (3/954)], Vrindaban1 f. 15v (3/94). The Sudhāsar presents this poem within the description of the mānī nāyak' (lover with wounded? pride).

9.4 देख] $G_eŚ_e$, देखु $Ṭ_e$ • देख] $G_eŚ_e$, देखु $Ṭ_e$ **10.1** जाम जाम] Σ, जीम जाम V_1 • घरी घरी] Σ, घरि घरि S_2 • होत] $B_1G_eV_1$, होति **S** • आवै] S_7^{ac}Σ, छावै S_7^{pc} • दोऊ] B_1G_e, दुहु **S**, दोउ V_1 **10.2** मोर] G_eV_1, मौन S_2, भौंर B_1, भौन S_7 • जिनि] Σ, मति B_1 • करियो] $B_1G_eV_1$, करि तौ **S** • हरावै] Σ, हटावै G_e **10.3** गोरी कहत] Σ, गोरी कहैत V_1 • जी] $B_1G_eV_1$, जू **S** • देखौ] V_1, देषि **S**, देख्यौ G_e • आम] G_eS_7, आव S_2, आंव B_1V_1 • अमलीन] G_e**S**, अबलीन B_1V_1 **10.4** झुमड्यौ] $B_1G_eS_2S_7^{ac}$, चुमड्यौ S_7^{pc}, झूमड्यौ V_1 • रितुराज] G_e**S**, राति राजा B_1V_1 • विरहीन] Σ, विरहान V_1

9.4 मौर [mukura-] m. bud, blossom; झौंर (झोंटा) [*jhomṭa-] Br. m. bunch, cluster. **10.1** झल [jhalā-] m.f. 1. heat; 2. fig. frenzy; छाना [chādayati] v.i. to spread; दीन [A] m. world; **10.2** हँकारना [*hakkārayati] v.i. to shout out; हरावै माननीन पै reg. they subdue the sulking women; हटावै var. v.t. removes (the pride). **10.3** आम [āmra-] m. mango; अमलीन f. pl. Br. 1. [āmla-] tamarind; 2. [cf. Br. abalī-] woman. **10.4** घुमड़ना [cf. H ghūmnā] v.i. to grow thick (as clouds) (here: the glare); घाम [gharma-] m.f. heat and light of the sun; glare झुमर- [cf. H jhūmar 'encircling, crowd'] reg. v.t. to conquer (KL); उमड़ना [*ummaḍḍ-] v.i. 'to swell, to boil up' to be enraged.

जालम जसीलौ भट मदन महंत को।
आतप-पवन के प्रपंचनि मिटावन है, 2
छाहरो बनावन है आनँद अनंत को।
ठाकुर कहत, हेती सुखद संजोगिन को, 3
बैरी बरियानौ, बीर, बिरही निहंत को।
कोकिल मधुप मौज-सौरभ के पायबे कों 4
बंदीजन भए बादैं बिरद बसंत को॥ R11॥

फूलि उठे सुमन, मधुप मधु गुंज उठे, 1
बोलि उठे कोकिला की बानी बर सर है।
जाग उठे जोगी भोगी, भूमि अनुराग उठे 2
भागि उठे बिरही बिलंद अवसर है।
ठाकुर कहत, मेरौ कहौ मानि, मेरी बीर, 3

---

11 Bharatpur1 f. 153rv (23), Granthāvalī B39, Sudhāsar [S_1 f. 223rv, S_2 f. 51rv (1/52), S_3 f. 50v (vasant 32), S_7 f. 169v (17/1616)], Vrindaban1 f. 6r (7/33). S_1 presents this poem as a description of Spring. 12 Z_1 ff. 30v, 31v (24).

11.1 **फुलावन**] $B_1G_eS_1$, **फूलांमन** $S_2S_3S_7V_1$ • **है**] Σ, **हैं** B_1 • **दूमन**] Σ, **दुमन** S_2 • **डुलावन**] Σ, **दुलामन** S_3, **झुलामन** S_7 • **है**] Σ, **हैं** B_1 • **जालम**] $B_1\mathbf{S}V_1^{pc}$, **जलसा** G_e, **जाम** (unm.) V_1^{ac} **11.2** **प्रपंचनि**] $B_1G_eV_1$, **प्रपंचन** **S** • **छाहरौ**] Σ, **छाहौरौ** S_2 • **बनावन**] Σ, **बनामन** S_7 • **है**] Σ, **हैं** B_1 **11.3** **ठाकुर कहत**] Σ, **ठा॰** B_1 • **हेती**] Σ, **हेरी** S_3S_7 • **संजोगिन**] S_1S_3, **⟨स/सा⟩जौगिनि** B_1, **संजोगनि** G_eV_1, **सजोगीनि** S_2, **संजोग** (unm.) S_7^{ac}, **संजोगन** S_7^{pc} • **बैरी**] $B_1G_eS_1S_2S_3$, **बरी** V_1, **बैर** S_7 • **बरियानौ**] Σ, **बरीपानौ** S_2 • **बिरही निहंत**] $B_1G_eS_1$, **बिरहीन हंत** $S_2S_3S_7V_1$ **11.4** **बादैं**] B_1, **बादौ** G_e, **बाँचैं** S_1, **बादै**] $S_2S_3V_1$, **बांधै** S_7

11.1 **फुलावन** (**फुलाना**) Br. m. the cause for (the flowers') blooming; **जलसा** var. [A jalsa] m. gathering, feast; **जसील-** [yaśa-] Br. adj. famous; **भट** [S] m. hero, soldier (Love's soldier: Spring). **11.2** **आतप** [S] m. 'heat' pain (of separation) (i.e. the lover is expected to return in the spring); **आतप-पवन** [S] m. (the spring destroys the expansion of) winds penetrated by the heat of the sun (i.e. the hot wind does not burn yet); **प्रपंच** [S] m. 1. expansion; 2. trick; **छाहरौ** [cf. chādayati] reg. adj. 'spreading' favourable (cf H chānevālā) (RSh); 2. [cf. H chāṃh] reg. m. shade, shelter. **11.3** **हेती** m. benefactor; **बरिया-** [bala-] Br. v.i. to become strong; **बरियानौ** Br. v.i. perf. (used as adj.) strong; **निहंत** [nihata-] adj. 'killed' wretched. **11.4** **कोकिल मधुप** poet. the cuckoos and the bees; **मौज** [A] f. 'surge' delight (of the fragrance); **बंदीजन** [P+S] m. bard; **बाद-** [vādayati] Br. v.t. to tell; to proclaim; **विरद** [S] poet. m. fame, glory. **12.1** **बोलि उठे कोकिला** Br. the cuckoos that started to sing; **बर सर** [vara svara] Br. best sound. **12.2** **भूमि** [S] m. obl. on the earth; **अनुराग उठे** affection arose; **बुलंद** [P] adj. great.

आयौ रितुराज, तोहि होत ना असर है।
4 सर कीनै लोक लोक, सर की नजर राखि
रंचक कै सर, पंचसर की पसर है॥ R12॥

1 गाए पिक जालनि करालनि सुरनि गान
ठाकुर रसालन की डारन पै झूलि झूलि।
2 आए पंचसाइक हरौल रति-नाइक के
जगत के घाइक मतंग-भौंर हूलि हूलि।
3 टेरि टेरि कहति रहति मुह फेरि फेरि
हेरि हेरि चहति लहति मांन भूलि भूलि।
4 बास बिरहीन के हुतास ज्यौं दहन लागें
आस पास बननि पलास रहे फूलि फूलि॥ R13॥

फाग

1 *केसर सुगंधहू के रंग मैं रँगोंगी हम

---

13 Bharatpur1 f. 133v (15). The quatrain is introduced as a poem on 'vasant' by Ṭhākur. The word 'ṭhākur'—although not in its usual place at the beginning of the third line—is not part of the syntactic structure of the sentence and should be understood as poetic signature.

12.3 मानि] *conj.* ⟨मा/म⟩नि Z_1 • बीर] *conj.* ⟨ची⟩र Z_1 **13.3** कहति] *conj.* कईति B_1

12.4 सर करना idiom. to subdue; सर की नजर idiom. glance piercing as an arrow (RSh); राखि [rakṣati] Br. v.t. imp. 1. defend, ward off; 2. keep (the eye on) (KL); रंचक कै 1. Br. making (their effect) small (by keeping an eye on them) (KL); 2. reg. adj. tiny (RSh); सर m. 1. [S] arrow; 2. [cf. H asar] poet. (small) part, effect (RSh); सरपंच var. [pañcasara-] m. 'the one with five arrows' Kāma; पसर [prasāra-] m. (here f.) expansion, attack. **13.1** जाल [S] m. 1. network, mesh; 2. (here:) group; करालनि सुरनि (Br. obl. pl.) on terrible voices. **13.2** पंचसायक [S] poet. adj. of five arrows (epithet of Kama); हरौल (हरावल) [Γ] Br. m. vanguard (of an army); रतिनायक [S] m. 'Rati's lord' Kama; घाइक [cf. ghāta-, H ghāy] m. wounder, killer; हूल- [*hūl-] Br. v.t. to drive or to urge (an animal forward). **13.3** कईति apa. चहति Br. v.i. (imperf.) she desires; भूलि भूलि Br. (abs.) occasionally forgetting (her love). **13.4** हुतास (हुताशन) [S] Br. m. fire;

और गुर लोगन की लाज कों पहेलिबौ।
गाइबौ बजाइबौ जू, हसिबौ हसाइबौ जू, 2
रसवश ह्वैकै सब सुखही कौ रेलिबौ।
ठाकुर कहत, लाल, होनी तौ करैंगी सब, 3
एक अनहोनी, कहौ, कौन बिधि झेलिबौ।
कर कुच पेलिबौ, गरे में भुज मेलिबौ जू, 4
ऐसी होरी खेलिबौ जू हम तौ न खेलिबौ॥ R14॥

---

14 Bharatpur1 f. 165rv (96), Kālidās-hajārā (H_e) 328, Hindī Sāhitya Sammelan, Allahabad 4364 (2030) (I_1) f. 54rv, Ṣaṭṛtu-hajārā (J_e) p. 18 (Vasant ṛtu varṇan), Mītal (M_e) p. 266 (Śiśir 146), Sudhāsar [S_3 f. 225r (31), S_7 129rv (2/1224)], Ṭhākur-satsaī (Ṭ) f. 4r (33), Vrindaban2 f. 71v. The Sudhāsar presents this poem within the description of the spring (vasant) within the 'ṣaṭṛtu' section in the chapter on 'uddīpan'. • The established text is based on S_7. • The eccentric readings of B_1 are occasionally followed by Ṭ. • I_1 shows traces of a phase of oral transmission.

14.1 केसर] $I_1J_eM_e$SṬ, केसरि $B_1H_eV_2$ • सुगंध] SV_2, गुलाब B_1, सुगंधि H_e, अबीर I_1, सुरंग J_eM_e, गुलाल Ṭ • हू] $B_1J_eM_e$SṬ, ही H_eV_2, हुं I_1 • के] Σ, सो I_1, को Ṭ • मैं] $B_1J_eM_e$SṬ, सौं H_eV_2, तो I_1 • रँगोंगी] $J_eM_eS_7$, सनैंगी B_1, रँगेंगे H_eI_1, रंगौ की S_3, रंगोगी Ṭ, रगेगी V_2 • हम] H_eSV_2, आजु J_eM_e, लाल I_1, आज B_1Ṭ • गुर] $B_1H_eI_1S_7$ṬV_2, गुरु $J_eM_eS_3$ • लोगन] $H_eJ_eM_eI_1^{pc}$SV_2, जनन B_1, जन (unm.) I_1^{ac}, लोकन Ṭ • की] Σ, कौ S_7 • कों] M_e, हू H_eV_2, को $B_1I_1J_e$Ṭ, रू $S_3S_7^{ac}$, हू S_7^{pc} • पहेलिबो] Σ, पहलबो I_1 **14.2** गाइबौ बजाइबो] Σ, नाँचिबौ नचाइबौ B_1, नाचबो औ गाइबो Ṭ • जू] $B_1H_eJ_e$ṬV_2, जु I_1M_eS • हसिबौ] H_eSV_2, गाइबौ B_1, नाचिबौ J_eM_eṬ, नचिबो I_1 • हसाइबौ] H_eSV_2, नचाइबौ $I_1J_eM_e$, बजाइबौ B_1Ṭ • जू] Σ, जु I_1 • ह्वै कै] Σ, है कै V_2 • सब] H_eSV_2, हमैं B_1, हम J_eM_eṬ, येक I_1 • सुखही कौ] S, सब सुख B_1, सुखहू कौ H_eV_2, सब बिधि M_e, संग मिलि I_1, सबी बिधि J_e, सबै सुख Ṭ • रेलिबौ] B_1H_eSV_2, झेलिबौ J_eM_e, मेलबो I_1, ठेलबो Ṭ **14.3** ठाकुर कहत] Σ, ठा° B_1, ठाकुर कहैत I_1 • लाल] B_1H_eSṬV_2, बाल J_eM_e, सब I_1 • करैंगी] S_7, सहैंगी B_1, करैंगे $I_1M_eH_e$, करौंगी J_eM_e, करैगी S_3V_2, करोगी Ṭ • सब] $B_1H_eJ_eM_eS_3S_7^{pc}$ṬV_2, लाल I_1, *om.* (unm.) S_7, सभ Ṭ • अनहोनी] Σ, अतिहोनि S_3 • कहौ] $B_1J_eH_eM_e$SṬ, ताह I_1, कहै V_2 • बिधि] $B_1H_eJ_eM_eI_1$ṬV_2, बिध SṬ • झेलिबौ] $B_1H_eI_1$SṬV_2, ठेलिबौ J_eM_e **14.4** कर] Σ, करि I_1 • कुच] Σ, कुचि I_1 • पेलिबौ] Σ, ठेलिबौ B_1 • भुज] $B_1H_eJ_e$SṬV_2, बांह I_1, भुजि M_e • जू] H_eM_eSV_2, सो B_1, जुं I_1, जो J_e, सु Ṭ • ऐसी] $H_eJ_eM_e$SṬV_2, ऐसैं B_1I_1Ṭ • जू हम] H_eM_eSV_2, तौ हम $B_1I_1J_e$Ṭ • तौ] Σ, सौं B_1

14.1 सुरंग हू var. Br. and also red; पहेलिबौं [cf. H pahal] v.t. fut. reg. I will push aside. **14.2** रेलना [cf. raya-] v.t. to push, to shove. **14.3** बाल [bālā-] f. voc. girl; होनी reg. adj. possible; अनहोनी reg. adj. impossible; झेलना var. [*jhelati] v.t. to endure, to tolerate. **14.4** पेलिबो [*prelayati] v.t. inf. reg. 1. to push; 2. to squeeze; ठेलना var. [*ṭhell-] v.t. to push; to shove; हम तौ न खेलिबो reg. then I do not want to play.

1 मच रची फागु और सब सबही पै घालैं
रंग औ गुलाल, लाल, ख्याल अबलोकों मैं।
2 मो पै तुही, ठाकुर, लगाये घात घूमै घेरि,
देखों, अब जात कितै इत उत रोकों मैं।
3 गहि लेहौं गाफिल कै छिन में, छबीले छैल,
छेदि कै, छली जू, निज नैननि की नोकों मैं।
4 ओटै ह्वै करत पिचकारिन की चोटै कहा,
सोंहै आव, साँवरे, सराहौं तब तोको मैं॥ R15॥

*ठाढी रहौ, न डगौ, न भगौ, तुम देखहु जो कछु खेलती ख्यालहिं।
2 गावन दे री, बजावन दे, सखि, आवन दै इतै नंद के लालहिं।

15 Ṣaṭṛtu-hajārā (J_e) pp. 18–19 (Included into the 'Vasant ṛtu varṇan' and attributed to 'Ṭhākur kabi prācīn'. 16 Sundarī-tilak (C_e) 393, Granthāvalī 93, Ṣaṭṛtu-hajārā (J_e) p. 18, Vidvanmod taraṅgiṇī (L_e) 87, Mītal p. 267 (śiśira, holī-bahār 153), Sudhāsar [S_3 f. 223r (18), S_7 127v (20/1208)], Śatak 90, Ṭhākur-satsaī (Ṭ) f. 4rv (34), Ṭhasak 99. The Sudhāsar presents this poem within the description of the spring (vasant) within the 'ṣaṭṛtu' section in the chapter on 'uddīpan'. • The Vidvanmod taraṅgiṇī introduces the poem as an example of the 'bhaviṣya suratigopanā' (heroine hiding her future pleasure).

15.1 घालैं] *conj.* घालै J_e **15.2** देखों] *conj.* देखो J_e **15.3** कै] *em.* कर (unm.) J_e • नैननि] *conj.* नैनान J_e **15.4** सोंहै] *conj.* सोहै J_e **16.1** ठाढी] Σ, ठाढौ Ṭ$_e$ • रहौ] Σ, रहौं C_e • न डगौ] **E**$J_eL_eS_7$, डगौं C_e, डगौ (unm.) M_e, न डरो S_3, न भगो Ṭ • भगौ] **E**$J_eL_eM_e$**S**, भगौं C_e, डगो Ṭ • तुम] L_e**S**Ṭ, अब C_e**E**J_eM_e • देखहु] S_7Ṭ, देखिहौं C_e, देखन **E**L_e, देखो J_eM_e, खेलहु S_3 • जो कछु] C_e**S**, जो है कछु M_e, जो हौ कछु J_e, देव जू **E**, देहु री L_e, जो कछू Ṭ • खेलती **S**Ṭ, खेलति C_eJ_e, कौतुक **E**, ख्याल जो L_e, खेल जो L_e^{vl}, खेलत M_e • ख्यालहिं] Σ, ख्यालह S_7 **16.2** दे री] Σ, देव **E** • दै सखि] **S**, दे सजि $C_eJ_eL_e$, देव जू **E**, दै सखी M_eṬ • आवन दै] Σ, आवन देव **E** • इतै] $C_eJ_eM_e$**S**Ṭ, जू **E**, इत L_e • के] Σ, को Ṭ • लालहिं] Σ, लालह S_7

15.1 मच रची (the celebration of spring) broke out; घालना [*ghalyati] v.t. to throw; ख्याल (खेल) [*khel(l)-] reg. m. (your) play; अबलोकों [avalokayati] Br. v.t. pres. I watch (from afar). **15.2** मो पै घेरि Br. besieging me, importuning me; तुही घूमै Br. it is you who go around; घात लगाना idiom. to look for an opportunity; देखों अब रोकों मैं Br. I will see now and I will stop you; जात कितै इत उत Br. where do you wander here and there. **15.3** गाफिल [P] adj. careless, negligent; गाफिल कै Br. distracting; छली जू reg. voc. o you deceiver! नैननि की नोकों Br. with side-glances. **15.4** सोंहै आव Br. come in front!. **16.1** देखिहौ [dṛkṣati, drakṣati] v.t. (Br. fut.) you will see (what I am going to play); ख्याल (खेल) [*khel(l)-] reg. m. (obl.) play, sport. **16.2** सजि var. 1. [P sāz] m. musical instrument; 2. [H sajkar] v.i. (abs. Br.) ornamented, well arranged.

ठाकुर, हौं रँगिहौं रँग सौं अँग ओडिहौं, बीर, अबीर गुलालहिं।
धूँधर मैं, धधकी मैं, धमार मैं हौं धँसिहौं, धरि लैहौं गुपालहिं॥ R16॥ 4

डार्‌यौ जौ गुलाल रंग केसर को अंग अंग 1
आन झकझोर्‌यौ मीडौ डौर मुख रोरी मैं।
चाहि चितवारी हितवारी नितवारी करी 2
काहे, कहौ, कौन अब जैहै ब्रजखोरी मैं।
ठाकुर कहत, ऐसे रस मैं निरस होत 3
कहा भयो छाती जौ छवीले छुई चोरी मैं।
अंक भरि लीनी तौ कलंक की न संक कीजै, 4
आज बरजोरी कौ न दोष होत होरी मैं॥ R17॥

*दृग मूँदिकै अंचर सौं कहतीं, पिचकारी हमारी, सखी, गहियो।

---

17 Granthāvalī 94, Ṭhasak 98, Śatak 57. 18 Granthāvalī 95, Jaipur1 f. 7r (23), Śatak 71, Ṭhasak 97, Udaipur (U) f. 126r (2). This savaiyā presents the words of a woman towards Krishna, whom she initially feigns to mistake for a companion and, therefore, forbids him to speak. In the end, however, when he is about to move away she cannot help calling him Krishna.

16.3 हौं] $C_eJ_eL_eM_eS_7$, त्यौं **E**, हौ S_3Ṭ • रँगिहौं] **E**$C_eJ_eM_eS_7$, रँगहौ L_eS_3Ṭ • अंग] M_e**SṬ**, अरु C_e**E**J_eL_e • ओडिहौं] $C_eM_eS_7$, मारिहौं **E**, ओडिहौ J_e, ओढिहौ L_eṬ, ओढहै S_3 • बीर] Σ, बौर C_e • गुलालहिं] Σ, गुलालह S_7 **16.4** धूँधर] **E**M_eS_3Ṭ, धूधुर C_eJ_e, धूँधरि L_eS_7 • मै] $C_eJ_eM_e$**SṬ**, की **E**L_e • धधकी] $J_eL_eM_e$**S**, धुधकी **E**, अब की C_e • धमार] **E**$L_eM_eS_7$Ṭ, धमारि C_eJ_e • हौं] Σ, *om.* (unm.) M_e • धसिहौं] C_e**E**$J_eL_eM_eS_7$, धसहौ S_3, धरहो Ṭ • धरि] C_e**E**$J_eL_eM_e$, धर **SṬ** • लैहौं] C_e**E**$J_eL_eM_eS_7$, लैहौ S_3Ṭ • गुपालहिं] C_e**E**$L_eM_eS_3$Ṭ, गोपालहि J_e, गुपालह S_7 **17.4** संक] $Ś_eṬ_e$, संकै G_e • लीनी] $G_eṬ_e$, लीनो $Ś_e$ **18.1** अंचर] J_1U, अंचल **E** • कहतीं] **E**U, गहिती J_1

16.3 ओडना var. [*oḍḍā-] v.t. 1. to cover (oneself) with a shield; 2. to ward off (a blow). **16.4** धुँधर f. 1. small drum; 2. darkness; धधकी f. tambourine beaten at Holi; धुधकी var. f. 1. 'dhu-dhu' sound, noise; 2. darkness, haze. **17.1** रंग केसर को Br. saffron colour; झकझोरना [cf. *jhakk(ol)- and *jholayati] v.t. to shake, to jolt; मींड- [*mṛñjati] Br. v.t. to rub; रोरी f. red clay used to mark tilak; मीडौ...मैं Br. running he rubbed red clay on my face. **17.2** चितवारी Br. what he desired; नितवारी Br. what he always does; करी v.t. perf. Br. he did; काहे Br. interr. for what? खोरी [*khora- or khola-] Br. f. lane. **17.3** छाती छुई Br. touched my breast; चोरी मैं idiom. Br. stealthily. **17.4** संक [śaṅkā-] Br. f. doubt; कलंक की न संक कीजै br. you shouldn't suppose that it was a sin; बरजोरी [bala- + P zor] f. violence, vigour. **18.1** मूँदिकै [mudrayati] v.t. abs. Br. covering (my eyes); कहतीं v.t. imperf. reg. I say (cf. H ham kahte haĩ); गहियो [grah-] v.t. imp. Br. hold!

2 अब बोलहु तौ खिसियैयै, सुनौ, फिरि रीझ-कुरीझ कछू कहियो।
कहि ठाकुर, कीजे फिराद कहा, यह दाद हमारी तुही लहियो।
4 मेरी आँखिन बीचि गुलाल गई, अब, लाल हहा, रहियो रहियो॥ R18॥

1 फागुन के औसर अनोखे बनि बानिक ह्वै
लीन्हे ग्वालबाल स्याम फाग आइ जोरी है।
2 पाइ सुधि डगरी नवेली राधिका के संग
रंग लै उमंग अंग अंग, बैस थोरी है।
3 ठाकुर कहत, प्यारी स्याम तन हेरि हेरि
मुरि मुसक्यात ठाढ़ी कुँवरि किसोरी है।
4 दौरी लै गुलाल ब्रजबाल चार्यौ औरन तैं,
होरी लाल, होरी लाल, होरी लाल, होरी है॥ R19॥

---

19 Granthāvalī 96, Śatak 58, Ṭhasak 95.

18.2 बोलहु] J_1, बोलिहौ **E**, बोलियै U • खिसियैयै] J_1, रिसियैहौं **E**, किसयैगे U • सुनौ] **E**J_1, महां U • फिरि] **E**J_1, अरु U • रीझ कुरीझ] **E**U, रीझि कुरीझि J_1 • **18.3** कहि] J_1, कवि **E**, कहा U • फिराद] **E**J_1, पुकार U • दाद] J_1, लाज **E**, दाहि U • तुमी] J_1, तुही **E**, तुम्हा U • **18.4** बीचि] J_1, माँझ **E**, बीच U • गई] J_1U, गयौ **E** • रहियो रहियो] **E**J_1U^{pc}, रहियो (haplography) U^{ac} **19.1** बनि] G_e, बन $Ś_eṬ_e$

18.2 बोलिहौ v.t. fut. Br. if you say anything; खिसियैयै [*khiss-] v.t. pass. or fut. pl. reg. I will be ashamed; I will be irritated; रिसियैहौं var. 1. [H risnā 'to be angry'] v.i. (Br. fut.) I will become angry; 2. (?) [caus. of H risnā 'to drip, to ooze'] poet. v.t. I will sprinkle you; कहियो [kathayati] reg. v.t. 1. pass. subj. may be called; 2. subj. you may say. रीझ कुरीझ कछू कहियौ Br. 1. our delight may be called (i.e. may turn into) some irritation; 2. you may say some good and bad things (because I am angry); **18.3** फिराद (फ़रयाद) [P] f. vulg. complaint; दाद 1. [S] m. (here f.) gift, boon; 2. [P] f. justice; (cf. dād-o-faryād 'appeal for justice or redress'); दाद लेना idiom. to administer justice; लाज लेना var. idiom. to protect one's honour. **18.4** गुलाल गई red powder fell (into my eyes); लाल [lālya-] m. voc. o dear child (i.e. Krishna). **19.1** बानिक poet. m. clothes; जोर- [H joṛnā] Br. v.t. to be celebrated. **19.2** पाइ सुधि Br. hearing the news; डगर- poet. v.i. to go, to set off; बैस थोरी हैं Br. though they are young.

*नीर सो माँचि रह्यौ रँग फाग पुरीं गलियाँ त्यौं गुलाल उलीच मैं।
जाय सकैं न इतै न उतै, सो घिरे नर नारि सनेह-रँगीच मैं।
ठाकुर, केतो बराउ कियौ पै उपाउ चल्यौ न सखीन के बीच मैं।
रंग भरी रसमाती गुवालि गोपालहिं लै गिरी केसर कीच मैं॥ R20॥

*होरी की हौंस हमैं ना कछू, हम जानती हैं तुम रार करैया।
फूलौ न मोहिं अकेली निहारि कै, भूलियो ना तुम गाय-चरैया।
ठाकुर, जौ बरजोरी करौ तुम, हौं हूँ नहीं कछु दीन-परैया।
फोरिहौ काहू की आँख, लला, रहु, नोखे गुपाल गुलाल डरैया॥ R21

---

20 Granthāvalī 97, Vidvanmod-taraṅgiṇī (L_e) p. 91 (90), Chaupasni Nr. 7249 f. 86r (4) (M_2), Ṭhasak 94, Ṭhasak 'Jīvancarit' (Ṭ$_e^j$) p. 22, Sundarītilak (U_e) 1273. The Vidvanmod-taraṅgiṇī presents this poem as an example of the 'vartamāna suratigopanā' (heroine hiding her current pleasure) within the 'Guptā' (hidden) or 'Suratigopanā' (heroine hiding her pleasure) subsection of the the 'Parakīyā' section. 21 Granthāvalī 98, Ṭhasak 96, Śatak 59.

20.1 नीर] $L_eM_2U_e$, रंग **E** • सो माँचि] Σ, कां रा⟨षी/ची⟩ M_2 • रह्यौ] *conj.* रही **E**, रह्यौ L_e, गई M_2, रहे U_e • रँग] L_eU_e, रस **E**, सुच M_2 • फाग] **E**, राचि L_e, मान M_2, राय U_e • गलियाँ त्यौं] **E**, गलिया औ L_e, गलिया यौ L_e^{vl}, गलियां जे M_2, गली आरग U_e • गुलाल] Σ, गुलाब Ṭ$_e^j$ • मैं] Σ, मै L_e **20.2** सकैं] **E**, सकै $L_eM_2U_e$ • सो] **E**L_e, *om.* M_2, सु U_e • घिरे नर] **E**, रहे घिरि L_e, बिदरे नर M_2, रही घिरि U_e • नारि] **E**L_e, नेह M_2, कान्हरे U_e • सनेह] Σ, बाल U_e • रँगीच] Σ, नगीच U_e **20.3** केतो] L_eU_e, ऐसो **E**, हां M_2 • बराउ] L_e, उमाह **E**, उपाइ L_e^{vl}, रंग सां M_2, बनाय U_e • कियौ] **E**U_e, मचो L_e, रंग हां M_2 • पै उपाउ चल्यौ न] L_e, भयो कौतुक एक **E**, कर कोतक हू M_2, पर दाव चलै न U_e • सखीन] Σ, सषियांन M_2 **20.4** °माती] Σ, मानी M_2 • गुवालि] **E**, वा L_e, ग्वालि (unm.) L_e^{vl}, गवाल M_2 • गोपालहिं] Ṭ$_e$$L_e$, गुपालहिं G_eU_e, गोपाल कां M_2 • लै] **E**M_2, लाल L_eU_e • गिरी] Σ, गई M_2 • केसर] Σ, केसरि L_e • कीच] Σ, बीच L_e **21.4** रहु] Ś$_e$, रहो G_eṬ$_e$ • गुपाल गुलाल] G_eṬ$_e$, गुलाल के लाल Ś$_e$

20.1 रँग-फाग poet. m. the joy of Holi; पुरीं गलियाँ Br. 1. the lanes are filled; 2. towns and lanes; उलीचना [ud-luñcana] v.t. to pour off, to throw; उलीच मैं Br. in pouring. **20.2** रँगीच [raṅgīta-] poet. m. colour; नगीच var. adv. postp. near. **20.3** बराव [cf. Br. barā- 'to hold oneself aloof'] m. guard (against); avoidance; **20.4** रसमाती [rasa-matta-] adj. intoxicated; **21.1** राड़ [rāṭi-] f. fight, disturbance, strife. **21.2** चरैया m. one who grazes (the cows), a rustic (H carānevāā). **21.3** बरजोरी [bala + P zor] f. violence; परैया poet. adj. coward (cf. H palāyan karnevālā). **21.4** फोड़ना [sphoṭayati] v.t. to make the eyes blind; रहु v.i. imp. Br. stop! नोखे- [anapekṣa-] reg. adj. uncommon.

मदमाते गुवाल गरूर भरे धिधकी दियैं ढोल बजावत है।
2 गहि लावत धावत धूरि भरे, जो पै गोपबधू कहूँ पावत है।
कहि ठाकुर, जौ पै चली तुम बाहिर कौन सयान कहावत है।
4 दई-मारे जिभार कछू को कछू हुरिहार दुवार पै गावत है॥ R22॥

1 एकन की कंचुकी चुपरि चारु चोवन सों,
एकन की आँखिन गुलाल मूठ मेलै है।
2 एकन के संग नाचै, गावै संग एकन के,
एकन के संग उर आनँद सकेलै है।
3 ठाकुर कहत, सहै एकन की गारी लाल,
एकन की पिचकारी अंगन पै झेलै है।
4 मोहिं कत लीन्हे जाति बावरी सी उतै, जितै
कान्ह रंगमातो रसमातो फाग खेलै है॥ R23॥

इत आए गुलाल सों बूडे गुपाल जू, चंदमुखी गहि बाँह रही।

---

22 Alvar 73v, Bharatpur1 f. 132v-3r (11), Bharatpur6 f. 7r, Granthāvalī 99, Vrindaban1 f. 9rv (1/53). 23 Granthāvalī 100, Ṭhasak 100. 24 Bharatpur1 f. 151r (11), Granthāvalī 101, Sudhāsar [S_3 f. 222r (13), S_7 f. 127r (14/1202)], Vrindaban1 f. 13v-14r (19/83). The Sudhāsar presents this poem within the description of phāg (the festival of Holi) within the 'ṣaṭṛtu' section in the chapter on 'uddīpan'.

22.1 मदमाते] $AB_1B_6V_1$, मदमान G_e • भरे] $B_6^{pc}\Sigma$, भरे मदमाते (unm.) B_6^{ac} • बजावत] Σ, बजावति B_6 • है] Σ, हैं B_6 **22.2** धूरि] $B_6G_eV_1$, धूर A, धूम B_1 • जो पै] AB_6V_1, लषि B_1, जु पै G_e • कहूँ] $B_1G_eV_1$, कहिं A, कोऊ B_6 • पावत] Σ, पावति B_6 • है] $B_1G_eV_1$, हैं AB_6 **22.3** जौ] Σ, ता B_6 • कौन] Σ, ⟨कै/कौ⟩⟨*/⟩ V_1 • सयान] Σ, सौ स्यान B_6 • कहावत] $B_1G_eV_1$, मनावत A, कहावतु B_6 • है] G_eV_1, हैं AB_1B_6 **22.4** दई] AB_1V_1, दै (unm.) B_6, दइ G_e • जिभार] Σ, जुह्वार A • को] AG_eV_1, के B_1B_6 • हुरिहार] Σ, फगुवारे B_6 • पै] Σ, मै B_6 • गावत] Σ, गावति B_6 • है] G_eV_1, हैं AB_1B_6 **23.1** चुपरि] G_e, चुपर $Ṭ_e$ **24.1** इत] Σ, यति॥ S_3 • आए] Σ, आअं V_1 • सों] Σ, स्सै V_1 • जू] Σ, जुं V_1 • गहि] Σ, गह S_3

22.1 धधकी (धुधकी) [cf. H dhū-dhū] f. loud noise. **22.2** गहि लावत धावत Br. he runs and catches; जो पै कहूँ Br. if somehow. **22.3** जौ पै idiom. Br. then if; ता पै var. idiom. Br. and what is more; सयान [sajñāna-] adj. (something) wise. **22.4** दई-मारे adj. unfortunate, wretched; जिभार [jihvā-] m. gossiper, a garrulous person; कछू कौ कछू Br. something or other (cf. H kuch na kuch); हुरिहार m.Br. f. one who plays Holi; दुवार [dvāra-] Br. m. gate. **23.1** चुपड़ना [*cuppa-] v.t. 'to oil' to smear; चोआ [cf. H cuānā] m. Av. fragrant paste of four ingredients. **23.4** कत interr. Av. Br. why? **24.1** बूडना [*buḍyati] v.i. to be immersed.

अब बारिये काम करोरन या छबि भाँति अनेक कबीन कही। 2
कहि ठाकुर, बानिक ताकि तिहारी, हमारी या दीठ-बसीठ कही।
'तन साँवरे, लाल कहावत हौ, परि लाल भए अबही हौ सही'॥ R24॥ 4

*होरी हो रही है, को रही है घाले घुंघत कों, 1
स्याम छबि देखि, सो न कोटिक अनंग मैं।
गावै गीत रस के, बजावै बाजे हँसि के, सु 2
चाहन के चसके निहारे अंग अंग मैं।
ठाकुर कहत, ब्रज-बालन के अंतर की 3
निरखि निरंतर की उमँग उमंग मैं।
बैठी निज संग मैं, सनेह के प्रसंग मैं, सु 4
तन लाल रंग मैं औ मन लाल रंग मैं॥ R25॥

*'कैसे ग्वार, बल कैसो ठहरै पसर कीनें, 1

---

25 Bharatpur1 f. 158v (53), Granthāvalī B42, Sudhāsar [S_2 f. 40rv (-/42), S_3 f. 18v (horī 47), S_7 131v (21/1243)], Vrindaban1 f. 4v-5r (12/25).

24.2 बारिये] Σ, **बारनै** G_e • **काम**] Σ, **का** G_e • **करोरन**] B_1**S**, **करौं** G_e, **करोरान** V_1 • **या**] Σ, **बारनिया** G_e • **कबीन**] Σ, **कबिन** (unm.) V_1 **24.3 ताकि**] $B_1G_eS_7$, **ताक** S_3V_1 • **दीठ**] B_1, **डीठि** G_eV_1, **डीठ S** • **बसीठ**] B_1**S**, **बसीठि** G_eV_1 **24.4 सावरे**] B_1V_1, **सामरे** G_e, **सामरो S** • **हौ**] Σ, **हों** V_1 • **परि**] Σ, **पर** S_7 • **अबही**] $B_1^{pc}\Sigma$, **⟨अ⟩बही** B_1 • **हौ**] Σ, **हौं** S_7 **25.1 घुंघट**] Σ, **घूंघट** S_7 • **देखि**] G_eV_1, **देषी S** • **कोटिक**] Σ, **कटक** S_7 • **अनंग**] Σ, **अन** (unrh.) S_2 **25.2 गावै**] $G_eS_3V_1$, **गामै** S_2S_7 • **बजावै**] $G_eS_3V_1$, **बजामैं** S_2, **बजावैं** S_7 • **हँसि**] S_2S_7, **हँस** $G_eS_3V_1$ • **चाहन**] $G_eS_2V_1$, **चाहत** S_3S_7 **25.3 अंतर**] Σ, **अंतरि** S_7 • **निरखि**] G_e, **निरषी निरंषी** (dittography) S_2, **निरखी** S_3S_7, **निरष** V_1 • **उमँग उमंग**] Σ, **उमग उग उमग** (dittography) S_2 **25.4 मन**] Σ, **मत** S_3 .

24.2 बारन (वारण) var. [S] m. prohibition; **का** var. Br. interr. what? **काम करोरान** var. reg. millions of Kāmas; **वारणीय** var. poet. adj. 1. worth to be sacrificed; 2. [varṇanīya-] worth to be described. **24.3 बसीठ** [vasiṣṭha-] m. messenger (said). **24.4 सामर- (सांवला)** var. [śyāmala-] Br. adj. black; **लाल भए** Br. you blushed. **25.1 को** Br. interr. who? **घालना** [ghalyati] v.t. to throw down; to keep. **25.2 चाह** [H cāhnā] f. 1. desire; 2. love; **चस्का** [cf. H casaknā] m. 1. relish; 2. ardent desire; **निहारना** [nibhālayati] v.t. 1. to look at; 2. to expect. **25.3 के अंतर की** the inner thoughts of; **निरंतर की** adj. permanent. **25.4 निज संग मैं** Br. alone; **सनेह के प्रसंग में** Br. in (a situation) love; **लाल रंग** 1. red colour; 2. Krishna's love.

सावधान भयें चाव चलत न चोरी को।

2 केसरि-गुलाल की, अबीर की चलाई आँधी,

खेलन न पावै स्याम खेल बरजोरी को'।

3 ठाकुर, बजाय बाजे धाइ धँसि पैठो ग्वार

होरी को दिवस, भयो हुकम किसोरी को।

4 चारु चित चल्ला होत, भारी प्रेम-पल्ला होत,

हरि कौ मोहौल्ला, पर हल्ला होत गोरी को॥ R26॥

---

26 Bharatpur1 f. 150v-151r (b8), Granthāvalī B43, Sudhāsar [S_2 f. 39v (5b/41), S_7 130v (13/1235)], Vrindaban1 f. 16r (16/96).

26.1 ग्वार] $B_1G_eV_1$, ग्वाल **S** • बल] $B_1S_7V_1$, बाल G_e, *om.* (unm.) S_2 • ठहरै] G_e**S**, ठहेरैं B_1V_1 • कीनें] B_1, कीने Σ • सावधान भयैं] Σ, भयो सवधान S_7 **26.2** केसरि] $B_1S_2V_1$, केसरी G_e, केसर S_7 • चलाई] Σ, चलाइ G_e **26.3** बाजे] Σ, बजि G_e • धसि] Σ, धस S_7 • पैठो] G_eV_1, बैठनो (unm.) S_2, बैठो S_7 • ग्वार] G_e**S**, ग्वारि B_1V_1 • होरी] Σ, होरि S_2 • हुकम] Σ, हुम्कमु S_7 **26.4** चारु] Σ, चार S_7 • पल्ला] Σ, प⟨ल्ल्वा⟩ S_2 • कौ] B_1V_1, के G_e**S** • मोहौल्ला] B_1V_1, मोहल्ला G_e, महुल्ल S_2, महल S_7 • पर] $B_1S_2V_1$, होत G_e, परि S_7 • हल्ला] Σ, ह⟨ल्ल्वा⟩ S_2 • गोरी] Σ, होरी S_7

26.1 ठहरना [cf. *stabhira-] v.t. 1. to remain; 2. (here:) to resist; पसर [prasāra-] poet. m. attack; सावधान भये Br. (But) if they are cautious (after an attack); चाव चलत न Br. 1. (then our) wish (for a concealed attack) won't work; 2. there is no temptation (to steal); चोरी [caurikā-] f. stealth, concealment. **26.2** केसरी [kesara-] f. saffron; गुलाल m. (red) powder; अबीर [A] m. red powder; आँधी [andhikā-] f. storm; खेलन ... को Br. (Radha ordered:) 'the Dark One should not be allowed to play a game of force.' बरजोरी [bala- + P zor] f. 1. overwhelming strength; 2. coercion. **26.3** बजाय बाजे Br. 'playing on instruments' with fanfare; बजि apa; पैठ- [praviṣṭa-] v.i. (perf.) to enter; ग्वार Br. (pl. obl.) among the cowherds; होरी को दिवस Br. It is the day of Holi; किशोरी [S] poet. f. Radha. **26.4** चल्ला [cañcala-] reg. adj. fickle; पल्ला (पलड़ा) [palla-] m. side, single part; 2. the pan of a scales; भारी प्रेम-पल्ला होत the pan of love is heavy (in the scales) (e.g. as against the pan of modesty); हल्ला [*halla-] m. 1. noise, uproar; 2. outcry; के मोहल्ला पर apa. It is in Hari's settlement but; (in order to keep the internal rhyme the word mohallā is not put into the oblique.) मोहल्ला होत apa.

*जानि झुकामुकी भेष छिपाय कै गागरी लै घर तें निकरी ती।
जानि परी न कबै केहि ओर तें आय जुरे जितै होरी धरी ती।
ठाकुर, दौरि परे मोहिं देखत, भागि बची जू कछ्छ सुघरी ती।
बीर, जौ द्वार किबार न देहुँ, तौ हौं हुरिहारन हाथ परी ती॥ R27॥

अखती

अखती की तीज तजवीज कै सहेलीं जुरीं,

---

27 Bharatpur1 f. 135v (28), Granthāvalī B44, Jaipur1 f. 3r (10), Rāmcandra Śukla (I$_e$) p. 438, Mītal (M$_e$) p. 267 (Śiśir 154), Ṭhasak 101, Ṭhasak 'Jīvancarit' (Ṭ^j_e) p. 4, Miśrabandhu Vinod (V$_e$) p. 730.

27.1 जानि] G$_e$J$_1$Ṭ$_e$V$_e$, हौं B$_1$, प्रात I$_e$M$_e$Ṭ^j_e • झुकामुकी] G$_e$Ṭ$_e$, सषियां कौ B$_1$, झुकामुकि I$_e$Ṭ^j_e, झुकामुको J$_1$, झुका झुकी G$^{vl}_e$M$_e$V$_e$ • भेष] B$_1$**E**I$_e$J$_1$M$_e$, बेष V$_e$ • गागरी] G$_e$Ṭ$_e$V$_e$, गागरि B$_1$, गागर I$_e$J$_1$Ṭ^j_e, गगरी M$_e$ • घर तें] G$_e$I$_e$J$_1$Ṭ^j_eV$_e$, जल कौं B$_1$M$_e$, घर से Ṭ$_e$ • निकरी] Σ, डगरी M$_e$ **27.2** जानि] B$_1$I$_e$Ṭ^j_e, जानौं G$_e$J$_1$Ṭ$_e$, जानी M$_e$ • परी न] B$_1$I$_e$Ṭ^j_e, नहीं मैं G$_e$Ṭ$_e$, कहां ते J$_1$V$_e$, गई न M$_e$ • कबै केहि] G$_e$Ṭ$_e$V$_e$, किती कौ B$_1$, कितीक I$_e$, कबै किहिं J$_1$, कितेक M$_e$Ṭ^j_e • ओर तें] G$_e$J$_1$Ṭ$_e$, बार तैं, अबार है I$_e$Ṭ^j_e, °ऊ बार तें M$_e$, बेर ते V$_e$ • आय जुरे] G$_e$J$_1$Ṭ$_e$V$_e$, आनि षरी B$_1$, आन जुरे M$_e$, जाय परी Ṭ^j_e • जितै] J$_1$V$_e$, जहाँ B$_1$**E**M$_e$, जहँ I$_e$ • धरी] Σ, षरी J$_1$ **27.3** मोहिं] Σ, मुहि J$_1$ • देखत] G$_e$J$_1$M$_e$Ṭ$_e$V$_e$, देखि कै B$_1$I$_e$Ṭ^j_e • भागि] Σ, भाग M$_e$ • जू] G$_e$Ṭ$_e$, री I$_e$Ṭ^j_e, सु J$_1$M$_e$, जु B$_1$V$_e$ • कछ्छ] B$_1$G$_e$J$_1$M$_e$Ṭ$_e$, बडी I$_e$Ṭ^j_e, कहूँ V$_e$ **27.4** जौ द्वार] G$_e$J$_1$, दुवार B$_1$, की सौं जो I$_e$Ṭ^j_e, जो दौरि M$_e$, जु द्वार V$_e$ • किबार न देहुँ] *conj.* किबार न दैंहु B$_1$, न देहुँ केबार G$_e$V$_e$, किबार न देउँ I$_e$M$_e$Ṭ^j_e, न देती किंवार J$_1$ • तौ हौं] B$_1$, तौ मैं **E**I$_e$, त तौ J$_1$, री तौ M$_e$, त मैं V$_e$ • हुरि°] B$_1$J$_1$M$_e$, होरि° **E**I$_e$V$_e$

27.1 झुकामुकी Bund. f. 'time when faces cannot be seen' dawn; भेष छिपाय Br. 1. hiding myself with my clothes; 2. having changed my clothes (RSh); गागरी (गागर) [gargara-] f. water-pot; निकरी ती (निकली थी) Bund. v.i. I was going out. **27.2** कितेक अबार है var. how inappropriate time it was; आय जुरे v.i. (Krishna) appeared; जिते (जितने) rel. pron. (ag.) all those who; (jite 'from where' is less possible since the line already had the expression 'kehi ora tē' in this meaning.) होरी धरी ती reg. perf. who played Holi. **27.3** भागि 1. [H bhāgnā] v.i. abs. Br. running away; 2. [bhāgya-] m. obl. (with) good luck; सुघरी Br. f. good moment. **27.4** केबार (कीवाड़) var. [kavāṭa-] m. reg. leaf of door; कीवाड़ देना idiom. to close the door; होरिहार one playing Holi.

वर के निकट ठाढीं भांवती कों घेर कै।
2 एक बेर समिट सम्हार सबही पै सब
बोदरें चलाईं मनभाई हेर हेर कै।
3 ठाकुर कहत, जब मुरकीं लली की ओर
लौदन-लफाई कह्यौ, लीजै नाम टेर कै।
4 स्याम कों बुलाय कें छिपाय कै सुनायो सुख
स्याम स्याम स्यामा सों कहायो बीस बेर कै॥ R28॥

*अखती रची राधिका मोहन सों बरजोरिहि नाम लिवावती हैं।

---

28 Chatarpur pp. 22v-23r (114); Granthāvalī 102, Śatak 48, Ṭhasak 104. 29 Granthāvalī 103, Ṭhākur-satsaī (Ṭ) f. 1v (9), Ṭhasak 102, Ṭhasak 'Jīvancarit' ($Ṭ_e^j$) p. 21.

28.1 अखती] **E**, अकती C • सहेलीं] C, सहेली **E** • जुरीं] **E**, जुरी C • ठाढी] **E**, ठाडी भई (unm.) C • भांवती] C, भावते **E** **28.2** समिट] **E**, सिमट C • सम्हार] **E**, समार कें (unm.) C • सब] **E**, *om.* (unm.) C • बोदरें] C, बोदर **E** • चलाईं] C, चलाई **E** • जुरीं] **E**, जुरी C • मनभाई] $G_eṬ_e$, मनभाइ $Ś_e$, सबही के मनभाईं (unm.) C • हेर हेर] **E**, हरें हेर C **28.3** लौदन] **E**, लोंद (unm.) C • लफाई] $G_eṬ_e$, लपाई $Ś_e$, लफाय C • कह्यौ] **E**, कहो C • टेर] G_eC, हेर $Ś_eṬ_e$ **28.4** बुलाय कें] C, बुलाइ **E** • छिपाय] C, पिय पाइ **E** • सुख] $Ś_e$C, मुख $G_eṬ_e$ • स्यामा] **E**, राधा C **29.1** बरजोरिहि] $G_eṬ_e$, बरयोबर (dittography) Ṭ, बधु को हठि $Ṭ_e^j$ • लिवावती] $Ṭ_e^j$, लवावती G_e, लवावत Ṭ, लेवावती $Ṭ_e$

28.1 अखती की तीज f. the Akṣaya Tṛtīyā festival on the 18th of Vaiśākha (April-May), when accounts are settled for the spring crop. At this occasion women worship small clay figures under a banyan tree. After the pūjā people may be asked to pronounce the name of their beloved. If they do not reveal it, they can be beaten by champa-twigs until they state the name; तजवीज़ [A] f. plot, scheme; जुड़ना [*juṭyati] v.i. to gather. **28.2 समिट-** (सिमटना) [samveṣṭayati, saṃvṛtta-] Br. v.i. to be drawn together; to gather; सम्हार [S] m. total destruction; समिट... सब Br. all drew together and attacked everyone (KL); बोदर m. (here: f.) stick; बोदर-चलाई var. reg. wielders of stick; मनभाई हेर हेर कै Br. f. looking again and again at the beloved woman; 2. searching for beloved women (i.e. for victims). **28.3 मुरक-** [*muṭati] Br. v.i. 1. to turn; 2. to return (BHK); लौद Bund. f. stick; लफाना (लपाना) v.t. to cause to bend or to move; लौदन-लफाई कह्यो reg. the brandishing of the stick indicated. **28.4 स्याम कों बुलाय कै** var. Br. calling Krishna to come; छिपाय कै Br. secretly; स्याम कों बुलाइ पिय पाइ कै Br. when they found that she calls out the name of Krishna as her beloved; सुनायो सुख var. Br. indicated the happy news; स्याम पिय var. Br. the dear Krishna. **29.1 अखती रची** (Radha) playing Akhatī.

झहरावती, भौंह झुकावती, फेरि कहौ जू कहौ जू सुनावती हैं।
कहि ठाकुर, काम-गुरू के कहे, उपमान के ओप बढावती हैं।
रस रीति के, प्रीति के, प्रीतम को बिसरे मनो पाठ पढावती हैं॥ R29॥

'गाँठ गँठीली चमेली की बोदर घालौ न, कोऊ अनूतरी कैहै।
ऊसइ नाम लेवावौ तो लैहैं, पै घाले ते, लाल, कहा रस रैहै।
ठाकुर, कंज कली सी लली, बलि, या जड-चोट सरीर न सैहै।
बाल कहै कर जोर 'हहा यह बोदर लाल हमैं लग जैहै'॥ R30॥

*पुतरीन पुजाय किसोरी सुजान सखीन समाज लिये उमही।
ब्रजचंद्र बिहारी बिराजो जहाँ अखती करी, यों सुख पाय सही।
कहि ठाकुर, लाल के आगे लता ललिता धरि अंजुलि जोरि रही।

30 Granthāvalī 104, I_2 f. 39r (1); Ṭhasak 105.   31 Granthāvalī 105, Ṭhasak 106.

29.2 झहर आवती] **E**, झिझकावत Ṭ • झुकावती] **E**, चढावत Ṭ • फेरि] Ṭ$_e^j$, फेर G_eṬ$_e$, है जु Ṭ • कहौ जू कहौ जू] G_eṬṬ$_e$, लिये कर लौद Ṭ$_e^j$ • सुनावती] G_eṬ$_e$, खिजावती Ṭ$_e^j$, कहावत Ṭ   **29.3** कहि] G_eṬ$_e^j$, कह ṬṬ$_e$ • उपमान के ओप बढावती] G_eṬ$_e$, कर लै कर लौद रिझावत Ṭ, कहौ जू कहौ जू सुनावती Ṭ$_e^j$ **29.4** रीति] Ṭ$_e^j$, रीत G_eṬṬ$_e$ • प्रीति] Ṭ$_e^j$, प्रीत G_eṬṬ$_e$ • को] **E**, के Ṭ • मनो] **E**, जनु Ṭ • पाठ] G_eṬ$_e$, अंक ṬṬ$_e^j$ • पढावती] **E**, पड़ावत Ṭ   **30.1** घालौ न] **E**, घालत हौ I_2 • अनूतरी] **E**, अनचित (unm.) I_2 **30.2** ऊसइ] **E**, ऊसैई I_2 • लेवावौ तो] **E**, लिवावत I_2 • लैहैं] **E**, लीजै I_2 • पै घाल ते लाल] **E**, बोदर घाल (unm.) I_2 **30.3** ठाकुर] **E**, कह ठाकुर (unm.) I_2 • कंज] **E**, चंप I_2 • बलि] **E**, ⟨प्रु/य⟩ह I_2 • या जड] **E**, बोदर I_2 **30.4** कहै] **E**, कहत (unm.) I_2

29.2 झहर- [cf. H jhallānā] Av. Br. v.i. 1. to be angry; 2. v.t. to scold. **29.3 काम-गुरू के कहे** Br. taught by Kāma, her guru (i. e. driven by love); **उपमान... हैं** [S] m. increases the beauty of the similes; **के** (**के लिए**) postp. Br. for; **ओप** [cf. *opp-] f. lustre; **लौद** Bund. f. stick; **कर लै कर लौद** var. taking sticks in their hands; **रिझावत** var. v.t. imperf. Br. they delight. **29.4 बिसरे पाठ** a forgotten lesson; **अंक पढाना** var. idiom. teach the characters. **30.1 गांठ** [granṭhi-] f. knot; **बोदर** m. stick, cane; **घालना** [*ghalyati] v.t. to beat; **अनूतर-** (**अनुत्तर**) [S] reg. adj. 'unanswerable' lowly (BHK); **कोऊ अनूतरी कैहै** reg. someone would say that it is a lowly thing; **अनचित** (**अनुचित**) var. [S] poet. adj. improper. **30.2 ऊसइ** (**वैसे ही**) reg. adv. in that way; just like this (i.e. without beating); **रैहै** v.i. (Br. fut.) will remain; **लेवावौ तो लीजै** var. Br. If you make me say the name then do it; **बोदर घाल** var. obl. from beating by the stick. **30.3 जड-चोट** f. the wound made by the insensitive stick. **31.1 पुतरी** [putrala-] f. clay figure worshipped at Akṣay Tṛtīyā; **पुजाय** [cf. pūjā-] v.t. abs. Br. having worshipped; **किशोरी सुजान** poet. f. the clever adolescent Radha. **31.2 सुख पाय सही** Br. imp. attain true happiness. **31.3 लता ललिता धरि** Br. Lalitā holding a twig.

4 मुसकाय मनोहर स्याम हरें सुख-साधा-पुजावन राधा कही॥ R31॥

1 लाँबी लचकारी लौद लीन्हे हौ, गोपाल लाल,
सो न घालि दीजो, घालें घनो रस घटहै।
2 छ्वै जौ जैहै काहू ब्रज बनिता नवेली अंग,
ऐंड की तिहारी, कान्ह, एकहू न सटहै।
3 ठाकुर कहत, टेक एकहू न रैहै धरी
संग में सहेली एक एक तें विकट है।
4 मेरे लग जैहै, तौ दोहाई बृषभान जू की,
ऐसी लौद घालिहौं की चौवर उपटहै॥ R32॥

ग्रीष्म

बीतो बसंत, मिलो नहि कंत सो आनंद मैं, तियं कौ लौं भरैगी।
2 जेठहू ज्वालन सों जरिहै तन, कामिनी काम सों कौ लौं लरैगी।
ठाकुर, जौ पै न आइहैं स्याम, अराम को कौन उपाय करैगी।

---

32 Chatarpur p. 22 (113), Granthāvalī 106, Ṭhasak 103, Ṭhasak 'Jīvancarit' ($Ṭ_e^j$) pp. 21-22.
33 Granthāvalī B50, Ṭhasak 108, Ṭhasak 'Jīvancarit' ($Ṭ_e^j$) p. 4 (5). (Bhagavāndīn presented this poem as an example of the poetry by Ṭhākur from Asni.)

32.1 लाँबी] **E**, लामी C • गोपाल] **E**, गुपाल C • घालि] $Ṭ_e^j$, घाल $CG_eṬ_e$ • घनो] **E**, घनेरों (unm.) C **32.2** छ्वै] $Ṭ_e^j$, छी $G_eṬ_e$, छ्रू C • की] $CG_eṬ_e$, को $Ṭ_e^j$ **32.3** धरी] **E**, घरी C **32.4** दोहाई] **E**, धुवाई C • घालिहौं] **E**, धालहों C • चौवर] $G_eṬ_e$, चौउर C, चौअर $Ṭ_e^j$ **33.1** बीतो] $G_eṬ_e$, आयो $Ṭ_e^j$ **33.2** जेठहू] $G_eṬ_e$, ⟨मेठ⟩हूँ $Ṭ_e^j$ • जरिहै] $Ṭ_e^j$, जरिकै $G_eṬ_e$ • कामिनी] $G_eṬ_e$, कामिन $Ṭ_e^j$

31.4 हरें [cf. H haule] reg. adv. slowly; सुख-साधा poet. f. wish for happiness; पुजावन [cf. pūrayati] Br. adj. fulfiller. **32.1** लचकार- [cf. H lacaknā] adj. supple, bending; लौद Bund. f. stick; घालना [*ghalyati] v.t. to beat. **32.2** छीना (छूना) var. [chupati] reg. v.t. to touch (BSK); ऐंड (ऐंठ) [cf. āveṣṭ(y)ate] f. 'twist' pride, arrogance (cf. H aiṃṭhnā); ऐंड की (your) arrogance (H aiṃḍ kī bāt); सटना [cf. saṃsthāti] v.i. 'to join together' to be effective, to work. **32.3** टेक धरना idiom. to insist on a matter; विकट [S] adj. fearsome. **32.4** मेरे लग जैहै Br. if it strikes me; चौवर Bund. adj. fourfold; m. four lines (cf. Varmā 2000: 55); उपटना [*utpaṭyati] v.i. to swell. **33.1** आनंद मैं poet. 1. (did not meet her beloved) happily; 2. (waiting) for happiness; (दिन) भरना idiom. to pass the time. **33.2** जेठहू [jyeṣṭha-] m. obl. even in (the heats of) Jyeṣṭha (May-June); जरिकै var. [jvalati] v.t. abs. Br. having burnt; कामिन var. [kāminī] reg. f. 'woman' I. **33.3** जौ पै Br. conj. if; अराम [ārāma-] poet. m. rest, ease.

खाय दरार रही छतिया यह, बूँद परे अरराय परैगी॥ R33॥ 4

सजनी, सुखद तें सुहाई दौरती है पौन 1
        कौन चार्‌यो ओर तें गुलाब आब छिरकै।
स्याबस है राखै तन, बातन बितावै खिन 2
        आपुस मैं मन मनभाइन कों झिरकै।
ठाकुर कहत, कोऊ जानत न भेद यह, 3
        घाम की घरेर रहैं दोऊ घर घिर कै।
आव, एक कौतिक अनूपम बिलोकि आई, 4

---

34 Bharatpur1 f. 153v (24), Sudhāsar [S_2 f. 17r (-/24), S_6 f. 81v (133/505), S_7 f. 56r (10/532)], Granthāvalī B25, Vrindaban1 f. 6rv (8/34). S_6 and S_7 introduce the poem as 'sakhī kī ukati sakhī prati. dampati kau saṅket maĩ lacchata kari bahiraṅga te antaraṅga bhayo cāhai hai. (A friend of the beloved woman talks to her friend. By indicating the place of the couples' meeting the outsider friend wants to become intimate.)

33.4 यह] $G_eṬ_e$, वह $Ṭ_e^j$ • अरराय] $Ṭ_eṬ_e^j$, अरण्य (unm.) G_e **34.1** सुखद] Σ, सुखेद G_e • तें] $B_1G_eV_1$, मै S_2, ते S_6S_7 • सुहाई] $B_1S_2^{pc}S_6S_7V_1$, सुहाइ G_e, सु⟨ष हो⟩ई S_2^{ac} • है] SV_1, हैं B_1, °यै G_e • पौंन] B_1**S**, त्यों न G_e, यौ न V_1 • चार्‌यो] Σ, चारौ V_1 • तें] $B_1G_eV_1$, ते **S** • छिरकै] Σ, छिरकैं S_6 **34.2** स्याबस] B_1S_6, स्वबस G_e, स्वांबत S_2, स्यम S_7, स्वाब⟨श्प/रूप⟩ V_1 • है] $B_1S_2S_6V_1$, ह्वै G_e, सह S_7 • आपुस] Σ, आपुसि S_7 • मैं] $B_1S_2V_1$, °यैं G_e, मै S_6S_7 • मनभाइन] Σ, मनभाइते G_e • झिरकै] Σ, झिरकैं S_6 **34.3** ठाकुर कहत] Σ, ठा° B_1 • कोऊ] Σ, कोउ V_1 • यह] $B_1G_eS_2V_1$, यहि S_6S_7 • रहैं] *conj.* रहै Σ • घिर] $B_1S_6S_7G_e$, घिरि S_2, घर V_1 • कै] Σ, कैं S_6

33.4 दरार [*darākāra-] f. crack, breach; दरार खाना idiom. to burst; छतिया f. 1. [cf. H chātī] heart; 2. [cf. H chat] roof; अरराना [āraṭati] v.i. to fall with a crash. **34.1** सुखेद var. [sva-kheda-] m. (because of) one's own pain; सुहा(य)- Br. adj. more pleasant (than anything agreable); दौरतीयै (दौड़ती हुई को) var. Br. v.i. imperf. obl. running (woman); पौन (पवन) [S] m. (here: f.) Br. (runs for) wind; त्यों न apa. यौ न apa. चार्‌यो ओर तें Br. from everywhere; आब [P] m. water; छिड़कना [*chiṭ-] v.t. to sprinkle. **34.2** स्याबस ह्वै राखै तन Br. (?) It is splendid as she keeps her body; स्याबास (शाबाश) [P] Br. interj. well done! स्वबस ह्वै राखै var. (?) Br. she controls (her body); स्याबति (साबित) var. [A] Br. adj. confirmed, proved (DB). स्वांबत apa. खिन (क्षण) [S] Br. m. moment; आपुसयैं (आपस में) var. reg. pron. obl. amongst themselves; मनभावन [mana- + bhāti] poet. m. lover; मनभाइत- var. [mana- + bhāti] reg. m. lover; झिड़कना [cf. *jhaṭati] v.t. 'to shake' to browbeat, to scold. **34.3** घाम [gharma-] m.f. the heat and light of the sun; घरेर [gharṣaṇa-] f. 'rubbing, friction' pain; रहैं... घिरकै Br. both of them stay confined in the house.

तौहूवै दिखाइ लाऊँ, देखि आऊँ फिर कै॥ R34॥

पावस

1 आए बढि-चढि से उघरि नभमंडल ते,
बेस करि डारे जिन द्यौस रतियान के।
2 खूंदि डारी धरनि, सरन जल पूरि डारे,
चूर करि डारे सुख बिरही तियान के।
3 ठाकुर कहत, प्यारे आनँद उमंग भरे,
कामिनि कै चोज-मौज ब्यौंत बतियान के।
4 देखि री, असाढ के ऊमैंडे ऐंडे-बैंडे झला
अजब अनोखे अलबेली बुँदियान के॥ R35॥

1 आग सी धँधाती ताती लपटैं सिराइ गईं,
पौन पुरवाई लागी सीतल सुहान री।

---

35 Bharatpur1 f. 176r (20), Datiya1 ff. 45rv (129), Granthāvalī 107, Śatak 54, Ṭhasak 123.
36 Datiya1 f. 47r (136), Datiya2 f. 9r (79), Granthāvalī 108, Śatak 55, Ṭhasak 107.

34.4 आव] B$_1$G$_e$S$_2$V$_1$, अब S$_6$S$_7$ • बिलोकि] B$_1$G$_e$S$_2$, बिलोक S$_6$S$_7$V$_1$ • तौहूवै] B$_1$G$_e$S$_7$V$_1$, तोऊवै S$_2$S$_6$ • लाऊँ] Σ, ल्यांऊ S$_7$ • देखि] Σ, देख S$_6$ • फिर कै] B$_1$G$_e$S$_7$V$_1$, फिरि मैं (unrh.) S$_2$, फिरकैं S$_6$ **35.1** बढि] B$_1$**E**, बड D$_1$ • चढि] B$_1$**E**, चढ D$_1$ • से] B$_1$D$_1$Ś$_e$, कै G$_e$Ṭ$_e$ • उघरि] B$_1$, उमै⟨ड⟩ D$_1$, उमंडि] **E** • ते] B$_1$, ⟨नै/मै⟩ D$_1$, मैं G$_e$Ṭ$_e$, तैं Ś$_e$ • बेस] B$_1$D$_1$, द्यौस G$_e$Ṭ$_e$, धूम Ś$_e$ • करि] B$_1$**E**, कर D$_1$ • जिन द्यौस] B$_1$, दिवस (unm.) D$_1$, जिन भेष **E** **35.2** खूंदि] B$_1$, ** D$_1$, खूँद] **E** • धरनि] B$_1$**E**, धरन D$_1$ • सरन] **E**D$_1$, सरनि B$_1$ • करि] B$_1$**E**, क* D$_1$ • तियान] B$_1$**E**, त्रीयान D$_1$ **35.3** ठाकुर कहत] **E**, ठा॰ B$_1$, ठाकुर क⟨हैं⟩त D$_1$ • प्यारे] B$_1$, प्यारौ D$_1$, प्यारी **E** • आनद उमंग भरे] B$_1$, है बिदेस सु न आयौ D$_1$, आनंद उमंग भरी **E** • कामिनि... बतियान] B$_1$**E**, ---र छुटे अबलान ---न के D$_1$ • कामिनि कैं] B$_1$, जोबन की **E** **35.4** देख... झला] B$_1$**E**, --- हट घन कांह⟨ट घु⟩रबान के ⟨छ/घ⟩टांन के D$_1$ • देषि] B$_1$, देख **E** • ऊमैंडे] B$_1$Ś$_e$, उमंडे G$_e$Ṭ$_e$ • अजब... बुँदियान] B$_1$**E**, *⟨म⟩काहट झमकाहट झलांन D$_1$ **36.1** सी धँधाती] D$_2$G$_e$Ṭ$_e$, सींधु धाती D$_1$, सी धधात Ś$_e$ • लपटैं] Σ, लपट Ś$_e$ • पौन] Σ, पवन (unm.) D$_1$ • लागी] D$_1$G$_e$Ṭ$_e$, लगै D$_2$, लागा Ś$_e$

34.4 तौहुवै (तुझे भी) reg. pron. obl. also to you; फिर कै Br. adv. again. **35.1** आए v.i. perf. (the clouds) came; द्यौस... के Br. who gave the garments of nights to the day; धूम var. [S] m. smoke, haze. **35.3** चोज [codya-] m. merriment; मौज [A] f. 'surge' delight; ब्यौंत [*viyavakṛntati] m.f. 1. style; 2. crookedness. **35.4** ऐंडे-बैंडे reg. adj. slanting (shower); झला [cf. H jhalnā] m. (here pl.) the first rain in monsoon; अजब [A] adj. astonishing. **36.1** धंधाना [*dhagg-] v.i. to blaze; पुरवाई [*pūrvavāta-] f. (here adj.) eastern (wind); सुहाना [śubhāyate] v.i. 1. to shine; 2. to please.

मृदुल अनूप चारु चाँदनी मलीन भई, 2
तापै छाँह छाई, छूट्यौ माननी को मान री।
ठाकुर कहत, आली, ग्रीषम गवन कीन्हो, 3
पावस-प्रवेस-बेस छवि सरसान री।
बद्दल बसन लागे, हिये हुलसन लागे, 4
मोर कुहकन लागे, बन हरियान री॥ R36॥

*कारे कारे बद्दल सुहाए कहूँ सेत सेत, 1
कहूँ लाल लाल, कहूँ आभा पीरी पीरी री।
ज्यों ज्यों होत चंचल दिखात चंचला की चौंध, 2
त्यों त्यों घन की धुकार होत धीरी धीरी री।
ठाकुर कहत, फिरैं चातक चढे से चाउ, 3
मोरन की अबली फिरत भीरी भीरी री।
कैसी नीकी लागत सोहाई सुखदैन आज, 4
मंद मंद बैहर बहत सीरी सीरी री॥ R37॥

*कारे लाल पीले धौरे धावत धुँवाँ के रंग 1
कितने सुरंग किते रंग मटमाढे हैं।

---

37 Granthāvalī 109, Ṭhasak 118. 38 Granthāvalī 110, Ṭhasak 120.

36.2 मृदुल अनूप] Σ, चैत D_1 • चाँदनी] Σ, चांदनी सो चंद स्यौ D_1 • मलीन] Σ, मलिन D_2 • तापै] Σ, तामै D_1 • छाई] Σ, छई D_1 • छूटौ] Σ, छूटे D_1 • को] Σ, के D_1 **36.3** आली] Σ, जहां D_1 • कीन्हो] Σ, कीन $Ś_e$ • छवि] Σ, °रि⟨न⟩ D_1 **36.4** बद्दल ... हरियान] D_1D_2, सावन सुहावन को आवन निरखि आली मेघ बरसन लागे हिय हुलसान **E** • बद्दल] D_2, बादर D_1 • हिय] D_2, हिये D_1 • कुहकन लागे] D_2, लागे कौहौकन D_2 • हरियान] D_2, हरआन D_2

36.3 **पावस प्रवेस बेस** Br. in the garment (form) of the coming of the monsoon; **सरसान** [sa-rasa-] v.i. 1. poet. perf. (in rhyming position) bloomed; increased; 2. poet. inf. (started) to bloom; to increase (the verb 'lāge' is provided in the next line. **36.4** **बसना** 1. [varṣa-] v.i. to rain; 2. [vasati] v.i. to stay; **कुहुकना** var. [cf. kuhu-] v.i. to cry (a bird); **बन हर** var. poet. m. in every grove. **37.1** **सुहाना** [śubhāyate] v.i. 1. to shine; 2. to please. **37.2** **चंचला** [S] poet. f. lightning; **धुकार** f. sound (of a drum etc.). **37.3** **चढे से चाउ** as if with increased desire; **अवली** [āvalī-] Br. f. flock; **भीड़ना** [cf. H bhīṛ] v.i. to gather. **37.4** **बैहर** [cf. vāyu-, vātāra- and P bahār] f. wind; **सीर-** [śītala-] Br. adj. cool. **38.1** **धौर-** [dhavala-] Br. adj. white; **धावत** [dhāvati] Br. v.i. imperf. (the cloud) running; **सुरंग** [S] adv. beautifully; **मटमाढा** [H miṭṭhī+māṛhnā] adj. dust-coloured.

2 कितने मही के रूप माधुरी करत घोर
सोर चहूँ ओर होत गहगहे गाढे हैं।
3 ठाकुर कहत, कवि बरनि बरनि थाके,
बरने न जात, यों बहसि-बर बाढे हैं।
4 मोहे लेत मनन जू ऐसी बने बनन जू,
आजु देखौ घनन घनेरे रंग काढे हैं॥ R38॥

घूमैं घटा, छटा छूटती हैं, उलहे द्रुम-बेलिन के पत्र नए।
2 सो हरी हरी भूमि मैं इंद्रबधू कँटिआइबे कौं जनु बीज बए।
कवि ठाकुर, यातें प्रतीत भई परदेसी कोऊ-कोऊ आइ गए।
4 अब साँझ-सवेरे कै काल-परौं, मनभावन आवनहार भए॥ R39॥

1 *चंडित मनोज कैसे झला झुमि झुमि आवैं,
घूमि घूमि डारैं अलबेली तन पानी हैं।
2 दामिनी दमंक ठौर ठौरन दिखाई देत,
मानौ इंद्रानी करै मेघ मिजुबानी हैं।
3 ठाकुर कहत, कूकि कूकि उठैं कोइलैं ये,

---

39 Granthāvalī 111, Ṭhasak 110, Śatak 49. 40 Granthāvalī 112, Ṭhasak 119.

38.4 मनन जू] G_e, मनन जो $Ṭ_e$ **39.2** कँटिआइबे] $G_eṬ_e$, कटि आइबे $Ś_e$ **39.3** कोऊ-कोऊ] $G_eṬ_e$, कोउ कोउ $Ś_e$ **40.1** अलबेली] $Ṭ_e$, अलबेलो G_e

---

38.2 मही के रूप Br. the forms on earth; **घोर** [S] 1. adj. deep; 2. m. thunder; **गहगह-** Br. adj. 1. rapturous, excited; 2. festive; **गाढ़ा** [gāḍha-] adj. 1. thick; 2. intense. **38.3 बहस** [A] f. 1. argument; 2. (?) (here:) claim (for good description); **बर** [bala-] m. (imaginative) power (of the poets). **38.4 मनन** [manas-] m. pl. Br. souls; **घनेर-** [ghanatara-] Av. Br. adj. many. **39.1 छटा** [S] f. 'splendour' lightning; **छूटना** [*kṣuṭati] v.i. 1. to be released; 2. to come forth; **उलह-** Br. v.i. to spring up, to shoot (vegetation). **39.2 इंद्रवधू** [S] f. 'Indra's wife' the red velvet-mite 'bīr-bahūṭī' [vīra-vadhūṭī], which appears during the monsoon and is believed to increase sexual desire; **कंटियाना** [kaṇṭaka-] v.i. 'to make one's flesh creep' to be excited. **39.3 प्रतीति** [S] f. conviction; **कोऊ-कोऊ (कोई न कोई)** pron. Br. some or other. **39.4 परौं (परसों)** [paraśvas] reg. adv. the day after tomorrow; **आवनहार (आनेवाला)** Br. adj. about to come. **40.1 चंडित** [S] poet. adj. angry; **कैसे (जैसे)** Br. adj. like (an angry Kāma); **झला** m. reg. the first (drop of) rain at monsoon; **तन** [tanaḥ] postp. Br. towards. **40.2 दमक** f. glitter, brilliance; **इंद्राणी** [S] kūṭ. f. 'Indra's wife' the red velvet-mite 'bīr-bahūṭī'; **मिजुबानी** [P mezvānī] f. entertainment of guests.

हूकि उठै बिरहा, निसंक उर मानी हैं।
धरा डारैं खूँदे, प्रेमफाँस कैसी फूँदें, आजु 4
लेती द्वार मूँदे, ऐसी बूदें बरियानी हैं॥ R40॥

*चौक-आसमान में अनेक सौक साहबी के 1
गाहक रिझाइबे के ब्यौंत-बिसतारे हैं।
कोई लाल पीरे, कोई सेत नीले धारीधार, 2
कोई रंग सेंदुर के, कोई धुँवाँधारे हैं।
ठाकुर कहत, देखि बादर अनेक रंग, 3
मन मनसूबा कै, बिचार ये बिचारे हैं।
बादर न होय बहु भांतिन के रेजा ये 4
असाढ-रंगरेजा रंग सुखिबे कौं डारे हैं॥ R41॥

दौरि दौरि, दमकि दमकि दुरि दामिनि यौं 1
दुंद देत दसहूँ दिसान दरसतु है।
घूमि-घूमि, घहरि-घहरि घन घहरात, 2
घेरि-घेरि घोर घनो सोर सरसतु है।
ठाकुर कहत, पिक पीकि पीकि पी कों रटैं, 3
प्यारौ परदेस, पापी प्रान तरसतु है।

---

41 Granthāvalī 113, Ṭhasak 117. 42 Granthāvalī 114, Ṭhasak 122, Śatak 53.

40.3 हूकना v.i. 1. to be felt (an ache or pain); 2. to cry out in pain; बिरहा [viraha-] m. (the pangs of) separation; निसंक (निःशंक) [S] adv. 1. (the cuckoos are) without fear; 2. (the pangs are) without reserve; (बात) मानी हैं they accepted this. **40.4** धरा [S] f. obl. the earth; खूँदे डारैं Br. v.t. pres. (the drops) trample; फूंड f. 'knot' trap; बरिया- Br. v.i. to be proud or arrogant; बरियान- [*balakāra-] reg. adj. strong (cf. H bariyār). **41.1** चौक [catuṣka-] reg. m. 1. painted decoration on a house-wall; 2. marketplace; शौक़ [A] m. 1. desire; 2. predilection; साहबी [P] f. 1. dominance, lordliness; 2. kind of silk cloth; ब्योंतना [cf. viyavakṛntati] v.t. to fit; बिसतार- [vistāra-] v.t. to extend, to spread; ब्योंत-बिसतारे reg. v.t. perf. (m. pl.) put out for display. **41.2** धारी [dhārā-] f. stripe; धुआँधार [dhūmra-] adj. dense (clouds). **41.3** मनसूबा [A] m. 1. intention; 2. plan, scheme; बिचार ये this idea; बिचारे हैं I (we) imagine. **41.4** रेज़ा [P] m. (five-six yard long) piece of cloth; रंगरेज़ [P] m. dyer. **42.1** दमकना v.i. to shine; to glow; दुंद [dvandva-] m. 1. quarrel; 2. uproar. **42.2** घहरना (घहराना) [? conn. *gharaghara-] v.i. 1. to rumble; 2. to roll, to surge (clouds); सरसना [sa-rasa-] v.i. 1. to increase; 2. to bloom. **42.3** पिक [S] m. the Indian cuckoo, papiha; पीकना (पिहकना) onomat. v.i. (the papiha) to call.

4 झूमि झूमि झुकि झुकि झमकि झमकि, आली,
रिमझिम झिमिकि असाढ बरसतु है॥ R42॥

पावस को परपंच बिलोकि अनंग ने बान निषंग तें काढे।
2 भूमि हरियै परी जहीं बूंद, उडे बगुला चपलै सुख बाढे।
ठाकुर, बोलि उठे मोरवा, घन घोरि उठे जितही तित गाढे।
4 कामरी माँझ छिपाए छबीली कों छाहरे कान्ह कदंब के ठाढे॥ R43॥

1 *पावस-प्रपंच को तमासो अबलोकत से
दामिनी के त्रास आय भूमि ना गिरत हैं।
2 मोरन मगन देखि, चातकन चाव पेखि,
लेखि पति आपनो न थाके से थिरत हैं।
3 ठाकुर कहत, हैं छिपत प्रगटत कहूँ,
भूले अनुकूले भटभेरे ना भिरत हैं।
4 मंद मंद देखिके नखत बदरान माँझ
मानो चौंधियाने चंद ढूंढत फिरत हैं॥ R44॥

पावस में परदेस तें आनि मिले पिय, औ मनभाई भई है।
2 दादुर मोर पपीहरा बोलत, तापर आनि घटा उनई है।

---

43 Granthāvalī 115, Ṭhasak 114. 44 Granthāvalī 116, Ṭhasak 116. 45 Granthāvalī 117, Rāmcandra Śukla (I$_e$) p. 444, Ṭhasak 157, Ṭhasak 'Jīvancarit' (Ṭ$_e^j$) p. 4.

42.4 झिमिकि] G$_e$Ṭ$_e$, रिमझिम (unm.) Ś$_e$ **44.4** देखिके] G$_e$, देखिये Ṭ$_e$ **45.1** में] **E**, तें I$_e$ • आनि] **E**, आय I$_e$ **45.2** पपीहरा] G$_e$I$_e$Ṭ$_e$, पपिहरा Ṭ$_e^j$

42.4 झूमना [*kṣubh- x *jhaṭ-] v.i. 'to sway' 1. to move imposingly; 2. fig. to be delighted; 3. to gather, to lower (clouds); झमकना (झिमिकना) v.i. to glitter; रिमझिम 1. adv. pitter-patter; 2. f. pattering sound (of rain). **43.1** प्रपंच [S] m. 1. expansion; 2. trick. **43.2** जहीं reg. adv. wherever (H jahāṃ bhī); बगला [cf. baka-] m. 1. heron; 2. ? crane. **43.3** जितही तित Br. adv. 1. here and there; 2. all around; गाढा [gāḍha-] adj. 1. thick; 2. intense. **43.4** कामरी (कंबल) [S] Br. f. blanket; छाहरे (छाया) [S] reg. m. obl. in the shadow of. **44.1** ना गिरत हैं Br. (out of fear of the lightning the stars) do not fall down. **44.2** लेखि पति आपनो Br. considering (the moon) as their husband; न... हैं they do not stop even when tired. **44.3** भूलना [*bhull-] v.i. to go astray; to err; अनुकूल- [anukūlayati w. H anukūl] Br. v.i. to be well-disposed. भटभेरा [bhaṭa-, + cf. H bhīṛ] m. clash, battle (cf. H muṭ-bheṛ); भिर- [cf. H bhīṛ] Br. v.i. to gather; अनुकूले... हैं Br. being friendly they do not clash. **44.4** नखत [nakṣatra-] Br. m. constellation, stars; चौंधियाने v.i. perf. dazzled (stars). **45.2** उनय- (उनव-) [ud+nam-] Br. v.i. to roll, to surge (clouds).

ठाकुर, वा सुखकारी सुहावनि दामिनि कौंधि कितै धौं गई है।
री, अब तौ घनघोर घटा, गरजौ बरसौ तुम्हें धूर दई है॥ R45॥ 4

*वा बरसै जलधारन सों, रसधारन याहु सतीत करी है।
घूमो रहै घुमडो वा मढो, यह लै मुरली अधरान धरी है। 2
ठाकुर, वाहि मिली चपला, अबला मिली याहि चरित्र भरी है।
देखत जोंई कहै धनि सो, घन सों घनश्याम सों होड परी है॥ R46॥ 4

देखि तमासो दिसा-बिदिसा बिरही उर अंतर काँपति सी है।
केकी पपीहन की बर बानि झिली झनकार कों झाँपति सी है। 2
ठाकुर, ठाढी मनोहर पास कहै बरबाल निसापति सी है।

---

46 Granthāvalī 118, Ṭhasak 113. 47 Bharatpur1 f. 149v (2), Granthāvalī 119, Ṣaṭṛtu (J_e) p. 167, Sudhāsar [S_2 f. 37rv (-/40), S_3 f. 215r (22), S_7 f. 122r (9/1159)], Ṭhasak 111, Vrindaban1 f. 5rv (2/28). The Sudhāsar manuscripts present this poem within the description of the rainy season (pāvas) in the 'ṣaṭṛtu' section of the chapter on 'uddīpan'. The Ṭhasak gives the first two lines in the reverse order.

45.3 कौंधि] I_e, कौंध **E** • धौं] **E**, कौं I_e **47.1** देखि] B_1**E**J_eS_2, देष $S_3S_7V_1$ • काँपति सी] B_1**E**J_e, कांमत सी S_2, काम बसी S_3, कांपत सी S_7V_1 **47.2** पपीहन] Σ, पपीहरा J_e • बर बानि] $B_1J_eS_2V_1$, बरबानी **E**, बर बान S_3, बर बात S_7 • झिली] Σ, झीली V_1 • झाँपति] $B_1G_eJ_eT_e$, झांपत **S**V_1 **47.3** ठाढी] **E**$J_eS_3S_7$, ठाटी S_2, ठाडी B_1V_1 • पास] Σ, पासि S_7 • कहै] Σ, कहैं B_1 • बर°] B_1**E**J_e, बल° **S**, बार° V_1 • निसापति] Σ, निसापत S_3

45.3 कौंध f. flash of lightning; कितै धौं Br. adv. who knows where. **45.4** री voc. Br. o cloud! ; धूर देना idiom. not to pay attention. **46.1** वा pron. Br. that one (i.e. the cloud); याहु pron. Br. this one (i.e. Krishna) also; सतीत [? sikta-] adj. wet, drenched. **46.2** घूमो रहै (घूमता रहता है) [*ghummati] Br. v.i. pres. keeps going around; घुमड़ना [cf. H ghūmnā] v.i. to gather, to grow thick (clouds); वा [S] conj. or; मढ़ना [cf. H maṛh 'difficult to move' (BHK)] v.i. to stop. **46.3** चपला [S] 'fickle' 1. lecherous woman; 2. lightning; चरित्र भरी adj. (f.) of good conduct. **46.4** जोंई [yuvatī-] Br. f. woman; धनी [S] m. husband; घन [S] m. cloud; होड [*hoḍḍa-] f. wager, rivalry. **47.1** दिशा-विदिशा adv. in every direction. **47.2** बर बानी [vara-vāṇī-] f. excellent sound; झिल्ली [S] f. cricket; झनकार f. chirping (as of a cricket); झाँपना [*jhaṃp-] v.t. to conceal (i.e. to overdo). **47.3** बरबाल [vara-bālā-] f. excellent woman (says); निशापति [S] m. 'the lord of the night' the moon.

4 काम-क्रिसान की डोरी चली चपला फिरै मेघन मापति सी है॥ R47॥

1 *केकी लागे नाचन, लगे री पिक बाचन, सु
झिल्ली झनकार, यौं बहार बन-बाग की।
2 पौन पुरवाई की अवाई अधिकाई, तामैं
तान गाई भारही-कलार चोखे राग की।
3 ठाकुर कहत, दुंद दादुर मचाई, बुंद
बडी बडी आई, छवि छाई अनुराग की।
4 सेत बग, कारे घन, पीरी बीज, हरी भूमि
धूम रंग धुरवा, ललाई लाल पाग की॥ R48॥

1 सखिन दुराई वृषभान की दुलारी राधे,
छाई दुचिताई अति नंद के नँदन मैं।

---

48 Bharatpur1 f. 149v-150r (3), Granthāvalī 120, Sudhāsar [S_2 f. 36rv ((48)/37), S_3 f. 212r (7), S_7 f. 120rv (6/1143)], Vrindaban1 f. 5v (29). The Sudhāsar manuscripts present this poem within the description of the rainy season (pāvas) in the 'ṣaṭṛtu' section of the chapter on 'uddīpan'. 49 Granthāvalī 121, Ṭhasak 112, Śatak 22.

47.4 क्रिसान] S_3S_7, **किसान** $B_1G_eS_2V_1$, **कृशानु** J_e, **कृपान** $Ṭ_e$ • **की**] Σ, **कि** $Ṭ_e$ • **चली**] Σ, **लिये** $Ṭ_e$ • **फिरै**] Σ, **फिरैं** B_1 • **मेघन**] Σ, **मेघत** S_3 **48.1 लागे**] $B_1G_eV_1$, **लगे** S • **वाचन सु**] S_7^{pc}, **पी पी कै** (unm.) B_1, **बाचन औ** G_e, **चाचन सु** $S_2S_3S_7^{ac}$, *om.* (unm.) V_1 • **झिल्ली**] $B_1G_eS_2V_1^{pc}$, **झिली** S_3S_7, **झल्ली** V_1^{ac} **48.2 पुरवाई**] Σ, **पुरवाइ** V_1 • **कलार**] B_1V_1, **मलार** $G_eS_2S_3$, **मल्हार** S_7 **48.3 कहत**] Σ, **कहैत** V_1 • **दुंद**] $B_1G_eS_3S_7$, **दुद** S_2, **इंद** V_1 • **बुंद**] $B_1^{pc}G_eS_3S_7$, **बूंद** $B_1^{ac}S_2$, **बंडु** V_1 • **बडी**] Σ, *om.* (haplography) S_2 • **आई**] Σ, **आइ** V_1 • **छाई**] Σ, **छाइ** V_1 **48.4 बीज**] Σ, **बीजी** V_1 • **भूमि**] $B_1G_eS_2S_7$, **भूम** S_3V_1

47.4 किसान [kṛṣāṇa-] m. farmer; **कृपाण** var. [S] m. dagger, sword; **कृशानु** var. [S] poet. m. fire; **कि** var. conj. or; **डोरा** var. [davara-] m. string, rope; **चपला** [S] poet. f. lightning; **डोरी चली चपला** poet. the lightning went forward as the thread; **मापति सी** Br. as if mapping (the clouds). **48.1 केकी** [S] poet. m. peacock; **पिक** [S] poet. m. Indian cuckoo; **बाँचना** [vācayati] v.t. to read, to utter; (here:) to make noise; **चाचना** apa. **बहार** [P] f. 1. spring; 2. splendour; spectacle; pleasure (BHK). **48.2 अधिका-** [adhika-] Br. v.i. to increase; **तामैं** Br. in that (wind); **भरही** [bharadvāja-] m. the small Indian skylark (Alauda gulgula); **कलार** (**कलवार**) [kalyapāla-] m. distiller or seller of spirits; **चोखा** [cokṣa-] adj. 1. pure; 2. delightful. **48.3 दुंद** [dvandva-] m. (here: f.) uproar. **48.4 बीज** [vidyuta-] Br. f. lightning; **धुरवा** [dhuravāha-] m. dense cloud; (here:) haze, mist (from the rain); **लाल** 1. [lālya-] m. dear one; 2. [P] adj. red. **49.1 सखिन दुराई** Br. her friends hid Radha; **राधे** poet. f. (not voc.) Radha; **दुचिताई** [dvi+citta-] f. doubt, confusion.

झूमि आए बादर, झमकि अँधियारी आई, 2
धाई फिरै दामिनी, दिखाई देत घन मैं।
ठाकुर कहत, चारु चातक चढे हैं चाउ, 3
आनँद उमंग मची मोरन के गन मैं।
राधे राधे टेर-टेर, पीरो पट फेर-फेर, 4
हेर-हेर हरि डोलै गेर गेर बन मैं॥ R49॥

*सगुन सुहावैं आवै भावतो हमारे ग्रेह, 1
मेह की निकाई भावै बूँद बौछरा की है।
सोऊ उर अंतर मैं सहल दिखान लागी, 2
काम के सरन की अवाई बेतरा की है।
ठाकुर कहत, फीकी दामिनी न लागै मोहि, 3
नीकियै लगत सोभा सबज धरा की है।
बाएँ अंग फरकत, दरकत कंचुकी री, 4

---

50 Bharatpur1 f. 156v (41), Granthāvalī B45, Sudhāsar [S_7 f. 93r (1/900)] Vrindaban1 ff. 9v-10r (4/56).

49.2 झूमि] Ś$_e$Ṭ$_e$, झूम G_e **49.3** हैं चाउ] G_eṬ$_e$, वा चारु Ś$_e$ **50.1** सगुन] $B_1S_7G_e$, सुगुन V_1 • सुहावैं] B_1, सुहावै $G_eS_7V_1$ • हमारे] $B_1G_eV_1$, हमारो S_7 • ग्रेह] $B_1S_7V_1$, गेह G_e **50.2** लागी] $B_1S_7V_1$, लगी G_e **50.3** ठाकुर कहत] G_eS_7, ठा° B_1, ठाकुर कहैत V_1 • मोहि] $B_1S_7G_e$, मोह V_1 • नीकियै] $B_1G_eV_1$, नीकीयै S_7

49.2 झमकना [cf. *jhamm-] v.i. 1. Br. to beat, to blow (wind or rain); 2. to spread; धा- [dhāvati] Br. v.i. to run. **49.3** चढे हैं चाउ Br. are overwhelmed with desire; गन [gaṇa-] m. multitude. **49.4** फेरना [*pherayati] v.t. to play with (his yellow garment); हेरना [*herati] v.t. to search; हेर-फेर m. 1. confusion; 2. wandering, roaming; 3. labyrinth; गेरना [cf. H girnā] v.i. to fall down. **50.1** सगुन [śakuna-] m. good omen; सुहावै [śobhā-] Br. adj. beautiful; सगुन सुहावै Br. 1. auspicious signs shine; 2. at an auspicious occasion; भावै है [bhāti] v.i. (pres. Br.) (the greatness of the clouds and the drops of the rain) look beautiful; बौछाड़ [vāyu- + chaṭā-] f. heavy shower. **50.2** सोऊ (वह भी) Br. pron. and he (i.e. my absent beloved) also; सहल [A] 1. adj. simple; 2. adv. in a simple way; शर [S] m. arrow; बेतरह (का) [P] adj. excessive. **50.3** फीका [*phikka-] adj. 'insipid' dull, uninteresting; फीकी... मोहि Br. I do not find the lightning dull; सबज [P sabz] adj. green; धरा [S] poet. f. earth.

सरकत घरी घरी फुंद घँघरा की है॥ R50॥

1 आई आई पावस अवाई छाई दिसन मैं,
फेर परि गयो रबि ससि के प्रकास मैं।
2 अवनि अनंद मान्यौ, सबन प्रभाव जान्यौ,
चातिक मयूर फिरैं बिमले बिलास मैं।
3 ठाकुर कहत, एतौ बधिक न धिक मानै,
देखन गई ती, भई अधिक उदास मैं।
4 अब तौ, भटू री, दिन पाँच-सात-आठक तैं
बादर बसन लागे दिनहू अकास मैं॥ R51॥

1 *पौन टेरै पानी काजै, पानी टेरै भूमि काजै,

---

51 Bharatpur1 f. 156v-7r (42), Granthāvalī B46, Sudhāsar [S_1 f. 196r, S_3 f. 25v (7), $S_7$155r (7/1472)], Vrindaban1 f. 10r (5/57). The Sudhāsar presents this poem within the 'pāvasa ritu varṇan'.

50.4 फरकत $B_1G_eV_1$, फरकति S_7 • दरकत] B_1G_e, दरकति S_7, दर कंत V_1 • सरकत $B_1G_eV_1$, सरकति S_7 • फुंद] G_e, फूंद $B_1S_7V_1$ **51.1** दिसन] Σ, देसन S_1 • परि] $B_1G_eS_1$, पर $S_3S_7V_1$ • के] $S_1^{pc}\Sigma$, *om.* (unm.) S_1^{ac} **51.2** अवनि] G_e**S**, अवन B_1V_1 • मान्यौ] B_1G_e**S**, मानौ V_1 • सबन] $B_1G_eV_1$, पवन **S** • फिरैं] Σ, फिरे S_7 • बिमले] $B_1S_3S_7$, बिमल G_e, बिमलैं S_1, चिमले V_1 • बिलास] $G_eS_1V_1$, बिकास S_3S_7 **51.3** ठाकुर कहत] G_e**S**, ठा° B_1, ठाकुर कहैत V_1 • मानै] Σ, मानैं S_1 **51.4** भटू] Σ, बटा S_3 • बादर] Σ, बादर×र× S_1 • दिनहू] $B_1G_eV_1$, निसहू **S**

50.4 फड़कना [phaṭ- x *spharati] v.i. 1. to flutter; 2. to be agitated; बाएँ अंग फरकत idiom. Br. 'the (woman's) left side to be agitated' it is a good omen; दरकना [cf. darayati] v.i. 1. to be torn, to split; 2. to throb; सरकना [sarati] v.i. to slip away; फुंद m. (here f.) tassel; घाघरा [gharghari-] m. an ample, ankle-length skirt. **51.1** अवाई [H ānā] reg. (the effects of) arrival; फेर [*phera-] m. 1. bartering, exchange; 2. rivalry. **51.2** अवनि [avanī-] poet. f. the earth; मान्यौ [manyate] v.t. perf. Br. accepted; मयूर [S] m. peacock; बिमले [vimala-] Br. adj. emph. pure. **51.3** एतौ (इतना) [cf. iyattaka-] adj. such big (hunter); बधिक [vadhaka-] m. hunter (i.e. the uddīpanas are lethal); न धिक मानना idiom. reg. 1. does not consider it contemptible; 2. is not influenced by contempt; गई ती reg. v.i. I went. **51.4** आठक [H āṭh + eka-] num. some eight; बसन लागे Br. started to dwell; निसहू var. Br. obl. even at night; दिनहू (दिन में भी) m. (Br. obl.) even during the day (it is said that clouds lower the most at nights in the month of Bhādõ.).

भूमि टेरै हरियारे-बसन सिँगारे कों।
दादुर झिली कों, झिली भारही पुकारत है, 2
भारही पिकन, पिक स्वाति सों सुखारे कों।
ठाकुर कहत, ऐसी टेराटेरी माँची तहाँ, 3
साँचियै जुबान प्यारी टेरै प्रानप्यारे कों।
रितु टेरै मोरन कों, मोर टेरैं मेघन कों, 4
मेघ टेरैं दामिनी कों, दामिनी अँध्यारे कों॥ R52॥

पावस के परस बियोगी सकुचौंहैं भए, 1
बरही नचौंहैं भए डगर मचौंहैं री।

---

52 Bharatpur1 f. 152v (19), Granthāvalī B47, Sudhāsar [S_1 f. 213v (81), S_2 ff. 49v-50r (2/50), S_3 f. 41v-42r (87), S_7 f. 164r (81/1571)] Vrindaban1 f. 15r (27/91). The Sudhāsar presents this poem within the description of 'bijurī', lightning, in the 'pāvasa ritu varṇan'. 53 Bharatpur1 f. 164r (88), Granthāvalī B48, Sudhāsar [S_1 f. 270v (4), S_2 f. 58rv (-/60), S_3 f. 145v (115), S_4 f. 70rv (122), S_7 f. 194r (4)], Vrindaban1 f. 8r (7/45). • The Sudhāsar presents this poem in the 'aur nānābidhi kī brijkelī barnan' (description of other various love sports in Braj) subsection of the 'Brajrasrīti' section.

52.1 टेरै] Σ, टेरैं B_1 • काजै] **S**V_1, काजैं B_1, की जै G_e • भूमि] $B_1G_eS_1S_7V_1$, भूंम S_2S_3 • काजै] Σ, की जै G_e • हरियारे] $B_1G_eS_1S_2$, हरिआरे S_3S_7, हैरिया (unm.) V_1 • बसन] Σ, बसना V_1 **52.2** झिली] $B_1S_1S_2S_7$, झिल्ली $G_eS_3V_1$ • झिली] $B_1S_1S_2S_7$, झिल्ली $G_eS_3V_1$ • पुकारत है] $B_1G_eS_3V_1$, पुकारै (unm.) S_2, पुकारत हैं S_7 • भारहि पिकन] B_1V_1, भारुही पिकनि G_e, *om.* (haplography) S_2, भारही पुकारै $S_1S_3S_7$ • स्वाति] $B_1G_eS_2S_7$, स्वात $S_1S_3V_1$ **52.3** ठाकुर कहत] G_e**S**, ठा° B_1, ठाकुर कहैत V_1 • टेराटेरी] B_1**S**, टेराटेर G_e, टेराटेरा V_1 • तहाँ] Σ, वहाँ G_e • साँचियै] $B_1G_eS_2$, साँचीयै $S_1S_3V_1$ • टेरै प्रानप्यारे] S_2^{pc}Σ, टे*रैं प्याँनप्यारो S_1^{ac} **52.4** मोर टेरैं] B_1S_1, मोर टेरै $G_eS_2S_3V_1$
53.1 बियोगी] Σ, बियोगि S_2 • नचौंहैं भए... मचौंहैं] Σ, नचौंहैं (eyeskip) S_4 • डगर] Σ, डूगर S_7 • मचौंहैं] Σ, नचौहैं S_7

52.1 टेरना [*ṭer-] v.t. 1. to shout; 2. to chant; काजै [kārye] postp. Br. for (water) (the wind is considered perfect when it brings rain); हरियारे (हरियाली) [cf. hara-] reg. m. greenery; हरियारे-बसन सिँगारे कों Br. for a decoration of clothes of greenery. **52.2** झिली (झिल्ली) [S] Br. f. cricket (DB); भारही [bharadvāja-] m. the small Indian skylark (Alauda gulgula); पिक [S] poet. m. papīhā, the Indian cuckoo; सुखार- [sukha-] Av. Br. adj. 1. happy; 2. pleasant; स्वाति सों सुखारे कों Br. for a thing as pleasant as svāti. **52.3** टेराटेरी [H ṭernā] f. shouting to and fro; साँचियै [satya-] Br. adj. emph. true; जुबान [A] f. (here:) voice. **52.4** अँधियारा [andha-] m. darkness. **53.1** बरही [varhin-] Br. m. peacock; डगर [*ḍag-] m. path, track; मचना [*macyate] v.i. 'to be produced' to break out (as rejoicing); मचौंहैं भए Br. became fixed (on the road).

2 लपटी लतान सौं तमालन के पुंज सोहैं,
पौन की झकोरन सो ह्वै रहे झुकौंहैं री।
3 ठाकुर कहत, आज प्रीति-रीति पेखिबे की,
धन्य घरी लेखिबे की, देखिबे की गौंहैं री।
4 घन बरसौंहें भये, सोहैं तोहि आवत, री,
आनन हँसौंहैं हरि जात कुंज सौंहैं री॥ R53॥

*सजि सूहे दुकूलन बिज्जु छटा सी अटान चढ़ी घटा जोवती हैं।

---

54 Hariaudh (A_e) p. 482, Bharatpur5 ff. 24v-25r (35), Sundarītilak (C_e) 410, Datiya1 f. 42r, Granthāvalī B49, Kālidās-Hajārā (H_e) 325, Rāmcandra Śukla (I_e) p. 436, Jaipur1 ff. 1v-2r (4), Ṣaṭṛtu-hajārā (J_e) p. 167, Marwar4 f. 26r (58), Mītal (M_e) p. 134 (Varṣā 207), Kasganj (N) f. 37r (164), Rasikvinod (O_e) 234, Pāvaskavitt-ratnākar p. 25 (111) (P_e), Sudhāsar [S_1 f. 212v (76), S_3 f. 40v-41r (82), S_7 f. 163v (76/1566)], Śatak 79, Ṭhākur-satsaī (Ṭ) f. 1v (11) Ṭhasak 115, Ṭhasak 'Jīvancarit' ($Ṭ_e^j$) p. 3, Vrindaban2 f. 70r. The Sudhāsar presents this poem within the 'pāvasaṛtu', Rainy Season section of the 'Pravāsaviraha uddīpana ṣaṭaritu varnana', description of the seasons as stimuli for emotions in physical separation.

53.2 सोहैं] $B_1G_eS_2V_1$, सोहै **S** • झकोरन] Σ, झकोरनि S_1 • रहे] $B_1G_eS_1S_3S_7V_1$, है (unm.) S_2, है रहै (dittography) S_4 **53.3** ठाकुर कहत] G_e**S**, ठा॰ B_1, ठाकुर कहैत V_1 • प्रीति] $B_1G_eS_2S_3S_4$, प्रीत $S_1S_7V_1$ • देखिबे की] Σ, *om.* (haplography) S_2 **53.4** सोहैं] $B_1G_eS_2V_1$, सोहै **S** • आवत] Σ, आवति S_3 • हँसौंहैं] S_1^{pc}Σ, ⟨हाँ/हर⟩सौंहैं S_1^{ac} • जात] Σ, जाति S_7 **54.1** सजि] $A_eB_5C_eD_1\mathbf{E}H_eI_eJ_1J_eM_eNO_eS_1V_2$, सज $M_4S_3S_7$Ṭ, छबि P_e • सूहे] $A_eB_5\mathbf{E}H_eI_eJ_1J_eM_4M_eN\mathbf{S}$Ṭ$V_2$, सोहे $C_eD_1P_e$, सूह O_e • दुकूलन] Σ, दुकूलनि A_eH_e • बिज्जु] $A_eB_5C_e\mathbf{E}H_eI_eJ_eM_eNS_1V_2O_e$, बिज (unm.) D_1, बीजु J_1, बिज्ज $M_4S_3S_7^{pc}$, में P_e, बि (unm.) S_7^{ac}, बिजु Ṭ • छटा सी] Σ, चुन कै P_e, छटनि $Ś_e$, छटा (unm.) Ṭ • अटान चढ़ी] Σ, अटा में चढ़ी C_e, अटानि चढ़ी O_e, अप आपनीते P_e, अटा पै चढि Ṭ • घटा] $Ṭ^{pc}$Σ, मग D_1M_4, घवा $Ṭ^{ac}$ • हैं] Σ, है $D_1S_3S_7$Ṭ

53.2 पौन [pavana-] m. wind; झकोर [*jhakkol-] f. blast of wind. **53.3** पेख- [prekṣate] Br. v.t. 1. to see; 2. to desire ; लेखिबे की poet. worth to be considered; गौंह [gama-] f. opportunity. **53.4** सौहैं तोहि आवत Br. 1. shine when you come; 2. they come towards you. कुंज सौंहैं Br. towards the grove. **54.1** सजि v.t. abs. Br. decorated (with red shawl); दुकूल [S] m. shawl; सूहा [conn. śubha-] adj. 1. bright red; 2. saffron coloured; बिज्जु [vidyut-] f. lightning.

सुचिती है सुनें सुर मोरन के, मदमाती सँजोग सँजोवती हैं।
कहि ठाकुर, वे पिय दूरि बसैं, हम आँसुन सों तन धोवती हैं।
धनि वे धनि पावस की रतियाँ पति की छतियाँ लगि सोवती हैं॥ R54॥

*ओपे से अमल झल झलक के टोपे से वे

54.2 सुचिती] $A_eB_5D_1H_eI_eJ_1M_4S_1$, रँगराती $C_eJ_eM_eP_e$, सुनती G_e, सुचती $NS_3S_7\text{Ṭ}^j_eV_2$, रंग राती O_e, सुनतीं $\text{Ś}_e\text{Ṭ}_e$, मधमाते Ṭ • है] D_1V_2, ह्वै $A_eB_5H_eI_eM_4\text{Ṭ}^j_e$, *om.* $C_eJ_eM_eO_eP_e\mathbf{S}\text{Ṭ}$, हैं $G_eN\text{Ś}_e\text{Ṭ}_e$, के J_1 • सुनें] $A_eB_5H_eI_eJ_1M_4M_eNO_e\text{ṬṬ}^j_eV_2$, सुनै $C_eD_1J_eP_e$, महा $G_e\text{Ś}_e\text{Ṭ}_e$, *om.* **S** • सुर] $B_5D_1G_eM_4NO_e\mathbf{S}\text{Ś}_e\text{ṬṬ}_eV_2$, धुनि $A_eC_eH_eI_eJ_1J_eM_eP_e\text{Ṭ}^j_e$ • के] $B_5D_1G_eM_4NO_e\text{ṬṬ}_eV_2$, की $A_eC_eH_eI_eJ_1J_eM_eP_e\text{Ṭ}^j_e$, के सुनि कैं S_1, की सुन कै S_3, कौ सुन कै S_7, कै Ś_e • मदमाती] $C_eD_1G_eJ_1J_eM_eO_eP_e\mathbf{S}\text{Ś}_e\text{Ṭ}_e$, रसमाती A_eI_e, मदमाते B_5M_4, रसमाते $H_e\text{Ṭ}^j_eV_2$, मन भांते N, रसराते Ṭ • सँजोग] $A_eB_5G_eH_eI_e\text{Ś}_e\text{Ṭ}_eV_2$, संयोग $C_eJ_eM_eP_e\text{Ṭ}^j_e$, सिगार D_1, सनेह J_1, सँजोव M_4, सिंगार NṬ, संजोग O_eS_1, सजोव S_3S_7 • सँजोवती] Σ, समोवती J_1 • हैं] $A_eB_5C_e\mathbf{E}H_eI_eJ_1M_4J_eM_eNO_eP_eS_1$, है $D_1S_3S_7\text{Ṭ}V_2$ **54.3** कहि] $B_5C_eD_1J_eM_eNP_eS_1S_7$, कवि $A_eG_eH_eI_eJ_1M_4O_eS_3\text{Ś}_e\text{Ṭ}_eV_2$, कह Ṭ • वे] Σ, वै A_eI_e • पिय] $A_eB_5\mathbf{E}C_eH_eI_eJ_eM_4M_eNP_eS_3S_7V_2$, पीय D_1S_1, पिया J_1, पी $O_e\text{Ṭ}$ • दूरि] $A_eB_5C_eH_eI_eJ_1J_eN\text{Ṭ}^j_eV_2$, दूर $D_1G_eM_4M_eP_e\mathbf{S}\text{Ś}_e\text{Ṭ}_e$, परदेस $O_e\text{Ṭ}$ • बसैं] $A_eB_5\mathbf{E}H_eI_eJ_eM_4M_eNO_eS_1S_7V_2D_1$, बसे $C_eJ_1P_eS_3\text{Ṭ}$ • हम] Σ, *om.* $H_eS_3S_7V_2$ • आँसुन] $A_eD_1\mathbf{E}I_eJ_1J_eM_4M_eNO_eS_1$, आसुन B_5, आँशुन $C_eM_eP_e$, असुवान $H_eS_3S_7V_2$, आस्वुन Ṭ • सों] $A_eB_5D_1\mathbf{E}H_eI_eJ_1M_4NO_eS_1S_7\text{Ṭ}$, से C_e, ते J_eP_e, तें M_e, सौं यौं S_3V_2 • तन] Σ, दृग $B_5J_1S_1$, तनँ M_4 • हैं] Σ, है $D_1S_3S_7\text{Ṭ}$ **54.4** धनि] $A_eB_5C_e\mathbf{E}H_eI_eJ_1J_eM_eNO_eP_eS_1V_2$, धन $D_1M^{pc}_4S_3S_7\text{Ṭ}$, अब M^{ac}_4 • वे धनि] $C_e\mathbf{E}J_eM_eNO_eS_1V_2$, वै धनि $A_eH_eI_eP_e$, वे धन $B_5D_1J_1M_4S_3S_7\text{Ṭ}$ • रतियाँ] Σ, रतिया $J_1S_3\text{Ṭ}$ • पति की] Σ, *om.* D_1, पिय की S_3, पत की Ṭ • लगि] $A_eB_5C_e\mathbf{E}I_eJ_1J_eM_4M_eO_eP_eS_3$, लगि नाह की D_1, लगी $H_eNS_1V_2$, लग $S_3S_7\text{Ṭ}$ • हैं] $A_eB_5C_e\mathbf{E}H_eI_eJ_1J_eM_4M_eNO_eP_eS_1$, है $D_1S_3S_7\text{Ṭ}V_2$

54.2 सुचिती [su-cit-] Br. adj. attentive, alert; सुर [svara-] Br. m. sound; मदमाता [mada-matta-] adj. lustful, in youth's bloom; सँजोना [saṃyojayati] v.t. 'to arrange, to collect' to acquire. **54.4** रतियाँ (रात) [rātri-] reg. f. pl. nights; छतियाँ (छाती) [*chātti-] reg. f. obl. breast.

बिधि-कारीगर ने बिचित्र बिसतरे हैं।
2 रंगन गरूरे लाल लहर ललाम लौने
छबि की उमंग के सुहाए जल भरे हैं।
ठाकुर कहत, पूरे पानिप के, मेरी बीर,
सुषमान भरे, ताके उपमान करे हैं।
4 पावस-फकीर के, कै मदन-अमीर के ये

---

55 Bharatpur1 f. 152rv (17), Granthāvalī B51, Sudhāsar [S_2 f. 37r (42/39), S_3 f 214rv (18), S_7 f. 121v (4/1154)], Ṣaṭṛtu-hajārā (J_e) p. 166 (Pāvasṛtu varṇan); Mītal (M_e) p. 158 (Varṣā 308), Vrindaban1 ff. 14v-15r (25/89). The Sudhāsar manuscripts present this poem within the description of the rainy season (pāvas) in the 'ṣaṭṛtu' section of the chapter on 'uddīpan'. (The text of J_e and M_e, representing a later phase in transmission, is considerably different from that of B_1, **S** and V_1.)

55.1 ओपे] B_1G_e**S**V_1, आये J_eM_e • झल] B_1G_e**S**V_1, झला J_eM_e • झलक के] B_1**S**V_1, °झल करैं G_e, झलहू के M_e, झलऊ के J_e • से वे] $B_1^{pc}J_e$, से बि° $B_1^{ac}S_7$, से कि G_e, स बि° S_2S_3, सबै M_e, सो बि° V_1 • बिधि] $B_1G_eJ_eM_eS_3$, बिध $S_2S_7V_1$ • कारीगर] Σ, कारिगरै S_2S_3 • बिचित्र] $B_1G_eJ_eM_eS_2V_1$, बचित्र S_3, बिचित्त्र S_7 • हैं] $B_1G_eM_eS_2S_7V_1$, है J_eS_3 **55.2** रंगन] $B_1G_eS_3S_7V_1$, रंगत J_eM_e, रंगना S_2 • लहर] $B_1G_eJ_eM_eS_3V_1$, लहरि S_2S_7 • लौने] Σ, लैन G_e • उमंग के] B_1G_e**S**, उमंगन J_eM_e, उमंगि के V_1 • सुहाए] $B_1G_eJ_eM_eS_3V_1$, सुहारा S_3, फुहारा S_7 • हैं] $B_1G_eM_eS_2S_7V_1$, है J_eS_3 **55.3** ठाकुर कहत] $G_eJ_eM_e$**S**, ठा° B_1, ठाकुर कहैत V_1 • सुषमान भरे] G_e**S**V_1, सुषमा भरे (unm.) B_1^{ac}, सुषमा के भरे B_1^{pc}, सुषमा भरे हैं J_eM_e • ताके] B_1G_e**S**, ताते J_eM_e, तीके V_1 • हैं] $B_1G_eM_eS_2S_7V_1$, है J_eS_3

55.1 ओपना [cf. H op 'lustre, polish'] v.i. to be polished; आये से var. as if coming (from far); अमल [S] adj. pure; झल [jhalā-] m.f. 1. heat; 2. radiance, brilliance; 3. strong desire, frenzy; झला var. reg. m. 1. the first (drop of) rain at monsoon; 2. f. brilliance; झलक के (झलकवाले) poet. shining (with brilliance); झलझल var. [cf. *jhal-] m. glitter, brilliance; झलाझल var. 1. m. f. lightning; 2. adj. glittering, brilliant; झलाझलहूँ के var. (?) they are also (like baskets) of lightning; टोपा [*ṭoppa-] m. 1. large hat, hood; 2. poet. large basket; विधि [S] poet. m. the Creator; कारीगर [P] m. craftsman; बिसतरे [cf. vistāra-] Br. v.t. perf. spread, expanded. **55.2** रंगत var. f. 1. disposition; 2. (good) mood; रंगन गरूरे Br. 1. proud of their own colours; 2. deep in their colours (KL); गरूर- [A gurūr] Br. adj. 'raised' haughty; लाल adj. red (cloud at sunrise or at sunset); ललाम [S] Br. 1. adj. red; 2. m. an adornment, a jewel; 3. fig. m. most excellent thing; लहर ललाम लौने poet. beautiful, most excellent waves; लैन apa.; उमंग के (उमंगवाले) poet. having surges; उमंगन var. [umaṅga-] m. (Br. pl. obl.) in surges; सुहाना [śubhāyate] v.i. 'to shine' to be attractive. **55.3** पानिप [S] m. 1. water; 2. radiance; सुषमा [S] f. splendour; उपमान m. simile; ताके उपमान करे हैं Br. they have been made the object of comparison.

बासन चिनी के नीके ठौर-ठौर धरे हैं॥ R55॥

*पावस की राति भारी, काजर तैं महा कारी, 1
जलधारा पारावार, परत न थाही सी।
धमकि धमकि धुकि धुरवा धमंकि धावै, 2
चपला चमंकि जिमि आनि असि बाही सी।
ठाकुर कहत, सन सन छ्नन छ्नन होत, 3
झन झन झर सो न परत सराही सी।
सुख बिरहीन के चुरत, दुख सींचे जात 4
बरसत मेह चढी काम की कराही सी॥ R56॥

---

56 Bharatpur1 f. 131v (3), Sudhāsar [S_1 f. 197r, S_2 f. 48r (-/48), S_3 f. 26v (12), S_7 f. 155v (13/1477)], Ṭhākur-satsaī (Ṭ) f. 3v (28). The Sudhāsar presents this poem within the 'Pāvasarṭu' section of the 'Pravāsaviraha uddīpana ṣaṭaritu varnana'.

55.4 चिनी] Σ, मनी G_e • हैं] $G_eM_eS_2S_7V_1$, है $B_1J_eS_3$ **56.1** राति] B_1**S**, रात Ṭ • काजर ते महा कारी] Σ, ×काजर तैं महा कारी× काजर तैं महा कारी (dittography) B_1 • तैं] B_1S_1, ते $S_2S_3S_7$Ṭ • पारावार] Σ, बारापर B_1 **56.2** धमकि धमकि] $B_1S_1S_2$, धमक धमक S_3S_7Ṭ • धुकि] $B_1S_1S_2$, धुक S_3S_7Ṭ • धमंकि] B_1S_2, धमंक S_1S_3Ṭ, धमङ्क S_7 • धावै] B_1Ṭ, धावैं S_1, धामैं S_2, धामै S_3S_7 • चमंकि] $B_1S_1S_2$, चमंक S_3Ṭ, चमङ्क S_7 • जिमि] *conj.* जिनि B_1S_2, जिन $S_1S_3S_7$Ṭ • आनि] $B_1S_1S_2$, आन S_3S_7, अत Ṭ • असि] B_1, अस Σ **56.3** सन सन] $B_1S_1^{pc}S_3S_7$Ṭ, सन सस S_1^{ac}, सन (unm.) S_2 • झर] Σ, *om.* (unm.) S_2 **56.4** चुरत] Σ, जुरत S_7 • सींचे] Σ, सींचैं S_3 • की] Σ, कैं B_1

55.4 फ़कीर के (cheap chinaware) of a fakir; वासन [S] m. 1. vessel, dish; 2. clothing; चीनी [H cīn] f. 1. china, porcelain; 2. silk clothes (cf. cīnāñśuka-); बासन चीनी के 1. china bowls (not thrown away as polluted having once been used); 2. silk clothes; मणि apa. [S] f.m. jewel; ठौर ठौर धरे हैं Br. are kept here an there. **56.1** जलधारा [S] f. stream, flow of water; पारावार [pāra- + apāra-] m. ocean; थाहना v.t. to sound, to plumb;. **56.2** धमक f. drumming or thumping sound; धुकना [cf. H. dhok 'bow in salutation'] v.i. to lower; धुरवा poet. m. cloud; धमकना v.i. 1. to make a loud sound; 2. to flash, to glimmer; धामना v.i. to run; आणि [S] poet. f. edge of a sword; जिमि Br. adv. like (H jaise); असि [S] f. scimitar, sword; बाहना v.t. to open out, to pull out. **56.3** सन [svana-] f. 1. a vibrant and insistent sound, whizzing, whistling, 2. thrill of delight; झन झन [cf. jhaṇ-] f. 1. chirring, 2. jingling, rattling; झर [S] m. flow, shower; न परत सराही Br. we cannot praise it enough; सी poet. (meaningless particle used here for rhyming). **56.4** चुरत [cf. H curānā] Br. v.t. imperf. (the raining cloud) boils (i.e. destroys); दुख सींचे जात Br. keeps sprinkling sorrow; चढ़ना [*caḍhati] v.i. to put on (the fire); कराही f. frying pan; चढी... सी poet. like Kāmadeva's frying pan put on the fire.

1 *कढ़ी दिशि दक्षिण ते, घोर घन घटा चढ़ी,
बढ़ी बिरही को दुख देन कौ न कम है।
2 ठाकुर, झरोखे ह्वै तनक ताकी तीय कह्यो,
तू री ताकि, आली, या उतंग रंग तम है।
3 कह्यो वाहि मेघ, सों न मानै, कहै, जानै तू न,
गरजत आवै या सु जान्यो जोग हम है।
4 है न बिज्जु, होत किरवारो, दंड चमचम
जीव आनै आवत जमात जोरे यम है॥ R57॥

1 *घन घहरान लागे, अंग सहरान लागे,
केकी कहरान लागे, बन के बिलासी जे।
2 बोलि बोलि दादुर निरादर सों आठों याम,
ग्रीषम की देन लागे बहुर बिदा सी जे।

---

57 Ṣaṭṛtu-hajārā (J_e) p. 166 (Pāvasṛtu varṇana), Mītal (M_e) pp. 157-158 (Varṣā 305), Pāvaskavitt-ratnākar (P_e) 52. 58 Ṣaṭṛtu-hajārā (J_e) p. 166 (Pāvasaṛtu varṇan), Mītal (M_e) p. 103 (Varṣā 74), Pāvaskavitt-ratnākar (P_e) 95.

57.1 दक्षिण] J_eP_e, दक्खिन M_e • ते] J_eP_e, तें M_e • को] J_eP_e, कों M_e • को न] J_eP_e, ही कों M_e • कम] J_eP_e, नम M_e **57.2** झरोके] J_eP_e, झरोखै M_e • ह्वै] J_eM_e, है P_e • कह्यो] J_eM_e, कहो P_e • ताकि] J_eM_e, ताक P_e **57.3** वाहि] J_eM_e, नाहि P_e • सों] J_eM_e, त्यों P_e • कहै] J_eM_e, कह P_e • तू न] J_eM_e, तन P_e • सु] J_eP_e, सों M_e • जान्यो] J_eM_e, जानै P_e **57.4** किरवारो] J_eM_e, कर वारो P_e • जोरे] J_eM_e, जोर P_e **58.2** कों] J_eM_e, की P_e • बहुर] P_e, बिरह J_eM_e

---

57.1 **कढ़ना** [*kaḍḍhati] v.i. to appear; **घटा** [S] f. dense cloud; **बढ़ी** [vardhate] v.i. perf. (the cloud) grew; **न कम** adv. 'not little' considerably. **57.2** **झरोखा** m. small window; **उतंग** [uttuṅga-] adj. adv. high; (here:) dense; **या उतंग रंग तम है** how dense the colour of the darkness is. **57.3** **कह्यो वाहि मेघ** Br. (her friend) called it a cloud; **सों न मानै कहै** Br. she does not accept it so and says **या** (**जो**) rel. pron. reg; **जान्यो जोग** (**जानने योग्य**) Br. suited, capable to know. **57.4** **बिज्जु** (**विद्युत्**) [S] Br. f. lightning (SBK); **किरवारो** [kṛpāṇa-] Br. m. sword, scimitar; **दंड** [cf. yamadaṇḍa-] m. Death's rod; **चमचम** adv. with a flash, brightly; **आनै** (**लेने**) [ānayati] Br. v.t. inf. obl. (in order) to take; **जमात** [AP] f. group; **जमात जोड़ना** idiom. to make a group. **58.1** **घहराना** [? *gharaghara-] v.i. 1. to thunder, 2. to roll, to surge; **सहराना** (**सिहराना**) [cf. śikhara-] v.t. to cause to thrill; **केकी** [S] m. peacock; **कहरा-** [? *kārayati] Br. v.i. to cry, to call (cf. H karāhnā). **58.2** **निरादर** [S] m. disrespect (for my lonely state); **की देन बिदा** Br. to say farewell to; **बहुर** [*vyāghuṭati] Av. Br. adv. once again; **जे** Bund. pron. they (KL).

ठाकुर कहत, देखो पावस प्रबल आयौ, 3
उड़त दिखान लागे बगुला उदासी जे।
दाबे से दबे से, चहुँ ओरन छपे से, बीर, 4
बर्बस रहन लागे बदरा बिसासी जे॥ R58॥

*भूमि हरी भई, पंथन सूझत नीर-प्रबाह, बहा बेबहा है।
स्याम घटान अँधेरो कियो, दिन-रैन मैं फेर कछू न रहा है। 2
ठाकुर, भौन तें दूसरे भौन लौं जात बनै न, बिचार महा है।
कैसे कै आवैं कहा करैं, बीर, बिदेसी बिचारेन दोस कहा है॥ R59॥ 4

---

59 Bharatpur1 f. 131v (2), Bharatpur12 ff. 118v-119r (129), Sundarī-tilak (C_e) p. 70 (415), Granthāvalī 155, Jaipur1 f. 4rv (13), Mītal (M_e) p. 137 ('Varṣā' 220), Pāvas-kavitt-ratnākar (P_e) p. 42. (198), Raskusumākar (R_e) p. 172 (465), Ṭhākur-satsaī (Ṭ) f. 3v (27), Sudhāsar [S_1 f. 212v, S_3 f. 40v (81), S_7 f. 163v (75/1565)], Śatak 52, Ṭhasak 121. The Sudhāsar presents this poem in the pāvasaṛtu section of the 'Pravāsaviraha uddīpana ṣaṭaritu varnana' and introduces it saying 'uttara taĩ prasna pragaṭ' (The question is manifest by its reply).

58.3 आयौ] J_eM_e, आई P_e **58.4** चहुँ] J_eM_e, चारो] P_e • छपे] J_eP_e, छये M_e • ब-र्बस] *conj.* बरबस (unm.) P_e, बसि बसि (unm.) J_eM_e **59.1** भूमि] $B_1B_{12}C_e$**E**$J_1M_eP_eR_e$, भूम **S**Ṭ • भई] Σ, हरी B_{12} • पंथन सूझत] B_1**S**Ṭ, गैलैं गईं मीटि $B_{12}C_e$**E**$J_1M_eP_eR_e$ • गैलैं] Σ, गैल B_{12} • गईं] Σ, गई B_{12}, गइ J_1 • मिटि] Σ, मीटि B_{12} • नीर] Σ, नी (unm.) J_1 • बहा बेबहा] B_{12}**E**J_1M_e**S**, ब⟨ह्यौ⟩ बेबहा B_1, बहाव बहा $C_eP_eR_e$, बहा सो बहा Ṭ **59.2** स्याम] $B_1J_1P_e$**S**Ṭ, कारी $B_{12}C_e$**E**M_eR_e • घटान] Σ, घटा ने C_e, घटानि R_e • अँधेरो] Σ, अँधेरी **E**, अंधारो Ṭ • कियो] Σ, कीयो Ṭ • दिन रैन] C_e**E**$M_eJ_1P_eS_1S_3$Ṭ, रैंनि B_1B_{12}, निसि द्यौस R_e, दिनु रैन S_7 • फेर] B_1**S**Ṭ, भेद $B_{12}C_e$**E**$J_1M_eP_eR_e$ • न] Σ, ना C_eṬ • रहा] Σ, लहा J_1P_e **59.3** लौं] B_1C_e**E**$J_1M_eR_e$, सु B_{12}, कौं **S**Ṭ, औ P_e • बनै] B_1C_e**E**$J_1M_eP_eR_e$, बनें B_{12}, ही मैं **S**, * Ṭ • न] $B_1B_{12}C_e$**E**$J_1M_eP_eR_e$, सु S_1, सो S_3S_7, आवै Ṭ **59.4** आवैं] Σ, आमै S_7, आवै Ṭ • कहा करैं] Σ, कहां करै S_7Ṭ • बिदेसी] Σ, बिचारे R_e**S** • बिचारेन] $B_1B_{12}C_e$, बिचारन **E**$J_1M_eP_e$Ṭ, बिदेसन **S**, बटोहिन R_e • दोस] B_1B_{12}**E**M_e**S**Ṭ, दोष $C_eJ_1P_eR_e$

58.3 उड़त (उड़ते हुए) [uḍḍayate] v.i. imperf. Br. flying; बगुल [baka-] m. 1. heron, 2. ? crane; उदासी [S] adj. (who had so far been) dejected. **58.4** दाबा [*dabb-] m. burden; दबना [*dabb-] v.i. to be pressed down; छपना v.i. to be pressed down; (here:) to be covered; बरबस [? bala- + vaśa-] adv. by force; रहन लागे Br. started to stay (here, in front of me); बिसासी [viśvāsa-] adj. treacherous. **59.1** पंथ न सूझत var. Br. the roads cannot be seen (because of the flow of water); गैल var. [cf. gati-] Br. f. path; बहा [H bahnā] v.i. perf. flowed; बेबहा poet. 'which normally does not flow' the water in the ponds (GSh, RSh). **59.2** अंधेरी var. f. darkness; लहा (लिया) var. [labhate] v.t. (reg. perf.) took. **59.3** भौन [bhavana-] Br. m. house; विचार [S] m. anxiety. **59.4** बिदेसी बिचारेन reg. the poor ones who are abroad.

सननात अँधेरी घटा, घननात छटा घन कौ, अरी, घेरत सी।
झननात झिली सुर सोर महा, बरही फिरैं मेघन टेरत सी।
कहि ठाकुर, कौन उपाय करौं तन मैन-मरूर अरेरत सी।
यह पीरि न पावत, आवत है फिर पापिनी पावस पेरत सी॥ R60॥

मोरन के मृदु मंजु मनोहर कुंजन कुंजन प्रेम लखे री।
चात्रग चाह भरे चरचान सौ चंचल चोर चलाचल के री।

---

60 Bharatpur1 f. 164r (89), Granthāvalī 156, Sudhāsar [S_1 f. 210r, S_2 f. 49r (-/49), S_3 f. 36rv (67), S_7 f. 162r (61/1531)], Śatak 50, Ṭhasak 109, Vrindaban1 f. 8rv (8/46). The Sudhāsar presents this poem in the pāvasaṛtu section of the 'Pravāsaviraha uddīpana ṣaṭaritu varnana'.
61 Datiya1 f. 42r (122), Vrindaban2 f. 68v (1).

60.1 सननात] Σ, ×स× सननात S_2 • अँधेरी] Y_eΣ, अँधियारी (unm.) **E** • घटा] Y_eΣ, छटा **E** • घननात] Y_eΣ, छननात **E** • छटा] Y_eΣ, घटा **E** • कौ] **S**V_1Y_e, कौं B_1, की **E** • अरी] Σ, अरि S_7 • घेरत] B_1**S**$V_1^{ac}Y_e$, घेरती **E**V_1^{pc} **60.2** झननात] B_1**E**S_1V_1, मिननात S_2, झिननात S_3S_7 • फिरैं] B_1**E**S_3V_1, फिरै मैं (unm.) S_2, फिरे S_1 • मेघन] B_1^{pc}Σ, मेहन B_1^{ac} • टेरत] Y_eΣ, टेरती **E** **60.3** कहि] B_1**S**V_1, कवि **E**, कह S_7 • कौन उपाय] B_1**S**V_1Y_e, वे पिय दूर **E**, कौन उपाव S_7 • करौं] $B_1S_1S_2V_1Y_e$, बसैं **E**, करौ S_3S_7 • मरूर] Σ, मरोर **E** • अरेरत] Y_eΣ, मुरेरती **E** **60.4** यह] Σ, यहि S_3 • पावत] Σ, पावति **E** • आवत] Σ, आवति **E** • फिरि] B_1, फिर **E**$S_1S_3S_7V_1$, पिरि S_2 • पेरत] Y_eΣ, पेरती **E** **61.1** मृदु] V_2, म्रद D_1 • मंजु] V_2, मज (unm.) D_1 • कुंजन कुंजन] D_1, मंदिर मंडल V_2 • प्रेम] D_1, पैम V_2 • लखे] (unrh.) D_1, लके V_2 • री] D_1, हैं V_2 **61.2** चात्रग] V_2चा⟨ब⟩क D_1 • °न सौ] D_1, करै V_2 • चोर] D_1, चोज V_2 • री] D_1, हैं V_2

60.1 सननाना (सनसनाना) [svana-] v.i. 1. to whistle; 2. to rustle; छननाना (छनछनाना) var. [*channa-] v.i. 1. to clink; 2. to hiss; घनना- (घनघनाना) [*ghanaghana-] v.i. to rumble; घेरत [*gher-] v.t. imperf. Br. (as if) encircling (the clouds). **60.2** झनना- (झनझनाना) [jhaṇ-] v.i. to jingle, to rattle ; मिननात var. [H minmin] v.i. to murmur; झिल्ली [S] f. cricket; सुर [svara-] m. sound; बरही [varhin-] m. (here: f.) peacock. **60.3** मैन [madana-] Br. m. Kāma, the god of love ; अरेर- (रगड़ना) poet. v.t. 'to rub' to torture; मरूरा (मरोड़) [cf. *muroṭati, H maroṛnā] poet. f. 'bending, twist' 1. ache, pang; 2. haughtiness. **60.4** यह पीर न पावत Br. it does not know my pain; फिर adv. again; पावस [prāvṛṣa-] m.f. rainy season; पेरना [prapīḍayati] v.t. 1. to crush, to grind; 2. fig. to afflict. **61.1** कुंजन कुंजन Br. the cries (of the peacocks) in the grove; लक var. (?) [lakṣati, Br. lakh] poet. v.t. to observe; लक्का (लक्का) var. [P] reg. m. the Indian fantail (a pigeon); प्रेम लखै Br. I observed with affection. **61.2** चात्रग [cātaka-] Br. m. cuckoo; चलाचल [S] 1. adj. swift; 2. m. 'moving and unmoving things' nature; चोज var. [codya-] m. wonderful words (of the nature); चंचल... चलाचल like a fickle (and) swift thief; के (in the manner of.

ठाकुर, जे बदरा बिरदैत बिलासी बिलंद बडे बल के री।
झूमैं, झुकैं, झमकैं, झर लावैं, झलाझलवारे झला झलके री॥ R61॥ 4

*मुरवा पुकारै हम जेहैं ऐ पहारन मैं, 1
दादुर पुकारैं हम जेहैं खँदरान मैं।
पीउ पीउ चात्रक पुकारैं द्रुम डारन पै, 2
झिल्ली झहनाती, पिक प्रेम मदरान मैं।
ठाकुर कहत, ऐसी पावस प्रभा कौ देखि 3
आयौ बिरहीन आजु, आली, गदरान मैं।
छम छम छम बाजै छम छूम छेई छेई 4
थेई थेई चंचला नचत बदरांन मैं॥ R62॥

*श्याम घटा देह जाकी, दंत पदश्वेत जाकी, 1
पौन पुरवाई की पुकार दरसतु है।

62 Datiyal ff. 44v-45r (128), Mītal (M_e) p. 100. (Varṣā 60). 63 Ṣaṭṛtu-hajārā (J_e) pp. 166–7 (Pāvasṛtu varṇan). Cf. Sūr's ocean 220, Sūrsāgar 3303.'

61.3 ठाकुर] V_2, कहि ठाकुर (unm.) D_1 • जे] D_1, ए V_2 • बिलासी बिलंद] D_1, बिलंद बिसासी V_2 • री] D_1, हैं V_2 **61.4** झमकैं झर] V_2, झर ⟨लै⟩वै D_1 • लावैं] *conj.* लामै V_2, झमकै (unm.) D_1 • झलके] V_2, बरसे D_1 • री] D_1, है V_2 **62.1** मुरवा पुकारै] D_1, बोलत मयूर M_e • जेहैं] D_1, ऐहैं M_e • ऐ] D_1, ये M_e • दादुर] M_e, दादुल D_1 • पुकारैं] D_1, कहत M_e • जेहैं] D_1, ऐहैं M_e • मैं] *conj.* में M_e, मै D_1 **62.2** पीउ पीउ चात्रक पुकारैं] D_1, चातक पुकारैं पीउ पीउ M_e • पै] D_1, में M_e • झहनाती] D_1, झमकानी M_e • मदरान] M_e, मदरंन D_1 • मैं] M_e, मै D_1 **62.3** कौ] *conj.* ⟨कौ⟩ D_1, में M_e • देखि] D_1, दुख M_e • आयौ] D_1, दैन M_e • बिरहीन आजु] M_e, बिरही ⟨जन कौ⟩ D_1 • आली] M_e, ⟨जीउ⟩ D_1 • मैं] M_e, मै D_1 **62.4** छम छम छम बाजै] M_e, घूंम घूंम ⟨छाम छाम⟩ D_1 • छम छूम छेई छेई] M_e, ⟨छेई छेई बा⟩जैं घन D_1 • मैं] M_e, मै D_1

61.3 विरदैत [ad. viruda-] Br. 1. m. brave warrior; 2. adj. famous (BSK, BHK); बिलंद (बुलंद) [P] poet. adj. high; बडे बल के powerful. **61.4** झुकैं v.i. pres. they hover, lower; झर [S] m. torrent; झर लावैं Br. they flow, shower; झलाझलवारे Br. adj. glittering, brilliant; वारे 1. [H -vāle] suff. Br. 2. [H bār bār] Br. adv. again and again; झला reg. m. (here pl.) the first (drop of) rain at monsoon. **62.1** मुरवा (मोर) [mayura-] reg. m. peacock; हम जेहै Br. (the peacock says) 'I'll go'; खंदर m. pond, puddle. **62.2** झिल्ली [S] f. cricket; झहनाना v.t. to chirr; पिक [S] m. koel, cuckoo (is intoxicated with love); मदरा [mada-] m. intoxication. **62.3** गदराना [H gadrā 'ripening'] v.i. to ripen, to bloom; आयौ बिरहीन गदरान में Br. (?) (the pain) of longing women has come to full bloom. **62.4** चंचला [S] f. lightning. **63.1** देह f. body; पदश्वेत m. 'white-footed' heron; पुरवाई adj. eastern; पुकार दरसतु है Br. the call is apparent (i.e. is heard).

2 मंद मंद दामिनि मदाइनि की झूल, तापै
अंकुश छटानन की कोन सरसतु है।
3 ठाकुर कहत, तापै मैन असवार भयौ,
हूलत है घरी घरी पौन भरसतु है।
4 प्रेम को सँघाती साथी बालम बिदेश छायो,
छाती पर घूमि घूमि हाथी बरसतु है॥ R63॥

1 पावस प्रवेस देखबे कौं कढे नदनंद,
झूमि आंई घटा आछीं चारहूकु घां तैए।
2 बेलिन सौं लपटीं तमालन कीं पातैं तहां,
पीउ पीउ रढैं चात्रकन कीं जमातैए।
3 ठाकुर कहत, धुन सुन कैं मयूर नाचे
बिचित्र रंग ल्याये धौ कहां तैंए।
4 कारे कारे घन देख, हरे हरे बन देख,
पीरी पीरी दामिनि, सुपेत बक पांतैए॥ R64॥

1 जान नीको पिय को मिलाप उर आन आन

---

64 Datiya2 f. 8v-9r (82).

64.1 घां] *conj.* धां D_2 **64.2** बेलिन] D_2^{pc}, बेल (unm.) D_2^{ac} • तमालन] *em.* तमाल (unm.) D_2

63.2 दामिनी f. 1. lightning, 2. a head ornament; मदाइनि 1. [eṇamada-, Br. madaeṇa] f. musk (RKS, Keśav); 2. (?) Bund. rainbow (KL); झूल [A] f. horse-cloth, cover of an elephant; छटानन [S] poet. m. lightning; कोन [koṇa-] m. staff, the lower part of the goad; सरसतु है v.t. imp. Br. is beautiful. **63.3** हूलना [H hūl] v.t. to drive, to goad; भरस- [H bharās 'anger, spleen'] Br. v.t. to vent one's anger. **63.4** संघाती adj. 1. damaging, hostile, 2. accompanying; बालम [vallabhatama-] m. lover, husband; घूमना v.i. to move in a circle; हाथी m. rain at the 'hasta' constellation, which is the 11th (13th) lunar asterism, represented by a hand containing five stars, identified by some with part of the constellation Corvus. **64.1** चारहूकु घां तैए poet. from all four directions. **64.2** रढ- (रटना) [*raṭyati] poet. v.t. to make a repeated sound; जमात [AP] f. group. **64.3** ल्याये (लाए) reg. v.i. perf. have (the rains) brought (this colour). **64.4** सुपेत [śveta- x P safed] poet. adj. white; पांत (पंक्ति) [S] Br. f. (pl.) lines.

मानिनी न मान्यौ उपदेस काम गुर को।
चंचला चमकिबे के चावन भरी है खरी, 2
मोरन को मन सुनि मोजन कों मुरको।
ठाकुर कहत, पौन, परम प्रमोद भर्‌यौ, 3
सीतल सुगंध मंद, तीन्यौं भाँति ढुरको।
देखि तौ असाढ की सुहाई साँझ, मेरी बीर, 4
आज आसमान मानो सेंदुर सों भुरको॥ R65॥

*घन ऐसे तन माँझ, बिज्जुल बसन माँझ, 1
बग मोतिमाल माँझ, चाह-मिल्यो दिल जा।
चातिक से स्रवन पियासे स्वाति-बातन के, 2

---

65 Bharatpur1 f. 149v (1), Granthāvalī 147, Sudhāsar [S_2 f. 36v (49/38), S_3 f. 212v-213r (11), S_7 f. 120v-1r (11/1147)], Vrindaban1 f. 5r (27). The Granthāvalī presents this poem in the 'māninī' section, the Sudhāsar manuscripts in the description of the rainy season (pāvas) within the 'ṣaṭṛtu' section of the chapter on 'uddīpan'. The Sudhāsar manuscripts introduce it with the following words: 'sakhī (kī ukti) nāyaka (prati)[sau], ritu dikhāya ruci upjāvai hai' (The words of a sakhī towards the man. She is arousing his interest by pointing at the season.)
66 Bharatpur1 f. 152v (18), Granthāvalī B24, Sudhāsar [S_2 ff. 12v-13r (21/15), S_7 ff. 48v-49r (60/462)], Vrindaban1 f. 15r (26/90).

65.1 पिय] Σ, पीय B_1 • आन आन] $B_1G_eS_3V_1$, आनि आनि S_2, आन नीकौ S_7 • गुर] $B_1S_3S_7$, गुरु $G_eS_2V_1$ • **65.2** चमकिबे] Σ, चमक्कवे S_7 • चावन] Σ, चावनि V_1 • है] Σ, हैं B_1 • खरी] Σ, षेरी S_2 • मन] Σ, मनि S_7 • सुनि] Σ, सुन S_3 **65.3** पौन] $B_1G_eS_2V_1$, यौन S_3S_7 • परम] Σ, परस S_3 • प्रमोद] Σ, पमोद S_3 • भर्‌यौ] $S_7^{pc}\Sigma$, भयौ S_7^{ac} • तीन्यौं] B_1, तीनो Σ • भांति] Σ, भाँत G_e • ढुरको] $B_1^{pc}G_eS_2V_1$, मुरकौ B_1^{ac}, टुरको S_3, तुरकौं S_7 **65.4** देषि] $B_1S_2S_7$, देख $G_eS_3V_1$ • असाढ] Σ, आसाढ V_1 • आज] $B_1G_eS_2V_1^{pc}$, आजु S_2S_7, *om.* (unm.) V_1^{ac} • भुरको] $B_1G_eS_7V_1$, भुरक्यौ S_2, ढरको S_3 **66.1** घन] Σ, धन V_1 • बिज्जुल] $B_1G_eS_2$, बिज्जुलि S_7, बिजुल V_1 • मोति°] Σ, मोती S_7 • चाह] $B_1G_eV_1$, चाहि **S** • मिल्यौ] Σ, झिल्यो G_e • दिल] Σ, झिल G_e

---

65.1 जान v.t. abs. thinking (of the meeting with the beloved as excellent); आन [ājñā-] f. vow. **65.2** खरी adv. well, a lot; मुरको [cf. muṭati] v.i. perf. Br. (the peacocks' minds) turned. **65.3** ढुरक- (ढलकना) [*ḍhalati] reg. v.i. 'to flow' to blow; टुरको apa. **65.4** सुहाय- [H suhāvanā] Br. adj. pleasant; सेंदुर [sindūra-] m. vermillion; भुरक- Br. v.i. to be sprinkled; **66.1** बिज्जुल [vidyullatā-] m. lightning; बग [baka-] Av. Br. m. heron; झिलना [cf. H jhelnā] v.i. to penetrate, to be immersed (in Krishna); चाह-मिल्यौ Br. adj. (heart) together with desire; चाह-झिल्यौ var. immersed in desire; दिल जा o my heart, go to Krishna.

मोर-मन भरौ घोर बाँसुरी की खिल जा।
3 ठाकुर कहत, रस-रोसन रसीले जग,
जाहिर जसीले हित-हौंसन सो हिल जा।
4 घाट पनघट बन बाग घर बाहिरहू
सबहू संकेत स्याम कबहूँ तौ मिल जा॥ R66॥

कजली

1 *घर के न बाहर के, काहे को करत घैर,
गरजी तमासे की हौं, बरजी न रैहौं मैं।
2 आजु सुभ सावन सलोने की परब पाइ
अंग अंग सुभग सिँगारन बनैहौं मैं।
3 ठाकुर कहत, संग संग ब्रजबालन के
रंग भरे राछरे उमंगन सों गैहौं मैं।
4 देखि रक्षाबंधन गोबिंद जू के हाथ साथ

---

67 Granthāvalī 123, Ṭhasak 125. The Granthāvalī presents this poem as the monsoon Raga 'Kajarī'.

66.2 चातिक] Σ, चतिक G_e • पियासे] Σ, पियोर G_e • भरौ] Σ, घिर्‌यौ S_7 **66.3** ठाकुर कहत] G_e**S**, ठ॰ B_1, ठाकुर कहेंत V_1 • रसीले] Σ, रसील G_e **66.4** पनघट] Σ, पनिघट V_1 • ॰हू] B_1**S**, जू G_e, ॰हु V_1 • सबहू] Σ, सबहि S_7 • संकेत] Σ, सेकेत B_1 • स्याम] $B_1G_eV_1$, कान्ह **S** • कबहूँ] $B_1G_eV_1$, कबही **S** • मिल] Σ, मिलि (unrh.) V_1 **67.2** की] G_e, ⟨की/को⟩ $Ṭ_e$ • सलोने] *conj.*, सलोनो **E**

66.2 **चातक** [S] m. the pied cuckoo (supposed to live only on raindrops fallen at the autumn asterism svāti); **प्योर** var. [ad. priya-] poet. m. husband, lover (BHK); **मोर-मन** poet. your peacock-mind (filled with the deep sound); **घोर** [S] f. deep sound; **खिलना** [*khil-] v.i. to open, to expand. **66.3** **रोस** [roṣa-] m. 'anger' enthusiasm; **रसीला** [rasa-] adj. 'savourous' charming, attractive; **जाहिर** [A] adj. evident; **जसील-** [yaśa-] Br. adj. 1. famous; 2. (here:) openly admitted; **हिलना** [*hillati] v.i. 'to become familiar' to be in love. **66.4** **संकेत** [S] m. meeting-place. **67.1** **कजरी (कजली)** [kajjala-] Br. f. a type of song sung throughout the month of Śrāvan related to the women's festival at Śrāvaṇ badī 3 (July-August), for which barley and oats are grown and then immersed in water accompanied by kajalī songs; **न** if not... then..., either... or...; **घैर** m. slander; **गरजी** [A garẓ] adj. restless, eager. **67.2** **सुभ सावन सलोने की** Br. of the auspicious and lovely Śrāvaṇ; **परब** [parva-] m. (here f.) festival; **सुभग** [S] adj. 1. fortunate; 2. beautiful. **67.3** **राछरा** [H rāch + H -rā] m. Kajalī song.

राधे की कजलियाँ सिरावन कौं जैहौं मैं॥ R67॥

तीज

वृंदाबन जुगुल किसोर परना के धाम, 1
स्याम अभिराम राधे ओर दृग जोरे हैं।
सावन की तीज तजवीज कै बसन सूहे 2
पहिरे बिमल, जामैं सौरभ झकोरे हैं।
ठाकुर कहत, देत दरस दयाल भए, 3
देखत देखैयन के चित लेत चोरे हैं।
बोलती हैं मोरैं, होती घनन की घोरैं, बीर, 4
दोनों गठजोरैं आजु झूलत हिँडोरे हैं॥ R68॥

हेमंत

आड़े न रहत, रोम ठाढ़े ही सदा रहत, 1
पच्छिम कौ पवन फेरि पाला सों कटत है।
कंपत करेज सेज सोइऐ सुखत अरु 2

---

68 Granthāvalī 122, Ṭhasak 124, Ṭhasak 'Jīvancarit' (Ṭ$^{j}_{e}$) pp. 22-23. 69 Mītal (M$_e$), p. 217 (Hemant 62).

68.1 वृंदाबन] G$_e$Ṭ$_e$, बिंद्रावन Ṭ$^{j}_{e}$

67.4 देखि v.t. abs. Br. seeing (the rākhī on Krishna's hand); रक्षाबंधन [S] m. 1. a festival on the last day of Śrāvan, when sisters tie 'rākhī' on the arm of their brothers and receive small gifts from them; 2. the 'rākhī' tied on the arm; राधे poet. f. Radha; कजली f. barley and oats grown for the kājalī festival; सिरा- Br. v.t. to immerse in water. **68.1** परना [parṇa-] m. 1. leaves; grove; 2. [H pannā] emerald; (According to Lala Bhagvandin this is also a reference to Panna, a princely state in Bundelkhand famous for its 'jhāṅkīs' and for its richly decorated temple of the divine couple.) राधे ओर poet. towards Radha. **68.2** सावन की तीज f. Bhādra (August-September) Śukla 3 (married women keep a fast on this day); तजवीज [A] f. scheme, plan; सूहा [śubha-] adj. bright red; झकोरना [*jhakkol-] v.t. to shake (as trees in the wind); 2. to beat (rain or wind). **68.3** दयाल भए Br. they became compassionate, they showed their grace; देखैया (देखनेवाला) [H dekhnā] Br. m. onlooker. **68.4** गठजोरे [H gāṇṭh + H joṛnā] m. pl. 'whose marriage knot is tied' husband and wife. **69.1** आड़े [cf *aḍḍ-] adv. 1. obstructed; 2. shielded, veiled; पाला [prāleya-] m. dew, frost.

गब्बर गरीबन की गरुता घटत है।
3 ठाकुर कहत, फेरि पानी तें परस होत,
होत तन पीर, नैम नाँहीं निपटत है।
4 ओढ़िऐ दुसाला तरैं तोसक बिसाला, बिना
लगै अंग बाला सीतकाला ना कटत है॥ R69॥

69.2 सेज सोइऐ सुखत Br. it pleases to sleep in bed; गब्बर adj. wealthy, powerful; गरुता [gurutā] poet. f. 1. weight; 2. fig. pride; गरुता घटत है Br. (their) pride decreases (since they are not able to cope with the cold, especially the poor, who during the summer did not need clothes). **69.3** फेरि Br. then (if); नैम [niyama-] Br. m. daily routine, custom. **69.4** दुसाला [duśālā-] m. a double shawl; तरैं adv. under; तोसक [P tośaka-] f. bedding, mattress; बिना लगे अंग बाला poet. without the embrace of one's beloved;

संसार और नीति

मानव-वैचित्र्य

*धन्य, बिधि, तेरी रचनान कौ न पारावार, 1
देखि देखि बिबिध बखान कीजियतु है।
केई रचे कूर, केई सुघर सरूप रचे, 2
केई रूपवंत, केइ बडाई दीजियतु है।
ठाकुर कहत, अंग-रंग सब न्यारे-न्यारे, 3
न्यारी-न्यारी प्रकृति सुभाव लीजियतु है।
बाजे बाजे मानस न देखे सुने भावत हैं 4

---

1 Granthāvalī 201, Jaipur1 f. 6v (20), Sudhāsar [S_1 f. 366r (93), S_2 ff. 71v-72r (-/81), S_7 f. 243r (74)], Śatak 5, Ṭhasak 36. • The Sudhāsar presents this poem within the 'Nīti' section. • The established text normally follows J_1 and not the Sudhāsar, which seems to be a revised text trying to eliminate the repetition and the clumsiness (sarūpa, rūpavanta) in the second line. The Sudhāsar's reading 'bibidha bidhāna' (various actions or creations) although alliterating and frequently used in literature does not make much sense in this line unless 'vidhān' is interpreted in the undocumented meaning of 'fancy, opinion'.

1.1 धन्य] Σ, धनि J_1 • बिधि] Σ, बिध **S** • °न कौ न] **S**, को है न **E**, की J_1 • पारावर] Σ, वारपार नांहि J_1 • देखि देखि] **E**S_2S_7, देख देख J_1S_1 • बिबिध] **E**S_7, बिबुध J_1, बिबिधि S_1S_2 • बखान] Σ, बिधान **S** • कीजियतु] Σ, कीजियत S_1S_2, कीजीयत S_7 **1.2** केई] J_1, कोई **E**, केतिक **S** • रचे] Σ, रचे हैं **S** • केई] J_1, कोई **E**, केतिक **S** • सरूप] *conj.* सरुप J_1, कुरूप **E**, *om.* **S** • रचे] $J_1S_1S_2$, कोई **E**, सूर S_7 • केई] J_1, कोई **E**, केतिक **S** • रूपवंत] Σ, सरूप **S** • कै] J_1, औ **E**, की **S** • बडाई] Σ, बढाई G_e • दीजियतु] **E**, भीजियतु J_1, दीजियत S_1S_2, दीजीयत S_7 **1.3** अंग रंग] J_1, रस रूप **E**, अंग अंग S_1S_2, अंगि अंग S_7 • सब] $J_1S_1S_2$, रंग **E**, सभ S_7 • न्यारे] S_7^{pc}Σ, *om.* (unm.) S_7^{ac} • प्रकृति] **E**S_2, प्रकृत $J_1S_1S_7$ • सुभाव] J_1, बिचार **E**, स्वभाव S_1, सुभाय S_2S_7 • लीजियतु] **E**J_1, लीजियत S_1, लीजीयत S_7

1.1 विधि [S, cf. vidhātā-] m. creator; पारावार [pāra-vāra-] m. limit; विबुद्ध var. [S] adj. 'awakened' wise; विधान var. [S] m. act, action; creation; (looking at the world again and again you created various things, KL). **1.2** केई [reg. pl. of Av. keu x H koī] pron. pl. reg. some people; कूर [krūra- 'cruel' x P kūr 'blind'] Br. adj. 1. base, vile; 2. benighted, dull; सुघड़ [cf. H gharṇā] adj. 'well formed' 1. beautiful; 2. skilled, intelligent; सरूप 1. [S sarūpa- x surūpa-] adj. attractive; 2. [svarūpa-] Av. Br. m. one's own form, character; रूपवंत [S] poet. adj. beautiful; कै Br. 1. conj. or; 2. pospt. for, to (H ke lie); बढाई var. [cf. H baṛhnā] f. increase. **1.3** सुभाव (स्वभाव) [S] Br. m. character, nature.

बाजे बाजे मानस निहारि जीजियतु है॥ N1॥

1 अनगढ बातें कहा कहियै, ये दई, तेरी,
मानस कौ प्रीति दीनी, प्रीति मैं बिछोह तो।
2 सुघरन सोच दीनो, कूरन कौं धन दीनो,
ऐसो नहीं कीनो कैसौ जैसौ जहाँ सोहतो।
3 ठाकुर कहत, जौ पै बिधि कौ बिबेक होतो,

---

2 Bharatpur2 ff. 5v-6r, Granthāvalī 202, Sudhāsar [S_1 f. 348rv (10), S_2 f. 67rv (10/77), S_4 f. 27v-28r (161), S_7 f. 214v-5r (13)], Ṭhākur-satsaī (Ṭ) f. 5v (47), Śatak 27, Ṭhasak 142. • The Sudhāsar presents this poem within the 'Nīti' section. B_2 introduces the quatrain as 'prastāvaka rūpa' ([?] introductory form). • RSh interprets this poem as the words of a messenger towards a woman whom she tries to persuade to visit her lover. • The Śatak uses the Bundeli 'jauna' and the manuscripts the Braj 'jāhi'. The phrase 'sone mẽ sugandha' in the last line evokes poem 18 in Padmākar's 'Jagadvinod'.

1.4 मानस] J_1**S**, मानुस G_e, मानुष Ś$_e$Ṭ$_e$ • हैं] S_1S_7, है J_1S_2, सु **E** • मानस] J_1**S**, मानुस G_e, मानुष Ś$_e$Ṭ$_e$ • निहारि] J_1S_1, न देखे **E**, निहारे S_2, निहार S_7 • जीजियतु] **E**J_1, जीजियत S_1S_2, जीजीयत S_7 • है] G_eJ_1**S**, हैं Ś$_e$Ṭ$_e$ **2.1** अनगढ़] B_2**ES**, अनगट S_4, अनघड़ Ṭ • कहा] **S**Ṭ, तेरी कहाँ लौं **E**, ये कहाँ (unm.) B_2 • कहियै] $S_2S_4S_7$, कहियैं B_2S_1, बखानौ G_e, बखानौं Ś$_e$Ṭ$_e$, कहीयत Ṭ • ये] $S_2S_4S_7$, *om.* B_2**E**Ṭ, हे S_1 • तेरी] S_1S_2Ṭ, *om.* B_2**E**, तरी S_4 • मानस] Σ, मानुस **E** • प्रीति] $B_2G_eS_1S_2$Ś$_e$, प्रीत ṬṬ$_e$$S_7$, प्रीत * S_4 • दीनी] B_2G_e**S**, दीन्ही Ś$_e$Ṭ$_e$, दीन Ṭ • प्रीति] Σ, प्रीत S_7Ṭ • बिछोह] Σ, बिछोहौ B_2 • तो] Σ, ⟨नी⟩ S_4 **2.2** सुघरन] $B_2S_1S_2S_4$, कूरन कौं **E**, सुघरन को (unm.) S_7Ṭ • सोच] Σ, धन **E** • दीनो] Σ, दीनी Ṭ • कूरन] B_2**S**, सुघरन **E**, मूड़न Ṭ • धन] B_2**S**, सोच **E**, धनी Ṭ • दीनो] Σ, कीनौ Ṭ • नहीं] $S_1S_2S_4$, पै न B_2**E**, नाहि S_7, नाह Ṭ • कीनौ] **S**Ṭ, दीनौ B_2**E** • कैसौ जैसौ] S_1, जाहि जैसौ B_2, जैसो **E**, कैसौ तैसौ S_2S_4, जैसो (unm.) Ṭ • जहाँ] $S_1S_2S_4$, कछू B_2, जहाँ जौन **E**, जाह S_7, जाहि Ṭ

1.4 बाजे बाजे [P bāz] pron. some; मानस (मानुष) [S] m. 1. human being, man; 2. person; सु 1. [S] adv. well, really; 2. [saḥ, H so] Br. conj. then, next; भाना [bhāti] v.i. to be liked, to seem good **2.1** अनगढ [cf. H gaṛhnā] adj. 'unformed, unfinished' disorganised, incoherent; दई [daiviya-] m. voc. God; मानस (मानुष) [S] m. 1. human being, man; 2. person; बिछोह [cf. H bichoṛnā] m. separation; तो adv. conj. then; while; बिछोहतो poet. m. separation. **2.2** सुघड़ [cf. H gharṇā] adj. 'well formed' 1. beautiful; 2. intelligent; कूर [krūra- 'cruel' x P kūr 'blind'] Br. adj. 1. base, vile; 2. benighted, dull; कैसौ जैसौ जहाँ सोहतो Br. as suits one; as pleases one; जाहि जैसो जहाँ सोहतो var. Br. as suits one; as pleases one.

सुर औ असुर, पसु, पंछी किह मोहतो।
रूपवंत आदिमी कसकवंत होतो, हुती 4
सोने मैं सुगंध, तौ सराहिबे कौं को हतो॥ N2॥

बार बीच अधिक अधीन ह्वै डरात फिरै, 1
बार बीच लगै याहि जम की न भीत है।
बार बीच परम धरम के करम करै, 2
बार बीच भावै याहि अधम अनीत है।
ठाकुर कहत, बार बीच रसरंगी, रस- 3
भंगी बार बीच, याहि कैसे कोऊ जीतहै।
मानुस हैं जे वे मन आपने ते जानत हैं, 4
मानुस के मन की निपट बाँकी रीत है॥ N3॥

---

3 Granthāvalī 186, Śatak 32, Ṭhasak 127.

2.3 कहत] Σ, कहति S_4 • बिधि] Σ, बिध Ṭ • कौ] **S**, मैं **E**, बिधना B_2, कै S_7Ṭ • होतो] B_2**E**$S_1S_2S_4$, हुतो S_7, होत Ṭ • औ असुर] **S**, नर मुनि B_2**E**, नर Ṭ • पसु] B_2**E**S_2S_7Ṭ, पछ्छ S_1, पस S_4 • पंछी] Σ, पछ्छी S_1 • किह] **S**, कैसो **E**, काहे कौं (unm.) B_2, कौन कांको Ṭ **2.4** आदिमी] B_2**S**$Ś_e$Ṭ, प्रानी जौ G_eṬ$_e$ • कसक॰] B_2**E**$S_1S_2S_4$, कसब॰ S_7, रसक॰ Ṭ • हुती] **S**, कहूं B_2**E**, होती S_7Ṭ • सोने] Σ, सौन S_7 • तौ] Σ, के **E** • कौं] Σ, मैं B_2 **3.1** जम] G_eṬ$_e$, जन $Ś_e$ • **3.3** जीत] G_eṬ$_e$, जीव (unrh.) $Ś_e$ **3.4** के मन] G_eṬ$_e$, की मन $Ś_e$

2.3 जौ पै Br. conj. if; बिधि [S, cf. vidhātā-] m. the Creator; किह (किसलिए) Br. interr. (?) for what reason? मोहतो [cf. moha-] v.i. cond. Br. (why) would (gods etc.) be enchanted (by the world?) (i.e. they could have focussed their attention on God and not on Maya.) **2.4** कसक [cf. kaṣati] f. pain; कसकवंत [H kasak + S -vat] adj. compassionate, sensitive (to others' pain) (cf. Krishna is insensitive to the gopīs' pain); सुगंध [S] f. fragrance; हुती (होती) v.i. cond. Br. if there was; कहूँ (कहीं) var. Br. adv. somehow; को [kaḥ] Br. interr. 1. who; 2. what (Keśav-koś); तौ... हतो 1. Who could then praise them? (i.e. they would be perfect beyond praise); 2. What could then be praised? (i.e. they would be so perfect that they would not need praise.) **3.1** बीच [*vīcya-] postp. during; बार बीच... बार बीच... adv. at one time... at another time...; भीति [S] f. fear. **3.3** भंगी [S] adj. destroyer; जीतहै (जीतेगा) v.t. (Br. fut.) will (or would) conquer. **3.4** मन [S] m. 1. mind; 2. heart; मानुस हैं जे वे Br. it is the humans who..; मन आपने ते poet. in their minds.

*कबहूँ वा सँयोग के भोग करै जिनकी सुरराज कों चाह सी है।
2 कबहूँ या बियोग बिथा कों सहै जु तौ जोगिन हूँ कौं अकाह सी है।
कहि ठाकुर, सोच बिचार यहै, सु तौ कैसी अलाहदी राह सी है।
4 यह मानस को तन, मेरी भटू, समयौ परे को बडो साहसी है॥ N4॥

1 ऐसो अंध, अधम, अभागो, अभिमान भरो
कौन सुख मानौ तन मानस धरे को यो।
2 लोचत फिरत, रंग रोचत, रुचा पै रुच,
सोच नहीं होत है बिधाता-बिसरे को यो।
3 ठाकुर कहत, दुक्खहरनी दया न होइ,
तौ लौं फल पावै निज करनी करे को यो।
4 पावहू पलक की न खबर घरी की एक,

---

4 Bharatpur1 f. 132v (9), Bharatpur8 f. 17v (50), Granthāvalī 188, Sudhāsar [S_1 f. 358v (57), S_2 f. 70v (-/80), S_7 f. 239v (39)], Ṭhākur-satsaī (Ṭ) f. 4v (39), Ṭhasak 128. • The Sudhāsar presents this poem within the 'Nīti' section. S_2 introduces it as 'dhutta saṃcārī'. S_2introduces the poem as 'dhut (i.e. dhruta) saṃcārī' (of fast motion). 5 Granthāvalī 204, Śatak 31, Ṭhasak 130.

4.1 वा] **S**, या B_1B_8, यौं **E**, *om.* (unm.) S_7, ब Ṭ • सँजोग] Σ, मन जोग S_7 • करै] B_1**S**Ṭ$_e$, करैं B_8G_e, कहै Ṭ • जिनकी] B_1B_8**E**S_1, जिनकौ S_2S_7, इनकी Ṭ • सुरराज] $B_1B_8^{pc}$Σ, सुरज (unm.) B_8^{ac} • है] Σ, हैं S_2 **4.2** या] S_2S_7Ṭ, वा $B_1B_8S_1$, यौं **E** • बिथा] Σ, ब्रिथा S_7 • सहै] Σ, सहैं **E** • जु तौ] $B_1B_8S_2S_7$Ṭ, जोऊ **E**, जुँ ती S_1 • जोगन] Σ, जोगिनु B_1 • अकाह] $B_1B_8^{pc}G_e$**S**ṬṬ$_e^{ac}$, अका⟨स⟩ B_8^{ac}, अगाह Ṭ$_e^{pc}$ • सी] Σ, * B_8^{ac} **4.3** कहि] B_1B_8**S**, कबि **E**Ṭ • सोच] $B_1B_8S_1S_2$Ṭ, देखौ **E**, चार S_7 • बिचार] Σ, बिचारि G_e • यहै] B_1S_1Ṭ, ⟨यी⟩ है B_8^{ac}, ⟨सी⟩ है B_8^{pc}, हिये **E**, इहै S_2S_7 • सु तौ] B_1B_8, कछ्रु **E**, नित **S**Ṭ • कैसी] Σ, ऐसी **E** • है] Σ, हैं S_2 **4.4** को बडो] B_1B_8**E**S_7, का बडो S_1S_2Ṭ

4.1 कबहूँ वा... कबहूँ या... Br. sometimes... at other times... भोग करैं var. v.t. pres. pl. (people) may enjoy; जिनकी rel. pron. (enjoyments) which. **4.2** अकाह [akathanīya-] poet. adj. ineffable. **4.3** अलाहदा poet. adj. 1. [A 'alā ḥida] distinct; 2. (the way) given by Allah; 3. lazy (RSh); राह [P] f. way. **4.4** समयौ m. emph. poet. the very occasion; परे को reg. 1. when arises; 2. when it is (time) how...? का (क्या) var. reg. interr. is it? **5.1** यो reg. 1. [H yõ] adv. in this way (the subject can be he or you); 2. [H yah] pron. he. **5.2** लोचना [locyate] v.t. to desire; रोच- [ruci-] v.t. to show interest; रुचना [rucyate] v.i. 1. to be pleasant; 2. to be longed for; रुच (रुचि) [S] reg. f. 1. brightness; 2. interest; रुचा पै रुच Br. is interested only in the pleasant. **5.3** दुखहरनी [duḥkha-haraṇa-] poet. 1. adj. (grace) which removes the pain; 2. m. 'remover of pain' God; करनी [karaṇīya-] f. 1. action; 2. misdemeanour.

बाँधत बँधेज जन्म कलप भरे को यो॥ N5॥

याही के निमित्त नित भोजन अनेक भाँति, 1
याही के निमित्त हय गय लीजियतु है।
याही के निमित्त चोज चातुरी बनाइ सबै, 2
याही के निमित्त धन धाम कीजियतु है।
ठाकुर कहत, देखो, याके राखिबे के हेत 3
नीम करू भेषज सु घोर पीजियतु है।
याही नर-देही कों परान छोड देतैं कैसे 4
जारि बारि करिकै पवार दीजियतु है॥ N6॥

कलियुग

दंभी दगाबाजन की बाढी है अधिक थाप, 1
ग्यानध्यानवारेन की बात बेप्रमाना है।
पूँछत न कोऊ कबि-कोबिद-प्रबीनन कों, 2

6 Granthāvalī 218, Śatak 104, Ṭhasak 131. Cf. 'jā dina mana-pāchi ura jaihai...' Sūrsāgar, vol. 1. p. 28 (86). 7 Granthāvalī 208, Ṭhasak 143, Hāfizullah Khān: Hazārā (X_e) p. 501 (Bhaṛauvā aur hāsī 75) (Collated from Dikshit's edition p. 606).

5.4 कलप] G_eṬ$_e$, पलक Ś$_e$ **6.1** है] G_eŚ$_e$, *om.* (unm.) Ṭ$_e$ **6.4** बारि] G_eṬ$_e$, बार Ś$_e$ **7.1** °वारेन] **E**, धारिन X_e • बेप्रमाना] G_eX_e, वे प्रमाना Ṭ$_e$

5.4 पाव adj. one fourth; घड़ी [ghaṭikā-] f. a period of twenty-four minutes; पावहू... घरी की एक Br. He is not aware of a few minutes or even of a quarter of a twinkling; बंधेज [*bandheyya-] m. 1. arrangement; 2. stability, permanence; कल्प [S] m. the period of a day of Brahma, 4320 million years, an aeon; यो reg. adv. like, as if; पावहु... यो (cf. idiom. 'sāmān sau baras kā, kal kī khabar nahīṃ.') **6.1** हय [S] m. horse; गय [gaja-] poet. m. elephant; लीजियतु v.t. (pass. Br.) is acquired. **6.2** चोज [codya-] m. wonderful saying; बनाइ v.t. 1. (Br. abs. used as adv.) well; 2. [cf. Br. banāvai] reg. pres./subj. make. **6.3** नीम [nimba-] m. the neem tree (known for its bitter fruit and for medicinal and antiseptic properties of its leaves); करू [kaṭu-] adj. bitter; भेषज [S] m. medicine; घोर- (घोलना) [gholayati] Br. v.t. to mix (into a liquid), to dissolve. **6.4** देही [S] poet. f. body; परान छोड देतैं Br. when it abandons life; जार- (जलना) [jvalati] Br. v.t. to burn; बार- Br. v.t. to burn; पँवार- [pravārayati] poet. v.t. to throw away. **7.1** दंभी [S] adj. 1. hypocritical; 2. arrogant; थाप [cf. *thapp-] f. authority, prestige; ग्यानध्यानवारेन poet. m. pl. obl. those with wisdom and consideration; बेप्रमान [PS] adj. inauthentic; वे var. 1. they (are its proofs); 2. [vai] encl. particularly, precisely.

नमकहरामी को हजारन खजाना है।
3 ठाकुर कहत, कलिकाल को प्रभाव देखौ,
झूठन की बातन पै जगत दिवाना है।
4 बडे बडे सूबा, तेऊ जात पाप डूबा, देखि,
जीव अति ऊबा, या अजूबा कारखाना है॥ N7॥

काहू प्रबीन नै प्रेम सौ सींचि सरीर-जिमीं गुन-खात लै डार्यो।
2 ता मधि बुद्धि को बीज बयो तनु तामैं कियो मन कों रखवारो।
ठाकुर, सो नर हात दिखात है, ऐसो कछू कलिकाल निहारो।

---

8 Bharatpur1 f. 185v (25), Sudhāsar [S_1 ff. 351v (24), S_4 ff. 30v-31r (175), S_5 f. 239v (21), S_7 f. 236rv (18)], Ṭhākur-satsaī (Ṭ) f. 4v (38). • The Sudhāsar presents this poem within the 'Nīti' section.

7.2 नमकहरामी] **E**, नकली हरामिन X_e • हजारन] **E**, हाजिर X_e • **7.3** झूठन की बातन पै] **E**, झूठी बात कहि कहि X_e • जगत दिवाना] **E**, जनम सिराना X_e **7.4** देखि] **E**, यह देखि X_e • जीव अति] **E**, जिय X_e • या] **E**, की X_e • **8.1** नै] Ṭ^{pc}Σ, * Ṭ^{ac} • प्रेम] Σ, नेम Ṭ • सींचि] B_1S_4, सीच $S_1S_5S_7$, पोख Ṭ • सरीर] Σ, सरीरि S_4 • जिमीं] Σ, तमी S_4 • खात] B_1S_7, खान $S_1S_4S_5$ **8.2** ता मधि] B_1, तानैं S_1, तामैं] $S_4S_5S_7$Ṭ • बुद्धि] B_1, सुबुद्धि S_1, सुबुध (unm.) S_4Ṭ, सुबुद्ध S_5S_7 • बीज] Σ, बीत S_4 • बयो] $B_1S_1S_4S_5$, बुयो S_7Ṭ • तनु] S_1S_5, तन $B_1S_4S_7$Ṭ • कियो] Σ, कीयो Ṭ • कों] S_1S_4, को $B_1S_5S_7$Ṭ **8.3** ठाकुर] Σ, ठाकुर ×कह× S_1 • सो] Σ, व्हां S_5 • हात] $B_1S_1S_5$, हाथ S_4S_7, खात Ṭ • है] Σ, हैं S_4 • ऐसो कछू] B_1, ता पर यौं Σ • कलि॰] Σ, कले S_4

7.2 कोविद [S] adj. expert; नमकहरामी [P] 1. f. ingratitude; 2. f. disloyalty; 3. adj. disloyal; नक़ली var. [A] adj. 1. false; 2. (here:) base, wicked; हरामी (हरामज़ादा) var. [AP] m. 1. bastard; 2. fig. scoundrel; ख़ज़ाना [P] m. 1. depository, store; 2. treasure. **7.4** सूबा [A] m. province; ऊबना [udvijate] v.i. to be dispirited; या (यह) pron. reg. this; अजूबा [A 'ujūba] 1. adj. wonderful; 2. m. miracle; कारख़ाना [P] m. 1. business; 2. way of action; 3. any place where public works are carried on. **8.1** जिमीं (ज़मीन) [P] Br. f. earth; तमी-गुन var. m. collection of qualities such as darkness; खात [khātra-] 1. m. pit (for compost); 2. f. manure, dung; खात डाल्ना idiom. to spread manure; खान var. [khāni-] f. (here:) m. 1. mine; store; 2. fig. abundance; खान (खनकर) var. [khanati] v.t. abs. to dig; लै डार्यौ (ले डाला) Br. v.t. perf. took and threw. **8.2** सुबुद्धि [S] m. good sense, intelligence; बोना [vapati] v.t. to sow, to plant; तनु [S] Br. adj. small, delicate (seed); तन तामैं var. [S] poet. m. (in) that body; तामैं... रखवारो Br. and in it he created the mind as protector. **8.3** हात [S] adj. abandoned; हाथ दिखाना var. idiom. to point (with a finger); ता धर्यौ var. Br. 'and following that' what is more.

रीझ-सनेह को, री, बिरवा जर-मूल तैं लोभ-तुसार नैं मार्‌यो॥ N8॥ 4

मीरजादे, पीरजादे, असल अमीरजादे, 1
साहेब-, फकीरजादे, गौसे तन गोर हे।
राइजादे, रावजादे, साहजादे, साहुजादे, 2
कुल के असीलजादे जातपन खो रहे।
ठाकुर कहत, कलिकाल के कहर बीच 3
पहर-पहर पीछे भारे भ्रम भो रहे।
दान किरवान समै, स्यान गुर-ग्यान समै 4
सब जादे मिटिकै हरामजादे हो रहे॥ N9॥

सुमृत पुरान बेद गीतहू गंवाये गए, 1

---

9 Granthāvalī 209, Sudhāsar [S_1 f. 380v-381r (24), S_2 f. 77r (-/87), S_7 f. 250v (150)], Śatak 75, Ṭhasak 145. • The Sudhāsar presents this poem within the 'prastāv hī kau aṅga bhaḍauvā' (mocking verse as part of the introduction) subsection of the 'Nīti' section.

8.4 सनेह] Σ, सनेहि S_4 • जर] Σ, तर S_4 • तैं] B_1S_1, ते $S_4S_5S_7$ • तुसार नै] Σ, तुसारन Ṭ **9.1** असल] Σ, असलि S_2 • साहेब] G_eṬ$_e$, साहब **S** • गौसे तन गोर हे] **S**, जादे आप खो रहे **E** **9.2** राइ°] **S**, राव° **E** • राव°] **S**, राइ° **E** • साह] **S**, साहु° **E** • साहु] **S**, साह **E** • जातपन खो] **S**, नींद ही में सो **E** **9.3** बीच] **S**, मांझ **E** • पीछै] **S**, पर **E** • भारे] **S**, भारी **E** • भ्रम] S_1S_7, मृम S_2, भय **E** **9.4** किरवान] S_1, किरपान **E**S_7, किरमाण S_2 • स्यान गुर-ग्यान] **S**, ग्यान गुन स्यान **E**

8.4 रीझ [cf. ṛdhyati] f. pleasure, delight; ए (यह) var. [eṣa-] reg. adj. (acc.) this; सनेही (स्नेह) var. [S] reg. m. love; बिरवा (वृक्ष) [S] reg. m. (acc.) tree; जड़-मूल से idiom. by the root, root and all; तुषार [S] m. frost. **9.1** असल [A aṣl] adj. real, genuine (nobles); जादे (ज्यादा) [P] adv. more; गौसे तन (गोशा-ए तन्हाई) [P] m. (obl.) in a solitary place; (here:) even when they are alone; गौर [A] m. close attention; care; गौसैं तन गोर है Br. they care for it even when they are alone; जादे आप खो रहे var. 1. they lost themselves a lot; 2. all the 'zādās' lost themselves. **9.2** रावजादा [HP] m. son of a nobleman; specific nobleman in Western India (cf. rāval); राइजादा [HP] m. son of a nobleman; higher nobleman (in general); असील [A] adj. of good origin; असीलज़ादा [P] adj. 'of real birth' of noble family; जातपन [jāti-, H -pan] poet. m. castism. **9.3** क़हर [A] m. 1. calamity; 2. rage, fury; पीछै reg. after; भो- (भीगना) [cf. bhiyagna-] poet. v.i. to be immersed in, to sink in. **9.4** किरवान [kṛpāṇa-] m. 'sword' war; स्यान [sa-jñāna-] Br. m. cleverness.

हौन लागे रैदसा कबीरा मति बाद रे।
2 को सुनै संगीत गीत धुरपद धरा पर
ठौर ठौर ठाकुर सुनन लागे दादरे।
3 बडे बडे मानस ते मौन साधि बैठि रहे
मानीं मसखरा ते करत रस बादरे।
4 करि कै निरादर अँगूरन कौ आछी भाँति
कूरन नैं ऊमर निपट अब आदरे॥ N10॥

लक्ष्मी

1 कहा कीजै, तू न आई उत तै उमंग, यातै
तेरे भांत भांत के बियोग सहनै परै।
2 आप मिल सुख दीजै, बिबिध बिलास कीजै,
मनवे मिलाय लीजै जे वै गहनै परै।
3 ठाकुर कहत, जे है रावरी मया मै लोग

---

10 S_1 f. 354r (35), S_6 f. 339v (39), S_7 f. 237v (28). The Sudhāsar presents this poem within the 'Nīti' section. 11 Bharatpur1 f. 176rv (21), Udaipur f. 127r (8).

10.1 सुमृत] S_1, सिंम्रत S_6S_7 • रेदसा] S_6, रेंदसा S_1, रैदास (unm.) S_7 • मति] S_1, मत S_6S_7 **10.2** सुनै] S_6S_7, सुनैं S_1 • धुरपद] S_6S_7, धुर्पद (unm.) S_1 • धरा] S_6S_7, धारा S_1 • पर] S_6S_7, परए (unm.) S_1 • सुनन] S_1S_7, सुनत S_6 **10.3** साधि] S_1, साध S_6S_7 • बैठि] S_1, बैठ S_6S_7 • मानीं] S_1, मानी S_6S_7 • मसखरा] S_1S_6, मसकरा S_7 **10.4** करि] S_1, कर S_6S_7 • भाँति] S_1S_6, भांत S_7 **11.1** कीजै] U, कहियै (unm.) B_1 • न] U, जौ न B_1 • उमंग] U, उमगि B_1 • भांत भांत] U, काज B_1 • के] U, ये B_1 **11.2** आप मिल सुख दीजै] U, आउ तेरे संग अब B_1 • बिबिध] U, बिबिधि B_1 • मनवे] U, मनए B_1

10.1 गंवाना [gamayati] v.t. 1. to loose, to waste; 2. to make useless, invalid (KL); बाद [ad. vāda-] m. speech, discussion. **10.2** धरा पर idiom. 'fell on the earth' collapsed, disappeared; धारा पर मारना var. idiom. 'to urinate on' to treat with contempt; दादरा [cf. H dādur] m. a type of song to a quick melody (common in Agra district and in Bundelkhand). **10.3** मसखरा m. joker, clown; 2. adj. amusing; बादर- Br. adj. happy (of expression, face). **10.4** अँगूरन [P] m. (Br. pl.) grapes; कूर [P] adj 'blind' benighted; dull; cruel; ऊमर [udumbara-] m. the wild fig Ficus glomerata and its fruit. **11.1** तू... उमंग you did not come (from there) with enthusiasm. **11.2** मनवे (मन) reg. m. (obl.) 1. (merge) into your soul; 2. (meet) his soul (H man ko); जे वै poet. emph. which indeed; गहने परै Br. falls to touch (one's feet);

तेऊ तेरी भांति ह्वै हमहू लहनै परै।
लच्छिमी तिहारे काजैं दीन औ अधीन ह्वै कै 4
बडे बडे चूतिया चतुर कहनै परै॥ N11॥

कापुरुष

*दगा देइ यार और माता उर बैर मानि 1
मारो चाहै पिता, तासों कौन बिधि जीजियै।
बसे जाकी बाँह, सो न बाँह को निबाह करै, 2
जान के अजान बनै, कैसे जान दीजियै।
चढै जाकी नाउ सोई जानबूझ बोरो चहै, 3
ठाकुर, अजान ता पै दिनै दिन छीजियै।
राजा ह्वै कै तजै न्याय, संगी ह्वै कै करै घाय, 4
बारी खेत खाय, तौ उपाय कहा कीजियै॥ N12॥

आपनो बनाइबे कों, और को बिगारिबे कों 1

---

12 Granthāvalī 192, Ṭhasak 154.

11.3 ठाकुर कहत] U, ठा° B_1 • हैं] B_1, है U • मया मै लोग] U, दया के लोग B_1 • तेऊ तेरी भांति] B_1, ति ×⟨भै⟩× ⟨भा⟩त ⟨भा⟩त U • ह्वै] B_1, के U • हमहू] U, हमैंहू B_1 • लहनैं] B_1, चहने U **11.4** लच्छिमी] *conj.* लछ्छिमी B_1, लक्ष्मी U • तिहारे काजैं] B_1, तिहारै निहारे काज (unm.) U • औ] B_1, ह्वै U • चूतिया] B_1, चुतिया U **12.4** न्याय] *conj.* न्याउ **E** • घाय] *conj.* घाउ **E**

11.3 मया f. 1. [dayā-] compassion, 2. [māyā-] illusion; 3. love; जे हैं... लोग Br. people to whom you are compassionate; तेऊ तेरी भांति ह्वै Br. (?) since they are also like you; लह- [labhate] m. 1. gain; 2. fate; 3. conflict (KL); लहना [labhate] Br. v.t. Av. to find; to receive; हमहू लहनै परै Br. I also have to receive wealth from them; चाहना var. [*cāh-] Av. Br. v.t. to see. **11.4** दीन ह्वै var. being wretched; चूतिया [H cūt] m. vulg. (acc.) 1. immoral person; 2. idiot. **12.1** दगा देइ यार Br. the friend cheats; माता... मानि Br. the mother cherishes enmity in her heart; तासों Br. adv. 'by these things' in this way. **12.2** बाँह [bāhu-] f. 'arm' protection; सो... करै Br. he does not carry through the protection; जान कै reg. adv. 'knowingly' on purpose; जान [P] f. 1. soul; 2. life; अजान [cf. H jānnā] adj. oblivious; **12.3** नाउ (नाव) [nāvā-] reg. f. boat; बोड़ना [*boḍayati] v.t. to cause to sink, to drawn; अजान [cf. H jānnā] adj. simple, innocent; ता पै Br. conj. therefore; छीजना [chidyate] v.i. to waste away, to deteriorate. **12.4** न्याउ (न्याय) var. [S] reg. m. justice; घाय (घाव) [ghāta-] Br. m. wound; बारी [vāṭa-, H bāṛ] Br. f. hedge, fence (BHK, RSh).

सावधान ह्वै कै सीखौ द्रोह सो हुनर है।
2 भूल गये दयासिंधु करुनानिधान राम,
जाको सब बिश्व मैं बनाव को बितर है।
3 ठाकुर कहत, लगे काम, क्रोध, लोभ, मोह,
जानत सरीर कै जौ अजर अमर है।
4 हाइ उन लोगन सों कौन सो उपाय जिन्हैं
लोक को न डर, परलोक को न डर है॥ N13॥

1 *अंध, अबिबेकीए, अभागे, अभिमान भरे
इनैं रचि रचि दिन नाहक गँवाए तैं।
2 सूमसि लवार सैठा हिजरा, हरामजादे,

---

13 Datiya2 f. 7v (66), Granthāvalī 194, Seondhal (O_1) f. 1r, Śatak 37, Ṭhasak 129.
14 Granthāvalī 203, Sudhāsar [S_1 f. 348v (11), S_2 f. 67v (78/11), S_4 f. 28r (162), S_7 f. 235r (14)], Śatak 74, Ṭhākur-satsaī (Ṭ) f. 5v (48), Ṭhasak 141. • The Sudhāsar presents this poem within the 'Nīti' section. • The first line is reminiscent of Tulsī's 'āṃdharo adhama jaḍa jājaro jarā javana...' (Kavitāvalī, Uttarakāṇḍa 76) but the overall sense of Ṭhākur's poem is devoid of the salvific nature of bhakti.)

13.1 सावधान] **E**, साहुधान D_2, सीषे साउधांन O_1 • ह्वै] **E**, हो D_2O_1 • सीषौ] D_2, पर **E**, *om.* O_1 **13.2** भूल गये] D_2, भूलि गे **E**, जानत ना O_1 • दयासिंधु] *conj.* क्रपासिंधु D_2, दया के सिंधु **E**, दयासिंध O_1 • राम] D_2, कहूं **E**, रामै O_1 • जाको] D_2O_1, जिन्हैं **E** • सब बिश्व] D_2**E**, तीन लोक O_1 • मैं] *conj.* मे Σ • बनाव] **E**O_1, बनाइ D_2 **13.3** लगे] D_2, रंगे **E**, भूले O_1 • काम क्रोध लोभ मोह] D_2O_1, लोभ मोह माया माँहि **E** • जानत] D_2O_1, कहत **E** • सरीर] **E**O_1, रीर (unm.) D_2 • कै जौ] D_2, यह **E**, जह O_1 • अजर] D_2**E**, अ अजर (dittography) O_1 • अमर] D_2**E**, अम (unrh.) O_1 **13.4** हाइ] D_2**E**O_1^{pc}, हा⟨हि⟩ O_1^{ac} • जिन्हे] D_2**E**, जिनै O_1 **14.1** अंध] $S_1S_4S_7$Ṭ, ऐसे अंध **E**, अध S_2 • अविवेकीए] **S**Ṭ, अधम **E** • इनै] Ṭ, यनै $S_1S_2S_4$, ये है S_7, तिन्हैं **E** • रचि रचि] Σ, रच रच Ṭ • गँवाए] Σ, बिताऐ $Ṭ^{pc}$, बिता⟨बो⟩ $Ṭ^{ac}$

13.1 सीखौ द्रोह Br. the hostility that was learnt; पर-द्रोह var. [S] Av. Br. m. hostility towards others; हुनर [P] m. (that hostility is considered) a skill (cf. H kalā); सोहु नर है var. reg. (the one who learnt hostility) is considered a man. **13.2 भूलि गे** (भूल गये) var. Br. v.t. perf. he forgot; बनाव [cf. H banānā] m. 1. composition, nature; 2. adornment; 3. harmony; बितर [vitarati, cf. vitaraṇa-, cf. vistara-] poet. m. 1. spread; 2. bestowing; distribution. **13.3 कै** (को) postp. reg; जानत... है reg. those who consider their bodies changeless and immortal; जह (जिस) var. pron. reg. obl. that (cf. Br. jihi). **14.1 यनै** (इन्हें) var. pron. reg. him; नाहक़ [PA] adv. in vain.

बुरिहा, दगैल, निज आँखिन दिखाए तैं।
ठाकुर कहत, ये अदानिया, अबूझ, भोंदू, 3
भाजन अजस के बृथाहीं उपजाए तैं।
निपट निकाम, काम काहू के न आवैं, ऐसे 4
सूरतहराम, राम, काहें कौं बनाए तैं॥ N14॥

मूढ सुनै कब रामकथा, कब दै धन पूजत बिप्र बिरागी।
सूमन को धन मूसत चोर कि लूटत भूप कि लागत आगी। 2
ठाकुर, धर्म के हेत सु तौ दुखपुंज कथै हरि के हित लागी।
आनन ऊँच उठाय ज्यौं रोवत संख सुनें सठ स्वान अभागी॥ N15॥ 4

---

15 Granthāvalī 195, Ṭhasak 161. The poem is about the miserly.

14.2 सूंमसि लवार सैठा हिजरा] **S**Ṭ, भकुआ भरंगी अरु हिरसी **E** • सूंमसि] $S_1S_2S_7$, सूंममि S_4, सूमसे Ṭ • सैठा] $S_1S_2S_4$, सैंबा S_7, सठ Ṭ • हिजरा] $S_1^{pc}S_2S_7$, हि⟨र⟩जरा S_1^{ac}, ढिजरा S_4, हीजरा Ṭ • हरामजादे] **E**$S_1S_2S_7$, हरामतादे S_4, हरामजादा Ṭ • बुरिहा] **S**, लबार **E**, दगहा (unm.) Ṭ • निज] $S_2S_4S_7$Ṭ, स्यार **E**, निजु S_1 • दिखाए] Σ, दिखाऐ Ṭ^{pc}, दिखा⟨बो⟩ Ṭ^{ac} **14.3** कहत] Σ, कहित Ṭ • अदानिया] Σ, अजांनी (unm.) Ṭ • भोंदू] **E**S_1S_2, भोह S_3, भोधू Ṭ • भाजन] **E**$S_1S_2S_7$, भातन S_3, भांडे Ṭ • अजस] Σ, अपजस Ṭ • **14.4** आवै] **E**Ṭ, आँवैं S_1, आमै S_2S_4, आ⟨वै/वैं⟩ S_7 • सूरत॰] **E**S_1S_7Ṭ, सूरति S_2, सुरति॰ S_3 • तै] Ṭ^{pc}Σ, ⟨॥⟩ Ṭ^{ac} • **15.3** सु] G_e, सो $Ṭ_e$ •

14.2 सूमसि (?) [? conn. A ś'um] poet. adj. very miserly; लबाड़ [cf. *labha-] reg. 1. adj. lying; 2. m. liar; सैठा (सीठा) 1. [śiṣṭa-] reg. adj. 'left over' insipid, useless; 2. [? śara-kāṇḍa-] m. 'the lower part of a reed stalk' useless man; भकुआ var. adj. stupid; 2. m. a fool; भरंगी var. [cf. H bhaṛauvā] adj. giving curses; हिरसी var. [A ḥirṣ] adj. covetous; बुरिहा var. 1. [cf. H burāī] m. slanderer; 2. [vṛddha-] adj. old; दगैल adj. 1. [P dāg] stained; 2. [P dagā] Br. deceitful; निज [S] adj. (to) my own (eyes); सियार var. [śṛgāla-] m. 1. jackal; 2. fig. (adj.) coward(ly); **14.3** अदानिया adj. 1. [cf. P dān 'knowledge'] dull; 2. [cf. dāna-] miserly; भोंदू [*bhonda-] adj. stupid; भाजन [S] m. 1. vessel; 2. fig. recipient; अजस [cf. yaśa-] m. disgrace; उपजा- [utpadyate] Br. v.t. to produce, to create. **14.4** सूरत-हराम [AP] adj. phoney, specious. **15.1** पूजत बिप्र बिरागी Br. 1. the priest worships the renunciant (by donations)? 2. (when does he) worship the priests and the renunciants? **15.2** सूम [? A ś'u'm] reg. m. miser; मूसना [mūṣati] v.t. to steal. **15.3** कथ- [kathayati] Av. Br. v.t. 1. to tell; 2. (here:) he considers; के हेतु (के लिए) postp. reg. for (the purpose of); लागि (के लिए) postp. reg. for; सु तौ दुखपुंज कथै Br. 1. he says that accumulated suffering (is needed) for righteouseness and for the love of God; 2. he calls (righteouseness and the love of God) accumulated suffering (dehrī dīpak). **15.4** ज्यौं adv. as; शठ [S] 1. adj. wicked; 2. m. a rogue; सठ स्वान अभागी Br. the wicked and wretched dog.

1 *राग कौ न रंग कौ, न जुद्ध जुरै जंग कौ, न
कामिन के संग कौ, अनंग न सतायौ है।
2 को कहै कुजस-जस, जानत न एकौ रस,
पसु कौ सौ जनम लिलाट लिखि पायौ है।
3 कूप कौ रहैया बेष जानैं कहा मानस कौ,
मानस कहाय ये तौ जगत ठगायौ है।
4 मेरे जान, सीतला के बाहन कौ जीव काढि
पाहन मैं मेलि कालबूत सौ बनायौ है॥ N16॥

अंक न जानत ओलंम को, कह आवत बात न पूरन की।
2 कहू गीत कवित सौ प्रीत नही, कह ठाकर, तान तंबूरन की।
तन जेब न देत पुसाक जिनै अर सूरत है जमहूंरन की।
4 अब भाग की बात कहा कहीऐ बन जात कहूँ-कहूं कूरन की॥ N17॥

16 Sudhāsar [S_1 f. 377r (6), S_2 f. 75r-v (-/85), S_7 f. 248v (132)]. • The Sudhāsar presents this poem within the 'prastāv hī kau aṅga bhaḍauvā' subsection of the 'Nīti' section. • This kavitt does not bear Ṭhākur's signature but the collection introduces it as a poem by Ṭhākur. The style with the reference to being human, the use of idiomatic expressions and strong vocabulary confirms this attribution. 17 Ṭhākur-satsaī f. 4v (35) (Ṭ).

16.2 लिखि] S_2, लष S_1^{ac}, लखि S_1^{pc}, लिख S_7 • है] S_1S_7, हैं S_2 **16.3** जानै] S_7, जानैं S_1S_2 **16.4** जान] S_1S_2, जाने S_7 • काढि] S_1S_2, काढ S_7 • मेलि] S_2, मेल S_1S_7 **17.3** हूंरन] *conj.* हूं⟨ठ/र⟩न Ṭ **17.4** कहीऐ] Ṭ[pc] कही (unm.) Ṭ[ac] • कूरन] *conj.* कू⟨ड⟩न Ṭ

16.1 राग कौ न... Br. The one who is neither for love nor... न कामिन के संग कौ Br. (who is not) for the company of women; सताना [saṃtāpayati] v.t. to torment. **16.2** को कहै Br. who would tell of his...? लिलाट लिखि पायौ है idiom. Br. is written on his forehead (i.e. in his fate). **16.3** कूप कौ रहैया idiom. reg. 'dweller of a well' an insular, parochial person (cf. H kūpmaṇḍūk); जानै कहा what does he know about? बेष m. custom, ways; मानस m. 1. [mānasa-] the Manasarovara Lake; 2. [mānuṣa-] human being. **16.4** मेरे जान idiom. to my mind; सीतला का वाहन (kūṭ) 'the vehicle of the goddess Sītalā' donkey; काढ़ना [*kaḍḍhati] v.t. to take out, to extract; पाहन (पाषाण) [S] reg. m. 1. stone; 2. ? clay; मेलना (मिलाना) [melayati] Br. v.t. to put in, to mix with; कालबूत [P kālbūd] Br. m. 1. mould; 2. frame. **17.1** अंक [S] m. letter, syllable; ओलम [cf. A 'ālim] reg. m. knowledge; कह... की he is not able to fully tell his words. **17.2** तंबूरा [P] m. tānpūrā, a stringed instrument used to accompany a singer; तंबूरन की (love) for tānpūrās. **17.3** तन [S] m. obl. on his body; जेब [P] m. 1. ornament; 2. beauty, grace; जमहूरा m. magician's assistant; **17.4** (की) बन जात idiom. Br. fortune to arise (for); कूड var. [cf. H kūṛā 'rubbish', P kūr 'blind'] adj. dull, foolish.

कृपन कंजूस बड़े, गुन के मंजूस, पै न 1
देवै कन नैंक, नीत राखत भिखारी में।
दान को न जाने, सनमान को न मानैं कबि, 2
राज को न माने, रहै शिष्णबरदारी में।
ठाकुर कहत, भली-बुरीहू न सोचै नेक, 3
राति-दिन सदा चित रहै मारामारी में।
राजी ना सिपाह औ न जंग की उमाह जिनैं, 4
जस की न चाह, ऐसी थूक सरदारी में॥ N18॥

बिन आदर पाय कै बैठि ढिगाँ अपनो रुख दै रुख लीजतु है।

---

18 Bharatpur1 f. 152v-3r (20), Hāfizullah Khān: Hajārā (X_e) p. 502 (Bhaṛauvā aur hāsī 79, Dikshit p. 607). 19 Sundarītilak (C_e) (300), Granthāvalī 190, Rasikvinod (O_e) (307), Ṭhasak 57. The same samasyā occurs in Ś83. Cf. also Bhikhārīdās: Śṛṅgār-nirṇay: 'āvai yahai aba daasa bicāra, sakhī, cali sautihu ke gṛha jaihai.' Vishvanathprasad Mishra (ed.): Bhikhārīdās granthāvalī, vol. 1. Varanasi: Nāgarīpracāriṇī sabhā, 1965, p. 105.

18.1 पै न] B_1, जेर X_e • देवै] *conj.* देवैं B_1, देहै X_e • कन नैंक] B_1, कननूस X_e • नीत राषत] B_1, राखे नियत X_e **18.2** जाने] X_e, जानैं B_1 • सनमान] $B_1^{ac}X_e$, सन आनाद B_1^{pc} • मानै] *conj.* मानैं B_1, आने X_e • कबि राज] B_1, गुणवान X_e • न माने] X_e, नानैं (unm.) B_1^{ac}, न मानैं B_1^{pc} • रहै] X_e, रहैं B_1 • °बरदारी] $B_1^{pc}X_e$, बर⟨धा⟩री B_1^{ac} **18.3** ठाकुर कहत] X_e, ठा° B_1 • °हू] B_1, को X_e • सोचै] B_1, सोच X_e • सदा] $B_1^{pc}X_e$, *om.* (unm.) B_1^{ac} • रहै] B_1, राखे X_e **18.4** जिनैं] B_1, जिन्हैं X_e • जस] B_1, यश X_e **19.1** अपनो] **E**O_e, अपनी C_e • दै रुख] **E**O_e, दै सुख C_e • है] C_e**E**, हैं O_e

---

18.1 कृपण [S] adj. 1. miserly, 2. wretched; कंजूस [H ?kān + cūs] adj. miserly; मंजूस [mañjūṣā-] poet. f. box, container; जेर var. [P] adj. 'inferior' small; कननूस var. m. deathsman; देहै कननूस var. Br. is deathsman in his body; नीत (नीयत) [AP] f. intention, resolve; पै न देवैं कन नैंक var. Br. but he does not give the smallest morsel; राखै नियत भिखारी मैं Br. he is resolved on begging. **18.2** सनमान (सम्मान) [S] reg. m. respect; न आने Br. does not bring (into his mind); शिश्न [S] m. penis; -बरदारी [P] m. 1. bearing; 2. caring; शिश्नबरदारी m. concern restricted to the bodily instincts. **18.3** मारामारी [H mārnā] f. wrangle, fight. **18.4** राजी ना is not pleased with; सिपाह [P] f. solderhood; उमाह Br. m. swelling, enthusiasm; थुक [onom. thu thu] interj. curse be on! **19.1** ढिगाँ [*ḍhigga-] reg. adv. near; रुख [P] m. 'face' 1. inner secret, emotion; 2. favour; रुख दै idiom. Br. telling his own (false) secrets; लीजतु reg. v.t. (pass. used as active) he takes; रुख लीजतु idiom. Br. 1. he receives favours; 2. he fathoms others' secrets.

2 अपमान औ मान परेखो कहा, अपनी मति में चित दीजतु है।
कबि ठाकुर, काम निकारिबे के लिये कोटि उपाय करीजतु है।
4 अपने उरझे सुरझायबे कौं सबही की खुशामद कीजतु है॥ N19॥

1 देखन के नीके और टेरै बडे आदर सो,
पेट मै न दांहें देखें, जीय मै जरे रहै।
2 भेदाभेदी पूछै तु संभारै, नाहि लाज मूचै,
पाप के समूह नितें चित्त मै मढे रहै।
3 ठाकुर कहत, वे तो बदी के तलासगीर,
घाटहूं मै बाट मै बजार मै खड़े रहै।
4 निंद्या को है नेम, चुगली अपार, परस्वार्थ
मिटाइ करिवे के खोज मै पड़े रहै॥ N20॥

1 कूर होते कुबरे, कुजाति होते कारे कारे,
भारे कछ्छ लंपटी लिलार भग भरतौ।

20 Ṭhākur-satsaī f. 5v (49) (Ṭ). 21 Bharatpur1 ff. 131v-132r (4).

19.2 **औ**] C_eO_e, **को** **E** • **अपनी**] C_eO_e, अपने **E** • **मति**] C_eO_e, हित **E** • **में**] C_eO_e, पै **E** • **है**] C_e**E**, हैं O_e **19.3** **काम**] C_eO_e, काज **E** • **के**] C_eO_e, कों **E** • **लिये**] C_eO_e, नित **E** • **कोटि**] C_e**E**, कोट O_e • **उपाय**] C_e**E**, उपाव O_e • **है**] C_e**E**, हैं O_e **19.4** **अपने**] C_eO_e, अपनी **E** • **उरझे**] C_eO_e, उरझी **E** • **खुशामद**] C_eO_e, खुसामति **E** • **है**] C_e**E**, हैं O_e **20.1** **दाहे**] ⟨दां/चां⟩⟨रे/हे⟩ Ṭ • **देखें**] *conj.* देख Ṭ **20.2** **समूह**] *conj.* संबूह Ṭ • **मूचै**] *conj.* मू* Ṭ • **चित्त**] *conj.* चितें (unm.) Ṭ **20.4** **परस्वार्थ**] *conj.* पर⟨स्वा⟩र⟨थ/ब⟩ (unm.) Ṭ • **मिटाइ करिवे**] *conj.* मिटाइ **वे Ṭ

19.2 **अपमान... कहा** Br. does he have any remorse for honour or dishonour? **अपनी मति में** in his own opinion. **19.3** **निकार-** **निकालना** [niṣkālayati] Br. v.t. 1. to take out; 2. to produce, to achieve; **करीजतु** v.t. (pass. used as active) poet. he makes (millions of schemes). **19.4** **खुशामद** [P] m. flattery. **20.1** **देखन के नीके** Br. he looks beautiful; **पेट** m. 1. stomach; 2. inside; **दाह** [dagdha-] f. 1. burning; 2. fault (KL); **पेट मैं दाहैं** Br. his faults within himself. **20.2** **भेदाभेद** [S] m. secret and open things; **तु** (**तो**) reg. conj. then; **मूच-** [mucyati] v.i. 1. Br. to release; 2. to extinguish; **मढ़ना** [*maḍ-] v.t. to cover, to spread. **20.3** **बदी** [P] f. evil, mischief; **तलाशगिर** [P] adj. searching for. **20.4** **निंद्या को है नेम** reg. 1. their regular activity is slander; 2. is there any rule (i.e. restraint) in slander? **चुगली अपार** poet. their slander is endless; **परस्वार्थ** [S] m. others' welfare. **21.1** **कूर होते कुबरे** Br. if the mean or cruel ones were hunchbacked; **भार-** [bhāra-] Br. adj. weighty; great; **कछ्छ** reg. adj. 1. [cf. Av. kac] very, a lot; 2. [cf. Br. kachu] a bit; **भारे कछ्छ** reg. adj. 1. very big; 2. big and small; **भग** [S] f. vulva; **लिलार भग भरतौ** Br. if the foreheads were filled with vulvas.

झूंठिनु की जीभन पै लांबे लांबे बार होते 2
गडी गडी अंखियां निलज्जन कैं धरतौ ।
ठाकुर कहत सिला होती सीस पापिन कैं 3
लपरा के करतार बूचे कान करतौ।
सूम होते मकनां मुछ्यारे सूरबीर होते 4
गांडू होते नकटे, नबेरो जानि परतौ॥ N21॥

ठाकुर

*मेवा बई घनी काबुल में, बिंदराबन आनि करील जमाए।
राधिका सी सुभ बाम बिहाय कै कूबरी संग सनेह बढाए। 2
मेवा तजी दुरजोधन की, बिदुराइन के घर छोकल खाए।
ठाकुर, ठाकुर की का कहौं, सदा ठाकुर बावरे होतई आए॥ N22॥ 4

काबुल जायके मेवा रच्यो, ब्रजमंडल आय करील लगाये।
मेवा तज्यो दुरयोधन के घर, सेवरी के फल जूठन खाये। 2

22 Granthāvalī 49, Ṭhasak 8. The word 'bāvare' in the last line is an emendation by Bhagavāndīn instead of a 'very harsh' (kaṭu) word. 23 Rasikvinod (O_e) 44. This poem is rather a variation on the previous quatrain than a conscious reworking of the same theme. It is probably a product of oral transmission, allowing substantial changes in poems.

21.2 निलज्जन] *em.* निलज्ज (unm.) B_1 **22.2** बढाए] G_e, भढाये $Ṭ_e$ **22.4** बावरे] *em.* $G_eṬ_e$

21.2 गडना [cf. H gāṛnā] v.i. to sink; कैं धरतौ poet. if they held. **21.3** लपरा (लबाड़) [cf. labha-] reg. m. 1. boaster; 2. liar; बूचे [*bucca-] adj. 1. earless; 2. defective. **21.4** सूम [? conn. A śu'm] reg. m. a miser; मकुना m. man without mustache; गांडू [gaṇḍa-] m. 1. male homosexual; 2. an impotent man; 3. fig. a timid or wretched person; नकटा [H nāk + kaṭā] adj. whose nose is cut (in disgrace); नबेरा (निबेड़ा) [cf. H nibeṛnā] m. 1. separation, distinction; 2. settlement, decision; नबेरो जानि परतौ Br. (then) they would appear distinct. **22.1** मेवा [P] m.f. dry fruit; बई (बोयी) [vapati] reg. v.t. perf. (f.) planted; घना [ghana-] Br. adj. plentiful, abundant; काबुल [P] m. Kabul; करील [karīra-] m. the thorny leafless caper-bush (which grows in deserts and is eaten by camels); जमाना [H jamnā] v.t. to fix, (here:) to plant. **22.2** बाम [vāmā-] Br. f. woman. **22.3** बिदुराइन reg. the wife of Vidura, Duryodhana's poor Brahmin minister, who was so much carried away by Krishna that she gave him the peel instead of the fruit; छोकल [śalka-] m. peel. **22.4** ठाकुर की का कहौं Br. what shall I tell of my Lord? सदा... आए Br. the lords have always been crazy. **23.2** सेवरी (शबरी) [S] f. a woman from the Shabara tribe (mentioned in the Ramayana).

कूबरी को पटराणी करी, तजि राधिका को चट द्वारिका धाये।
4 ठाकुर को मत कोऊ कहो, सदा ठाकुर चूकत ही चले आये॥ N23॥

1 *छिपिया को दूधभात, खीचरीहू करमा की,
चक्करा रैदास जू चमारहू के खाए हैं।
2 विदुर की भाजी रोटी बथुआ समाँ की रुची,
बिदुरैन केर छोल छिकुला खवाए हैं।
3 करिकै करार आय बौध अवतार लेइ,
आपनी पुरी मैं एक पातरी जिमाए हैं।
4 नीच परसंगी, जात-पाँत के न अंगी, ऐसे
ठाकुर दोरंगी तौ सदा तें होत आए हैं॥ N24॥

सेवा

1 *सुकबि सिपाही हम उन रजपूतन के

---

24 Granthāvalī 50, Ṭhasak 7.

24.4 पाँत] G_e, पाँति $Ṭ_e$

23.3 चट [*caṭa-] adv. 'with a crack' swiftly. **23.4** मत कोऊ कहो Br. no one should say anything (about the lords but...) चूकना [*cukk-] v.i. to blunder, to err. **24.1** छिपी Bund. m. tailor (i.e. Nāmdev) (BHK); दूध-भात [S] m. rice boiled in milk; कर्मा (कर्मा बाई) f. (Name of a saint who used to prepare food for God early in the morning without having her bath); चक्करा [cakra-, ? conn. H. cikkaṭ] m. pakora made of pulse; चमार [carmakāra-] m. leather-worker. **24.2** भाजी [bharjita-] f. fried vegetables; बथुआ [cf. vāstu-] m. 1. fat-hen (a herb like spinach that grows without planting); 2. a herb (growing in January) of which raita is made; समाँ [śyāmaka-] m. a quick growing millet (or rice) (Panicum fumentaceum); भाजी रोटी बथुआ समाँ की fried fat-hen and chapathi of millet (krama alaṅkāra); केर (केला) [kadala-] reg. m. banana; छोल [*choll-] v.t. abs. having peeled; छिकुला (छिलका) [cf. chilla-] m. skin, peel. **24.3** क़रार [A] m. 1. determination; 2. peace; बौध अवतार [S] m. incarnation as Buddha; पुरी f. (in her) abode; पातरी [cf. pātrā-] f. courtesan (i.e. Ambapālī); जिमाना [H jimnā 'to eat'] v.t. to feed, to receive to a meal. **24.4** परसंगी (प्रसंगी) [S] reg. m. (commensal) companion; जात (जाति) [S] f. caste; पाँत [paṅkti-] f. 1. line; 2. rank; अंगी [S] poet. m. companion दुरंगी [dvi-, raṅgin-] adj. capricious.

दान जुद्ध जुरै जे न कबहूं सु मुरके।
नीति देनहारे हैं मही के महिपालन के, 2
नेही उनहीं के जे सनेही साँचे उर के।
ठाकुर कहत, हम बैरी बेवकूफन के, 3
जालिम दमाद हैं अदेनिया ससुर के।
चोजन के चोर रस-मौजन के पातसाहि 4
ठाकुर कहावत पै चाकर चतुर के॥ N25॥

*प्रथमे मेहिरि कैया होइ, दूसरे देवैया, 1
तीसरे सरूपवत नैनन लहत है।

---

25 Datiya2 f. 9v (84), Granthāvalī 5, Rāmcandra Śukla (I_e) p. 440, Jagannāth Prasād (Q_e) (98), Sudhāsar [S_1 f. 378v (13), S_2 f. 75v (-/86), S_7 f. 249v (139)], Śatak 73, Ṭhasak 14, Ṭhasak 'Jīvancarit' ($Ṭ_e^j$) p. 12, Miśrabandhu Vinod (V_e) p. 729. • The Sudhāsar presents this poem within the 'prastāv hī kau aṅga bhaḍauvā' (mocking verse as part of this context) subsection of the 'Nīti' section. D_2 introduces the poem as 'bisara ko aṅgaka' (part of mockery [KL]). It may have been considered a bharauvā because of the harsh words in the third line. With the word 'sukavi' at the beginning the poem is more about being a poet rather than a man in general in the world suggested by the word 'sevaka' in the printed editions. 26 Sanjay Sharma Sangrahalay (J_2) 753-23 ff. 12v-13r. Strangely, this poem is included into the 'śṛṅgārras-barnan' section.

25.1 सुकवि] D_2**S**, सेवक **E**I_eV_e • सिपाही] Σ, सिपाई S_1 • उन] Σ, उनि S_2 • रजपूतन] Σ, राजपूतन V_e • जुद्ध] Σ, जुध्ध G_e • जुरै जे] **S**, जुरिबे Σ • न] **S**, मैं $D_2G_eI_eṬ_eV_e$, कौं $Ś_e$ • कबहूं] **S**, जे न D_2, नेकु **E**I_eV_e • सु] **S**, जे न $G_eI_eṬ_eV_e$, कहूँ D_2, नहीं $Ś_e$ • मुरके] Σ, सुरके S_1 **25.2** नीति] Σ, नीत S_1S_7 • दैनहारे] D_2**S**, देनवारे $G_eI_eṬ_e$, दै निवारे $Ś_eV_e$ • हैं] Σ, है S_1 • महिपालन] D_2I_e**S**$Ś_eṬ_eV_e$, महिपाल D_2, महीपालन G_e • के] **S**, कौं Σ • नेही...जे] Σ, हिये के बिसुद्ध हैं I_e • नेही] D_2**S**, कवि **E**V_e **25.3** कहत] S_1^{pc}Σ, क (eyeskip) S_1^{ac} • बेवकूफन] Σ, बेवकूपन **S** • के] Σ, पे S_2 • हैं] Σ, है S_2S_7 • अदेनिया] **S**V_e, अदानियाँ D_2**E**I_e **25.4** चोर] **ES**V_e, चोजी D_2I_e • रस] D_2**E**$S_1S_7V_e$, महा I_e, स (unm.) S_2 • पातसाहि] **E**V_e, बादसाह D_2, महराज I_e, पातसाह **S**$Ṭ_e^j$ • ठाकुर कहावत] Σ, हम कविराज हैं I_e • पै] **E**I_eV_e, पर (unm.) D_2, हैं S_1, है S_2S_7 **26.1** प्रथमे] प्रथे (unm.) J_2 • सरूपवत] *conj.* सनूपुवत J_2

25.1 जुर- (जुड़ना) [cf. *yoṭayati] Av. Br. v.i. to join (with), to be involved (in); मुड़कना [cf. muṭati] v.i. 1. to turn away; 2. to be broken. **25.3** दामाद [P] m. son-in-low (conceived as pretentious). **25.4** चोज [codya-] m. 1. wonder; 2. wonderful saying; मौज [A] f. wave; surge of emotion. **26.1** मेहिरि [P mehr] reg. m. benevolence, kindness; कैया (करनेवाला) Br. doer; देवैया (देनेवाला) [cf. H denā] Br. m. 'giver' generous. स्वरूपवत poet. adj. according to the thing's own form.

2 चौत्रे परवीन होइ, पँचए हमारो काम,
छठए छली न होइ, बेदु यो कहतु है।
3 ठाकुर कहत, सातै आपन सुजसु चाहै,
अठए एऐ उदार बोलनि बरतु है।
4 नवए सुचाह करै, दसए दरिद्र हरै,
हम गुनवान लोग ताहि के रहत है॥ N26॥

1 दुखवारे सुखवारे जुग जुग जो मन सो
कैयो रूप धरे हैं, यौं कैयो रूप धरैंगै।
2 हारी कला जीती करी, भरि भरि रीती करी,
रीती मन आये फेरि भरे कै न भरैंगै।
3 ठाकुर कहत, ऐसे समरथ स्वामी वे तौ
आपने चरित्रन मैं आप जानि परैंगै।

27 Bharatpur1 f. 164v (93), Granthāvalī 217, Sudhāsar [S_1 f. 421r (24), S_2 f. 83r (-/93), S_3 f. 276/67rv (10), S_7 f. 270v-1r (157)], Vrindaban1 f. 8v (11/49). • The Sudhāsar presents this poem within the 'Bhaktapada' (S_1) or 'Bhaktipantha' (S_3) subsection of the 'Devstuti, bhaktapakṣa, nirveda, karunā, binaya' section.

26.2 छली] *conj.* छेली J_2 **27.1** जुग जुग] Σ, जुग जुण S_2 • जो] B_1S_2, S_7V_1, जों S_1, जोई (unm.) G_e • सो] Σ, सूं B_1 • कैयो] Σ, कईयो (unm.) S_3S_7 • धरे हैं] G_eS_3, धरै है $B_1S_1S_2S_7V_1$ • यौं] B_1, औ Σ • धरैंगे] $B_1G_eS_1S_2$, धरैगो S_3S_7, धरैगे V_1 **27.2** भरि भरि] Σ, भर भर S_3S_7 • आये] $G_eS_1V_1$, आऐं B_1, आई $S_2S_3S_7$ • फेरि] $B_1G_eS_1S_2V_1$, फेर S_3S_7 • भरे] B_1**S**, भरि G_e, भर V_1 • भरैंगै] $B_1G_eS_1$, भरैगौ (unrh.) S_2, भरैगो S_3S_7, भरैगे V_1 **27.3** ठाकुर कहत] Σ, ठा° B_1 • जानि] $B_1G_eS_1S_2V_1$, जान S_3S_7 • परैंगे] $B_1G_eS_1$, परैगौ (unrh.) S_2, परैगो S_3S_7, परैगे V_1

26.2 हमारो काम (मेरे काम का) Br. useful for me; छली [S] adj. deceitful; छेली (छेरी) apa. [chagalikā-] reg. f. nanny-goat; बेदु यो कहतु है Br. the Veda tells it so. **26.3** बरत एऐ (बरत आए) v.i. conj. should use (noble words). **26.4** सुचाह करै Br. to be of goodwill; गुनवान लोग poet. m. pl. 1. (used for singular) 'virtuous man' artist; 2. (belong to those) virtuous men. **27.1** दुखवारे सुखवारे painful and blissful (forms); जो rel. pron. the one who (takes on forms); जोई (जो) var. rel. pron. (those) who; मन सो Br. with affection; कैयो (कई) [cf. *kiyatta-] adj. several (SBK); (of) various (kinds) (BSK); **27.2** कला [S] f. 1. game; 2. through his sport; जीती करी reg. he made victorious; भरि भरि रीती करी Br. emptied what was full to the brim; रीती 1. [rikta-] reg. adj. f. empty; 2. f. emptiness; भरे आये v.t. perf. he filled. **27.3** समरथ (समर्थ) [S] adj. powerful; चरित्र [S] m. action; मैं postp. Br. in, (here:) through; आप (अपने से) [ātman] pron. Br. 'yourself' on your own part; जानि परैंगै reg. will be recognised.

याही मति गाह्यौ है, सराह्यौ है सबन, उन 4
　　　चाह्यौ है सो कीयौ है, औ चाहैंगे सो करैंगे॥ N27॥

मर्दानगी

वेई नर निरनैं निदान पै सराहे जात, 1
　　　सुखन अन्हात, प्यालौ प्रेम को पिये रहैं।
हरि जस चंदन चढायैं सब अंगन मैं 2
　　　चौप को तिलक बेंदी रस की दिये रहैं।
ठाकुर कहत, कंज मंजु तें मृदुल महा, 3
　　　मोहनी सरूप धारैं, हिम्मत हिये रहैं।
भेंट भए समये-कुसमये, कुचाल-चाल 4

---

28 Sudhāsar [S_1 ff. 347v (5), S_2 ff. 66v-67r (-/75), S_4 ff. 26v-27r (156), S_7 f. 234v (8)], Granthāvalī 184, Rāmcandra Śukla (I_e) p. 440, Ṭhasak 132, Ṭhasak 'Jīvancarit' (Ṭ^j_e) p. 11–12. • The Sudhāsar presents this poem within the 'Nīti' section. • The variants in the Sudhāsar put emphasis on love, while the edited text downplays it.

27.4 याही] $B_1G_eS_1S_2V_1$, यही S_3S_7 • मति] $S_1S_2S_3$, मत $B_1G_eS_7V_1$ • गाह्यौ] B_1V_1, गायौ G_e, गाहा **S** • सराह्यौ है] B_1, सरायौ है G_e, सराहा है **S**, *om.* (unm.) V_1 • चाह्यौ] B_1V_1, चायौ G_e, चाहा **S** • कीयौ] $B_1G_eV_1$, किया S_1S_2, कीआ S_3S_7 • चाहैंगे] $B_1G_eS_1S_2$, चाहेगो S_3S_7, चाहैगे V_1 • सो] Σ, सु S_2 • करैंगे] $B_1G_eS_1$, केरैगे S_2, करेगो S_3S_7, करैगे V_1 **28.1** निरनैं] **S**, निन्नय G_eṬ$_e$, निर्नय I_e, निरनय (unm.) Ṭ^j_e • पै] **S**, में **E**I_e • अन्हात] S_1S_2, अनाहत (unm.) S_4, अनात S_7, अघात **E**I_e • प्यालौ] $S_1S_2S_7$, प्याला **E**I_e, षालो S_4 • रहैं] **E**$I_eS_1S_4$, रहै S_2S_7 **28.2** हरि] I_e**S**Ṭ^j_e, राम G_eṬ$_e$ • जस] $S_1S_2S_4$, रस **E**I_e, जसु S_7 • चढायैं] S_1, चढाय **E**I_e, चढावै S_2S_7, चटावै S_4 • सब] **S**, अंग **E**I_e • चौप] **S**, नीति Σ • रस] **S**, जस Σ • रहैं] **E**$I_eS_1S_4$, रहै S_2S_7 **28.3** कंज मंजु] **S**, मंजु कंज **E**I_e • तें] Σ, से S_7 • महा] **S**, मन **E**I_e • मोहनी] Σ, मोहनौं S_1 • धारैं] S_1S_4, धारे **E**$I_eS_2S_7$ • हिम्मत] Σ, हिमत (unm.) S_4 • रहैं] **E**$I_eS_1S_4$, रहै S_2S_7

27.4 याहि मति गाह्यौ है (इस मत को ग्रहण किया) Br. this is the opinion accepted (by everyone); उन (उन्होंने) Br. ag. God; **28.1** निरनैं (निर्नय) [S] (m. obl. used as) adv. truely (cf. H niścay hī); निदान पर in the end; सराहे जात v.t. pass. Br. are praised; अन्हा- (नहाना) [snāti] reg. v.i. to bathe; सुख न अघात var. Br. are not satisfied with happiness, there is no end to their happiness. **28.2** चौप var. Br. m. 1. desire; 2. delight. **28.3** मोहनी(य) सरूप enchanting form.

दूनी चाह राखैं, आँखैं एक सी किये रहैं॥ N28॥

1 *जौ लौं काहू पारखी तें भेंट होन पाई नाहिं,
तौ लौं तेई लागत गरीब से सरीरा हैं।
2 पारखी तें भेंट भए दामहू चढत लाख,
कीमत के आगरे औ बुद्धि के गँभीरा हैं।
3 ठाकुर कहत, नाहीं निंदौ गुनबानन कों,
रंक से दिखात पै सहूर सूर-बीरा हैं।
4 ईस की कृपा तें होत ऐसे कहूँ कहूँ नर
मानुस सहूर भरे धूर भरे हीरा हैं॥ N29॥

1 *बैर प्रीति करिबे की मन मैं न संका राखै,
राजा-राव देखि कै न छाती धकधक री।
2 आपनी उमंड के निबाहिबे की चाह जिन्हैं,

---

29 Granthāvalī 185, Ṭhasak 140. 30 Hariaudh (A$_e$) p. 483, Rasikvinod (O$_e$) p. 5. (22), Sudhāsar [S$_1$ f. 356r (43), S$_2$ f. 69v (-/79), S$_4$ f. 36rv (194), S$_7$ f. 238rv (36)], Hāfizullah Khān: Hazārā (X$_e$) p. 533 (Bhaṛauvā aur hāsī 49 and Phuṭkar 4). • The Sudhāsar presents this poem within the 'Nīti' section.

28.4 भेंट] Σ, भट S$_7$ • कुसमये] **S**Ṭ$_e^j$, असमये] G$_e$I$_e$Ṭ$_e$ • कुचाल चाल] **S**, अचाहे चाहे **EI**$_e$ • दूनी चाह राषैं] **S**, ओर लौं निबाहैं **EI**$_e$ • राषैं] S$_1$S$_7$, राषे S$_2$ • रहैं] **EI**$_e$S$_1$, रहै S$_2$S$_7$ **29.4** हीरा] *em.* हीरो (unrh.) G$_e$Ṭ$_e$ **30.1** बैर...राखै] Σ, बनी बेबनी की कछू परवा रहै न जिन्है O$_e$ • बैर] **S**A$_e$, बैरी X$_e$ • की] Σ, कौं S$_1$ • संका राखै] X$_e$, संका मांनि S$_1$S$_2$S$_4$, संका मान S$_7$, राखै संक A$_e$ • राव] Σ, रंक X$_e$ • कै] Σ, *om.* (unm.) O$_e$ • °धक री] S$_1$S$_2$S$_4$X$_e$, धा करी A$_e$, पकरी O$_e$, °धक्क री S$_7$

28.4 भेंट भएँ Br. if they meet one; कुचाल [S] 1. f. misconduct; wicked conduct; 2. adj. of bad conduct; चाल [*cālya-] f. behaviour, conduct; (here:) good conduct; ओर लौं var. idiom. Br. till the end; निबाहना var. [nirvāhayati] v.t. to fulfill; to carry through; दूनी चाह राखैं Br. their enthusiasm is doubled. **29.1** भेंट होन पाई नहीं reg. (until) one does not meet. **29.2** पारखी [cf. *pārīkṣya-] 'discerning' m. 1. tester; 2. connoisseur; आगर- [agra-] adj. increased, excessive; कीमत के आगरे poet. more valuable than their price; बुद्धि के गंभीरा are of serious intelligence. **29.3** निंद- [nindati] Br. v.t. to blame, to abuse; सहुरि [S] f. earth. सहूर [A śu'ūr] Br. m. wisdom. **30.1** बैर प्रीति Br. enmity and love; शंका [S] f. 1. doubt; 2. fear, awe; न राखै Br. the one who does not keep; छाती [*chātti-] f. obl. in his heart; धकधक m. f. palpitation, tremour, anxiety.

एक से दिखात, यारौ, बाघ अरु बकरी।
ठाकुर कहत, या बिचारी है बिचार करि, 3
यही मरदानगी की रीति एक अकरी।
गही तौनि गही, और छाँडी तौनि छाड़ी दई, 4
करी तौन करी, और न करी सु न करी॥ N30॥

*सामिल हो पीर मैं, सरीर मैं न राखि भेद, 1

30.2 आपनी] **S**X_e, अपनी O_e, आपने A_e • उमंड] $S_1S_2S_7$, अमेंड A_e, उमेड O_e, डमंड S_4, उमंग X_e • के] Σ, की X_e • निबाहिबे की] Σ, निबाहि की है X_e • जिन्हैं] A_eX_e, तिन्हैं O_e, जिनें **S** • से] O_e**S**, सो A_eX_e • दिखात] Σ, लगत O_e • यारौ] **S**, तिन्हैं A_eX_e, यार O_e • अरु] S_2S_4, और $S_1A_eX_eO_e$, अर S_7 • बकरी] Σ, बाकरी A_e, बक्करी S_7 **30.3** ठाकुर] Σ, कवि ठाकुर, (unm.) O_e • कहत] Σ, कहति S_4 • या] **S**, मैं A_eX_e, ये O_e • बिचारी है] $S_1S_2S_4S_7^{pc}$, बिचारि कै A_eX_e, काम ना O_e, बिचा (unm.) S_7^{ac} • बिचार करि] $S_1S_2S_4S_7^{pc}$, बिचारि देख्यौ A_eX_e, हरेकन को O_e, र कर (unm.) S_7 • यही] **S**, यहै A_eX_e, मुरक (unm.) O_e • मरदानगी] O_e**S**, मरदानन A_eX_e • रीति] $S_1S_2S_4$, रीत S_7O_e, टेक A_eX_e • एक] $O_eS_1S_2S_7$, बात X_e, औ A_e, धक S_4 • अकरी] Σ, अटाकरी A_e, अक्करी S_7 **30.4** तौनि गही] $S_1S_2S_4$, तौन गही $A_eS_7X_e$, जोन गही O_e • और] **S**, फेरि X_e, जौन A_e, फिर O_e • छाडी] A_e**S**, छोड़ी X_eO_e • तौनि छाडी] S_2S_4, तौन छोड़ि X_eO_e, तौन छाड़ी A_eS_1, तौन छाड़ S_7 • दई] Σ, जौन A_e • करी तौन करी] Σ, हां करी सु हां करी O_e • तौन] Σ, तौनि S_1 • और न] **S**, जौन न X_e, बात ना A_e, ना O_e • सु] O_e**S**, सो A_eX_e • न करी] $S_1S_2X_e$, ना करी A_eO_e, नक्करी S_7

30.2 उमंड (उमड़) [cf. *ummaḍḍ-] f. overflowing of emotion, desire; उमेद (उम्मीद) var. [P] f. expectation; निबाहना [nirvāhayati] v.t. to carry through, to fulfill; एक से दिखात Br. (for him the goat and the lion) look alike (i.e. does not fear either of them). **30.3** या बिचारी है reg. this has been deliberated; मुरक var. f. twist, bend, crookedness (the unattested reading maraka f. 'sign' is also possible); एक adv. alone, only; अकरा [cf. eka-] Av. Br. adj. 1. unique, sole; 2. precious, 3. good, sound, pure, genuine. **30.4** तौनि pron. reg. 1. what (H jo); 2. that (H vah); जोन (जो) var. pron. reg. what; फिर var. adv. then.

अंतर कपट जो उघारै सो उघरि जाइ।
2 ऐसो ठान ठानै तौ बिनाहू जंत्र मंत्रन सौं
साँपहू को जहर उतारै, तौ उतरि जाइ।
3 ठाकुर कहत, कछू कठिन न जानौ, देखौ,
हिंमति करे तें कौन काम न सुधरि जाइ।
4 चारि जने चारिहू दिसा तें चारि कोने गहि

---

31 Alvar f. 68v, Hariaudh (A_e) pp. 483-4, Bharatpur1 f. 132rv (7), Sudhāsar [S_1 f. 367r (98), S_2 f. 72v (-/83), S_7 f. 243v (79)], Granthāvalī 187, Kālidās-Hazārā (H_e) 331, Vrindaban1 f. 2r (9/9), Vrindaban2 f. 70rv, Hāfizullah Khān: Hazārā (X_e) p. 494 and Dikshit p. 597 (Bhaṛauvā aur hāsī 47). (Dikshit's text is collated here), Z_1 ff. 26v, 27v (19). • The Sudhāsar presents this poem within the 'Nīti' section.

31.1 सामिल] Σ, स्यामल ×में× A • हो] $A_eB_1G_e\mathbf{S}V_1Z_1$, है A, में $H_eV_2X_e$ • सरीर मैं] Σ, *om.* (unm.) S_2 • राषि भेद] B_1S_1, राखै भेद AG_eZ_1, भेद राखै A_e, भेद राषि $H_eS_2S_7V_2$, राष भेद V_1, भेद राखैं X_e • अंतर] $AB_1G_e\mathbf{S}V_1Z_1$, हिम्मत A_e, हिंमिति V_2, हिम्मति H_eX_e • कपट] $AB_1H_e^{vl}\mathbf{S}V_1V_2Z_1X_e$, कपाट A_eH_e, कपन G_e • जो] $AB_1H_eS_2S_7$, को A_eX_e, जौन G_e, तो $H_e^{vl}V_2$, जों S_1, जोनि V_1, कछु Z_1 • उघारे] $AA_eH_eS_2S_7V_2X_e$, होय $B_1G_eV_1Z_1$, उपारेइं (unm.) H_e^{vl}, न होइ S_1 • तो] $AA_eH_eS_2S_7X_e$, सो $B_1G_eZ_1S_1$, तें $H_e^{vl}V_2$ • उघरि] $A_eB_1G_eH_eH_e^{vl}S_2V_2X_e$, उघर AS_7Z_1, उथर S_1 **31.2** ठान] $A_eB_1G_eH_eS_2S_7V_1V_2X_e$, साच AZ_1, ठाठ S_1 • ठानै] Σ, ठाँनिकें S_1 • तौ] $AA_eB_1G_eH_eV_1V_2$, जौ **S**, तै Z_1 • बिनाहू] Σ, बिनाँ S_1 • मंत्रन $B_1G_eV_1$, मंत्र $AA_eH_e\mathbf{S}V_2Z_1X_e$ • सौं] $B_1G_eV_1$, कियें $AA_eH_eV_2X_e$, °हू के S_1, करै S_2S_7, मंसै Z_1 • साँपहू] $B_1G_eS_1Z_1$, सांप $AA_eS_7H_eX_e$, स्याप $H_e^{vl}S_2V_2$, सापहु V_1 • को] Σ, के A_eX_e • जहर] $B_1G_eS_1V_1Z_1$, जहर जो] AH_eV_2, जहर को A_eX_e, जहर तौ H_e^{vl}, जहर यौ S_2S_7 • तौ] Σ, ⟨तै/सै⟩ Z_1 • उतरि] $A_eB_1G_eH_eS_1V_2X_e$, उतर $AS_7V_1Z_1$, उत× ⟨नि⟩ × रिर (dittography) S_2 **31.3** ठाकुर कहत] Σ, ठा° B_1 • कछू] $B_1G_eH_eS_1Z_1$, कछु $A_eV_1X_e$, अरे A, यह S_2, यहि S_7, इह V_2 • कठिन न] $A_eB_1H_e\mathbf{S}V_2X_e$, कठिन G_eV_1, सोच मत A, अगम न Z_1 • जानौ] $A_eS_2V_2$, बिचारि B_1, बिचार G_eV_1, कर A, जानै H_e, बूझौ S_1, जानी Z_1 • देखौ] $B_1G_eV_1$, मन A, अब $H_eV_2X_e$, मीत A_e, याहि S_1, कछू S_2S_7, जात Z_1 • हिंमति] $B_1G_eH_eS_2V_2X_e$, उद्यम A, साहस A_e, हिम्मत $S_1S_7V_1Z_1$ • करे] $B_1G_eZ_1$, किये $AA_eH_e\mathbf{S}V_2X_e$, कर V_1 • तें] Σ, तो A • कौन] $B_1G_eS_1V_1$, कहो $AA_eH_eV_2Z_1X_e$, कहा S_2S_7 • काम] $B_1G_eS_1V_1$, कहा $A_eH_eV_2Z_1X_e$, का⟨हा⟩ A, कहौ S_2S_7 • न] Σ, नां A • सुधरि] $A_eB_1G_eH_eV_1V_2X_e$, सुधर $AS_1S_7Z_1$, सुधारि S_2

31.1 सामिल हो पीर मैं reg. who is present at one's pain; भेद न राख- idiom. Br. does not see a difference between (two men); अंतरकपन var. [antar-kampana-] poet. m. inner pain; कपाट var. [S] m. door; जौन (जो) var. conj. if; सो pron. Br. he; उघड़ना [udghaṭati] v.i. to appear. **31.2** ऐसो ठान ठानै Br. 1. if one is resolved on such principles; 2. if such a man is resolved; बिनाहू... उतारै (i.e. if they drink it.) उतारना [uttārayati] v.t. to drive out (poison) (i.e. to treat a snake-bite).

मेरु को हलाइ कै उखारैं, तौ उखरि जाइ॥ N31॥

जानि पर्‌यो जग पेखनो है, तिहि की अब छाक छके रहनौ है।
मंत्र यहै निरधार निरंतर अंतर की न कहूँ कहनौ है।
ठाकुर, दोस लगाइयै कौन कों, पाइयै भाग लिख्यौ लहनौ है।
काम इही मरदानगी को, सिर आनि परै सु लिये रहनौ है॥ N32॥

---

32 Bharatpur1 f. 132v (8), Granthāvalī 189, Rasikvinod (O_e) 146 pp. 32-33, Sudhāsar [S_1 f. 348r (8), S_2 f. 67r (-/76), S_4 f. 27rv (159), S_7 f. 234v (11)], Śatak 86, Ṭhākur-satsaī (Ṭ) f. 4v (37), Ṭhasak 134. • The Sudhāsar presents this poem within the 'Nīti' section. • The second and the third lines are in the reverse order in O_e.

31.4 चारि] $A_eB_1G_eH_e$**S**$V_1V_2X_e$, च्यारों A, चार S_7Z_1 • चारिहू] Σ, च्यारहू A, चारौं S_1 • दिसा तें] Z_1^{pc}Σ, *om.* S_1, दिसा तौ Z_1^{ac} • चारि] $B_1G_eS_2$, च्यार A, चारो A_eX_e, चार V_1Z_1, चार्यौ H_eV_2 • कोने] Σ, कोन H_eX_e • गहि] Σ, गहै A, गहि चारौं ओरन तें S_1 • मेरु] $A_eB_1G_eH_e$**S**V_1X_e, मेरू A, मेर $S_7V_2Z_1$ • को] Σ, कूं A • हलाइ कै] Σ, हालावे तौ Z_1 • उखारैं] Σ, उखारै S_7 • तौ] Σ, तै Z_1 • उखरि] $A_eB_1G_eH_eS_2V_1V_2X_e$, उषर $AS_1S_7Z_1$ **32.1** जानि] **E**, आनि B_1, जान O_e, यह जांनि (unm.) S_1S_2, यहि जांनि S_4, यहि जान (unm.) S_7, यह जान (unm.) Ṭ • पर्‌यो] B_1S_1Ṭ, परो **E**O_e, परी $S_2S_4S_7$ • जग] Σ, जुग O_e • पेखनो] B_1**E**S_1Ṭ, देखनो O_e, पेषना $S_2S_4S_7$ • है] B_1**E**$S_1S_2S_7$Ṭ, तो O_e, हैं॥ S_4 • तिहि] $B_1S_2S_4Ś_e$, जिहि B_1, यहि G_eṬ$_e$, मिलतेहु O_e, तिह S_1S_7Ṭ • की] Σ, तें **E** • अब] **S**Ṭ, नित B_1, इहि **E**, *om.* O_e • छाक] Σ, भाँति **E** • छके] B_1**E**$S_1S_2S_4$Ṭ, छको O_eS_7 • रहनौ] S_1^{pc}Σ, रहने **E**, रहैनौं S_1^{ac} • है] **E**S_1S_7, *om.* (unm.) O_e, हैं $B_1S_2S_4$ **32.2** मंत्र] $B_1S_1S_4S_7$Ṭ, बात **E**, धार S_2, मिंत O_e • यहै निरधार] B_1O_e, यही निरधार $S_1S_4S_7$Ṭ, *om.* **E**S_2 • निरंतर] Σ, निर्नरं S_2^{ac}, निनरं S_2^{pc} • अंतर की] B_1S_1Ṭ, अंतर की अपने दिल की **E**, अंतर कौ O_e, *om.* (unm.) S_2, अंतरि की S_4S_7 • कहूँ] Σ, कछू O_e • कहनौ] Σ, कहने **E** • है] **ES**, हैं B_1S_4, *om.* (unm.) O_e **32.3** दोस] Σ, दोख S_4S_7 • लगाइयै] **ES**, लगायै (unm.) B_1, लगाईऐ Ṭ • पाइयै] B_1**E**$O_eS_1S_2S_7S_7$, पाईये S_4Ṭ • भाग] **E**$O_eS_1S_7$Ṭ, भागि $B_1S_2S_4$ • लिख्यौ] B_1**S**, लिखे **E**, लिखो O_eṬ • लहनौ] Σ, लहने **E** • है] **ESṬ**, हैं B_1S_4, *om.* (unm.) O_e **32.4** काम] Σ, अब चिंत O_e • इही] B_1, इहै **E**, यह O_e, यही **SṬ** • को] Σ, कौं S_4 • आनि] S_2S_4, आ⟨चि⟩ B_1, आन **E**$O_eS_1S_7$Ṭ • परै] B_1**E**$S_1S_2S_4$Ṭ, बनै S_7O_e • सु] Σ, सो B_1 • लिये] **ES**O_e, लियैं B_1, लीऐ Ṭ • रहनौ] B_1, बहने **E**, बहनौ $S_1S_2S_7$ṬO_e, ⟨ब⟩हिनो S_4 • है] **ESṬ**, हैं B_1S_4, *om.* (unm.) O_e

---

31.4 हला- (हिलाना) [*hillati] reg. v.t. to shake; उखड़ना [utskṛta-] v.i. to be uprooted. **32.1** पेखनो [prekṣaṇa-] Av. Br. m. spectacle; यहि तें var. Br. conj. therefore; छाक [*chakka-] f. 1. satisfaction; 2. quantity of food sufficient for one time; छके रहनौ है reg. one must be satisfied. **32.2** अंतर की adj. (f.) 'of the heart' internal, private. **32.3** पाइयै भाग लिखे Br. what one receives written as one's fate; लहनौ है reg. (that) should be accepted. **32.4** काम [karma-] m. work, task; मर्दानगी [P] f. manliness; सिर आनि परै Br. whatever befalls to one('s head); बह- [vahati] Av. Br. v.t. to carry.

उदारता

1 *बिधना बडाई दई, ताहि तकि आवै कोई,
ताके काज दौरि कै दया के हेत ढरिये।
2 ताहि धन दीजै, जस लीजै जग जीवन को,
सदा मत दौरि दुख दीनन को हरिये।
3 ठाकुर कहत, जौ पै गाँठ सों न दयो जाय,
देतहू न बनै उपकार सों न टरिये।
4 आपने कहे तें काहू दूसरे को भलो होय,
भलो कहिबे में कछू गाफिली न करिये॥ N33॥

1 *दस बार, बीस बार बरजि दई है याहि,
एते पै न मानै जौ, तौ जरन बरन देव।
2 कैसो कहा कीजै, कछू आपनो करौ न होइ,
जाके जैसे दिन ताहि तैसेई भरन देव।
3 ठाकुर कहत, मन आपनो मगन राखौ
प्रेम, निरसंक रस-रंग बिहरन देव।
4 बिधि के बनाए जीव जेते हैं जहाँ के तहाँ
खेलत-फिरत, तिन्हैं खेलन-फिरन देव॥ N34॥

1 छानि बसुधा है, सुधा बिष को सवाद चाख्यौ,

---

33 Granthāvalī 191, Ṭhasak 139. 34 Granthāvalī 198, Rāmcandra Śukla (I_e) p. 443, Śatak 36, Ṭhasak 24.

34.1 बरजि] I_e, बरज **E** • याहि] **E**, जाहि I_e • जौ तौ] $G_eI_eṬ_e$, जौ पै $Ś_e$ **34.3** नि-रसंक] **E**, निहसंक I_e

---

33.1 विधिना [vidhi- (S instr.)] m. the creator; **बडाई दई** Br. gave (you) greatness; **के हेतु** postp. for; **ढर-** (**ढलना**) [ḍhalati] v.i. 'to flow' to incline, to show favour. **33.2** मत (मति) poet. f. (obl.) (hastening in your) mind. **33.3** गांठ [granthi-] f. 'knot in a dhoti' purse; देतहू न बनै Br. if you cannot give; उपकार [S] m. beneficence, favour. **33.4** ग़ाफ़िली [PH] f. negligence. **34.1** बरज [varjaṇa-] reg. f. prohibition; बरजना [cf. varjita-] v.t. to forbid; **बरजि दई** Br. I forbade (the matter). **34.2** कैसो कहा कीजै Br. whatever one does in whatsoever way; करौ (v.t perf. used as a noun) Br. m. deed; भरना [bharati] v.t. to pass, to live out (one's days). **34.3** मगन [magna-] Br. adj. immersed, absorbed; निरसंक (निःशंक) [S] poet. adv. fearlessly; बिहरना [viharati] v.i. 'to wander' to delight, to revel. **34.4** जहाँ के तहाँ adv. exactly there where they are.

तप बेद भाख्यौ, अभिलाख्यौ-भेद जान्यो री।
छोभ-छल-छिद्र मैं लगावत का टोभ-गोभ, 2
लोभ की लहर आएँ को न ललचान्यो री।
ठाकुर कहत, दुख-सुख हीर-पीर जानैं 3
जान्यौई परत यह अकह कहान्यो री।
तन-धन-जोबन नगर-बन-गाँउ सोऊ 4
अपनो सो अपनो, बिरानो सो बिरानो री॥ N35॥

काव्य-कला

*मोतिन कैसी मनोहर माल गुहै, तुक अच्छर जोरि बनावै।

---

35 Bharatpur1 f. 159r (56), Granthāvalī 219, Sudhāsar [S_1 f. 300rv (42), S_3 f. 172v (254), S_4 f. 100rv (267), S_7 f. 209v (103)], Vrindaban1 f. 11rv (2/67). • The Sudhāsar presents this poem within the 'uddhava kau braj mẽ āyabau' (Uddhava's coming to Braj) subsection of the 'Brajrasrīti' section. 36 Granthāvalī 6, Śatak 72, Ṭhākur-satsaī (Ṭ) f. 5v (46), Ṭhasak 13, Ṭhasak 'Jīvancarit' (Ṭ$_e^j$) p. 10.

35.1 छानि] S_1S_4, छावन G_e, छान $B_1S_3S_7V_1$ • बसुधा] Σ, सुधा G_e • सुधा] Σ, छुधा V_1 • बेद] Σ, भेद S_3S_4 • अभिलाख्यौ] $B_1G_eS_1V_1$, अब लख्यो $S_3S_4S_7$ **35.2** छिद्र] Σ, छिद्द्र S_3S_7 • मैं] Σ, भै S_4 • का] B_1S_1, को G_eV_1, क $S_3S_4S_7$ • गोभ] Σ, लोभ S_7 • लहर] Σ, लहरि S_4 • आएं] Σ, आइ S_4 **35.3** ठाकुर कहत] G_e**S**, ठा° B_1, कहैत V_1 • जानैं] $B_1G_eS_1S_4V_1$, जाने S_3S_7 • यह] Σ, यहि S_4 • अकह] Σ, अकहि S_4 **35.4** गाँउ] B_1G_e, गाँव S_1, गाम $S_3S_4S_7$, गा⟨उं/ऊ⟩ V_1 • अपनो सो अपनो] $B_1G_eV_1$, आपनौं सो आपनौं $S_1S_3S_4$, आपन सो आपनो S_7 • बिरानो] Σ, बिरान S_7 • सो] Σ, सु S_1 **36.1** कैसी] **E**, की सी Ṭ • माल] G_eṬṬ$_e$, माँग Ś$_e$ • गुहै] **E**, जुरे Ṭ • अच्छर] Ś$_e$Ṭ$_e$, अक्षर G_e, अछर (unm.) Ṭ • जोरि] **E**, जोर Ṭ • बनावै] **E**, रिझावै Ṭ

35.1 छानना [*kṣānayati] v.t. (perf. poet.) 'to sift' to search through; छावन var. [chādayati] 'spreading' m. protector; सुधा... चाख्यौ Br. 1. (but) nectar tasted poison; 2. I tasted nectar and poison; छाख- (चखना) [cf. *cakṣati] v.t. to taste; भाख- [bhāṣate] Av. Br. v.t. to tell; तप बेद भाख्यौ Br. the Veda spoke of ascetic heat; अभिलाख्यौ [cf. abhilāṣā-] (v.t. perf. used as a noun) Br. m. desire. **35.2** छोभ [kṣobha-] Av. Br. m. ill-will, malice; छल [S] m. 1. deceit; 2. trick; छिद्र [S] m. 1. hole; 2. defect; को Br. interr. who? टोभ Br. m. stitching; गोभ [cf. gobhnā] m. piercing. (who would pierce what was cut by others? i.e. why to increase pain?) **35.3** हीर [S] m. 1. energy; 2. delight, joy; जानै जान्यौई परत Br. (they) are known only by experience; कहानो [kathānaka-] Br. m. tale, story. **35.4** वन [S] m. forest, uncultivated land; अपनो सो अपनो Br. what is one's own is one's own. **36.1** कैसी [cf. H kī sī and jaisī] poet. adv. like of (pearls); गुह- [guphati] Br. v.t. to thread; अच्छर जोरि 'joining syllables' 1. (creates rhymes) on the basis of syllables (i.e. makes pure rhymes); 2. (makes rhymes) of several syllables.

2 प्रेम को पंथ, कथा हरिनाम की, बात अनूठी बनाइ सुनावै।
ठाकुर, सो कवि भावत मोहिं, जो राजसभा मैं बडप्पन पावै।
4 पंडित-लोक प्रबीनन को जोइ चित्त हरै, सो कबित्त कहावै॥ N36॥

1 *सीख लीने मीन, मृग, खंजन, कमल, चंद,
सीख लीने जस औ प्रताप सरसानो है।
2 सीख लीने चिंतामनि, मेरु अरु कामतरु,
सीख लीने रस को सवाद उर आनो है।
3 ठाकुर कहत, याकौ कठिन बिचारि देखौ,

---

37 Granthāvalī 7, Rāmcandra Śukla (I$_e$) p. 443, Sudhāsar [S$_1$ f. 372v (127), S$_2$ f. 74r (-/84), S$_5$ f. 245v (48), S$_7$ f. 246v (104)], Ṭhākur-satsaī (Ṭ) f. 4v (36), Ṭhasak 12, Vrindaban2 f. 68v. • The Sudhāsar presents this poem within the 'Nīti' section. • Manuscript S$_7$ on its margin introduces the poem as 'kabittana ko hāsabe ke' (to mock poetry) • I$_e$ and Ṭ$_e$ prefer more Sanskritic spellings than the other sources.

36.2 हरि॰] **E**, हर Ṭ • बात] **E**, युगत (unm.) Ṭ **36.3** भावत] **E**, भावै Ṭ • मोहिं] **E**, हमै Ṭ • जो] **E**, सोई Ṭ • बडप्पन] **E**, बडपन (unm.) Ṭ **36.4** लोक] Σ, और Ṭ$_e^j$ • को] G$_e$Ṭ$_e$, की Ś$_e$, के Ṭ • जोइ] **E**, जोऊ Ṭ • चित्त] **E**, चित (unm.) Ṭ • कबित्त] **E**, कबित (unm.) Ṭ **37.1** सीख] G$_e$I$_e$S$_1$S$_5$S$_7$ṬṬ$_e$, सीषि S$_2$V$_2$ • लीने] **S**Ṭ, लीन्हो G$_e$I$_e$, लीन्हों Ṭ$_e$, लीनैं V$_2$ • मीन...चंद] Σ, दाता ग्याता कलि मैं कलपतरु V$_2$ • मीन मृग] Σ, *om.* Ṭ • चंद] **S**, नैन **E**I$_e$, मृग जैस नैन Ṭ • सीख] G$_e$I$_e$S$_1$S$_5$S$_7$ṬṬ$_e$, सीषि S$_2$V$_2$ • लीने] **S**Ṭ, लीन्हो G$_e$I$_e$, लीन्हों Ṭ$_e$, लीनौ V$_2$ • जस औ] **E**I$_e$S$_1$S$_2$S$_6$, सुजस S$_5$, प्रबल ṬV$_2$ • सरसानौ] **S**, को कहानो **E**I$_e$, अधकानौ ṬV$_2^{pc}$, अधिकौनौ V$_2^{ac}$ • है] Σ, हैं V$_2$ **37.2** सीख] G$_e$I$_e$S$_1$S$_5$S$_7$ṬṬ$_e$, सीषि S$_2$V$_2$ • लीने] **S**Ṭ, लीन्हो G$_e$I$_e$, लीन्हों Ṭ$_e$, लेने V$_2$ • चिंतामनि मेरु अरु कांमतरु] **S**, कल्पबृक्ष कामधेनु चिंतामनि **E**I$_e$, ग्याता दाता कल मै कलपतर Ṭ, षंजन चपल मृग ऐसे नैंन V$_2$ • चिंतामनि] S$_2$, चिंतामन S$_1$S$_5$S$_7$ • मेरु अरु] S$_2$S$_5$, मेरु और S$_1$, मेरू अर S$_7$ • कांमतरु] S$_1$S$_2$S$_7$, कामतरू S$_5$ • सीख] **E**S$_1$S$_5$S$_7$Ṭ, सीषि S$_2$V$_2$ • लीने] **S**, लीन्हो G$_e$I$_e$, लीन्हों Ṭ$_e$, लीनो Ṭ, लीनौं V$_2$ • रस को सवाद उर आनो] **S**, मेरु औ कुबेर गिरआनो **E**I$_e$, सुजस सुंगंध मरसानो Ṭ, सरस सुगंध सरसानौ V$_2$ • गिरआनो **E**, गिरि आनो I$_e$

36.2 युगत (युक्ति) var. [S] Br. f. combination, means, strategem; अनूठा [*anna-uṭṭha] adj. uncommon, wonderful; बनाइ (v.t. abs.) adv. well-(formed). **36.4** पंडित-लोक प्रबीनन Br. connoisseurs (patrons) in the world of the learned. **37.1** कहानो var. [kathānaka-] Br. m. tale, story. सरसा- [cf. sarasa-] Br. v.i. to be luxuriant, to abound. **37.2** मेर (मेरु) var. [S] m. the mount Meru; उर आना idiom. Br. 1. to clasp to the breast or heart; 2. (here): to experience. गिर आनो var. 1. ('gira' taken as m.) brought in the mountain (of Kubera); 2. [girvāṇa- 'delighting in invocations'] poet. m. god;

ताकौं भूलि कैसैंहूँ न बाँधियत बानो है।
डेल सो बनाय आन मेलत सभा के बीच, 4
लोगन कबित्त कीबो खेलकरि जानो है॥ N37॥

*बेदमत सुम्रत पुरानन पुरानन तें 1
हेम के हलास इतिहास परसत है।
सीलमय, सोभामय, रीतिमय, प्रीतिमय, 2

---

38 Bharatpur1 f. 157v-8r (48), Granthāvalī 199, Ṭhasak 185, Vrindaban1 f. 3v (4/17), Yājñik.

37.3 याकौ] **S**, याकी **E**I_e, यह ṬV_2 • कठिन बिचारि देषौ] **S**, बड़ी है कठिन बात] **E**I_e, काम सभ ही को नाह Ṭ, काम सब ही कौ नाहि V_2 • बिचारि] S_1, बिचार $S_2S_5S_7$ • ताको... बाँधियत] **ES**, मूड़ कहा जांनै कठन जांको Ṭ, जानत जिहांन हैं कठिनि यह V_2 • ताकौं] **S**, वाको **E**, याको I_e • भूलि कैसैं हूं न] **S**, नहीं भूलि कहूं **E**I_e • भूलि] $S_1S_2S_7$, भूल S_5 • कैसैंहूं] $S_1S_2S_7$, कैसहू S_5 **37.4** डेल] **E**$I_eS_1S_2S_7V_2$, डेलो S_5, ढेल Ṭ • सो] **E**$I_eS_1S_7$ṬV_2, स S_5, सौं S_2 • बनाय] Σ, बना कै V_2 • आन] S_1Ṭ, आय **E**$I_eS_2S_5S_7$, आनि V_2 • के] Σ, कैं V_2 • बीच] Σ, मद्ध Ṭ • लोगन] **E**$I_eS_1S_2S_5V_2$, लोकन S_7Ṭ • कबित्त] Σ, कबित Ṭ • कीबो] Σ, कैबौ V_2 • खेलकरि] $I_eS_1S_2S_5$Ṭ$_eV_2$, खेलकर G_e, हासी खेल S_7Ṭ • जानो] Σ, जान्यौ S_2 • है] Σ, हैं S_2 **38.1** सुम्रत] V_1, स्मृत (unm.) B_1, संमत **E**, सुम्र (unm.) Y_e • °न पुरानन] $B_1V_1Y_e$, उपुरानन Ṭ$_e$, °ऊ पुरानन G_e • तैं] $B_1V_1Y_e$, को **E** • हैंम के हलास] $B_1V_1Y_e$, संभु को बिलास **E** • हुलास] B_1, हलास V_1Y_e, बिलास **E** • इतिहास] B_1**E**, इतरास V_1Y_e • परसत] $B_1G_eY_e$, ⟨के⟩ परसत V_1, तरसत Ṭ$_e$ • है] Σ, हैं B_1

37.3 याकी (इसकी) var. pron. Br. its (of poetry); कठिन विचार [S] difficult idea. बांधना [bandhati] v.t. (Br. pass. used as active) to bind; to confine; बाना [varṇa-] m. manner, way; style. **37.4** डेल सो poet. like lumps (i.e. useless things); मेल- [melayati] Av. Br. v.t. to put in, to throw in; लोगन (लोगों ने) m. pl. obl./ag. people. खेलकरि (abs. used as a noun) m. playing, an easy task. **38.1** वेदमत 1. [S] m. 'the teachings of the Vedas', the Shruti; 2. (it is a smriti) according to Vedic teachings; सुम्रत (स्मृति) [S] f. the Smriti, secondary revelation; संमत var. [*sammata-, cf. sahamata-] poet. adj. agreeing; पुरानन पुरानन Br. poet. the old Puranas (the plural marker on both the adjective and the noun is ungrammatical); उपुरानन (उपपुराण) var. [S] poet. m. the 18 secondary Puranas; पुरानऊ पुरानन को var. Br. and also the Purana of the Puranas; तें (से) postp. Br. (is) more than; हेम kūṭ [S] m. (gold, S suvarṇa-) good letters, good writing; हलास 1. [cf. H hulasnā] m. deligh; 2. radiance (RSh); संभु को बिलास var. Br. (the story of) Shiva's sport; इतरास apa. परसत [parasatya-] poet. m. 1. supreme truth; 2. truth which is beyond; 3. [cf. sparśa-] Br. v.t. imperf. as soon as (history) touches it (it acquires the brilliance of gold).

नीति के प्रमानन प्रसिद्ध दरसत है।
3 ठाकुर कहत, धन्य तुलसी तिहारी बानी,
अकह कहानी रससानी सरसत है।
4 चंद सी, चमेली सी, प्रबाह गंगधार सम,
मघा मेघ भई रामजस बरसत है॥ N38॥

38.2 सीलमय सोभामय] B_1, सोभामई सीलमई **E**, मीलमय सोभामय V_1, सोभामय सील-मय Y_e • रीतिमय प्रीतिमय] $B_1V_1Y_e$, रीतिमई प्रीतिमई **E** • प्रसिद्ध] Σ, प्रसिद्धि B_1 • है] Σ, हैं B_1 **38.3** ठाकुर कहत] ठ° B_1 • धन्य] Σ, धन्नि B_1 • रससानी] B_1^{pc}**E**, रससनी B_1^{ac}, रसानी (haplography) V_1, रसानीर Y_e • सरसत] B_1**E**, सरसरसत (dittography) V_1 **38.4** चंद] Σ, चंद्र B_1 • प्रबाह] $B_1V_1Y_e$, गिरा सी **E** • °धार] **E**, धारा B_1V_1 • सम] $B_1V_1Y_e$, कैसी **E** • मेघ] Σ, मेह° Y_e • भई] B_1V_1, °मई **E**

38.2 शीलमय [S] adj. agreeing with moral principles; रीतिमय [S] adj. agreeing with the tradition (i.e. with the shastras); प्रसिद्ध [S] adj. 1. renowned, celebrated; 2. proved; नीति के प्रमानन प्रसिद्ध Br. 1. (exhibits) the well-known proofs of moral conduct (i.e. the nītigranthas) (KL); 2. (it appears) proved by the proofs of moral conduct (RSh); 3. it is celebrated because it shows the right conduct. **38.3** रस-साना [rasa-, H sānnā] adj. saturated by emotions. **38.4** चंद सी [candra-] m. (pure and bright) as the moon; चमेली सी [campavelli-] f. (bright) as jasmine; मघा [S] f. name of the tenth lunar asterism (in which rains are the most beneficient).

संदिग्ध कबित्त
Quatrains of uncertain authorship

करीस सो पील देख पीठ पानीपत देत 1
...दिल्ली डरात है।
कालपी कनार कंच कनवज लौ हुरदंग 2
सबलगढ़ साहन सतारी लों सतात है।
आगरो नजीमगढ़ मेरठ मस्तुलाबाद 3
तेरी धाक सुन कलकत्ता भय खात है।
राजन कौ राज भूप पारीछत महाराज 4
हिन्दुवान राज तेरे हाथ ही दिखात है॥ U1॥

गैल में छैल कढ़ै जितही तहि बंसी बजावत ही यह टेक है।
गेह सों नेह भरी कढै कामिनी दामिनी सी छुटि जात बिवेक है। 2
देखती वे खनि खेल न लावति लेखती या जग ठाकुर एक है।

---

1 Barsãiyā p. 26. Dr. Gangaprasad Barsaiya collected this quatrain from an elderly pandit in Jaitpur (Jaitwara) claiming it to have been written by Ṭhākur in praise of his patron, Rājā Parīkṣit (d. 1842) of Jaitpur. 2 Sundarī-tilak (C_e) p. 18 (104). The word 'ṭhākura' in the third line can be the poet's signature since words like 'prītama' or mohana' would have been more natural in this context.

1.1 करीस सो पील] *conj.* करी सपील (unm.) B_e • देत] *conj.* देश B_e • डरात] *conj.* दरात B_e **1.2** हुरदंग] (unm.) B_e • सबलगढ़] (unm.) B_e **1.3** तेरी] *conj.* तेरो B_e

---

1.1 करीश [S] m. king of elephants; पील [P] m. elephant; सपील (स-पालवान) adj. together with its mahaut; पीठ देना idiom. to run away; देश apa. [S] m. country. **1.2** कालपी N. of a town near Kanpur; कनार (कन्नड) reg. m. Karnataka; कंच (कांचि) reg. m. Kanchipuram; कनवज [kānyakubja-] reg. m. Kannauj; हुड़दंग [H hūṛ, daṅgā-] m. commotion; सबलगढ़ m. N. of a town in the Dekkan; सतारी (सितारा) N. of Śivajī's capital; सतात है v.t. imperf. Br. (you) torture. **1.3** नजीमगढ़ m. (Name of a place); मस्तुलाबाद m. (Name of a place); धाक [*dhākka-] f. 1. fame; 2. awe, dread. **1.4** हिन्दुवन राज Br. the kingdom of the Hindus. **2.1** गैल [cf. gati-] Br. f. lane; जितही Br. adv. wherever; तहि (वहाँ) reg. adv. there; बंसी बजावत ही Br. he does play his flute. टेक [cf. H ṭeknā] f. 1. sthg on which one insist; 2. habit (RSh). **2.2** दामिनी सी poet. (the woman appeared fast) like lightning. **2.3** खनि (क्षण) [S] Br. m. (obl.) (not even) for a moment; खेल न लावति Br. she does not indulge in (other) sports; लेख- Br. v.t. to consider;

4 होति निहाल महा सो बड़ी अँखियान सों जाहि निहारत नेक है॥ U2॥

1 तेरे द्रग तीच्छन हैं, तीच्छन कटाच्छ करैं,
अधिक अदां के ये सदां के जंग जोर है।
2 अंजन के हीन ह्वैकै रंजन करै है चित्त,
खंजन गुन गंजन कटारि है कि कोर है।
3 धाय कै करै हैं घाय, चाहि कै चलाय सेंन,
घूंघट की ओट चोट काजै ढुके दोर है।
4 खड्ग है कि खंजर है, तीर है कि सेल सांगि,
ठगि है कि ठाकुर, डकैति है कि चोर है॥ U3॥

धनि हैं तुव तात औ मात जनी, जिहि देह धरी सु घरी धनि है।

3 Bharatpur4 f. 15v. The word Ṭhākur does not appear in the usual position at the beginning of the third line and it is uncertain whether it is a poetic signature or not. 4 Bharatpur1 f. 154v (31), Barasaiya (B_e) p. 26, Jaipur1 f. 1r (1), Marwar3 f. 1r (1) and Marwar3vl f. 1r (2), Marwar5 f. 32v (5), Marwar6 f. 35v (17), Rasikvinod (O_e) pp. 147–8 (691), Ṭhākur-satsaī (Ṭ) ff. 1v-2r (11b), Udaipur f. 126r (7), Hāfizullah Khān: Hazārā (X_e) p. 448 (Siṃhāvalokan 30). Manuscripts B_1, M_3, M_6, Ṭ and U present the second and the third lines in the reverse order.

3.1 करैं] *conj.* करै B_4 • अदा] *conj.* अदां B_4 **3.2** ह्वैकै] *em.* हैकै B_4 **3.3** ढुके] *conj.* ⟨ढु⟩के B_4 **3.4** खड्ग] B_4^{pc}, खड्ग⟨ए⟩ B_4^{ac} **4.1** धनि] $B_1J_1O_eX_e$, धन $B_eM_3^{vl}M_5$ṬU, धिन M_3M_6 • हैं तुव] B_1, वै जिहि X_e, वे (unm.) B_e, है वह J_1, हे अरु M_3, है जीये M_3^{vl}, री वहे M_5, है जिन M_6, हैं उन O_e, *om.* ṬU • तात] Σ, मात M_3M_5 • औ] $B_1J_1X_e$, अरु (unm.) B_e, रू $M_3M_3^{vl}$, सो M_5, र M_6, जे O_e, °ह Ṭ, वहै जिह U • मात] Σ, तात M_3M_5 • जनी] $B_1J_1M_3M_3^{vl}M_5M_6O_e$ṬU, जनौ B_eX_e • जिहिं] $B_1B_eX_e$, यह J_1, धिन M_3M_6, धन M_5, जीये M_3^{vl}, जब O_e, जिनही जिह Ṭ, जिह U • देह धरी] $B_1B_eJ_1M_3M_5M_6$ṬUX_e, देह घरी M_3^{vl}, जन्म लियो O_e • सु] $B_1M_3^{vl}M_6$ṬU, सो $B_eJ_1M_3M_5X_eO_e$ • घरी] Σ, धरी B_e, धनी M_5 • धनि] $B_1J_1O_eX_e$, धन $B_eM_3^{vl}M_5$ṬU, धिन M_3M_6 • है] Σ, हैं O_e

2.4 निहाल adj. gratified, happy; होति ... सो Br. that (woman) becomes very happy; नेक [? na + eka-] Br. adv. (even) a little, just; जाहि ... है Br. on whom (Krihna) casts even his slightest glance. **3.1** अदा [A] f. flirtatious gestures; अधिक अदा के of many flirtatious gestures; **3.2** गंजन [S] m. 'destruction for' destroyer; कटारी [*karttāra-] f. small dagger; कोर [koṭi-] f. tip, edge (of the eye). **3.3** चाहि कै Br. v.t. abs. looking; सैन [saṃjñā-] Br. f. sign, signal; घूंघट की ओट (obl.) from behind the veil; काजै [kārya-] postp. Br. for; ढुक- [*ḍhukyati] Av. Br. v.t. to hide in wait; ढुके दौर है Br. they hide in wait and then run (to attack). **3.4** सेल [S] m. spear, javelin; सांगि [? śaṅku-] f. spear. **4.1** जनना [janayati] v.t. 1. to give birth to, 2. to beget; उन तात जे मात जनी apa; तातह मात जनी apa; देह [S] f. m. body; घड़ी [ghaṭikā-] f. moment.

धनि हैं जेहि ठाकुर धाम बसौ, जहँ डोलो, लली, सो गली धनि है।
धनि हैं दृग जेउ तुमै दरसैं, परसैं कर तेउ महा धनि है।
धनि है, धनि तू, धनि तेरो हितू, जिहिं की धन तू सो धनी धनि हैं॥ U4

4.2 धनि] $B_1J_1O_eX_e$, *om.* B_1, धन $B_eM_3^{vl}M_5$ṬU, धिन M_3M_6 • हैं जेहि] O_e, *om.* B_1, है कवि $B_eJ_1M_3UX_e$, री कवी M_5, है कव M_6Ṭ • धाम] $B_1B_eJ_1M_3M_5M_6$ṬU, धा⟨म⟩स X_e, ग्राम O_e • बसौ] O_e, *om.* B_1, वहीं B_eX_e, बड़े J_1, वोंही M_3, ऊहां M_3^{vl}, वहे M_5, उहि M_6, वहै ṬU • जहँ] J_1U, जहां सए जिहि (unm.) B_1^{ac}, जहां सबए जिहि (unm.) B_1^{pc}, जंह B_eO_e, जांहां M_3, सो M_3^{vl}, जहे M_5, जिन M_6, जहां X_e, जिह Ṭ • डोलो] O_e, डोलैं B_1U, डोल B_e, डोलै $J_1M_3M_5M_6$ṬX_e, डोलत M_3^{vl} • लली] Σ, अली B_1, गली M_3 • सो] $B_1B_eM_3O_eX_e$, सु $J_1M_3^{vl}M_5M_6$Ṭ, स॰ U • गली] Σ, गलि M_6 • धनि] $B_1J_1O_eX_e$, धन $B_eM_3^{vl}M_5$ṬU, धिन M_3, धीन M_6 **4.3** धनि हैं] $B_1J_1O_e$, धन है B_eM_3ṬU, धिन हे M_3M_6, धन री वहे M_5, धनि है X_e • दृग जेउ] O_e, दृग वे जु B_1, जो तुम्है B_e, दृग तेवै J_1, दृग वे स M_3, द्रग सु सो M_3^{vl}, जो द्रि⟨से⟩ M_5^{ac}, जो द्रिग से M_5, द्रग⟨न्वै सो⟩ M_6, द्रिग वै जु Ṭ, द्रग तेरे U, उनको जो X_e • तुमैं] B_1O_e, दरसै B_e, दरसें J_1, तुंहीं M_3Ṭ, तो ये M_3^{vl}, *om.* M_5, तो प M_6, तुही U, तुम्हैं X_e • दरसैं] $B_1O_eX_e$U, हरसै B_e, दरसें J_1, दरसे $M_3M_3^{vl}M_5M_6$Ṭ • परसैं] B_1O_eU, परसै $B_eM_3^{vl}M_6$Ṭ, परसे J_1M_5, कर से M_3, कर सों X_e • कर] $B_1B_eJ_1M_3M_5M_6O_e$ṬU, पर M_3, परसैं X_e • तेउ] O_e, सैं सु B_1, से सो B_e, तेवै J_1, बेस M_3U, सुं सो M_3^{vl}, सुं जो M_5, ⟨न्वै⟩ सो M_6, वे जु Ṭ, सो X_e • महा] Σ, बड़े O_e, माहा M_6 • धनि] $B_1J_1O_eX_e$, धन $B_eM_3^{vl}$ṬU, धिन M_3M_6 • है] Σ, हैं B_1O_e **4.4** धनि है] J_1, *om.* B_1, धन मैं B_e, धिन हे M_3M_6, धन री $M_3^{vl}M_5$, धनि हौ O_e, धनि मैं X_e, धन है Ṭ, धन है कब ठाकुर (eyeskip) U • धनि] $B_1J_1O_eX_e$, धन $B_eM_3^{vl}M_5M_6$ṬU, धिन M_3, ⟨धी⟩न M_6 • तू] $B_1B_eJ_1O_e$ṬUX_e, तो M_3M_6, तुं $M_3^{vl}M_5$, ⟨वै⟩ M_6 • धनि] $B_1J_1O_eX_e$, धन $B_eM_3^{vl}M_5$ṬU, धिन M_3 • तेरो] $B_1B_eJ_1O_e$UX_e, तोय M_3, तोप M_6, तिहारो M_3^{vl}, तेरी M_5Ṭ • हितू] U^{pc}Σ, हितू सजनी B_1, भटु M_5, हीतुं M_6, हीतू U^{ac} • जिहि की] B_1J_1, धना B_e, जिनके M_3, जिन की $M_3^{vl}M_5O_e$, जीन⟨के⟩ M_6, जिह की ṬU, अरु जाकी X_e • धन तू] J_1U, तू धनी B_1, जाकी हो B_e, धिन तुं M_3, तुं बधू M_3^{vl}, धीन तु M_6^{ac}, धन तुं $M_5M_6^{pc}$, धन हौ O_e, धन है Ṭ, धना X_e • सो] $B_1B_eJ_1M_3M_3^{vl}M_5M_6O_eX_e$, सु Ṭ, ज×ध× (dittography) U • धनी] Σ, धन ही (unm.) B_e • धनि] $B_1J_1O_eX_e$, धन $B_eM_3^{vl}M_5$ṬU, धिन M_3, धीन M_6 • है] Σ, हैं O_e

---

4.2 जेहि ठाकुर धाम the house of the lord in which; डोलना v.i. 1. to swing, 2. to move about; लली [lala-] f. girl. **4.3** जेउ (जो भी) pron. reg. whichever; दरस- v.t. [darśati] Br. to see; कर [S] m. hand. **4.4** हितू [cf. hita-] m. friend; धन [dhanikā-] Br. f. young woman, beloved; धनी [S, cf. dhanya-] m. husband.

सखि, आई है मोह मनावन को कहा, मोह को और-सी तैं परमानी।
वे अपने घर के जिम ठाकुर मै अपने घर की ठकुरानी।
जो जिय माँह भई सो गई, कहा होत सखी तू जान अजानी।
जाहु जू जाहु, कहा नही मानत का, जू, मै काहू के हाथ बिकानी॥ U5॥

कान्ह, सुनी, अहो राजा भए, नित नेह की नीति बिचारत औडी।
प्रीति करी पुर-नारिन सौं, ब्रजनारि गंवारिन जानि कैं भौडी।
ऊधौ, महा कपटी वह ढीठ, हमैं कियौ चाहत प्रेम-कनौडी।

---

5 Ṭhākur-satsaī f. 1r (2) (Ṭ). This poem is included into a collection of Thakur's quatrains, The word 'ṭhākur', however, may have been mistakenly perceived as a signature. (The compiler of the Satsaī was not strict in his selection since he also included a savaiyā by Raskhān.) Yet, there is no other signature in the poem and some other poems where his signature is used as a meaningful part of a sentence (mudrā alaṅkāra) have been accepted as Ṭhākur's by early and modern editors. CITE EXAMPLES Gr131! The use of two idiomatic expressions in the last line strongly suggest his authorship. 6 Sudhāsar [S_1 f. 295r (20), S_2 f. 59v (65), S_3 f. 167r (226), S_4 f. 94v (239), S_7 f. 206v (74)]. This poem does not bear Ṭhākur's signature but some manuscripts ($S_3S_4S_7$) introduce it as a poem by Ṭhākur. The style with the sharp words of the cowherd women and the use of a strong idiom at the end would confirm this attribution. However, the manuscript representing the earliest version of the anthology (S_1) as well as S_5 (not collated here) attribute this poem to Ṭhākurdās. The poem is given within the description of 'Braj mahimā'.

5.1 सखि] *conj.* सख Ṭ **5.3** जिय] *conj.* जीअ Ṭ **6.1** कान्ह] S_1S_2, कान S_3S_7, कांनु S_4 • भए] **S**, भयौ S_1 • नीति] S_2S_3, नैति S_1, नीत S_4S_7 • बिचारत] **S**, बिचारति S_3 **6.2** प्रीति] $S_1S_2S_3$, प्रीत S_4S_7 • नारिन] **S**, नारिना (unm.) S_2 • गंवारिन] $S_1S_2S_3$, गमारग S_4, गमारनि S_7 • जानि] $S_1S_2S_4$, जान S_3S_7 • भौडी] **S**, मौडी S_2 **6.3** वह] **S**, वहि S_7 • ढीठ] **S**, ढी⟨ढ़⟩ S_2

5.1 मोह (मुझ) Br. obl. (me); परमानी (प्रमान की) [cf. pramāṇa-] Br. v.t. perf. 'accept (as authentic)' to consider; मोह को… परमानी Br. you considered me something else. **5.3** जान (जान-बूझकर) v.t. (abs.) on purpose; जान अजानी Br. 1. (why do you) pretend to be ignorant? 2. even if you are intelligent (why have you become) unaware (of it). **5.4** का (क्यों) Br. interr. why? कहा नहीं मानत का Br. why don't you mind what I said? मैं काहू के हाथ बिकानी Br. am I under the power of someone? **6.1** सुनी [śṛṇoti] v.t. perf. I heard this matter (i.e. bāt sunī); औडी adv. in a twisted, crooked or unfavourable way. **6.2** गंवारिन [cf. H gaṃvār] f. 'village woman' uncouth or ignorant woman; भोंडा [*bhoṇḍa-] adj. 1. ugly; 2. uncouth. मौडी var. [H moḍā, ad. ? *moḍḍa-] Bund. f. girl, lass; **6.3** कपटी वह ढीठ poet. he is cunning and insolent; प्रेम-कनौडी poet. grateful for his love.

राज कौं पाय निलाज नैं कैसी दई अब लंगर लौडि की डौडी॥ U6॥ 4

गाइयै सुजस बिसराइयै कुजस धर 1
धाइयै सदाई सतसंग सुषकारी कौं।
कीजियै भलाई तजि दीजियै बुराई जग 2
जीजियै जिहान मैं जपत बनबारी कौं।
ऐंठियै अरी कौं पुनि पैठियै प्रबीन पैंठ 3
बैठियै सुठांम ठीक ठाकुर उचारी कौं।
खोदियै तलाव कूआ बावरी बसुंधरा पै 4
चोदियै जरूर ही कुपंच की कुवारी कौं॥ U7॥

रूसनहारी घनेरी हुती, पै कहां लग रावरी कीजै बडाई।

7 Bharatpur1 ff. 133r (13). The style of this kavitt is different from that of the other poems although the last line is reminiscent of the indecent ending of some other verses. The poem is included into a sequence of Ṭhākur's quatrains in the manuscript. 8 DAV 1580 f. 48r (P), Sudhāsar [S_1 f. 98r (35), S_2 f. 21v (3/28), S_7 f. 67r (7/668)]. This savaiyā is included into the 'māninī' (woman with wounded pride) section of the Sudhāsar. Although it does not have a signature it is attributed to Ṭhākur in the S_2 and S_7 manuscripts. It is also present in the other Sudhāsar manuscripts without attribution, where it is introduced as 'benisān' (without signature). The attribution of S_2 may rather refer to savaiyā Ś108 'yaha komala ka.mja sau a.mga...', which the scribe apparently started to copy and then merged it into this poem. Since the DAV collection contains no other poem by Ṭhākur and all the other poets included into it lived earlier than Ṭhākur, it is likely that the collection itself predates Ṭhākur and thus this savaiyā was written by someone else. The word play with the idiom in the fourth line may have reinforced the attribution of S_2 and S_7.

6.4 डौडी] **S**, लौडी (dittography) S_4 **8.1** रूसनहारी] PS_1S_7, यह कं सौ कोम रूमनहारी (unm.) S_2 • हुती] S_1S_7, लषी P, हतीS_2 • लग] **S**, कहि P

6.4 राज [rājya-] m. kingship; निलाज [nirlajja-] adj. shameless; लंगर adj. poet. 1. mischievous; 2. brash; लौंडी [*lavaṇḍa-] f. 1. (servant) girl, 2. promiscuous woman; डौंडी [ḍiṇḍima] f. small kettledrum; डौडी देना idiom. 'to beat a drum' to proclaim. **7.3** ऐंठना [āveṣṭ(y)ate] v.t. 1. to twist; 2. to squeeze; 3. (here:) to trouble; पैंठ [pratiṣṭā-] f. shop, stall; पैठियै प्रबीन पैंठ poet. enter into the shops of the skilled ones; उचारी (उच्चारित की) [uccārayati] v.t. perf. (f. used as m.) as indicated; ठीक ठाकुर उचारी कौं poet. exactly as the Lord (Ṭhākur) indicated. **7.4** चोदना [*coddati] v.t. to have sexual intercourse with; कुपंच [S] m. 1. bad arbitrator; 2. bad person. **8.1** रूसना [ruṣyati] v.i. 1. to sulk; 2. to quarrel; घनेर- [*ghanatara-] Av. Br. adj. many, much; बडाई f. praise.

2 रूसे समै पिय के जिय की, तिय, काहू नै या बिधि पीर न पाई।
रीझी हौं तेरी या बूझणि ऊपर, तेरी सौं, तैं बहुतै हौं रिझाई।
4 भांवतौ भोर कौ भूखौ हुतौ, तैं भली करी, नेक हहा तौ खवाई॥ U8॥

दान दया बिन दीबो कहा, अरु लीबो कहा जब आपु तें माँगो।
2 प्रान गए रस पीबो कहा, पग छीबो कहा उर प्रेम न जागो।
नारि कहा जेहि लाज तजी, गुरु कीबो कहा भ्रम दूरि न भागो।
4 वा जग में फिर जीबो कहा, जब आँगुरी लोग उठावन लागो॥ U9॥

कूट कबित्त

1 हरि हित नामै ये वचन सुनि मोहन के
दस रस भूषन सँवारि चलु गेहरी।
2 सुर-अरि-गुरुवर-वाहन के अरि अरि

9 Granthāvalī 178, Ṭhasak 149. Ṭhākur's poetic signature is missing from this poem. The worthlessness of a shameless woman in the third line contradicts Ṭhākur's other poems. The last line with an idiom about slander may have caused this savaiyā to be linked to Ṭhākur.
10 The following six poems are all found in Dr. Hiralal: Twelveth Report (1923-5) (S_e), p. 1471 (426), place of deposit: Ṭhākura Naunihāla Simha (descendant of Śivsiṃh Seṅgar), Kānthā, Unāo Distr. (VS 1842).

8.2 रूसे] **S**, रोस P • समै] **S**, समें P • के] PS_1S_2, की S_7 • तिय काहू नै] **S**, अब P • या] PS_1S_7, ⟨पा⟩ S_2 • बिधि] PS_2, बिध S_1S_7 • पीर] **S**, काहू की पीर P **8.3** रीझी] **S**, तेरी P • तेरी या] **S**, पावति P • बूझनि] S_2, बूझन PS_1S_7 • तें] PS_1, तै S_2S_7 **8.4** भोर] **S**, तेरो हे भोर P • हुतो तैं] S_1S_7, हतौ तै S_2, *om.* P • करी] **S**, भई P • नेक] $S_2S_7^{ac}$, नेह S_7^{pc}, नैंकु S_1P • हहा] $S_1S_2S_7^{ac}$, कहा S_7^{pc}, हाहा P

8.2 तिय काहू नै reg. 1. o woman, nobody... 2. no woman... **8.3** बूझनि Br. f. understanding; तैं हौं रिझाई Br. you pleased me. **8.4** भांवतौ Br. m. beloved; भोर कौ Br. from the morning; नेक [na + eka-] Br. adj. a little; हहा खाना idiom. to beg, to entreat. **9.1** आपु तें pron. 1. by himself (H apne se); 2. from you (i.e. God) (H āp se); माँगो [mārgati] v.t. perf. Br. asked. **9.2** छी- (छूना) [chupati x ? kṣipati] Bund. v.t. to touch. **9.4** वा adj. such; उंगली उठाना idiom. to slander; लागो [Br. perf. lāge distorted for the sake of rhyme] v.i. perf. Br. (people) started. **10.1** हरि हित नामै (kūṭ) the name of God's friend, Sugrīva 'of beautiful neck or throat'; (hearing these words from Mohan's) beautiful throat; रस [S] m. (kūṭ) six; दस रस num. (kūṭ) 'ten plus six (rasas)' sixteeen; गेहरी [gṛha-] reg. m. home.

ता पत पिता कों रिपु दाहत है देहरी।
कैसे मन कैसे लगै अजहू यो मानतु प्यारो 3
बेगिही सिधारौ को करौ ना मनु नेह, री।
दई सेंवरी होती वाम की कुमारी 4
आज कूं सो छबि वानवै वर देह, री॥ 1॥ U10॥

अजौं चलु प्यारो तोहि तातैं बोलैं खगपति- 1
पति कै बियोग भौन तेरे मैं जु आई री।
दादुर के रिपु, ताको पति, ताको तात, वाको 2
अरि कारने निहोरि हौं पठाई री।
रविसुत-रिपु, ताके पतिय गोपाल लाल, 3
ताके सुत सुत की घरनि होति, माई री।

---

11 The poem describes the words of a messenger.

10.3 यो मानतु] (unm.) S_e • वेगिही] *conj.* वेगिहो S_e • मनु] *conj.* नमु S_e **10.4** दई सेंवरी] (unm.) S_e **11.1** पति] *em.* पतिय (unm.) S_e • कै] *em.* कई (unm.) S_e • भौन] *conj.* मौन S_e **11.2** ताको तात] *conj.* वाको तात S_e **11.3** सुत की] *conj.* सुत को S_e

---

10.2 सुर-अरि (असुर) m. pl. (kūṭ) 'enemies of the gods' the Asuras; (असुर का) गुरुवर (शुक्र) m. (kūṭ) 'the great guru of the Asuras', Śukra; (शुक्र का) वाहन (दादुर) m. (kūṭ) the vehicle of Śukra, frog; (दादुर का) अरि (साँप) m. (kūṭ) the enemy of frog, snake; (साँप का) अरि (मोर) m. (kūṭ) the enemy of the snake, peacock; (मोर का) पति (कार्तिकेय) m. (kūṭ) the lord of the peacock, Kārtikeya; (कार्तिकेय का) पिता (शिव) m. (kūṭ) Kārtikeya's father, Shiva; (शिव का) रिपु (कामदेव) [S] m. (kūṭ) 'enemy of Shiva' Kamadeva, Love. **10.3** कैसे... प्यारो (?) यो मानतु (ऐसे मानते हुए) (?) बेगिही [vega-] Br. adv. quickly; **10.4** सेंवरी (सेमल) [śaimbala-] reg. f. 1. the silk-cotton tree; 2. a kind of sweetmeat; वाम (?) [S] adj. left; Shiva; वानवै (?) **11.1** अजौं (आज ही) Br. adv. right now; तातैं poet. adv. quickly (KL); बोल- (बुलाना) Br. v.t. (pres.-subj.) to call; खगपति (गरुड) [S] m. (kūṭ) 'the lord of the birds' Garuḍa; खगपति-पति (कृष्ण) [S] m. (kūṭ) 'Garuḍa's lord', 'Vishnu' Krishna. **11.2** दादुर के रिपु (साँप) (kūṭ) 'the enemy of the frogs' snake; ताको पति (बलदेव) (kūṭ) 'its lord' Baladeva; ताको तात (कंस) (kūṭ) 'his uncle' Kansa; वाको अरि (कृष्ण) (kūṭ) 'his enemy' Krishna; कारने [kāraṇa-] adv. 1. because of, 2. for the sake of; निहोर- Br. v.t. to beseech; हौं पठाई Br. I was sent. **11.3** रविसुत (कर्ण) [S] m. (kūṭ) 'the son of the Son-god' Karṇa; रविसुत-रिपु (अर्जुन) [S] m. (kūṭ) 'Karṇa's enemy' Arjuna; ताके पतिय (कृष्ण) (kūṭ) 'his lord' Krishna; ताके सुत (प्रद्युम्न) (kūṭ) 'Krishna's son' Pradyumna; सुत (अनिरुद्ध) [S] m. (kūṭ) '(Pradyumna's) son' Aniruddha; घरनि (ऊषा) [cf. H gharvālī] Br. f. '(Aniruddha's) wife' Ūṣā (i.e. dawn).

अब को हौं आई, मोहि दीजिये विराट-सुत
तारो मुख इंदु-रिपु जोहत कन्हाई री॥ 2॥ U11॥

अंबु-तनै-हित नेक रह्यौ, तब तें तुम्हरे ढिंग बैठी कुमारी।
वारुनी श्रौन-पितू दृग जाम गई निसि भौन फिरी अभिसारी।
तो बसु भूप दिसान दई, खगपाधिप की जननी करि हारी।
जोह न ऐन, सरोरुह-नैन, चलौ, मघवा रिपु जाहुँ तिहारी॥ 3॥ U12॥

...

पास अहार जो सिंह मरै, कबहूं न मरै खर के वह खाये।
कागद धूप दिखाये गरै, कबहूं न गलै जल मांहि सडाये।
निसि आये से चंद मलीन लगै, कबहूं न मलीन लगै दिन आये।
मानुष सुधारस पीये मरै, कबहूं न मरै विष के वह खाये॥ 7॥ U13॥

मीन मरै जल के परसे, कबहूं न मरै वह पावक लाये।

14 The first line is identical with the second line of Hāfizullah Khān: Hazārā (X_e) 'gūḍh arthvāle chand' 20 (p. 614 in Dikshit's edn).)

11.4 अब] *conj.* कब **12.2** पितू] *em.* पितु (unm.) S_e **12.4** जोह न] *conj.* जोहन S_e

11.4 अब को adv. now; विराट-सुत (उत्तर) [S] m. (kūṭ) 'Virāṭa's son' Uttara (i.e. answer); तारो (तेरा) pron. reg. your; इंदु-रिपु (कमल) [S] m. (kūṭ) 'the enemy of the moon' lotus (which closes down at night); इंदु-रिपु (राहु) [S] m. (kūṭ) 'the enemy of the moon' Rahu; Br. rāhu way, coming. **12.1** अंबु-तनै (अंबुज) (kūṭ) 'born of water' lotus; अंबु-तनै-हित (दिन) (kūṭ) 'the friend of the lotus' daylight; नैक [na eka-] Br. adv. little; अंबु... रह्यौ Br. (since) daylight decreased; ढिग [*ḍhigga-] postp. Br. near. **12.2** वारुणी [S] poet. f. west; श्रौन-पितु (कर्ण का पिता) m. (kūṭ) 'Karṇa's father' the sun; दृग (दो) [S] poet. m. (kūṭ) 'eyes' the number two; दृग-याम (दोपहर) [S] poet. m. two watches (i.e. midnight); वारुनी... जाम Br. two watches after the sun set in the west; गई निसि Br. (late) at night. **12.3** तो... दई Br. the lord entruted to your power the ten directions (i.e. his ten senses); खगपाधिप (गरुड का अधिपति) [S] m. (kūṭ) 'the lord of the birds' lord', 'the lord of Garuḍa', 'Vishnu', Krishna; जननी (विनती) [S] f. (kūṭ) '(his) mother, Vinatā' vinatī (i.e. entreaty); खग°... हारी Br. I am exhausted entreating you. **12.4** ऐन (अयन) 1. [S] m. way; (2. [A] f. eye); जोह न ऐन idiom. Br. do not wait for her; सरोरुह-नैन (कृष्ण) [S] m. voc. poet. 'lotus-eyed one' Krishna; मघवा-रिपु (बलि) [S] m. 'Indra's enemy' Bali (i.e. sacrifice); मघवा... तिहारी Br. 'I sacrifice myself for you' I beg you. **13.1** अहार [āhāra-] Av. Br. m. food; खर [khaṭa-] reg. m. grass, straw. **13.2** गर- (गलना) [galati] Br. v.i. to dissolve; सडाना [śaṭati] v.caus. to allow to rot. **14.1** जल के परसे by touching water; पावक [S] m. fire.

फूल जू फूलै सिला महं, कंज कबौ नहिं फूलै तडाग लगाये।
बोलत सर्द में कोकिल है, कबहूं नहि बोलै बसंत के आये।
दोषा प्रकास करिअ दिन में, कबहू न प्रकास करै निसि आये॥ 8॥ U14॥

दादुर ग्रीषम बोलै, कहूं नहिं बोलत हैं बरषा रितु आये।
भानुहि राहु गहै, कबहूं नहिं घेरत है निज अवसर पाये।
भोजन खाये ते जीव मरै, कबहूं न मरै बिन अन्नहिं खाये।
ठाकुर चंद पताल उवै, कबहूं न उवै जु अकासहिं ठाये॥ 9॥ U15॥

15.2 **है**] *em.* *om.* S_e **15.4**]

14.4 **दोषा** [S] f. night. **15.2** **भानु** [S] poet. m. sun; **निज अवसर पाये** Br. when it has its proper opportunity (i.e. at the constellation expected). **15.4** **उव-** [udgāti, H ugnā] Br. v.i. (pres.) to rise; **ठा-** [cf. sthā-] Br. v.i. (perf. used as imperf.) stay.

प्रकीर्णक

Miscellanea

1. Ṭhākur-related samasyāpūrti

धनि वे जिन प्रेम समे पिय के उर में रस-बीजन बोवती हैं।
धनि वे जिन पावस में पिसि कै मेंहदी कर-कंज मलोवती हैं।
धनि वे जिन सूरति साजि सजैं, हम लाज के बोझ कों ढोवती हैं।
धनि वे धनि सावन की रतियाँ पति की छतियाँ लगि सोवती हैं॥ M1॥

निज नैनन को बरषा बरषा तरसा तन आंसुन धोवती हैं।
कहुँ रामचरित्र न रोवति हैं, दिल की दिल ही बिच गोवती हैं।
हम तो नित पावस की निशि में, सखि, सूनी ही सेज टटोवती हैं।
धनि वे धनि पावस की रतियाँ पति की छतियाँ लगि सोवती हैं॥ M2॥

धनि वे जिन पावस की रितु में नित प्रीति में प्रीति सँजोवती हैं।
धनि वे जिन कारी घटा में अटा बिच बिज्जु छटा छबि छोवती हैं।

---

1 This is a poem by Sūrati (? Sūrati Miśra, fl. VS 1766-1800) published in Rasikvinod p. 76 (356), in Mital 1961 p. 134 (208) and in Hāfizullah Khān: Hazārā (X_e) (Pāvas ṛtu 38, Dikshit 2006, p. 443). The last line is shared with Ṭhākur B49. 2 This is a poem by Rāmcaritra published in Rasikvinod p. 76 (355) and in Hāfizullah Khān: Hazārā (X_e) (Pāvas ṛtu 37, Dikshit 2006, p. 443). The last line is shared with Ṭhākur B49. 3 This is a poem by Rāmcaritra published in Rasikvinod p. 76 (357), Mital 1961 p. 134 (209) and in Hāfizullah Khān: Hazārā (X_e) (Pāvas ṛtu 39, Dikshit 2006, p. 443). The last line is shared with Ṭhākur B49.

1.3 सूरति] O_e, सूरत M_e

1.2 मलोना (मलवाना) [*malati] v. caus. poet. to cause to be rubbed. **1.3** सूरत 1. [A ṣūra] Br. form, appearance, face; 2. [cf. smṛti-] f. remembrance; साज [sajya-, sajjā-] f. (obl.) (with) decoration; सजना [cf. sajjayati] v.i. to be adorned; ढोना [ḍhaukayati] v.t. 'to carry' to bear (as suffering). **2.1** बरषा बरषा (वर्षा बरसकर) poet. raining. **2.2** कहुँ (कहीं) poet. adv. somehow; दिल की दिल m. (here f.) obl. in the heart of her heart; बिच (बीच) [vīcya-] postp. reg. in; गो(व)- [gupta-] Br. v.t. to hide. **2.3** टटोना (टटोलना) v.t. to grope. **3.1** सँजोना [saṃyojayati] v.t. 1. to lay out (as things on a tray); 2. to decorate. **3.2** कार- (काला) [kāla-] Br. adj. black; छटा[S] f. brilliance (of the lightning); छो- (छूना) [chupati] reg. v.t. to touch; छोह- [cf. kṣobha-] Br. v.i. to feel affection for (to be moved by).

धनि वे जिन रामचरित्र हियैं हिलि हौंसन हर्षित होवती हैं।
धनि वे धनि पावस की रतियाँ पति की छतियाँ लगि सोवती हैं॥ M3॥

हम सै तो बनी बिगरी, हरसै, तुमकौ परी बात चलायबे मै।
हम तौ अपनौ मन मार लयौ, तुमै का मिल झूठि मिलायबे मै।
उत लाडलौ कूबरी संग रमौ, वह जानती खूब रिझायबे मै।
तुम सै इह बात सै काम कहा बुनबे मै न बीन बजाइबे मै॥ M4॥

जा दिन ते परदेस गये पिय ता दिन ते तन छीजतु है।
निसिवासर भौन सुहात नहीं, सुध आये उसासन लीजतु है।
अब और उपाय बनै न कछू अनुभौ इतनो सुख कीजतु है।
उन प्यारे पिय की उन्हारी, सखी, ननदी मुख देखिकै जीजतु है॥ M5॥

कंज मरै रबि के दरसे कब हूँ न मरै वह चंद्र दिखाये।
मीन मरै जल के परसे, कबहूं न मरै वह पावक पाये।
नारि मरै पिय के दरसे कबहूँ न मरै परदेस सुनाये।
संत जो पाप करैं तो तरैं कबहूँ न तरैं हरि के गुन गाये॥ M6॥

राति द्यौस हाजर हुकमहूं न लोपैं कोपे
बिन काम और औगुन गहा करैं।

---

4 Allahabad2 (I_2) f. 40(2)rv (5). The last line is similar to Ṭhākur Ś133 and Ś134. 5 M_4 f. 44v and B. Dikshit, ed. Prayāganārāyaṇ-vilās, Lucknow: Navalkiśor Press, p. 40. The last line is shared with Ś 84. 6 Hāfizullah Khān: Hazārā (X_e) (Dikshit p. 614) (Gūṛh arthvāle chand 20). Cf Kūṭ kabitt 7-9. The second line is shared with U14 (Kūṭ kabitt 8a, S_e). 7 M_4 f. 46r. The phrase 'ṭhākura pai cākara' in the last line is shared with N25. This may be a coincidence rather than a samasyāpūrti.

3.3 हर्षित] O_e, हरषित (unm.) M_e **4.3** उत] *conj.* *om.* (unm.) I_2 • वह] *conj.* वे (unm.) I_2 **4.4** इह] *conj.* या (unm.) I_2 **6.2** पाये] X_e, लाये S_e

---

3.3 हिलना [*hillati] v.i. (reg. abs.) to be close to; हौंसन [A havas] f. (Br. pl. obl.) (with) desire; हर्षित [S] poet. adj. delighted. **4.1** हरसै [cf. harṣa-] v.i. pres. pl. (used as sing.) Br. I am delighted (i.e. I am happy with it); तुमको परी idiom. Br. you are interested in. **4.2** का मिल (क्या मिलेगा) reg. what do you get (from)? झूठि मिलायबे में (सच में झूठ मिलाने से) Br. from mixing lies (in the truth). **4.3** रमौ [ramati] v.i. pres. Br. sports (Br. ramai); जानती v.t. imperf. poet. 'knowing' clever. **4.4** बुनबे [*vunāti] v.t. (Br. inf.) to weave; बुनबे... बजाइबे मै idiom. Br. 'You are good neither in weaving nor in playing the vina', you do not have anything to do with it. (cf. H tum na tīn mẽ ho na terah mẽ). **6.2** जल के परसे by touching water; पावक [S] m. wind, air.

2 रीझ कहा पैवौ तापै कठिन बितैबो दिन
सुख को न लेस है कलेसन हहा करैं।
3 चाकरी न सूझै सेख खैबे की न बात बूझै
रोजगार मांगें रोज गारी ही रहा करैं।
4 हां करि न जानैं एक नां कर पढे हैं नाम
ऐसे ठग ठाकुर पैं चाकर कहा करैं॥ M7॥

2. Poems Erroneously Attributed to Ṭhākur

1 लाल लाल लोचन सकोचन सकुचि रहे
घूघट उघारि नेंक ससि सौ उगन दै।
2 अगिया उतारि गज मोतिन कौ हार डारि
बेसरि उतारि ओठ ओठ सों लगन दै।
3 कहै कबि बाकूराय, सुनि लीजै चित लाय
प्यारी अब तन की धों बुझन दै।
4 बतियां मती बिरमें रतिया बितीत होति
हेत्या मति लेइ नेंक छतियां छुवन दै॥ M8॥

कोइल कान सुनै उमगै मन और सुभाव भयौ अब ही कौ।
2 मुरली लता द्रुमु कुंज सुहात लगै अलि गुजत भांवतौ जी कौ।
कारन कौनु भयौ सजनी यह ष्याल लगै गुडियान कौ फीकौ।

---

8 Bharatpur5 ff. 36r-37r (55). Although this kavitta's rhyming is similar to N34 and Ś55 its signature is Bākūrāy (? for Ṭhākurāy). 9 Datiyā1 ff. 105v (341). This poem is the ninth in a sequence of twelve quatrains, where all other poems bear the signature 'Ṭhākura'. It's inclusion into the sequence suggests that the scribe perceived it as a poem by 'Ṭhākur' in spite of the fact that the word 'muralī' can be a signature of another poet in it. According to Dr. Kishorilal, its style is different from that of Ṭhākur. This poem would come under the category of 'ajñāta-yauvanā nāyikā', heroine unaware of (the coming of) her youth within the 'vayaḥsandhi varṇan' description of the transition from childhood to adolescence.

8.2 ओठ ओठ] B_5^{ac}, होठ होठ B_5^{pc} **9.1** मन] *conj.* *न D_1 **9.2** मुरली] *conj.* ⟨षु/घु⟩रली D_1 **9.3** गुडियान] *conj.* ×बिन बुय कतै आचि नीकौ× गुडियान D_1

8.3 धों [dava- 'fire'] reg. f. (forest-)fire. **8.4** बतियां मती बिरमें reg. don't be hindered by words; बितीत [vyatīta-] adj. passed; हेत्या (हत्या) var. [S] f. (do not take on the sin of) murder; **9.3** ष्याल] *conj.* खेल D_1

काहे तै सांवरौ अंग छवीलौ लगै दिन द्वैक तै आँषिन नीकौ॥ M9॥ 4

परि चली कछुक ढीली घांघरी की फूंद 1
थिरताई पाँवन कढी है छवा छाई सी।
हरिकेस केसन चिलक चढि आई 2
वचन मिठाई यो चखन चंचलाई सी।
लागी सी सुहान सूही ओढनी सहज ही मै 3
छाती यो सुहाती कुकरोंही उठि आई सी।
ठोर चित्त करों, ब्रज-ठाकुर-कुवर, कांहा, 4
हों न अब चाहत तिहारे मन भाई सी॥ M10॥

बैठी माननी गहि मौन।
मनहुं सिद्ध समाधि सेवत सुरन साधै पौन। 2
अटल आसन पल न टरई गुफा गूंघट-भौन।
रोस ही कौ ध्यान कीनौ टेक टारै कौन। 4
लेहू जाय मनाय, मोहन, करि सुरस हित गोन।
सुर के प्रभु तुमही देषत करैगी रिस वौ न॥ M11॥ 6

---

10 Sūkar Kṣetra Śodh Sansthān, Kasganj ms. without number (N), ff. 37v-38r (170). This is a savaiyā by Harikeś containing the word Ṭhākur as part of the epithet of Krishna.
11 Vrindaban1 f. 11r (12/64), Sūrsāgar (S_e) vol. 2. pp. 1107-8 (2574/3162) (Rāga kedārau). This pad was included into a manuscript devoted exclusively to Ṭhākur.

9.4 द्वैक] *conj.* दुयक D_1 • आँषिन] *conj.* आषिन D_1 **10.1** ढीली] *conj.* ठीली N • कढी है] *em.* क⟨ढी⟩ हे N • पाँवन] *conj.* पवन N • छवा] *conj.* छुवा N **10.2** चढि] (unm.) *conj.* चठि (unm.) N **10.3** यो] *conj.* पो N **11.1** माननि] V_1, मानिनि S_e **11.2** मनौ] V_1, मनहूं V_1 • सुरन] V_1, सुरनि S_e **11.3** अटल] V_1, अचल S_e • पल न टरई] V_1, पलक तारी S_e **11.4** कीनौ] V_1, धारैं S_e **11.5** लेहू] V_1, अबहिँ S_e • मोहन] V_1, लीजै S_e • करि सुरस हित] V_1, अवसि कीजै S_e **11.6** सूर] S_e, सुर V_1 • तुमही] V_1, जाय S_e • देषत] V_1, देखौ S_e • करैगी रिस वौ न] V_1, चित्त चौंधी जौन S_e

---

10.1 परि चली (चल पड़ी) v.i. perf. Br. became (loose) (i.e. my waist is so slim); फूंद [cf. H phundnā 'tassel'] poet. f. knot, string; कढी [cf. *kaḍḍhati] v.i. perf. (firmness) appeared; छवा poet. m. ankle. **10.2** चिलक [cf. *cilla-] f. 1. glitter, brilliance; 2. shooting pain; चखन [cakṣu-] m. pl. obl. Br. in the eyes. **10.3** लगी सी सुहान poet. started to look very attractive; सूहा [śubha-] adj. bright red; कुकर- poet. v.i. to shrink; कुकरोंही उठि आई सी Br. what was shrunk appeared clearly. **10.4** ठोर चित्त करों कांहा Br. where can I fix my mind? (i.e. find peace); हों... सी (seeing you I blossom but) I do not want what pleases you.

3. Poems by Ṭhākurdās

1 छोंडि दिहे संग पिआवा हो, के करे घर जैबे।
2 पाच पचीश तीश चबतीश लेइ एनके शंग मे सेयीबे रे।
3 इहबा आए नात हीत चिंधे वशार शशुर अब शाशु हो।
4 जानत हौ हम नाही मरबै शीर पर बएठा काल हो।
5 दुऔ जुन सठ खायो कशि के घीबगुरू ⟨गो⟩द दालि हो।
6 हरि की गति बिंधवन हे नर जे न एह शम कछु देत रे।
7 टेढी ताज दिहे शीर उपर बोलत अनुचित बात रै।
8 ठाकुर कहत चेतु शषि उलटी करौ मप दान हो के॥ M12॥

1 आपुही नारि हौ, पुरुश आपै भयो,
आपही करौ मन कर्मकारा।
दह दिशा जाय जग कर्म देखते,
आपही मया करू चर्मकारा॥
2 आपही सूति रहौ, जागते आपही,
आपही करौ ⟨ज⟩म ×∗× स्वप्नकारा।
स्वप्न के बीच जग मर्म ना⟨र⟩चत हौ,
लींग भगु नयन मोह धारा॥
3 आपही साहु हौ, चोर आपै भयो
आपही आप को लुटि डारा।
आपही समर बिच भोग भटकन लागा
आपही बयठि धन धर्म धारा॥
4 शकल जग कर्मणा छोंड
बेकूफ मन होहु एक रंग हीप बयठि धारा।
दाश ठाकुर कहै, छोंडु मन डगमगी
बए केरतन क्षर जन नसारा॥ M13॥

---

12 Ṭhākurdās padāvalī NPS 833, f. 18r. 13 Ṭhākurdās padāvalī NPS 833, f. 21r.

English Translation of Selected Poems

ABOUT THE TRANSLATION

A selection of poems is given below in English translation. They are close English renderings of the main text with a minimum amount of notes. Their aim is to provide help in grammatically interpreting the quatrains and they only distantly reflect the poetic intensity of the originals. Several features of the Brajbhasha versions had to be sacrificed in order to keep the clarity of the English translation. The most conspicuous of them is poetic forms. The only metrical element normally retained is the caesura in the middle of the *kavitta* lines. Brajbhasha poetry in general puts extraordinary emphasis on how a poem sounds. For this reason, the verses are often packed with repetition of sounds, alliteration, internal rhyming, punning, homonyms or word play. Moreover, the poems' imagery and vocabulary are firmly rooted in South Asian traditions, elements of which may find their origins in millennia past. The traditional layers of meaning of specific words may be absent from their English equivalent.

Other characteristics can only be partially reflected. Ṭhākur had a penchant for idioms and it is not always possible to give back Hindi idiomatic usage. Nevertheless, when the grammatical structure of a Hindi idiom is clear then equivalent English idioms or phrases may be used in the translation. (For example, "troglodyte" for the phrase "dweller of a well" referring to the Hindi word designating a parochial person: *kūpmaṇḍūk,* "frog in a well".) The poems maintain a high level of immediacy and their composer invites the listener or the reader to be part of the event the cowherd girls are witnessing. Krishna-poetry often speaks through the mouth of the cowherd girls and tends to use exclamations and vocatives normally addressed to a female companion. Exclamations, such as *rī*, *re*, *arī*, can be translated as "oh", "hey" but also as "look", "listen", "you see", etc. If exclamations are the rhyme words, they may only be translated once, usually in the first line. In translation, the etymological meaning of vocatives is not maintained and words originally meaning "hero" *(vīr, bhaṭu)* or "mother" *(māī)* are translated as "my friend", "my companion" or "my sister".

Another peculiarity of the originals is that conventional epithets sometimes stand for actual nouns. For example, the word "white-footed" refers to herons, the name "Intoxicator" refers to the God of Love. In such cases, I included both the epithet and the designated noun into the translation: "white-footed heron", "the Intoxicating God of Love ". The poems often use conventional epithets for divine figures known by only one name in English, such as Dear Child, Dear One, Dark as a Cloud, Dark One, Enchanter (of the Mind), Cowherd, Cowherd Boy, Moon of Braj, Lord of Braj, for Krishna, the Fair One for Radha, the Creator for Brahma, etc. Epithets standing for names are capitalised in English. Even when referred to by these epithets, however, in most of the poems Krishna is not as much a mythological figure as the exemplary lover. In this context Radha remains the exemplary beloved and Brahma would stand for fate.

A further difference in translation is that obscurities of the grammatical person in Hindi need to be spelt out in English. Hindi may use the same pronoun *(ham)* and same verbal endings for the first person in singular and in plural thus leaving it unclear whether a particular cowherd girl is speaking or the cowherd girls as a group. Sometimes the lack of pronouns leaves the Hindi reader or listener uncertain whether a poem is told in the first or the third person.

The translations here are linear translations of what I judged to be the most prominent variant and meaning. There are usually more possible meanings and variations than the translations reflect. Anyone interested in further possible interpretations or meaningful variants of a specific quatrain should consult the annotation to the originals.

Since notes on the poems are concentrated in the section presenting the originals, I kept the number of notes here to the minimum necessary for a reader unfamiliar with the originals to access these poems.

The text in various places is obscure and the translation is uncertain. It is hoped that further research will clarify many obscurities and to improve on these English renderings.

DEVOTION AND GOD'S SPORTS IN THE WORLD

No good fortune seems to be written for those who have not tasted the emotions of Braj.
The effect of not finding Krishna's fame is that they stay thirsty at holy waters.
If their minds are not under their control, says the poet Ṭhākur, are they to attract the Enchanter?
Why have they refused to sing the praise of Hari? Fie, fie on their tongues! (B6)

Ram is my pandit who finds the unmistakably auspicious day for the medicine;
Ram is my guru and I keep repeating the name of Ram.
It is Ram and Ram that I sing, Ram and Ram that I meditate on
By hearing only Ram, every hour of the day is blissful.
Ṭhākur says, I have true hope only for Ram,
my only concern is Ram and my wealth and home is Ram.
Ram is my doctor and my rest is Ram, O brother;
Ram is my medicine and my efforts are for Ram. (B12)

My mind has become a mad elephant and sunk into the sea of illusion.
Neither the goad of modesty nor the chain of scruple of its mahout, knowledge, has controlled it.
Ṭhākur, I have also tried tricks but it does not come under control—it has settled in bad company.
Ignoring death behind its shoulder, it has been trapped in the mud of delusion. (B14)

God in the World: The Divine Sports

I saw him coming! How beautiful is the flute on his lips!—
just like a dark neck-rope on a red cow's calf.
It is he whom the endless serpent Śeṣa praises; it is he whom the Vedas expound;
the story of Pūtanā's embrace is about him.
Ṭhākur says, nobody, not even the primordial unborn Brahma,
has any hint that it is he who gathers up and expands the universe.

Some were ensnared, others assailed—
no one could fathom the guts of this dark son of a herdsman. (B27)

THE LIFTING OF MOUNT GOVARDHANA

On the cowherds, women and men, on the cows, on Braj and on its inhabitants;
Indra's wrath is on them—people are watching speechless.
Seeing the commotion, He said "Come here from everywhere!"
He saved all through his extraordinary fervour.
Ṭhākur says, lovely women watch his dark body
and call themselves fortunate.—Seeing this, who would not be enchanted?
On his little finger gleams the hill, and torrents of rain above the hill
and above the torrents charming clouds shine. (B30)

THE LOVE OF THE DIVINE COUPLE

Why are you so restless in your mind?
Watch, laugh, and speak!—Why do you look so miserable?
Your body is emaciated, your eyes spread clouds of tears.
Just look, it is the same manner everywhere in the city of love.
Ṭhākur says, have a look at us here, then
look at him—it is the same condition for both of you.
As you started off hearing the sound of the flute
so has Krishna been wounded by the tinkling of your anklets. (B35)

Why is the border of his garment scattered,
his flute tucked in upside-down, his body languid,
and his turban bound misshapen with coils hanging loose?
Nanda's son is beautiful in his ill-disciplined finery.
Ṭhākur says, Krishna with lust and desire,
careless of his belongings, is bewildered in his mind—
Call your fate blessed and look at the exquisite splendour of this happiness!—
He saw the fair-complexioned Radha and goes around as if possessed. (B37)

One of them says, "It's this way!", the other "It's that way!" "It's neither like this nor like that! Your body is crooked!"[1]
She looks at him and laughs, delightfully catches his arm and stares at him as the partridge stares at the rising moon.
Ṭhākur: Pārvatī and Shiva with excitement watch the spectacle and listen to its racket.
Look, the Fair One is cross with the Cowherd Boy as the row over the gamble progressed on both sides. (B42)

THE POWER OF KRISHNA'S FLUTE

I do not know who Govinda is or where Gopāla or Kanhāī comes from.
I only heard that a boy cowherd played the flute, so yesterday I ran to see it.

[1]Suggesting "how can then Krishna's mind be straight?"

Ṭhākur, where is the waywardness in that?—Tell me clearly.
Look, why have you started to slander me everywhere, my friend? (B44)

My body may leave me but not my love for the Enchanter;
look, I broke with my elders and lost delight in all.
You may call me promiscuous, defamed and bad woman;
if you want, call me a human or a beast.
Ṭhākur says, who will listen to your teaching?
think about it yourself, has anything remained in my power?
His name on my tongue, his form has settled within me,
his beauty is in my eyes and his flute in my ears. (B45)

Love in Separation

He cheated many like Radha in Vrindaban,—can, therefore, a cowherdess touch his body with love?
Her heart became like a ship in a whirlpool—now I know that the world considers only power.
Ṭhākur, he is the Lord of Braj and, be it good or not, everything goes well with Krishna.
Where the biggest leaders are washed away who would carry across a lowly drummer? (B49)

Had he been true to us, even then we would not have believed it.
Since the time he cheated Bali as a dwarf[2] *we have been apprehensive in our hearts.*
Ṭhākur says, yet our eyes were delighted and they relished meeting him.
As for you, worship him as your king Rama, but for us Krishna is as familiar as our utensils. (B51)

Krishna's Messenger Rebuffed

The Dear Child is just as great an enthusiast as the company he acquired is valuable.
He abandoned a shining beauty like Radha and talked lovingly to the hunchback.
Ṭhākur, what shall we say to you? It's better to remain speechless with a vow of silence.
In a blind man's house, there is a difference of thousands even in an account of farthings. (B54)

Repeatedly searching for new tastes, he uprooted them from their fields: their families.
Then secretly had them to his fill but he did not tell anyone whether he liked them or not.
Ṭhākur, thus speak the women of Braj, listen, Uddhav, to this story soaked with love.
Some he ate, some he threw away—Hari treated the cowherd girls like some slave's carrots. (B55)

'Fie on the ear that listens to someone else's words; we have been dyed and assimilated in only one colour.
'If ever another name is on our tongues, then tear it out and throw it into poison.'
Ṭhākur, they have learned just one thing of importance; the nature of the people of Braj is so simple.

[2]This is a reference to the Puranic story of the dwarf incarnation of Vishnu.

'Dear Uddhav, let our eyes burn if instead of the Dark One they look at some fair person.' (B56)

Without any reason my heart became infatuated and glimpsing his beauty trusted it; it did not get frightened seeing his black colour.
It became so dyed in the colour of delight that kinsmen and outsiders failed to dissuade it.
Ṭhākur, it has received its fruit: it abandoned joy by day and by night.
Dear Uddhav, it is not your fault or his; it is I who threw a stone at my own feet. (B59)

All others knew about him, but his sidelong glance fell on me.
I bore the insults of the slanderers and I bore their words sharper than arrows.
Ṭhākur, now the same Hari abandoned me and garrulous women say "Shame on you!"
Dear Uddhav, it is not your fault or his; it's I who took a scorpion into my own hand. (B60)

Dear Uddhav, our fate is against us while good times have come for them.
He drew his arms away from our shoulders and put them on those of the hunchback.
Ṭhākur, this saying of someone else has also turned out to be valid for us:
My companion, why would a bird pounce on another bird?—a nobleman, however, is expert in hunting. (B61)

If he himself had come, then would he also have taught yoga to us?
Would he have cast away pleasure and spoken of swallowing strings?
He sent you, and you have been verbose;
now we do not know who is inimical and who is friendly.
Ṭhākur says, banish the visible form yourself
and meditate on the Imperceptible—how difficult it is!
These two jobs are done by one's own hands:
is there seasoning by others and is there farming by messages?[3] (B62)

The hunchback woman has loved Krishna: Allah is wonderful in every aspect.
What shall we do when we are angry? Let us remain silent staying at the foot of love.
He sent Uddhav to give a message, but we are not afraid of the fuss of Yoga.
A person gets what he deserves: the broken mosque there has a blind mullah.[4] (B64)

He did not recognise the proper ways of emotions, but studied from a slate in the school of trickery.
The Lord has abandoned us; no sooner has he gone away than he entered into relationship with a hunchback.
Earlier he expounded openly his theft[5] *but now desire has become our powerful deception.*
We thought that our beloved was at least suffused with infatuation but that brazen Hari turned out to be a friend only at the spring harvest. (B65)

[3]The cowherdesses' meaning is that Krishna cannot teach them through an intermediary about how to achieve him.

[4]The mosque as a feminine noun would stand for the hunchback woman and the mullah for Krishna.

[5]A reference to Krishna as the butter-thief.

We do not know what to do concerning Krishna,
others blame him without reason.
Once we drank like nectar the Enchanter's words
but now we sit and drink separation like poison.
Ṭhākur says, Uddhav, what were we able to do
when falsely and shamelessly he made a vow?
Then we thought who would live until his promised time?
And look now, after passing that time, we are still alive. (B66)

At daybreak, my friend, it occurred to me to write and send a letter to my lover.
Now he is sending excuses to explain and sweet words are on his lips.
Ṭhākur says, this is the way of love, Uddhav, my heart breaks just as the cool breeze comes.[6]
Since he so suddenly left Braj for Dvaraka, the night has become the enemy of the cowherd girls. (B68)

LOVE

Being in Love

Hearing its sound, I rejoiced in my mind, "Oh, I should go there to experience its excessive delight."
Getting near I saw that sometimes its rhythm was confused, sometimes its melody.
Ṭhākur says, my eyes made a mistake; why should one fall in love with it?
Let's go away, my friend, I pined for it with no point. Drums from afar, you know, always sound attractive. (Ś1)

I saw that his love is full of merriment, trusting him is blissful,
and his emotions are joyful—I considered him a man of great passion.
But all this turned out to be false. Only one thing was extraordinary
and I believe only one to be true: he trapped those who were to be trapped.
Ṭhākur says, this maxim has thus been proven:
"a guideline that has been accepted should by no means be altered."
One cannot leave it since it is tasty and one cannot swallow it since it is curved:
my love for the Enchanter became a sickle coated in jaggery. (Ś3)

Who is as highly accomplished as he is? How much he boasts of his disrepute!
What happened today has happened and it happened well. Now who would say anything and take the dispute forward?
Ṭhākur, there is one concern in my mind: who would now make mud by pouring water on it?
Thinking of this I fell into a dilemma: who would now release worms by breaking a wild fig?[7] (Ś5)

[6]The cool breeze is considered *uddīpan*, an inciting factor for love.

[7]The wild fig is often full of worms. Taking the idiomatic meaning the second half of the line would translate as "who would create confusion by revealing what is hidden?"

FEMALE BEAUTY

Waves of enthusiasm rise on her body and she goes around radiating the intoxication of her youth.
She looks sideways with her big eyes and she goes around excited when she sees a friend.
Ṭhākur says, her hands and her beautiful upper arms do not stop; she goes around swaying.
Her head covered with her shawl, her breasts tight in her bodice, she goes around flapping the smaller shawl she wears. (Ś13)

He took the tenderness of a lotus, the fragrance of a rose,
the light of the moon and made brightness manifest;
And he took the beauty of Rati's[8] *features, the cleverness of the cultivated ones,*
the water, its brilliance, from reservoirs—and accomplished this wonder;
Ṭhākur says, seeing with one's own eyes these raw materials
of the craftsman Creator who would not be overwhelmed by them?
Taking the colour of gold, the taste of the nectar
and plundering the joy of the earth he has created your face. (Ś15)

THE WONDER OF THE EYES

They are in me but they are always apathetic towards me,
set on not learning they do not accept any teaching.
As if startled or astonished, as if sometimes animated by obsession, sometimes
tired they look in so many ways.
Ṭhākur, my mind is confused by his wonder-making words,
it does not know what it is saying to Hari.
Look, this bright, knowledgeable and cautious mind of mine,
has been fooled by my eyes. (Ś18)

They have been the two trusted guards of my heart;
tell me, has anyone reached his aim by eluding or bypassing them?
I have been living under the watches of these two, but alas,
the watchman ate the crop! Things have become so topsy-turvy.
Ṭhākur says, when interrogated they keep shedding tears,
they do not give the least information about whom they have given it to.
It seems, O my friend, that my mind
is gone because of the treachery of the bandits, my eyes. (Ś19)

Believe what I say and hurry there, my lady, what good does it to you to vacillate?
You wounded him, and you can remove it, no one is skilled for this but you.
Ṭhākur says, they were sharpened on the whetstone of the blacksmith Kāma, I have observed it.
Your glances, arrows shot from the bow of your eyebrows, have penetrated deep into the heart of your dear one. (Ś22)

[8]Rati, 'Delight', is the beautiful wife of the God of Love, Kāma. In *rīti*-poetry her role is normally to be a point of reference for comparisons.

Love in Union

My mind, besieged and surrounded by her skirt in its fullness, was entangled in the drawstrings and rumples.
It was trapped in the lane of the three folds of her skin and seeing the beauty of her navel reached out to it.
Ṭhākur says, leaving that place it went away, then it fell and sank into the caves of her hills.
Oh, give me back my mind that is hiding among your breasts. When you were binding the string of your bodice, I myself became bound. (Ś28)

'My wretched sister-in-law roams like a lion searching for noises.
If I don't forbid you to come, people will say "Get away, you rascal!"
The wives of your elder brothers are
also awake; and people still roam on the streets here and there.'
Ṭhākur says, while she was making thousands of pleas
the Dear One embraced the girl by force.
'Please get on the bed without making the bedstead crack;
O Hari, and without letting my necklace or ankle chain rattle.' (Ś30)

My sisters-in-law are all awake . . . people at home will hear us . . . don't grab my arm!
Let me sleep . . . Is there any pressing need? Just listen to me, O my lord!
Ṭhākur says, why are you agitated? Be patient in your heart.
The whole night is ahead . . . Don't cause me to talk so much! Out of a kilogram, not even a handful of wool has been spun yet. (Ś31)

Separation—Uncommunicated Love

"Who are you?" "I'm an astrologer, and I tell the future.
After all, my name is known everywhere."
"Come, sit down, let me touch your feet, take some paan, and then,
concentrated and relaxed, make your calculations."
Ṭhākur says, "In this test of love let me carry
your advice in my heart as a proof of my desires.
My mind is attached to the Enchanter in millions of ways;
now find out whether his will be attached to me." (Ś36)

While He who is dark as a cloud was standing there, I went up to the rooftop and looked at him.
You also know the ways in Braj; love does not remain concealed even for a twinkling of an eye.
Ṭhākur says, so has his sidelong glance penetrated me that I am not able to forget him.
Sitting at home doesn't please me for a moment. What is the use of a veil? What good is modesty? (Ś42)

That beautiful girl without love, who superficially probably thinks about me
looking at me again and again all the time must at least recognise my face.
Ṭhākur says, my mind trusts her yet she probably does not feel love for me.
She always appears for me—She must at least be aware of this. (Ś44)

On the one hand you want to maintain your family honour, on the other you muse over Nanda's son;
Yet if somehow he appeared on his usual way, you can't look at him from your window.
The poet Ṭhākur says, there is no remedy, when being apprehensive you try to make your apprehension true.
Seeking love and being concerned about reputation, tell me, can these two things happen at the same time? (Ś53)

Why are you listening and stand speechless? Find out, whom did he go away with?
Delighting us by playing on his flute, look, he went somewhere in the grove to milk the cows.
Ṭhākur says, it seems, my friend, that he went to thread a garland of guñj*-berries.*
Oh, somebody please run, stop him and turn him back! That charming Enchanter of Nanda is gone. (Ś54)

I explained it through millions of crafts but it is so angry that it doesn't understand.
Having once acquired a taste for the nectar of his beauty, it doesn't recognise right and wrong any more.
Ṭhākur, it doesn't care at all for slander, public disgrace or odium.
What can I do? Without seeing the face of the Enchanter of the Mind, my mind doesn't heed me. (Ś62)

He has turned clever and sagacious and has become somewhat different to everyone.
On tasting, he tastes very sweet but he's learnt to always change his nature.
Ṭhākur says, can I say anything to anyone now? That mind and that affection were at those times.
Those days, that happiness, such enthusiasm—all this, my companion, has been lost. (Ś65)

When one's true heart is set on something, it takes the person right there.
I tell you, the wild goose plucks pearls and the cuckoos receive svāti *drops.*[9]
Ṭhākur says, listen to this true mystery: the one who entangles people also gives a solution.
God is famed for the fact that he gives exactly what one wants. (Ś66)

SEPARATION—DISTANCE

O my Dear Child, though you gave up your love and forged enmity, I still think of you.
I know no other face at all. It's your name that I chant to live on.
Ṭhākur says, all fault is mine; therefore, I don't blame you.
My mind wants me to talk falsely but since I am in love, I pay no heed. (Ś68)

In my dream, I went to a flower garden, where Hari put his arms around my neck and embraced me.
I was embarrassed lest another girl glimpsed us and shook his arms from me.
Ṭhākur says, as day broke so did my dream and I found myself alone in my room.

[9]The pied cuckoo *(cātaka)* is conventionally supposed to live only on raindrops fallen at the autumn asterism *svāti.*

As I opened my eyes, the Dark One was not by my side, neither were the trees and creepers of that wretched garden (Ś71)

Look, he either fell into the clutches of someone or became afraid of the elders.
I've been watching for his coming at the door since lamps were lit but he didn't remove my anguish.
Ṭhākur says, the agreed time was sunset—he fixed the hour of his coming when he left.
It's past midnight but Hari hasn't come. He trapped me like a worm in a fig. (Ś73)

It seems, O Dark One, that she remains immersed
in the multitudes of delight of the moments spent in union with you.
She doesn't open her eyes to look around, she is unable to;
she keeps watching for your coming with the sight of her heart.
Ṭhākur says, she is awake yet in a deep absorption like a yogi,
and ignorant people near her think that she sleeps profoundly.
Weeping restlessly day and night
she keeps washing her body with a flow of tears. (Ś79)

Go, Beautiful Boy, crash the pain of separation of the woman
at whose brilliance the beauty of Rati[10] *suffers continuous defeat.*
Since she heard the rumours of your departure from here, O Dark One,
she has been passing her days as if struck mad.
Ṭhākur says, her eyelids never close
and she keeps looking dazzled and confused.
The streams of tears that she drenches her sari with
keep distressing and squeezing your heart. (Ś80)

I cannot live without seeing the charming face of the dear Enchanter.
Therefore, I listen to everything, good and bad in this world, and consider it to be a lesson.
Ṭhākur says, in order to see the Dear Child I do not reply to anyone.
What can I say when I have been entangled? I flatter all the people. (Ś83)

Since my Dear Child went abroad, my companion, my body is continuously wasting.
Without the one who is as dear as my life, the breasts in my bodice are drenched with streams of tears.
Ṭhākur says, such is my condition, O my sister, that only you console me:
I live on looking at the face of my sister-in-law, my friend, which is like that of my lover. (Ś84)

With firm resolution and control, I have managed to live so far but now every moment has become difficult.
Only a woman who sleeps without her dear lover will know this suffering.
Ṭhākur, whom shall I approach and ask when the Creator has bestowed this distance?
One does not know, my sister, how many days are left in this separation from the Cowherd Boy. (Ś85)

[10]See note 8.

At that time, you ran to meet me without pretence, so you ought not to bring someone else into your mind now.
You were subject to that emotion. So having once shown desire, do you now need to keep me waiting?
The poet Ṭhākur: it's all right that you grasped my arm but then you should fulfil its promise.
If you set this boat of love afloat, you should pull it to the other shore. (Ś86)

Separation—Wounded Pride

When the tender woman, once the abode of happiness, was sitting
filled with intense fury her beauty glowed.
When pleaded with, she swayed her beautiful head,
and then another companion invented a matter to placate her:
Ṭhākur says, 'Your face, your eyes, your nose
and your nose-ring suggest four wonderful similes:
On a lotus, there are wagtails, between two wagtails a parrot,
and the parrot seems to swing a cluster of pearls.' (Ś90)

Is it Love's ardour? Or the conceit of your power, or rather
your intoxication with affection that looking at them is so precious for you?
Is this the proper way of emotions? Or have you been testing love?
Or are you untying the knot of affection that was tied in your heart?
Ṭhākur says, O you cunning expert on love, are you so much
dazzled and astonished that you dither in confusion?
Mistaking them for me, you lift the veils of other girls, my Dear Child,
but mistaking me for others, you never say a word to me. (Ś93)

When you saw that her house was empty, you left,
—she was up on the roof to take some fresh air.
Learning that it was you she was embarrassed, and didn't she say with much love:
"O my friend, doesn't my lover enjoy my love?"
Ṭhākur says, listen, O intelligent Enchanter,
No one is clever enough to please you.
No one knows the secret of how to convince you,
but everyone is ready to criticise others. (Ś95)

Counsel

Whenever I see you, I say to myself that you should keep increasing your love.
Radiant lady, give up your worry and enjoy delight—why go around with wounded pride?
Ṭhākur says, your Beautiful Boy is hiding somewhere among your co-wives—gain back your married bliss.
Appear before him and make him happy, let separation pass, look at him, look at him!
(Ś96)

Oh, look at the charming light emanating from the moon of your face spreading all around.
The wealth of your youth is a guest of four days,[11] *so consider this counsel.*
Ṭhākur says, if Krishna made a mistake, then rectify the wrong.
Who knows whether an opportunity remains or not—wash your hands in a stream that is flowing now. (Ś97)

Like a bullock stringed with a nose-rope your lover is under your control, why do you torture him? Won't you heed reason?
The water runs downwards, my friend, you cannot carry on with love in this way.
Ṭhākur says, if you are to go on with it, then why do you harass the Enchanter of the Mind?
Will the day not dawn, my sister, if there is no cockerel in the village? (Ś101)

To whom did you make a vow of physical torment? After all, your mind is united with him like water in milk.
What concealment remains from the one whose love you accepted in your mind?
You should consider this humble request of your lord—Who can say harsh words naturally?
My clever love, dear as my life, how can you keep your veil when you live in my heart? (Ś103)

I bought her along by lure, O Enchanter, and you first pleased and then irritated her.
She left you with dislike and embarrassment—what's all this that you have done?
Ṭhākur, the proper way of love is for delight to continuously increase.
There is no difficulty in engaging one in an affair, but parting with love is difficult. (Ś106)

The Cowherd Boy's body is like a tender lotus—but you know all this.
I'm telling you, it withers from the slightest roughness, haven't you even realised this much?
Ṭhākur says, he talked to you with folded hands but you don't listen to his entreaty.
Your eyes are arrows, your eyebrows a bow; oh say, stretching them up to your ears what are you aiming at? Why are you cross? (Ś108)

Manners are no longer the same; neither the talk is the same nor the skills, neither the ways of emotion nor the flow of love.
Truth decreased and falsity increased in the world; people run everywhere out of their greed.
Ṭhākur, the Cowherd Boy is the same, we are the same—but could the same wind blow everywhere?
The whole of Braj has changed for the worse, my companion, in front of my very eyes. (Ś109)

Commitment

It is my condition day and night that my mind is to roam in your lanes.
Why did you harden your mind so much? It is not your wish either.

[11] A variant based on a cluster of apparently later sources has the meaning "I say, your dear lover has become subject to you".

Ṭhākur says, you haven't shown yourself at all; why do you want to be praised by hypocrites?
Do, Sujān, whatever pleases you – I am to fulfil my love's commitment. (Ś116)

ADULTEROUS LOVE

When she glimpsed her paramour going to the well, she could not contain herself.
Considering that her pot stand was full, she hatched a plot saying that she was doing what others had asked.
Ṭhākur, she pays no heed to what they say and is not afraid to go to the house of others.
Angry at custom and excited by desire she brings water to her neighbours. (Ś119)

I gave up bridal chastity and fell in love. I didn't carry it through and became a laughing stock.
I had to remain silent and had to tell it,[12] *and all will hear the same thing.*
The maxim I heard, says Ṭhākur, has turned true.
"I received neither love, nor the Lord," in my dilemma, listen my companion, I lost both. (Ś120)

I knew that my beloved is not mine but of someone else—this is what the Vedas sing.
Neglecting this, I fell in love and discarded the family honour propagated by the elders.
That lord has not become mine. Whom shall I blame for this, my sister?
The bee is visible in the milk, my friend; I have seen it and, alas, I have drunk it. (Ś122)

Can I explain this now? Who would understand? I've already sowed the seeds of my disgrace.
Just reflect on this—tell me, has anyone who fell into this trap been released?
Ṭhākur says, I am dyed in the ways of this emotion—fallen in love, I have lost my bridal fidelity.
Good and bad were written in my fate—all that had to happen has now happened. (Ś123)

She never comes out of her house, but appears at the gate with her glittering toe-ring.
Hiding in her veil, she wounds me and sings flirtatiously from behind her balcony.
She does not stop for a moment and incites my mind by displaying a multitude of coquetries.
Coming into sight, she goes into my heart but my lovely neighbour does not come into my hand. (Ś124)

How many times have I told you to come often, but you didn't. This fills me with pain.
By chance, we met, Enchanter, so let's turn this entanglement into a good bondage.
Ṭhākur, the cows roam scattered: listen to my request and round them up to graze.
Do come twice for the work of binding, milking and releasing them. (Ś127)

[12]This apparent contradiction may be interpreted in several ways. For example, "I had to tell that I had to remain silent", "though I was originally silent about it I had to tell it" or "I could not help telling it through my silence".

Everyone of the house went out for a feast but I remained at home pretending to be ill.
My lord, there is only one deaf servant around, whom I put at the gate on purpose.
You have done well to come through the window,—exactly what I wanted.
Today, my dear, my love, let's make love sport all night without anxiety. (Ś128)

O my sister, whom should my husband approach to make money?
Not even a king's intellect can find a solution.
My body and wealth became lean, my mind fouled,
my soul, restless and troubled, is never at peace.
Ṭhākur says, compulsion overwhelms this world.
My mind is stained, show me some way out!
Now when I have nothing but oaths in my mouth, I can do nothing but sin,
I have disgrace to take and false love to give. (Ś131)

A Woman for Everyone

That girl proud of her enormous wealth of good looks wobbles like an elephant.
Her body is filled with the waves of Love's splendour; she appears satisfied in every way.
Ṭhākur, what simile can describe her when she looks at everyone with the same emotion?
She delights her male friends—she, the trader's radiant wife when offering ritual donations. (Ś132)

Slander

Now there is nothing left to say or to hear; don't be troubled by good or bad.
We must resign ourselves to remain always according to his wishes.
Ṭhākur says, this is the counsel to follow in order to see the Dear Child:
Living amongst these troublemakers, my friends,[13] *we should keep aloof from the bad times.* (Ś136)

How carelessly you are setting off! Do not keep putting your arm on everyone's shoulders!
Deceitful women will cheat you with their trickery, if not in a moment or a minute, then an hour.
Ṭhākur says, they have gathered and are about to make some plot in Braj.
My Dear Child, can you see the recent wicked conduct of the slanderers or not? (Ś139)

When I saw the One who is Dark as a Cloud I said that I liked his beauty.
Hearing this you assume I'm involved with the Cowherd Boy and start to wrangle.
From that day my sisters-in-law have plunged into strife against me
and even people who live nearby come and quarrel.
Ṭhākur says, how can one remain in such a village
where people always create new gossip?
I see how the people of Braj are these days: I
talk of the field but they think of the granary. (Ś148)

[13] The word *vīr* translated as 'my friends' originally means 'hero(es)' and thus fits the context of the legend associated with this poem.

I am in love with the Enchanter of the Mind—what will people achieve by slander?
I have already gained disrepute in Braj. Should I be afraid that my elders learn of it?
Ṭhākur says, in order to see the Dear One, I've forgotten the entire Braj and abandoned my home.
You should mind your own business; would someone fall in a well on purpose? (Ś150)

You should not tell your own mantra to others but meditate on its wonder in your inner self.
You should call good good and bad bad. This rule should always be born in your mind.
Ṭhākur says, listen, my dear connoisseur, and remove the confusion from your heart.
Slander and slur has arisen all around, keep it in mind, my friend, and be careful. (Ś151)

I did not make any acquaintances or smile at anyone.
In spite of this, people come up with so much slander.
My mother-in-law keeps account of my every sigh, my sister-in-law is treacherous and enemies dwell nearby—I suffer double pain.
Ṭhākur says, think it over in your mind:
why would one destroy the jewel of one's heart?
May the country burn down where looking is seen as theft!
Shall then people lock up their eyes? (Ś152)

These slanderers should not ascertain anything; the fear of anger from all around should disappear.
In this way, if he did not like our union and now the metal rods of separation burn my body,
Ṭhākur, no one should be inimical and no libel should arise in the houses of the slanderers.
Tell me a way, my friend, to embrace Hari but not to incur stain. (Ś154)

THE SEASONS

Spring

Mango flowers are his crown, Flame-of-the-forest his bracelet,
the buds are his golden jewellery and pollen adorns his clothes.
Ṭhākur, his banners the leaves, his throne the red lotus;
the variety of groves has become palanquins, elephants and chariots.
The wind his wedding procession and the trees its members;
the buzz of the bees, the mace-bearers, is his music.
Enchanting for the spectator, he has his bride, the Breeze, with him—
the shining Spring has become like a bridegroom. (R3)

On the blossoming mango branches, the cuckoo is cooing—it cannot stay silent.
Ṭhākur, the swarm of bees buzzing around in every grove cannot be still.
When the cool, slow and fragrant breeze touches it, O my friend, my body cannot help being stirred.
The spring has completely overcome me.—Won't anyone go and tell my lover? (R7)

Look at the leaves of the forest-creepers, at the buds and flowers—
this beautiful radiance spread all over the groves and gardens.
Feel the pain one has when hearing the cooing of the cuckoo—
how people spend their days and nights in such circumstances?
Ṭhākur says, ponder clearly in your heart,
in such a time, you shouldn't distress the Dark One.
Look at the blossoming mango-tree, look at the bunches of flowers,
and how pleasantly the bees buzz among the bunches. (R9)

Every day, every watch, every hour, every moment
it comes in frenzy and spreads in the two worlds.
The cuckoo coos loudly, the peacock cries out:
"Do not sulk", and they subdue the sulking women.
Ṭhākur says, the fair woman says to the Cowherd Boy,
"Look at the beauty of the mangos and tamarinds in the groves and the gardens!
Everywhere the glare of the sun thickens, Love wanders in conquest,
the king of the seasons goes around attacking those without their lovers." (R10)

Lord Kāma's famous cruel soldier
causes the flowers to bloom and the trees to sway.
It prevents the surreptitious expansion of the burning winds,
and prepares kind shade for endless bliss.
Ṭhākur says, it is the pleasant companion of those in union with their loved ones,
and is the powerful enemy, my friend, of the wretched women without lovers.
The cuckoos and the bees in order to attain its fragrance, the delight,
became bards proclaiming the glory of Spring. (R11)

Holi

To dye myself in saffron and in red,
to push aside modesty kept for the elders.
To sing and play music, to laugh and make others laugh,
governed by emotion to press for all delights.
Ṭhākur says, my Dear Child, I am to do whatever is possible.
Only one thing is impossible; tell me, how to tolerate it.
Putting your hands on my breast and your arms around my neck—
if Holi is to be played like this, then I am not meant to play. (R14)

Stay where you are, don't move, don't run!—Now, you'll see all the sports I play.
Allow me to sing, O my friend, allow me to play the music, allow Nanda's Dear Child to come.
Ṭhākur, I will be coloured with colours and covered, my companion, in red powder.
I will enter the haze, the noise of tambourines and of dhamār *songs and will get hold of the Cowherd Boy.* (R16)

Covering her eyes with the end of her sari she says "My friend, hold my water syringe.
"If you talk now, I will get angry, listen, later you can say good or bad things."

Ṭhākur says, "Why shall I complain? You should administer justice to me.
"Red powder fell into my eyes, stay with me, my Dear Child, please stay."[14] (R18)

The colours of Holi were celebrated with water. The lanes are doused in pouring red powder.
Since they cannot go anywhere men and women are wrapped in the colour of love.
Ṭhākur, enthusiastic but without means among her companions
A cowherdess full of passion and intoxicated with emotion caught the Cowherd Boy and fell into the mud of saffron. (R20)

I am not at all keen on Holi.—I know that you are a troublemaker.
Don't presume to see me alone, don't forget that you are a cowherd.
Ṭhākur, if you exert force, then I am not one to be subjugated.
Whose eyes are you blinding, my Dear Child ? Stop, O matchless Cowherd, throwing red powder! (R21)

It is Holi now, who remains under veil? Look at the beauty of the Dark One,
nothing like that in millions of Love-gods.
He sings amorous songs, smilingly he plays the music and
recognises the taste for love in each one.
Ṭhākur says, he perceives the inner thoughts of the girls of Braj
in every bit of continuous elation.
Still you sit alone penetrated by love:
your body coloured red and your mind coloured in love for the Dear Child. (R25)

"You know how the cowherds are, how they resist attacks,
and if they are cautious then our wish for a concealed attack won't work.
Unleashing a storm of saffron and red powders,
the Dark One should not be allowed to play a game of force."
Ṭhākur, they entered with fanfare among the cowherds—
it is the day of Holi and the adolescent Radha wields power.
Her charming mind is quick, the scales of love are heavy—
It is Hari's domain but the uproar comes from the Fair One. (R26)

Considering that it was dawn, hiding myself in my clothes, I took the water pot and went out.
I did not realise when and whence all those appeared who were celebrating Holi.
Ṭhākur, glimpsing me they started to run, I was fortunate to get away in time.
My friend, if I hadn't shut the gate, I would have fallen into the hands of Holi-players.
(R27)

Akhatī—The Festival of the "Undiminishing"

Radha plays with the Enchanter on Akhatī and forces him to utter the name of his beloved.

[14]This poem presents the words of a woman to Krishna, whom she initially feigns to mistake for a companion.

She scolds him, frowns at him and says, "Tell me, tell!"
Ṭhākur says, as taught by her guru, Love, she increases the brightness of this simile:
It seems as if she makes her lover repeat the forgotten lesson of the ways of emotions and of love. (R29)

After worshipping the clay figures, the clever adolescent Radha eagerly took along a group of her companions.
They played Akhatī where the playful Moon of Braj happened to be and truly enjoyed it.
Ṭhākur says, Lalitā holding a twig put her hands in salute in front of the Dear Child.
The Dark Enchanter, the fulfiller of the wish for happiness, smiled and slowly uttered "Radha". (R31)

Rainy Season

Look, black clouds shine here, white ones over there,
red ones somewhere else and others are bright with yellow.
As the dazzle of the fickle lightning is sudden,
so is the rumbling of the thick clouds slow.
Ṭhākur says, the cuckoos wander as if with increased desire
and bigger and bigger flocks of peacocks gather.
How great, how pleasing and delightful it feels today
as the cool breeze blows gently. (R37)

They run black, red, yellow, white and smoke-grey—
How beautifully the dust-coloured clouds take on hues.
How sweet the sound of thunder renders the forms on earth!
It becomes festive and lush in every direction.
Ṭhākur says, poets fail to depict it,
it can't be described; it's beyond any imaginative power.
The groves thus transformed enchant the minds—
Look, the clouds today appear in so many colours. (R38)

The first rain comes swaying like an angry Love-god
Lowering, it showers water on the beautiful woman.
Every here and there one can see flashes of lightning
as if red velvet-mites[15] *are entertaining clouds as their guests.*
Ṭhākur says, these cuckoos keep cooing,
people cry out in their pangs of separation, their hearts are without fear.—
They dig tiny mounds on the earth, which are like traps of love, today
they shut the doors—so powerful are the raindrops. (R40)

On the marketplace of the sky with immense predilection for silk
in order to please his costumers he put them out on display—

[15] The etymological meaning of the code word for the red velvet-mite, called indravadhū, is here *indrānī* is "Indra's wife". Therefore, the secondary meaning of the line is "as if the wife of the Rain-God Indra is entertaining clouds".

Some are red and yellow, some striped white and blue
some are of the colour of vermilion, others like smoke—
Ṭhākur says, looking at the clouds of many colours
I thought about this secret plot to myself:
They are not clouds but various pieces of cloth
put out to dry their wet dyes by their dyer, the monsoon. (R41)

They seem to watch the spectacle of the rainy season's expansion
but out of fear of the lightning they do not fall on the earth.
They see the affection of the peacocks and the desire of the cuckoos
and considering it their husband they do not even stop when tired.
Ṭhākur says, here they appear, there they hide—
erring but well-disposed they do not clash.
Looking for it slowly among the clouds, the dazzled stars
seem to search for the moon. (R44)

That one showers torrents of waters,—he also drenches girls in emotions.
That one keeps going around, lowers and covers one,—he holds a flute to his lips.[16]
Ṭhākur says, that one is accompanied by capricious lightning,—he by a young girl with integrity.
Seeing this, a woman tells her husband that the dark cloud and the One who is Dark as a Cloud are engaged in rivalry. (R46)

The peacock started to dance, the cuckoos to coo and
the crickets to chirp—such is the splendour of groves and gardens.
The eastern wind gets stronger and stronger and in it
the skylark has struck up the tunes of a delightful Malhār *raga.*
Ṭhākur says, frogs create an uproar, drops of rain
are falling and love's beauty has spread.
White herons, black clouds, yellow lightning, green earth,
a dense grey haze—and the ruddiness of the Dear One's red turban. (R48)

Auspicious signs show that my loving one will come to my house,
the size of the clouds and the drops of shower look beautiful.
And He simply started to appear in my heart,
the flow of Kāma's arrows is excessive.
Ṭhākur says, the lightning doesn't seem dull to me,
and the radiance of the green earth is magnificent.
My left is agitated, my bodice throbs
and the tassels of my skirt slip away every moment. (R50)

The wind cries out for water, the water for earth,
and the earth for the garment and ornaments of greenery.
The frogs call to the crickets, the crickets to the skylark,
the skylark to the cuckoos, the cuckoos for something as pleasant as svāti drops.

[16]The powers of the two are compared here.

Ṭhākur says, where such shouts are exchanged
the beloved calls out for her lover in a true voice.
The season calls to the peacocks, the peacocks to the clouds,
the clouds call to the lightning and lightning to darkness. (R52)

Donning an ochre shawl, which is like the flash of lightning, I have climbed on the rooftop
and I am watching the clouds.
I attentively listen to the cry of the peacocks as they lustily enjoy their union in love.
Ṭhākur says, my dear one is far away and I am soaking my body in tears.
Blessed indeed are the monsoon nights in which I sleep on the chest of my lord. (R54)

They are like well-polished, pure baskets shining with brilliance
spread spectacularly by their craftsman, the Creator.
Proud of their colours, beautiful and attractive with their red waves,
they surge with beauty and they contain pleasant water.
Ṭhākur says, filled with radiance, my companion,
abounding in splendour, I made them the object of a comparison:
scattered here and there they are the chinaware
of Monsoon, the fakir, or of the Love God, the nobleman. (R55)

The monsoon night is heavy and darker than lampblack;
the streams of water are an endless ocean—one cannot sound it.
Drumming and thumping the clouds thunder and lowering they run;
the lightning flashes like the edge of an unsheathed scimitar.
Ṭhākur says, whizzing and whizzing is heard constantly;
and the continuous patter of the rain is beyond all praise.
It boils away the peace of lonely women and sprinkles pain—
the raining cloud is like the Love God's frying-pan put on the fire. (R56)

When it appeared on the southern sky mounting on a terrible thick cloud,
it advanced to afflict great pain on the lonely woman.
Ṭhākur says, looking a bit through the window the woman said,
"Look, my companion, how dense this colour of darkness is."
When one says that it is a cloud, she does not accept it and states "You don't know
I am able to recognize what is coming with thunder.
"It is not lightning; it's his sword, his glittering rod—
Death is coming with his retinue to take away my life." (R57)

As the clouds started to roll my body was thrilled,
the peacocks, who take their pleasure in the groves, started to cry.
Disregarding me, the frogs croak day and night
as if repeatedly wanting to say farewell to the hot season.
Ṭhākur says, look how the powerful monsoon has come,
the previously dejected herons are seen flying.
As if weighed down by burden and pressed from every side, my companion,
the treacherous clouds started to stay with me. (R58)

The earth turned green; the roads are invisible under streams of water: even things that
do not flow, flow now.

Black clouds have caused darkness and no difference remained between day and night.
Ṭhākur, it is impossible to go from one house to another: I am deeply concerned.
How could they come? What can they do? My friend, is it the fault of the poor travellers? (R59)

The peacock cries out saying "I'm going to the hills."
the frog calls out saying, "I'm going to the crevices."
The cuckoo on the tree-branches calls out saying "my love, my love"[17]
the cricket chirps and the koel is intoxicated with love.
Ṭhākur says, seeing this beauty of the monsoon,
the pain of longing women, O my friend, has come to full bloom.
As the music plays "cham cham cham cham chum chei chei
thei thei" the lightning dances among the clouds. (R62)

Its body is the dark cloud, its teeth are the white-footed herons
and the call of the eastern wind resounds.
It has beautiful head-ornaments, the lightning, and a cover of rainbow;
and the staff of its goad, the flash, is fair.
Ṭhākur says, mounted on it is the Intoxicating Love-god;
and venting its constant anger the wind urges it on.
When my beloved is abroad, this hostile companion of love,
the elephant-asterism-rain, falls and tramples my heart. (R63)

Cloud in his body, lightning in his garment,
herons in his pearl-necklace.[18]*—Go to him with eager heart!*
Your ears, like the cuckoo, are thirsting for his svāti-*raindrop-words,*[19]
open up your peacock-mind filled with the deep sound of his flute![20]
Ṭhākur says, the world is savoury with passionate emotions,
so join him with frank, openly admitted fervour.
The riverside, the pond, the grove, the orchard, the in and outside of the house—
all are meeting-places for the Dark One—meet him sometime! (R66)

KAJALĪ[21]

You are neither from the family nor from outside. Why are you involved with slander?
I am eager for spectacle; no one can keep me back.
Today on the feast of the auspicious and lovely Śrāvaṇ
I am adorning my body with beautiful ornaments.

[17] The cuckoo's perceived call *piu piu* means "my dear, my dear" in Braj.

[18] The cloud, the lightning and the herons are conventional *uddīpan*s, stimuli to excite the emotion of love.

[19] This image is slightly inappropriate in a verse about the rainy season since the asterism *svāti* refers to the autumn. However, the cuckoo's connection to the raindrops overshadows this slip.

[20] The deep sound also refers to the sound of the thunder that makes peacocks dance.

[21] *Kajarī* or *Kajalī* is a type of song sung throughout the month of Śrāvaṇ related to the women's festival at *Śrāvaṇ badī* 3 (July-August), for which barley and oats are grown and then immersed in water in the accompaniment of *Kajarī* songs.

Ṭhākur says, together with the other girls of Braj
I will enthusiastically sing Kajalī-songs full of emotion.
Seeing her rākhī-bracelet bound on the arm of the dear Cowherd
I will go with Radha to immerse in water the barley and the oats.[22] (R67)

THE WORLD AND PROPER CONDUCT

The Ways of the World

Blessed are you, Creator; there is no end to your works;
looking at them over and over again, one describes them in varied ways.
Some people you made dull, others sophisticated and attractive,
some are beautiful and bestowed with greatness.
Ṭhākur says, bodies and characters—all different;
people receive varied natures and dispositions.
One is very pleased not to see and not to hear some people, at the same time one lives on looking at others. (N1)

What can I say of your incoherent ways, O Creator,
You bestowed love on man and separation on love.
You gave trouble to the intelligent and wealth to the dull;
You did not work in a way that is suitable.
Ṭhākur says, if the Creator had any brains,
would then gods, demons, men and animals be enchanted?
If a beautiful man was sensitive to others' pain
and if there was fragrance in gold, who could then praise them? (N2)

Sometimes it enjoys delights of love in union that even the King of Gods may desire.
Sometimes it suffers such pangs of separation that may be beyond expression even for ascetics.
Ṭhākur says, I have pondered how distinct its ways may be.
This human body, my companion, becomes truly valiant when need arises. (N4)

For its sake, one constantly takes all kinds of food; for its sake, one takes horses and elephants.
For its sake, everyone makes clever remarks; for its sake, one collects wealth and makes an abode.
Ṭhākur says, look, in order to preserve it one drinks the bitter medicine of neem.
Look, how it is burnt and thrown away as soon as this body abandons life. (N6)

The prestige of arrogant cheats has increased greatly
the words of the learned and thoughtful are treated as inauthentic.
No one consults poets, experts or connoisseurs
while thousands host ingratitude.
Ṭhākur says, look at the power of the Dark Age;
the world is mad for the words of the false.

[22] The festival of *Rakṣābandhan* nowadays is eleven days later, on the last day of *Śrāvaṇ*.

Look, even the greatest places keep sinking into sin;
The soul is utterly dispirited—this is the industry of the bizarre. (N7)

A BAD PERSON

Your friend cheats you, your mother has enmity in her heart
and your father wants to kill you—how can one live like this?
The lord whom you serve doesn't protect you,
his eyes glaze over—how can you offer your life for him?
The ferryman whose boat you boarded wants to sink it on purpose.
Ṭhākur says, the unsuspecting, therefore, wastes away day by day.
When your king abandons law, when your companion strikes you,
when your fence eats your field—what is then the way ahead? (N12)

You passed your days uselessly when you created
blind, dull, wretched and arrogant people.
Couldn't you see with your own eyes the rogues, idlers,
liars, eunuchs, bastards, slanderers and crooks?
Ṭhākur says, you have created to no avail these
miserly, thick and obtuse receptacles of disgrace.
Absolutely hopeless, they're no use to anyone,—o my god,
for what purpose have you fashioned such phonies? (N14)

A person who is not for passion, love, fighting in a battle,
or the companionship of women; who has never been tortured by Kāma,
What would he tell of glory or disgrace? He knows no emotion.
Animal fate is written on his forehead.
What does a troglodyte[23] *know of the human world?*
He deceived the world by being called human.
To my mind, he was made by taking the soul of Śītalā's donkey,
and casting it in stone. (N16)

THE LORDS OF THE WORLD

In Kabul, he sowed nuts[24] *in plenty—when he came to Vrindaban he planted caper-bush.*[25]
Foregoing a fair woman like Radha he fell in love with his hunchback.
He discarded Duryodhana's dry fruits—to eat the banana peels of Vidura's wife in his house.[26]
Ṭhākur, what shall I say of my Lord? Lords have always been crazy. (N22)

[23]Troglodyte—"dweller of a well" in the original—refers to the Hindi phrase designating a parochial person: *kūp-maṇḍūk*, "frog in a well".

[24]The Hindi word *mevā* is a collective name for dry fruits, such as peanuts, almonds and cashew nuts valued high in India.

[25]Caper bush *(karīl)* is a thorny plant found in abundance around Vrindaban.

[26]This is a reference to a popular story developed from an event described in the *Udyoga Parva* of the Mahabharata (5.39). When Duryodhana offered Krishna a stay in his guest house, Krishna chose to be with Vidura in his home. When Krishna entered his house, Vidura was not there. His wife seeing Krishna standing at their door was utterly overjoyed. She offered Krishna a seat and treated him with bananas. In her elation, she peeled the banana, gave the skin to Krishna and threw the fruit down.

He ate the tailor's rice boiled in milk[27], *Karmābāī's khichri*[28]
and the pulse-pakora of Raidās, though he was a leather-worker.
He fancied Vidura's fried fat-hen and chapati of millet,
and his wife gave him banana peels to eat.
With peaceful determination he came as the incarnation of Buddha,
and was received for a meal by a prostitute in her town.[29]
A companion of the lowly, unrelated to castes and ranks,
the Lord has always been capricious. (N24)

TRUE SERVICE

I am the poet and soldier of Rajputs
who never turn away from gifts and battles.
I give prudent counsel to the kings of the earth;
I am fond of the true-hearted lovers.
Ṭhākur says, I am the enemy of the stupid;
the cruel son-in-law of the miserly father-in-law.
I am the thief of wonders and the emperor of the surges of emotion;
called Lord but I'm the servant of the intelligent. (N25)

Firstly he is benevolent, secondly generous;
Thirdly, he has eyes to perceive things as they are;
Fourthly he is a connoisseur, fifthly of my interest;
Sixthly he should not be a deceiver—this is what the Scriptures say.
Ṭhākur says, seventhly he seeks good repute;
Eighthly he should only use noble words;
Ninthly he is of goodwill, tenthly destroys poverty—
It is such men that I serve as an artist. (N26)

MANLINESS

Those men are eventually praised and bathe in happiness who keep drinking from the cup of love,
Who always apply the sandalwood of God's fame on their entire body and put on the sectarian mark of delight and the bindi of emotions.

[27]The tailor is the Maharashtrian saint Nāmdev, popular throughout North-Western India. The story of his feeding milk to God is already referred to in his earliest hagiography in the sixteenth century. See W. M. Callewaert and M. Lath, *The Hindī Padāvalī of Nāmdev: A Critical Edition of Nāmdev's Hindi Songs with Translation and Annotation,* Delhi: Motilal Banarsidass, 1989, p. 17.

[28]According to a popular legend, Karmā used to prepare khichri for God early in the morning without having her bath. Her name is taken when puri is eaten with khichri.

[29]This is a reference to the courtesan Ambapālī of Vesāli inviting the Buddha. The story is already present in the *Khuddaka Nikāya,* part 9 *(Therigāthā)* Canto 13 and the *Dīgha Nikāya* 16 *(Mahāparinibbānasutta)* 2, 16-26. Her figure has captured popular Indian imagination beyond Buddhism and is present even in Indian cinema.

Ṭhākur says, they are far gentler than a delicate lotus
and holding the form of the Enchanter they keep courage in their heart.
Whether they meet one at appropriate or inappropriate time, whether of good conduct or not,
their enthusiasm is doubled and they view the world consistently. (N28)

Until they meet some connoisseur
they look poor in their body.
When a connoisseur finds them their worth also increases millionfold;
they are more valuable than their price. They are of sharp minds.
Ṭhākur says, do not abuse the virtuous ones:
they look like lowly men but they are the heroes on earth.
In a few places, by God's grace, there is a man like this—
men full of wisdom are gems covered by dust. (N29)

He does not fear to make friends or enemies;
he does not tremble in his heart before a king or a prince;
Lion and goat look alike, O friends,
to one who is resolved to fulfil his desire.
Ṭhākur says,—I have thought it over thoroughly—
this is the only genuine way of manliness.
What one seized, is seized, what he left is left,
what one did is done and what one didn't do, is not. (N30)

If a man who is present in one's pain and doesn't look at the difference between people
exposes one's hidden crookedness, then it is exposed.
If a man has a resolution, then without charm or incantation
he is able to drive out the poison of snakebite and it is driven out.
Ṭhākur says, do not consider anything difficult in your mind—
what is there that cannot be resolved by brave acts?
If four men from four directions grab its four corners
and shake to uproot mount Meru, then it is uprooted. (N31)

Generosity

If the Creator gave you greatness, and seeing it someone approaches you,
then you should hasten with compassion to favour him.
Give him wealth and acquire fame for your life in this world,
be always prompt in your mind to remove the suffering of the needy.
Ṭhākur says, if you cannot donate from your purse,
even if you cannot give, do not refrain from beneficence.
If someone profits from your words,
do not be negligent in saying good words. (N33)

Forbidden ten times, twenty times—
and if in spite of this he does not mind it then let him burn in hell.
Whatever one does in whatsoever way is not one's own deed.
Let everyone live out their days as they have them.

Ṭhākur says, keep your mind immersed
in love and let it revel fearlessly in the colours of this emotion.
There are so many souls made by the Creator; in every place
playing and rushing—let them all play and rush. (N34)

THE ART OF POETRY

The one who strings it like a charming necklace of pearls and produces it by joining rhymes and syllables;
Forming the matter in an excellent way speaks of the path of love and of the story of God's name;
Ṭhākur: I like the poet who earns greatness in a royal assembly—
And the thing that enchants the mind of the connoisseurs among the scholars is called poetry. (N36)

They have learnt the imagery of fish, deer, wagtail, lotus or moon;
They have learnt to say 'fame and valour abound';
They have learnt about the wondrous jewel, Mount Meru or the wish-granting tree;
they have learnt to say that aesthetic delight should be tasted within the heart;
Ṭhākur says, consider how difficult it is
words can never, not even accidentally confine it.
Still they churn it out and introduce it to the assembly:
people think composing poetry is an easy game. (N37)

It is taken from the ancient ideas of the Vedas, the Smriti and the Puranas,
has the brilliance of good writing, of history and of the supreme truth.[30]
It is morally right, beautiful, agrees with proper tradition and is filled with love;
it exhibits the well-known proofs of proper conduct.
Ṭhākur says, blessed is, Tulsī, your literature:
unutterable story saturated with overwhelming emotions.
It is like the moon, like the jasmine, it flows like the Ganges,
like the cloud of the Magha[31] *asterism it showers Rama's glory.* (N38)

[30]This line can also be interpreted as 'It radiates gold when touched with (the touchstone of) history.'
[31]*Magha* is the name of the tenth lunar asterism in which rains are the most beneficent.

Bibliography

'Ali, Sayyid Azhar, ed. *Safarnāma-i Mukẖlis: The Diary of the travel of Anand Ram Mukhlis,* d. 1164 AH, Rampur, 1946.

'Barsainya', Ganga Prasad "Bundelkhaṇḍī kavi ṭhākur (ṭhākurdās kāyastha) aur unkā kāvya." *Bundelī basant* (2002): 25-9.

'Shankar', Gaurishankar Dvivedi. *Bundel-vaibhav athavā bundelkhaṇḍ ke hindī kaviyõ kā sāṅgopāṅg itihās (sacitra aur saṭippaṇ),* 3 vols. Bundelvaibhav Granthamālā. Agra: Śānti Press, vols. 1-2: 1935, vol. 3 n.d.).

Andhare, B.R. *Bundelkhand under the Marathas, 1720-1818 A.D.: A Study of Maratha-Bundela Relations,* Nagpur: Vishwa Bharati Prakashan, 1984.

Avasthi, Vandana. *Kavi ṭhākur: kavitt evaṁ racnākār*. Lucknow, 1990.

Bangha, Imre. *The First Published Anthology of Hindi Poets: Thomas Duer Broughton's Selections from the Popular Poetry of the Hindoos – 1814*. New Delhi: Mahatma Gandhi International Hindi University and Rainbow Publishers, 2000.

———. "Lover and Saint: The Early Development of Anandghan's Reputation." *Journal of the Royal Asiatic Society* 11, no. 2 (2001): 175-90.

———. "Political Contextualisation, Individualism and Search for a New Style in Late Brajbhasha Court Poetry: The quatrains of Ṭhākur from Bundelkhand." In *Bhakti in Current Research 2000-2003: Procedings of the Ninth International Conference on Early Devotional Literature in New Indo-Aryan Languages, Heidelberg, 23-26 July 2003*, ed. Monika Horstmann, 1-13. New Delhi: Manohar, 2006.

———. "Romantic poetry in the Era of Convention? The Emergence of the Idea of a Rītimukt Trend within Hindi Mannerist Literature." *South Asia Research* 25, no. 1 (2005): 13-30.

Bangha, Imre and Balázs Déri. *Ánandghan: A Jótudásúhoz: a nőhöz és istenhez*. New Delhi: Hungarian Information and Cultural Centre, 1996.

Bansal, Umarani. *Kavivar dayānidhi aur unkā kāvya*. Kasganj: Sūkarkṣetr Śodh Saṁsthān, 2001.

Bayly, C.A. *Empire and Information: Intelligence Gathering and Social Communication in India, 1780-1870*, Cambridge: Cambridge University Press, 1996.

Bhagavandin, Lala. *Ṭhākur ṭhasak*. Benares: Sāhitya Sevak Kāryālay, 1924.

Broughton, Thomas Duer. *Letters Written in a Mahratta Camp During the Year 1809: Descriptive of the character manners domestic habits and religious ceremonies of the Mahrattas*. London: Murray, 1813. Reprint, Westminster: Archibald Constable and Company, 1892—A new edition with an Introduction by the right Honourable Sir M.E. Grant Duff G.C.S.I. F.R.S.); New Delhi and Madras: Asian Educational Services, 1995.

———. *Selections from the popular poetry of the Hindoos*. London: Whittingham and Rowland, 1814.

Bryant, Kenneth E. "Three-three-two versus Four-by-four: Metrical Frames for the Padas of Surdas." In *Devotional Literature in South Asia: Current Research 1985-1988*, ed. R. Stuart McGregor, 209-24. Cambridge: Cambridge University Press, 1992.

Busch, Allison. *Poetry of Kings: the Classical Hindi Literature of Mughal India*, New York: Oxford University Press, 2011.

Callewaert, Winand M. and Mukund Lath. *The Hindī Padāvalī of Nāmdev: A Critical Edition of Nāmdev's Hindi Songs with Translation and Annotation*. Delhi: Motilal Banarsidass, 1989.

Chaturvedi, Javaharlal. *Brajbhāṣā rītiśāstra granth koś*. Prayag: Hindi Sahitya Sammelan, 1965.

Chaturvedi, Shivdatt, and Vidyanivas Mishra. *Dev kī dīpśikhā*. 2nd edn. New Delhi: Vāṇī Prakāśan, 1988.

Cheler, Janardan Rav, ed. *Vṛnd granthāvalī*. Agra: Vinod Pustak Mandir, 1971.

Das, Syamsundar. *Annual Report on the Search for Hindi Manuscripts for the Year 1904*. Allahabad: United Provinces Government Press, 1907. Reprint, Varanasi: Nāgarīpracāriṇī Sabhā, 1995.

———. *Annual Report on the Search for Hindi Manuscripts for the Year 1905*. Allahabad: United Provinces Government Press, 1908. Reprint, Varanasi: Nāgarīpracāriṇī Sabhā, 1995.

Dikshit, Bandidin, ed. *Prayāganārāyaṇ-vilās*. Lucknow: Navalkiśor Press, 1906.

Fairbanks, Florence. "Hindi Stress: A New Approach thru Meter." Paper presented at *Linguistics Club*, University of Minnesota, 1987.

Garcin de Tassy, J.H. *Histoire de la littérature hindoui et hindoustanie,* vols. 1-3. Paris, 1870-1. Reprint, New York, Franklin, 1968.

Grierson, George Abraham. *Linguistic Survey of India*. Calcutta: Office of the Superintendent of Government Printing, India, 1903.

———. *The modern vernacular literature of Hindustan*. Calcutta: Asiatic Society, 1889.

Gupta, Kishorilal. *Saroj sarvekṣaṇ*. Allahabad: Hindustānī Ekeḍemī, 1967.

Hawley, John Stratton. *Sur's Ocean*, Harvard Oriental Series. Cambridge: Harvard University Press, (forthcoming).

Hiralal, ed. *The twelfth report on the search of Hindi manuscripts for the years 1923, 1924 and 1925*. Varanasi: Nāgarīpracāriṇī Sabhā, 1944.

Hunter, W.W. *Imperial Gazetteer of India: Indore to Kardang,* 2nd edn. vol. 7. London: Trübner & Co., 1886.

The Imperial Gazetteer of India. New edn. 26 vols. Oxford: Clarendon Press, 1907.

Imperial Gazetteer of India: Central India. Calcutta: Superintendent of Government Printing, 1908.

Islam, Khurshidul, and Ralph Russell. *Three Mughal Poets*. London: Allen & Unwin, 1969.

Jatav, Ramkishan, Devkumar, and Vinodkumar. *Rājasthānī-hindī hastalikhit granth-sūcī*. Jodhpur: Rajasthan Oriental Research Institute, 1995.

Kellogg, Samuel H., and Thomas Grahame Bailey. *A grammar of the Hindí language: in which are treated the high Hindí, Braj, and the eastern Hindí of the Rámáyan of Tulsí Dás: also the colloquial dialects of Rájputáná, Kumáon, Avadh, Ríwá, Bhojpúr, Magadha, Maithila, etc.: with copious philological notes*. 3rd edn. London: K. Paul, Trench, Trubner and Co., Limited, 1938.

Kishorilal, ed. *Gvāl kavi kṛt kavi-darpaṇ*. Delhi: Anaṅg Prakāśan, 2007.

Kolff, Dirk H. A. *Naukar, Rajput and Sepoy: The Ethnohistory of the Military Labour Market in Hindustan, 1450-1850*, Cambridge: Cambridge University Press, 1990.

Losensky, Paul. "Moḥtaśam Kāśānī". *Encyclopaedia Iranica* (2004), *http://www.iranica.com/articles/mohtasham-kashani*.

Malviy, Lakshmidhar, ed. *Dev sampūrṇ granthāvalī*, 3 vols. Delhi: Āditya Prakāśan, 2002.

Mathur, Surendra. *Kavi ṭhākur aur unkā kāvya*. New Delhi: Young Asia Publications, 1969.

Mishra, Chandrashekhar, ed. *Ṭhākur granthāvalī*. Varanasi: Nāgarīpracāriṇī Sabhā, 1973.

Mishra, Satyaprakash, ed. *Rahīm racanāvalī*. Allahabad: Lokbhārtī Prakāśan, 1994.

Mishra, Sureshdatt. *Kavivar gopālrāy aur unkā kāvya*, Ph.D. dissertation, 1982.

Mishra, Vishvanathprasad, ed. *Bhikhārīdās granthāvalī*, vol. 1. Varanasi: Nāgarīpracāriṇī Sabhā, 1965.

———, ed. *GhanĀnand (granthāvalī)*. Varanasi: Vāṇī Vitān, 1952.

———, ed. *GhanĀnand aur Ānandghan (granthāvalī)*. Varanasi: Vāṇī Vitān, 1945.

———. *Hindī sāhitya kā atīt*, vol. 2. Varanasi: Vāṇī Vitān, 1960.

———, ed. *Padmākar: Jagadvinod*. Varanasi: Vāṇī Vitān, 1965.

———, ed. *Rāmcaritmānas*. Varanasi: Kāśīrāj, [1962].

Narayan, Pitambar and S. Bhaskaran Nayar. *Hindī-sāhitya-sāriṇī: Hindī mẽ san 1964 ke ant tak prakāśit sabhī granthõ kā vaijñānik prakriyānusār vargīkṛt evaṁ kramabaddha vivaraṇ*, vol. 1. Vishveshvaranand Indological Series. Hoshiarpur: Vishveshvaranand Institute, 1971.

Pachauri, Bhagavan Sahay. *Mahākavi gvāl: vyaktitva evaṁ kṛtitva*. Mathura: Rājyaśrī Prakāśan, 1973.

Pandey, Gopalsharan. *Kavi ṭhākur*. Ranchi: College of Commerce, 1990.

Pandey, Sudhakar, ed. *Bihārī satsaī: lālcandrikā se yukta*. Varanasi: Nāgarīpracāriṇī Sabhā, 1977.

Pauwels, Heidi Rika Maria. "New Indo-Aryan Poetry in Performance: Metre and Oral Formulae as Exemplified in the Poetry of Harirām Vyās." In *Studies in early modern Indo-Aryan languages, literature, and culture: research papers, 1992-1994, presented at the Sixth Conference on Devotional Literatrure in New Indo-Aryan Languages, held at Seattle, University of Washington, 7-9 July 1994*, ed. Alan W. Entwistle, Carol Solomon, Heidi Pauwels and Michael C. Shapiro, 311-38. New Delhi: Manohar, 1999.

Pinch, William. "Who was Himmat Bahādur? Gosains, Rajputs and the British in Bundelkhand ca. 1800." *The Indian Economic and Social History Review* 35, no. 3 (1998): 293-335.

Pinch, William R. *Warrior ascetics and Indian empires*. New York: Cambridge University Press, 2006.

Prasad, R.C., ed. *Tulasidasa's Shriramacharitamanasa: The Holy Lake of the Acts of Rama*. Delhi: Motilal Banarsidass, 1990. Reprint, 1999.

Rao, Velcheru Narayana, and David Shulman. *God on the Hill: Temple Poems from Tirupati*. New York: Oxford University Press, 2005.

Ratnakar, Jagannathdas. *Ghaṇākṣarī-niyam-ratnākar*. Varanasi: Bhārat Jīvan Press, 1897.

Ray, Vijay Shankar. *Svacchand kāvyadhārā aur kavi ṭhākur*. Varanasi: Manīś Prakāśan, 2008.

Sharma, Jagdev Kumar. *Rītimukt kavi ṭhākur aur unkā kāvya*. New Delhi: Sañjay Prakāśan, 2006.

Sharma, Vinaymohan, ed. *Hindī sāhitya kā bṛhat itihās*, vol. 8*: Hindī sāhitya kā abhyutthān: bhāratendu yug saṁ 1900-1950*. Kāśī: Nāgarīpracāriṇī Sabhā, 1972.

Shyamsundardas. *Hasatalikhit hindī granthõ kī khoj kā vivaraṇ san 1905 (Annual report for the search for Hindi manuscripts for the year 1905)*. Allahabad: United Provinces Government Press, 1908. Reprint, Varanasi: Nāgarīpracāriṇī Sabhā 1995 [vs 2052].

Singh, Amarjit. *Rīti kavitā ke sandarbh mẽ ṭhākur kā kavittva-kṛtitva*. Amritsar: Guru Nanak Dev University, 1985.

Singh, Baburamdin, ed. *Sundarītilak*. Bānkīpur (Patna): Khadgavilās Press, 1892.

Singh, Saheb. "Provincialisation of the Vernacular: Navīn's Sudhāsar in the Gurmukhi Script." M. Phil. dissertation, University of Oxford, 2009.

Snell, Rupert. *The Hindi Classical Tradition: A Braj Bhāṣā Reader*, London: School of Oriental and African Studies, 1991.

Tripathi, Rampher. "Rītimukt śṛṅgār kāvya: Pramukh kavi." In *Hindī sāhitya kā bṛhat itihās (Rītikāl: rītimukt)*, ed. Bhagirath Mishra, 59-110. Varanasi: Nāgarīpracāriṇī Sabhā, 1972.

Vajpeyi, Nandadulare, ed. *Sūrsāgar*, 2 vols. Varanasi: Nāgarīpracāriṇī Sabhā, 1950-2.

Varma, Krishna Chandra. *Kavivar ṭhākur*. Delhi: Niraj Book Centre, 2000.

Varma, Siddheshwar. *G. A. Grierson's Linguistic Survey of India: A summary*, 3 vols. Hoshiarpur: Vishveshvaranand Institute, Panjab University, 1972.

Vidyarthi, Devinder Singh. *Pañjāb ke darbārī kaviyõ ke paripekṣya mẽ kavi gvāl ke kavitva kā adhyayan*. Patiala: Bhāṣā Vibhāg, 1983.

Index of Poems

Quatrains translated into English are marked with asterisk.

अंक न जानत ओलंम को N17

*अंध, अबिबेकीए, अभागे N14

अंबु-तनै-हित नेक रह्यौ U12

अखती की तीज तजवीज R28

*अखती रची राधिका मोहन सों R29

अजौं चलु प्यारो तोहि U11

अद्धर को है अधार हरी B13

अनगढ बातें कहा कहियै N2

अपने अपने निज गेहन B32॥

अब का कहियै, किहि सों Ś64

*अब का समझावती को समझै Ś123

अब न अटोकि मोहि Ś55

*अरे लाल सनेही, सनेह तज्यौ Ś68

*आँखिन देखत ध्यान मैं Ś96

आए बढि-चढि से R35

आइ अगीत पछीत गई Ś41

आई आई पावस अवाई छाई R51

आऔ, चलौ, देखियै जू B33

आग सी धँधाती ताती R36

आगी बीच दैकै कहूँ Ś98

आजु यहि कौतुक छको B34

आपनो बनाइबे कों, और को N13

आड़े न रहत, रोम ठाढ़े R69

आनि जुरीं बिजुरी सी B53

*आप सूनो सदन बिलोकि Ś95

आपने रूप गुमान छकी Ś126

आम-मौर झौरैं R4
*आवत हैं देखे कैसी B27
*आवते जौ आप तो B62
आवहु, लाल, दिखाय Ś49
*आवै चली गजचाल सों बाल Ś132
इत आए गुलाल सों बूडे R24
*इतै राखी चहैं Ś53
*ऊधौ जू, भाग हमारे लटे B61
एकन की कंचुकी चुपरि R23
*एक समै सुख की सदन Ś90
*ए कहैं ऐसी है B42
एक ही सों चित चाहिये Ś111
एकै खिन खिन माँझ B7
एकै नंदगांव के झपट B40
ए तो ब्रजमंडल-बसत Ś113
*एरी मेरी बीर, कंत Ś131
ए री, सुन, चारु B23
ऐसी इह चाह की Ś57
*ऐ सुंगहा कछु सोधु न पावै Ś154
ऐसे, कहौ, कहा कारज होत है B36
ऐसो अंध, अधम, अभागो N5
*ओपे से अमल झल झलक R56
*कढ़ी दिशि दक्षिण ते R57
कढौ जिन बाहिर, बढौ न Ś153
*कबहूँ वा सँयोग के भोग करै N4
करीस सो पील देख U1
कहा कीजै, तू न आई N11
कहते न बनै कछु Ś135
कहि आई इहाँ की कुरीति लखें Ś134

कहिबे की कछू न, कहा कहिये B50
*कहिबे सुनिबे की कछू न इहां Ś136
का करियै तुम्हरे मन को Ś117
का करियै पराधीन भई Ś56
का कहि, बाल, गोपालहि Ś102
का कहियै, कोऊ पीरकौ नाहिनै Ś137
का कहियै, परी नेह अधीन Ś87
काजर की रेख नैन Ś59
काठ तें एतो कठोर भयो Ś88
कान्ह, सुनी, अहो राजा भए U6
काबुल जायके मेवा रच्यो N23
*काम कर तेज Ś93
काम के तीर सी Ś23
*कारे कारे बद्दल सुहाए R37
कारे लाल करहे पलासन R2
*कारे लाल पीले धौरे R38
काल्हि कहूँ हँसि बोली Ś35
काहु के होइ तौ कैसी Ś46
काहू प्रबीन नै प्रेम सौ सींचि N8
काहे, अरे मऩ, साहस Ś72
*काहे को बिकल होती B35
कीरतिकुँवरि कहें B10
*कूबरी कान्हर का B64
कूबरौ नीकौ मिलौ है B67
कूर होते कुबरे N21
कृपन कंजूस बड़े N18
*केकी लागे नाचन R48
*केसर सुगंधहू के R14
*कैइक बेर कह्यो नित ऐहै Ś127

*कैसे ग्वार, बल कैसो R26
कैसी करौं, कासों कहौं Ś138
*कैसे पीत-पटवारो B37
*कैसे सुचित्त भए निकसौ Ś139
*को उनसों परबीन बडो Ś5
*कोटि कला करिकैं Ś62
*कोमलता कंज तें Ś15
कौंल को महल Ś33
कौन गुनाह परो हम सों Ś114
कौन से केलि के मंदिर ते B41
*कौन हौ जू, जोतिसी हैं Ś36
*खेत-कुटुंब तें B55
*गति मेरी यही Ś116
गाँठ गँठीली चमेली की R30
गाइयै सुजस बिसराइयै कुजस U7
गाए पिक जालनि करालनि R13
गावैं पिकबैनी, मृगनैनी R1
गुनगाहक सों बिनती Ś10
गैल में छैल कढ़ै U2
*गोपी-गोप-गाइन पै B30
ग्वारन को यार है B22
*घन ऐसे तन माँझ R66
*घन घहरान लागे R58
*घर के न बाहर के R67
घर पास परोसिनि घैर Ś142
घर-बाहर, पास-परोस Ś52
घर बाहर लोग लुगाइन Ś141
घूमैं घटा, छटा R39
घैर करै सगरै Ś58

घैर भयौ सिगरी नगरी Ś143
घैरवारी, बैरवारी Ś50
*चंडित मनोज कैसे झला R40
*चलिये, छबीले छैल Ś80
*चारहूँ ओर उदै Ś97
*चाल न वा, चरचा न वा Ś109
*चाह देखी चोजवारी Ś3
*चीन्हत नाहिनै, को है गुविंद B44
*चौक-आसमान में R41
चौचँदहाई जरैं ब्रज की Ś144
चौहट को मिलिबो तौ रह्यौ Ś145
छबि देखत ही बनि आवति Ś32
*छल छोडि कै दौरि मिले Ś86
*छिपिया को दूधभात N24
छानि बसुधा है, सुधा N35
छोटे कों छोटो B4
*छोडि पतिव्रत प्रीति Ś120
जगर मगर जरबाफिये Ś29
जब तें निरखे मनमोहन जू Ś146
जब तें बिलोकि गई Ś51
*जब ते, अली, लाल बिदेस गयो Ś84
जा दिन जान लगे परदेस B48
जान नीको पिय को मिलाप R65
जाउ न कुंजन मैं B29
जाकी लगी हुती रावरे Ś105
*जानत ही अपने नहीं Ś122
*जान-पहचान मुसक्यान नाहि Ś152
*जानिऐ न जाति B66

*जानि झुकामुकी भेष छिपाय R27
जानि पर्यो जग पेखनो है N32
*जानी जात रावरे Ś79
जाने जौन काज कों B15
*जारहीं जात लखो Ś119
जिन बलबीरहि बिलोक्यो B46
जिहि भाँति निहारत आनि हते Ś69
जीव को जीव है Ś11
*जैसई लाल बडे B54
जैसो मंजु माथे पै B28
जो छबिता कछु देखियै Ś115
जो सुख देइ तो B2
जोतिषी बिचार कहै Ś37
जौ चाहौ तौ मेल कै B52
*जौ लौं काहू पारखी तें N29
झूम देइ झूला में B25
झूलत पाट की डोरी Ś14
ठाढे हूजै, यामैं Ś48
*ठाढी रहौ, न डगौ R16
डारत कै पग-पाँवडे Ś27
डार्यौ जौ गुलाल R17
डीलदार, सीलदार Ś16
*तन को तरसाइबो कौने Ś103
तन देखि, बन देखि Ś107
तान लगे, तरवार लगे Ś17
तुमही बिचारौ निरधारौ Ś67
तेरे द्रग तीच्छन हैं U3
थिगरी न लगै, ऊधो B59
*दंभी दगाबाजन की बाढी N7

*दगा देइ यार और माता N12
*दस बार, बीस बार N34
दहने परी देह बियोग Ś63
दादुर ग्रीषम बोलै U15
दान दया बिन दीबो कहा U9
*दिन दिन, जाम जाम, R10
दिन बीसक तीसक तें B47
*दिल साँचो लग्यौ जिहि को Ś66
*दिवरानी जिठानी सबै Ś31
दुखवारे सुखवारे जुग जुग N27
दूरि है बतात कहा Ś118
*दृग मूँदिकै अंचर सौं R18
देखत ही चित लेइ Ś34
देखती ती ललितादि जहाँ B38
देखन के नीके और टेरै N20
देखि तमासो दिसा-बिदिसा R47
*देखें घनस्याम मैं Ś148
देखे अकेले किते दिन ह्वै गए Ś147
*देह मेरी छूटै B45
दौरि दौरि, दमकि दमकि R42
दौलत या दीजै B16
धनि धनि कहत B21
धनि हैं तुव तात औ मात U4
धना और सदना B8
*धन्य, बिधि, तेरी रचनान कौ N1
धम धम धौंसन की B26
*धिक कान जे आन की B56
नलिनी बिधु बीच Ś61
*नाथ नथो है तिहारे Ś101

*नाहर सी ननदी Ś30
*निज मंत्र न औरन सों कहने Ś151
*नीर सो माँचि रह्यौ रँग R20
*न्यौते गए घर के सिगरे Ś128
*पत्र बन-बेलिन के R9
*परि गे किधौं काहु Ś73
पास अहार जो सिंह मरै U13
पावस के परस बियोगी R53
पावस को परपंच बिलोकि R43
*पावस-प्रपंच को तमासो R44
पावस प्रवेस देखबे कौं R64
पावस में परदेस तें R45
पिय प्यार करैं जेहि पै Ś8
*पिय मोहन कौ वह Ś83
*पुतरीन पुजाय किसोरी सुजान R31
*पौन टेरै पानी काजै R52
पौन के पुंज धरा तें R8
*प्रथमे मेहिरि कैया होइ N26
प्रनव प्रसिद्ध B1
*परभात भयैं सुधि आवै B68
प्रानन प्रेम की B18
फागुन के औसर अनोखे R19
*फूलन फुलावन है R11
फूलि उठे सुमन, मधुप R12
बन जाइ बने, बिगरे बिगरे B57
बरुनीन में नैन झुकैं Ś74
बाँके बनैत पटैत Ś20
बार बीच अधिक अधीन ह्वै N3

*बाहर लौं न कढै Ś124
*बिधना बडाई दई N33
बिन आदर पाय कै बैठि ढिगाँ N19
बिन बूझें ही ऊतर Ś110
बिप्र की बानी सुने Ś39
बीतो बसंत, मिलो नहि कंत R33
बुरो मानती जो सिख देत Ś133
*बृंदा सी बृंद B49
बेदन के भेदन तें B11
बेदन को सार B9
*बेदमत सुम्रत पुरानन N38
बैठे पटा पर Ś38
*बैर प्रीति करिबे की N30
*बौर मौर, किंसुक सु R3
*बौरे रसालन की चढि डारन R7
भवन तें कढि, बढि R6
भावती, रूप महाछवि Ś43
*भूमि हरी भई R59
भूलि न प्रीति करौं Ś60
भूलि गई खेल Ś25
मच रची फागु R15
मदमाते गुवाल गरूर भरे R22
मन-धन बिससे से Ś94
*मन मेरो मतंग भयौ B14
मरद मुछारे, गभुवारे Ś21
*मानि कही, चलि बेगि Ś22
मीन मरै जल के परसे U14
मीरजादे, पीरजादे N9
*मुरवा पुकारै हम जेहैं R62

मूढ सुनै कब रामकथा N15
मेंहदी लपेटे लाल B19
मेरी कही मान B5
मेरी कही कर मो जिय Ś75
*मेवा बई घनी काबुल में N22
मैं हू सुन्यौ, मेरी B24
*मोतिन कैसी मनोहर माल गुहै N36
*मोहीं में रहत Ś18
मौरन लगे हैं आम R5
*यह कोमल कंज सौ Ś108
यह को है, कहाँ को B43
यह प्रेमकथा कहियै Ś7
यहि प्रीति-अजार के Ś6
याही के निमित्त नित N6
येई हैं वे बृषभानुसुता B20
ये जे कहैं, ते भले कहिबो Ś140
*येही हिय द्वार के Ś19
*रस नाँही मिल्यौ B6
*रस रीति की प्रीति कौं B65
राखे हते हम रावरे को Ś91
*राग कौ न रंग कौ N16
राधा, न नोहरिया लगै Ś47
राधिका स्याम लसे पलका पर B39
*राम मेरो पंडित B12
रूप अनूप दई दयौ Ś99
रूपमान सुंदरी सुजान Ś100
रूपवारी, जोबन-अनूप- Ś112
रूप है न, रस है न Ś78
रूसनहारी घनेरी हुती U8

रोज न आइयै जू, मनमोहन Ś129
रोज न आईऐ जू, मनमोहन Ś130
रोजही आनि हरावत बातन Ś92
लगी अंदर की, करै जाहिर Ś76
लहरैं उठैं अंग Ś13
लाँबी लचकारी लौद लीन्हे R32
*लाई ही हौं फुसलाय Ś106
लाख हजार चुबाइन Ś24
*वह घेर कै घाघरे Ś28
वा निरमोहिनि रूप की रासि Ś44
*वा बरसै जलधारन सों R46
वृंदाबन जुगुल किसोर R68
वेई नर निरनैं निदान पै N28
वे तो हुते गोप B63
वे तौ नैन बान मारि Ś40
वे तौ छबि धाम Ś82
वे परबीन बिचच्छन लोग Ś65
*वे सब जानती हीं B60
*श्याम घटा देह जाकी R63
सखि, आई है मोह मनावन को U5
सखिन दुराई वृषभान की R49
*सगुन सुहावैं आवै R50
सजनी, सुखद तें सुहाई R34
*सजि सूहे दुकूलन बिज्जु छटा सी R54
सद है, अबही हद है B3
सननात अँधेरी घटा R61
समुझाइ सिखाइयै कासु Ś4
*साँचे करार करे हमसों B51
*सापने हौं फुलवाई गई Ś71

*सामिल हो पीर मैं N31
*साहस कै कस कै Ś85
*सीख लीने मीन, मृग N37
*सुकबि सिपाही हम N25
*सुनती कहा ठाढी भई Ś54
*सुनिकै धुनि चाह बढी Ś1
सुमृत पुरान बेद गीतहू N10
सुरझी नहीं केतो Ś12
सोक को समुद्र, बिरहागि Ś77
सोभा सुहात बिलोकत भावती Ś89
हम एक कुराह चली तौ चली Ś9
हम तौ परनारी भईं Ś121
*हम से मनमोहन से हित है Ś150
हम सौं हसि बोले, सुनें Ś155
हरिजू की गैल मेरी पौरि Ś149
हरि लाँबी औ चौरी Ś70
हरि हित नामै ये वचन U10
हैं मृदु बैनन Ś26
हारि पर्यौ लरि B17
हिलिमिलि लीजिये प्रबीनन Ś104
होत कहा काहू Ś81
*होरी की हौंस हमैं ना R21
*होरी हो रही है R25
हौं करिहौं हित Ś2
हौं बरजी बर बीसक Ś45
हौं ही समै लखि कै Ś125
हौ तुम यातैं भली B31

Index of Names and Works

Abhaivilās, 73
Airāvat, 35, 46
Ajīt Siṁh, 60
Akbar, 17
Ālam, 35, 47n, 73, 74
Ali Bahādur, 16
Allah, 23, 329
Amareś, 69
Ambapālī, 348n
Ānandghan (Ghanānand), 13, 14, 23, 35, 37, 41, 47n, 48, 51n, 55, 73, 75, 76
Ānandrām Mukhlis, 52
Annamayyā, 33
Anūpgiri (Himmat Bahādur), 15, 16, 18, 19, 20, 23, 24, 25, 27, 28, 29, 71
Arjun Siṁh, 16

Balavant, 76
Bali, 328
Balibhadra, 70
Bansal, Umarani, 60, 61
'Barsainya', Ganga Prasad, 9, 18, 77
Bayly, C.A., 30
Bhagavant, 71
Bhagvandin, 17, 18, 24, 26, 27, 29, 31, 36, 38, 39, 54, 55, 56, 58, 59, 78
Bhikhārīdās, 47n
Bhīma, 35
Bhramargīt, 31
Bhūṣan, 73, 76
Bihārī, 13n, 24, 25, 27, 29, 44, 52, 56, 69, 72
Bihārī-ratnākar, see *Satsaī* (of Bihārī)
Bīr Siṁh Dev, 16
Bodhā, 35, 72
Bohra, Shivnarayan, 72
Brahma (poet), 74
Brahma (the Creator), 45, 47, 75, 325, 326, 331, 334, 344, 346, 349, 350
Brajbhāṣā sūr koś, 38, 39, 98
Brajbhāṣā sāhitya kā ṛtu-saundarya, 59, 77
Brajbhūṣan, 21
Brajdūlah, 70
Brajnidhi, 70
Broughton, Thomas Duer, 13n, 51, 52
Bryant, Kenneth, 49
Buddha, 348
Bundel-vaibhav, 79
Bṛhat hindī koś, 38, 95, 97

Cain, 71
Cand, 77
Catur, 18, 71
Chatrasāl, 15
Chaturvedi, Shivdatt, 44
Chaturvedi, Vishnuvirat, 9
Comparative Dictionary of the Indo-Aryan Languages, 95
Cowherd, *see* Krishna
Cowherd Boy, *see* Krishna
Creator, *see* Brahma

Dagar, Vasifuddin, 51n
Dampati-vākya-vilās, 61
Dark as a Cloud, *see* Krishna
Dark One, *see* Krishna
Daryāv Siṁh, 17n, 18
Dayānidhi, 56, 60, 61n, 69, 76
Dear Child, *see* Krishna
Dear One, *see* Krishna
Debendra, 52, 53
Derashri, R.S., 76
Dev, 13n, 14, 41, 44, 47n, 48, 52, 56, 69, 72, 76, 92
Devakīnandan, 24, 71
Devakīnandan commentary, 24, 25, 36
Devendra Singh, 61
Devīdās, 73
Deviprasad, 17
Dhīraj, 70
Dictionary of Bhakti, 98
Dictionary of Urdu, Classical Hindi and English, 98
Dīgha Nikāya, 348n
Digvijay bhūṣaṇ, 77
Dīndayāl Giri, 29
Dubey, Udaya Shanker, 9, 71
Dūlah, 71
Duryodhana, 27, 352
Dvijbaldev, 47n
Dvijdev, 35, 44

Enchanter (of the Mind), *see* Krishna

Fair One, *see* Radha
Fairbanks, Florence, 49

Gaj Siṁh, 16
Ganesha, 26, 72
Gaṅg, 74
Garcin de Tassy, J.H., 28, 30
Ghaṇākṣarī-niyam-ratnākar, 50
Ghanānand, *see* Ānandghan
Gillābhāī, Govind, 72
Gobardhan līlā melā saḍan, 26
God of Love, *see* Kāma
Gopāla, *see* Krishna
Gopīnāth, 72
Goswami, Atulkrishna, 74
Goswami Babulal, 18n
Govinda, *see* Krishna 331
Granthāvalī, see *Ṭhākur granthāvalī*
Grierson, G.A. 24, 38
Gulābrāy, 17
Guṇ nāṭikā, 26n
Gupta, Kishorilal, 25, 61, 63, 77
Gurucandroday-kaumudī, 61
Gurudatt, 71
Gvāl, 60, 61

Hanumān, 47n, 60
Hari, *see* Krishna
Hariaudh, 14, 59, 77
Harikeś, 56, 74
Hariścandra, Bhāratendu, 31, 44, 47n, 60, 77, 78, 94
Harsevak, 17
Harsukh Singh, 74
Haṭhī, 71
Hawley, J. S., 46
Hazārā (of Hāfizullah Khān), 33, 78
Himmat Bahādur, *see* Anupgiri
Hindī sāhitya kā itihās, 77
Hīṅgan Khān, 72
Hirde Śāh, 15
Histoire de la littérature hindoui et hindoustani, 28
Hulās, 71

Indra, 35, 327, 342n
Intoxicator, *see* Kāma
Īś, 61, 62
Iśklatā, 75
Īśvar kavi, 48

Jagannathprasad, Babu 53n
Jagat Rāj, 15, 16
Jagat Siṁh (of Jaipur), 28
Jasvant, 71
Jasvant Siṁh (of Nabha), 61, 62
Javān Siṁh (of Udaipur), 69
Jñāngītā, 26

Kabīr, 70
'Kālidās-hazārā', 25, 77, 94
Kālikāprasād, 71
Kāma (God of Love, Love, Love-god), 34, 45, 325, 331, 335, 338, 340, 341, 342, 343, 344, 345, 347
Kamlājan, 71
Kanh, *see* Krishna
Kanhāī, *see* Krishna
Karam Siṁh, 60
Karmābāī, 348
Karnārjunī, 26
Kashiprasad, 58, 78
Kāśināth, 76
Kāsīrām, 76
Kavīndra, 71
Kavitāvalī, 43, 46, 47
Kavitta sār saṅgrah, 71
Kavitta ratnākar, 79
Kellogg, Samuel H., 38
Keśavdās, 13n, 41, 52, 62, 72
Kesrī Siṁh (of Bijawar), 16, 18, 27
Kesrī Siṁh (of Jaitpur), 16, 18, 26
Khaḍgarāy, 17, 18, 60
Khān, Hāfizullah, 33, 77, 78
Khemrāj, 76
Khoj Report, 26, 56, 60n, 61n, 62, 73, 78
Khūbcand, 76
Khuddaka Nikāya, 348n
Kishorilal, 9, 10, 38, 71, 77, 98
Kiśor, 69, 71
Kiśor (or Kiśorī) Siṁh (of Panna), 16, 20, 21, 27
Krishna (Cowherd, Cowherd Boy, Dark as a Cloud, Dark One, Dear Child, Dear One, Enchanter [of the Mind], Gopāla, Govinda, Hari, Kanh, Kanhāī, Lord of Braj, Moon of Braj, Nanda's son), 11, 13, 14, 18-20, 25, 27, 29-35, 38, 43, 46, 48, 52, 53, 56n, 63, 74, 93, 325-343, 345, 346, 347n
Kūṭ kabitta, 43, 56, 78, 92
Kuvalyānanda, 40
Kuvera, 36, 355
Kṛṣṇa (poet), 24

Lāl (poet), 71
Lāl, Lallū, 29n
Lalitā, 34

Letters Written in a Mahratta Camp, 51, 52
Lord of Braj, *see* Krishna
Love or Love-god, *see* Kāma

Mādhavdās, 73
Mahabharata, 26, 35, 347n
Mahadji Shinde, 16
Mānak hindī koś, 98
Mathur, Surendra, 38, 44
Matirām, 47n, 73, 74
McGregor, R.S., 11, 49, 95
Mīrābāī, 70, 73, 78
Mishra, Chandrashekhar, 36, 58, 77
Mishra, Sureshdatt, 60
Mishra, Vishvanath Prasad, 31, 36, 37, 58n
Mishrabandhu, 78
Miśra, Gaṅgāprasād, 76
Miśra, Rāmbakhś, 60
Miśrabandhu vinod, 78
Mital, Prabhudayal, 59, 77
Moon of Braj, *see* Krishna
Motīrām (poet), 71
Motīrām, Sevag, 73
Muhammad Śāh, 24
Murlī, 56

Nādīr Śāh, 29, 52
Nāgarīdās, 69, 73
Najaf Khan, 16
Nakhśikh saṅgrah, 79
Nakhśikh-hajārā, 78
Nāmdev, 348n
Nanda's son, *see* Krishna
Nanda, 327, 333, 340
Nandadās, 31
Nandan, 74
Nāth, 73
Naṭnāgar, 56, 69
Navaleś, 18
Navīn, 23, 25, 57, 60-63, 64n, 74, 78
Nehnidān, 61
Nidhi, 77
Nipaṭ, 71
Nīti-satsaī (*Satsaī* of Vṛnd), 44, 45, 46, 47
Niẓām ul-Mulk, 29, 52

Padmākar, 13, 14, 18, 27, 28, 41, 45, 47n, 51, 56, 69-73, 76, 77
Pad-saṅgrah (of Brajdūlah), 70
Pajaneś, 71
Paramānand, 70
Parīkṣit, 16, 18, 21, 27
Pārvatī, 327
Pāvas-kavitta-ratnākar, 59, 77
Pinch, William, 16
Prasad, R.C., 47, 57
Pratāp Siṁh, 28, 76
Prayāgnārāyaṇ-vilās, 42
Pravīn, 60, 62
Prem-pacīsā, 70
Priy-pravās, 14
Puranas, 35, 350
Pūtanā, 326
Pṛthvīrāj Sāndū, 73

Radha (Fair One), 23, 25, 30, 31, 70, 93, 325, 327, 328, 341, 342, 346, 347
Rahim, 23
Rahīm, 29, 51, 70, 71, 72
Rahman, 23
Raidās, 348
Rājasthānī hindī śabdkoś, 98
Rājasthānī sabad kos, 98
Rājnīti rā kavitta, 73
Rama (Ram), 22, 326, 328, 350
Rāmbakas, Kuṁvar, 72
Rāmbakas, Lālā, 77
Rāmcandra-vilās, 26n
Rāmcandrikā, 72
Rāmcaritmānas, 33, 46, 47, 57
Rāmcaritra, 42
Rāmpratāp, 72
Raṅgtaraṅg, 61
Raṇjīt Siṁh, 76
Ras Ānand, 69
Rasik-vinod, 54, 55, 57, 77, 94
Raskhān, 35, 47n, 56, 71, 75
Raskusumākar, 78
Raslīn, 27, 51
Rasrāj, 71
Ras-sāgar, 62
Ratan Siṁh (of Bijawar), 16
Rati, 331, 334
Ratnākar, Jagannāthdās, 50, 63, 78
Rāv Rājā, 17
Riṣināth, 25
Rītikāvya śabdkoś, 98
Rukminī-maṅgal, 26n

Śabd satguru ke, 26n
Safar-nāma, 52-53
Śāh, 71
Sāhityik brajbhāṣā koś, 39, 98
Śāhzādī, 23

Sambhu, 76
Śaṅkar Prasād, 17n
Saraiya, Kamata Prasad, 71
Sarasras, 61
Sarasvati, 26
Saroj Sarvekṣan, 25
Śatak, see *Ṭhākur śatak*
Satsaī (of Vṛnd), see *Nīti-satsaī*
Satsaī (*Bihārī-Ratnākar*), 24, 27n, 29n, 44
Satsaī (of Ṭhākur), see *Ṭhākur-satsaī*
Satsaiyā varanārtha, 24
Ṣaṭ-ṛtu-hajārā, 59, 77
Ṣaṭ-ṛtu-kāvya-saṅgrah, 77
Sekh, 72
Senāpati, 74, 76
Śeṣa, 326
Sevag Motīrām, 73
Sevak, 24
Sharma, Govind, 9, 98
Shastri, Dharmeshvar, 71
Shiva, 11, 327
Shuja ud-Daula, 16
Shukla, Ramchand, 24, 59, 60, 77
Shukla, Ramdeo, 9, 98
Sindia, Daulat Rao, 51
Singh, Baburamdin, 40, 55, 60, 78, 94
Singh, Bhairav, 55, 77
Singh, Naunihal, 78
Singh, Raghuvir, 9, 71
Śītalā, 33, 347
Śivsiṁh Saroj, 18, 23, 24, 25, 48, 77
Śivsiṁh Seṅgar, 18, 25, 29, 60
Snell, Rupert, 29n
Somnāth, 70, 76
Śrīpati, 71
Śṛṅgār kavitta, 74
Śṛṅgār saṅgrah, 77
Śṛṅgār sudhākar, 77
Sudhāsāgar, 75
Sudhāsar, 23, 25, 31, 39, 40, 53, 59-71, 74, 75, 76, 78, 92, 96
Suhane, Paramanand, 59, 77, 78
Sujān, 19, 21, 23, 54, 55, 337
Sundar Kavirāy, 27, 51
Sundarī sarvasva, 60, 79
Sundarī-tilak, 40, 55, 59, 60, 77, 78, 94
Sūr śabd-sāgar, 98
Sūrati, 42
Sūrati Miśra, 42n
Sūrdās, 31, 33, 45, 49, 56, 70, 76
Sūrsāgar, 38, 45, 46n, 76n
Syām kavi, 76

Tejā sipāhī, 74
Ṭhākur (author of the *Karnārjunī*), 26
Ṭhākur (of Asni), 23-26, 36
Ṭhākur (prācīn), 23, 25
Ṭhākur granthāvalī (the *Granthāvalī*), 36, 39, 53n, 54, 55, 56, 58, 59, 73, 77, 94
Ṭhākur śatak (the *Śatak*), 39, 43, 58, 59, 78, 94
Ṭhākur-satsaī (Satsaī), 53n, 56, 57, 63, 75, 76
Ṭhākur ṭhasak (the *Ṭhasak*), 17, 19n, 31, 36, 39, 54, 55, 56, 58, 59, 60, 78, 94
Ṭhākurāy, 70
Ṭhākurdās, 25, 26, 48, 73
Ṭhākurdās (author of *pads*), 26
Ṭhākurdās (of Gauspur), 26
Ṭhākurdās Brahman (of Jhansi), 23, 25
Ṭhākurdās Kāyastha (of Charkhari), 26
Ṭhākurdās of Ṭīkamgaṛh, 26n
Ṭhasak, see *Ṭhākur ṭhasak*
The Oxford Hindi-English Dictionary, 11, 95
Therigāthā, 348n
Tipu Sultan, 30
Tivari, Keshav Kishor, 71
Tripathi, Rampher, 62
Tulsīdās, 33, 43, 46, 47, 48, 71, 73, 74, 76, 350
Turner, L.R., 95

Uddhav, 31, 37, 47, 52, 53, 68, 328-30

Vāgvilās granth, 24
Vaid, Bhai Mohan Singh, 75
Vairāgyamañjarī, 76
Vajpeyi, Shankarlal, 72
Varma, Krishna Chandra, 38
Vedas, 31, 326, 337, 350
Vidura, 30, 35, 347, 348
Vidvanmod taraṅginī, 77
Vṛnd, 29, 44, 45
Vṛndāvandhāmānurāgāvalī, 61

Yajnik, Bhavanishankar, 53n
Yajnik, Mayashankar, 40, 53n, 59, 60, 61n, 62, 73, 78